Back to the Seventies

The 1870's

Through the Eyes of Two Country Newspapers

by Jerry Michael

HERITAGE BOOKS
2017

HERITAGE BOOKS

AN IMPRINT OF HERITAGE BOOKS, INC.

Books, CDs, and more—Worldwide

For our listing of thousands of titles see our website
at
www.HeritageBooks.com

Published 2017 by
HERITAGE BOOKS, INC.
Publishing Division
5810 Ruatan Street
Berwyn Heights, Md. 20740

Copyright © 2017 Jerry Michael

Heritage Books by the author:

Back to the Seventies: The 1870's Through the Eyes of Two Country Newspapers

It Was Different Then: 1870 to 1885 Through the Eyes of the Loudoun County, Virginia Press

International Standard Book Number
Paperbound: 978-0-7884-5777-7

It can be argued that in recording history, the average citizen is often forgotten. Powerful iconic leaders, cataclysmic disasters, great political movements, wars, sensational crimes, magnificent achievements, etc. are the common news subjects. The eccentric, the colorful and the unusual occupy the most written space.

All of which is understandable. Actuality, meaning the mundane, is often boring. "Little people" like you and I require some boost in our attention span away from the humdrum. Perhaps something like this is what Andy Warhol meant when he said every person will have his "fifteen minutes of fame." I always thought that the man and his quotation were not all that important – an offhand comment recorded by some media person that somehow caught on. But maybe Warhol was onto something.

The problem for the historian is that an overemphasis on dramatic events and personages presents a skewed picture of the past. Like today, "little people" and their conventional lives should be recognized. After all, they vastly outnumber the "celebrities" of the time. One goal of this book is to recognize this aspect.

How to do this and retain the reader's interest is difficult. Actually, however, the simple passage of time comes to our rescue. The ordinary of 130 years ago is unique to our modern experience. The reader of the following pages may enjoy following the common events of the "little people" such as camp meetings, stolen horses, buggy accidents, impassible roads, harvest news, the humor, new inventions, etc. The ads of the day are truly unique and the old societal attitudes and methods of expression also provide interest. This local news is first-generation reportage copied directly from the microfilm. The more dramatic and important subjects are not neglected, however.

Loudoun has recently been declared the richest per capita county in the nation. Professionals, lobbyists, political appointees and all manner of successful folk have migrated from the crowded D.C. environs and purchased rural acreage which once grazed cows or grew corn. The so-called mega-mansions proliferate. Their lawns are often the size of football fields fostering a burgeoning lawn care industry. Many newcomers purchase horses, not the Belgians or Percherons of yesteryear, but the riding kind. This has also prompted service businesses of fence building and horse boarding. Some traditional farming is still prevalent with a few beef operations but a lot of acreage is rented out for free to corn and soybean farmers just to escape the high land use taxes. All of this affluence is in many ways positive as the new homes are well kept, their entrances often exquisite. The population growth, the increased traffic is, however, altering the quaint rural landscape.

Contrast this with the Loudoun of the 1870's. Leesburg, once a town, is now a small city. The county's population for 120 years remained nearly static, never varying more than 10% decade by decade. Farming, of course, as with everywhere was the main occupation. Horses were common, but they were necessities for work and travel and rarely for sport. Loudoun was a superior agricultural region even then. In later years, it became one of the nation's leading orchard grass producers and at another time a state leader in milk production. Today only one dairy farm remains.

Its boundaries were still the Blue Ridge to the west, the Potomac and Maryland to the north, and equally historic Fairfax to the east which it had broken off from in 1757. Thirty-five miles to the east was the nation's capital. The counties to the south were like Loudoun, part of Mosby's Confederacy with its attendant guerrilla activity during the war.

We shall skip over most of Loudoun's rich history and proceed to 1870, the first year of the ten year span covered by these pages. There was probably still animosity prevalent, which was created by the federal burning raids of 1864, but even this seemed to be dissipating. Reconstruction was being completed and in 1876 troops were removed from the Deep South. Loudoun, which had several enclaves of Union sentiment, probably adjusted better than most.

Problems remained as they always do – a long lasting economic downturn which began in 1873, Indian problems in the west, the contentious Hayes-Tilden election for 1876 and its extraordinary settlement, and towards the end of the decade there was an increase in labor and racial strife.

Still the county progressed. In the opinion of the writer, the benevolent and intelligent influence of the local press had a lot to do with this. Though originally defenders of secession (one editor was a Confederate officer) they adjusted to the new realities. Hopefully, the reader will find my arbitrary selections informative and interesting. A "feel" for the life and times is my main objective.

THE WASHINGTONIAN.

Dates at least back to 1808. It was edited by former Confederate veteran Captain William Lynch and published in the county seat of Leesburg. Both The Washingtonian and The Mirror had to suspend operations during the Civil War.

THE MIRROR.

Began publishing in 1855, but like its Leesburg neighbor above, voted the democratic line. It was edited by Benjamin Sheets, whose son took it over later. Both The Washingtonian and The Mirror joined forces in 1904 and became an ancestor of the present Loudoun Times Mirror.

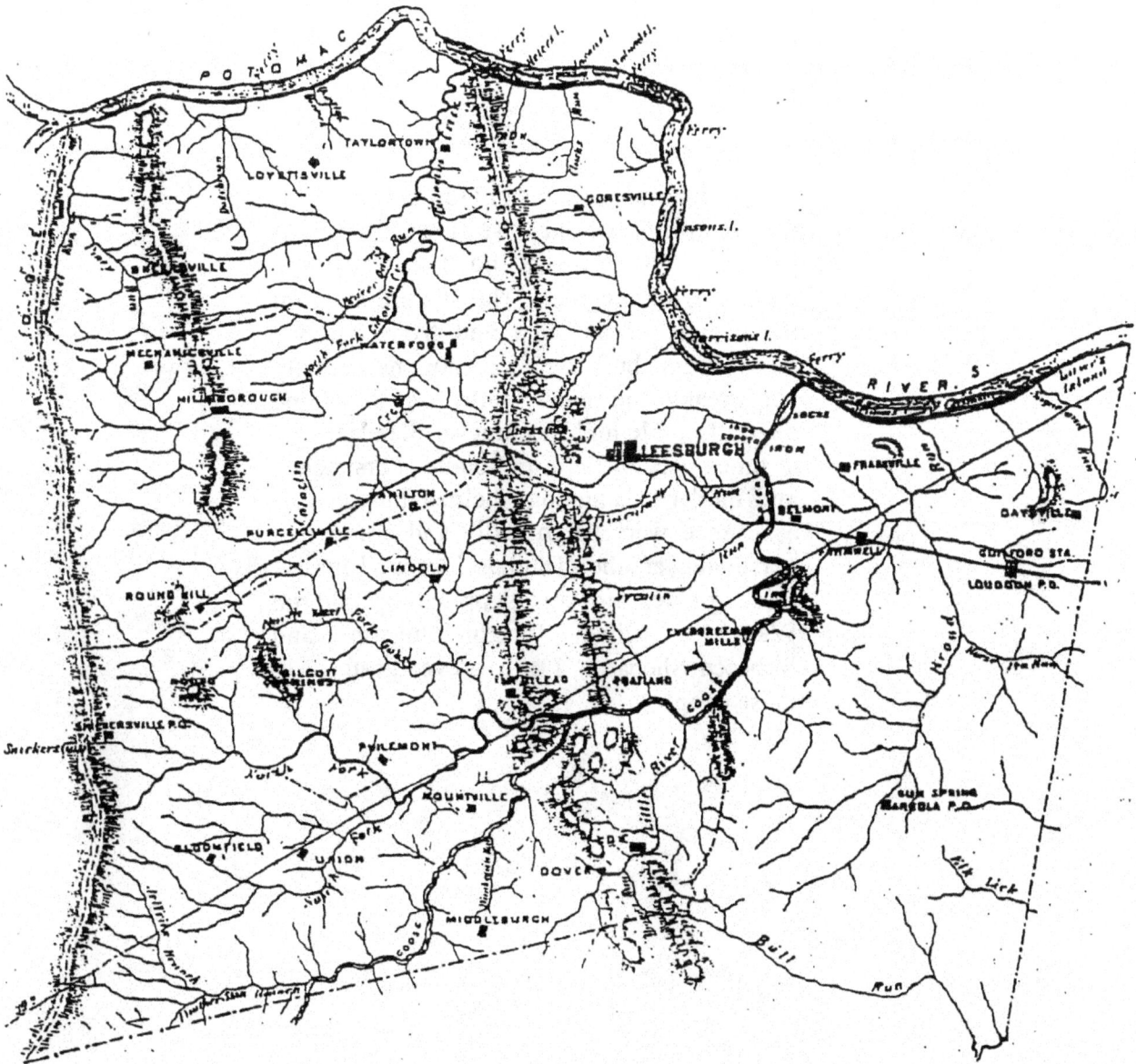

MAP OF LOUDOUN CO. VIRGINIA.

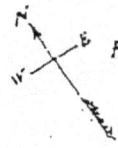

1883. H.H.HARDESTY, PUBLISHER.

The following pages contain copies from the microfilm of the two local Leesburg papers. The articles move in a rough chronological manner. The ads are all from the decade of the 70's and from the two newspapers but they do not necessarily accompany the news items on the same page. Legible and meaningful material was at times very difficult to obtain. Persistence and modern technology helped but also of assistance were the friendly and competent personnel at the Thomas Balch Library. Even greater aid was supplied by Sharon Warren, Trillian Wright-Johnston and Rebecca Shepard. I am forever grateful to these people.

There is no microfilm data for early 1870, so our journey begins in July of that year.

7/8/70 Washingtonian

STEAMBOAT RACE ON THE MISSIS-SIPPI.

The great steamboat race from New Orleans to Cairo, between the steamers R. E. Lee and Natches, is creating quite a furor in fancy circles out West. Several hundred thousand dollars have been bet. The boats left New Orleans at 5 o'clock, P. M., last Thursday. The R. E. Lee passed Memphis one hour ahead of her competitor, and will probably win the race. This is grand amusement, and in all probability will lead to a grand explosion, and a still grander flight in the air, of the carcases of a hundred or more individuals, as was the case when steamboat racing was the rage many years ago. Well, if they prefer that mode of "going up," we don't know that we dry-land mortals have any cause to be fretting about it.

The result—the R. E. Lee victorious.

St. Louis, July 4, 1870.

The steamer R. E. Lee arrived at 11.25 A. M. making the run from New Orleans in three days, eighteen hours and fourteen minutes, beating the time of the steamer Natches on her last trip three hours and forty-four minutes, and the Jas. W. White's famous time about five hours. The Natchez is detained by a heavy fog 120 miles below, and had not arrived at 6 P. M. A million dollars changed hands on the result. Thousands of people were out to witness the arrival. The arrival has been a complete ovation from first to last. The steamer Lee is a Louisville boat, and as stated heretofore the Natches is a new Cincinnati boat, built expressly to beat the Lee, which was notedly fast before this contest.

This event was recorded by the press, later historians, and even musical composers.

7/8/70 Washingtonian

GEN. LEE.

"Your correspondent did not send you last spring any account of the action of the Board in reference to making General Lee's position more comfortable because he did not think it proper to publish it. As, however, it got into the Lynchburg papers in rather an exaggerated form and went the rounds of the press, I have, upon consultation with friends of the College, determined to send you the facts. It is generally known that Gen. Lee has always refused to receive gratuities of any kind—that just as during the war he refused to receive a house from the city of Richmond, and nobly said to the council: "If you have benefactions to bestow, give them to my private soldiers, who are more needy and more deserving than myself," so since the war, though robbed of his patrimony, he has steadfastly refused to recieve presents that have been offered him. His conduct in this respect has been very strickingly like that of Washington.

The board of Trustees of the College have found it, therefore difficult to make such provision for General Lee as they have felt due alike to him, themselves, and the public. He has declined to receive such salary as the Board thought he ought to have, and they have been puzzled to know what to do.

During his absence they had a meeting, at which they settled upon Mrs Lee for life the house in which the General now lives and an annuity of $3,000.

At their recent meeting the Board received a letter from Gen. Lee in which (on behalf of Mrs. Lee) he very respectfully but firmly declines the proffer.

After a full consideration of the matter the Board have, as delicately as possible, decided that they must adhere to their original action—that they cannot suffer the risk of any contingency in which the family, of our loved and honored chieftain might suffer. They insist that this is not a "gratuity," but the payment of a very small part of the debt which the College, the State, and the country at large, owe to the distinguished patriot who has devoted himself to earnestly and so successfully to the education of the youth of the land.

The Board have also elected a private secretary to the General.

[Most people know that after his death Washington College was eventually renamed Washington and Lee University.]

2

10/21/70 Washingtonian

Last Hours of Gen. Lee.

10/21/70 Washingtonian

Lexington, Va., Oct. 13.—This community was plunged into profound sorrow upon the announcement of the death of Gen. Lee. The various church bells were tolled, and a general suspension of the duties of Washington College, the Virginia Military Institute and the minor schools followed. They will not resume until after the final interment of the great chieftain. Every business house in the community was closed, and crape affixed to the door. Even the colored barbers shut up their shops, and an expression of deep grief was visible in every face. Washington College, the College Chapel, the Virginia Military Institute and the Episcopal Church, of which Gen. Lee was a communicant were draped in mourning a few hours after his death. Gen. Lee had been almost entirely unconscious since Monday night last, and expired very peacefully and quietly at half-past nine on Wednesday morning.

He was first taken sick on Wednesday evening, September 28th, while just about to sit down to tea, when he suddenly sank in his chair insensible. A reaction soon took place, and in the course of the next ten days he steadily improved until it was hoped he was out of danger, but on Monday evening last he became suddenly and rapidly worse, and continued to sink until Wednesday morning. During the early part of his sickness he slept much and spoke but little, but was rational when awake, and always recognized those who approached him. At times his mind seemed to wander, and on several occasions reverted to the army.

He once ordered his tent to be struck, and at another time desired that "Hill" should be sent for. He suffered comparatively little pain during his whole sickness, and died without a struggle. He will be buried on Saturday, October 15th, at 12 o'clock. The place selected for his interment is a vault beneath the college chapel, which stands in the midst of the college grounds. This was the first building he had erected after his removal to Lexington, having declared that it was proper the first thing the college did should be to dedicate a house to the service of religion.

Here he will appropriately rest, surrounded by the monuments of his late years, his remains sentineled by the mountains of that Virginia on which he had conferred such imperishable fame. The corpse was removed to day from his residence to the chapel, where it will lay in state until midday on Saturday next. To-day the Faculty of Washington College, the faculty of the Virginia Military Institute and the students of Washington College held meetings and passed appropriate resolutions of condolence and respect to the memory of the illustrous deceased, who asserted at the surrender of Appomattox Courthouse, that "Human virtue should be equal to human calamity."

DEATH OF GEN. LEE.

"A great and good man is gone," has been, during the past week, echoed with the profoundest grief, from millions of voices, from the Potomac to the Rio Grand. And as the fame of the hero and patriot, whose death his countrymen now laments, is limited only by the verge of civilization, the same common eulogy, upon the announcement of the sad intelligence, comes unbidden from every enlightened heart. Wherever the nobler virtues of humanity are properly appreciated—one who has so completely and splendidly exemplified them in his life, must be entered upon that role of the immortal, whose fame is claimed as the common heritage of mankind. No one nation can be the custodian of the renown of those, whom Providence has raised up, for the sublime purpose of blessing mankind with an example of pure devotion to duty in all its relations—with a self-sacrifice which is alone in its grandeur among the distinguished names of history.

No one act, no single brilliant victory, no grand civil achievement, called forth the universal homage paid to his memory. It is a tribute, won by a life in which, at every stage, were beautifully blended those principles, which form and mature the character of the great and good. It comes from a well spent youth and glorious manhood, which, like the golden fruits of Autumn, was matured and ripened by seasonable culture in the practices of the purer virtues of our nature.

A Tribute of Respect.

At a meeting of the citizens of Leesburg and vicinity held at the Courthouse on Saturday evening, the 15th inst., to take suitable action relative to the death of Gen. R. E. Lee, Capt. JAS. WM. FOSTER was called so the Chair and W. N. WISE appointed Secretary. The chairman by appropriate remarks stated the object of the meeting, and was followed by Maj. J. M. Orr, who paid a fitting tribute to the memory of the illustrious dead, and upon his motion a committee of three, to which was added the Chairman, was selected, to frame resolutions in conformity with the object of the meeting.

PUBLIC SALE.

THE undersigned having quit farming, will sell at public sale, at the Limestone Mill,

On MONDAY, OCTOBER 24th, 1870,

the following articles, viz:

8 head of No. 1 Work HORSES,

among which are six good brood Mares, several of them with foal, 3 valuable Colts, two of them by the horse Georgia,

Six Milch Cows,

one fresh at this time, 4 fat Steers, 6 young Cattle, 2 sets Breech band, 4 sets front Gear, 6 sets Plow Gear, Bridles and Collars, 1 Wagon Saddle and Line, 2 Government Wagons, 1 Fifth Chain and Stretcher, 1 two-horse Spring Wagon and Harness, 2 pair Hay Carriages, 2 three-horse Plows, with tripple, double and single Trees, 1 Harrow, 3 single and three double-shovel Plows, 1 pair Wood-Ladders, 1 new Cutting Box, (Sinclair's make,) 1 Buggy Rake, self-discharging, Forks, Rakes, &c.

oct 14-ts   T. A. CRAMPTON.

AT the same time and place, E. G. MARLOW, (intending to close his business on the first of January,) will sell the following property, viz : 1 fine riding and driving

HORSE,

1 blooded Colt, 3 years old next Spring, handsome, and promising to be fast, 1 Yearling Colt, 1 Sucking Colt, by horse Georgia, one Buggy and Harness,

Eleven Fat Hogs

1 thorough-bred Essex Boar, 1 Sow and 8 fine Shoats, 1 of them the Essex stock.

TERMS.—All the above property will be sold upon a credit of six months, for all sums of $20 and upwards, the purchaser giving bond with approved security, bearing interest from date. Sums under $20 cash.

Sale to commence at 10 o'clock, A. M.

J. L. RINKER, Auct.   E. G. M.
oct 14-ts

THE FREE SCHOOL SYSTEM OF VIRGINIA.

The law providing for the adoption of the free school system of this State, is being put in execution in most of the counties. The preliminary arrangements require time and careful attention—the system is new to our people, and such a policy has to be pursued as best to avoid unnecessary opposition, and to mature its organization in that manner which will bring to it, the strongest popular support. The law provides, that the annual amount for schools, should be distributed among the counties in proportion to the number between the age of five and twenty-one years of age, to be expended in teachers salaries—all the other expenses, school-houses, &c., to be paid for by a tax upon the people. The amount apportioned to the county from the State, cannot be applied, until enough has been raised by the counties or townships, to make the necessary arrangements, by the erection of school-houses, &c., for a judicious application of the States' funds to teachers salaries. The county or township appropriation, is to be made by a vote of the people—the election to be ordered and controlled by instructions from the State Superintendent of Schools.

*   *   *

Again, the Public School system is no longer optional with us. The Constitution, as ratified by our people and Legislature, has made it obligatory upon us, and we can not reject it, if we would. It is the dictate of common sense to accept it, and direct it to good ends. In the light of recent events the free school is necessary and progressive. It was bad enough for any liberal-minded man to advocate ignorance of the masses in the good old times, when we had pure and patriotic public men to protect the interests of their constituents. Surely, now that our people are at the mercy of any demagogue who may be shrewd enough to take advantage of ignorance and easily deluded artlessness, it is of unquestionable importance that all voters shall have sufficient education to at least read and write, that they may thus and otherwise have every facility for judging wisely for themselves. The Public School system is then a fixed fact, and if we who have been appointed to organize it in our county do not succeed in introducing it, another set of officers will be appointed in our place, and the system may, by default, assume a less agreeable status among us then to some it now exhibits. Let us then throw aside every prejudice against the free school and waive all objections to it, and determine to give it a fair, prompt, and cheerful trial.

1/25/71 Washingtonian

COMMUNICATED.

A meeting of the Overseers of the Poor of Loudoun County was held at the Almshouse on Tuesday, the 19th January, 1871, for consultation and reorganization under the new law. There were present

Henry Hibbs, Superintendent.
Geo. Wire, Overseer Jefferson District.
Isaac Piggott, " Lovettesville "
Jas. G. Otley, " Mt. Gilead "
Sam'l Orrison, " Leesburg "
None representing Overseer Broadrun "

After a good dinner, embracing everything available at this season, the object of the meeting was entered into; Wm. Hough, late President of the Board, handed over to the Superintendant $10,700.00, in the bonds of individuals, which, when the investment was made, was considered the safest procurable, but unfortunately now, some of the signers are not much better than the inmates of the Almshouse, and $2,300 00 may be considered a total loss, leaving $8,400.00, the interest of which when paid, is the only fund, besides the proceeds of the farm, applicable to the maintenance of paupers at the Almshouse, and keeping the buildings in repair.

The number of paupers at present, in the Almshouse, are 15 white and 14 negroes, mostly blind, idiotic, or helpless through extreme age, or infancy. The negroes receive more assistance generally than the white population, but from their erratic habits, they remain only long enough to receive medical service when sick, and get necessary clothing, when they straggle to some point that in a distribution of plunder, they may get sustenance, with other gratifications of the gregarious life. The white paupers as a rule, are idiots or helpless from age—and if the length of time some of them have been in the hands of the Overseers, is a test of care, there can be little cause of complaint.

The buildings, fencing and land have been placed in somewhat better condition than that in which it was left by the vandalism of the federal troops, and, it is hoped means may be produced for replacing the barn and stables, as these buildings are necessary for the protection of the stock and produce of the farm.

Mr. Hibbs is exhibiting his reputation as a judge of stock, by his selections, to replace the worn out beasts he found upon the place.

The question was discussed as to the propriety of disposing of the present farm, and replacing it with the improvement requisite for the age, including a work house at some point near the Railroad, now available for supplies and with greater facilities of access. Though all were agreed as to the necessity of the change, yet each thought it must be somebody else's business to carry it out, and left the matter for another generation to act upon. As it is, considering the time since the little "unpleasantness," the scarcity of money, and the physical weight of the Board, I think all things are doing well for the

PAUPER.

TO WHOM IT MAY CONCERN.

The ferry, where the Georgetown and Leesburg Turnpike crosses Goose Creek, will shortly be abandoned and all facilities for crossing vehicles of every description, sheep, hogs, &c, be suspended. Therefore, I wish to call the attention of the Supervisors to the above fact, that they may make some arrangements with the owner of the boat, by which the ferry can be kept open, until the bridge can be rebuilt. Should the ferry be closed for a limited time it would subject a large number of citizens to serious inconvenience. As a bridge at the above named point is indispensible, it should be rebuilt as soon as practicable. The county will appropriate $1,200 to repair the piers and rebuild the superstructure, provided $800 can be raised by private subscription. Those who are interested and wish to contribute to the erection of the bridge, can find a subscription paper with

HENRY SAUNDERS, Jr.
Commissioner of Roads for Leesburg Township.
jan. 25th, 1871.

1/25/71 Washingtonian

A STEAM BUGGY.—A new invention in the form of a common open buggy, propelled by steam, is exhibited in New York. The machinery is the same as that of a locomotive. Beneath the seat and occupying the body of the vehicle is the boiler, which holds three pails of water. The cylinders and other parts of the machinery are placed between the axle trees. The inventor claims that, with the fire produced by a single hod of coal he can run 33 miles.— The pressure of steam required on an ordinary road is about 29 pounds

1/25/71 Washingtonian

"You have lost your baby, I hear," said one gentleman to another. "Yes, poor little thing, it was only five months old. We did all we could for it. We had four doctors; blistered it head and feet, put mustard poultices all over it, gave it nine calomel powders, leeched its temples, had it bled, gave it all kinds of medicines and yet, after a week's illness, it died."

2/22/71 Washingtonian

A Welcome for Northern Settlers.

Governor Vance Concerning the Treatment of Northerners—North Carolina Needs Imigrants, and Especially Colonies—Great Advantages Offered to Settlers.

What Gov. Vance so well says, in the following letter, of North Carolina, can be truely said of Virginia and Virginian people.

To the Editor of the N. Y. Tribune

Sir—A gentleman of your city sometime ago wrote me that a considerable number of persons from the State of N. Y. contemplated buying a large tract of land in Western North Carolina, but before doing so would be glad to have my opinion as to whether a colony of Northern settlers would be welcome and entirely safe in that region. It is mortifying in the extreme to have such questions asked, as they very often are, by intelligent citizens of the United States. It is a sad commentary, either upon the state of lawlessness which it presupposes to exist here, or upon the unscrupulous representations of partizan newspapers, which give false impressions to strangers. I earnestly desire, on behalf of the real interests of my State, to address a few through your columns to those who ask such questions. I am intimately acquainted, socially and politically, with the feelings and disposition of the people of North Carolina, and have been for many years. If there has been a single instance of resistance to legal process since the Government of the United States resumed its authority over them, I have never heard of it. If any outrage, or even insult, such as one man would offer to another on equal terms, has ever been offered to a bonafide settler from the North, come to live and be a citizen among us, I have never heard of it. If there is a portion of the State where such persons would not be eagerly and gladly welcomed, when they came to buy our vacant lands and cast in their lot for good and for evil, I know not which or where it is. On the contrary, I know that the universal desire of our people is to secure the filling up of the land with emigrants, Northern, European, or any other that can bring capital thrift, and good citizenship with them. And I know that all such will be welcomed gladly, and will be as safe as they can be anywhere on earth.

It is true we have no love for a class of adventurers called "carpet-baggers," by which term we mean those who come for political ends only; not those who come to plow the earth, to build the mill, to wield the hammer, to trade, &c. Many of the former have acted so as to render themselves justly odious to our people, and caused us, in giving expression to that dislike, to be suspected of unfriendliness is incorrect. It is true that we have inconsiderate people among us—especially young men who were soldiers—who have not learned to refrain from the use of intemperate language. Nor do I pretend to deny that there are some of the old bitterness of the war still rankling in the hearts of many. But cannot sensible people North, with but a small grin of charity, make some allowance for this? Can they not, with victorious magnanimity, consider the bruises and festering wounds of defeat? And on the whole, I ask you as a candid, generous mir a title which you have fairly earned among the southern people—on the whole, has there not been less of bitterness, less of violation of law, less of social disorder among us than any statesman, however farseeing, could have hoped. Is there any instance in history of a more thorough submission to events and a more rapid return from a state of bloody and chaotic disorder to a state of law and quiet labor? In giving rebuke to such acts of violence as now and then we have committed, have not the Northern people failed to give us due credit for the progress we really made toward the old channels of industry and peace? Do any of us sufficiently thank God for the safety which has attended our footsteps returning through the demoralized surroundings of disbanded armies, the bitter hatreds and bloody memories of civil war? Political hate should not blind our eyes to these things, for they will form a glorious page in our annals.

Therefore, sir, I appeal to all who desire to live in North Carolina to come on with perfect confidence both as to welcome and protection. The fields of industry that open to them here are unbounded, the soil rich, cheap, and producing abundantly almost every article known to the North Temperate Zone. The climate is unsurpassed on the American Continent.

ZEBULON B VANCE.

2/22/71 Washingtonian

DR. SHUMAN SENTENCED.

He Appeals for Mercy for his Help-less Wife.

TWO YEARS AND SIX MONTHS IN THE PENITENTIARY.

In the Criminal Court yesterday Dr. Septimus T. Shuman, who was lately convicted of killing Henrietta Paddon by administering to her certain medicines, from the effects of which she died, was brought into court to receive sentence. The Court asked him if he had anything to say why the sentence of law should not be pronounced upon him.

Dr. Shuman in reviewing his case, said in conclusion I shall have to beg of your honor to be as lenient with me as possible. I have got A HELPLESS WIFE AND LITTLE BABES, with no one to provide for them at all. If you will do so, I promise that I will not prescribe again for man or woman, I shall go into a different business altogether. I have lived ten years in Washington, and my reputation has been unblemished during the whole of that time. I had no notion of producing any such a thing as abortion. If I had desired to do such a thing I could have given her medicine put up in such a way that she could have taken it home with her."

Judge Humphreys asked: "Have you concluded your statement?"

The Prisoner. "I have.

The Judge after a short address to the prisoner, pronounced the following sentence:

The sentence is that you, Septimus T. Shuman, shall be confined at labor in the penitentiary at Albany for the period of two years and six months from the date of this sentence.

The *Chronicle* says:

Our whole community will, we trust, be gratified at the conviction and sentence of Dr. Shuman. We hope to see all practitioners in the same line join him inside the penitentiary walls.

2/22/71 Washingtonian

"My lord," said the foreman of a Welsh jury, when giving in the verdict: "we find the man who stole the mare not guilty.'

A paper recently made the statement that "two thousand cart-loads of cats had been shipped over a certain Western railroad." The editor meant to say "oats."

2/22/71 Washingtonian

[*From the Nashville Banner, Feb. 7.*]

A CORPSE DRIVING A HORSE THROUGH THE STREETS.

Dr. William Burdett, who resided at No. 330 South Cherry st., died at 6 o'clock last evening under the most peculiar circumstances. About half an hour previous to his demise he had driven to the residence of Conductor Edward Wellis, near the Decatur depot, who lay very ill of inflammatory rheumatism. After saying some instructions with his patient he got into his buggy and started his horse homeward.

Sudden death, like a stroke of lightning, overtook him, probably before he had driven more than a few hundred yards, and the late living, speaking human being, who a few moments before had talked calmly and quietly, after his usual manner, to a patient and that patient's family, and had even joked with a little boy whom he met by the street side as he entered his buggy, still sat stark and stiff upright upon his seat, the reins clutched in his hands, staring eyes looking out upon the street driving homeward—a corpse. Father of us all! what was it that those who met that horse and vehicle saw in the face of the driver that made them shudder and hurry on a little faster? Death looked out from those lifeless eyes, and it was he who guided the unknowing horse, plodding on to his late master's door, and those who looked into that vehicle felt a something awful and indefinable, and made them shudder, perhaps, and hasten involuntarily forward.

The horse drew up at the familiar hitching post, but no master descended and he stood gently pawing the ground, anon jerking the lines, but he got no answer to these signals, however oft repeated. No familiar voice which had so often chided or cheered him in long jaunts. Then he pricked back his ears and jerked the reins a little harder, and listened, but there was no response, save the grating of the leather over the dash board. What could it all mean. And now Mrs. Burdett looks out of the window and says, "Well, I declare, the Doctor's come, but why don't he get out?" She looks a moment, but he does'nt move, and she says, perhaps he wants something, and then she trips out to the street, looks up into the buggy and says, "Well, William, what is it?" No answer. And then she bends forward a little, and the light shines fuller on the figure there. It is her husband, but the face is livid and the eyes blindly staring. "William! oh, William!" And she grasps him by the hands, still clutching the reins; they are cold and stiff. He is dead.

Through the assistance of several gentlemen Dr. Burdett's body was taken into the house, where Coroner Brien held an inquest over his remains. The jury returned a verdict that he came to his death from disease of the heart.

3/31/71 Washingtonian

WASHINGTONIAN.

Local Items.

The History of White's Battalion.—We have procured from the Agent a copy of this history, which will be read with interest by those who will wish to read the story of the adventures of this gallant Battalion. It is told in a pleasant and agreeable manner by the author—at times sketching in a lively and graphic manner the adventures and achievments of those who composing the command. It is well printed and neatly bound in cloth.

(Lige White's batallion was called the "Comanchees" and they fought often with the local pro northern group, the Loudoun Rangers. Hard feelings persisted among these groups after the war, and this book, written by confederate officer Frank Myers, had most of its 1ˢᵗ edition stolen.)

"The Comanches."

THE publishers will shortly issue the history of the 35th Battalion Virginia Cavalry C. S. A. familiarly known as "White's Battalion, from its commander, Col. Elijah V. White.

It is a work of over 300 pages and contains the history of this famous command during in the period of its existence, from the formation of its first Company in 1861, to the Surrender of Gen. Lee's army.

It shows the operations of the "Ashby Brigade" during the two years that the 35th Va., Cav. formed a portion of that gallant command, giving the only published account of the great expedition of Gen. W. E. Jones through West Va., when the Kanawha river was set on fire, and also the connection of the cavalry with the campaigns of the A. N. V.

The history of the Battalion as partizan rangers on the Potomac border, and along the army lines of Banks, Pope, McClellan and other Federal commanders, together with the experience of its men as Scouts, guides and couriers for Generals Jackson and Ewell is given, and the MSS. is highly endorsed by the officers of the Battalion who have examined it. Written by FRANK M. MYERS, Late Capt. Co. A. 35th Va., Cav.

Orders addressed to the author will be promptly attended to. The price of the work is $2.00. Agents wanted: For terms &c., address

F. M. MYERS,
Waterford, Loudoun Co., Va.

3/31/71 Washingtonian

The New Ku-Klux Bill.

The *Alex. Gaz.* gives the following synopsis of this bill

The bill reported by the Select Committee in relation to alleged "outrages" in the South, provides additional powers for the President, authorizing him to declare when insurrection shall exist in the contemplation of the act and to so declare by proclamation, and to then use the military at his discretion, and declare martial law as exigencies may require. It further provides that the President need not await a requisition from the State for troops, but that he may be the judege as to whether the State authorities are powerless or neglectful in the premises,

The Ku-Klux Epidemic.

Admitting that there are disorders in the South, says the New York Herald, and particularly in South Carolina, it is worthy of notice however, that the reported Ku-Kluk terrible outrages are always made to assume a formidable character at the time of elections in the North, and when radical politicians are pressed for issues before the people. Conservative men who have just come through the Southern States were astonished to hear when they arrived at the North the frightful stories of Ku-Klux enormities. We are inclined to think there is much more political smoke than real fire in these reports.

Troops in South Carolina.

The Carolina Spartan, in noticing the arrival of a company of United States soldiers at Spartansburg, on Thursday, says:

"—We are certain they have never seen a more quiet place than our town has been since their arrival. We are not informed at whose instance they were sent here, or the cause of their comeing. Our county has been very quite for several weeks, so far as we know, and we had concluded that bayonets were hardly necessary preserve law and order' here. However, we do not object to their presence, as they are a gentlemanly and well-disciplined body of men under the command of an accomplised officer, whose stay among us we hope will be pleasant."

8

HARD TIMES.

"Hard Times," the Richmond *Enquirer* says "has been the cry since Jacob set out to make his way in the world." Times doubtless are hard where there are many daughters in a family. Times are obliged to be hard when our women spend so much on dress. If they would be content to dress as their mothers dressed, we would hear less about the expense of living. A woman's head-gear in town costs now about $100 a year—and what do they look like? They go on the streets encompassed about the head with the weight of twenty horse-tails. Our young men, too, on $600 a year smoke cigars at ten, fifteen, and twenty cents apiece, with gloves at $3 a pair.

It is evident to us that the South is rallying and that, although we make no cotton in Virginia, that Virginia is rallying. There has been a silent, steady progress. Of course men have to struggle—they always have struggled; but we are getting along and overcoming difficulties. Our white people have gone to work, they are learning not to be above working in the fields; many farmers are gradually introducing white labor on their farms: The movement in railroads is an evidence of the healthy state of things in Virginia. We are doing more in this respect than we ever did before the war. By next Christmas we shall have an all-rail line from Richmond to Washington. We shall have soon a great and quick through line from the South to Richmond. The Chesapeake and Ohio company, in twelve months, will have established a communication between Richmond and the far West. General Mahone is pushing his line into Kentucky. The Pennsylvania Central is at work on the Shenandoah Valley railroad. We shall soon have a line from from Danville to Lynchburg and from Danville to Bristol. The Valley road will soon be completed to Lexington. The James River and Kanawha canal begins to see day-light. In addition we shall ere long have narrow gauge roads affording facilities to regions of country not traversed by the the main lines. There are signs, too, that the Republican party is on the wane.

These things ought to encourage us. We have much to be grateful for. in the place of our perpetual grumbling. Every man who is free from the tooth-ache ought to feel thankful. How much worse things might have been; how much worse it seemed a few years ago.

Our Farmers are now in the midst of harvest. Throughout the county, the reapers are busily engaged in gathering the golden sheaves, and from all quarters comes the gladdening assurance that the yield is "very good," and the quality of the grain greatly better than for several years. The season too, is most auspicious. The past week we have had several delightful showers that have infused life and vigor to the growing corn and oats, and afforded the harvesters a cool and pleasant atmosphere for the prosecution of their labors. From present indications the industrious husbandman is this year reaping rich rewards from the fruits of the earth.

DEATH OF C. L. VALLANDIG-HAM

The death of this gentleman, the particulars of which are given in another Column, will cause a pang of sorrow in the breast of every one throughout the land who appreciates great intellect—sterling worth, and bold and fearless independence. The New York Herald says:

With the bold and robust character of the Western man there was united the high tone, generous impulse and refinement of the old Southern school of statesman. He may have erred during the rebellion; but are we sure that he erred?

CINCINNATI June 16.—Mr Clement L Vallandigham, of the counsel for the defense of Thos. McGahan, now on trial at Lebanon, Ohio for murder, accidentally shot himself to-night.

CINCINNATI June 18 — A later despatch from Lebanon says Mr. Vallandigham was vomiting which was regarded as an unfavorable symptons, and one of his physicians said there were indications of internal hemorrhage. The doctors ceased their fruitless search about an hour after the accident. They then closed the wound, and placed the patient on his right side. He was calm and collected.

It appears that no one was present with Mr. Vallandigham when the accident occurred but ex-Lieutenant Governor McBurney who has been associated with him in the defence of McGehan. Mr. McBurney had expressed some doubts as to the theory that Myers had shot himself. Mr. Vallandigham picked up a pistol from a table saying he would show him in a half a second.. Two pistols were on the table one unloaded, and he by mistake took up the loaded one, and put it in his pocket and withdrew it, keeping the muzzle next to his body

Just as it was leaving his pocket it was discharged, it is reported at nearly the same part of the body where Myers was shot. He ejaculated, "Oh, murder" and said he had taken the wrong pistol. While the examination was going on, he watched the surgeons with eager eyes and even assisted them in searching for the ball.

LEBANON Ohio June 18 — Hon. Clement L. Vallandigham who accidently shot himself on Friday, died at 9.45 o'clock on Saturday. He went down very rapidly after three o'clock, having no pulse scarcely after that hour. Mr. Dawson, of Cincinnati, arrived at 3 o'clock, but was too late to do any good for the dying man. Judge Haynes, his law partner, from Dayton, reached Lebanon Saturday morning with other personal friends, who were with him in his last hours. McGehan in prosecution in whose case he lost his life, was taken from jail on Saturday morning to the bedside, and shed tears as he beheld the dying friend who had appeared during the progress of the trial to surrender all his energy and legal acumen in his defense.

Wednesday Morning, June 28, 1871

The funeral of the late C. L. Vallandigham took place at Dayton on Tuesday 20th and was of the most imposing character.—The procession was two miles long, and was composed of persons of all political parties and professions. Business in many parts of the city was suspended during the passage of the cortege.—The county, city and many private buildings were draped in mourning. Many distinguished gentlemen from all parts of the Union were present.

Not the least of the sadness that attaches to the melancholy event of Mr. C's death, is the fact that Mrs. Vallandigham, who was absent at the time, attending the funeral of her brother, John Y. L. McMahon, has returned to her home so completely prostrated that the most serious consequences are feared. She fails to recognize her most intimate friends watching by her bedside. By many it is feared she has lost or will lose her reason, while others declare that her death is merely a matter of brief time. A telegram of the 23d says "Mrs Vallendigham is much worse to-day, It has been deemed necessary to summon additional medical aid. She has repeated spasms, and her mind wanders to such an extent that her friends are apprehensive of the most serious consequences. To-day she is constantly calling for Clement, asking friends by her bedside "Why don't Clement come home."

In nearly every large conflict, the civil liberties of the citizen suffer, often to the extent of the war's duration and degree of violence. Consider our Civil War and the suspension of the writ of *habeas corpus*. Vallandigham was the leader of the Copperheads, a vociferous antiwar group who severely criticized Lincoln's policies. At one time he was arrested by General Burnside, but the sentence was commuted by the President. Copperhead influence waned as the North's fortunes improved.

6/21/71 Mirror

GREELY on CARPET BAGGERS

Horace Greely has just completed an extended tour in the South and upon his return to New York met with quite an ovation from the Republican Association of that city — He made them a speech, in the course of which he said —

Well, gentlemen, the thieving carpet-baggers are a mournful fact; they do exist there, and I have seen them [Laughter] They are fellows who crawled down South in the track of our armies, generally a very safe distance in the rear, some of them on sutlers wagons, some bearing cotton permits, some of them looking sharply to see what may turn up.

Some of them got elected Senators, others Representatives some sheriffs, some Judges and so on. And there they stand right in the publics eyes stealing and plundering, many of them with both both arms around negroes and their hands in their rear pockets seeing if they could pick a paltry dollar out of them, and the public looks at them, does not regard the honest Northern men but calls every "carpet-bagger" a their, which is not the truth by a good deal. But these fellows — many of them long faced and with eyes rolled up are greatly concerned for the education of the blacks and for the education of their souls. [Great laughter] Let us pray," they say. But they spell pray with an e.

CARPET-BAGGERS and SETTLERS

We observe that ex-Governor HUMPHREYS of Mississippi, has been interviewed by a New York *Herald* reporter, and are struck with what he is reported as saying about the disposition of the Southern people towards Northern men who come among them. He makes the distinction between the the mercenary carpet-bagger and the honest settler, which all right-minded Southern people make.

"How can the people of the North expect that embers of the rebellion, will ever be quenched so long as they pile that foul mess of driftwood from the North known as the carpet-baggers, on those embers. Withdraw that 'driftwood' and restore local self-government to the people of the South is all that is needed to quench the embers of rebellion forever."

THE MIRROR.

WEDNESDAY,...............JULY 5

LIME! LIME!!

Messrs. H. K. Smith & Co, take pleasure in announcing to the public that they now have completed every arrangement for conducting the Lime business—that hereafter they will continue to manufacture at their Kilns on the Potomac, the best quality of Lime, which can be had at their Warehouse in Leesburg.

The Fourth.—Although our business houses were not closed on Tuesday, business generally was at a stand still. There was a celebration at Guilford Station, to which point some of our citizens repaired, while others hied then to the mountains or the river.

Destroyed by Lightning.—We are sorry to hear that the barn on the farm recently owned by the late JOHN JONES, Sr., on Broad Run, a few miles below Leesburg, was struck by Lightning about 7 o'clock on Saturday morning last, and entirely destroyed. Whether there was any other loss of property we did not learn.

A "loose horse," made his appearance on King street, one day last week, and after a few wild antics, made a rush through the back door, for BASSELL's Cheap Store, in a manner "most fearful to see." He mounted the counter, and taking a survey of the establishment must have become disgusted with what he saw, as he soon thereafter yielded to surrounding circumstances, and was led hence, no doubt to the great relief of the knights of the yard-stick.

The Leesburg Academy.—The final exercises of this Institution, for the past scholastic year, were held at Academy Hall, on Friday night last, June 30th. The exercises were opened with an appropriate prayer from the Rev. Dr. HEAD, after which the Principal, Mr. THOS. WILLIAMSON, gave a brief but exceedingly clear statement of the management of the school, and the proficiency and standing of each scholar.—A handsome gold medal was awarded to Master EDWARD STANSBURY, for punctuality and good behavior. Rev. Mr. DAVIS made the presentation speech, and accompanied it with a few happily conceived and excellently expressed suggestions, calculated to inspire the young minds.

More Horse Stealing—We understand that two horses were last week stolen from a couple of gentlemen living in the Lovettsville neighborhood immediate chase was given, and on Friday, a young man named CHARLES COPPER, was arrested and lodged in the jail of Jefferson county. W. Va., charged with the offence, where he is now confined, awaiting the requisition of the Governor of this State, when he will be returned to Loudoun for examination and trial.

Small-Pox and Taxes—Our august legislators, in framing the present Public School law of the State, very properly determined that those who enjoy the benefit of a free education must at least pay taxes and keep clear of the Small-pox,—and therefore provided, that no child shall be admitted into the public schools "whose father, if he be alive, and resident within the school district, and not a pauper, shall not have paid the capitation tax in aid of public free schools last assessed on him." —and that "no pupil shall be admitted unless they have been vaccinated " The public schools of this county will be resumed about the first of September, and we are authorized to say that the above requirement will be rigidly adhered to.

A Free University.

The Richmond *Enquirer* learns from the University of Virginia, that the Society of Alumni, at its recent meeting, had under discussion a proposition looking to the conversion of this institution into a Free University for the young men of this State. The idea suggested was to have the University made a part of the Free School system of the State, to increase the annuity from $15,000 to $30,000, and to admit all young men from Virginia to the schools of the University without charges for tuition The *Enquirer* warmly urges the adoption of such a course and says. At present the poor young men of the State are, to a great extent, cut off from the higher education, because they cannot raise some $300 or $400 a year to spend at the University. Of course all who go there must be expected to board and clothe themselves.

13

7/5/71 Mirror

Hamilton & Rawdon's combined Exhibition, gave two entertainments in this town on Saturday, both of which were well attended. After the performance at night, the Indians gave themselves up to the sports of frontier life, and for awhile blows fell thick and fast among them, which finally resulted in the Chief's being carried to the little caboose over the hill, where he was detained until Sunday afternoon. After the arrest of the Chief, everything remained "serene," until the departure of the entire Company at daylight Monday morning.

7/8/71 Washingtonian

SECRETS OF THE CIRCUS.

A Chicago reporter has penetrated behind that mysterious curtain whence all the splendors and wonders of the circus issue, and thus sets down what he discovered —The dressing room was occupied by a dozen or fifteen performers in the operation of preparing for their respective acts. Some were naked, and upon their bodies, in every conceivable place appeared formidable bandages and plasters. They were from strains and bruises, of which every one had his share at that. One of these gentlemen a well-known bareback and four-horse rider while in the act of putting on a pair of elastic knee-caps, to strengthen his knees, explained that the most serious strain resulting from riding and tumbling came upon the kidneys, which were often badly injured. The breast was also strained at times, though not so frequently. Such trivial matters as shoulder and ankle sprains were continually occurring and unworthy of notice. Heaps of porus plasters and quantities of glycerine enough to stock an apothecary's shop were used by a circus company in one season. There are at present, he said, forty travelling circuses in the United States, involving a capital of several millions, and affording employment for several thousand people, most of them trained to fit as a trade. The complete outfit of a first class circus includes all the necessaries for the foundation of a colony. The number of people employed is generally about 100. From 100 to 150 animals make up the complement of live stock when there is no menagerie attached.

Traveling companies lay out their campaigns with all the care that an army takes in preparing for a long march. The minutest details, which would be entirely overlooked by an inexperienced person we arranged with the utmost precision. Even the arrangements for feeding and watering the stock are made with a wonderful nicety The tour of a circus during six months, extending over thousands of miles is sometimes made with little deviation from the plan laid out before the start.

Before starting, each individual his an opportunity to eat what is called breakfast. He then gets on the most convenient wagon, generally knowing by experience the most comfortable loads for sleeping purposes as the only time which the circus man gets for indulging in the balmy is while the caravan is on a move.

The clown of to-day is generally an old performer, who, having matured in the circus business, has adopted this easier branch of the trade. His jokes are carefully prepared by another and committed to memory, and his very antics are but the ghostly spectres of his past agility. The salary of a circus performer is about equal to that of an actor, although it is larger per week during the season, which is generally thirty weeks. Stars get sometimes as high as $150, but of course this is exceptional. The average of riders and acrobats is $40 per week. Clowns get an average of $50. The drivers of eight, six and four horses receive from $30 to $50 a month, and the less important of the assistants in all the departments from $15 to $30 a month, according to the value of their services.

THE MIRROR,

WEDNESDAY,..............AUGUST 23

The Camp meeting for Hillsborough circuit, in this county, was commenced on Friday last. We understand that there are between thirty and forty tents, and that the meeting grows every day more interesting. On Sunday an immense crowd was on the ground, many of them doubtless attracted thither under the expectation of hearing a sermon from Rev. Dr. Munsey, a report to that effect having been generally circulated. In his absence, however, Rev. Dr. Bennett preached in the morning; Rev. Dr. Granberry, in the afternoon, and Rev. Dr. Head at night—thus amply repaying those who had endured the dust and heat of the day in anticipation of listening to the great Munsey. A number of the ablest divines of the church are expected to be present during the continuance of the meeting. So far, the best of order has been observed.

Sudden Death on the Camp-Ground —We regret to learn that the Camp-Ground near Hillsborough, was on Sunday the scene of a most sad and melancholy event. It seems that Mr. Robt White, an old and much esteemed citizen of Georgetown, a gentleman upwards of eighty years age, of had visited Loudoun a few days previous for the purpose of being once more present at an old fashioned Methodist Camp-meeting at the home of his early life. He was in the altar attending morning love-feast, in which he seemed much interested, and gave in his religious experience. At the conclusion of his remarks he took his seat, and in five minutes was a corpse. His sudden death cast a gloom over those present, and much sympathy was manifested for his immediate relations and friends, many of whom were on the ground.

Mr. White was for many years a successful merchant in Georgetown,—at different periods Mayor of the city, and Collector of the Port, and in all the relations of life maintained the character of a high toned, christian gentleman.

9/27/71 Mirror

—A man broke a chair over his wife's head a week or two ago. When he got to jail, and the clergyman undertook to talk with him, he displayed a good deal of penitence. He said he was very sorry that he had permitted his anger to obtain the mastery of him, and to suffer him to do such an act, because it was a good chair, one of those old fashioned chairs which was an heirloom in his family, and he was sure he could never replace it.

Leesburg
Female Institute,
1871-'72:

THE FOURTH ANNUAL SESSION of this School will

Open Wednesday, Sept. 20th, 1871, and

Close Wednesday, June 22th, 1872,

embracing a period of forty weeks.

The services of Miss LATHAM in the English and Mathematical Departments, and those of Miss NEY in Music and French, both these ladies having heretofore given eminent satisfaction, have been secured for the ensuing session.

THE CURRICULUM COMPRISES:

The English Department, including:

1. The Primary Division—Spelling, Reading, Writing, Dictation, Definitions. Grammar, Geography, Arithmetic and History.

2. The Collegiate Division—The foregoing studies continued, Rhetoric, Composition, Analysis, History of English Literature, Natural Philosophy, Chemistry, Physiology, and Astronomy.

The Department of Ancient and Modern Languages, including, particularly, the Latin Language with selections from authors of the Augustan Age, Mythology, History of Roman Literature, Roman Antiquities, and Ancient Geography; and the French Language and Literature. Greek, German, and Italian, if desired.

The Department of Mathematics, including a full course of Oral and Written Arithmetic, Algebra, Geometry and Plane Trigonometry.

The Ornamental Department, including Music as a Science, Solfeggio or Singing at Sight, Vocal Culture, Music on the Piano, Drawing, Painting and Embroidery.

A Normal Department, in which young ladies will receive instruction specially designed to fit them for the profession of Teaching, will hereafter be added.

Parents are invited to consider well the propriety of keeping their means and influence within their own neighborhood, building up home institutions, and patronizing schools near their own doors, rather than commit themselves to the policy of sending abroad they know not where, committing their dearest interests to they know not whom, incurring unnecessary expense, and at last procuring superficial embellishments, instead of that true adorning that wears and wins.

Young Ladies that Board with the Principal, will have the benefit of his constant supervision, and to secure a place in his family, immediate application should be made.

THE SESSION IS DIVIDED INTO TWO TERMS OF TWENTY WEEKS EACH.

CHARGES PER TERM,
Payable in Advance

Preparatory Department	$20 00
Collegiate	25 00
Ancient and Modern Languages, each.	12 50
Drawing Painting and Embroidery, each	12 50
Music on Piano	25 00
Use of Piano, for practice	5 00
Sacred Music, no charge except for books, say	1 00
Board, with Washing, Fuel and Lights	100 00

N. B.—Unless in compliance with parents' wishes to the contrary, boarders in his family will be expected to attend Church and Sabbath School with the Principal.

Parents must designate what visitors, if any, from home, or elsewhere, their daughters are to be permitted to see.

july 29 tf   WM. B. CARR, Principal.

LOVETTSVILLE SCHOOL FOR
Girls,

WILL be re-opened the 2nd MONDAY in SEPTEMBER, (the 11th.) Charges made from this date. Board and Tuition at $150 for ten months—$50 in advance.

Extra charge for washing and for fuel used in school rooms; also, for any incidentals.

Application made to
     Miss CLAPHAM, Principal.

N. B.—Music (Piano) taught in the village.

july 22-tsept8

9/13/71 Mirror

THE SUNDAY QUESTION.

From the Louisville Ledger.

The question concerning the compulsory observance of the Sabbath is exciting discussion in the secular press. and at some points it will shape the contest between the political parties. It seems like a waste of time to discuss the question in its strictly ecclesiastical relations. The Bible speaks in no dubious language on this subject. The Sabbath day is so interwoven with the very existence of the church. and so necessary to the observance of the ordinances of the church. that to dispute its binding authority over the consciounces of Christians is simply to dispute the authority of Christianity itself.

But the passage of laws and ordinances by the State. compelling it observance after a certain fashion. is quite another question. Our view of Christianity in its practical operation as a remedial scheme and promoter of virtue among men. embraces the idea of free acceptance on the part of all who are to obey its precepts. It addresses itself to the free and untrammeled choice of men. There can be no acceptance that is pleasing to its author but a willing acceptance. Now. while it would be a happy thing if all men would accept it, and live in obedience to its requirement. yet the fact stares us in the face that they do not do it. To force upon men the outward observance of what they inwardly detest would not and could not make them virtuous. This being the case. it is scarcely worthwhile for the arm of the law to be raised with its penal sanctions to legislate piety into men.

8/12/71 Washingtonian

☞A number of highly respectable ladies. of Washington, who take an active interest In public affairs, have discovered that a bill has been quietly passed through the Territorial Council which substantially adopts for Washington what is known as the St. Louis system for regulating houses of ill-fame. These ladies strongly oppose this measure and have set to work to defeat it in the Lower House of the Legislature.

9/13/71 Mirror

COLORED BISHOPS ON THE RACE QUESTION

The Indiana Conference of African Methodists held its yearly session in Chicago last week, and the white Methodist pastors sent a committee of their number to extend a fraternal welcome. The Chairman of the committee Rev. Dr. Reid, of the Northwestern Christian Advocate, in the course of his speeches expressed a hope and belief that the white and black Methodists would soon be united under one roof-tree. This brought up Bishop Brown, who said that for fifty years the colored body had been on the defensive. They were willing to bury the tomahawk. But there would have to be a deal more courting before the proposed marriage could be consummated. All he wanted was freedom to do as he pleased in a free country. There had been a damnable heresy in the Church which prevented the black man from kneeling at the same alter. or attending the same church. and for his part he really needed a great deal of grace from God to forget all the injuries received at the hand of the white man He did not like to see his white brethren dodge from one sidewalk to the other when they saw him coming. His people were willing to exchange visits with the white people, but he feared he might backslide some if forced to remain under the same roof-tree. Bishop Campbell followed in the same vein. He loved the Methodist Church. But he was not educated yet up to the point of union with it — nor were his white brethren. He believed, however, that the time would come when the latter would recognize the fact that Brother Brown and Brother Campbell could preach a tolerably good sermon.

9/13/71 Mirror

A man in Galveston the other day who complained of being over-heated effected a permanent cure by drinking six glasses of ice water without the aid of a physician He was cool when the coroner came.

Newspaper-writers will thoroughly appreciate the following o'er true tale, which we take from the Philadelphia *Dispatch* :

"A week or two ago one of our reporters had occasion to refer to a certain woman whom we will call Hannah Smith, as a denizen of the Eleventh Ward.' A day or two afterward a huge man entered the office with his brow clothed with thunder. In his hand he carried a fearful club, and at his side trotted a bull dog whom hunger had evidently made desperate.— With that quick appreciation of the situation which is creditable to the superior intelligence of educated men, the editor of this paper and the proprietors darted to the window, climbed outside, slid down the lightning-rod, and went across the street to watch the bloody fray through a spy glass. With the fearlessness of conscience innocence we sat still, merely inserting our legs in two sections of stove pipe to guard against any misapprehension of facts on the part of the bull-dog. The man with the club approached.

"Are you the editor?" he asked, spitting on his hand and grasping his club. We told him that the editor was out—that he had gone to the North pole with Captain Hall and that he would not return before 1876, in time for the centennial celebration.

"Are you the proprietor?" asked the man.

We explained to him that we were not ; that the proprietors were also out ; that they had gone to South America for the purpose of investigating the curative properties of cundurango, and they expected to remain there for several years.

"Well, whoever you are." exclaimed the warrior, "my name is Smith !"

We told him we were glad ; because, if there was one thing better than the possession of the name of Smith, it was the privilege of knowing a man by that name. "But Smith," we said, "why this battle array ? It is absurd for a man to put on the panoply of war and frisk into editors' sanctum fumbling a club and accompanied by a disheartening bull-dog simply because his name happens to be Smith "

"He said he called in to burst the head of the man who had insulted his sister.

"It is impossible, Smith, that such a thing could have been done by any one in this office."

"Is, but it was, though ; and her name was published, too ! Miss Smith—Miss *Hanner* Smith !"

"May we be permitted to inquire, Mr Smith, what was the precise character of the affront offered to Hannah ?"

"Well, you see," said Smith "the black-guard said she was a denizen. And I want you to understand." exclaimed Smith, becoming excited, and brandishing his club in a wild manner over our head, while the bull-dog advanced and commenced to sniff up and down our stove pipe— I want you to understand that she is a decent young woman, with a good character, and none of your denizens and such truck. The man who says she is a denizen is a blackguard and a thief and I'll smash him over the nose if I get a chance. They may say what they please about me, but the man who abuses my sister has got to suffer." And Smith struck the table in a violent manner with his club, while the bull-dog put his fore-legs upon the back of our chair.

We pacified Smith with a dictionary. We pointed out to that raging warrior that the Websterian definition of the word "denizen" gives such a person an unoffending character and deprives the term of everything like reproach. Smith said he was satisfied; and he shook hands and kicked the bull-dog down stairs.

CHICAGO.

10/18/71 Mirror

Full Particulars of the Conflagration

A Connected Narrative—Origin and Progress of the Fire—Vivid Description—Scenes, Incidents, &c.

The following is a report of the fire and its incidents, specially described for the Associated Press by those who witnessed and fought the flames throughout :

Late on Sunday evening a boy went into a stable on DeKaven street, near the river, on the west side, to milk a cow, carrying with him a kerosene lamp.

This was kicked over by the cow, and the burning fluid scattered among the straw. This was the beginning of the great fire. A single extinguisher on the ground, or active work by the police in tearing down one or two shanties would have prevented the spreading of the flames, but the engines were waited for, and when they arrived

THE FIREMEN. STUPEFIED

by their exertions at the first fire, on Saturday night, worked slowly and clumsily. Their effo is were unavailing. The wind blew a gale from the southwest.

Rapidly the flames shot from house to house and from board yard to board yard having meanwhile crossed the river north of Twelfth street to the south side, and made for the brick and stone business blocks, the railroad freight depots and manufacturing establishments — The full extent of the danger was now realized for the first time.

The fire department, already tired out, worked like heroes and the mayor and city government, that had supinely rested now began to exert themselves, but the opportunity had been lost.

A LOST OPPORTUNITY.

The time when thorough organization could have blown up the buildings or prepared for emergency was neglected, and it was now a fight for life.

The wind blowing a stiff gale had possession of the flame , and the beautiful buildings, Chicago's Glory, lay before them, Harrison, Van Buren, Adams, Monroe and Madison streets were soon reached, the intervening blocks from the river to Dearborn street on the east being consumed. Three-quarters of a mile of brick blocks were consumed as if by magic.

UNCONSCIOUS VICTIMS

It being Sunday, proprietors and employees were at home utterly unconscious of what was taking place. Those who saw the flames supposed it was the remains of Saturday night's fire and having confidence in the fire department, were unconcerned, but between eleven and twelve o'clock a rumor got abroad that the fire was in the business-portion of the city.

Then the people commenced moving. Horses were brought into requisition to take proprietors and others to the conflagration. What a scene met their gaze! The board of trade court house, West on Union Telegraph and Associated Press office, and hundreds of other buildings were all in flame

The air was filled with live coals, which were hurled to north and east a becon of destruction. Fire engines were powerless for saving: All that the men could do was to blow up buildings, but this availed but little.

The Times Tribune, Post, Republican, Journal, and other newspaper offices, Western News Company, Black, Field & Lettler's establishment, the Drake block, recently built, and Farwell & Co's. all were soon in ashes

QUICK DESTRUCTION.

It seemed that no sooner had the flame struck a wall then it went directly through, and a very few minutes sufficed to destroy the most elaborately built structures. The walls melted and the very bricks were consumed. The wooden pavements took fire, making a continuous sheet of flame two miles long and a mile wide. No human being could possibly survive many minutes. Block after block fell, and red hot coals shot higher and higher and spread farther and farther until the north side was a vast sheet of flame from river to lake. At one time it so hemmed the people that it was expected thousands must perish. The Sherman, Tremont and other hotels were emptied of their guests.

A patrol of men, under Samuel Medill, swept off live coals and put out flames inside the walls and another lot of men under the direction of Hon. Joseph Medill.

watched the roofs. At half past seven o'clock this appeared safe, and most of the men went to get rest and food. A number went to sleep in the Tribune building. But there was

A CHANGE OF THE WIND

The flames reached Wabash avenue, State street and Michigan avenue. Soon after Mc-Vicker's Theatre caught fire. In a few moments the Tribune building was in flames, and at the last moment the sleeping men were aroused and rescued from the flames. By ten o'clock in the forenoon this remaining block was in ashes.

Now was to be seen the most remarkable sight ever beheld in this or any country. There were from 50,000 to 75,000 men, women and children fleeing by every available street and alley to the southward and westward attempting to save their clothing and their lives.

Every available vehicle was brought into requisition for use, for which enormous prices were paid, and the streets and sidewalks presented a fearful sight. Thousands of persons and horses inextricably commingled.

The Fire Still Raging.

Scarcely had the flames of the above fire been suppressed than another conflagration, more terrible than the first, made its appearance in the western section of the city, which soon spread with the rapidity of lightning, until almost the whole city was enveloped in flames. We glean the following from dispatches.

CHICAGO, October 9—2 A.M.—The fire is still raging with increased fury, and spreads with almost the velocity of the wind. The district already burned embraces an immense number of lumber yards and the freight depots of the Chicago and St. Louis and Pittsburg, Fort Wayne and Chicago railroads.

The property already destroyed counts up many millions of dollars, and perhaps half is not told

The task of arresting the flames now seems five-fold greater than an hour ago, and no one dares venture the opinion as to where and when it will stop.

The flames are raging with increased fury in every direction, and God's mercy can only save the city from utter destruction.

A fearful panic prevails through the streets where the people are rushing to and fro, weeping and wailing.

The prospects are that the gas-house will be destroyed and the city wrapped in darkness It now looks as if the whole city will be destroyed. Large numbers of lives have been lost but how many cannot be known till the fire is arrested.

Vessels in the river are catching fire in every direction, and all in South river will probably be destroyed.

A raging, roaring hell of fire envelops twenty blocks of the city, and is already within a block of the Western Union Telegraph office, where this dispatch is written sweeping onward as a whirlwind of flame, against which human efforts are powerless and it is impossible to tell where it will stop.

The bridge across Van Buren street is burned.

The cars on the Chicago and Alton and Fort Wayne railroads, with the freight houses, have been swept away.

NEW YORK October 9.—There is no telegraph communication with Chicago. The flames reached the telegraph office, which was abandoned at 2.15 A.M. Chicago time, and since which no telegraph has been received.

The Awful Work of Destruction.

CHICAGO. October 9—5 o'clock P.M.—The awful work of destruction still goes on with relentless fury from Harrison street in the south to Division street in the North, and from the river to the lake, an area of four miles long by one mile wide. The flames have swept everything before them. It is estimated that at least 100,000 people are homeless and in a suffering condition. The streets in the districts still unburned are lined for miles with such household goods as have been saved from destruction. Most generous offers of assistance in money, food or anything wanted, are coming in from almost every city or town throughout the country by telegraph.

Reliable gentlemen just arrived from the north division bring the joyful intelligence that the water works are uninjured. God grant that it may prove true.

PILLAGE AND EMPLOYMENT.

Fears are entertained that the desperate distress of so many will create squads of pillagers and that life will not be safe. To relieve these Gen Sheridan is telegraphing for more troops, and special public forces are being organized by the citizens. The only effectual remedy is to find employment for the thousands who would work if they could.

20

The following proclamation has been issued by the Mayor of Chicago:—

The Mayor of Chicago is happy to be able to announce that the city remains quiet and peaceable. There is no lawlessness, incendiarism or riotous conduct, and order reigns supprime. Life and property are secure as before the burning of the city. The Government, in all its departments, is in full and comple operation. None of our inhabitants are without shelter of some kind.

CHICAGO.

10/25/71 Mirror

The Chicago *Tribune*, of October 19th, has the following:

WHAT IS SPARED US.

"Our columns have been so extensively occupied during the past week with reports of the enormous losses of life and property in the late fire that there is some danger that the damage sustained will be over-estimated. True, we have seen 2,500 acres in the most central portion of the city swept bare, 20,000 buildings destroyed, and 100,000 persons rendered homeless, the total pecuniary loss being not less than

THREE HUNDRED MILLION DOLLARS.

but we have still a great deal left. We may roughly estimate the situation as follows:

"Above 50,000 persons have left the city; population remaining, 280,000.

"Five grain elevators were burned, with 1,800,000 bushels of grain; leaving us with eleven grain warehouses intact, containing 5,000,000 bushels.

"One-half of our stock of pork products were burned up, with the same proportion of flour.

"Of lumber, 50,000,000 feet were burned; the stock remaining is 240,000,000 feet.

"Of coal, 80,000 tons were burned up; we have 76,000 tons on hand.

"Our stock of leather was decreased one-quarter, the value of that burned up being $95,000.

"The greater portion of the stocks of groceries, dry goods, and boots and shoes were burned up, with more than one-half the ready made clothing; but the quantities destroyed were scarcely equal to more than a three weeks' supply, and are now being rapidly replaced.

NOT MORE THAN TEN PER CENT

of the currency was destroyed by the fire, we have 30,000 houses left standing, and our real estate could not burn up.

"A careful average of these larger items, with smaller ones that need not be enumerated, shows that the city of Chicago has suffered a loss of not less than 20, nor more than 25, per cent. on her total assets—real and personal.

CHURCHES DESTROYED IN CHICAGO.—A list of the churches destroyed in the Chicago fire shows the following classification: Baptist 4, Congregational 3, Protestant Episcopal 6, Evangelical and Lutheran 9, Jewish 2, Methodist 10, Presbyterian 8, Roman Catholic (including convents) 14, Swedenborgian 2, Unitarian 1, Universalist 1—total 60. There were also several mission establishments not included in the above enumeration.

The *Bath-Rooms* at the Leesburg Barber Shop, are open every day. Those who wish to enjoy the luxury of a delightful bath can be accommodated by calling at this establishment, which is kept in the best manner. Good health and comfort require frequent bathing this season of the year.

THE MIRROR.

WEDNESDAY,...................Oct. 11

TELEGRAPH TO LEESBURG.

The wires of the Virginia Telegraph Company, reached this place on Saturday, and the battery was at once placed in position—the following telegram, received at this office about 7 o'clock, p. m., from the wide-awake Secretary of the Company, signalizing the event:

By Telegraph from Alexandria:

B. F. SHEETZ.—Alexandria greets your town and hopes that Loudoun will appreciate her enterprise, and treat her better in the next Convention. The line is in operation now and we want it sustained by a liberal use of its wire.   G. C. WEDDERBURN.

Leesburg acknowledges the friendly greeting, and Loudoun rejoices with unselfish joy at each new evidence of Alexandria's enterprise, but cannot acknowledge bad treatment on her part in the late Convention. However, now that communication with our venerable sister is secured by electricity as well as steam, let us hope that the necessities of each may be better understood by the other, and that "peace harmony and fraternal love" may hereafter direct us in all our intercourse.

J. B. McCabe, son of Mr. C. F. McCabe, of this town, had his arm broken last week playing base ball. Wouldn't be surprised to hear next of a juvenile funeral from the same cause.

A youth named ALEXANDER was thrown from the stage in Middleburg on Saturday and his leg broken.

We regret to learn that Mr. Thos. E Taylor, one of the recently nominated candidates for the State Senate, was either thrown from or knocked down by his horse on Saturday night last, and had his shoulder dislocated, and received other painful, though we believe not serious injury.

More Light.— Mr. J. J. Stansbury, to whom was awarded the contract for lighting this town with lamps, has workmen engaged in planting the posts, and as every thing else is in readiness, by the close of the present week, our streets may be traversed "in the night as well as day." Telegraph and street lamps will do for one week.

DIED

Of Diphtheria, on Friday October 13th, 1871, ADA BLANCH, daughter of Thomas B., and Mary J. Camp, aged 5 years, one month and one day.

At Aldie. Va., on the morning of the 22d inst., CHARLES F BERKELEY, in the 38th year of his age.

It affords the writer a melancholy satisfaction to be instrumental in paying a deserved tribute to the memory of the deceased. Brave, generous and just, he never uttered a falsehood, suppressed a truth, or perpetrated an unmanly act. No mean or sordid motive ever actuated him in any of his acts, for he loved right, scorned meanness, and was truly an honest man. In 1861 when the thunder of war was heard, and the chivalry, the valor of the South, was being marshaled in the order of battle, he left the home where his early years were passed in peaceful and tranquil enjoyment, and joined the 8th Va., Regiment, where, for four long years, he discharged his duty as a brave man only can, and won the confidence and respect of his associates, by whom the intelligence of his death will be received with much sorrow. That the great issue of the future was definitely settled in his mind, the writer cannot doubt. His labors now ended, we trust and hope that his spirit may be with him who gave and took it.   P.

(There were four Berkeley brothers in the Eighth VA Regiment which was composed mostly of Loudoun volunteers.)

11/1/71 Mirror

BAYONET RULE IN SOUTH CAR-OLINA.

The proclamation of martial law in South Carolina is already doing its work. More un-just high-handed outrages were never perpe-trated in the name of "liberty," not even in the bloody days of war, than are now being practis-ed in the proscribed counties of South Carolina. No man is safe, and yet the President of the United States, sworn to support its constitution and protect its citizens, is himself the author of this wholesale barbarous exercise of power, by his hireling soldiery. We have not room for all the revolting details of this reign of radical terror, but the following is sufficient :

The Columbia, S .C., *Phœnix*, of October 24, published an extract from a private letter from a prominent citizen of Yorkville, addressed to a gentleman in that city. His letter, which we reprint below, will give some idea of the scenes enacted in York and other counties where the writ of *habeas corpus* has been suspended. No one can fail to appreciate the indignation evinced by the writer, who is known to be a quiet, law-abiding citizen :

YORKVILLE, S. C., October 21, 1871.

* * * * Although I feel secure in my own innocence of any complicity in the causes which have made the pretext for the infamous proceeding inaugurated here by the party in power, yet I cannot but be shocked and feel uneasiness at the total overthrow of all my preconceptions of Republicanism, freedom, and law. Indeed, no stranger to our community could remain here unaffected by the prevailing gloom and sense of insecurity. Every bulwark of civil protection seems leveled, and personal liberty appears now to depend entirely upon the absence of malice on the part of the igno-rant and depraved. No warrants are issued, no charges specified, no authority exhibited; a soldier under arms, sometimes a commission-ed or non commissioned officer, sometimes merely a private, presents himself and orders a march to jail. Arrived there, the prisoner is searched, and then locked up in a cell and told that he can have no source of amusement to while away the time, as he is placed there for punishment and not for pleasure. In some ca-ses a little consideration has been shown, such as time to take leave of wife and children, when convenient; in many others, the "summary process" is most scrupulously adhered to. A case of this kind took place in town to-day.

A Mr Mitchell, highly esteemed as a straight-forward, upright man, by all who know him, came to town last night to attend a Masonic meeting. This morning, while standing in a store, he was arrested by a common soldier, who, after cocking his musket and putting on a fresh cap, ordered him to hold up his hands, and told a negro to search his pockets and dis-arm him. This being done, the doughty sol-dier, with his able assistant, carried the pris-oner to jail. What adds poignancy to this shameful indignity, is the fact that the black ras-cal who took part in it has been strongly sus-pected of having been one of Rose's gang of barn-burners. There are now thirty-two or three in jail; but this number will doubtless be largely increased by morning, as nearly all of the cavalry companies are ranging over the country, and night arrests seem to be in special favor.

All this is bad enough, God knows, but there are consequent evils to be apprehended, which dwarfs it into petty annoyance. The county is being depopulated. Numbers of far-mers and other citizens innocent as well as guil-ty, appalled at the prospect of a long incarcera-tion, a packed jury, an unscrupulous judge, and a ready host of accusing witnesses, eager to swear *according to instructions*, for $2 a day and expenses paid," have left homes and fami-lies just as the threatened danger found them. The matured crops are but half gathered, and unprotected farms stand as tempting baits for the idle negro. It will not be long before lar-ceny, arson, and outrage of every sort will be committed throughout this helpless section. Already the signs of exultation are shown on the faces of the negroes. The town is daily filled with them—many coming to tell their concocted tales of Ku-klux injuries, or to seize the chance of easy vengeance upon those whom they dislike.

It is needless to add that all business and in-dustry are paralized. Through all this, A. S. Wallace, directing and controlling spirit of this scheme of infamous outrage, remains in our midst. He daily airs himself upon our streets, here in the very heart of murder and conspira-cy, as he calls it, and gloats over the verifica-tion of his prophetic threat that "he would yet have this people beneath his heel."

And all this suffering, misery, ruin and des-olation, has been brought about to establish a lie, as is evidenced by the presentment of the grand jury of Chester county, composed of

SIX WHITES AND SIX NEGROES,

who have made a presentment embodying the result of their investigation of the alleged Kuklux outrages there, which concludes as follows "We, the grand jurors, upon our oaths, are compelled to say from the testimony which we have taken, and from our knowledge of the different parts of the county, that the

ALLEGATIONS CONTAINED IN THE PROCLAMATION OF THE PRESIDENT OF THE UNITED STATES ARE WITHOUT FOUNDATION.

and must be the result of falsehood communicated to him by persons equally regardless of good order and the peace of society."

11/15/71 Mirror

EQUINE SAGACITY.—The Layfayette (Indiana) *Courier* gives the following:

A well-known citizen hired a pair of horses and buggy from Nick Hank's livery stable and drove them the direct road to the vicinity of Stockwell, a distance of twelve miles southeast of the city. The horses were hitched to the fence while the gentleman took supper at the residence of a friend. After supper, when ready to start home, it was found that the horses had broken their halters and disappeared. The young man came to the city by the early morning train from Stockwell, and the first thing went to the stable to report the loss of the team. Imagine his suprise at learning that the horses had come to the stable at 3 o'clock in the morning without a driver, and with everything intact, the buggy not even being scratched in the least. They had come alone and undirected except by instinct, twenty-eight miles, that being the distance from Stockwell by the route they had taken. Between Yorktown and Jefferson there is a bridge, out of the floor of which two or three boards had been taken. The horses, instead of trying to cross the bridge, went down one side of the road, crossed the stream and up the bank on the other side, in a track nobody had ever taken before. Mr. Hank informs us that to his knowledge the horses had never passed over the road but once, and that several years since, as they have been in his possession quite a long time.

24

The Democratic Mirror

BENJ. F. SHEETZ, Editor.

Wednesday Morning, Nov. 8th, 1871

A SAD PICTURE.

The Richmond *Enquirer* draws the following sad picture of the condition of affairs in South Carolina. It says : "South Carolina has a Republican governor, a negro for lieutenant-governor. It has four (we believe it is) negro representatives in Congress. It has a Republican Supreme Court, one of whose judges is a negro. The legislature consists of 157 Radicals to 23 Conservatives or Democrats. The whites number in the State 289,000. The negroes amount to 415,000. The negroes have 35,000 majority on the registration books.

The inferior judges, justices, clerks, sheriffs, constables, supervisors, collectors, school trustees, road commissioners, &c., &c. are black or white Radicals.

Is it any wonder the people are flying the State? Was there ever such a state of things before on the face of the earth? The British crown appoints the executive officials in Jamaica, and there is a large property qualification required to vote,

And yet the best thing the government can find to do with these poor, ruined people is to put them in jail, to haul them before negro juries, to govern them with the bayonet and the provost-marshal.

The writ of habeas corpus is suspended in Chester county, and a grand jury of six whites and six blacks, summoned before a Republican judge, by a Republican deputy sheriff, declares that "the allegations contained in the President's proclamation are without foundation, "and *must be the result of a falsehood communi-* "cated to him by persons equally regardless of "good order and the peace of society."

The astonishing thing to us is, that there is any "order" at all. We wonder the land is no a theatre of universal disorder and confusion. We wonder the people do not march away to other homes.

It is one of the cruelest and bitterest pages in history. Where is there a parallel to South Carolina? We hardly know anything like it except the fate of the Jews."

11/15/71 Mirror

More Martial Law in South Carolina.

The New York *Herald* has the following dispatch from its special correspondent in South Carolina, dated Columbia, 8th inst. :

I have just arrived from Union Court-house this morning. The arrest of citizens was resumed at an early hour. The infantry which arrived on Monday last picketed all the roads leading into the town, and refused to permit any person to leave or enter. Leaving my room I found drawn up on the street in front of the hotel a body of soldiers, with United States Marshal Johnson and his assistant on the porch. Mr. Hughes, proprietor of the hotel, was called out and summarily arrested. Another man, whose name I have not learned, was immediately after taken into custody. Squads of troops were then sent with deputy marshals to various parts of the town to make arrests.

From the list of names on the paper I saw in the hands of the deputy marshal, I expect that a large number were taken up. To-day the spectacle was one I hope never again to see. It was painful in the extreme.

When I left Union on the cars for Columbia the town was being secured by the troops. As fast as the prisoners were arrested they were taken to the depot under guard, and no person allowed to approach them. They will be sent to Spartanburg to-day.

To the time I left not the slightest opposition had been made by the citizens, but the feeling throughout South Carolina, and especially in the counties under the ban, is exceedingly bitter. If the present troubles end in bloodshed I should not be surprised at all.

11/29/71 Mirror

RAILROAD EXTENSION TO SNICK-ERSVILLE.

The Washington and Ohio Rail Road Co. proposes to extend its road to the foot of the Blue Ridge immediately, provided a liberal amount in bonds is taken by citizens of Loudoun county. We understand four thousand dollars in these bonds have already been taken by some of our citizens, and that an agent has been dispatched to the upper part of the county to canvass for them.

11/29/71 Mirror

VIRGINIA'S DEBT TO DR. HORACE GREELEY.

Dr. Greeley's kindly feelings toward the South were never manifested more strikingly than in the important part he played in the reconstruction of Virginia, the facts respecting which have never been made public until now.

The Convention that framed the present Constitution of Virginia was not only Republican, but extremely Radical. As that instrument came from their hands, it contained a test-oath and a clause disqualifying all from holding any office who had taken any part in the rebellion or aided it in any way whatever. Of course these provisions would have excluded from office ninety-five out of every hundred white Virginians.

The Convention ordered the Constitution to be submitted for ratification as a whole. The people of the State were greatly alarmed, but did not know what to do. By refusing to ratify the Constitution they would doom themselves to continued military government; and if they ratified it as framed they would put the State government absolutely in the hands of the newly-enfranchised blacks, who were in a minority of over 30,000 in the State. Their only hope was an appeal to Congress to permit a separate vote to be taken on the obnoxious clauses. But how to get at Congress in such a way as to secure favorable action was the question.

Just in the midst of their perplexities three Virginians—Gen. Mahone, Gen. Imboden, and Col. Flournoy—happened to meet in New York, and in discussing the situation at home it occurred to them to see Dr. Greeley and seek his counsel and advice, as he was then known to be influential with the President. They met Dr. Greeley at his office by appointment, the conference lasting from 6 till 11 P. M. The result was that Dr. Greeley cordially adopted their views in regard to the obnoxious features of the Constitution, and said that he would go and see President Grant at Long Branch, and endeavor to induce him to recommend to Congress the passage of an enabling act or joint resolution to take the separate vote desired by the Virginians.

He went to Long Branch, and spent a long time with the President, but returned little encouraged. After a further conference with the Virginians, he advised them to call in the aid of several leading Republicans of this city. They attempted to do this, but failed. Dr. Greeley then went a second time to Long Branch, spent the night there, and next day reported his belief that his mission had been successful, as afterward proved to be the fact. The President sent a short message to Congress on the subject, which resulted in the immediate passage of a joint resolution, under which the vote on ratification was taken; the Constitution purged of its odious features, and the State rehabilitated, with the best government in the South.

The President's mind was known to be inclined against this course before Dr. Greeley saw him. It is almost certain that but for the earnest efforts of Dr. Greeley a separate vote would not have been allowed. So great was the desire in Virginia to reestablish civil government that the Constitution would perhaps have been adopted as it was framed. Had that been done, three fourths of all State officers would be filled to day by the ignorant blacks; for in many counties there was not a single white man who could have taken the oath prescribed to fill any office. This conduct of Dr. Greeley has endeared him very much to liberal minded Virginians.—*New York Sun.*

11/29/71 Mirror

THE SOUTHERN DEAD.

Oration by General Jubal Early.

The annual oration before the Survivors' Association of South Carolina, delivered last Friday evening at the Baptist Church, in Columbia, by Lieutenant-General Jubal A. Early, has been published in full in the Columbia *Phoenix* by authority of the Survivors' Association, and is well worth perusal. After a review of the principal events of the war, General Early said:

"No man could look upon that scene at Appomattox Courthouse, and for a moment, in his heart, believe that the followers of Robert E. Lee were traitors or rebels. But, my comrades, the 'victor' on that occasion had not the remotest conception of the true meaning of the word 'magnanimity,' much less of the sentiment. Talk of Grant's magnanimity on that occasion, in conceding the terms that he did to General Lee's demands! I scout the idea. General Lee went to that interview with the firm resolve to cut his way out with the small remnant left, if terms were not granted him deemed honorable in war. Grant saw the blue mountains not far off—he had sad experience of what that little army was capable—he was afraid General Lee might make his way into those mountains, and then he would lose the supreme glory of terminating the war by the surrender to him of his great antagonist, and he granted the terms, without which he could not have procured that surrender.

"Call you this magnanimity? But it is said he prevented General Lee from being prosecuted for treason. He had, then, fortunately for him, a mentor who forced the idea into his dull brain, that his own honor and glory were in some way connected with that matter, in maintaining inviolate the parole granted General Lee and his soldiers, and he acted in accordance with the suggestions made to him. That mentor has since gone, and what has been his course, as the head of a powerful Government, towards General Lee and his followers? Compared to what has been done to our people, it would have been mercy to have hung all our leaders, civil and military, and then granted peace and amnesty so the masses. Jeffrys, himself, could not have devised more exquisite torture and cruelty than has been inflicted on all our people."

The oration concluded as follows:

"We must and will preserve, green and fresh, the memories of our dead heroes.

11/29/71 Mirror

"Yes! I am a free lover! I believe I have an inalienable right to change my husband every day if I like. I trust I am understood, for I mean what I say and nothing else. I claim that freedom means to be free.

The above disgusting sentence was the utterance of Mrs. Virginia Woodhull, as she addressed a crowded audience last week at Steinway Hall, New York, setting forth her "free love" and "woman's rights" doctrines. With ignorance, vice and corruption controlling the highest positions in the world of politics, and women harranghing fashionable audiences that applaud such vulgar sentiments, so revolting to all the finer sensibilities of humanity, and so utterly debasing to every womanly virtue, it is high time that something was done to restrain the one and correct the other, if we would maintain a semblance of that moral excellence which "exalteth a nation." The entire lecture of Mrs. Woodhull, was replete with sentences as revolting to virtue and good morals as the one quoted, and yet the *Rev.* THEODORE TILTON, introduced her to the crowd, and sat upon the stage while she delivered herself of her base fanaticism.

(In a couple of years the "Rev." Tilton would be involved in a much larger controversy.)

12/27/71 Mirror

A College Lark.

The following capital story is told by "one who knows" of Dr. Maxcey, and cannot fail to amuse our readers: On one occasion several students of South Carolina College resolved to drag the Doctor's carriage into the woods, and fixed upon a night for the performance of the exploit. One of their number, however, was troubled with some compunctions visitings, and managed to convey to the worthy president a hint that it would be well for him to secure the door of his carriage-house. Instead of paying any heed to this suggestion the Doctor proceeded on the appointed night to the carriage-house and esconced his portly person inside the vehicle. In less than an hour some half a dozen young gentlemen came to his retreat and cautiously withdrew the carriage into the road. When they were fairly out of the college precincts they began to joke freely with each other by name.

One of them complained of the weight of the carriage, and another replied by swearing that it was heavy enough to have the old fellow himself in it. For nearly a mile they proceeded along the highway, and then struck into the woods, to a cover which they concluded would effectually conceal the vehicle. Making themselves infinitely merry at the Doctor's expense and conjecturing how and when he would find his carriage they at length reached the spot where they had resolved to leave it. Just as they were about to depart—having once more agreed that "the carriage was heavy enough to have the old Doctor and all his tribe in it"—they were startled by the sudden dropping of one of the glass door pannels, and the well-known voice of the Doctor himself thus addressed them:

So so, young gentlemen, you are going to leave me in the woods, are you? Surely, as you have brought me hither for your own gratification, you will not refuse to take me back for mine. Come, Messrs.——, and —— and ——, come to; and let us return; it's getting late!"

There was no appeal for the window was closed and the Doctor resumed his seat. Almost without a word the discomfitted young gentlemen took their places at the pole, at the back of the vehicle, and quite as expeditiously, in with less voice, did they retrace their course. In silence, they dragged the carriage to its wonted place, and then retreated precipitately to their rooms to dream of the account they must render on the morrow. When they had gone, the Doctor quietly vacated the carriage and went to his house, where he related the story to his family with much glee. He never called the heroes of that nocturnal expedition to an account, nor was the carriage ever afterwards dragged at night into the woods.

WEDNESDAY.................Dec. 27,

CARRIER'S ADDRESS.—The carrier of the Mirror requests us to say that he will be around bright and early on New Year's morning with his annual address and counting-house calendar. He has served his patrons punctually the past year, and trusts that he may be remunerated generously.

Our teacher friends at the Academy were the recipients of well chosen Christmas gifts from their pupils. A goose and turkey for the older, (a married man); a picture for the younger, who is only a candidate for matrimonial honours.

During the cold snap last week most of the Ice Houses hereabouts were filled with excellent ice.

Christmas Day, as usual, witnessed a considerable number of people on our streets. Good cheer and good humor were the prevailing features of the day,

One or two bellicose demonstrations were promptly suppressed by the arrest of the offenders,

To all Whom it may
CONCERN!

An Act to Prevent the Sale of Fire Crackers in the Town of Leesburg.

WHEREAS the peace and good order of the Corporation of Leesburg is frequently disturbed and broken, and the property and lives of its inhabitants frequently endangered by the firing of Guns and other explosion of Gunpowder, in other ways,

Be it therefor enacted, by the Mayor, Recorder, and Common Council of the Town of Leesburg, in Common Hall Assembled, that it shall be unlawful for any persons within the Corporation of Leesburg to sell, vend, give, or otherwise dispose of to Boys or others, any Fire Cracker or Crackers, and that any person or persons who shall be guilty of such offense shall for every such offense, forfeit and pay, a fine of $10, to be recovered with costs, by warrant before the Mayor, Recorder, or any Justice of the Peace within the Corporation.

Sec. 2d. And be it further enacted, That one half of the fine imposed by this Act shall go to the informer, the other half to the Corporation.

WASHINGTONIAN.

LEESBURG, LOUDOUN COUNTY, VA.

SATURDAY, JANUARY 13 1872.

DEATH OF JOHN JANNEY.

Mr. JANNEY, after a protracted illness, died at his residence in Leesburg, on Friday night, the 5th instant, in the 74th year of his age. He was born in Alexandria, on the 8th of November, 1798. In 1810, he removed with his father, ELISHA JANNEY, to Loudoun, who located in Hillsborough, where he was raised, and trained for the distinguished part he has performed in the events and scenes which go to make up the history of his county and State.

In the memorable campaigns of HARRISON and CLAY, in '40 and '44, he was among the most popular and conspicuous orators in the country, and his speeches added no less to the fame of his State than to his own renown.

He was elected to represent this county in the Convention of '50 and 51, to remodel the State Constitution, and with Wise, Summers and Steuart, he ranked as one of the leading members of that body.

In '60 and '61, he was again called to represent his county in that memorable Convention. Composed as it was of the most distinguished men of the Commonwealth, he was elected to preside over its deliberations, and to control by his dignity of character and admirable judgment, the proceedings of a body, upon whose decision hung the fate of the State. His speeches in that body were but few, but won the plaudits of his countrymen. He came up to the full measure of the wise and able statesman in every trust committed to him, and his constituents were proud to know that he reflected more honor upon the offices he filled, than they conferred upon him.

It is sad to see those who were conspicuous actors in the most prominent and brilliant epochs in the history of the State and whose names form the connecting link between the present and the days of Virginia's glory passing away, leaving so few competent to take up the splendid role they have played in the history of their State and Nation. But though dead, their example lives to perpetuate their virtues and guide those who are to be the actors in the events and scenes of the present and future—and but few nobler examples are left than that given in the life of the subject of this notice.

Mr. JANNEY belonged to that school of public men, whose ambition it was to discharge their duty conscientiously, regarding the plaudits of the populace second to the approval of their consciences. He stood upon that high plane of public honor, to which but few reach at this time—regarding official position only as a means to serve his State and Country, and to promote the common wellfare.

(The distinguished Loudoun citizen who would have become vice president had he voted himself in the Whig election of 1840. Janney chaired the two Virginia secession conventions. He, however, voted in the negative both times.)

1/3/72 Mirror

A Large Hog.—The largest hog, the untimely death of which we have been called upon to record, was slaughtered recently by Mr. GEO. M. WOODS, of lower Loudoun—it weighed *eight hundred and twenty-one pounds*, which would indicate that that section of country can't be beat in producing *swine*. Mr. W., however, is a good farmer, a clever gentleman, and an excellent manager generally, which after all may account for his big hog.

THE MIRROR,

WEDNESDAY,................Jan. 24,

W. & O. Railroad.—We are glad to notice that active preparations are now making for pushing the work on this road, at least to the base of the Blue Ridge at Snickersville. The contractor, Mr. McClure, last week passed through this town with horses, carts and hands, and on Monday the first dirt was broken on its westward course from Hamilton.

The intelligence cannot be otherwise than gratifying to the entire large and wealthy section of country soon to be penetrated by the iron horse, which will place them within speedy and easy connection with the great centres of trade and travel of the world; and we hope that every reasonable facility will be accorded those engaged in this long expected and much desired improvement, in the prosecution of their labor Let no petty jealously, nor narrow-minded selfishness, interfere to arrest its progress, but rather let each one put his shoulder to the wheel and do what he can in the interests of the work. The construction of the road to Snickersville, even, will render it a paying institution, advantageous alike to the stockholders, the people and the State. At that point it will attract an immense local trade from the right and the left, and even from the adjoining county of Clarke, beyond the Ridge.

FREE SCHOOLS.

A bill has been passed to its engrossment in the House of Delegates providing for the organization of county school boards, and prescribing the powers and duties of said boards, &c. It forms into a body corporate, under the style of "The County School Board of—— county."

1/31/72 Mirror

Fred Douglas, the Colored Orator, Refused Admission to the Planters Hotel, in St. Louis

St. Louis, January 24, 1872.—The city of St. Louis is just now greatly exorcised over the refusal of the proprietor of the Planters Hotel to entertain or harbor Fred Douglass, the celebrated colored orator and abolitionist. Mr Douglass came to the hotel yesterday and entered his name on the register the same as any guest; and shortly afterwards came and said he would like some dinner. The clerk remarked in substance that he thought the Planters Hotel would be damned before he could get any dinner there, and then pointed to the book, where his name had been erased.

"What is the meaning of this outrage? sternly asked the old man pulling indignantly at his *distingue* gray moustache.

"It means simply this: that the Planters House don't keep niggers; if you want anything you will have to go elsewhere," said the intelligent clerk.

Here the crowd thickened, and a rush was made towards the book to see the name of the man who was the subject of the row. Each man as he saw the name, either gasped approval or grunted dissent. The majority grunted. The crowd read upon the books simply the name, "Fred. Douglass, Washington, D. C."

This name seemed to be enough to damn the man in the estimation of nine out of ten who read and sympathized with the clerk.

Mr Douglas made a short speech, in which he denounced in very indignant terms the procedure. He said he had travelled over all the civilized countries of Europe, had been received by the highest, and nowhere had he been where he had met with such shameful treatment.

The crowd listened, and sneered, and laughed, when Mr. Douglass retired to find quarters elsewhere.

2/17/72 Washingtonian

THE INDIAN NOT CIVILIZABLE.

To those who advocate the application of the laws of civilization to the Indian, it might be a profitable study to investigate the effect which such application produces upon the strength of the tribe as expressed in numbers. Looking at him as the fearless hunter, the matchless horseman and warrior of the Plains. where Nature placed him, and contrasting with the reservation Indian, who is supposed to be revelling in the delightful comforts and luxuries of an enlightened condition, but who in reality is grovelling in beggary, bereft of many qualities which is in his wild state tended to render him noble, and heir to a combination of vices partly his own, partly bequeathed to him from the paleface, one is forced even against desire, to conclude that there is unending antagonism between the Indian nature and that with which his well-meaning white brother would endow him. Nature intended him for a savage state; every instinct, every impulse of his soul inclines him to it. The white race might fall into a barbarous state, and afterwards, subjected to the incidence of civilization, be reclaimed and prosper. Not so the Indian, He cannot be himself and be civilized; he fades away and dies. Cultivation such as the white man would give him deprives him of his identity. Education, strange as it may appear, seems to weaken rather than strengthen his intellect. Where do we find any specimens of educated Indian eloquence comparing with that of such native, untutored orators as Tecumseh, Osceola, Red Jacket, and Logan; or, to select from those of more recent fame, Red Cloud of the Sioux, or Sa-tan-ta of the Kiowas?—"*My life on the Plains,*" *by Gen. Custer, in February Galaxy.*

1/31/72 Mirror

A Party of Fort Wayne young gentlemen dined sumptuously at a restaurant, and each one insisted on paying the bill. To decide the matter it was proposed to blindfold the waiter, and the first one he caught should the bill. He hasn't caught any of them yet.

THE MILX TRADE

We understand that an effort is making by a number of persons residing along the line of the W. & O. Railroad if the necessary arrangements can be perfected, to have some special accommodation for transporting milk to Alexandria and the District. For the benefit of such we publish the following extracts from a letter upon the subject written by B. Catford, Dairyman, of Fairfax C. H., giving instructions as to the preparation of milk, &c.

GENERAL INSTRUCTIONS TO MILX PRODUCERS.

In curing milk, a spring of running water at a temperature of 55 degrees or lower is a necessity. A tank set near the spring made deep enough to raise the water over the breast of the can is a necessity. The tank should be large, the more water the better.

Keep the covers off the cans of milk while in the spring. Never put a can of milk into the spring until the milk is in the can that you intend to put it in. The vat or spring house should be as near the spring as possible, so that the water may not become warm by running a long distance in the pipe. It will be found better and easier to drive the cows to a yard near the spring to milk than to carry the milk after it is milked. Fill the can to the neck, so that the flange of the cover dips into the milk, as this will prevent its churning. When carting to the depot in warm weather the cans should be covered with a wet blanket or with fresh grass.

MANNER OF CLEANSING MILK CANS.

When cans are brought home at night they should be well rinsed with cold water, then left to stand over night with a bucket of cold water in them. In the morning empty out the water and wash them thoroughly with hot water and soft soap, after which they must be thoroughly scalded with steam or scalding water; it is well to put in one teaspoonful of sal-soda to each can when you wash them. After the cans are thoroughly scalded they should be again rinsed and turned down to sun.

No matter how good cows are, stingy feeding and shiftless management will soon run down the stock, and dissipate all hopes of profit. Everybody knows that when a cow is driven rapidly on her way home to be milked, the milk is lessened in quantity, becomes hot and is more liable to sour. Cows should be driven as leisurely as they will walk, never harassed, annoyed, or irritated by man boy or dog, as harsh treatment of every sort has a very injurious effect on the milk. Poor milkers dry up cows. Ground oats and peas, or oats and corn meal or wheat bran and corn meal will give a better flow of milk and conduce more to the health of the cow giving milk than ear corn meal, which seems to be of too heating a nature.

PRICE OF MILK

Fluctuates with the season; and, probably, will range from 12cts. per gallon in summer, to 25cts. in winter, that is a higher price than is averaged in New York City.

MARKETING

My experience for the last year has convinced me that this is the most defective part of the business, the unreliability and irresponsibility of milk-men, is aggravating and sometimes detrimental to the interest of the farmer. I have come to the conclusion that an agent, some one that we shall have confidence in, must be established in Washington, who shall wholesale for cash our milk and other produce.

CANS

will cost about $6 each for the 40 quart size, freight added. Every farmer might do with three sets, although four would do better; as once missing might cause the agent to lose the sale of that brand. Every person should have their name and station stamped in plain letters on copper plate and soldered to the can.

(The coming of rail connections to western Loudoun suggested to farmers a shift from grain or subsistence farming to the milk trade.)

2/14/72 Mirror

Fruit Culture and Dairy Farming.—By reference to a communication in to-days paper, it will be seen that a meeting of the farmers of this county, is called at Hamilton, at 11 o'clock on Saturday, the 2nd day of March, for the purpose of organizing a Farmers and Dairyman's Association. The objects of this association are too clearly set forth in the communication itself, to need recapitulation, and must, we think, commend themselves to every intelligent tiller of the soil who reads them. We understand that the President of the W. & O. Railroad company, has promised, as soon as it is ascertained that a sufficient number of our people will take hold of the matter to justify it, to erect a switch at the Washington Junction, place upon the road a regular milk car, to be run in connection with the freight train, with the schedule so arranged that the milk, butter, eggs, poultry, fruit, fresh meats, etc., thus transported will be run into Washington about 8 o'clock each evening—thus affording the denizens of that city a regular supply of the rich products of our teeming fields and well stocked dairies, and ensuring to our farmers the market value of their industries. We are glad to witness this disposition on the part of the farmers of Loudoun to avail themselves of the means thus presented for utilizing their farm labor. Experience has demonstrated that it will not do longer to trust to the uncertain and precarious yield of cerials alone for profitable husbandry,—we must pay more attention to the cultivation of those smaller articles of the farm, which enter so largely into the world's consumption, and which pay so much better for the time and labor bestowed upon their growth. We have one of the most superb grass growing regions in the State, and a climate and soil unexcelled for fruit growing.

2/10/72 Washingtonian

The Arlington Estate.

The following from the Baltimore American, the leading Radical paper of Maryland, is creditable alike to the head and heart of the writer:

The application of the widow of General Robert E. Lee for payment for the Arlington estate has been before Congress for more than two years, and we regard the delay as in no way honorable or creditable to the nation.

Mrs. Lee has suffered from the rebellion as no other woman now living has suffered. This also was her own private property, which she inherited from her parents. There as been no systematic confiscation of the property of those engaged in the rebellion, and the Government has no right to make an exception in her case, where accidental circumstances have given possession. She has put in a claim for reasonable compensation, and wisdom, justice and common honesty require that it should be promptly settled. We agree with *The Cincinnati Gazette* that the present attitude of the Government with regard to the Arlington estate is "contemptible," and that "persons may make savage declarations against Rebels to stave off reflection in this affair, but an honorable nation cannot maintain the position which ours holds as to this estate. Sooner or later compensation will be made. The sooner it is done the sooner will the Government relieve itself from a position which will not bear examination."

(During the war, under the pretext of nonpayment of taxes, the Lee estate was seized.)

2/21/72 Mirror

LIFE IN BROOKLYN.—A gentleman, while walking in Atlantic avenue. Brooklyn, on Saturday evening, was jostled by a stranger, and after proceeding a few yards felt in his pocket in vain for his watch. He hastened back, overtook the thief, and pointing his revolver sternly demanded, "Give me that watch!" The stranger surrendered it without a word and hurried away. On reaching home the gentleman was startled in the middle of his narrative of his desperate encounter with a highwayman by an interruption from his wife, "Why, John, you left your watch on the bureau this morning, and I have been wearing it all day.

2/14/72 Mirror

BEECHER AND HIS FLOCK

Rev. Henry Ward Beecher has given his congregation, in a social way, the "cut direct."— Awakened to a sense of neglected social duties by the complaints of the female members of his flock, he attempted to carry out a scheme of pastoral visits by devoting each Tuesday to that purpose, announcing from the pulpit on Sunday what district he intended to visit on the succeeding Tuesday. Beginning work on New Year's day he got through with sixty visits, finding everybody ready to receive him. The next Tuesday was consumed in thirty visits, and fourteen was the utmost he could manage the third Tuesday whereupon he abandoned the project in disgust and despair. Sunday before last he thus delivered himself of his indignation. The ladies kept him waiting without regard to the calls upon his time, in order to array themselves in all the paraphernalia and gewgaws of fashion their wardrobes could afford, and in no instance were they ready to receive him. Besides, when they did come down they would talk of nothing but servants, children's ailments, and family genealogies until it got to be fearfully monotonous; and he thought unproductive of spiritual benefit.

(Henry Ward Beecher, the most prominent preacher of the day, was a brother of Harriet Beecher Stowe who wrote Uncle Tom's Cabin.)

3/6//72 Mirror

A CURIOUS STORY ABOUT MRS. LINCOLN REIT-ERATED.—A few days ago a paragraph in the *Herald*, based upon what was known to be good authority, announced that Mrs. Abraham Lincoln had recently visited Boston, and, *incognito* and closely veiled, attended a public *seance* of a well-known lady medium on Washington street, on which occasion the spirit of her lamented husband appeared, and by unmistakable manifestations revealed to all present the identity of Mrs. Lincoln, which she had attempted to keep secret. We have now the best authority for saying that the report was in all respects accurate; that Mrs. Lincoln did visit Boston on the 4th instant; that she took lodgings at the Parks House, registering her name as Mrs. Linder; that she remained there ten days, during which time she made frequent visits to the medium above mentioned, and and that while at the hotel her identity was discovered by a person who had often seen her in Washington.

4/3/72 Mirror

GHOSTS.

The editor of the Lexington *Gazette*, is telling his readers what he knows about ghosts.

We copy an account of an occurrence well known to some of our citizens.

Of course ninety-nine out of a hundred cases of curious sound and sight are either fancies or of easy explanation. In a few instances after careful investigation by competent persons, the mystery remains. Of the latter class is the

SMITH CRADLE ROCKING.

This is one of the most remarkable and best authenticated phenomenon of its kind on record. It occurred in 1840 in Lynchburg, at the residence of the late William A. Smith, D. D., for many years President of Randolph Macon College. In that year he was pastor of a Lynchburg church. An empty cradle in his house was noticed rocking of its own accord. It continued its motion for an hour. The next day it commenced rocking at the same time, kept it up, and stopped as on the day before. Thus it continued daily for over a month. Many intelligent citizens and ministers witnessed the wonderful affair and made repeated efforts to solve the mystery without success. It was moved to different parts of the room without any change in its behavior. It was removed to other apartments in the dwelling with the same result. It was taken to pieces and each part scrutinized and refitted, yet there was no change in its motion.

The Methodist clergy selected one of their number to hold the cradle and prevent, if possible, its movement. The Rev. Dr. Penn, one of the purest men of his time, was chosen for this purpose. While it was rocking he grasped it. It wrenched itself from his grip! He seized it more firmly. The timbers cracked and the cradle would have been broken in the struggle to release itself, had he not loosened his hold.

It was not further hindered in its daily exercise. After thirty or more days it stopped and never commenced again.

3/27/72 Mirror

Melancholy.—On Monday last, a little daughter of Mrs. EMILY LLOYD, of this town, aged about 4 years, died after a brief illness. About four years ago, the father, Mr. CHAS. E. LLOYD, died of phneumonia, leaving a wife and four children, two boys and two girls. A few months after his death, the two boys sickened and died, rather suddenly. Four or five weeks ago, one of the girls also sickened and died, and on Monday the fourth, and last child, died, as before stated, after two days' illness. All of the children were similarly affected, and all of them died, apparently from the same cause, —leaving the widow and mother to mourn the loss in four short years, *of her entire household treasures.*

P. S. On Tuesday, after the above was in type, at the instance of R. M. Bentley, Recorder, Officer B. R. Attwell, summoned the following jury of inquest to investigate the matter.

4/3/72 Mirror

Not yet concluded —At the date of our last paper, we left the jury in session over the dead body of the little child, whose rather sudden and mysterious death we announced at the time. A number of witnesses were examined and the fact developed that upon several occasions, arsenic had been purchased by the mother of the children: it was therefore determined to have the stomach analyzed. Accordingly, a post mortem examination was made by Drs. MOTT & CROSS, and the stomach of the child, properly sealed up was delivered to R. M. Bentley, acting Mayor, who proceeded directly to Baltimore, and turned it over to Prof. Tonery.

Grand Concert.

THE EXCELSIOR CHORALS OF AL-EXANDRIA will give a GRAND CONCERT at the Colored M. E. CHURCH, in Leesburg, on

MONDAY AND TUESDAY EVENINGS, APRIL 6th and 7th

The proceeds to be given to the Sabbath School of that Church.

The entertainment will afford a rich musical treat, and the public generally are invited to attend.

The galleries will be reserved for white persons exclusively.

ADMISSION, 20 cts.   Children 10 cts.

The Lloyd Poisoning Case

SUDDEN DEATHS OF THE FATHER AND FOUR CHILDREN.

THE MOTHER PURCHASES POISON,

The Deaths of the Victims.

The Coroner's Inquest.

A POST MORTEM EXAMINATION.

REPORT OF PROF. TONERY.

Arsenic Found in the Stomach of the LAST CHILD

THE ARREST OF THE MOTHER.

Her Commitment to Jail Upon the HORRIBLE SUSPICION.

Our usually quiet community is this morning convulsed as by a terrible moral earthquake, the vibrations of which, as they echo back from the lips of the witnesses examined before the coroner's inquest, send a thrill of horror, and tell a tale of circumstantial guilt, the enormity of which is almost unparalled in the annals of human depravity. We have heretofore noticed the singular deaths of the various members of the Lloyd family, in this town, and the terrible suspicions which they occasioned. The subject has now reached that point of definiteness, in which it will be sifted by a legal prosecution. Numerous vague and indefinite rumors have been set afloat in regard to it, and with the view of giving a clear and accurate account of the circumstances which led to the arrest of the mother upon the charge of administering arsenic to and producing the death of her last and only child, we have compiled the following summary, sincerely cherishing the hope that a fair and impartial investigation of the subject may fully acquit her of all complicity in the transaction, and result in placing her where the virtue, the morals, and the innoce.e of the female character should ever be—above suspicion.

DEATH OF THE FATHER.

In December, 1868, Mr. CHARLES E. LLOYD, the keeper of a Drinking Saloon in this town, a man of high temper, and said to have been unkind to his family, but by no means a bad citizen, otherwise, was taken sick and for ten days suffered from a severe attach of typhoid pneumonia. He had become convalescent, however, and his physician pronounced him out of danger. The Doctor visited him on the morning of his death, and found him sitting up, and so much better that he stated he would be at his business next day. In a short time, perhaps less than an hour, he was again summoned to his assistance, but the vital spark had fled before he reached him. Lloyd had in the meantime partaken of some slight refreshment. The death was so sudden and unexpected, that his friends were startled but his physician attributed it to disease of the heart with which he was afflicted, and next day his remains were interred in Union Cemetery, where in a few months, they were followed by

AN AUNT OF MRS. LLOYD.

In April, 1870, Mrs. HAMMERLY, of Washington, an aunt of Mrs. LLOYD, and by whom she had been raised—paid her a visit, and in two or three weeks after her arrival, another grave was dug, and another form laid beneath the clods —but as the aunt was old and quite infirm, and had been known to express a desire to return and be buried at the home of her early life, her death occasioned little else than sympathy for the again bereaved widow.

THE DEATH OF THE TWO LITTLE BOYS.

The father died, leaving his wife in moderately comfortable circumstances, with four children, two boys and two girls, (one of the girls, Maud, was born a few weeks after the father's death) all of them fine, healthy, robust children, who became, apparently, the almost idolized objects of the widowed mother's affections. In July 1870, the two boys, George, aged 9 years, and Henry, aged 6 years, in company with one or two other children, and a negro girl, some 12 or 14 years of age, living in Mrs. Lloyd's family, were permitted to go blackberrying. They returned in the evening, uncomplaining, but that night both boys were taken seriously ill, and the family physician, Dr. A. R. Mott called in. He found them suffering from the effects of poison, but as their mouths, both inside and out, were covered with irruptions, he attributed it to their having, in their ignorance, eaten poison-oak leaves with their berries. Their condition grew worse and Dr. Cross was called in, but the children both died, Henry on the 24th of July, and George on the 25th,—the mother manifesting all the evidences of sorrow natural to the maternal heart lacerated by the sudden taking off of two of her first-born. These sad events were the subject of much comment at the time, and an examination of the stomachs was talked of, but no one was bold enough to charge foul play on the part of the mother, because no one was willing to believe, from her previous character, that so revolting a crime could have originated in her breast. Two little graves were dug beside that of the father,— two little coffins were consigned to their narrow embrace—and day after day the mother's form might have been seen bending over the fresh mounds, seemingly with all the loving tenderness of a mother's heart, and each time as she turned her back upon those little graves there might have been seen resting upon their cold bosoms a bunch of flowers, those sweet-scented mementoes of woman's constancy and affection— thus disarming the credulous of their suspicious, and strengthening the incredulous in their convictions of the mother's entire innocence.

CHANGES HER HOME.

Shortly after the death of the two boys, Mrs. Lloyd left her old home, the scene of so many painful memories, and took up her residence in a neat little story-and-a-half stone house, situated on the West end of London Street, fronting immediately on the street. Here it was hoped, that her and her surviving little ones, would be spared the withering touch of the Angel of Death, which seemed to brood like an evil genius over her household. But not so.

THE DEATH OF ANNIE.

On the 11th of February, 1872, the Doctor was summoned to administer to little Annie the eldest of the two girls — whom he found suffering from what he thought to be the effects of an attack of cholera morbus, superinduced by the eating of oysters. The usual treatment was resorted to, but without avail, and on the 16th of the same month the little thing died, as the Doctor supposed, from congestion of the stomach. The next day she was assigned her place by the side of those who had gone before, in the silent city of the dead. One more suspicion was aroused. Expressions of doubt and misgiving were no longer uttered in secret; still, the moral sense of the community was so shocked, and so unwilling to recognize as the source of all this woe that one toward whom all the circumstance seemed to point, that again no inquiry was instituted.

MAUD DIES

But scarcely had the echo of the dull thud of the cold clods that rattled on the coffin of Annie been borne away by the passing breeze are Maud, the last lovely flower left blooming on the family stem, began to droop and in three short days, withered and died. She was taken sick on Saturday, March 23d, 1872, and died on Monday the 25th.

THE MOTHER BUYS ARSENIC.

Another circumstance that fed the flame of suspicion, was the fact, that just prior to the death of each of the children, it was ascertained that the mother had purchased arsenic. What disposition was made of it is stated in her testimony before the coronor.

THE CORONOR'S INQUEST.

The announcement of Maud' death fell upon the public ear with stunning effect. A mighty wrong, or a terrible fatality had fallen upon a household and swept away the last of its treasures, as ruthlessly as chaff before a whirlwind, and there came an appeal from almost every christian heart, seconded, as it were, by a mighty voice from an unseen world, pleading in behalf of a score of new made graves, for investigation. Accordingly, on Tuesday, the 26th of March, Coroner R. M. Bently, summoned a jury of inquest, and repairing to the House of Mrs. Lloyd, where the dead child was still lying, examined a number of witnesses, from whom he elicited, briefly, the following facts:

THE TESTIMONY.

Mrs. Emily E Lloyd, sworn, testified, that the child was sick 48 hours, previous to its death. That it threw up,—and when its sick spell, came on, was very pale, but did not appear to suffer much. Sent for Dr. Mott on Saturday evening—who saw what it threw up.

Two weeks previous child was sick,—gave it Frey's Vermifuge, and it passed two worms. It had gotten well and its appetite was good until Saturday. Eat a little old ham, and some toast. Put it in warm bath, just before it died. Died easily and calm.

Dr. A. R. Mott—When he first saw child Saturday evening, did not think it seriously sick—gave it calomel every 2 or 3 hours and lime water, found it worse on Sunday evening—gave Bismuth powders, one every 3 or 4 hours; thought it presented every appearance of congestion of the stomach—was uneasy from the continual vomiting. On Monday morning found the child much oppressed with every evidence of congestion—was very uneasy then from the fact that it was so much like last child's sickness, and at his suggestion Dr. Cross was called in, who gave a little morphine and oxalate cerium; also proposed Huxam's tincture of Bark. Child died of intense congestion. Was of that opinion from the first. Saw what it threw up always—it was of a little bilious appearance—no blood—tongue all right: Pulse always small. No pain. Sunday evening it threw up. This is not the natural state of a healthy child. It may be brought on by any irritants, or indigestible food. Have attended her (Mrs Lloyd's) children, from time to time, always irritable of stomach—the weak organ All the children were the same. Came to death from natural causes. No reason to believe otherwise at all. Her death was not similar to that of the two who died of poison. It was more like the death of the last child.

Dr. Wm. Cross—Saw the child on Monday morning—regarded it as in *articulo, mortis.* Advised immediately, as the only possible means to save it, stimulents, both internally and externally, with immediate use of antimecties. The pupils of the eyes were very much dilated. This showed irritation of the brain.

Dr. Edwards—Testified—never sold Mrs. Lloyd any medicines. On the the 8th of February she bought ½ an ounce of arsenic, as she said, to kill rats. (The Dr. then described the affects of arsenic poisoning.)

B. R. Attwell—Testified that he called on Mr. Samuel Orrison, the guardian of the child, and told him of the reports about its death, and Mr. O. agreed with him as to the propriety of an examination They together visited Mrs Lloyd on Monday night, and Mr. Orrison told her the object of their visit. She refused her consent. Told her it ought to be done for her own sake. She again refused. I started out.

She called me back and gave her consent.— Said Wm. Lloyd (a brother of Charles) had a spite against her. Said she got milk from that old rascal Gill, and implied that something was wrong with the milk. This morning she again called my attention to the milk, and again intimated that something was wrong with it and Gill. Delphy told Mrs. L. in my presence, that they all drank of the milk and it didn't make her sick. Mrs. Lloyd exonerated Delphy from all suspicion.

Delphy, the colored girl was next examined; the most of her testimony related to the sickness of the child as detailed by the other witnesses. She said the child took no medicine except from its mother. Was living with Mrs. L. when the other children died.— Have not many rats, but heaps of mice. Have never used arsenic since I lived here, to kill rats She was afraid the children would get it. No trouble with rats since I lived here. No one else lived with Mrs. Lloyd but me, for nearly two years. Ain't any poison here at all. I do all the dealing for Mrs. Lloyd for the children—never bought anything at Dr. Edwards. She has not sent me to the apothecaries. This child was taken just like the last child that died: Mrs. L. did not think the child would die until Sunday morning. Mrs. L. appeared surprised at the death of the child, and was much distressed.

Julian A. Hutchison—Sworn,—Am a Druggist. Don't recollect of selling Mrs. Lloyd but one article in my life; that was one ounce of arsenic a few days before the death of the two boys, summer before last. She said it was to poison rats.

Mrs Lloyd was recalled. Bought all her medicines from Dr. Mott. Bought Arsenic and Frey's Vermifuge from Dr. Edwards.— Bought arsenic there about a month ago to kill rats with, but never got it home—lost it on the way. Rats are bad here—run about the house —Got more arsenic from Dr. Mott but never used it—afraid the children would get hold of it, and burnt it. Lost that I got from Edwards and burnt that I got from Mott.

Delphy (col.) recalled. Never saw any rats here. Never had any here—nothing but mice. No rat holes here at all. Never bothered with rats. Ain't any here. Mrs. Lloyd would not get arsenic without letting me know it. Never used any at the other house. She talked of it but never did get it. I never smelt anything like onions or garlic about the house.

At this point, the jury of inquest having determined that a post mortem examination of the deceased child should be had, adjourned until 6½ o'clock, p. m. At the appointed hour the jury re-assembled, and

Mrs. Lloyd was again re-called. Bought first arsenic of Dr. Edwards while living at other house. Bought of Edwards again and lost it. Bought of Mott two or three weeks after that was lost. Bought it for rats. Did not burn it the same day I bought it. I bought the last, I think, about the first of this month, of Dr. Mott—more than a week, I think, before this child was taken sick. Bought none between the first sickness of this child on March 11th, and its last sickness on March 23d, of which it died. Bought all of it myself—never sent any body for it.

Dr. Mott, again testified that the last arsenic bought of him was on March 18, 1872, as recorded on his register.

B. R. Attwell testified. when I asked Mrs. Lloyd to have an examination, she said: "What's the use, the child is dead now," and that "all the Lloyd family had died in the same way."

Here the post mortem was entered into by Dr. Mott and Cross, after which

Dr. A. R. Mott testified; on post mortem examination of the child, I find Omentum and Duodenum very much engorged; the stomach seemed free from inflamation—lung and liver normal. To question by juror—Stomach does not exhibit evidence of congestion. There is great congestion of the Omentum. Before post mortem I thought it died of congestion of the stomach.

Dr. Wm. Cross testified—I have seen nothing in my examination of the vicera to make me think there is sufficient inflamation, or engorgement, to cause death. In articuls mortis, or about the period of life becoming extinct, the blood may pass from the irritated vicera, leaving it blanched, or in that state that would indicate no inflamation having existed. Still, there may have been enough inflamation in the vicera that looked this way, to show what it is, in fact, the cause of death.

The stomach was then placed in a glass jar, properly sealed and delivered to coroner Bently, to be conveyed by him to Prof. Tonery, or some other reliable chemist in Baltimore, for immediate analysis, and the jury adjourned to reassemble at the call of the coroner. For nearly three weeks our people were held in a state of feverish excitement awaiting the result of the analysis, until Saturday last, when the jury was assembled

In SECRET SESSION

and a telegraphic dispatch from Prof. Tonery, read in which he stated that he had found in the stomach,

GRAIN AND A HALF OF ARSENIC, (ARSENOUS ACID)

Drs. Mott, Cross and Edwards, were sum-

moved before the jury, and questioned as to what was considered the usual dose of arsenic, and each concurred in saying from the 10th to the 16th part of a grain; after a lengthy and patient consideration of the whole matter, the jury rendered the following

VERDICT.

CORPORATION OF LEESBURG

Loudoun County, to wit.

At an adjourned inquisition taken at the house of Emily E. Lloyd, in the Corporation of Leesburg, of the County of Loudoun, on the 13th day of April, 1872, before R. M. Bently, a Coroner of the said Corporation, of Leesburg, upon the view of the body of Maud Lloyd, then lying dead, the jurors sworn to inquire when, where, how, and by what means the said Maud Lloyd came to her death, upon their oaths do say, that upon the testimony of witnesses and other evidences taken by them. it is their belief, that the said Maud Lloyd came to her death on or about the 25th day of March, 1872, by reason of the administration to her of Arsenic, and that the said arsenic was administered to said Maud Lloyd by her mother, Emily E. Lloyd. In testimony whereof the said coroner and jurors hereto set their hands this 13th day of April, 1872.

R. M. BENTLY, Coroner.

H. O. CLAGETT, JOHN GRAY, W. H. THOMAS, JOHN HAMMERLY, C. A. JOHNSON, E. J. CRISSER, WM. CLINE. C. P. McCABE, W. W. DIVINE, F. W. SHAFER, R. S. DOUGLAS, J. J. STANSBURY. Jurors.

ARREST OF THE PRISONER.

Whereupon, a warrant was at once issued for the arrest of the unfortunate woman and placed in the hands of Sergeant Attwell, and the jury adjourned. The news of this action spread like wild-fire; and the most intense excitement prevailed. By the time the carriage arrived containing the prisoner, the street in front of the Mayor's Office was almost completely blockaded. The coroner's functions having ended, the further management of the case was turned over to Justice JAMES M. WALLACE.

THE PRISONER AT THE MAYOR'S OFFICE.

At about 9½ o'clock, Mrs. Lloyd entered the Mayor's office, escorted by officer Attwell. There was nothing remarkable in her appearance, except that she looked a little pale. She is of medium height—is about 35 or 36 years of age, and dresses in black. She was much more composed than might have been expected, though in the course of the proceedings, once or twice she was deeply affected, and moved to tears Messers. M. Harrison and J. W. Foster appeared as her counsel, and in the absence of the Prosecuting Attorney, Maj. Chas. H. Lee was retained to look after the interests of the Commanwealth.

The Leesburg Poisoning Case.

At the date of our last paper, we left the accused murderess of her own flesh and blood, occupying a felon's cell in the county jail, awaiting the action of the grand jury in June, where she still remains.

The day after her incarceration, upon the suggestion of the Commonwealth's Attorney, Sheriff Barrett repaired to Union Cemetery, where the victims of the accursed crime were entombed, and proceeded to have them disinterred. There lay the tastily arranged lot—side by side lay the father and the two little boys—beautiful tombstones marking the spots of their last repose—and the green grass of early spring spreading, like a mantle of velvet, over their peaceful graves; while at their feet, the fresh turned earth of two little mounds, spoke more plainly than words could utter, the untimely taking off of AN- NIE and of MAUD. In the presence of a group of curious spectators, who gathered around the opening graves, over and about which there hovered a solemn stillness, the work of disinterment proceeded. At length the coffins were reached, and that of HENRY who died on the 24th of July, 1870, was gently raised and in the presence of Drs. MOTT, CROSS and FAUNTLEROY, the lid was removed, only to reveal a body so far decomposed and covered with the mosses of death, that nothing remained save the skeleton frame, which was fast crumbling to pieces and returning to the dust from whence it came No further investiga- tion was deemed desirable in this case,—the lid was replaced, the coffin lowered, and the lit- tle sleeper was once more at rest. The remains of George were not disturbed. Then came the opening of the grave of ANNIE, the child that died on the 16th of February, 1872. The cof- fin was raised and opened, and there lay the childish form, beautiful even yet, though for two months locked in the silent grave. Every portion of her grave clothes was bright and perfect, from the white ribbon that held back the golden curls from the brow of death, to the tiny slippers that first encased her icy feet, while the bracelets upon her arms, and the gol- den chain that girdled her neck, placed there by a mother's hand, sparkled in the calm sun-

light of that April evening, in saddening con- trast with the condition of that mother to-day. The body was in an almost perfect state of pre- servation,—and the stomach and liver were dis- sected, placed in a glass jar, securely sealed, and turned over to Mr. Barrett, who next morning carried them to Prof. Tonery, of Baltimore to be analyzed, who promised to execute the task as soon as possible. The result of his investi- gation will have a material bearing in the fu- ture unravelling of this most mysterious case, and will be awaited by the public with no or- dinary degree of interest.

THE PRISONER IN HER CELL.

The prisoner is comfortably quartered in her cell on the first floor of the jail—and appears to be perfectly resigned to her imprisonment. Her apartment is well furnished with her own furniture, while a few pictures hung upon the rough walls, and two or three flowers growing in the window, serve to re- lieve the room of much of its gloom, and lend to it an air of comparative comfort. The pri- soner seems cheerful—converses with calmness and apparent composure—speaks warmly of the treatment she receives at the hands of those who have her in charge, and says, now that she is in jail, she has NO DESIRE TO BE BAILED. That if released upon bail, and in her own house, she would have no disposition to go out, and does not therefore feel, that she is any more a prisoner where she is; besides in her present quarters, she is quiet, and relieved from hear- ing much that would probable be disagreeable, were she elsewhere.

We have thus far given the facts in this case, with such incidents as we supposed would be interesting to the public, without expressing any opinion as to the guilt of the prisoner. The cir- cumstances attending the entire transaction have woven a dark cloud, that now rests with por- tentious fury over her head: yet it is possible, that the penetrating eye of the law may peer through the accumulated mists, and in so do- ing purify the moral atmosphere of the taint that rendered investigation a necessity. Un- til then, let us not judge too harshly, but en- deavor to exercise towards the unfortunate woman—who, if even guilty, we are bound to pity,—those cardinal virtues "Faith, Hope and Charity".

An Interview.

A correspondent of the N. Y. *Herald*, who visited this town and interviewed Mrs. LLOYD, publishes the following account of what he saw and heard.

MRS. LLOYD'S DWELLING.

She resides in a little single story attic-finished stone house, with a steep old fashioned roof, the shingles of which are curling with age, which sits hard out upon one of the principal streets of this country village. A coat of white-wash covers up the rough and ungainly exterior of the undressed rock of which it is composed, and two windows, with green shutters, one upon each side of a little white porch, extending out upon the sidewalk let in the light of day to this stricken household. These shutters are closed hard down to-day, as if to exclude the rude gaze and curious villager who might chance to pass that way, and an air of solemn stillness seems to pervade the whole surroundings. Even the two locust shade trees that stand in front of the house, take an unnatural importance and seem grim sentinels guarding the entrance of this unhappy household, instead of being ornaments to its surroundings. In my visit to this little home of sorrow yesterday I was accompanied by Mr. Samuel Orrison, who was the guardian of the children and is a sincere friend of Mrs. Lloyd. He is a solid member of this community, and a bluff, good natured, intelligent Virginian, who believes firmly in the innocence of the accused. He became her bondsman when she was bailed on Saturday night, and declares his intention of seeing her out of this difficulty. From him I learned many interesting facts in relation to the family, and by his kindness was enabled to see the accused lady. As we stood together before the home I have described he pointed me to the other little properties belonging to the family, which constitute quite a competency.

A GLANCE WITHIN.

After a moment's delay we stepped upon the porch. Mr. Orrison rapped and a negro girl answered the summons. We stepped inside the narrow hall that runs through the house, turned to our right and stood in a neat little parlor literally strewn with beautiful children's trinkets, neatly arranged upon mantels, tables and whatnots. Large, nicely framed pictures of the family hung up on the walls, those of the four children being the most prominent and elaborate of them all. After a moment's delay, which was occupied in looking at the pictures of the four beautiful children, we were invited into the room on the opposite side of the hall, where the unfortunate lady would receive us.

AS WE ENTERED SHE AROSE.

received us kindly and asked us to be seated, and she resumed her chair near the old fashioned fireplace, upon which was burning a sickly wood fire. The shutters had been slightly parted, and a little stream of daylight lit up the room like the flicker of a single candle. At the opposite side of the window was a bed, the rumpled appearance of which indicated that the accused lady had been seeking upon it rest from the tortures of mind and body that were now upon her. Under the window sat a sofa, and upon it a basket containing the squares of a pretty bed quilt the mother was piecing for her lost child, when it was taken away. Upon the black mantel piece over the fireplace were two lamps, between which was an old-fashioned clock, which had ceased to pace off the steps of time, and around the room stood a few chairs, a small stand, upon which rested the family Bible, and upon the walls hung a few dresses and the wrappings of the woman who sat before me.

THE ACCUSED LADY.

After a moment's contemplation of the surroundings I turned to the lady who has been so suddenly dragged from the seclusion of her country home before the gaze of the whole reading people of our country. She was dressed in deep mourning, with a light shawl thrown over her shoulders; for she had arisen from her bed to receive us. Her hair was *combed plain and caught up in a knot behind*, with no attempt at ornamentation at all. As she sat for a moment quiet before me, her her fingers listlessly playing with the fringe of her shawl, I had an opportunity to study well her countenance. Her features are sharp and a little irregular, but a well-formed mouth and a pair of dark, expressive eyes make up for any deficiency in the outline of the face.

EMILY LLOYD'S STATEMENT.

After a moment's silence she asked if it *were not bad weather out, to which I replied.* "Terrible," for it had been snowing all morning. Conversation then turned upon the subject that was an all-important one to her, and she expressed herself much gratified that I had called to see her; for said she, "thee are so many terrible, untrue stories told, that I feel glad to be able to have them set right, and I know that you will do justice."

"Yes," said I, "Mrs. Lloyd, I shall be glad to state fairly whatever you may desire to give me for that purpose?"

THE DEATH OF HER HUSBAND.

"Well," said she, "so much has been said about the death of my husband that I will begin by telling you of his death. He died in December, 1868; he had been sick for some time with the pneumonia, and on the morning he died seemed better, and about seven o'clock, expressed a desire to have a roasted apple. I immediately sent to the boy who attended the restaurant for some apples, and as soon as possible prepared them. After they were ready he asked me to take the rind off and the core out and stir it up with some current jelly, which I did, while he sat up in bed near me. When they were prepared he eat them, and after that received some company, and a gentleman had just left him whom he told he was much better, when he dropped back and died suddenly. Every one that knew him knew that he had been long a sufferer with misery in his right breast.

THEY SAY I KILLED MRS. HAMMERLY.

Mrs. Hammerly, of Washington, an aged aunt of mine, they even say I killed, who came, as she often said, home to die. I took the best care of her while sick, and waited upon her all the time, besides taking care of my children. I did for her all that it was possible for one human being to do for another. Yet I am accused of killing her. She died in April, 1870. But I know I am innocent and God knows it, and I do not fear the result of this inquiry.

BUT MY DEAR CHILDREN,

Is it not hard enough to lose them, without being accused of such a terrible crime as this?" said she, while her large eyes filled with blinding tears and coursed down her pale features as she affectionately told me of their taking off.

"After Charles, my husband, died, I lived for my children; they were smart, bright children, and I set great store upon them, I often denied myself for them and took great pleasure in doing so. George W. was the oldest child; he was eight years, while Charles Henry was the next eldest, and was six. They had never been blackberrying, and had often asked me, so I promised them, and one day in July, 1870, Delpha, the nurse, and the two boys started for the field before sunrise; and I cautioned them to return early. They came back before the sun was hot, about nine o'clock, I think.

THAT NIGHT THEY WERE TAKEN SICK

and broke out around the mouth and hands, and the doctor thought it was poisoned oak. They were sick for nearly two weeks, George dying on the 24th of July and Charles on the 26th. Annie, aged six, and Maud aged three years, were then left to me, and I felt in my sorrow that I had much yet to live for, and I was happy in doing for them." (Here again the poor woman's utterance became choked, and she wept bitterly.) "For a time all went well," said she, "and I was feeling happy, when Annie was, on the 11th of last February, taken ill and lingered until the 16th, and died.

But I still had one left, and contented myself with doing the best for the dead and caring for my living child."

SHE WAS A BEAUTIFUL CHILD,

too, and, although she could not talk plain

she could say Bible verses and hymns. At last, on March 25, little Maud, the last I had, was taken sick, and died in two days after, and when I lost her I felt that I had nothing more to live for. I have no relatives here, and although the members of my church are very kind and come to see me, yet I feel that I am now alone in the world."

The poor woman seemed much affected and said, "It is so hard to be suspected of doing such horrid things; but, as I know and God knows I am innocent, I can bear it all."

DID DELPHA DO IT?

Knowing that Mrs. Lloyd knew the worst in relation to her case I asked if she did not believe the servant, Delpha, was the cause of her trouble.

She quickly replied, "No, sir; Delpha loved the children as I did; she seemed to be perfectly wrapped up in them."

I then asked to see Delpha and she was called. She is a bright mulato girl, apparently about twenty years of age.

DELPHA'S STORY.

She told her simple story to me in relation to the sickness of the children which completely corroborated the above statement of Mrs. Lloyd. She seemed to feel very bad, and said that she would rather have all the trouble on her than that "Miss Em!" as she called Mrs. Lloyd, should have any.

She said Mrs. Lloyd had been more than a mother to her, and she would rather die than see her get into trouble. After some further general conversation I left, deeply impressed with what I had seen and heard.

4/24/72 Mirror

Among the gentlemen of the quill in quest of information who were attracted to this town on Tuesday last by the preliminary examination of Mrs. LLOYD, was a "special correspondent" of the Alexandria *Gazette*, who bears a closer relation to that paper than that of an ordinary reporter, and for which reason, we were particularly anxious, as a matter of journalistic courtesy, to put him in possession of all the facts we had at hand. He reached here at 11 o'clock, after Court had opened, and left at one, before it closed, and had little time to collate facts for himself. Accordingly, just before leaving, and at his own request, we cheerfully furnished him with *advance slips* of our own paper, of the next morning, supposing that he would use them as the basis of his own letter, or that, in the event of substituting our report for one of his own, he would give the proper credit. Our surprise and chagrin may be imagined when we next morning read in the *Gazette nearly two columns of our own brain work*, published as the contribution of its enterprising "special." Had the matter rested there we might have been silent, and consoled ourself with having enlivened the pages of that journal with two columns of interesting *original matter*—but when we find it copied into several of our exchanges, credited to the Alexandria *Gazette*, justice to ourself seemed to demand that we should "rise to explain," especially as the *Gazette* gave it to the world twelve hours in advance of the *Mirror*. Such practices may be common in big cities like Alexandria, and on great dailies like the *Gazette*, and their perpetrators may regard them as "huge jokes"—country folks, however, in their rural simplicity, have a different name for them. We do not claim for the article in question any special merit, but what is worth copying is generally regarded by journalists, worth crediting.

P. S. A few hours before going to press, but after the above paragraph was in type, we received from the "special" aforesaid a letter of explanation, but as we already knew "how it was," and our sole object being to relieve ourself from the natural imputation of having "cribbed" from the *Gazette*, we know that our friends of that Journal, usually so scrupulous in the matter of credits, will excuse us for endeavoring to set ourself square upon the record.

4/27/72 Washingtonian

The Condition of the South.

Henry Ward Beecher in the Christian Union.

It is needless here to trace the political history of reconstruction, or to apportion the blame for its mistakes. It is enough to say that in point of fact the State governments of the South have very largely fallen into the hands of ignorant and knavish men. Public money has been wasted and stolen by wholesale. A proud and high-spirited population have seen their places of trust filled by foreign adventurers and uneducated freedmen. The old political leaders in whom the people had confidence and who alone had experienced in the conduct of affairs, have been excluded from office by Congress. The course of politics has tended the antagonism between the former masters and the blacks, and to still further allieniate the former from the national authority. This is a gloomy picture. One feature remains to be added. Into this weakened and distracted community there has been no infusion of new, healthy blood. I was hoped that immigration would renovate the South. But there has been no immigration, or but little. The old elements are left to work out their way unassisted. Of the present duty of the nation at large towards the South we shall here say but a word. The best service that can be rendered to the Southern people politically is to to let them alone.

5/8/72 Mirror

THE CONDITION OF THE SOUTH.

The manner in which the Southern States have been plundered since the conclusion of the war is a reproach to the American name. And it is especially a disgrace to the country that the adventurers who have preyed upon the conquered and defenceless communities of the South, without mercy and without compunction, have steadily received support and encouragement from the Administration.

It will not be till the existing Administration has gone out of power that we shall know the full extent of the wrongs that have been perpetrated in the Southern States. But the revelations made in the report of the Committee "on Alleged Outrages in the Southern States," of whom a majority are Republicans, though probably falling short of the truth, will be likely to astonish fair-minded men in the North.

From statistics given in this report it appears that in the ten States where carpet-bag domination has had full sway, their debts and liabilities have been increased since the close of the war by the enormous amount of more than two hundred and forty millions of dollars. In Texas, which had no debt in 1861, the present debt and liabilities amount to $17,000,000. Georgia in 1860 owed $3,000,000. To-day its debts and liabilities—exclusive of $6,000,000 deemed fraudulent, and which will probably not be paid—sum up over $44,000,000. South Carolina has increased its debt since 1861 from $4,000,000 to $39,158,544. Alabama's debt has increased since 1861 from less than $6,000,000 to more than $38,000,000. Arkansas, under carpet-bag rule, has added nearly $16,000,000 to its debt. The little State of Florida, whose total assessed value of real and personal estate only amounts to $22,480,843, has had $15,542,447 added to its indebtment since it has fallen into the hands of Grant's friends. Throughout the South the same story is told.

Wherever the carpet-baggers have had power there has been, without exception, extravagant, wasteful expenditure and shameless acts of plunder.

It is no wonder that the Claytons, the Pavises, the Scotts, the Clarks, the Bullocks, the Blodgetts, the Holdens, and all their kind ardently desire Grant's re-election, for it would be an impossibility that any other President could ever be induced to support and protect them as he has done.—*N. Y. Sun.*

5/1/72 Mirror

THE CASE of the Long Island lady who apologized to her guests for the breakfast being late by saying that a babe had been born to her during the night, is paralleled by the Western wife who sent her husband his washing with the message "Dear John, I have only had time to do up two of your shirts, its a boy and weighs twelve pounds"

5/15/72 Mirror

THE CINCINNATI NOMINEES.

The Cincinnati Convention met on Wednesday, organized promptly, deliberated briefly, commenced balloting at an early hour on the third day, and nominated amid a storm of applause on the sixth ballot, HORACE GREELEY, of New York, for President, and on the second ballot, B. GRATZ BROWN, of Missouri, for Vice President.

Thirty years ago Mr. GREELE established the *Tribune*, and from that hour to the present has allowed no opportunity to pass unimproved in the interests first of Abolitionism pure and simple secondly of more advanced Republicanism—thirdly of Union-saving Radicalism, and latterly, of modern Liberal Republicanism. Albeit somewhat crotchety, he is generally credited with ability, consistancy, and honesty—traits that ought to insure him the support of his party friends, but elements, we regret to say, not often duly appreciated by Radicals.

5/18/72 Washingtonian

Greeley, with his present position, is far preferable to Grant. It is a choice between these two—a Democratic ticket would not stand the shadow of a chance, and would only secure Grant's election. With the past issues dead to memory as they are to the politics of the country, Greeley upon his present platform of principles, can be taken by the country as a mighty change for the better, in comparison with this administration, with its "Ku-Klux laws, its suspension of the habeas corpas, its packing of the Supreme Court, its interference with the States and their free elections, its military government, its St. Domingo jobs, and its favorites and nepotism."

(In retrospect, this newspaper editor seemed to be an unlikely choice for president. He appeared to be an eccentric intellectual rather than a successful politician. Grechley, though a former abolitionist, had offered to post bail for Jefferson Davis and he was sympathetic to many southern complaints during Reconstruction.)

5/15/72 Mirror

MOSBY AT THE WHITE HOUSE.

A special from Washington to the Philadelphia Press gives the following, under the head of "A Pleasant Interview," of a number of distinguished personages at the White House on Wednesday :

Col. J. S. Mosby, ex-Confederate ranger, called to-day upon the President, in company with Senator Lewis, of Virginia, and was kindly received. They talked for some time upon public affairs, and during the interview Col. J. W. Forney, of Philadelphia, came in to pay his respects to the President. He was, of course, introduced to Col. Mosby. The latter had his little son with him, to whom he introduced Col. Forney, saying: "Here is the man who has abused your father in his newspaper;" to which Col. Forney responded, "Not half as much as you deserved."

"Well," said Mosby, "what are you going to do about the Cincinnati convention?"

To which Col. Forney replied :

"I am going to stand by the old flag and follow the old leader, Gen. Grant. We shall settle our difficulties in Pennsylvania, if there is any wisdom in our party leaders, and so help to secure a good editor for the New York Tribune and a good President for the country."

"Then," said Mosby, turning to Grant, "I will never vote for Horace Greeley. I will stump Virginia against him. I will undoubtedly support a democratic candidate if my party nominates one, and if it don't I will vote for President Grant."

The President was very much pleased with the interview, and after Mosby left remarked that "*he looked like a man who could ride a horse boldly and freely.*"

COL. JOHN S. MOSBY'S POSITION.—The Alexandria *Gazette* says—We have seen a letter from Col. John S. Mosby to a friend in this city, in which reference is made to a reported conversation between Col. Mosby and President Grant. Referring to that report Col. M. says, "I see I am reported as saying to Gen. Grant that I would support him 'even if a Democrat were nominated against him. I do not care about coming out in the papers to correct this, but I hope my friends will not think that I said any such thing. On the contrary I expressly told Gen. Grant that I would support the Democratic nominee, but as between him and Greeley I was in favor of the South going for the one that would offer us the most generous terms i. e., that the Philadelphia Convention must out bid Cincionati "

(His friendship with former foe Grant began when in the weeks following the war his wife went personally to the General to apply for his parole while Mosby was still hiding out.)

The Drought is becoming serious—from all sections of the country we have most discouraging accounts of its effects upon the wells and springs, and even the weakening of the volume of water in streams and rivers. New York is greatly exorcised lest the supply from which that great city is fed, should prove inadequate. And such is the case almost everywhere. Here at home, the famous Rock Spring, which for nearly a half a century, has supplied the citizens of Leesburg with a superabundance of pure water, and hitherto regarded as inexaustible, begins to give signs of weakness. and is lower by nearly two feet than it was ever known before, while numerous wells and springs in the surrounding country give forth uncertain flows,—and we hear of many persons who have been compelled to haul water a considerable distance for ordinary domestic uses. If such things are seen this early in the season, what may we not look for by midsummer, unless in the meantime we are blessed with abundant showers. The pastures are backward—the stock lean—vegetation sickly—the earth dry and parched, and the heavens wear the appearance of brass.

Another Terrible Warning.—A negro girl aged about fifteen years, living with her parents three miles from Leesburg, was so seriously burned on Saturday night last by the explosion of a coal oil lamp, that she died before daylight Sunday morning. She was in an upper room of the house dressing for a ball, and it is supposed attempted to fill the lamp while burning. The explosion occurred about 8 o'clock in the evening, and death followed at four the next morning.

The same night, a lamp exploded in the house of Mr. SAMUEL ORRISON, in this town, but fortunately with no more serious consequences, than a terrible fright and an ugly spot of grease. These lamps, now in such general use, cannot be handled with too much caution.

Poe and the Juleps.

In the "Monthly Gossip" of *Lippincott's Magazine* for May, we find this story of the author of "The Raven":

John R. Thompson succeeded Edgar A. Poe, as editor of the *Southern Literary Messenger*. Fresh from the University, well to-do in the goods of this world, and justly proud of his position—for the *Messenger* then was the oldest, and certainly one of the best, magazines in the Union—Thompson lived *en prince* in a suite of apartments in Main street. One of them, furnished handsomely as a reception-room, contained a beaufect well stocked with the choicest liquors. Into this room came one morning about eleven o'clock a handsome, very intellectual-looking man, who, bowing formally, asked if he had the pleasure of addressing Mr. John R. Thompson.

"Yes," said Mr. Thompson, who had already risen.

"My name," said the stranger, "is Poe."

It may be taken for granted that the youthful editor, who was never lacking in courtesy, gave his predecessor just such a reception as the occasion and the man required. If Thompson felt honored by the visit, Poe was more than gratified by the cordiality and unfeigned respect manifested by the young poet. The author of "The Raven" was now seated in an easy chair. Conversation flowed freely and pleasantly, Poe, of course, taking the lead, and an hour or two slipped away seemingly in as many moments.

Poe rose to take leave. Thompson entreated him to remain. No, he had an engagement. As he turned toward the door, Poe's eye fell upon the beaufet with its glittering array of silver and cut-glass, and a change passed over his grave, handsome face. In an animated tone he said, "Ah! you have a nice little arrangement there, Mr. Thompson. Perhaps you can give me something to drink?"

"Indeed I can," said Mr. Thompson, "What will you have?"

"That depends upon what you've got."

Thompson enumerated several kinds of wine, whiskey; and French brandy, commending the last as very superior.

Poe chose brandy. Selecting a tumbler of the ordinary size, he lifted the decanter with steady hand and began to pour—one finger, two fingers, three fingers, four fingers, five!

Thompson became alarmed. "Excuse my seeming incivilty," said he; "such it really is not, I assure you—but, Mr. Poe, are you—are you not taking a little—just a little—too much for your own good?"

"No, sir, not at all," was the reply. "I know myself thoroughly well, Mr. Thompson, and can gauge myself to a hair. I have had some experience in these matters, and I have discovered about brandy, good French brandy, this remarkable peculiarity, that it is least injurious when you fill the glass as nearly full as possible, and leave room for as little water as possible." And the pouring went steadily on till the tumbler was full to the very brim. "Now a drop—just a drop—of water, if you please."

The drop of water—it was barely more than that—was added, and then, to Thompson's amazement and horror, Poe drained his glass to the bottom.

He lingered awhile, and Thompson, fearing the brandy might tell upon his distinguished guest after he got into the street, suggested, as adroitly and respectfully as he could, that a few moments of repose on the sofa would be of service to him.

"Oh, no," said Poe, "you need have no fear for me. The brandy is nothing. *I've already had thirteen juleps;* and now I think I'll step across the way and get my breakfast."

Extending his hand in farewell, he bowed stiffly and was gone.

How Poe's "Annabel Lee" Came to be Published.

"Paul Peebles" writes in the *Home Journal:* A pleasant little story of John R. Thompson and Edgar A. Poe appears in the "Gossip" corner of "Lippincott's Magazine" for May. Probably the readers of the *Home Journal*—especially those who "dote" upon the author of "The Raven"—have already enjoyed the account of poor Poe's "thirteen juleps" and the agreeable titillation of the midriff created by his tumblerful of fine French brandy, taken neat. But the anecdote reminds me of another one, which I do not remember to have seen in print: perhaps you can find space for it.

While Mr. Thompson was conducting the *Southern Literary Messenger*, Poe was a regular visitor to the editorial sanctum of that excellent magazine—or, rather, he was an exceedingly irregular dropper-in; his normal condition being, so to speak, always abnormal if judged by the ordinary human standards. Generally under the combined influence of poetic frenzy and of strong alcoholic stimulant, he was likewise celebrated for a perpetual impecuniosity. Money seemed to drill holes through his pockets, and, by some curious inversion of the laws of Nature, the hard cash he was able to obtain (for his day was the day of gold and silver) underwent a summary process of liquefaction. Like an excellent sponge, he was always absorbent and soon dry.

One day, entering Thompson's room—the same in which the *buffet* with the fine French brandy stood—Poe requested a small loan, saying that he had received a sudden call to Philadelphia, and was out of funds—"would Mr. Thompson oblige him with five dollars?"

The editor of the "Southern Literary," accustomed to Poe's peculiar ways, met the demand with the easy grace and open hand for which he is noted; and Poe, bowing his thanks, retreated toward the door; but, pausing at the threshold, he carelessly flung to Thompson a small bit of writing, with the remark:

"By the way, Thompson, there is a little thing I knocked off last night—it's not much, but you've been very kind to me, and perhaps you can make room for it in the magazine!"—saying which he turned and left.

Thompson opened the paper and found the manuscript of "Annabel Lee"—one of the most charming of love-songs. It appeared in the next number of the "Southern Literary Messenger." Thompson, I believe, still preserves the autograph copy as a memento of Poe.

5/22/72 Mirror

Decoration Day.

THE ANNUAL Decoration of the graves of the Confederate Dead in the Union Cemetery will take place on Saturday next, June 1st, 1872, at 4 o'clock, P. M. All interested in this labor of love are invited to assemble at the COURT HOUSE at that hour, and bring with them all the flowers they can.

MEMORIAL ASSOCIATION

LECTURE.

REV DR. W. E. MUNSEY,

BY INVITATION of the CENTRAL MEMORIAL ASSOCIATION of Loudoun, will deliver an ADDRESS in LEESBURG, on

TUESDAY, JUNE 4th, 1872

at 3 o'clock, P. M., for the benefit of the Association.

TICKETS, 50 Cts.

THE PROCEEDS will be applied to the ERECTION OF THE PROPOSED

MONUMENT

TO THE CONFEDERATE DEAD. Members of the Association are requested to hand in their Annual dues to the Treasurer as soon as convenient.

J. W. FOSTER, President.
H. O. CLAGETT, Sec'y. and. Treasurer
may 29 1872.

Strawberry Festival.

THE LADIES OF THE PRESBYTERIAN Congregation, Katoctin Church. will hold a GRAND FESTIVAL AT WATERFORD, WEDNESDAY, MAY 29th, 1872. The public are cordially invited to attend, and aid the Ladies in their charitable work. Everything tempting to the appetite will be procured, such as STRAWBERRIES, ICE CREAM, LEMONADE, &c. A STRING BAND will be in attendance, and no pains will be spared to make the occasion pleasant and delightful to all.

Festival will commence at 3 o'clock, and continue late in the evening.   (may 29

AMUSING SCENE ON A STREET CAR.

The passengers on one of Riker's street cars laughed some yesterday morning at a scene between the conductor and a well-dressed young man from Georgetown. As the car was passing down the Avenue, the young man at the time standing on the platform taking it easy, with one foot on a trunk, he was approached by the conductor and his fare demanded. He quietly passed over his five cents.

Conductor.—I demand 25 cents for that trunk.

Young Man. (hesitating.)—25 cents? Well, I think I will not pay it.

C.—Then I shall put the trunk off.

Y. M.—You had better not, or you may be sorry for it.

Conductor pulls strap, stops car, dumps trunk on the Avenue, starts car, and after going some two squares, approaches the young man, who was still as calm as a summer morning, and in an angry mood says: "Now I have put your trunk off, what are you going to do about it?"

Young Man. (coolly.)—Well, I don't propose to do anything about it; it's no concern of mine; it wasn't my trunk.

Conductor (fiercely.)—Then, why didn't you tell me so?

Y. M.—Because you did not ask me, and I told you you'd be sorry for it.

C. (furiously.)—Then go inside the car.

Y. M.—Oh, no! you're good enough company for me out here.

At this juncture a portly German emerges from the car, and angrily says; "Mine Gott! you feller, where is mine drunk?"

Young Man.—My friend, I think that is your trunk down on the avenue there.

German.—Who puts him off? I hafe de monish to pay him. I will see about dot.

The car was stopped, and shortly afterwards the conductor was seen to come sweating up with the trunk on his back—a part of the performance he did not enjoy half as well as did the passengers.— *Washington Star.*

LOOK OUT!

MUSEUM

OF LIVING

CURIOSITIES!

WILL EXHIBIT IN

LEESBURG,

ON

MONDAY

AND

TUESDAY

JUNE, 10 & 11,

ON THE

COR. MAKET & LIBERTY STS.,

NEXT TO M. E. CHURCH SOUTH

WONDERFUL LEOPARD CHILD,

OR

SPOTTED BOY!

AND HIS COMPANION, A HUGE

Boa Constrictor.

This astonishing specimen of humanity, a connecting link of the brute creation, was captured, with his strange companion, in the wilds of Africa, by an exploring party in the service of Her Most Gracious Majesty, Queen Victoria, in the spring of 1868, and brought to London and exhibited at the Zoological Gardens, and in the short space of ten months they were visited by one million, five hundred thousand curious sight-seers. At a special medical examination in the city of Paris, gentlemen of the highest educational standing, of London, Glasgow, Vienna, St. Petersburg, and of the French Capital, failed to account for this most wonderful freak of nature, and mysteriously constituted mortal. This Leopard Child is supposed to be about nine (9) years of age, and is entirely covered by regularly-formed white and black spots, similar to the leopard. The white spots are as clear as the purest Caucasian skin, whilst the black is of that jetty hue of the Congo African. His companion—a huge Boa Constrictor—is not a poisonous reptile, but is of that ferocious species who destroy their victims by strangling and crushing them to death. This huge monster seems perfectly delighted with the caresses and familiarities of the Leopard Boy, permitting him, at any and all times, to handle him with the greatest freedom—the two seemingly appear to be inseparable companions, even to sharing beds. Their attachment is so mutually strong, that occasionally it is even very difficult to separate them, each showing the affection of a mother and child.

PROF. PADGETT

The Great

CIRCASSIAN

WONDER

The only Male Circassian in America. He can entertain an audience for hours with thrilling narratives of his escape from bondage.

THE

HAPPY FAMILY,

CONSISTING OF VARIOUS SPECIES

OF

ANIMALS!

Living together in Perfect Harmony.

The Democratic Mirror

BENJ. F. SHEETZ, Editor.

Wednesday Morning, June 5, 1872

A SHORT time ago it was announced that the Second Vice President of the Pennsylvania Railway Company, had been sent to an Insane Asylum, on account of impaired mental faculties, resulting from hard and incessant labor. Recently we have been informed that the President, Mr. J. EDGAR THOMPSON, had sailed for Europe in search of necessary rest, and that Colonel THOMAS A. SCOTT, the First Vice President, had been ordered by his physicians to cease his arduous labors, if he desired the ordinary prolongation of life vouchsafed to mortals. The successful management of a gigantic corporation like the Pennsylvania Central unquestionably requires an inconceivable amount of labor. Yet the sacrifice of valuable lives even in the pursuit of a laudable ambition is scarcely justifiable, when, by a proper division of labor, the terrible risk incurred in overtaxing the brain and body, might easily be avoided.—*Balt. Gazette.*

A very interesting case of the successful transfusion of blood from one person to another is described by Professor Judgeson, of Berlin, in a recent number of a medical journal published in that city. His patient was a man twenty-eight years of age, who had been poisoned by phosphorus, having taken a solution of the ignition mass of eight bundles of matches on the 9th of December. On the 11th of February, the activity of the heart having been excited by champagne, a transfusion of 580 cubic centimetres of blood, which had just been taken from three persons in good health, was affected, into a vein of the arm, 500 cubic centimetres of the patient's own blood being at the same time taken from an artery. An improvement in his condition at once set in and he was able to leave his bed early in March.

6/26/72 Mirror

The Murder of the Buffalo.

From the N. Y. Evening Post.

Few persons probably know how rapidly the American bison is disappearing from the Western plains. At one time, it is said they were to be found everywhere west of Lake Champlain and the Hudson river; but for many years they have been extinct east of the Mississippi river. The work of destruction, however, appears to go on more bravely in proportion as they are driven into narrower and narrower limits and it is not unlikely that the fate of the European bison, which once abounded in the woody wild wilderness of Germany, Northern Gaul, and neighboring parts of the continent, but which is now to be found alone and rarely in the forests of Lithuania, will soon be theirs.

Some idea of the extent of this ruthless slaughter may be formed from the fact that twenty-five thousand bisons were killed during the month of May south of the Kansas and Pacific railroad for the sake of their hides alone, which are sold at the paltry price of two dollars each on delivery for shipment to the Eastern markets. Add to this five thousand—a small estimate—shot by tourists and killed by the Indians to supply meat to the people on the frontier, and we have a sum total of thirty thousand as the victims for a single month.

If the bison were a wild and savage animal—if to kill one required any special skill, or bravery, or nerve—there might be some justification for this enormous slaughter. But the fact is, that the bison is an exceedingly mild dispositioned animal. His looks indicate ferocity and malignity, but his nature does not correspond with his appearance. Even in the breeding season, when the common bull is frequently dangerous; when the stag and the elk attack everything that comes in their way; and when most animals are pugnacious, the bison will go by on the other side to avoid a man. It is only when he is wounded by a blundering aim, or irritated by a persistent pursuit, that he shows fight enough to make hunting him enjoyable. Besides, the Indian ponies are trained to dodge his onset, when maddened beyond endurance, so that the hunter who can manage to stick to his horse has little to do but sit still and keep firing until he makes a fatal shot.

Every one remembers how Prince Alexis under the leadership of General Sheridan, participated in this "sport," to the intense gratification of his royal father, and to the profit of the special correspondents. It is doubtful, however, whether even a royal precedent can justify this kind of so called hunting. However this may be in the Eastern States, the following paragraph from the letter of an army officer shows that in the Western States this kind of "sport" is estimated at its true worth, while at the same time, its reference to the number of persons who are following the Russian Princeling's example confirms the apprehension that the American bison will soon become as fabulous an animal as the dodo:

"'To shoot buffalo' seems to be a mania. Men came from London—cockneys and nobles—and from all parts of the Republic to enjoy what they call sport. Sport! when no danger is incurred and no skill required. I see no more sport in shooting a buffalo than in shooting an ox; nor so much danger as there is in hunting Texas cattle."

Imposing Ceremonies.

Seven hundred and eighteen Confederate soldiers, disinterred at Gettysburg recently and taken to Richmond, were interred at Hollywood Cemetery on Thursday last, amid the most impressive and solemn funeral ceremonies. The procession, two miles in length, consisting of the First Virginia Regiment, the Richmond Howitzers, detachments of police, sixteen wagons with boxes containing the dead, followed by ex-Confederate comrades, was headed by Geo. Gen. E. Pickett, to whose division the dead belonged. Next came the Society of the Southern Cross Brotherhood, the rear being brought up by carriages extending a mile in length. Along the line of procession the streets were draped in mourning, the stores closed, and business generally suspended. An immense concourse of persons lined the streets.— The spectacle is said to have been the most imposing witnessed in that city since the close of the war.

The Ideal Art Music.—On Tuesday evening next, July 2d, at the M. E. Church, South, in Leesburg, Rev. Dr. W. E. MUNSEY, will by invitation of the Confederate Memorial Association, deliver a Lecture on the above subject, the proceeds to be applied to the fund for the erection of a monument in Union Cemetery to the memory of the Confederate dead who there lie entombed. The object itself should be sufficient to guarantee a crowded house, but when to that is added the pleasure of listening to one of the most remarkable literary geniuses of the age, it should be overflowing—and if the two together are not sufficient to attract every body who has a kindly regard for the dead heroes of a Lost Cause,—or a soul to be stirred by the eloquent notes of an intellectual prodigy.

A Father Shoots his Daughter's Alleged Seducer.

Considerable excitement was created in Georgetown on Thursday last, by the shooting of a man named Davis, a real estate agent of Washington, by Edward T. Hardy, a merchant of New York, but formerly of Norfolk. It seems that Hardy stepped into the store of Bradly & Carter, and walking up to Davis, asked if his name was Davis. Receiving an affirmative reply, he drew a revolver and fired, striking Davis in the side, inflicting a slight flesh wound. Davis at once fled, halloring for help, and Hardy was arrested by a policeman. When questioned as to why he did it, Hardy replied that Davis had ruined his daughter, that he came there to kill the villain, and he intended to do it. He was carried to the Police Court, and there appearing to be no danger of life from the wound of Davis, Hardy was bailed in $3,000, Mr. Joseph H. Bradly, jr., becoming his bond man. The cause of the difficulty is thus stated by the *Patriot:*

While Mr. Hardy was doing business in Norfolk he married Miss Pickerille, of Georgetown, the daughter of Mrs. Ann Pickerille. The daughter of the couple, Miss Hardy, an accomplished and pretty girl, frequently made visits to the house of her aunt, sometimes staying for month at a time. It is alleged that on one of these visits she became acquainted with Davis, and that he accomplished her ruin. It is said also that in order to cloak his villainy, Davis introduced Mr. Henry Bradley to the young lady, and that on the 2d of last November Mr. Bradley was married to Miss Hardy at Christ Church, Rev. Dr. Williams officiating

About five months after the young couple were married —the testimony is, that up to that time they had lived happily—Mrs. Bradley was suddenly taken sick, and, unexpectedly to Bradley and his friends, gave birth to a healthy and full developed child. Bradley, as soon as his wife was strong enough, sent her home to her father, and, it is said, instituted a suit for a divorce in the County Court of Montgomery county, Md., which is now pending. At first Mrs. Bradley denied that Davis was the father of the child, but it is reported that she has lately confessed to her father the fact, upon which he immediately took action.

The Alexandria Gazette of one day last week, says: Mrs. Adrain, an old lady, resident of Loudoun county, who has spent two or three months in Philadelphia having her eyes operated upon for cataract, passed through this city this morning on her way home entirely blind.

THE MIRROR.

WEDNESDAY................................July 10.

The Fourth.—The Fourth of July was hot—excessively so. The fervent patriotism of our people gave vent to its inspiration through drops of perspiration, that played the dial with the aristocracy of starched shirts and paper collars. The doors of our business houses were open, but few were the customers and short the profits.

The Sabbath School attached to the M. E. Church, South, hied to Vandevanter's woods at an early hour in the morning, but a threatning cloud about one o'clock terminated their enjoyment, and they returned home dustier if not better children.

About 11 o'clock a special train from Alexandria, landed at the depot a small number of excursionists who brought with them a drum and fife and two copies of the American flag. A baker's dozen of the stalwart sons of Ham marched into town rigged out in costumes the flashy colours of which outraged the most approved Dolly Varden. They demeaned themselves with much propriety, however, and at a seasonable hour left for their homes, pleased, we hope, with their day's enjoyment.

The larger and wiser portion of our own people, who wished to observe the day in quiet enjoyment, fled to the Potomac, and on its shady banks and in its cooling waters, passed their time in eating, drinking, bathing, rowing fishing, and dreaming of the good time coming.

At night, the firing of rockets, the burning of barrels, and "music by the Band," enlivened the otherwise monotonous routine that characterised the town, until a late hour.

At the depot there was a slight jarring among the "amendments," but a black eye and a bloody nose or two restored the equilibrium in that quarter, while later at night, a couple of usualy undemonstrative young men, became unduly enthused with too much 4th of July and bad whiskey, and had to be put in the lock up until they simmered down—which they did by morning. Otherwise all went merry. The celebration at Guilford, under the management of Mr. Longcore attracted a good many from hereabouts, and we understand was quite a success. Horace was not present to tell the crowd "what he knew about farming," but his place was supplied by the ever ready J. Mort Kilgour and Dr. J. C. Hitt, of Alexandria, the possible future Congressman from this district. Both gentlemen acquitted themselves serenely, and the programme in other respects was well filled.

Strangers.—Our hotels and boarding houses are pretty well filled with summer visitors from the cities. We have not for several years seen more strangers in our midst than at present, and we have no doubt that with proper accommodations the number would be largely increased. We are within a couple hours ride of Washington city, and there is no place, when reached, more pleasant, more healthy, or more desirable generally as a quiet summer resort for those who with their wives and children seek relief from the dust and heat of a large city, than Leesburg.

7/10/72 Mirror

John Robinson's circus met with an accident on the 3d instant, at West Haven, Conn., on the railroad. While going under the bridge the bridge settled, and the menagerie cages on the platform cars struck it. Six cages were knocked off and broken up. The lion and tapir escaped, but were soon secured. The zebra was fatally injured. A cage of birds was also broken up, but all were saved. A cage containing fifty monkeys was among those wrecked and the monkeys are now loose in West Haven woods. The loss is estimated at $10,000.

Alexandria vs. Falls Church.—There was a colored excursion to Vienna station on the W. & O. R. R., from this city yesterday, and one from Falls Church to the same station. Things passed off very pleasantly until near 11 o'clock, when a fight took place, and in a very few minutes it became general. The females left the scene of conflict and took refuge in the woods. Pistols, knives, razors, hatchets, and axes were used freely and many of the combatants were severely wounded. The fight lasted some time, but finally ended in a victory for Falls Church as the Alexandrian retreated to the cars. Many in their fright and eagerness to get on board, came near being killed as the train was starting from the depot at the time.—*Alex. Sentinel of the 3d*

6/26/72 Mirror

The Board of Supervisors of this county met in Leesburg on Friday for the purpose of taking some action toward improving the Poor House farm, which was seriously injured during the war. The barn was wantonly burned by federal soldiers, with a full knowledge of its uses, and should long since have been repaired by the general government, the attention of which has been repeatedly called to it. It has not done it, however, and as will be seen by notice in to-day's paper, the Board advertise for Proposals to re-build the barn and repair the other buildings on the farm.

7/10/72 Mirror

A Cleveland woman not long ago modestly requested her husband to go to the dressmaker and tell her that she (the wife) had changed her mind and would have the watered silk made up instead of the poplin, and "then if she thinks it would look better with ten bias flounces without puffing and box-plaited below the equator, which should be gathered in hemstitched gudgeons up and down the seams, with a gusset stitch between, she can make it up in that way, instead of fluting the bobinette insertion and piecing out with point applique as I suggested yesterday.

6/8/72 Washingtonian

Base Ball — On June 1st, 1872 a match game of base ball was played at Middleburg between the Loudoun B. B. C., and the Dolly Varden of Leesburg— When after 6¼ hours' play the score stood as follows:

LOUDOUN B. B. C.

		Runs.	Outs.
McKensie,	C.	6	5
Yellet,	P.	10	3
Stone,	S. S.	7	5
Pryor,	1 B.	12	0
Taylor,	2 B.	8	5
C. Yellet,	3 B.	6	6
McVeigh,	L. F.	10	2
Brooks,	C. F.	9	1
Brown	R. F.	10	0
Totals		73 R.	27 O.

DOLLY VARDEN B. B. C.

		Runs.	Out.
W. Shafer,	C.	4	4
Harvey,	P.	6	2
Fountleroy,	S. S.	6	3
A. Lynch,	1 B.	4	4
Wildman,	2 B.	6	2
Grimes,	3 B.	5	5
Cline,	L. F.	4	5
Manson,	C. F.	7	5
Hough	R. F.	5	5
Totals		46 R.	27 O.

The Leesburg Club return their thanks to their successful contestants.

7/13/72 Washingtonian

Horace Greeley's Interview with President Johnson.

From the Courier Journal.

Soon after Johnson was installed for President, he sent a gentleman to New York to solicit an interview with Horace Greeley. Unable to leave the Capital. Greeley must come to him at once at the White House. Greeley promptly complied with the request.

Johnson opened the conversation by saying that he found himself in a most trying position. The nation was convulsed with passion in consequence of Mr. Lincoln's assassination; the situation was new and embarrassing to him: he felt inadequate to the task to which he had been so unexpectedly called, and he felt the need, as he had never before felt it, of the counsel of some cool and sagacious man. He had, therefore, sent for Greeley. What course to pursue, how to stem the torrent of Northern frenzy, how to manage the reins of government in a crisis so awful, was a problem too deep for him to solve. Placing himself in Mr. Greeley's hands, he asked:

WHAT MUST I DO?

Thanking him for the confidence thus reposed in him, Mr. Greeley replied that his best course was to call to his assistance, a few of the wisest and best men in the country. They should be representative men from the two great sections. On the part of the North he would suggest Gov. Andrew of Massachusetts, Gerrit Smith of New York, and Judge Spalding of Ohio. A like number of Southern gentlemen should be called; they should be invited to the White House as guests of the President, there to remain and deliberate as long as they thought fit; and having agreed on some policy, they should submit it to the President for his approval, and if approved by him, as Mr. Greeley doubted not it would be, it should be, faithfully and rigidly pursued. despite the popular clamor which might for a time ensue.

Mr. Johnson thought with the suggestion. "But what Southern men should I invite, Mr. Greeley, to meet the gentlemen you have named from the North?"

"First and foremost," said Mr. Greeley, "Robert E. Lee, of Va."

"Great heavens!" exclaimed Johnson; "he is the very head and front of the rebellion."

"I know that," said Greeley. "and for that reason you should invite him. , He knows, if any man does, the wants of the Southern people; he of all men possesses the confidence of the entire South; he is upright and pure; he would not recommend a single action on your part which would not meet the approval of your advisers from the North, and the result of the deliberations in which Robert E. Lee. Judge Campbell, of Alabama, and a third man like them, from the South took part, would not only insure the approbation of the disaffected States but in the course of a few months would, I am firmly pursuaded, bring to your support every right-minded and right-hearted man at the North. The pacification of the estranged sections, your main difficulty, would thus be solved. and your path made clear towards the solution of minor difficulties. How are you to discover the true sentiments of the South and the wants of its people if you do not consult her representative will that be in the plan of which the South has no part whatever? It must of necessity be one-sided, partial and unjust. Be persuaded, Mr. President, and call to your aid men of the standing, position, and temper I have suggested, and by all means call them from both sections."

In this strain Mr. Greeley continued until he

FAIRLY WON THE PRESIDENT

over to his way of thinking. The interview ended with the assurance of the President that he would adopt the views of Mr. Greeley, and follow them exactly. He would, however, make a single modification—he would substitute Horace Greeley in place of Gerrit Smith.

"Very well," said Mr. G., "if you call me I will come gladly and aid you to the best of my ability."

They parted, and ten days afterward Johnson threw Greeley's suggestions to the wind, adopted "My policy," and pursued it; with what result the country is too sadly aware.

Thus it will be seen that the *role* of pacificator is

NO NEW THING

with Mr. Greeley, but is only a part which he has systematically pursued ever since the close of the war. So also his confidence in the integrity and good sense of the Southern leaders, and his willingness to trust the Southern people is no new thing. What he is to-day he was years ago; and what better guarantee do we want for the future? At a time when the North was wild with rage against the South, when the execution of every one of her political and military chiefs, and the confiscation of the entire property of her people would hardly have atoned in Northern eyes for Lincoln's assassination, then Greeley, with the wisdom of the statesman and the sympathy of a great heart, stood up for the South alone in his party recommending a line of policy which would have brought peace and happiness to the country and exhibiting traits of character which do credit to and commend humanity.

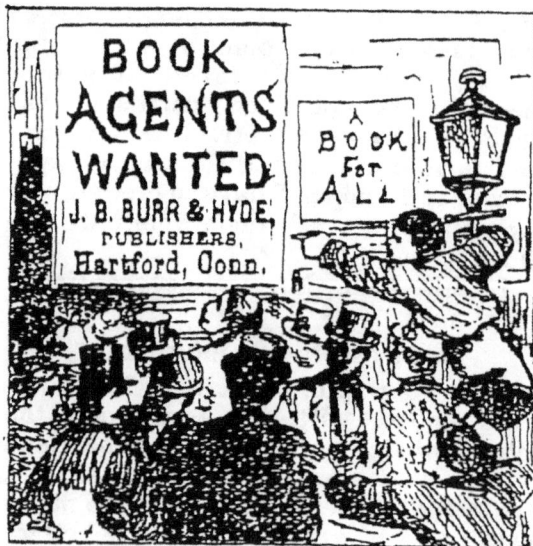

7/31/72 Mirror

Equalizing Whites and Blacks in Restaurants, Saloons, &c.

The Legislature of the District of Columbia recently passed a "social rights bill," which went into operation on Saturday. It has reference to restaurants, ice-cream saloons, barber shops, and the like, and is stringent in its terms.

The act requires that keepers shall display conspicuously in their places of business a scale of prices to be charged for articles or services, and provides a penalty of not less than $20 nor more than $50 for a failure to do so. Any proprietor of any such place of business *for refusing to sell to or wait on any respectable, well-behaved person, without regard to race, color, or previous condition of servitude, or refusing under any pretext to serve any well-behaved, respectable person in the same room and at the same prices as other well-behaved and respectable persons are served, shall be deemed guilty of a misdemeanor,* and upon conviction fined $100 and forfeiture of license.

The dealers have united in a sort of protective association, and in order to prevent their houses from being crowded with negroes they have fixed their tariff of prices as follows, which is posted in a conspicuous place in almost all of saloons:

The bill of fare is as follows:

"Steak, $2; chops, $2; ham and eggs, $3; boiled eggs, fried eggs, coffee, tea, bread and butter, $1 each; fish of all kinds, $2; raw tomatoes, 50 cents."

"A liberal deduction made to our regular patrons."

9/4/72 Mirror

THE LOUISVILLE CONVENTION

On yesterday, the 3d of September, the Convention of "straight-out" democrats. gentlemen opposed to both Grant and Greeley, was to have met in Louisville, Ky., for the purpose of putting in nomination a third candidate for Presidential honors. What their action was we have not yet learned, but it seems to us that any steps they may have taken in that direction can but lead to the re-election of Gen. Grant. As an original proposition we can understand how many men might have hesitated before choosing between them, and as long as there was a ghost of chance of electing any body else, might have striven for the accomplishment of that end. But such a consummation is no longer even possible. The action of the Baltimore Convention, in committing the great democratic party of the country to the support of HORACE GREELEY, has rendered it certain that for the next four years. either Grant or Greeley is to be president of the United States—the fiat has gone forth, and the result is as certain as if the election had already taken place, and no nomination that may be made at Louisville or anywhere else, can alter the decree. This the participants in this new movement understand as well as any body else. They do not pretend to claim that they can elect the man of their choice,—the most they can do, and all they can do, is possibly to compass the defeat of Greeley and insure the success of Grant. That this must be the inevitable result of their movement is fully demonstrated by the active co-operation they are receiving from the friends of Grant and Radicalism, and yet, it is to this feast that they are inviting "simon-pure" democrats.

We want to see the present corrupt ring of radical officials broken. and Horace Greeley, although himself a radical, is capable at this time of dealing a heavy blow in that direction.

(Unfortunately, Greeley's victory was not to be. Grant in fact would carry Loudoun by a slim margin. It was not known at this time that it was General Grant who gave the final orders for the infamous burning raids in Loudoun in 1864. It was thought to be the hated Phil Sheridan who had conducted similar raids in the valley.)

9/4/72 Mirror

The Largest Show in the World.—OLD JOHN ROBINSON's Mammoth Show will exhibit in ALEXANDRIA, on MONDAY, the 9th of September. It is universally conceded to be the Largest and most Complete in all its Departments, of any similar exhibition now travelling. In order that the show may be visited by all in this section disposed to do so, the W. & O. Railroad will transport the people on the line of their road from any station for one-half the regular fare. Hundreds will no doubt avail themselves of this cheap fare to visit the Largest show in the world.

THE MASTODON SHOW!

OLD JOHN ROBINSON'S
MENAGERIE! AQUARIUM! MUSEUM! HIPPODROME AND MONSTER CIRCUS
At Alexandria, on Monday, September 9, 1872
TEN SHOWS IN ONE. SEVEN ACRES OF TENT. ONE TICKET FOR FIFTY CENTS.
Passes to all the Tents. Children Half Price.

SPECIAL NOTICE.—The W. & O. Railroad will run Trains on that day (see time-table) at ONE HALF FARE from any Station on the road. Remember, Monday, Sept. 9, 1872:

A SEDUCER SHOT IN HIS CELL

Miss Fewell's Brother Shoots Clark, Her Seducer, and Mortally Wounded Him

Dying Declaration of the Prisoner

Surrender of Fewell to the Authorities

[Special telegram to the Dispatch.]

Second Dispatch.

BRENTSVILLE, via MANASSAS JUNCTION, VA, August 31,—At about 9 o'clock this morning some men sitting on the porch of Mr. Kincheloe's store, which commands a view of the court-house and jail, discovered a man creeping on his hands and knees towards the front door of the jail which at that time happened to be open. On getting to the door he was observed to enter, but taking him to be the brother of the jailor, the spectators give him no farther thought until in a very few minutes firing was heard in the jail; whereupon several citizens ran from different parts of the village to the jail, and Major W. W. Thornton, who was the first to arrive there, seized the intruder, who proved to be Miss Fewell's brother, by the right arm. Fewell had a pistol in each hand—one supposed to be a navy pistol, the other a smaller one. Major Thornton attempted to drag him away and begged him to stop, but Fewell told him to go away, that he did not want to hurt him (Thornton). The Major, however, did not succeed in taking him away, as Fewell had his left arm bent inside of the iron-grated door, and with the pistol pointed toward Clark discharged another shot. He then walked to the door, ran out and jumped over the fence of the Court green and down into the woods about a hundred yards behind the jail.

Medical aid was at once secured and a warrant immediately issued for the arrest of Fewell who in the mean time walked back into the village and drove off to Manassas in a carriage which happened to be here from that place.

Clark was at first placed in the debtors' cell, which is in the upper story of the jail, but owing to some remarks made by him that he could easily get out, he was yesterday morning taken out and placed in a cell on the ground floor and close to the front door. It appears that Fewell had been up the Orange road putting up lightning-rods, and came down this morning. He got off at Bristow, and walked to Brentsville unperceived by any one until it was too late to prevent this supposed fatal affair.

Clark thought that he had received but one wound, which, on examination, was discovered to have passed about an inch below the left side of the heart and penetrated the backbone. Upon subsequent examination, however, the physicians, Doctors Barbour and Leary, found that another ball had entered the back, but so far have been unable to discover its location. The doctors think that he will die in the course of twelve hours, as internal hemorrhage has taken place.

The following is the dying declaration of the wounded man:

"I was lying on the bed about half asleep. I was aroused by hearing the room door open. On looking I saw a pistol, pointing through the inside door in Rody Fewell's hand. I jumped up and run to the corner on the right-hand side of the door. As I was going to the corner he fired on me and missed me. I ran to the corner on the other side of the door, and he shot at me again. I saw him poke the pistol again through the door, and I grabbed it. It was about the size of a navy pistol. I tried to wrest it from him but failed. He then drew a smaller one, and with that shot me in the breast. Just before he fired the last shot Major Thornton came and endeavored to stop him from firing.

MANASSAS, VA., August 31.—Advices just received from Brentsville state that Clark's condition is easier. Dr. Simpson, his attending physician, pronounces his wound not mortal, and says with proper care he will stand a good chance of recovery. One ball has been extracted; the other is still in him.

A correspondent of the Baltimore *Sun*, writing from Brentsville after the shooting, says that Clark had announced before its occurrence that if there was any shooting to be done he would have the first shot. He says:

Clark has once before been wounded in the lungs as now. He was shot very much in the same manner during the war. His father a Baptist clergyman, came up on the night train, and he is now surrounded by his friends. They are very indignant at the loose way in which the jail was guarded.

Fewell expresses no fear of the result to himself. He is a young man of remarkably excitable disposition and determined character. Some months since he was found lying in an alley at Alexandria literally cut open, and for some time his life was despaired of, but he now bears no marks of his injury.

9/7/72 Washingtonian

DEATH OF CLARK.

[Special to the Alexandria Gazette.]

BRENTSVILLE, Sept. 3, 1872.—Clark is dead! and whether the enormity of his guilt was as great as is is now generally believed to have been, is only known to the unfortunate survivor of the elopement in which he was implicated for. so far as is known, he never breathed a word about the part the young lady took in that affair, except to say that he had not taken her away, and had not seduced her. Soon after he was shot he was removed to the debtor's room on the second floor of the jail, the same in which he had been confined when first incarcerated. The iron bed stead and shuck mattress, upon which he had laid when in there before, were removed, and the room furnished with a wooden bed stead and feather bed, upon which he was propped up, for his wounds would not allow him to lie down. Here he received the assiduous attention of his physicians, Drs. Leary and Barbour, and the constant and unremitting care of numerous residents of the village, who vied with each other in anticipating and supplying his every requirement. His brother-in-law, J. Milton Weedon, was with him from Saturday morning, soon after he was shot, until he died. His father, who had been with him on Saturday and Sunday, returned to him again on Monday, and his mother also reached here a few minutes before he died. Mr. Weedon and Dr. Leary, came to Brentsville last Saturday morning to be present at Clark's examination, which had been set for that time, and both expected that blood would be shed that day, but not until after the trial. They reached here a half an hour after the shooting had occurred. Clark commenced sinking on Sunday morning and life gradually wasted away.

9/18/72 Mirror

Bush Meeting.—The negroes of this town and neighborhood, held a Bush Meeting in the beautiful grove of Mr. JAMES THOMAS about a mile from town. The meeting commenced on Friday and continued over Sunday. The congregations were large and well-behaved, and the best of order maintained throughout. A negro man, JACK BARNES, was arrested about a mile from the ground on Saturday, by the colored police, charged with selling liquor. and carried before Justice WALLACE, who fined him $5 for the offence. The meeting was under the control of Revs. Lane and Robey of this town, assisted by several ministers from a distance.

The first of the Season.—Orrison and Spinks both regaled their customers on Saturday night with fresh Oysters—the first of the season.

THE MIRROR.

WEDNESDAY................... Oct. 2,

MR. ASBURY M. NIXON, familiarly known as "Judge Nixon," died at his residence near Leesburg, on Wednesday night last, in the 63d year of his age. He was an honest, upright man, and enjoyed the confidence and respect of all who knew him.

THE COMMITTEE appointed for the purpose, have secured the services of the Hamilton Cornet Band for the Loudoun Agricultural Fair.

A GOOD HAUL.—Messrs SAMUEL ORRISON and ROBT. MOORE, a few days ago drew from the Potomac, with hook and line, between 40 and 50 bass, the finest caught this season—some of them weighing between three and four pounds.

THE W. & O. RAILROAD.—We are glad to learn that the work on the extension of this road westward is being gradually pushed forward. The grading is now completed from Hamilton to a point within half or three-fourths of a mile of Purcellville. Here they encountered a ledge of shally rock, through which they will have to blast for perhaps fifty yards

SOME PUMPKIN.—Our friend, Mr. THOS. E TAYLOR informs the *Washingtonian* that he this year raised a pumpkin, measuring five feet ten inches by four feet eleven, and weighing 98½ pounds, which in rotundity was about the size of the Senator himself.

10/2/72 Mirror

IMMENSE WHEAT FARMS.

Everything seems to be on a grand scale in California. The big trees have for some time been classed with the wonders of the world. Now they are, according to the San Francisco *Bulletin*, rivalled by the vast wheat farms. That journal declares that there are three wheat farms in the San Joaquin Valley, with areas respectively of 36,000, 23,000, and 17,000 acres. On the largest of these farms the wheat crop this year is reputed to be equal to an average of forty bushels to the acre, the yield running up on some parts of the farm to sixty bushels. The product of this farm for the present year, is 1,440,-000 bushels. The boundary on one side of this farm is about seventeen miles long At the season of ploughing, ten four-horse teams were attached to ten gang-ploughs, each gang having four ploughs—or forty horses, with as many ploughs were started at the same time, the teams following in close succession. Lunch or dinner was served at a midway station, and supper at the terminus of the field seventeen miles distant from the starting point. The teams return on the following day. The wheat in the immense field was cut with twenty of the largest reapers, and we believe, has now all been thrashed

COUNTY FAIRS.

10/9/72 Mirror

From the New York Evening Post:
The holidays of the farmers are none too numerous, their opportunities of social intercourse with each other and with other people are too limited at best, and in this point of view the fall festivals and cattle shows have a significance and value beyond their obvious purpose of promoting better breeds of cattle and horses, and exhibiting the largest turnips and the fattest hogs. The farmers need to exhibit themselves, to come in contact with one another, to compare notes, to see machines and talk with their inventers, to see and talk with all classes of men, to get out of themselves, to find out what is going on, to talk a snatch of politics while looking at the poultry, to see to if in short, that while the breeds of horses are improving the breed of men who drive them shall not degenerate.

The truth is, that the world is moving a little faster than the secluded cultivators of the soil are well aware of and they need a nudge at the elbow now and then to jog them along. They get it at the cattle show. When we say that the speeches there do not amount to much we mean no desrespect to Mr. Greeley or Dr. Loring. both of whom have done their best on such occasions. The true and lasting instruction at such times come in at another point, it comes by impact, it breaths through the crowds: it speaks in the Machinery, the rough joke voices it and the sharp repartee ; old ideas get jostled ; prejudices loosen up a little; new methods are suggested ; old experience is talked over, and the farmers are lifted out of the rut in which they otherwise are sure to run.—They wake up and drive back to their endless work wiser than they went.

These festivals have a fascination for the farmers and for others which show how really useful they are. They never seem to die out; their return is greeted with a fresh interest; the crowd is as great as ever ; and the institution seems rooted in human nature and in the wants of a vastly important class of men.—Such festivals are now in full career or celebration all over the country. We wish to say a good word for them, and to advise the people to frequent them. both for the sake of what they can give and for what they can get there.

10/16/72 Mirror

Revival of an Old Discovery in Loudoun.

The following communication is from a gentleman of intelligence, who knows whereof he speaks. The story of a silver mine at Hillsborough, discovered years ago, and abandoned, has long been a tradition in that neighborhood, and it would be a little remarkable, if after the lapse of so many years the mine should now be reopened, and prove as rich and profitable as we hope it may.

HILLSBOROUGH, Oct. 10th, 1872.

MR. EDITOR:—There has been a tradition, handed down from generation to generation, to the effect that a silver mine existed in the gap in the Short Hill mountain at Hillsboro'. It has been the general belief, as well as the general report in this community, that a mine was opened and that silver in valuable quantities was discovered at this place prior to the revolutionary war. In consequence of these reports, a party was formed, some thirty or forty years ago to look for this hidden treasure. Operations were begun at the spot tradition had located the mine on the land of Jas. C. Janney Esq., and after digging to the depth of eighteen or twenty feet an old windlass, picks, buckets and other mining tools were discovered. The bottom of the excavation was solid rock of a white sand stone formation, containing a substance pronounced silver by all who saw it. The search was then abandoned and nothing more than to talk of the undeveloped wealth in our mountain has been done since. A few days ago two men, entire strangers to all in town, made their appearance and asked for board for a few days. They represented themselves as coming from Illinois, and in reply to questions from the curious, stated that that the object of their visit was to see the lands of Loudoun, of which they had heard a great deal said. This statement did not suit the inquisitive disposition of our villagers; some thought they were land buyers, some that they were manufacturers and were looking for a location, others thought them miners looking after minerals, while a very few thought they might be after running voters into Pennsylvania. Our Mayor interviewed them, but failed to elicit anything; other good questioners were sent to them but without results. In the meantime our visitors were quietly going about looking at, and enjoying our fine mountain scenery, criticizing the town, the way farming was done in this county and things generally. After keeping us on the rack for several days they informed one of our citizens that a long time ago, before the old French War, their great grandfather, an old miner, had discovered silver and opened a mine at this place. They stated that an opening to the depth of eighty feet was made by him and silver in large quantities found, but just at the time he was to receive the reward of his labor he was driven off by the officers of the colonial government who claimed the silver as belonging to the crown of England in consequence of a reservation made in all charters and grants of land, of all minerals and metals. The old miner made a careful plat of the place, intending to return at some future time and go to work again, but the french war breaking out at that time, and this place being in the line of Gen. Braddock's march, and other causes unknown now, prevented his return. The description of the place where the silver was found has been carefully kept by his descendents and now after the lapse of a century they come to the scene of their ancestor's discoveries for the purpose of reopening the mine. Mr. Janney offered them liberal terms,—which they have under consideration—and is anxious for them to go to work and develop what had been talked of for so many years. Respectfully,

EXCHANGE.

THE HORSE DISEASE.

This terrible malady, which has caused so much annoyance and inconvenience to the business public generally, in all our larger cities, and inflicted so much misery upon the poor dumb brutes, as well as loss to their owners, is still raging, in various sections. In Baltimore on Saturday and Sunday scarcely a horse was to be seen. Street cars stopped running, and pedestrians were abundant. In some instances engines were attached to the trains usually drawn through the streets by horses, while the accumulation of freight about the various railroad depots and steamboat wharves almost completely barricaded the streets.

11/13/72 Mirror

Since the date of our last paper, nearly every horse owner in the county has had more or less of it among his animals. In this town almost every horse you encounter is an invalid. For several days our livery stables have been closed, and the stalls, with their close blanketed steeds, and strong smelling drugs, resemble the wards of a hospital.

The attendance at Court on Monday was quite slim, owing in great part to the horse disease.

11/20/72 Mirror

THE HORSE MALADY

Still prevail extensively throughout this county. Almost every stable has had one or more diseased animals.

NEW HORSE DISEASE.
TREATED SUCCESSFULLY BY
Dr. M. MORIARTY

I RESPECTFULLY inform the public that I am prepared to treat this disease with entire success, having had much experience with the horse influenza—which this is.

Persons wishing pamphlets, descriptive of this disease, mode of treatment, &c., can be supplied with them, by calling upon, or writing to me.

I have correspondence with leading Veterinary Surgeons upon this subject, and have all the desired information for its successful treatment.

☞ Office on King street, Leesburg, two doors south of the Post-Office.

M. MORIARTY,
nov 13-tf   Leesburg, Va.

(John Kelly's recent popular column in the Washington Post gives a very interesting description of the effects of this epidemic in the big city. Horse drawn locomotion for a time was paralyzed. One delivery wagon was found to be pulled by a bull. Over 80% infection rate, but only 2% died in this fall of 1872.)

11/6/72 Mirror

THE LLOYD TRIAL.

ACQUITTAL OF THE PRISONER.

The trial of Mrs EMILY E. LLOYD, in the Circuit Court for this county, charged with the murder by poison, of her child, MAUD, on the 25th day of March, 1872, was brought to a close on Thursday night, and resulted in the acquittal of the prisoner.

At the close of our report last week, the testimony was nearly all in—that which followed on the afternoon of Tuesday was immaterial, and would lend no additional interest to the case by publication now.

On Wednesday, morning Major ORR opened the argument for the prosecution in a well arranged argument of considerable length. He was followed by

POWELL HARRISON, Esq , on the part of the defence, who based his argument, on the following points,, each of which he forcibly elaborated. We give them below, as indicative of the foundation upon which the defence rested their case :

He said: The Commonwealth must prove first that Maud Lloyd was murdered by poison. Second, that the prisoner at the bar committed the murder. Both must be proved beyond all reasonable doubt. In this respect the law knows no distinction between circumstantial and direct evidence. The Commonwealth has failed in both branches of the inquiry. They have not proved that Maud Lloyd was murdered by poison: First, because the symptoms of arsenical poison were not exhibited in her last illness, or on the post-mortem examination. Second, because the analysis made at the instance of the Commonwealth, and the result shown on the trial, was made either by an incompetent chemist or one lacking in integrity. Third, because the analysis was improperly conducted from the exhuming of the body at the cemetery till its close. Fourth, because the arsenic found the analysis could readily be accounted for by the arsenic proved to be in the bismuth administered in Maud's last illness. Fifth, because the arsenic found could readily be accounted for as being in the carbolate of lime sprinkled on the body when exhumed, on the rag used by Dr. Tiffany on that occasion, in the water. also used thereon, and on his old

dissecting knives. Sixth, because there is nothing in the case proved inconsistent with the hypothesis that the child took the poison by accident.

Mr. H. was followed by General HUXTON, also for the defence, in a lengthy and argumentative speech, in which he analyzed the testimony—witness by witness—and made a touching appeal in behalf of the almost friendless widow and childless mother who stood arraigned as the murderess her own offspring. On Thursday morning, MATTHEW HARRISON, Esq , spoke for the defense, and J. MORT. KILGOUR. Esq , Attorney for the Commonwealth, closed the argument for the prosecution. The effort of each of these gentlemen was unusually fine. Each did his duty, the one to the prisoner and the other to the Commonwealth, with a power of logic and a beauty of eloquence worthy the best bars of the State.

At 5½ o'clock in the evening the case was submitted to the jury, who retired to their room, and after an absence of about twenty minutes, returned into Court with a verdict of

"NOT GUILTY"

Upon its announcement the Judge thanked the jury for the patience with which they had for eight days listened to the details of the case, and told them, if it was any gratification to them to hear it, he would say, that the Court fully concurred in the correctness of the verdict upon the testimony before them ; whereupon the jury was discharged, and

THE PRISONER,

leaning upon the arm of Sheriff Nixon, but no longer held by the stern grasp of the law, left the Court-House a free woman.

Thus closed one of the most remarkable trials ever witnessed in Loudoun—one that has occasioned more excitement among our own people, and occupied a larger space in the public mind than any ever before tried in this county. And here the curtain falls. God grant that we may never be called on to record its like again, even though the accused, as in this case, be pronounced by the law and the testimony "not guilty,"

From a correspondence of the Baltimore *Sun* written from Leesburg the morning after Mrs Lloyd's acquittal, we take the following :

After the rendition of the verdict, Mrs. Lloyd was observed to smile frequently No person approached her or congratulated her, and during the trial she was wholly unnoticed. Not even a relative came near her. She frequently laughed at the witty remarks of counsel and witnesses during the trial.

During Mr. Kilgour's pathetic remarks in connection with her buried children she was evidently weeping, with her handkerchief to her eyes. She returned alone to the jail, where she still remains.

Early this morning, before breakfast, she went to the cemetery to see the graves of her husband and four children, all of whom have neat marble tombstones. Her four children are buried in double graves—two of each together. She immediately sent to the court-room for the plate of Maud's coffin, (which was used in the evidence) to have it restored. The graves will be enclosed with an iron railing, which she has paid for, the stone base being already prepared

Mrs Lloyd was visited this morning by Drs. Mott, Taylor and Wilson, and another, and received them in the parlor of the jailer's residence. She declared her innocence, and that she never feared the result. She heard she was to be prosecuted again. (It was publicly stated that a warrant had been applied for to arrest her on the charge of poisoning her other daughter, Anna.) She would not evade arrest, and did not fear another trial. She showed the photographs of her children, and cried over them. She said they closely resembled their father. She proposes to stay with a friend near Leesburg for a short time ; after that she will resume her work at tailoring in some other place. Public opinion here was too strong against her, but it was unjust. She also said, although it was reported that she was indifferent to the proceedings, that all the testimony and the arguments were indelibly fixed on her mind, and she could detect any errors that had been made in the reports of the case ; that her indifference arose from the consciousness of her innocence. It was heart-rending to hear the lawyers speak of the mangling of the body of her child and cutting it up.

Notwithstanding the strong feeling in this community against Mrs. Lloyd, the verdict of acquittal was generally anticipated, on the ground of insufficient evidence. If the friendless woman is innocent, and her counsel affirm personally as well as professionally, their solemn belief that she is innocent of any crime, she is certainly much to be pitied for the wrongs she has endured. She is said to possess property to the amount of about $3,600. The expenses of her trial, the counsel, witnes-

ses, &c., will probably be about $1,000, and she owes some debts of about $750, as was stated in the evidence.

Dr. Mott, Mrs. Lloyd's family physician, declared most solemnly to the writer, this morning, that she is wholly innocent of crime; that her daughter Anna died of intersusception of the bowels ; that her two boys died in 1870 from eating poisoned oak leaves, while gathering and eating strawberries in the woods, and that Maud died from a disease resembling cholera morbus.

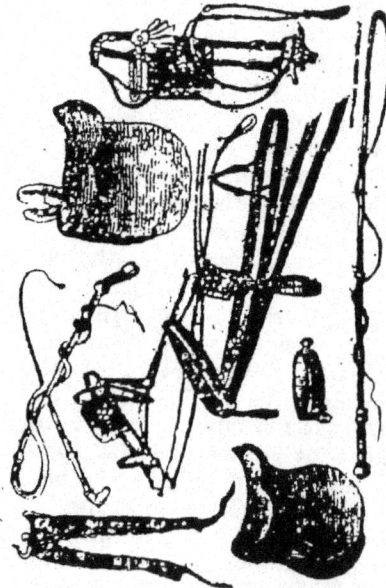

The Democratic Mirror

BENJ. F. SHEETZ, Editor

Wednesday Morning, Nov 13, 1872

THE ELECTION LAST WEEK.

An election was held in the United States last week, for President. Ulysses S. Grant was a candidate for the position, and we rather think he got it. We have a vivid recollection of the preparations made for the contest, and an indistinct notion that we recorded our suffrage on Tuesday for a gentleman by the name of Greeley, Horace, we believe, of New York.— Since then our knowledge is cloudy—the newspapers are filled with election returns, but Greeley's name is so rarely mentioned in them, that we sometimes fancy the whole thing a myth—that he was no candidate after all—or at all events "not much of a one."

Seriously, however, the defeat of Mr. Greeley is complete. His own State, New York, the theatre of his political achievements since 1830, repudiates him by nearly 50,000 majority, while Virginia, for the first time in thirty years, goes back on the nominee of her party, and suffers Gen. Grant to add her name to his pyramid of victories.

VOTE OF LOUDOUN.

	For President GREELEY.	For President GRANT.
Leesburg Township.		
Leesburg	241	221
Goresville	83	46
Mt. Gilead Township		
Hughesville	138	174
Silcott's Springs	65	99
Snickersville	104	26
Jefferson Township		
Hillsborough	89	63
Waterford	49	128
Purcellville	50	65
Woodgrove	50	4
Mercer Township		
Middleburg	111	97
Aldie	74	36
Blakeley's Grove	48	22
Unison	90	49
Lovettsville Township		
Lovettsville	42	248
Water's	36	51
Luckett's Store	26	101
Broadrun Township		
Guilford	85	64
Gumspring	131	55
	1516	1549

Grant's majority, 33.

11/27/72 Mirror

THE HEALTH OF MR GREELEY.

A dispatch from New York yesterday stated that it was currently reported that Hon. Horace Greeley had become insane. We learn from Washington that the rumor created a profound sensation there, but private dispatches received in that city from New York stated Mr. Greeley was in a dangerous condition from excessive nervous prostration, brought on by the excitement and anxiety of the late campaign, and by the death of his wife and by an affliction which has overtaken his eldest daughter. He has performed no mental labor since writing the card announcing his return to the Tribune, but it does not appear that his intellect is impaired, though his mental and physical organization are seeking much-needed rest out of New York. —*Balt. Sun, of Tuesday.*

12/4/72 Mirror

THE DEATH OF HORACE GREE-
LEY

We publish elsewhere in our paper, an account of the sickness and death of this eminent American citizen and journalist. We do not propose to write either his obituary or a fulsome eulogy to his memory. These offices of love and admiration have already been performed by hundreds of abler pens than ours, who doubtless felt all they wrote. But to our mind there hangs around the death of Horace Greeley a melancholy sadness, that impresses us with the instability of earthly friendships, and the vanity of worldly ambition.

Almost from the moment of his appearance in New York, more than forty years ago, a penniless, friendless youth in search of employment, he made an impression upon the public mind of that great city. Since 1841, when he established the *Tribune*, the name of Horace Greeley has been as familiar to the people of the whole country, as that of any man who ever figured in its history.

Eccentric in appearance—irrascible in temper—fanatical in his views, he was yet a bold, free thinker, of vigorous mind, a forcible and polished writer, and wielded an influence over the politics of the nation, second to no man of his generation; and however honest his convictions, we are sorry to believe, not always for his country's weal.

Amid the cares, and anxieties of his treadmill toils in the *Tribune* office, there lurked in his bosom a burning thirst for office: a thirst rarely gratified, it is true, but none the less intense and hopeful, and which even the decrepitude of three score years failed to assuage.

By a most wonderful combination of circumstances, Mr. Greeley became a candidate for the Presidency of the United States, not made so by the party which he had done more than any other living man to mould into form and build up and sustain, but mainly by that party upon which he had heaped his bitterest anathemas, and at which he had hurled his most poisoned shafts. Once a candidate, his whole soul was thrown into the contest, and all the powers of his great mind were exerted in the effort for victory. He saw political friends who held high positions mainly through his influence, turn their backs upon him, and denounce him for his apostacy from a creed to which he had never subscribed. Still, he labored on confident of success.

But as the day of conflict drew near, there came a messenger from the unseen world, and spreading its dark pinions over the home of Horace Greeley, bore hence the partner of his sorrows and his joys—one around whom entwined the holiest affections of his nature. The old man staggered under the blow, but mastering his feelings, with philosiphical calmness he again entered the arena of strife, and on the fifth of November, beheld himself deserted, not only by his political friends of forty years association, but by a race for whom he had battled from his youth—and in behalf of whose rights he had contended when there were few bold enough to render him homage for his fidelity.

Death and defeat weighed heavily upon him—how heavily, none but the great tongue of Him who "moves in a mysterious way" can ever tell. But the cup was not yet full. A few days later the affianced husband of his favorite daughter is lost on board the ill-fated Missouri. The burden was too heavy.—the effort to rise under it was too great—death at his own door, and disasters by land and by sea, had dethroned the once strong intellect of Horace Greeley, and like the sturdy oak riven by the lightning's blast, the old man bowed his head, AND DIED—with his last expiring breath exclaiming—"It is Done." Politically, Mr. Greeley was never a favorite of ours, and we bitterly lamented the necessity that seemed to demand his candidacy at the late election, though we are bound to believe that had he been elected, his administration would have been characterized by an honest endeavor to reestablish peace and good will between the sections, and a restoration of the government to a policy of honesty and justice in its dealings with its subjects. That he was a man of strong mind, indomitable energy, and eminent ability, the entire record of his checkered life, from the days of his obscurity and poverty, to his years of affluence and almost world-wide renown, bears ample testimony, and now that he has gone, we can but feel a sympathy for his memory, when we consider the blackness of the night of grief under which the sun of his existence sank forever to rest, and trust that he now has an everlasting realization of one of his own death-bed utterances, "I know that my Redeemer liveth."

☞ The public will read with mournful interest the following touching letter from Horace Greeley, which appeared in the Philadelphia *Press* of the 5th inst. The date, it is said is the last day the great journalist ever visited the *Tribune* office, and was one of the last letters written by its lamented author :

New York, November 10.

My Dear Friend : I am a man of many sorrows, and doubtless have deserved them : but I beg to say that I do not forget the gallant though luckless struggle you made in my behalf. I am not well.

Yours,　　　　Horace Greeley.
Colonel A. K. McClure.

12/4/72 Mirror

It must have been with infinite amusement that Henry Ward Beecher, during a late vacation, heard one of his own published sermons delivered in an obscure village. At the close of the service he accosted the divine, and said : "That was a fair discourse ; how long did it take you to write it ?" "Oh, I tossed it off one evening when I had leisure," was the reply. "Indeed," said Beecher, "it took me much longer than that to think out the very framework of the sermon." "Are you Henry Ward Beecher?" "I am," was the reply. "Well, then," said the unabashed preacher, "all that I have to say is that I ain't ashamed to preach one of your sermons anywhere."

12/11/72 Mirror

A sad story is told of Judge Rice in the Staunton *Spectator*, which is very good:— About the commencement of the war he made a speech in North Alabama in which he said that the Southern soldier could whip the Yankees with pop-guns. Since the war he chanced to make another speech at the same place. A big double-jointed fellow was present who heard and remembered the former speech, and being in no amiable frame of mind, concluded to go for Sam. Rolling up his sleeve and popping his fist in the palm of his hand, he propounded the fearful question :

"Sam Rice, didn't you make a speech here in 1861?"

"I did," said Sam.

"And didn't you say we could whip the Yankees with pop-guns?"

"Certainly I did, but the d———d rascals wouldn't fight us that way."

12/4/72 Mirror

ANECDOTE OF GEN. GRANT.

The election being over, anecdotes of the President, we suppose, are now in order, and as we desire to give him full credit for all the good qualities he may possess, we copy the following, furnished the Ravenna (Ohio) *Democrat* over the signature of L. V. Pierce :

General Grant is said to be a bad man. Perhaps he is ; I don't know. If he is be has changed wonderfully since he left the army. As proof of this I will give an incident which came under my observation.

While our army lay at City Point on the James river, at the mouth of the Appomattox, in Virginia, my duties as Assistant Adjutant-General of the United States volunteers, called me there to consult with General Grant. One afternoon, while walking out with the General, (he being in military undress, with nothing to indicate his rank.) we passed a boy 10 or 12 years of age fishing.

Grant—Bub, have you good luck to day ?

Boy—Not very ; they don't bite to day.

Grant—You have got a few here ; won't you give them to me?

The tears started in the little fellow's eyes, as he said : "I have had no breakfast to day, and no dinner, and if I don't sell my fish I shall have nothing to get me a supper."

General Grant enquired as to his history.

The boy was a native of Michigan, and *his mother was a widow.* To obtain money to support his widowed mother he went into the army as a waiter for a captain of the Michigan troops, whose name I cannot recollect. The captain was dead, and he had not a friend left.

Grant—Bub, you know where Grant's headquarters are ?

Boy—Yes, sir.

Grant—Bring your fish up there at 10 o'clock and he will buy them.

Punctually at the time the boy was on hand, with his string of fish, but was promptly stopped by the orderly in front of the quarters. General Grant, overhearing the order, stepped out, took the little fellow by the hand, led him into his quarters, and, becoming satisfied with the truth of his story, procured for him a suit of clothes, a hat, a free pass on the railroads home, and gave him $50 in money.

Now, Grant may be a bad man—I am not going to argue that question—but I don't believe you could make the mother of that boy believe it.

12/25/72 Mirror

HOW I ESCAPED BEING KILLED IN A DUEL.

EY MARK TWAIN.

The only merit I claim for the following narrative is that it is a true story. It has a moral at the end of it, but I claim nothing on that, as it is merely thrown in to curry favor with the religious element.

After I had reported a couple of years on the Virginia city (Nevada) Daily Enterprise, they promoted me to be editor-in-chief—and I lasted just a week, by the watch. But I made an uncommonly lively newspaper while I _did_ last, and when I retired I had a duel on my hands, and three horse-whippings promised me. The latter I made no attempt to collect; however, this history concerns only the former. It was the old "flash times" of the silver excitement, when the population was wonderfully wild and mixed: everybody went armed to the teeth, and all slights and insults had to be atoned for with the best article of blood your system could furnish. In the course of my editing I made trouble with a Mr. Lord, editor of the rival paper. He flew up about some little trifle or other that I said about him—I do not remember now what it was. I suppose I called him a thief, or a body-snatcher, or an idiot, or something like that. I was obliged to make the paper readable, and I could not fail in my duty to a whole community of subscribers merely to save the exagerated sensitiveness of an individual. Mr. Lord was offended, and replied vigorously in his paper. Vigorously means a great deal when it refers to a personal editorial in a frontier newspaper. Duelling was all the fashion among the upper classes in that country, and very few gentlemen would throw away an opportunity of fighting one. To kill a person in a duel caused a man to be even more looked up to than to kill two men in the ordinary way— Well, out there, if you abused a man, and that man did not like it you had to call him out and kill him; otherwise you would be disgraced. So I challenged Mr. Lord, and I had hope he would not accept: but I knew perfectly well that he did not want to fight, and so I challenged him in the most violent and implacable manner. And then I sat down and suffered and suffered till the answer came. All our boys—the editors—were in our office, 'helping' me in the dismal business, and telling about duels, and discussing the code with a lot of aged ruffians who had experience in such things, and altogether there was a loving interest taken in the matter, which made me unspeakably uncomfortable. The answer came— Mr. Lord declined. Our boys were furious, and so was I—on the surface

I sent him another challenge, and another and another and the more he did not want to fight the bloodthirstier I became. But at last the man's tone changed. He appeared to be waking up. It was becoming apparent that he was going to fight me, after all. I ought to have known how it would be—he was a man who never could be depended upon. Our boys were exultant. I was not, though I tried to be.

It was now time to go out and practise. It was the custom there to fight duels with six-shooters at fifteen paces—load and empty till the game for the funeral was secured. We went to a little ravine just outside of town, and borrowed a barn-door for a target—borrowed it from a gentleman who was absent—and we stood this barn door up, and stood a rail on end against the middle of it, to represent Lord, and put a squash on top of the rail to represent his head. He was a very tall, lean creature, the poorest sort of material for a fuel—nothing but a line shot could "fetch" him, and even then he might split your bullet. Exaggeration aside, the rail was of course a little too thin to represent his body accurately, but the squash was all right. If there was any intellectual difference between the squash and his head, it was in favor of the squash.

Well, I practised and practised at the barn-door, and could not hit it; and I practised at the rail, and could not hit that; and I tried hard for the squash, and could not hit the squash.

At last we began to hear pistol shots near by in the next ravine. We knew what that meant. The other party were out practising, too. Then I was in the last degree distressed: for of course those people would hear our shots, and they would send spies over the ridge, and the spies would find my barn-door without a wound or a scratch, and that would simply be the end of me—for of course that other man would immediately become as bloodthirsty as _I_ was. Just at this moment a little bird, no larger than a sparrow, flew by, and lit on a sag-bush about thirty paces away; and my little second, Steve Gillis, who was a matchless marksman with a pistol—much better than I was—snatched out his revolver, and shot the bird's head off? We all ran to pick up the game, and sure enough, just at this moment, some of the other duelists came reconnoitering over the little ridge. They ran to our group to see what the matter was;

and when they saw the bird, Lord's second said :

"That was a splendid shot. How far off was it ?"

Steve said, with some indifference :

"Oh, no great distance. About thirty paces.'

"Thirty paces ! Heavens alive, who did it?"

"My man—Twain "

"The mischief he did ? Can he do that often ?"

"Well—yes. He can do it about—well—about four times out of five."

I knew the little rascal was lying, but I never said anything. I never told him so. He was not of a disposition to invite confidence of that kind, so I let the matter rest. But it was a comfort to see those people look sick, and see their under jaw drop, when Steve made these statements. They went and got Lord, and took him home, half an hour later, there was a note saying Mr. Lord peremptorily refused to fight !

It was a narrow escape. We found out afterwards that Lord hit his mark thirteen times in eighteen shots.

I have written this true incident of my personal history for one purpose, and one purpose only—to warn the youth of the day against the pernicious practice of dueling, and to plead with them to war against it. If the remarks and suggestions I am making can be of any service to Sunday-school teachers, and newspapers interested in the moral progress of society, they are at liberty to use them.

12/4/72 Mirror

A K. Philips, Esq. of this place, we learn, found fourteen hundred and fifty dollars' worth of silverware, which had been buried over ten years. It appears that at the approach of the Federal army it was thought best to put the valuables out of sight in order to insure their safety, and the silverware was entrusted to an old faithful servant by the name of John Haydon. After the war, or perhaps during the war, John took a notion to go North, and settled in New Bedford, Mass. The ware was almost given up for gone, as no one but John Haydon knew where it was buried, and none of the family knew where John was. The other day John sent a diagram of the spot and its surroundings and, following the directions given, the treasure was found without the slightest trouble, much to the gratification of its owner. It had been buried just in rear of Mr. Philips's store, where it never would have been found except by accident, if the directions had not been given.

1/1/73 Mirror

Another of the Lowery Gang Turned Under.

This band of North Carolina desperadoes, which a year ago consisted of five persons; Henry Berry Lowery, the leader; "Boss" Strong, Andrew Strong, Steve, Lowery and Tom Lowery, and who ruled affairs generally in Robeson county, has been pretty well disposed of by "*Providence and Buckshot.*" Andrew Strong, of the notorious outlaws was shot dead last week, by a young man named Wilson whom Strong warned to leave the place. The body was delivered to the Sheriff, who immediately paid Wilson $1,000 for it, which is the standing reward offered by the county for any of the Lowery gang, dead or alive. Wilson is also entitled to $5,000 reward from the State, as the only villain of the gang now alive is Steve Lowery.

1/22/73 Mirror

GAME IN THE VALLEY OF VIRGINIA.—The Staunton Vindicator of the 10th instant says: "Last week there were shipped from Winchester, Virginia, seventeen thousand rabbits. The wagons arriving there daily are laden down with them. One wagon Saturday had twenty-seven hundred. Pheasants, partridges and wild turkeys are shipped in proportion to Baltimore and Washington. The rabbits sell at six dollars per hundred, skin and all.

2/12/73 Mirror

General Pardon of Ku-Klux.

A correspondent writes to the Baltimore *Sun* from Washington as follows:

It is believed that nearly all the Ku-Klux prisoners who are now in prison will be pardoned within a very short time, and particularly those of the more ignorant class, convicted for crimes of that character. The government will, however, prosecute vigorously all new instances of Ku-Klux persecutions.

The 22d in Alexandria—An Extra Train for Leesburg.—Extensive preparations are making in Alexandria for a grand celebration of the 22d of February.

The Oration will be delivered and Washington's Farewell Address will be read at Sarepta Hall. This will be the largest celebration that has taken place in Alexandria since the war.

(Washington's birthday of course. George Washington continued to be a venerated figure north and south.)

2/22/73 Washingtonian

FROM WASHINGTON.

The Report on the Credit Mobilier Briberies—Scene in the House of Representatives.

A MEMORABLE DAY IN THE HOUSE.

WASHINGTON, February 18.—The intense feeling that has been excited both in and out of Congress by the Credit Mobilier investigations was well illustrated in the House of Representatives this afternoon. It having been announced that Judge Poland's committee would probably report to-day, a large crowd of spectators filled the House galleries at an early hour. Messrs. Brooks and Ames had both been advised beforehand that the committee would recommend their expulsion.

The former; pale emaciated and feeble, a mere shadow of his former self, was in his seat examining books and papers, and evidently preparing for an elaborate self-defence. The latter, insisting upon his innocence, and claiming that he had done no wrong, moved about restlessly, however, from desk to desk, and was frequently seen in consultation with his colleagues from Massachusetts and other friends. Up to half-past one the House was in committee of the whole, engaged in the consideration of the sundry civil appropriation bill. When at that hour Mr. Poland entered with a large roll of paper in his hand and a motion was made that the committee rise, every one knew what was coming.—Speaker Blaine called Mr Cox to the chair, and the floor outside the outer row of benches was filled with persons privileged to be there. All the Clerks and employees of the House seemed to be gathered on the floor for the time being. The galleries were crowded, and the corridors were thronged with persons who had not arrived in time to gain admittance. Mr. Cox as Speaker pro tem., rapped once with his gavel, and an unusual stillness pervaded the entire assembly as Clerk McPherson commenced the reading of the report which covered ninety eight pages, and occupied over an hour and a half, and it is doubtful whether the House was ever before so quiet for such a length of time.

Mr. Ames seemed very unconcerned, and even smiled when the passages were read which reflected on him most severely. No one who knows Mr. Brooks could fail to see that he felt profoundly his position, even though the House should not adopt the resolution of expulsion. It was with deep regret that his friends saw him rise after the report had been read through, for in the few brief words he uttered he said nothing to improve his situation.

☞ A grocer had a pound of sugar returned, with a note attached to it, saying "Too much sand for table use, and not enough for building purposes.

2/12/73 Mirror

Murder in Loudoun.

A MAN SHOT AND KILLED.

The Deceased a Victim of An Old Grudge.

Coroner's Inquest, &c.

DAVID BROOKS THE SUPPOSED MURDERER.

THE ACCUSED ARRESTED AND LODGED IN JAIL.

It this morning becomes our duty to record the particulars of one of the most cold-blooded murders that has ever stained the history of this county, showing that there are those in our own peaceable midst, in whose breast the demon of revenge lurks with as blooody purpose, as ever stirred the passions of the most lawless and depraved criminals of our large cities.

On Sunday morning last, the dead body of a white man, named WM. D. SMITH, was found lying along the W. & O. Railroad, about four miles above Leesburg, with unmistakable evidence of having been murdered by gun-shot wounds. Information was at once given to Coroner H. O. CLAGETT, and Sheriff BARRETT summoned a jury of inquest to ascertain how, when and by whom the deed was committed. In the afternoon the Local of the *Mirror* accompanied the jury to the scene of the bloody tragedy, and here is what he saw—

At a point on the railroad, just beyond what is known as Bowie's cut, and about one mile above Clarke's Station, we found the body of the murdered man, lying on its back, and within two feet of the railroad track. The mouth and eyes were both open, one leg drawn up rather under the body, and the other extended—both hands were resting in an apparently careless, natural manner, all indicating that death must have speedily followed after he fell. There were no signs of the slightest movement of the person after it was down. Only a few drops of blood were visible any where near him, and none immediately around the body, except on the left hand, which he had probably placed to his breast when first shot.

An examination of the body revealed a wound produced either by a buckshot or a slug, most probably the latter, just about the juncture of the right clavicle with the sternum, and another in the lower part of the right groin. There were one or two other slight abrasions of the skin, but the first named wound, was, in the opinion of Dr. W. H. JAMES, who made a post mortem examination, the fatal one. The ball, or slug, after entering the body, had lodged in the region of the heart, but without touching it. The bleeding was all internal, great clogs of which were found coagulated in the left breast.

Smith was a laboring man, about forty years of age, and was well known in the community where he was murdered, and is said to have had a colored mistress, the wife of a negro man named Brooks, who is now living at Hamilton.

REASSEMBLING OF THE JURY.

At 9 o'clock on Monday, after the above was in type, the jury reassembled in the Council Chamber in Leesburg, at which time a number of witnesses were examined, several of whom testified to having heard between 9 and 10 o'clock Saturday night, the report of a gun, in the direction of where the dead body of Smith was found.

C F. McCoy—Knew Smith. Saw him last on the 3d inst. Never had any trouble with him. Had never driven him from my place nor cautioned him about coming there. Never gave me any annoyance or trouble. Never heard his (Smith's) life threatened by any one. Have no reason to believe Smith has been coming to my house for any improper purpose.

George Holland (colored) testified that while cutting wood for Mr. Hamner, about the 7th of January, David Brooks told him that he had ordered Smith from his house, and that he wanted him to stay away—that he had a man watching Smith. Brooks did not say what he would do with him. Smith was in the habit of staying at Brooks house. Did not know whether he slept there. Brooks had a single-barrel shot gun in his house—never saw him load it.

Reuben Johnson, (colored), Lived on David Carr's farm near Hamilton. Knew Smith, but knew nothing of his death. Have heard his life threatened by David Brooks. Heard Brooks tell Margaret Gilbert, who lives in same house with me, that he intended to kill Smith whenever he found him.

Harriet Brooks,—colored.—Am the wife of David Brooks. Knew W. D. Smith. Saw him last going on two months. Have lived for the last two months at Mr. McCoy's, at Hamilton Depot. My husband lives in Mr. Bush. Fox's house, which he rents. He drove me away from his house—gave no reason for doing so. Said I did not do the work properly for him. Mr. Smith had been in the habit of coming to his house while I lived there for the last two or three years. Did not board there; I did his washing; he staid there several weeks, with the consent of my husband, when he was sick; he brought Mr Smith to the house and brought his clothes to me to wash; he never found any fault to me about Mr S's staying there, but he did to other people; said I did not wash his clothes as well as I did Mr Smith's; he never drove Mr Smith away from the house. Have not seen my husband for sometime until two or three Sundays ago, when I saw him at my mother's, who lives on Mr David Carr's place; have always lived on good terms with my husband until this year; had a fuss with him just before Christmas; he wanted to go over the river and I would not go with him; he knocked me down twice, for dead; he gave no other reason for the attack; have heard him threaten to take Smith's life; about two weeks ago, when I was at my mother's, he said that I left home on Smith's account; he swore that he would kill him the first time he caught him if it took him fifty years; saw my husband on last Saturday—he was at Mr McCoy's; it was before dinner; Did not speak to him; he had a gun at home, a single barrel shot gun; he told my brother he had gotten some ammunition, but had no caps; my brother gave him some caps; I saw him give them to him; he swore he would kill Mr Smith if he never saw his own by it—if it took him fifty years; he told me this when he was standing in my mother's yard.

David Brooks, colored.—Live in Mr. Fox's house, above Mr. T. M. C. Paxson's. Knew W. D. Smith. Saw him last on Thursday.—Knew nothing of his death. On Saturday was at Hamilton. Went to Margaret Gilbert's on Mr. Carr's place, and then went home, by sundown. Did not see Mr. Smith on Saturday. Have never heard Mr. Smith's life threatened. Have never had any falling out with Smith.—Told him at Christmas to hunt a washer-woman. Never ordered him him away from my house. My wife washed for him with my consent. Was sick there for several weeks. Did not board there, and never paid me anything. Complained to my wife about her coldness to me, and her intimacy with Smith. When I told her to stop washing for Smith, she left my house. Never told my wife nor any one else, that I was going to kill Smith. Never had any one watching for him. Passed by the cattle-stop on Saturday, on my way to Hamilton with my little boy—early in the day. Left the boy with his grand-mother. Have had no talk with my wife but once since Christmas—then at her mother's. Got nothing from her brother that day. The gun I have is a cut off musket. Shoots big caps. Got some two or three caps from her brother. Got some powder from Mr Titus, sometime ago. Have got no shot lately. Have not shot my gun since New Year's Day; don't know whether it shoots close or wide; [The gun from which the fatal shot was fired was evidently of the "wide" kind—Reporter.] I never told him (Smith) to leave on account of any intimacy with my wife, although my boy (aged six years) had told me he had seen him in bed with her; he told me this last Wednesday, after my wife left me.

This closed the testimony, and the jury, after carefully considering all the circumstances rendered the following

VERDICT :

"The jurors sworn to enquire when, how and by what means, the said Wm. D Smith came to his death, upon their oaths do say: That the said Wm. D Smith came to his death by reason of a gun-shot wound, and that the gun by which said wound was inflicted, was in the hands of DAVID BROOKS.

Whereupon the accused was turned over to the Sheriff, and by Justice Wallace committed to jail to await the action of the grand jury on the 2d Monday in March.

Brooks is a large man, quite black, and we suppose, 60 years of age. He has hitherto borne a good character among those who knew him: His wife, Harriet Brooks, is rather a neat negro woman, and we should judge, not more than 30 years of age.

2/22/73 Washingtonian

Good News for the South.

"The President is showing a disposition of increased friendliness to the South. It is an auspicious sign, and we hope much from it. Congress falling short of the popular wish and expectation—for thus far in the session scarcely anything generous has been done for the Southern States—we look to the president to make good the deficiency to the extent of his power. The first benefit promised is the withdrawal of most of the troops. The presence of Federal soldiery at the South, even though they rest on their arms and fraternize with people, is a menace and an annoyance to to a high spirited race, who are conscious of doing nothing to deserve continued military surveillance.

They do not feel that this is place, or that the Union is re-established in sentiment as well as in fact, while part of the Northern people (not many in number) demand of their representatives that the South shall still be treated as an alien. It is given out that the proposed removal of the troops is not to be made because they are wanted in Utah (which might explain it to some minds,)but because they are not required longer at the South.

3/5/73 Mirror

Mosby in a New Role.

The Washington Star of Thursday gives the following interesting little episode:

The Southern claims commissioners had just heard the claim of Josiah B. Bowman of Fairfax county. Va. for $6,700 yesterday, and were hearing the closing statements of Mr. James L. Gardner, of Loudoun county. Va. in support of his own claim for $1,500 for property taken from his farm by Union soldiers, when Col. J. S. Mosby, the ex confederate came into the room to file a claim before the Commission for a client. Mr. Gardner was reciting at the time how he escaped from the rebels during the war under command of the notorious Mosby, and how he saved his property, to be kept, only, however, until the Union soldiers came along and gobbled it up. Mosby, who was an attentive listener throughout, turned quietly to Mr. Benjamin, the chief clerk of the commission and asked "Who is this witness? what is his name." He was informed, to which Mosby replied, "Oh, yes I know him to be a loyal man, too; there was a good many after him." The counsel for Gardner immediately asked him if he would give in evidence of Mr. Gardner's loyalty. Mosby then, to the surprise of Gardner, who never in his life had seen him before took the stand and testified that he himself had never seen him, (Gardner) during the war, though he had often tried to catch him, as one of the few union men in Loudoun. The claimant and Mosby then shook hands over the bloody chasm, the former remarking, "Good God! how people change places!" Thats so.

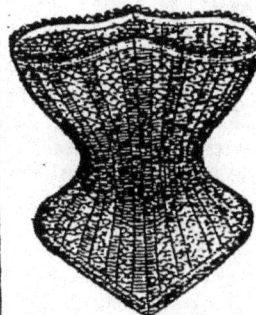

3/5/73 Mirror

THE CROWD IN WASHINGTON. From all sections of the country living masses of human beings are pouring into Washington, to witness the second inauguration of President Grant, see the sights and undergo the tortures in such cases inevitable. Gentlemen who were in that city on Monday inform us that even then it was difficult to thread the crowd on the Avenue Up to Saturday it was estimated that an addition had been made to the resident population of 18,000 souls. Every train that has arrived since has tended to swell the numbers. On Sunday sixty-five car loads of people passed over the Washington stem of the B. & O. Railroad freighted with passengers for the grand event, and the hotels and boarding houses were overflowing—many who arrived on Sunday being unable to get accommodations.

On Monday the train from Leesburg, on the W. & O. Railroad was crowded with men, women and children, of all shades of politics and color. The demonstration in Washington will no doubt be the grandest seen there for many years, and as inauguration day comes but once in four years, why not enjoy it, even if it is to see U. S. G. installed.

3/8/73 Washingtonian

PRESIDENT GRANT'S INAUGURATION.

The inauguration of Gen. U. S. Grant for the second term as President of the United States took place at noon yesterday, and was witnessed by many thousands of people, comprising a representation not only of all classes of citizens, but of many of the collective bodies in the country. It was a handsome but cold affair.

The President occupying an open carriage, accompanied by Senators Sprague, Logan and Bayard, joined the procession soon after the starting, taking position in the third division. The carriage in which he sat was drawn by four closely-clipped mouse-colored horses and his appearance was the signal of hearty cheering, waving of handkerchiefs and other demonstrations of applause as he rode along. Immediately preceding his carriage was his escort, the First Troop Philadelphia City Cavaly.

The first formal ceremony of the day was the installation of the Vice-President elect, Hon. Henry Wilson, of Massachusetts, which took place in the Senate Chamber a few minutes before noon.

The Vice-President elect was escorted to a seat near the Vice President, and shortly after the diplomatic corps and the justices of the Supreme Court entered.

Just before noon the President, President elect, came into the chamber, escorted by the committee of arrangements, and followed by his cabinet.

The President took his seat in front of the Secretary's desk, with the Committee of arrangements, and the cabinet took seats on the left of the Vice-President's chair.

There was a deep hush on the floor and in the galleries when the President, escorted by Senators Cragin, Bayard and Logan, came down the aisle and took the seat assigned him in front of the Secretary's table. Everybody in the galleries and on the floor arose and did not take seats until the President had taken his seat and the gavel of the Vice President fell. The Vice-President (Colfax) then read his farewell address, amid an impressive silence.

Vice-President Wilson then addressed the Senate, after which the oath of office was administered to him by Mr. Colfax.

THE INAUGURATION CEREMONIES.

The ceremony in the Senate chamber was concluded at twenty minutes past 12 o'clock, and the procession then proceeded by way of the main entrance to the platform on the central portico of the capitol.

At half-past twelve o'clock, the President arose to take the oath of office prescribed by the constitution. As Chief Justice Chase held the Holy Book in his hand and repeated the text of the oath, every head was uncovered, and deep silence pervaded the multitude.

TAKING THE OATH.

As the Chief Justice concluded, President Grant raised the Bible to his lips, upon which there was a simultaneous outburst of cheers from the assembled thousands in front of the stand, and at the same moment a battery of artillery stationed on the north of the Capitol thundered forth a salute, flags (many of them tattered and war-worn) waved in the breeze, and the fire department added to the general acclamation by sounding their gongs.

The scene in front of the grand inauguration stand, was one of exceptional brilliancy. The varied and gay uniforms of the visiting and home organizations, the bright colors waving in the breeze, the polished apparatus of the fire department, and the immense concourse of ladies and gentlemen stationed on the plaza below the stand, all attired in holiday apparel, served to render the scene one of extraordinary beauty and impressiveness.

THE MIRROR.

WEDNESDAY............... April 23.

Mr. John W. Wildman, with his wife and little daughter, Katie, had a narrow escape on Friday last. They started for Waterford, and just after reaching the top of the mountain, the buggy wheel ran off, throwing Mr. and Mrs. W. to the ground with great force; the child clung to the vehicle for perhaps a hundred yards farther, when she too was thrown out, and our old friend "Mack" took to the woods at frightful speed. The occupants of the buggy, who were all more or less severely bruised but none of them, fortunately, seriously injured, were brought to town by Mr. Bernard Taylor, who happened to be passing that way at the time. The fugitive horse was recaptured without a scratch. The buggy itself however, is undergoing divers repairs.

In passing through Union Cemetery a few days ago, our attention was attracted by a beautifully arranged lot, recently enclosed with a handsome iron railing. As we approached, we read in letters of bronze, stamped upon its enduring entrance, the word "Lloyd." Within the enclosure was the grave of Charles E Lloyd, a massive tombstone marking the spot of his repose, while close by his side were two double mounds, a beautiful double stone at the head of each, upon which were the names of "George and Henry," and "Annie and Maud." The iron railing had just been put in place, the green grass was growing over the family of graves—the flowers of early spring were blooming around, and nothing seemed lacking, that the heart of most devoted affection could suggest, to lend an air of quiet, melancholy beauty to the sacred spot. And yet, as we gazed at this group of graves and read in their tender surroundings so many seeming evidence of a mother's love, we could scarce realize that for more than half a year, the wife and mother had occupied a felon's hands, planted that dead colony of her own flesh and blood. These graves received her last attention ere she was hurried to prison, and these same sad spots, received her first attention, when a jury of her countrymen pronounced her "not guilty," and set her at liberty; and to-day we find her in a distant city, toiling with her own hand for the necessaries of life.

75

5/14/73 Mirror

DUEL NEAR RICHMOND.

The Richmond papers of Monday contain full particulars of an affair of honor, that was fought near Oakwood Cemetery, on Friday evening at 3 o'clock, between Page McCarty, Esq., and J. B. Mordecai, Esq. As usual in such cases there was a woman behind the scene. A few weeks ago there were published in the *Enquirer* some verses of poetry, written by Mr. McCarty, to which Mr. Mordecai objected as reflecting, in his opinion, upon the lady called "Mary." A challenge passed at that time, but the matter was arranged by mutual friends. Subsequently, however, a personal rencontre took place between the beligerents, which led to the duel.

From the *Whig* we learn that the principal seconds called in each another, second and surgeons, being as follows: for Mr. McCarty, Col. W. B. Tabb, of West Virginia, and John S. Meredith, of this city, with Dr. J. S. P. Cullen, surgeon; and for Mr. Mordecai, Messrs. W. L. Royall and W. R. Trigg, both of this city, with Dr. Hunter McGuire, surgeon. The affair had gone too far to talk of an accommodation without an appeal to arms, and no time was wasted in that vain endeavor. The preliminaries were promptly arranged, and the whole party, in carriages, were carried to the field of honor Friday afternoon late, attracting no attention beyond that aroused by the ordinary sight-seers that are continually driving about our city environs. The place selected was a sequestered vale southeast of Oakwood Cemetery. The weapons were Colt's navy revolvers, carrying army balls, and the distance ten paces.

The choice of pistols fell to Mr. McCarty, and his friend, Col. Tabb, also won the privilege of giving the words of command. The revolvers were loaded and the principals put face to face. Messrs. Mordecai and McCarty were both perfectly cool and collected; neither showed the least sign of agitation or slightest mark of excitement, and when placed in position, faced each other in a manner that indicated their determination to make a desperate fight.— There was absolutely no advantage in position, though the choice had fallen to Mr. McCarthy. They stood on a line running

north and south, and the sun just sinking in the west, fell aslant of each of them.

It was about 6 P. M., when the first shots were exchanged, neither taking effect. A second exchange of shots followed, on the demand, it is said, of Mr. McCarty's side, both the combatants falling on the earth — Mr. McCarty severely wounded in the right hip, and Mr. Mordecai dangerously, if not mortally, wounded in the abdomen, the ball penetrating near the navel.

The affair was managed so quietly that the authorities knew nothing of it until it was all over.

The wounded men, after having their wounds temporarily dressed, were placed in carriages and brought to the city at a late hour of the night. On Saturday morning the Seconds were bailed in the sum of $500 for their appearance on Monday. Warrants were issued for both the principals, and executed on Mr. McCarty, who gave $5,000 bail. Mordecai's condition was too critical to admit of his being disturbed.

THE PARTIES.

Mr. John B. Mordecai is a nephew and the law-partner of Colonel John B. Young, of this city. He was a gallant Confederate officer. Mr. Page McCarty is a grandson of Congressmen McCarty, who killed Mason in a duel fought with muskets. He was a Lieutenant of artillery attached to Wise's brigade in the late war, and was known as a brave and spirited man. He is engaged in the tobacco trade.

The following ambiguous and unpretentious poetry appeared in the *Enquirer* on the 5th of February, and out of them grew the "late unpleasantness."

We have received for publication the following poem. A loving swain who, doubtless, has been kicked by his sweetheart.

When Mary's queenly form I press,
  In Strauss' latest waltz,
I would as well her lips caress,
  Although those lips be false.

For still with fire love tips his dart,
  And kindles up anew;
The flame which once consumed my heart
  When those dear lips were true.

Of form so fair, of faith so faint,
  If truth were only in her
Though she'd be then the sweetest saint
  I still feel like a sinner

5/14/73 Mirror

LICENSE VS. LICENSE. At the April term of the County Court, Mr. C. F. McCoy, who for a year past has been keeping a house of public entertainment at Hamilton Depot, made application for a renewal of his license to retail ardent spirits. Strong opposition was brought to bear against the granting of the same, by residents of the neighborhood, and the subject was continued until the present term. Accordingly, the motion was again considered on Monday, Messrs. R. H. Lee and Powell Harrison appearing for the applicant, and Mr. Henry Heaton for the opposition.—As this was the only licensed house for the sale of the "ardent" in the village of Hamilton, a determined effort was made to have it suppressed. A number of witnesses were summoned on both sides, and the entire afternoon consumed in the hearing of testimony and the argument of counsel,—the Court-house the meanwhile being literally crowded with curious spectators, without regard to "race, color or previous condition," eager to hear the end.

At the conclusion of the argument, Judge Ball, declared in a few brief terms, that while in contests of this sort his sympathies were always on the moral side of the question, as he had demonstrated two years ago, when the law left it discretionary with the Court—now, the law was changed : the applicant in this case filled every requirement contemplated by the provisions of the law,—he was proven on both sides to be a man of excellent character and of the strictest sobriety : and in the eye of the law the place was a proper one for the sale of liquor ; the Court therefore had no discretion in the matter, and the license was granted accordingly.

Upon the rendition of the decision a slight demonstration of applause was attempted by some one in the house, which was promptly squelched by the Court, and the crowd quietly dispersed, and for another year, at least, King Alchohol holds dominion in the vicinage of the Hamilton Depot.

5/21/73 Mirror

WAYSIDE THOUGHTS.

For the first time in two or three years we last week journeyed from Leesburg to the Point of Rocks, and during our ride several thoughts suggested themselves to our mind, the first of which was, that in the perfection of Nature God never grouped together in the same number of miles, a superior soil and a lovelier landscape: and the next was, that man ought to be ashamed that he has done so little to lend additional beauty and attractiveness to the scene. As a general thing the soil is the richest and most fruitful of our rich Loudoun lands, and some of the handsomest and most elegant residences to be found in this or any other county, are visible from the Point of Rocks road. But, ye gods, what a road, especially in the winter season.

THE MIRROR.

BENJ. F. SHEETZ, Editor.

Wednesday Morning, May 28.

LET US HAVE PEACE.

Friday next is the day set apart for the decoration of the graves of the federal soldiers buried in the various national cemetries of the country, and extensive preparations are making by the Grand Army of the Republic for its due observance. To this nobody objects. It is a fitting tribute to the memory of the dead, the sacredness of which few would interrupt if they had it in their power. But the following extract from a notice by the executive committee of that body of immaculate loyalists breathes such a spirit of malignant hate and fiendish depravity, that we would fain hope that a "decent respect for the opinions of mankind" would repress every responsive echo in each manly breast. We merely wish to call attention to the utter loss of shame and decency displayed in the language. It needs no comment. After announcing the day, and the "purpose of strewing flowers upon and decorating the graves of the deceased Union soldiers, they continue—"any attempt by the friends " of the rebel dead to strew flowers on " *their* graves, will be regarded as an inter- "ference with the programme of the day, " and will not be tolerated."

6/11/73 Mirror

MEMORIAL DAY.—The annual meeting of the Memorial Association of Loudoun county, was held at the Court House on Saturday. A larger number of persons were in attendance than we remember ever to have seen together on a similar occasion.

After music by the Leesburg Brass Band, an appropriate prayer was offered by Rev. Mr. Follinsbee. J. Wm. Foster, President of the Association, then stated the object of the meeting; and in a few neat and becoming remarks paid a fitting tribute to the memory of the departed heroes whose graves were about to be decorated with the choicest flowers of spring.

THE PROCESSION.

The services at the Court-House concluded, the procession, composed of several hundred persons of all ages and both sexes, and extending more than three squares, presented a very beautiful and imposing appearance, and gave gratifying evidence of the reverence with which the memory of the Confederate dead is cherished in the hearts of the living. The silver locks of age, some of whose hearts had been pierced with sorrow when the graves just about to be strewn with flowers, first opened their jaws to receive their victims, and the sunny curls of childhood, too young to remember the evil days that filled a nation with gloom, united in the same holy mission of bearing to the tomb, and placing upon the "long ago" made graves, their floral tributes of love.

The procession thus formed, and preceded by the Leesburg Band, playing in sadly mournful strains a funeral dirge, proceeded to the Cemetery, where the work of decorating the soldier's graves was at once begun

THE PHILOMONT CORNET BAND.— On Saturday morning last Leesburg was favored with a visit from the Brass Band recently organized at Philomont in this county. Under the instruction of Prof. TURNER, of Staunton, they have made commendable progress, performing sweetly and with remarkable exactness. They are provided with a full set of new instruments, and a handsome Band wagon, which on this occasion was drawn by four black horses.— They drove through the principal streets of the town, attracting much attention. They were made the guests of our citizens, and during their stay were entertained by them at the "Osburn House." In the afternoon, at the invitation of the Ladies of the Memorial Association, they partook of Strawberries and Cream at Academy Hall.

During the evening the Leesburg Brass Band met them on the Court-green, and poured forth some of their choicest pieces, which they executed in good style— indeed we don't think we ever heard them perform more sweetly. The visiting Band left about four o'clock for their homes, (well pleased, we hope, with their brief stay) much to the regret of our people that they could not remain to participate in the ceremonies incident to the decking of the Soldier's graves.

6/4/73 Mirror

DEPOT AT PURSELLVILLE.—The officers of the W. & O. Railroad Company are persistent in their endeavors to push forward the work with as much speed as their limited means will allow. On Friday, President McKenzie, accompanied by Engineer BLYTHE, HENRY HEATON, of this place, one of the Directors, and others, visited Purcellville, and located the site for the Depot at that place. We understand that a thorough survey of the surrounding grounds was made, and the most eligible spot,—damages, facilities for access, cost of leveling, &c., considered—was found in the strip of woods at the upper end of the village, about 200 yards north of the turnpike, at a point where the county road leading to Hillsborough crosses the railroad, and on the lands of JOHN R. SMITH and JOHN J. DILLON.

We also learn that the Company is in possession of the necessary cross-ties to lay the track to Purcellville, and that the 101 tons of iron recently purchased by the President, will arrive in a few days, and be immediately laid as far as it will go. But that stops far short of Purcellville.

6/18/73 Mirror

SIXTY HOURS TO EUROPE.

Prof. Wise, the veteran aeronaut, who proposes a balloon trip to Europe, is in New York endeavoring to raise $16,000 to complete his outfit. A few days ago he was interviewed by a Herald correspondent; and in reply to his question the Professor expressed his conviction that the trip can be made in sixty hours,—that an easterly current prevails in the upper atmosphere of sufficient force to carry a balloon not only across the ocean, but even around the globe. He continued—The balloon itself will be globular in shape. A balloon of 100 feet in diameter is of ample size to cross the ocean, and one of 150 feet would be sufficiently large for the purpose of circumnavigating the globe. I am certain that if I can cross the ocean I can go around the globe. This would require probably eight or nine days.

HERALD REPRESENTATIVE—What capacity would you have, Professor, for passengers or mails?

Professor WISE—In a balloon 100 feet in diameter we could take 10,000 pounds of disposable ballast. In the transatlantic trip we should take a great deal of this in the shape of provisions, cooked and canned meats and fruits. A large quantity of quicklime would be taken, and we should use it for warming coffee and boiling eggs.

Should the balloon encounter the brave west winds on the ocean with the aid of a drag line we could go right along without the loss of gas or ballast.

HERALD REPRESENTATIVE.—Am I to understand that you will have a line in the water from the car?

Professor WISE—Precisely so. The balance or drag rope, about one thousand feet in length, relieves the balloon of weight exactly to the extent of the rope's emersion in the water. It does not materially retard its progress, and gives us the exact direction in which the balloon is travelling.

HERALD REPRESENTATIVE—Please describe the car in which the passengers will travel?

Professor WISE—We shall have a large wickerwork car, with strong canvass sides and roof to protect us from the weather—In these will be glass windows. This car will be of two stories in height. We shall live on the upper floor, and in the lower we shall store our provisions. Underneath the car will be an open gallery for taking observations of the sun. It will be put as far below as practicable, so as to avoid as much as possible the shadow from the balloon. Below this gallery the life-boat will be suspended. This will be of metal and decked over.

HERALD REPRESENTATIVE—What are the possibilities of the future should your trip prove successful?

Professor WISE—Everything imaginable in the way of transportation

HOW HE PREPARED HIS CASE.

Among the stirring recollections of the history of the New Orleans bench and bar during the past twenty-five years, there has been unearthed one touching two high legal luminaries, who, a quarter of a century ago, were among the first at the bar, but who are now, alas, gone the way of all earth.

The chief characters in the story were a certain district judge and a certain district attorney; and the occasion was the trial of a very important case in which the district attorney represented the Government, being sued for claims amounting to many thousand dollars. The case was fixed for trial by a jury; on the appointed day and at the appointed hour, the judge was on his bench, the jurymen were in their places, and the district attorney came not.

An hour two hours—passed, and the patience of court and jury was well nigh exhausted. Messengers had been dispatched in all directions for the laggard, but he could not be found, when lo, as the court was about to adjourn in despair, the governmental representative appeared on the scene, blowing like a porpoise. The court, in ruffled temper, demanded why the wheels of justice had thus been ruthlessly stopped—in short, "Why had not the distinguished gentleman come at the appointed hour, and did he choose to treat the court with contempt?"

To this the gentleman offered profuse apologies, disavowing any disrespect of the court, and offering in extenuation that, having been engaged the whole night long in preparing for this case, his labor had prostrated him, and the slight rest he sought after his arduous task was done became prolonged slumber, from which he had just awakened.

His honor looked daggers, but used none—rather expressing himself satisfied with the explanation, and then without delay, the case was ordered to proceed, and proceed it did vigorously to a termination, marked by an elaborate and exhaustive argument at the hands of the district attorney; and a verdict in his favor after only a short deliberation.

After adjournment of court, the foreman of the jury dined with the judge, when quite naturally there came up the subject of the recent suit, and the foreman dwelt at length in terms of ardent praise on the faithfulness, sacrifice and devotion to the interests of his office of the district attorney, instancing his labors of the night before as an evidence of "what sort of man he was."

The judge smiled at his friend's remarks. "Why do you laugh?" said the other. "Because the story is enough to make a horse laugh. That stuff he told about laboring all night was a confounded lie. I know it, for (now this is a secret) I was with him myself all last night and we played poker from early dark until long after daylight this morning, and that was the way he prepared himself for the great case."

Trial of Reapers and Mowers Combined, Before a Committee of the Loudoun County Agricultural Association.—In response to the announcement last week, by the executive committee of the Loudoun county Agricultural Society, five combined reapers and mowers were presented on Wednesday last in Mr. Thomas Burch's grain field, adjoining the town of Leesburg, to compete for the premium offered by our agricultural association for the best implement of their class:

The grain selected was well-adapted to test the merits of such machines. It was heavy and very much tangled by the recent storms and heavy rains. The true merit of the contestants were brought out, and they did their work well. It was a gratifying and pleasing sight to see with what ease and skill the three leading machines moved on thro' the tangled grain.

Four machines were entered: the Champion the Hubbard, the Kirby, and the Superior.

The *Champion* was entered by Mr. Henry Vanderhoof, agent Leesburg, assisted by Mr. Moore of Baltimore. It performed its work with much ease and precision; all its parts answered to the satisfaction of those present It has a net cut of four feet, eight and a half inches, and is manufactured at Springfield, Ohio.

The Champion also entered as a drop-machine and did its work in that class admirably well.

Trial of Mowers.—On Thursday morning, all the reapers which entered on Wednesday, were tried as mowers, in Mr Shafer's lot near this town.

As some importance was attached to the time it took to change them from the mower to the reaper, they were timed by the committee.

The HUBBARD was changed in 7 minutes. The KERBY in 7½, and the CHAMPION in 11½. The SUPERIOR was not timed.

All these reapers mowed beautifully—the grass being up and in good condition. We will have to leave to the committee to decide, which did best. Their opinion will be known at the Fair.

They are the AGENTS for Loudoun of the celebrated HUBBARD REAPER AND MOWER, which never fails to take the premium when brought into competition with order Machines by trial in the field.

They will also furnish the WOODS, McCORMICK, and other Machines. also BUGGY RAKES of the best styles: BARNEY OUTT & FORSYTH GRAIN CRADLES, FRY and other HAND RAKES, CRADLE and GRASS-SCYTHES, FORKS, RIFLES, &c. &c

Their stock is large and composed of none but first class goods.

SHROFF & CO.,
Leesburg, Va.

The Three Richest Men in America.

The three richest men in America are W. B. Astor, A. T. Stewart and Commodore Vanderbilt—all residents of New York city. Astor's wealth is mainly in real estate and its revenues; Vanderbilt's is mainly in railroad stocks and their dividends; Stewart's is in goods, houses, stores, factories, lands and stocks. The aggregate wealth of each of them is seventy-five and one hundred millions which looks rather heavy. Nobody knows exactly they couldn't tell themselves within a million or two. Those who know most about their affairs put their figures higher, and say that the income tax returns of a few years ago, which showed each of them to be worth between twenty and thirty millions, gave no proper idea of their real wealth.

Astor lives unostentatiously; Vanderbilt lives in a three story on a third-class street and Stewart lives in a marble palace on Fifth avenue, more magnificent than any other residence on the American continent, and equalled by but few of the great cities of Europe. Astor is a large, heavy man of seventy, with strong features and a rubicund face, indicative of high living; Stewart is a medium-sized man, rather slender, and tall, of seventy three, with a face like a parchment, and gives the impression of being hard up; Vanderbilt is a tall, slim, handsome, proud looking man of nearly eighty, straight as an arrow. Astor has heirs to his estates; Vanderbilt has children to whom he can leave his fortune; Stewart is childless. Astor's public benefactions are confined to something like a couple of hundred thousand dollars, which he gave to the Astor Library, and the two golden candlesticks nine feet high, which he recently gave to Trinity Church. Vanderbilt has never made any public benefactions, excepting a steamship to the government during the war till very recently, when he gave a million dollars for educational purposes—one half of this sum to found a University in Tennessee, and the other half to another educational institution. Stewart has always had the reputation of being pretty close fisted; but he must be credited with his million dollar "Home for Women," which will be completed next year. Astor is an Episcopalian. Vanderbilt is a Methodist, Stewart is said to be inclined to thinking for himself— Stewart is a scholarly man. Vanderbilt is not. Astor is an accomplished man of the world.

7/30/73 Mirror

The Balloon Mania.

If Professor Wise is successful in crossing the Atlantic in a balloon, the newspapers will have to add to "marine news" "aerial news," and will be relative as the steam-car is to the telegraph. Carrier-pigeons, it is stated, find no trouble in flying from a balloon three miles high, but above that point they die. The balloon ascension made in September, 1864 by Professor John La Mountain, (not the one who was killed on the Fourth,) accompanied by John A. Haddock, of Watertown, N. Y., turned out in a very perilous manner for the two voyagers. Before they were aware of it they were drifting over an immense extent of wilderness in Canada which stretches away to regions of endless cold and night. So they concluded to come down. The balloon had to be abandoned, and after two days of wandering and extreme hardships they encountered a party of men from Ottawa who were hunting timber tracts. They there learned that the balloon had taken them one hundred and fifty miles beyond the boundaries of civilization.

One who has been up in a balloon thus describes the sensation:

"I could not realize that I was moving. I seemed to be standing still and the earth to be falling away. As we rose higher the illusion was lost, though there was still no consciousness of motion. The objects below dwindled until the men and women, horses and vehicles in the streets of the city looked like pigmies, then insects, and then faded from sight. The trees and houses looked like toy villages, the river appeared corrugated, the waters boiling. The towns on both sides of the river became invisible. We steadily mounted and floated to the east over fertile fields and rich farms. Vast inclosures seemed like small garden-beds, as regularly laid out as checker-boards. We were now a mile high, but we could hear very distinctly the cries of the people below us."

The absence of a sense of motion in balloon traveling, either up, down, or side-wise, even though the "vessel" is moving at a speed of a hundred miles an hour, is a distinctive peculiarity of this mode of travel. Upon this point a balloonatic who has tried it says —

"We could not tell whether we were going up or down, except by tearing bits of tissue paper and dropping them out of the car. If we were ascending the paper would fall, if descending it would mount. We saw the sun set three or four different times, our steady ascent giving us new points of vision. We began to feel chilly and donned our overcoats. The mercury had fallen twenty-five or thirty degrees. We were over two miles high, and we could plainly perceive the earth's sphericity."

The first fire-balloon went up ninety years ago last month in France, and in the same year two men made successful ascents. The "fever for balloon ascensions broke out in England and America the same year and in each country men went up in gas-balloons. A year or two later the English channel was safely crossed in a balloon. The distance in air-line is fifteen miles, and it was then thought a wonderful achievement.

Balloons were used with great success during the siege of Paris, often carrying several hundred pounds weight in dispatches.

A Colorado Character.

7/30/73 Mirror

A Colorado correspondent of the St. Louis *Globe* has come across quite a character, who is known as Judge Baldwin. He is an old settler and has endured more hardship, alarms, and startling experience than fall to the lot of many men. Barnum, who was here last summer, offered him ten thousand dollars to go with him, but was indignantly refused. He has been twice scalped. Every distinct tribe has its own method of performing that delightful operation.— Some take a strip off from front backwards; some a round piece off the side ; some the crown, &c. Only one or two ever take the whole scalp.

At the massacre three years ago, above referred to, he was attacked and fought valiantly against overwhelming odds. His amunition giving out, he fought with the stock of his gun until it was broken, and then took off his boots and fought with them. Overpowered at last, he was left for dead, scalped, the sinews of his arm taken out for arrow strings and so mangled and injured that when found and cared for, it was four months before he recovered. Last week, when the Utes were here, he took off his hat one day, whereat they clapped their hands gleefully and cried out, "Apache! Apache!" signifying what tribe had scalped him. He replied with the witticism: "Yis, ye rid divils, ye'll ne'er do't agin." As two tonsorial operations had left him but very little scalp, there was evidently a fine point to the remark.

8/6/73 Mirror

The "Graphic" Balloon.

Work on the great trans-Atlantic balloon of the *Daily Graphic* has been rapidly pushed during the past weeks, and every portion of the apparatus is now in an advanced stage of progress. From eight to twelve machines of the Domestic Sewing Machine Company have been constantly employed in sewing the seams and uniting the immense strips of cloth. Last evening 1,500,657 stitches had been made, and over four of the eight miles of sewing required had been accomplished. The force will be further increased on Monday, and by the close of next week all the sewing will have been finished. The work of attaching the doubling, or second thickness of cloth, to the crown of the balloon is a delicate operation, requiring much skill and experience- is being performed under the immediate supervision of Miss Inling, the neice of Prof. Wise. Nearly one half the netting is finished. Profs. Wise and Donaldson are superintending every step of the preparations.

At the Brooklyn navy yard the strips which have already been finished are being coated with varnish, consisting of linseed oil boiled very thick, which is reduced with benzine and laid on with calciming brushes. Six painters are engaged in this portion of the work. The strips will require three coats of varnish one inside and two outside. The varnishing and drying will probably occupy these six men during the next two weeks. It is the most tedious and slow part of the work.

The construction of the car has already been commenced. The making of the hoops as well as of the valve, requires most careful manipulation, and has been intrusted to R. Hoe & Co. The car will be made in great part of ropes and duck, and will be put together and finished at the Domestic building.

The life-boat has been commenced, and will be finished on the first Monday in August. It is building at the establishment of the most experienced boat-builder in the city; and in accordance with the best approved plans.

It seems highly probable that the balloon will be ready to start by the 20th of August.

(Lotteries were popular even then.)

TERRIBLE DISASTER ON THE POTOMAC.

Burning of the Steamer Wawas set,

Between Forty and Fifty Lives lost

Recovery of Bodies Statement of One of the Rescued—A Frightful Spectacle—The Passengers—Death in the Waves, &c.

The steamer Wawasset, running on the Potomac river, between Washington city and Currioman, took fire about twelve o'clock on Friday, at Chatterton landing, and was destroyed. She had about one hundred and fifty passengers on board, and between forty and fifty lives were lost.

Doc Kenney, bar-keeper of the Wawasset, who reached Washington Friday night, on the steamer Express, with an excursion party from Piny Point, the latter vessel having sighted the wreck about four o'clock this afternoon, and picked up Kenney, who had been sent out in a small boat to come up to Washington, the passengers and crew of the Wawasset being at that time all cared for at Stewart's wharf, near the scene of the disaster.—Kenney states that the Wawasset left Washington at six o'clock Friday morning on her regular weekly trip to Cone river with one hundred and seventeen registered passengers, and quite a large cargo of freight for river landings.

Just before reaching Chatterton's Landing five miles below Aquia Creek, and after the whistle of the boat had been blown as a signal of her approach to that landing, the steamer at the time being about a third of a mile from the shore.

FIRE WAS DISCOVERED

in the hold, and the hose was attached immediately, but before the men could reach it the conflagration became general, as the fire had been burning for some time. The fire had been smouldering, it is supposed, for some hours, and upon opening the hatches it burst forth with great fury, driving the men from the hold, and completely baffling all attempts to subdue it.

THE WILDEST CONFUSION

prevailed on the vessel, the passengers becoming panic stricken and frantic with fear, very few having presence of mind sufficient to take care of themselves. The steamer was, without a second's delay, headed for the shore.

ON THE VIRGINIA SIDE,

and in a few minutes ran aground about two hundred yards from the Virginia shore. By this time the flames had spread with fearful rapidity; and in the excitement many jumped overboard, several of them, jumping into the water before the steamer struck the bottom. She was provided with but two small boats, and in the frenzy of the moment one of these boats was thrown overboard and lost by the passengers, who, uncontrolled, were endeavoring to launch her.

Captain Wood, of the ill-fated steamer, and his assistants are said to have used every effort to control the passengers, but without avail, and but for this

DISOBEDIENCE OF ORDERS

many who were lost would have been saved. The vessel was well provided with life preservers, but in the panic it seems that none of the passengers secured them.

(Circus ad in The Washingtonian.)

A Towering Giant Among its Fellows

The Great 12 Centre-Pole Tent

AND

$100,000 CHALLENGE SHOW

WILL EXHIBIT AT

Leesburg, Monday, September 15th.

THREE PERFORMANCES.—10 A. M., 2 and 5 P. M., DOORS open one hour previous.

ADMISSION...75cts.

CHILDREN UNDER 10 YEARS...........................50cts.

A TICKET WAGON WILL BE OPEN on the street from 9 A. M. to 12 M. when tickets can be purchased, thus avoiding a rush on the ground.

Great Eastern Menagerie.

Museum, Aviary, Circus, Roman Hippodrome,

AND

EGYPTIAN CARAVAN.

Its augmentation the past winter makes it four times larger than last year, and then it was confessed the Monarch Masterdon of the road. Over a million dollars have been expended to make this the most stupendous and greatest World Exposition ever attempted; and an immense Twelve Centre-Pole Pavilion, covering over four acres of ground, and measures 168,000 yards of canvass, is required to exhibit is thirty-one dens of living Wild Beasts, breathing Sea Monsters, Plumaged Birds, Flesh-eating Reptiles, and the colossal

DUAL CIRCUS EXHIBITION.

MAKING IT A

Grand Combination More than
Equal to Twelve Shows in One.

To transport this Goliah of Shows, 100 cars, 6 passenger coaches, and 4 engines are brought into requisition, and the services of over 200 men and horses are necessary to the success of this unprecedented enterprise.

EVERY ACT DOUBLE,

In 2 RINGS AT THE SAME HOUR, UNDER ONE GRAND PAVILION

A DOUBLE GRAND ENTREE.

Grand Combination More than
Equal to Twelve Shows in One.

To transport this Goliah of Shows, 100 cars, 6 passenger coaches, and 4 engines are brought into requisition, and the services of over 200 men and horses are necessary to the success of this unprecedented enterprise.

A GRAND TRIPLE MENAGERIE.

In 4 Separate Tents, combined with the COLOSSAL MUSEUM, AVIARY of Tropical Birds, and Caravan of Elephants, Camels, Dromedaries, Elks, Buffaloes, etc., etc.

TWO STUDS OF RING HORSES, DUAL CORPS OF EQUESTRIENNES, MALE RIDERS, ACROBATS, GYMNASTS, CLOWNS, ETC., GREATEST ACHIEVEMENT IN ARENIC ANNALS EVER WITNESSED! EVERY DAY AT 10 O'CLOCK. A. M., AN UNPARALLED

Pageant & Procession Over Two Miles Long!

With emerald, crimson and gold dens, three brass and reed bands, grand Steam Piano, and a full Martial Band; as in the days of '76; Twenty Beautiful Women, and one hundred horsemen and pages, mounted, and followed by the Cavalcade with their flags, banners and paraphernalia, mounted Gods and Godesses, in original costumes, with Living Tigers, Lions, Panthers and Jaguars loose in the Streets. Before each exhibition a

GRAND BALLOON ASCENSION

will be given. All the Railroads running into the city have been arranged with to bring people at greatly reduced fare.

CHAS. SIVALLS, Agt.

aug 30-3

9/10/73 Mirror

CATCHING THE TRAIN.
—Moral : Don't be in a Hurry.

One of the greatest delights of boarding in the country for the Summer, is the pleasure a man derives from his efforts to catch the early morning train by which he must reach the city and his business. When he gets out of bed he looks at his watch, and finds he has plenty of time ; so he dresses leisurely, and sits down to breakfast in a calm and serene state of mind. Just as he cracks his first egg, he hears the up-train. He starts, jerks out his watch, compares it with the clock, and finds that it is eleven minutes slow, and that he has only four minutes left in which to get to the depot. In a fearful hurry he tries to scoop the egg out of the shell, but it burns his fingers ; the skin is tough, and after fooling with it for a moment it mashes into a hopeless mess, and he gets his fingers smeared; he drops the whole concern in disgust, grabs a hot role, and scalds his tongue with a quick mouthful of coffee; then he stuffs the roll in his mouth, while his wife hands him his satchel, and tells him she thinks she hears the whistle. He plunges madly around the room looking for his umbrella : then kisses his wife as well as he can with all that unswallowed bread distending his cheeks, says good-bye to the children in a lump, and makes a dash for the door.

Just as he gets to the gate he finds that he has forgotten his duster, and he charges back after it, snatches it up, and tears down the gravel walk in a frenzy. He doesn't like to run through the village, because that would be undignified, but he walks furiously. He goes faster and faster. Half way down he does hear the whistle, for certain. He wants to run, but he knows that he will start up that yellow dog there by the sidewalk if he does. Then he actually sees the train coming into the depot, and he feels that he must make a rush. He does. The yellow dog becomes excited, and tears after him. Six other dogs join in the chase one after the other, and bark furiously and frolic around his legs. Small boys contribute to the excitement as he goes past, by whistling on their fingers, and the men at work on the new meetinghouse knock off to look at him and laugh. He feels ridiculous, but he must catch that train. He gets desperate when he has to slacken up until two or three women, who are on the sidewalk discussing the servant girl question and the price of butter, scat-

ter to let him pass. He arrives within one hundred yards of the depot with duster flying in the wind, coat-tails horrizontal, and the yellow dog nipping his heels just as the train begins to move. He puts on extra pressure, and resolves to make that train or to perish. He reaches it as the last car is going past. He seizes the hand-rail, is violently jerked around once or twice, but finally lands on the steps on his knees, and is hauled in by his coat-collar by the brakeman, hot, mad, dusty, with his trousers torn across the knees, his shins bruised, and three ribs in his umbrella broken.

Just as he gets comfortably into the car the train stops, backs up on the siding, and lays there for half an hour while the engineer fixes a broken valve.

9/17/73 Mirror

A SENSATION.—The advent of the Great Eastern Circus, on Sunday last, created quite a sensation in our town. Thirty-two cars, drawn by three engines, the whole under the management of Capt. PRICE, rolled the mammoth concern from Washington on Saturday night, and carried it back after the performance Monday night. The display of canvass, and the procession on the street were scenes not usual here, as was attested by the thousands who flocked from all sections of the county to behold. Just before the afternoon exhibition, there was a balloon ascension in front of the pavillion ; the youthful æronaut rose to an altitude of several hundred feet, and after sailing over the town in a northerly direction, landed in an open field about half a mile from where he started.

9/13/73 Washingtonian

Washington Irving once when picking up an apple under a tree in his orchard, was accosted by an urchin of the neighborhood, who, not recognizing him as the proprietor, offered to show him a tree where he could "get some better apple than those." "But," said the boy, "we must take care that the old man dosen't see us" "I went with the boy," said Irving, "and we stole a dozen of my own apples."

"Put down your umbrellas! You'll scare this engine off the track!" screamed the engineer on the Western North Carolina road, to a crowd of country people who had gathered to see the train come in. They were all lowered at once.

9/17/73 Mirror

Bursting of the Graphic Balloon —Statement of Prof. Wise— What the Graphic Says.

The collapse of the "Graphic" balloon at Brooklyn, N. Y., on Friday last, while being inflated ostensibly for the long-promised trans-atlantic voyage, via the easterly air current, was announced on Saturday by telegraph. The New York Post says:

The inflation of the Graphic balloon at the Capitoline Grounds, Brooklyn, was begun at 3 o'clock Friday morning, and continued until 4 o'clock P. M. Thousands of persons visited the grounds and waited to see the proposed ascension. Professor Wise arrived at about 10 o'clock with his son Charles, who was ordered out of the inner enclosure containing the balloon by Chaales Goodsell, proprietor of the Graphic. This led to an altercation between Mr. Goodsell and the elder Wise, which terminated in a private conference at the ticket office.— Professor Wise left the grounds after predicting, it is said, that the balloon would not stand the strain of inflation.

At 4 o'clock, when the amount of gas forced into the balloon amounted to 300,000 cubic feet, three rents suddenly appeared in the great bag, running from the valve at the top to the bottom, and in a moment the whole structure had collapsed. The disappointed spectators then gradually left the grounds.

Professor Wise publishes a card in which he defends his theory of the easterly air current, and announces his readiness to start for Europe at any time in a gas-tight silk balloon. Such a balloon, he says, was promised to him by the Graphic Company, but was not furnished, that supplied being a rotten cotton structure, which was manufactured without regard to his advice. He also censures attempts to turn a great scientific experiment into an enterprise for money-getting.

Well, we hope we will hear no more about going to Europe in a balloon. We begin to suspect that Wise's theory like the Graphic balloon, is "too thin" to serve the great purpose predicted by the Professor.

9/17/73 Mirror

Northern Men in Virginia.

The Richmond *Enquirer*, in an article upon the reception and social standing of Northern men in Virginia, candidly says : "There have been, and there are still, some Northern men in Virginia who, while they are treated civilly, are not taken by the hand with that cordiality which is extended to others. It is not because they are Northern men ; not because they are not natives here ; not because they thought and fought against us in the war ; but because they have been busy in the business of the demagogue, the adventurer, the self-seeking politician poisoning the mind of the negro against his former master—creating bad feeling on the part of the colored race toward the white race ; and thus disturbing the harmony of our society, retarding the progress of our people, and impairing the prospect of prosperity for our State. Such men would not, and could not, command the confidence and esteem of their fellow-men any more in Massachusetts than in Virginia. They are workers only in the ways of evil.

Virginia has appealed, and still appeals, not only to Northern men, but to men from foreign lands, to come and establish themselves and their families here in happy homes amid a hospitable people. She means all she says. She wants them, and willingly numbers them among her sons when they come. All she asks of them is their duty to her ; and she will do her duty to them."

9/24/73 Mirror

THE FINANCIAL CRASH.

The announcement of the failure of the Banking House of JAY COOK & Co., which was first made public on Thursday last, has created a panic in the financial world, the like of which has not been felt in this country for years. The blow came suddenly and unexpectedly, and in every direction, banking institutions of high and low degree, have toppled over, like brick piled on ends. Not less than fifty houses have succumbed to the pressure in the three cities of Washington, Philadelphia and New York,

The panic, however, appears already to be subsiding, and the probabilities are that in a short time it will be numbered among the things of the past, and the business affairs of the country again resume the even tenor of their way.

The Jay Cooke Financial Disaster—Washington Comment —View of the Situation, &c.

WASHINGTON, September 18.—A little before noon to day faint whisperings of rumors that the houses of Jay Cooke & Co., in New York and Philadelphia, had suspended payment were heard in the vicinity of the telegraph offices. In a very short time the rumors had spread to all public places, and were spoken more loudly. At first there was a great deal of incredulity on all sides. The firm of Jay Cooke & Co., was popularly supposed to be possessed of abundant resources for all emergencies, and confidence in it was not easily shaken. Even when telegrams were publicly exhibited stating the fact many still doubted. Several parties who had accounts at the house here, and who were early advised of the rumors, as a matter of precaution presented themselves at the counter of the house here and handed in their checks for the amounts standing to their credit. This action speedily solved all doubts. Payment of the checks was declined, the doors of the banking house immediately closed, and a notice announcing the suspension of the firm was posted up. A few minutes after the doors of the First National Bank were also closed. Mr. H. D. Cooke, the resident partner of the house here, is also president of the First National Bank, and the two concerns are intimately connected.

(While the effects of this were not immediately apparent in Loudoun County, it initiated a country wide depression which did not abate until 1878.)

10/1/73 Mirror

THE LOUDOUN NATIONAL BANK.—Amid the general wreck of bonds and crash of Banks, it must be gratifying to the people of Loudoun to know that their own home institution is "all right." It is run by gentle of much financial ability,—of high integrity, and prudence—and under the almost universal suspension of banks elsewhere, the loss of this one, if anything, is merely nominal. As an evidence of the faith of the directors in the sound condition of the institution, we heard one of them say on Monday, that the Board was ready, individually to obligate themselves to make good every dollar for which the bank is responsible. They are able to do it.

9/24/73 Mirror

Mr. Hopley, of Danbury, Undertakes to Put on a Clean Shirt to See the Graphic Balloon.

One of those distressing accidents, which no amount of precaution can guard against, occurred on Pine street yesterday. Mr. Hopley, the insurance agent, intended going to New York at 9.45 A. M., to see the Graphic balloon. A friend suggested it to him just about a half hour before the train would leave, and Mr. Hopley hastened home to change his clothes and tell his wife. When he got to the house he found it vacant, but hoping that his wife would come in before he departed, he got out his Sunday suit and began disrobing. He had got on his clean shirt and was adding the collar, before drawing on the pants, when he remembered that his sleeve-buttons were in the stand drawer in the dining-room, and he cautiously moved in there after them. He found the buttons and secured them, when the hall door opened and his wife's voice and the voice of a feminine friend were heard approaching. He would have fled back to the bedroom, but he could not leave the apartment he was in without being seen by them. For one instant it seemed as if he would drop dead and run into the carpet. The next, he perceived the open door of the china closet, and immediately bolted in there and closed the door. Mrs. Hopley and the lady friend came into the room, and remarking on the heat; drew their chairs close to the open window and brought out their sewing. Then they fell to talking about the weather, and Mrs. Robbin's black corded silk, and the remedies for worms, and other topics of engrossing interest. Mr. Hopley hung to the door with awful tenacity, and perspired and thought. The darkness was intense and to add to the unpleasantness, a mouse or rat was heard in among the papers on the floor. Mr. Hopley was not a timid man, but he was bare-legged and barefooted, and when a man is thus situated a mouse is about the last thing he wants to think of. Still the voices outside continued, and greater grew the heat in the china closet. Mr. Hopley did not dare to make the least noise to alarm his wife, because of the presence of the other lady, whose voice he could not recognize. How he did curse that balloon and the man who suggested his going to see it, and Professor Wise, and how bitterly he regretted that he could not think of that other aeronaut's name (Donaldson) that he might curse him too But still the two ladies glided on through the mazes of the neighbor's affairs, without the least sign of abatement. He heard the clock strike ten and also eleven. Once or twice the mouse came quite close to his feet, starting the perspiration afresh until he could feel it trickle from his chin and down his body. Then he moved his foot to rest himself and it struck against something very soft and covered with hair, and he uttered a half stifled shriek and jumped up, striking his head against a shelf, and bringing a piece of some kind of crockery to the floor. His wife sprang to the door in alarm, but Hopley caught the knob and clung to it with the grip of death. Mrs. Hopley tried in vain to open it. Then she thought of a burglar being concealed in the closet, and screamed for help, still clinging to the door to prevent the ferocious intruder from dashing out and braining both of them and burning up the house. Her screams, added to those of the female friend, alarmed the neighborhood in an instant, and among those who dashed in was old Mr. Stocton with a double-barrelled gun, and as soon as he learned the trouble, he turned the dreadful weapon full upon the door. There was a stunning report, a chorus of feminine shrieks, mingled with a terrific howl from the other side of the door, and the next instant the unhappy Hopley, with both legs full of shot, was writhing on the floor of that closet. The door was opened, the women pushed up to get a sight; got it, and immediately dispersed with another shriek. Hopley was put to bed, and Dr. Myers summoned, who picked out the shot, which had merely pricked through the skin, and applied the needful remedies, and the patient to-day is quite comfortable, and will be at his office this week.—*Danbury News.*

(The author of these humorous Danbury stories was James Montgomery Bailey. He should be rediscovered.)

10/15/73 Mirror

A Cock-Fight in Danbury.

[*From the Danbury News.*]

Rev. Mr. Pinkney, bought a game rooster from a Danbury dealer Saturday. Mr. Pinkney informs us that he was not aware the fowl was of the game species; he bought it because of its shapely appearance. We believe this statement, and are confident that the good people of Slawson will acquit him of all blame in the unfortunate affair of last Sunday morning, the particulars of which are as follows: At the time the trouble commenced Mr. Pinkney was engaged in arranging his neck-tie preparatory to putting on his vest and coat. Happening to look out the window he saw his new rooster and a rooster belonging to the widow Rathburn squaring off in the street for a fight. Surprised and pained by this display, he immediately started out to repel the disturbance, but was too late. When he got there half a dozen young ruffians with cigars in their mouths and evil in their eyes had surrounded the birds which were already in the affray. They would thrust their heads out at each other and ruffle their necks and then dance around and strike out with their spurs and jump back and thrust out their heads again. And when the boys saw him they shouted out, "Hurry-up, baldy (Mr. Pinkney is a little bald), or you'll miss the fun." Mr. Pinkney was inexpressibly shocked. It was Sunday morning; the homes of two of his deacons and several of his most prominent members were in sight, and here were those roosters carrying on like mad and a parcel of wicked and profane boys standing around shouting their approved and noisily betting on the result. He made an effort to secure his fowl, but it eluded him. The perspiration streamed down his face, which burned like fire, his knee trembled, and he

felt, as he saw the neighbors gathering, that if the earth would only open and swallow him he could never be sufficiently grateful. Just as he attempted to catch his rooster a rough-looking individual, with his pants in his boots, and a cap with a drawn-down fore-piece, came up, and taking in the scene at a glance, sided in with the other rooster. "Fair play," shouted the new comer for the benefit of the crowd, and "Don't step on the birds, old codger," for the particular benefit of Mr. Pinkney, who, crazed beyond reason, was jumping about, swinging his arms, and muttering incoherent things, to the great danger of stepping on the combatants. "Good for old Pinkney's rooster," screamed the boys in delight, as that fowl knocked a handful of feathers from his opponent's neck. "The parson knows how to do it," said a one-eyed man gleefully. Mr. Pinkney could have swooned. "I'll go you five dollars on the Widder," said the rough man, earnestly winking at the clergyman. "Take him, Pinkney; take him, Pinkney," chorused the crowd of ragmuffins. "My friends," protested the unfortunate minister in a voice of agony, "I cannot, I cannot —." "I'll back you, sir," said an enthusiastic man with a fish-pole; "I'll put up for you, and you can let me have it from your donation." The clergyman groaned. "Catch the Widder," shouted the rough man to Mr. Pinkney, indicating that lady's bird by a motion of his finger.

Mr. Pinkney clutched it, dropping on his knees as he did so. At the same time the rough man, by a dexterous move, caught the clergyman's bird, and also dropped on his knees opposite. Just then Mr. Pinkney looked up, and there saw two of his deacons and several of the members staring down upon the scene with an expression that brought the blood to his face, and with a groan of intense pain the unhappy man dropped Mrs. Rathburn's fowl and darted into the house. As soon as he recovered from his mishap he sent in his resignation; but as a critical examination had been made in the mean time, and it transpired that as far as the worthy man was concerned there was not the least blame, the resignation was not accepted.

10/25/73 Washingtonian

THE SCOURGE OF MEMPHIS.

A Year of Misfortunes—and scenes on the street —Heart-Rending Details—Graphic Description of what is going on in the Stricken City.

[Memphis Cor. of New York World.]

During the year Memphis has been peculiarly unfortunate. For two months the river was so choked with ice as to prevent commerce. When the river became navigable the epizootic broke out and raged so virulently that trade and industry were paralyzed. Then came the small-pox; then "indigenous cholera," the ravages of which among the already discouraged people were as severe as those of the small-pox; and before the cholera had run its full course came this most terrible of all scourges, to decimate the inhabitants of the doomed city, and spread sorrow, death and despair on every hand. These unparalleled calamities have drawn to us the sympathy and aid of all the land. Had we been left to ourselves we would have been swept utterly out of existence. for the plague is deadly, swift and sure. and to be fought successfully only by the most untiring vigilance, ceaseless energy, and all the resources of medical and sanitary science which wealth can place at our disposal.

The city has entirely changed in life and appearance within the brief lapse of thirty days. The shops are closed, not one being open north of Exchange street.

THE STREETS ARE NEARLY DESERTED.

save by those who are engaged in sanitary work and in burying the dead. There is no promenading and the women who once made the sidewalks brilliant with life and color are either in their graves or have fled from the town for their lives. The few who remain. when they are seen at all, flit rapidly and silently through the emptied street. their white and haggard faces telling the rueful story of breaking and broken hearts. Whole families have been hurried into the vaults and tombs of the cemetary within a few hours. The city swarms with helpless little children

whose parents are dead, and to provide anything like comfortable temporary homes for these is one of the most difficult tasks of benevolent societies, which have done and are doing such noble work. The money which is sent to them from all parts of the Union disappears rapidly—even more promptly than it comes in—and there is ever an urgent necessity for more.

THE PRICE OF PROVISIONS

has enormously increased, and for bread which one bought for five cents a loaf fifteen cents are now demanded; the milkmen have ceased their daily round; meat can hardly be obtained at all; and it really seems as though to the horrors of the pestilence the gnawing pangs of hunger are to be added. The most pressing demands for aid are made by able-bodied men upon the resources of the disbursing authorities. These poor creatures would be willing enough to work, but unfortunately there is no work for them to do for buisiness is stagnated and they have been thrown out of emloyment. On Saturday last ninety applications for relief were made at the commissary depot, and not less than 2,500 rations were distributed to the sick. Wanness and misery, sickness dispair. and death deface this once beautiful city. All day long the noise of hearses is rattling through the street— for they are driven almost as fast as the horses can go, and even then cannot dispose of the corpses rapidly enough—is heard and a night fires cast their glare upon the sky as though Death were celebrating his victory, and the sound of wailing and sobbing in place and hovel strikes the appalled sense of him who ventures abroad in this unhallowed time. The yellow-fever has been confined to no particular locality. and rich and poor have suffered alike.

Of all the inhabitants perhaps not 10,-000 sleep at night within the city limit; the rest leave in the evening and remain in the country till morning. Many of those who thus have left have been seized on the cars and perished miserably at the various stations, for so intense is the fear of the disease that the country people turn from citizens as from lepers, and will have nothing to do with those who have any appearance of being infected. Indeed,

THE HEARTLESSNESS AND INHUMANITY

which generally accompany such terrible plagues as this have been conspicuous here. The blood of Satan—thieves, pickpockets, and burglars—seem to have been about the only persons who have thriven during the past month. They have come from other cities to prey upon the dead and dying as upon the living. Singularly enough, the drinking-saloon have not found their account in the plague, although during such visitations drunkeness and debauchery generally hold high carnival, the people becoming reckless and ready to drown their fears in the diversion of alcoholic drinks. Out of between thirty and forty of such saloons, which commonly are openly from one years end to the other, all are close but one, and this by no means does a thriving business. The boldness of the desperadoes is something simply wonderful. Unhappily where all are dying, the dead have often to be left for hours without attention, and in such instances it is often found that, after death, their persons and rooms have been robbed. Several arrests of men and women accused of such dreadful work have been made, and it is likely to go hard with the sacrilegious villains. Some undertakers, in the press of business, have refused to make returns to the Boards of Health, and others are accused of hurrying corpses off to the shops and keeping them there until they should find time for burial. There are not, indeed, hearses enough for the work, and sometimes as many as nine corpses are placed in one wagon and driven at all speed to their last resting place. The

HORRIBLE SPECTACLE

of the horses of such a wagon running away with their ghastly burden is said to have been witnessed, the dead being thrown from the tumble into the road, and some caught by their clothing dragging on after the clattering wheels.

10/1/73 Mirror

Died With My Face to the Foe.

A single shot, followed by a loud shriek, told us that one of our best men, Bradley, was wounded. He proclaimed his agony with a loud voice, turning over on his back, and commenced kicking so vigorously that the surgeon had difficulty in getting in reach of him. "Poor fellow," said the doctor, as he saw a whitish liquid oozing out. "shot in the bladder : I am afraid it's fatal," and he commenced opening his coat. "Oh, my God," said Bradley, "I'm a dead man ; I'll never get over it." "Keep up your spirits, my boy : never say die," said Captain Johnson, kneeling kindly over him.

"Doctor," asked the wounded soldier feebly, "will you write to my mother and tell her that I died bravely doing my duty, with my face to the foe, and that I thought of her when I was dying ?"

"Yes, yes," said the doctor, with dim eyes and a husky voice, "I will write to her and tell her, too," but suddenly springing to his feet with an indignant and angry voice added—

"Why, confound it, man, you are not hurt a bit : it's only your canteen that's shot, and that's the water from it : get up, will you."

Bradley raised up slowly, felt himself all over, and with an exceedingly foolish countenance, crawled back to his position, amid the uproarious laughter of the whole regiment.

For months after that, on the march or in camp, and sometimes in the stillness of the night you would hear a voice in one direction demanding "what shall I tell your mother ?" And perhaps a half dozen responses would be heard. "Tell her I died with my face to the foe," and then "Canteen" Bradley would come out and angrily hunt for the man that said it. He seldom found him, but when he did there was certain to be a fight.—*Rebelliana in the Courier Journal.*

11/12/73 Mirror

President Grant and His Cabinet at the Loudoun Fair.

Thursday last was a grand day in Loudoun. The morning opened delightfully, and at an early hour the throng commenced pouring into Leesburg, from whence they wended their way to the Fair Grounds.— Humanity of every shape, size, sex, age and color comprised the multitude, the whole producing a scene of life and animation rarely excelled.

At 11 o'clock, the train from Washington arrived, bearing a special car, containing President Grant; Secretary of War, Belknap Secretary of State, Fish; Secretary of Navy, Robeson; Secretary of interior, Delano; Secretary of Treasury, Richardson; Attorney General, Williams; Assistant Secretary Interior, Cowan; Surgeon General, Barnes; General Babcock; Commodore Ammen; Gen. Pitcher; Col. Casey, brother-in-law of the President, and a number of distinguished visitors, and strangers. This was the first time that Gen. Grant had ever been attended by so "full a Cabinet" in his jaunts of pleasure— every member of that body being present except Creswell, which may be considered quite a compliment to Loudoun.

The party was met at the depot by Col. J. W. Fairfax, President of the Agricultural Society, and a deputation of the Committee of Reception, and conveyed at once to the Fair Grounds, the President riding in an open carriage drawn by four horses. The cavalcade was escorted through town by a number of citizens on horseback, and the Tankerville Band.

When the President reached the judges' stand, he was greeted with three long, loud cheers. On the stand, he was met by Thos. W. Edwards, Esq. who received him in the following APPROPRIATE SPEECH:

"In compliance, Mr. President, with the desire of officers and members of the Agricultural Society of Loudoun county, and in entire accordance with my own pleasure, I am here to greet and bid you welcome. As the President of the United States and the head and representative of

this great nation, you are welcome, and I am happy to assure you that, in your individual and private character, you are most cordially welcome, and we hope that your first visit to Loudoun will prove to you and your companions as agreeable as it is gratifying to us all."

The President bowed his thanks and shook hands with the hundreds who pressed around him, and then, escorted by the President of the Society, the whole party made a circuit of the grounds, viewing the stock and other articles of interest on exhibition, and receiving the welcome of the people.

At one o'clock the admirable address of Clinton Lloyd, Esq., which will be found entire in to-day's paper—was delivered— the President and his party occupying prominent seats near the speaker during its delivery.

At the conclusion of the speaking, lunch was served on the ground. Later in the evening the Presidential party and a number of invited guests, were conveyed to the residence of Col. Fairfax, where an elegant dinner was in waiting, and soon dispatched, great good humor prevailing throughout. At 9 o'clock the party proceeded to the depot, and at 10 o'clock, amid the huzzahs of the attending crowd, and the music of the Leesburg Band, they started on their return trip, apparently much pleased with their visit to Loudoun.

11/1/73 Washingtonian

LOCALS.

Rev. W. W. Reese will preach at Christ Church, Gonesville, to-morrow, Sunday morning at 11 o'clock.

Do an Act of Charity, by purchasing an Article of Domestic Use.—Mrs. Sanford I. Ramey has had left at the store of Messrs. Douglas & Sellman, Leesburg, a number of "Mops," neatly and handsomely made, which she asks her friends in Leesburg and vicinity to purchase, as the small amount she realizes from their sale, is all she has, upon which to support herself and her afflicted child. We are sure there is no acquaintance of Mrs. Ramey, who knows her destitute condition, will refuse to give the little aid she asks at their hands in this way. Our liberality cannot be bestowed upon one more in need, and who will more feelingly appreciate the kindness shown.

Immense Yield of Corn.—Mr. William Benton has on his farm, near Middleburg, a forty acre field of corn, which averages 17 1-3 barrels per acre, and twenty-five acres of the same field averages 18 1-3 barrels. This field has been carfully examined by a committee of farmers, and an acre measured, and the corn husked, shelled and weighed, and the above is the result. There is no bottom land included in the estimate. It has been entered for the premium of the State Fair at Richmond, and we have no doubt Loudoun will again take the premium for the best field of corn in the State.

Sidewalks.—The order of the Council some weeks since, obliging the property-holders of the town to re-pave the sidewalks in front of their residences, &c., has started many to work, and those who have not already complied with the order, are getting ready to begin the work, and by the first of December, the walking will be greatly improved, and the safety and convenience of pedestrians greatly advanced.

11/26/73 Mirror

A Hundred-Mile Trip on the Truck of a Railroad Car.

On the arrival at Camden station yesterday afternoon of the 5:10 western train, Baltimore and Ohio railroad, a man was discovered lying upon the truck of one of the passenger cars. At first it was supposed he was dead, but upon investigation it was found that he was alive, but sadly used up, and suffering greatly from the cold. His face and clothing were covered with smoke and dust. After thorough ablution he stated that he had secreted himself on the truck under the car yesterday morning while the train was at Martinsburg, W. Va., one hundred miles from Baltimore, and in that perilous position had ridden the whole distance without food and in imminent peril of his life to this point; thus accomplishing one of the most desperate journeys ever recorded. He gave his name as George Allender a native of Pittsburgh, Pa., and said that a few days ago he received a letter from a friend in Washington stating that he could obtain employment in that city. Being out of employment he determined to visit Washington and invested what money he had in a ticket calling for passage from Pittsburgh to Martinsburg. Upon arriving there and being out of funds he concluded to steal a ride for the rest of the journey, and selected the truck of one of the cars as his seat. His account of the trip from West Virginia to Baltimore was a thrilling one. He was in great danger several times of falling from the truck in consequence of his body becoming benumbed with cold. The space between the truck and the bottom of the car where he rode was about twelve inches in height, and as a consequence he was forced to extend his body along the four timbers which constituted the frame-work of the truck. While relating his story the young man referred to his inability to obtain employment and shed tears. Several gentlemen who heard the story of the trip contributed a sum of money for his relief, and after a good dinner furnished him by Mr. Hassan, of the depot restaurant, he proceeded to Washington. The daring of the adventure and its prompting motive are sufficient commentaries on the desperation of the times.—*Baltimore Sun, 19th.*

11/5/73 Mirror

A Soap Man Makes Trouble in Danbury.

We see by the Troy-Whig that Frank D. Hatfield, the agent for the soap house of McKeon, Van Haagan & Co., has received a vote of thanks from the board of aldermen of that city, for a gift of soap. Mr. Hatfield is appreciated in Troy, and had better stay there. At least, he should keep away from Danbury. Several weeks ago some of his soap was left at a house on Liberty street, where it gave satisfaction, we learn. Two weeks later, the lady of the house bought a box of fancy soaps of the same manufacture. The cakes were of three colors, yellow, white and pink. She took the box home, and meant to have laid it away, but it caught the eye of her child, some three years old, and so exercised the throat of the youngster, that she was obliged to give up the box and the contents. Subsequently, being engaged in baking, she lost sight of the affair. In the meantime, the child looked over the box, and finding the contents to be unusually attractive, undertook to eat them; but failing in this, used them as blocks for laying out townships, erecting towers, and performing a variety of other engineering feats. Pretty soon it fell to knocking them down with its hand, and then to kicking them around the room with its foot, and when this amusement lost its attraction, it suddenly set up a dreadful howl of agony, and started for the kitchen. It was about this time that the man of the house, who had been abed up stairs, came down stairs in pants and shirt, to get some shaving water. When within four steps of the bottom, he stepped on something which immediately disappeared with astonishing celerity, and deposited him on the floor below without the aid of the other steps. He got up on his feet at once, and looked about for the cause of the accident. It was a cake of that soap. He picked it up, and with wonderful presence of mind, hurled it through the glass of the first window. Then he gathered up the shaving cup

and brush, and went into the room. He went into it just as any man would who had missed four steps in coming down stairs; and lighting on another cake just as he was about to kick the door shut, that leg shot away so violently as to hurt the roof of his mouth, and he came down on one knee, with his head against the bureau. The top of his scalp was somewhat bruised, and one drawer was without its complement of knobs, and he had bitten a piece from the tip of his tongue, although no one would have suspected that last by the flow of conversation that followed as he bounded to his feet. The appearance of his wife, with her face depicting emotions of the liveliest alarm, was welcomed as a providential escape valve for the wrath boiling within him, but he found his rage turning to astonishment as he saw her suddenly change her motion, and dash towards him with her head down and uttering a hysterical scream. As the instinct of self-preservation is the loudest, he immediately proceeded to move out of the way of his sliding spouse, when he encountered another cake of soap, and was twisted completely around, and hurled headlong against the centre table, and immediately across her line of march. What became of her or the centre table in the crash that followed he cannot tell. He remembers when striking the table of seeing some twenty-five new planets with a pyrotechnic display in the back-ground, and thinks he must have heard a million fire crackers go off under a barrel. When he came too, he was abed in a darkened room, with two persons whispering in a corner, and the air thoroughly impregnated with a flavor of castor oil. If Mr. Hatfield can obtain reasonable board in Troy, within five minutes walk of the depot and post office, he will find it a bargain.—*Danbury News*

12/17/73 Mirror

ALEX. H. STEPHENS ON THE SALARY BILL.

The event in Congress Thursday last was the speech of Hon. Alex. H. Stephens on the salary bill. He held that a member of Congress should command the highest salary, commensurate with the responsibilities imposed upon him.

A Washington correspondent of the *Sun* says: "There was probably never a man on the floor who was listened to with more attention. His prominence in the councils of the nation years ago, the important position he held in the southern Confederacy, and his conceded great ability, all had the effect to direct great attention to him. The members of the House, gathered about his seat, in order that they might hear every word, and it no sooner became known that he had the floor than Senators came pouring into the hall of the House of Representatives, while the Senate galleries were speedily depleted.

Mr. Stephen's very appearance is bound to attract attention. Physically he is the most diminutive man in Congress, but he is considered a giant in intellect, and has a most wonderful voice. His language is pure and classic and his enunciation is so clear that every word could be heard in all parts of the hall. While speaking he wore a plum colored velvet smoking cap, and leaned for support upon a crutch under his left arm. With his right he added force to his language by his gestures, and at times very forcibly struck the desk just behind him. While speaking he faced the republican side of the House and prominent among these who paid the most marked attention were Messrs. Dawes. Garfield, B. F. Butler, G. F. Hoar, Kelley and other republican leaders. Gathered around him and in his immediate vicinity were at least twenty-five members who had served with him in one capacity or another in the southern Confederacy. The whole scene was one which those who witnessed it will not soon forget. After he had finished his speech Gen. Butler walked up to him and warmly congratulated him.

(Alex Stephens was the former Vice President of the Confederacy.)

12/3/73 Mirror

BOSS TWEED IN THE PENITENTIARY.

On Saturday last, Wm. M. Tweed, who but a little while ago, occupied a high position in the city of New York, and from his great influence in the city government, was generally known as "Boss Tweed," was incarcerated in the penitentiary at Blackwells Island. In response to the usual questions he answered that he was aged fifty, occupation, a statesman, no religion, but as his family are Protestants he was entered as a protestant. He weighed 263 pounds. He was taken to the bath, then had his head shaved in penitentiary style, and was arrayed in the full striped uniform. He had two letters from New York city physicians recommending that he be placed in the hospital, but after examination by the penitentiary physician he was removed to a common cell, like all the other felons, and number 39. The jacket given him to wear is known as the larceny jacket. His son staid by him until he was led away to his cell, when he and a few friends and reporters left the island.

(Boss Tweed was put behind bars because of the efforts of certain magazines, newspapers, and "the acid pen" of illustrator Thomas Nast. Governor and future presidential candidate Sam Tilden and New York Attorney General Charles Fairchild also played a significant part. Back in the days when a dollar was worth $20 of today's money it was estimated that he and his "ring" had stolen 45 million out of public funds.)

12/10/73 Mirror

Mrs. Stephen Treadway, of Mt. Sterling, Ky., has recovered a saddle-mare, which was taken from her by some Federal soldiers during the war, and was gone nine years and nine months to the very day, when the affectionate animal astonished the whole family and whole neighborhood by returning home by herself and of her own accord.

1/3/74 Washingtonian

|By Request.

The Richmond *Whig* says:

Intemperance among the young men Christmas day seems to have generally prevailed. It was noticed here, and we find that our exchanges make the same complaint about the young men in their various localities. It is an ugly sign. Our young men cannot afford to begin life under the crushing burden of intemperance. If they thus begin life, how will they end it? That is a question for them to ponder.

Let the old men set the young ones a good example in this direction. In the past they have not done it. Let the year 1874 witness a radical change in this direction. Keep the boys out of the drinking saloons. Prosecute all who sell liquor to minors. If the law officers fail to enforce the laws, indict them for a violation of their oaths.

THE MIRROR.

WEDNESDAY............... Jan. 7

BOLD THEFTS.—ELEVEN HUNDRED DOLLARS STOLEN FROM A BED-ROOM.—A bold thief or thieves seem to be investing this section of country, whose skill in their rascally art would put to blush the veterans of the Five Points—and we would advise those encumbered with Uncle Sam's promises to pay, to bolt well their "chamber doors," and sleep with one eye open.

A month or two ago, the bed-room of Mr. JNO. ALDRIDGE, near Mt. Gilead, was entered, his secretary opened, and between three and four hundred dollars abstracted, and that was the last of it so far as Mr. A. was concerned.

MONEY, WATCH, BOOTS AND BREECHES.

On the night of the 21st of December some one hoisted a window, and passing through a pantry, and the dining-room entered the chamber of Mr. SAMUEL CARR, about two miles from Leesburg, and while Mr. C. was enjoying "balmy nature's sweet restorer," the thief gathered up his watch, his boots and his pantaloons, in the pocket of which latter was a purse containing $70 in money and a lot of papers. In the dining room the rogue investigated the purse, and generously left on the floor the papers, retreating with watch, boots, pants and money. The pantaloons were found a few days after concealed in a straw rick about a mile from the house. The other articles, however, are still going.

THEY STRIKE ILE

The latest exploit was equally daring and much more remunerative. On Friday night, Mr. WM. LOWE, a cattle drover, who lives some two miles south of Leesburg, came up from Washington on the evening train, having in his possession about $1100 in money, and a note for $110. The train reached Leesburg at 6½ o'clock, after which Mr. L. walked home, and before retiring placed his money and note, (which were rolled together in a pocket-handkerchief) in a box, and set it on a table near the foot of his bed, intending to use the money next day. Weary and tired, he soon fell asleep, and awoke in the morning to find that the box and its contents was missing. The box was afterward found a short distance from the house, broken open and rifled. Immediate steps were taken to stop the payment of the note, but so far nothing has been heard of the money, nor any clue obtained as to who "struck the ile."

As will be seen by advertisement in another column, Mr. Lowe offers a reward of $200 for the detection of the thief.

1/10/74 Washingtonian

WASHINGTONIAN·

MIXED SCHOOLS

[From the Richmond Dispatch.]

The Lynchburg *Press*, the Republican organ of that city, has an earnest and forcible editorial upon the subject of the proposed mixed schools of the civil rights bill now pending in the House of Representative of Congress. The *Press* declares itself most emphatically against such schools, and expresses its belief that the majority of the negroes of the State are also opposed to them.

The *Press* declares that the Public Schools of Virginia are now conducted fairly and impartially—the negroes having as good teachers as the whites—the whites paying the bulk of the taxes that support the schools—and it inveighs against any obstacle being thrown in the way of their harmonious and successful operation by "those who live a thousand "miles from us, and whose interest in our "people, both white and colored, *extends no* "*further than the advancement of their own* "*ends.*" This is very true, but nevertheless very frank talk for a Republican journal, and in which we know has stood up for the Republican party of Virginia with steadiness and vigor.

The *Press* predicts that to mix the colors in the schools would be to take away the impartiality that now distinguishes the system. The bringing the races together would do violence to the feelings of both, as the *Press* believes, and produce "discord, tumult, and open rupture." It boldly predicts the ruin of the system of education in Virginia should the races be required to enter the same schools.

Mayor's Office,

LEESBURG. JAN. 12, 1874.

WHEREAS, many citizens complain that they are greatly annoyed by disorderly persons Whooping and Hallooing about the streets of the Town, and by other improper conduct, whereby the peace and good order of the same is disturbed and broken; and whereas, it has been deemed necessary by the Council that additional Police be appointed, that the repose of the citizens be not disturbed.

Now, therefore, I, GEO. R. HEAD, Mayor of the town of Leesburg, by authority in me vested, (and at the request of the Council,) do hereby appoint BENJ. F. HEAD, SPECIAL POLICE, until further orders, and all citizens will respect him as such.

The newly-appointed officer is assigned to NIGHT DUTY, and is required to arrest any and all persons, without regard to age or sex, who may be found violating the following

ORDINANCE:

Be it Enacted by the Mayor. Recorder and Common Council of the Town of Leesburg, in Va., That if any person after night, in the streets of Leesburg. or in any other part of the Corporation, shall disturb the good order of the town, or the repose of the citizens thereof, by raising clamour, by loud Whooping, Hallooing, or in any other way whatsoever.— Or if any person shall, in the streets or any other part of the town, assemble after night and shall tumultuously behave themselves so as to alarm the citizens, or disturb the quiet of the town, he or they, upon conviction of either offence, shall pay a fine of not less than One nor more than Five Dollars; upon failure to make present payment, he or they shall be committed to jail.

jan. 14- GEO. R. HEAD, Mayor.

1/28/74 Mirror

Lightning Trains

Perhaps there is no popular delusion which obtains so generally, even among people who ought to know better, as that regarding the speed of railroad trains. A striking example of this is given in the report of a train in a Northern State, in which the claim for damages rested upon the speed at which a certain train was driven. Several witnesses among them a clergyman testified that it was running at the rate of sixty miles an hour, and undoubtedly believed they were telling the truth. Any practical railroad hand, however, could have told the jury that the speed, even of an express train, rarely exceeded thirty-five miles an hour and was oftener less than more than that. There have been instances where trains have attained a rate of fifty miles an hour, but authentic ones are as rare as centenarians.

THEN AND NOW.

1/10/74 Washingtonian

One of the New York papers has revived a little reminiscence in the career of the notorious Tweed which shows the manner in which those men lived who plundered the great city of New York of more money than Warren Hastings bore off from the Indian empire. The reminiscence in question is one of the wedding of Tweed's daughter two years ago in princely style:

There were forty silver sets, any one of which would have attracted a crowd if placed in a jeweler's window, and one single one contained two hundred and forty separate pieces, Mr. James Fisk, jr. sent a frosted silver contrivance representing an iceburg, evidently intended to hold ice cream, or some equally frigid substance. The association was beautifully sustained by the presence of arctic bears reposing on the icicle handle of the bowl, and climbing up the spoons. There were forty pieces of jewelry, of which fifteen were diamond sets. A single one of the latter is known to have cost $43.000. It contained diamonds as big as filberts.

A cross of eleven diamonds, pea size, a pin of sixty diamonds, representing a sickle and sheaves of wheat; diamond bracelets of fabulous magnificence; a ring with a tiny watch as the seal; bronzes, thread lace, cashmere shawls, rare pictures, everything that could be conceived which is rare and costly filled the room with splendor. The trousseau of the bride included fourteen dresses, varying in price from $300 to $3,200 each, though her wedding dress of white gross grain cost $1,000, to which $4,000 worth of point lace was added. A black silk walking suit was decorated with 382 bows, and others were elaborated correspondingly.

1/14/74 Mirror

—"There, now," cried little Bessie the other day, rummaging a drawer in the bureau. "grandpa has gone to heaven without his spectacles."

From Field's Memory of Men and Women.
MR. LINCOLN'S DEATH.

At last, at just 7.22, he ceased to breathe. When it became certain to all that his soul had taken its flight, Dr. Gurley dropped upon his knees by the bedside and uttered a fervent prayer. Never was a supplication wafted to the Creator under more solemn circumstances.

When it was finished most of the persons assembled began slowly to withdraw from the chamber of death. I, however, with a few others, remained. We closed the eyes completely, and placed silver coins upon them, and with a pocket hand-kerchief we tied up the jaw, which had already begun to fall. Mr Stanton threw open the two windows of the room. Just then Peterson entered, and rudely drawing the upper pillow from under the head of the dead, tossed it into the yard. Shortly afterward we retired from the room. Mr. Stanton locked the door, and stationed a sentry in front of it. I then went into the front parlor, where I found Dr. Gurley again praying. Mrs. Lincoln was lying upon a sofa, moaning, and her son Robert was standing at her head. When Dr. Gurley had finished his prayer Robt. Lincoln assisted his mother to rise and together we walked to the front door. The President's carriage was standing before the house in the dripping rain as it had stood there all through that terrible night. As Mrs. Lincoln reached the door-steps she cast a hurried glance at the theatre opposite, and three times repeated, 'Oh, that dreadful house!" She was then helped into the carriage, which drove away.

Perhaps the most affecting incident connected with this drama occurred an hour later. Mr. Lincoln's body, inclosed in a plain wooden box, around which was wrapped the American flag, was borne from the house by six private soldiers, then placed in an ordinary hearse behind which the soldiers marched like mourners, and so carried it to the Executive Mansion. As the cortege passed along it attracted but little attention, for but few persons knew what burden was being carried past their doors. It was fitting that this great man of the people—plain Uncle Abe, then, as in years gone by in his Western home—should pass through the silent streets of the capital under the escort of common men.

This contrasted strikingly with the following account of the manner in which the dead President was tricked out for public show on his passage to his last home.

As I saw Mr. Lincoln lying in state in the East room of the Executive Mansion his appearance was quite unlike what it had been immediately after his death. The black had gone from his eyes and his face, which had resumed a natural color. This I was informed was the work of an artist. The pencil had been employed to produce the change. While his corpse was being carried in procession through the cities of the land, before it was exposed to public gaze the coffin was opened, the dust was brushed from the face and the discolored parts were retouched. And so he went to his rest.

2/4/74 Mirror
Dr. Wm. E. Munsey.

A correspondent of the Staunton *Vindicator* writing from Salem, Roanoke county, on the 25th of January says :

It was announced that on the evening of the 16th inst., Dr. W. E. Munsey would deliver a lecture in the Town Hall of Salem ; at an early hour a large audience had gathered to partake of the intellectual feast which the well-earned reputation of the reverend divine warranted ; the subject of the lecture was "*Man.*" It was not your correspondent's good fortune to hear this lecture, but he was informed of its being one of the Doctor's master efforts. On Sunday morning Dr. Munsey preached in the Methodist Church : a great many persons could not be admitted for want of room to seat them. 'Tis useless to attempt a description of his sermon ; for an hour and a half the audience was held spell-bound by the magic of his eloquence : it was replete with acute reasoning, brilliant flashes of imagination and a more than oriental richness of illustration : clothed in such eloquent drapery *the Church* was raised from stage to stage until at last crowned by the grand climax of its final triumph over error. In his description of the final judgment, the lurid scenes portrayed seemed to pass before the mind's eye leaving an impress never to be forgotten. It was in Salem that those detrimental reports in reference to the reverend gentleman first gained publicity. Proud indeed must have been his feelings, when, with his still steady eye, his calm and thoughtful face and the native fire of his eloquence he proclaimed their utter falsity ; showing that true greatness can never be *permanently* tarnished by the lying tongue of slander.

(The Rev. Munsey mentioned above must have been quite a speaker. Newspaper accounts often referred to him as "the great Munsey".)

2/2/74 Washingtonian
Pardon of the Virginia Duelist.

RICHMOND, VA., Feb 17.—Page McCarty, recently convicted of dueling, who has been in jail under a sentence of six months's imprisonment imposed by the courts, in addition to the fine of $500, was to-day pardoned by Governor Kemper. The pardon sets forth that the sole ground upon which executive clemency is extended is that physicians certify that further confinement would be fatal to McCarty he having been very ill since his incarceration.

HILLSBORO', Feb. 2d, 1874.
MR. EDITOR:—The notice of the arrest of Wm. Corrie, in the last issue of the Loudoun Enterprise and copied from that paper by the Washingtonian, does that unfortunate gentleman great injustice. He was not the worthless character that he is represented. That he lived alone, and in a hut of his own making for a short time, is true, but that was more his misfortune than his fault. He was a quiet, peaceable citizen, honest in his dealings, prompt in payment of his debts, industrious as a laborer, trusty and efficient and a general favorite with the farmers in the locality in which he resided. He was unfortunately addicted to the use of strong drink, and an occasional "spree," but never molested any one during their continuance, and until he *lost his mind* was considered harmless.

This statement is due an unfortunate man and a stranger. JUSTICE.

105

2/11/74 Mirror

Women Fighting Liquor.

Queer things are happening in these latter days, and the queerest of them all, is what is called the Ladies League in Ohio, the object of which is to crush out the liquor traffic, and the weapons used — songs and prayers, not offered up in secret, but in the bar-rooms of the villages where the Leaguers hold sway. They go from one grog-shop to another, and either in the house or on the pavement in front of the door, hold prayer-meetings, lasting in some instances all day through. So far they appear to have met with success, nearly all the dealers having abandoned the traffic altogether and smashed in the heads of the "red-eye," or at least capitulated for the present. Some idea of their procedures may be formed from the following occurrence in Franklin—it is but one of many related by the papers:

On Saturday the women went early in the morning to the saloon of Ph. Weber and began to sing and pray. They dragged with them an old lady of ninety years who could hardly walk, and they were hardly in the saloon before three parsons also put in an appearance. They remained in the saloon until 6 o'clock in the evening. Mr. and Mrs. Weber quietly permitted them to go on with their songs and prayers: but in a pause Mrs Weber told them to betake themselves away, as she wished to close the saloon; but, instead of answering the women *returned a jeering, spiteful laugh*.

Mrs. Weber, nevertheless, attempted to close the saloon: but Jacob Scherzer took a seat before the door. The powerful woman thereupon attempted to pull him away, and two men sprang forward, and one of them *struck the woman across the hand with a slung-shot* with such violence as to send the key flying out upon the sidewalk, so that it was long before it could be found. The woman thereupon hastened to the Marshal, but he only laughed at her, and said, "I belong to the other party."

On Monday morning early the women returned and besieged the Weber saloon. On Tuesday morning they again sung and prayed all day in front of the house. On Wednesday the scene was repeated. As it was cold they had a small stove, which they placed upon the sidewalk, so that they could warm themselves.

The object of the Ladies League is unquestionable good — whether their mode of attaining it is exactly the thing, may well be doubted.

2/21/74 Washingtonian

GEORGETOWN NO MORE.

The Alexandria *Sentinel* of Wednesday says:—"A bill to extend the limits of the city of Washington, providing for the extension of the present boundary, so that the territory heretofore known as Georgetown, shall be embraced within the same, was introduced in the House of Representatives on Tuesday, by Mr. Chipman, and it further provides that the property within the late corporate limits of Georgetown shall not be taxed for the payment of any debt heretofore contracted by the corporation of Washington, nor shall the property within the limits of the city of Washington be taxed for the payment of any debt heretofore contracted by the city of Georgetown. The second section provides that the port of Georgetown shall hereafter be known as the port of Washington, and the customs laws are hereby amended to conform to the provisions of this act. The third section provides that the office of postmaster in Georgetown be abolished, and the postmaster general is directed to extend the free-delivery system within the boundaries of the city of Washington as herein defined. The fourth section changes the name of the streets running north and south, so as to conform to the Washington streets,

(Georgetown existed long before the federal capital was established adjacent to it. Some of these old newspapers referred to it as West Washington.)

2/4/74 Mirror

THE COURT HOUSE FENCE.—The Court-house yard will soon be entirely enclosed with a handsome iron railing—the contract for the purpose having on Friday last been awarded by the Board of Supervisors, to Messrs. COCKEY & Co., iron Founders of this town,

THE MIRROR.

WEDNESDAY.....................March 4

A LITTLE BOY, some four or five years of age, son of Mr. Samuel McAnther, residing near Hillsborough, in this county, was killed one day last week by a kick from a horse.

MEETING THEM HALF WAY.—By reference to proceedings in to-day's paper, it will be seen that the Township Board, Leesburg Township, propose to meet their Broad Run neighbors half-way in building a Bridge over Goose Creek on the Leesburg and Alexandria Turnpike. We hope this action of the Board may meet with a hearty and prompt response. The absolute necessity for a Bridge at the point indicated, is too seriously felt to need any argument in its favor. Let Broad Run Township and those citizens most deeply concerned in the improvement, put their shoulders to the wheel, and before the close of the coming summer, have the work completed.

THE GENERAL R. E. LEE MONUMENT.—The collossal monument to the memory of Gen'l Lee which is now rapidly being constructed under the direction and skill of Prof. Volentine, will, when completed, be the greatest triumph of art and mechanical skill ever produced in this country. The structure will be surmounted by a reclining figure of Gen'l Lee enveloped in his military cloak.

DOGS.—The Legislature has under consideration the tax on canines. The public have little idea of the amount of revenue that came from this levy. In forty counties where the dogs were taxed. $40,000 were collected from this source alone. Rockbridge raised on this item nearly $2,000.

[Well, last year Loudoun collected within a fraction of $2,000 from the tax on dogs, and after paying out of it for all the sheep reported killed by dogs during the year, turned over nearly $1,000 for the benefit of the public schools of the county.]

THE RAILROAD TO PURCELLVILLE.—From present indications the completion of the W. & O. Railroad to Purcellville, will mark an era in the history of that hitherto quiet little village—and the first train is to be greeted with a grand ovation by the hospitable and intelligent citizens of that neighborhood.

WASHINGTONIAN.

LEESBURG, LOUDOUN COUNTY, VA.

SATURDAY. MARCH 7, 1874.

POINT OF ROCKS BRIDGE.

The Bridge at the Point of Rocks over the Potomac, we are glad to learn, is now the subject of Legislation, in this State and Maryland, preparatory to the reorganization of the company, and the issuing of preferred stock, to be used in rebuilding it. The most expensive part—the piers—are there, in good and substantial condition—the abutment on the Virginia side, will need repairs. It is proposed to issue about $80,000 worth of preferred stock—the net income of the bridge, to go to paying interest on this stock, and if there be any residue, to be applied to the payment of interest on all the stock. The importance of this improvement is highly appreciated by the people of Loudon

(The bridge was burned down early in the war by General Jackson. Eventually, it was replaced but it was swept away by the flood of 1889 (the Johnstown flood). Today, thousands of cars use it.)

2/18/74 Mirror

The Danbury Man Who Has a Horse and Carriage.

The man across the way has a horse and carriage. We have none. Three sadder words we never saw. The man across the way drives gaily forth every pleasant afternoon with his wife beside him. And we envy him and can't help it. There are others of the neighbors who envy him, and could we reach each other's hearts we would find that our thoughts were following the lucky horseman in his various turns about town, in his cantering here and trotting there, and in the shine of his carriage and the proud bearing of his horse. But if it is a sadness to see him drive away, yet there is a pleasure in seeing him come back. For it is dark when he returns, the sunshine is gone, and in its stead is darkness with frost in it. He smiled complacently when he handed his wife into the carriage, but he doesn't smile when he hands her out.— Perhaps the operation requires so much care and attention that it would not be right to smile. We know his nose is red, because we can see it as he drives by the lamp. We know that his feet are frigid and that his legs are asleep, by the way he gets down to the ground. We are beginning to see how wrong it is to envy our fellow man. He looks at her as she runs into the house and into the arms of the genial base-burner, and gloomily wonders why heaven so favors her above him. He stumbles painfully along to the stable with the horse, which he now thoroughly despises, ambling behind him. His hands are so numb he can hardly undo the fastening of the door, his legs have awakened, and appear to be reproaching him; his eyes are full of water, and his soul overflowing with discontent. No harness was ever before so difficult to remove as is this. He feels the wrath bubbling up to the highest water-mark, and he could scream out—he is so mad. We are seeing now how wicked it is to envy our fellow man. He hears footsteps on the sidewalk, and sees the flash of warm light shoot out into the cold air as the various neighbors, having returned from their work, and having no horse, disappear hastily within and take with them the bright, cheerful light. He gets the horse in the door, and starts to look up the lantern. He bumps various parts of his anatomy against articles it is too dark to learn the nature of. He would cry out in his pain and mis-

ery were he not awed by the astonishing profusion of things he is falling over. He gives up the lantern and pulls off the harness to hang it up. The straps dangle down and get under his feet, and trip him, and the impatient animal suddenly bolts into the stall before it is fully undressed. Then there is another search for the lantern, and during it he raps his head against a beam, and the blow is so violent that it stirs up every one of his ideas, including the one which tells him that the lantern was taken into the house last night to be cleaned. He stumbles back over the frozen clods and into the house, where the bright light and warm air render him more gloomy and morose. He vouchsafes no information to the appropriate query from his wife if it is cold out, but darkly hints of impending retribution to whoever doesn't quit fooling with that lantern; and then stalkes back to the stable. And here for the next fifteen minutes he employs himself in arranging the bedding, mixing the feed, and pondering on the advantage he has over his neighbors in having a horse and carriage of his own.

3/11/74 Mirror

LINCOLN

An Anecdote Told by Charles Dickens,--A Remarkable Dream upon the Eve of the Assassination.

In the New York *Herald's* review of the third volume of "Forster's Life of Dickens" we find the following anecdote of Lincoln :

It will (says Mr. Forster) be no violation of the rule of avoiding private detail if the very interesting close of this letter (one written by Dickens from Washington) is given. Its anecdote of President Lincoln was repeatedly told by Dickens after his return, and I am under no necessity to withhold from it the authority of Mr. Sumner's name: "I am going to-morrow to see the President, who has sent to me twice. I dined with Charles Sumner last Sunday, against my rule ; and, as I had stipulated for no party, Mr. Secretary Stanton was the only other guest beside his own secretary. Stanton is a man with a very remarkable memory, and extraordinarily familiar with my books. He and Sumner having been the first two public men at the dying President's bedside, and having remained with him until he breathed his last, we fell into a very interesting conversation after dinner, when, each of them giving his own narrative separately, the usual discrepancies about details of time were observable.

"Then Mr. Stanton told me a curious little story, which will form the remainder of this short letter. On the afternoon of the day on which the President was shot there was a Cabinet council, at which he presided. Mr. Stanton, being at the time commander-in-chief of the Northern troops that were concentrated about here, arrived rather late. Indeed, they were waiting for him, and, on entering the room, the President broke off in something he was saying, and remarked : '· Let us proceed to business, gentlemen.' Mr. Stanton then noticed with great surprise, that the President sat with an air of dignity in his chair, instead of lolling about in the most ungainly attitudes, as his invariable custom was, and that instead of telling irrelevant or questionable stories he was grave and calm and quite a different man. Mr. Stanton, on leaving the council with the Attorney General, said to him 'That is the most satisfactory Cabinet meeting I have attended for many a long day. What an

EXTRAORDINARY CHANGE.

in Mr. Lincoln !'' The Attorney General replied : 'We all saw that before you came in. While we were waiting for you he said, with his chin down on his breast : "Gentlemen, something very extraordinary is going to happen, and that very soon." To which the Attorney General had observed : "Something good, sir, I hope," when the President answered very gravely : 'I don't know, I don't know ; But it will happen, and shortly too."' As they were all impressed by his manner, the Attorney General took him up again. 'Have you received any information, sir, not yet disclosed to us?'' 'No,' answered the President, but I have had a dream, and I have now had the same dream three times. Once on the night preceding the battle of Bull run, once on the night preceding such another, (naming a battle also not favorable to the North.) His chin sunk on his breast again, and he sat reflecting. 'Might one ask the nature of this dream, sir ?' said the Attorney General. 'Well,' replied the President, without lifting his head or changing his attitude, 'I am on a great, broad, rolling river, and I am in a boat, and I drift and I drift—but this is not business,' suddenly raising his face, and looking round the table as Mr. Stanton entered. 'Let us proceed to business, gentlemen ' Mr. Stanton and the Attorney General said, as they walked on together, it would be curious to notice whether anything ensued on this, and they agreed to notice. He was shot that night."

(A well known incident reported by most biographers.)

3/25/74 Mirror

THE NORTH CAROLINA VOLCANO—*Additional Reports of the New Wonder.*—The Charlotte and Asheville (N. C.) papers give letters from persons residing in the neighborhood of Bald mountain that confirm the telegraphic accounts. The Raleigh News says :

"The people of that section are becoming much alarmed about a rumbling noise that has been heard daily for some two months proceeding from this mountain, houses being jarred for miles in every direction The Asheville Expositor publishes letters from reliable parties in the vicinity of the disturbed mountain, who all give the same report in substance, and the inhabitants of the section are preparing to leave from fear. We met, a couple of days since, the editor of the Expositor, and he assures us, upon the strength of the assertion of gentlemen from the vicinity of the disturbance whose word he could not question, that no doubt existed of the fact that the mountain was in terrible throes from some cause, the rumbling noise and the attendant quaking of the earth being anything but pleasant, while there are positive indications that the mountain is on fire. The recent snows have melted as rapidly as they fell upon the mountain. Would it not be well for some scientist to look into this matter, as a correspondent writing from there says : "The people are going to leave if it is not stopped.

The Charlotte Observer of the 15th has further confirmatory details :

"This terrible subterranean thunder has been heard distinctly at Marion and Old Fort, a distance of eighteen or twenty miles. Consternation prevails among the inhabitants of the section of the country lying around Bald Mountain. The editor is informed by "a reliable gentleman just from the front that an "old blockade whiskey distiller, who had been making whiskey in contempt of revenue officers for five or six years, heard the mumbling of the mountain, and supposing the day of judgment had come, came out of his hole and abandoned his distillery and called in his neighbors to pray for him. For the last several days a grand prayer meeting and revival has been going on in the neighborhood of Bald Mountain. These whiskey sinners believe that the day of judgment is close at hand, and are praying fervently."

4/1/74 Mirror

Latest from the North Carolina Volcano—The Opinions of a Scientist.

The volcano, incipient earthquake, or whatever else it was that recently convulsed the mountains of North Carolina, and struck terror to the surrounding inhabitants, seems most likely to be a veritable "mountain in labor" with no greater progeny than that produced in the aphorism. A correspondent of the New York *Herald* who visited the scene, in his special to that paper says :

I reached here this morning, after riding all night, from Chimney Rock. Friday afternoon I found myself able to make the ascent of Stone Mountain, which is now established as the seat of the most serious disturbance.—Stone Mountain is of the same range as the Bald Mountain, lying seven miles northeast, and the shocks have extended between the two. With a guide I crossed Stone Mountain, and at one minute past 4 I experienced quite a shock, which

FRIGHTENED MY HORSE AND GUIDE

so much that both seemed about to leave me. Descending upon the southern side, I made the circuit of the Knots, and joined a party of students, professors and reporters at the Widow Nan's, on the north side of the mountain. Here we experienced a second shock, which shook preacher Logan off a rail fence upon which he was sitting, and a ladder, which was resting against the side of the house, was thrown down. Great excitement prevailed among the people, and some

FORTY-FOUR CANDIDATES FOR BAPTISM

on the following Sunday began to be douced at once despite the cold and rain.

Friday evening the party seperated in order to get accommodation at the different farmhouses, with the stipulation that we should meet the following morning at Chimney Rock to interview Professor Dupre, Professor of Natural Science, Wofford College, Spartanburg, S. C.

Brother Logan here asked the Professor if he thought there was any danger, to which there was a negative reply.

3/4/74 Mirror

LAST OF THE LOWRY GANG.

The Wilmington (N. C.) papers furnish full details of the death of Steve Lowry, the last of the outlaws who for a long time, was a terror to the people in Robeson county. He was shot and instantly killed, about 4½ o'clock Monday morning by three young men named Daniel Halcombe, Thomas Sutton and McNeill Patterson at a point on the Carolina Central Railway about sixteen miles west of Lumberton, the county seat of Robeson.

The reward for the killing of Steve Lowry amount, in all, to $6,200, and this amount will be paid over to the three young men who killed him.

The manner of his taking off is thus related by the Wilmington *Journal*:

"The three young men approached the outlaw and began to converse with him.— He made many boasts of what he had done and what he could do, and said that he could show more gold than any man in Robeson county. After a while the young men arose and bade Steve good night, saying that they were going home. After getting well out of the range of the camp they made a detour and crept up to within twenty yards of the outlaw. Here they remained quiet for a long time, waiting for a shot, but were deterred for more than an hour by the fact that that there were others near him. Finally they all separated, and Steve picked up a banjo, thrumming it.— One colored individual crept near him, so as to more readily get his fill of the music, and was so near Lowry that for some minutes the young men hesitated to fire for fear of injuring him. But the opportunity was not to be lost, and so, at a given signal, they all three fired. There was but one report from the three guns; and the outlaw sprang into the air and fell dead on the ground.

Black Warrior.

THIS CELEBRATED SADDLE and Harness STALLION will stand the ensuing season, commencing April 1st, 1874, in Loudoun county, Va., at the following places viz : Leesburg, Mountsville, Philomont and Upperville. He will be in Leesburg on Monday of April Court. For full particulars see handbills, or address either of the proprietors at Leesburg, Loudoun county, Va.

AARON DAILY.
THOS. BURCH.

april 1-3t

3/18/74 Mirror

Death of Chas. Sumner.

We last week recorded the death of MILLARD FILLMORE, an ex-President of the United States, before his mortal remains were consigned to the grave an arrow sped from the unerring bow of the insatiate archer, found lodgment in the breast of another, who for many years had occupied a prominent position in the counsels of the nation, and whose name will fill a conspicuous page in the country's history. The death of Hon. CHARLES SUMNER, a United States Senator from the commonwealth of Massachusetts which occurred at his residence in Washington city at 3½ o'clock on Wednesday afternoon, thrilled the people with a shock of surprise, and fell with crushing force upon the hearts of his admirers who regarded him as the embodiment of all that was pure, and good, and wise. In view of the open grave of the dead Senator, we can respect the grief of those who thus believed but the honest conviction of thousands of his fellow countrymen is that the interests and glory of this land, at least would have suffered no detriment had he never been born. He was a man of commanding presence and unquestioned learning, but his statesmanship was based upon an intense hatred and prejudice of the people and institutions of the South, and in its frenzy, he contributed much to inflame the sectional passions which ultimately culminated in blood, and after the close of the struggle, he was unceasing in his efforts to force upon a brave and generous people, measures that were unwholesome and objectionable, the natural fruits of which were bitterness, and sorrow, and discontent. But however misguided they may have believed him to have been, few doubted the sincerity of his convictions— and all are willing to acknowledge his greatness and ready to bury in the grave of his mortal remains, whatever feelings of resentment they may have felt toward him in life.

THE MIRROR.

WEDNESDAY............... March 25

THE IMPROVEMENTS in our town progress satisfactorily. Mr. Jno. Hammerly has laid the wooden curb on the entire front of his lot from King to Wirt street, a distance of about 420 feet, and has graded the side walk and is covering it with white gravel.

We note also, near the Cemetery, three posts, mortised at the top, into which it is designed to insert rails making a rack 50 feet long to which horsemen coming to a funeral can hitch their horses.

WESTWARD HO!—The celebration of the Purcellville Extension of the W. & O. R. R. will take place on Tuesday, March 31st.—

ECCENTRICITIES.—Tom Brown, larceny of wood from Mr. Jno. McCabe; Thirty days in jail. Tom said he preferred the lash, but the barbarian could not be found to wield it

William Honesty, alias Cupid Robinson, house-breaking and stealing from Mr. Beuchler. Warrant issued, but Honesty came up a-missin'.

4/1/74 Mirror

A Touching Obituary.

The *Daily Argus*, of Leavenworth, is no more. The editor of the *Argus*, in writing the obituary of his paper, sums up the history of his enterprise in the following racy fashion :

About four months ago we took possession of this paper. It was then in the very act of pegging out, and we breathed in it four months more life than it otherwise would have had had we not taken possession of it. Having neither friends, money nor credit, we put into it all our surplus cash, and every dollar of our friends that we could get, but as everybody will see, it is no go. We presume our enemies will rejoice, especially Simon Abeles, D. R. Anthony, and W. McNeil Clough; but we have had the satisfaction of ventilating Simon and Daniel to our fullest extent. We did it because we believed them both to be villains of the deepest dye. Either the people of the city don't appreciate our efforts, or we don't know how to run a paper. We went into the business determined to run it or bust. We have busted. During our connection with the *Argus* we have made some friends and numerous enemies. The former will have our gratitude while life lasts : the latter are affectionally requested to go to hell. With these few remarks we take our leave of public life, and now propose to enter into a field of more usefulness, and if God is willing we will never go into the newspaper business again."

4/9/74 Mirror

THE RAILROAD opening to Purcellville Tuesday, notwithstanding the unfavorableness of the day appears to have been quite a success. As we indicated last week, there was a considerable gathering of people from a distance as well as the surrounding country. Three Bands, Philomont, Hamilton and Leesburg enlivened the occasion with music, and the committee of arrangements strengthened the inner man of those present with a capital dinner.

Eloquent and practical speeches were made by Messrs. Ed. Nichols, of Leesburg. Col. F. M. W. Holliday, of Winchester; J. Mort. Kilgour, of Hamilton, Lewis McKenzie, President of the road, and Henry Heaton, of this town—each of whom took a hopeful view of the future prospects.

PURCELLVILLE.—The running of the trains to this point on the W. & O. railroad has set the little village aglow with life and activity. The scene around the depot on Saturday reminded us of accounts we have read of towns and cities along western railroads springing up as it were, in a night.

A TEXAS FARM.

The main rancho, Santa Gertrudes, is situated on a high hill between the Santa Gertrudes and San Fernando creeks. A tower or lookout, erected on the top of a large brick warehouse, commands an extended view, the eye taking in at one glance a scope of country for twenty miles around. The sight is delightful, combining the pleasant with the picturesque. On this hill the Captain has erected a large and commodious dwelling, with the necessary outhouses. He has also a stable built for the use of his rancho, capable of accommodating from fifty to sixty head of animals at a time. The houses for his vaquerous are constructed with a view to comfort and durability, at a respectful distance from the main house. A neat and substantial picket fence encloses several acres of Bermuda grass around his dwelling; its appearance in spring resembling a well-cultivated park, interspersed here and there with beautiful shade trees. Several immense brick cisterns furnish an abundance of water for the residents of the rancho, while the stock is supplied from the tanks and the adjacent creeks.

The Santa Gertrudes tract of land contains 78,225 acres, and originally was an old Spanish grant, the title from the Spanish Government running back through a long series of years. Of this tract about 65,000 acres are under fence, embracing within its folds grazing lands unsurpassed in the known world for its abundance in producing and in point of quality. An almost impenetrable belt of mezquit timber borders on both sides of the Santa Gertrudes creek, within the pasture, extending for a distance of twelve or fifteen miles, and abounds in wild game—deer and turkeys predominating in numbers.

The entire fence is forty miles in length, a portion of which is constructed of first-class heart pine planks, sawed in accordance with orders to a specified size, say twenty-four feet in length by six inches wide and one and a quarter inches in thickness. The posts used are mezquit, the majority of which are from ten to fourteen inches in diameter, calculated to last a life time.

The stock of the rancho consists mainly of cattle, horses, and sheep although a great number of jacks and jennets, goats and hogs are included in the grand total. The cattle stock number about 50,000 head, out of which are branded annually 15,000 head of calves. Great efforts have been made by Capt. King to introduce a fine breed of cattle, in which we believe he has succeeded.

Next comes the horse stock, consisting of mares, colts, mules, jacks, and horses, numbering about 6,000 head, out of which, in favorable seasons, are branded from 1,400 to 1,500 head of colts. Like the cattle stock, large sums of money have been expended in the introduction of fine stallions and jacks, until the stock has attained to a degree of fineness unsurpassed in that portion of Texas.

The sheep stock number 30,000 head improved Merino, yielding an average of four pounds of wool to the head. In this, as in his other stock, the owner has spared no pains nor means. To improve the texture and staple of their fleeces and increase the size of their bodies has been his great aim, which frequent importations of fine bucks amply testify.

This last but not least of the stock of this rancho consists in an unknown number of hogs. Five years ago 1,000 head were purchased and turned loose upon the range, since which time but few have been slaughtered or molested in any manner. They will probably now number between 6,000 and 7,000 head.

(King Ranch was legendary then and it is equally so now. It is still composed of over 800,000 acres in Texas and Florida. The founder Richard King who was a teenaged runaway, made part of his fortune as a river boat captain before investing in his ranch.)

WASHINGTONIAN.

LEESBURG, LOUDOUN COUNTY, VA.

SATURDAY, APRIL 11, 1874.

Dissipated Officials.

In the appointment of officers to take charge of the Financial Department of the State Government, *freedom from dissipation of all kinds* should be made a *sine qua non.* It should be an essential condition in the appointment of any officer whatever, but more especially for those officers who have charge of the Finances of the State. Whisky and card playing are fatal to a faithful and correct management of the monetary affairs of any institution, but more especially of a State, and whenever the least suspicion, with reference to the indulgence of such vices attaches to the incumbent of these offices, he should be quickly and promptly expelled from office—and those who have the power to dismiss them and do not, under these circumstances, do it, ought to be impeached and expelled themselves.

Pensions to the Soldiers of 1812.—The law giving pensions to the soldiers of 1812, which we published two weeks ago, as it passed the House, has become a law. All interested, by referring to the paper of that date, can see the law, as it passed. All who participated in the war, without regard to the late war, are entitled to a pension. The grant of a land warrant is taken, as evidence, that the party to whom it was granted, was in the war. This law is liberal and just.

Mr. Henry Heaton had recently, fourteen sheep killed by dogs on his farm near Round Hill.

The CHORALS, a company of colored singers from Washington, D. C., gave two concerts in Leesburg, Monday and Tuesday nights. We have rarely heard better music. Their bass and tenor is not easily surpassed.

THE MIRROR.

WEDNESDAY............April 29

ROBBING AN ORCHARD. —We understand that a few nights ago some one visited the orchard of Mr. Geo. W. Heater, not far from Bethel, in this county, and pulled up and carried off, all the young trees, set out last fall. This is the most wholesale case of orchard robbing that we ever heard of.

RANAWAY.—On Sunday afternoon, while Mr. JOHN DE BUTTS was driving his fine carriage horses to an open buggy on the public road between his house and Wheatland, the animals became unmanageable, and ranaway—overturning the buggy and throwing Mr. DeB. violently to the ground. The buggy was made a complete wreck, and Mr. DeButts, we are sorry to learn, had an arm broken, and was otherwise severely injured.

SOMEBODY fired a gun in the streets of this town one day last week, the report of which frightened the four horse team of Mr. CHAS. HENDERSON. Despite the efforts of the driver, who was in his saddle, the horses ran about half a square, carrying away a lamp post, and almost demolishing a pump. This brought the team to a halt, no further damage being done than a slight injury to one of the horses, but illustrates the wisdom of the corporation ordinance which imposes a heavy fine for firing in the streets. The man who fired the gun, however, like the fellow that "struck Billy Patterson," hasn't been found.

LOOK OUT FOR YOUR COWS.—The freight train on the W. & O. Railroad, when a short distance below town, on Tuesday morning, ran over a fine cow belonging to Wm. Robey, and cut off her leg.

4/29/74 Mirror

WOMEN'S PRAYERS AND SUFFRAGE.

Mark Twain, writing to the London *Standard* of the prayer crusade, says : "Would you consider the conduct of these crusaders justifiable ? I do—thoroughly justifiable. They find themselves voiceless in the making of laws and the election of officers to execute them. Born with brains, born in the country, educated, having large interests at stake, they find their tongues tied and their hands fettered, while every ignorant whiskey-drinking, foreign-born savage in the land may hold office, help to make the laws, degrade the dignity of the former, and break the latter at his own sweet will. They see their fathers, husbands, and brothers sit inanely at home and allow the scum of the country to assemble at the 'primaries,' name the candidates for office from their own vile ranks, and, unrebuked, elect them. They live in the midst of a country where there is no end to the laws and no beginning to the execution of them. And when the laws intended to protect their sons from destruction by intemperance lie torpid and without sign of life, year after year, they recognize that here is a matter that interests them personally, a matter which comes straight home to them. And since they are allowed to lift no legal voice against the outrageous state of things they suffer under in this regard, I think it is no wonder that their patience has broken down at last, and they have tried to persuade themselves that they are justifiable in breaking the law of trespass when the laws that should make the trespass needless are allowed by the voters to lie dead and inoperative. The present crusade will, doubtless, do but little work against intemperance that will be really permanent, but it will do what is as much, or even more, to the purpose, I think. I think it will suggest to more than one man that if women could vote they would vote on the side of morality, even if they did vote and speak rather frantically and furiously ; and it will also suggest that when the women once made up their minds that it was not good to have the all powerful 'primaries' in the hands of loafers, thieves, and pernicious little politicians, they would not sit indolently at home as their husbands and brothers do now, but would hoist their praying banners, take the field in force, pray the assembled political scum back to the holes and slums where they belong, and set up some candidates fit for decent human beings to vote for. I dearly want the women to be raised to the political altitude of the negro, the imported savage, and the pardoned thief, and allowed to vote. It is our last chance, I think. The women will be voting before long, and then if a B. F. Butler can still continue to lord it in Congress, if the highest offices in the land can still continue to be occupied by perjurers and robbers ; if another Congress, like the Forty Second, consisting of 15 honest men and 296 of the other kind, can once more be created, it will at last be time, I fear, to give over trying to save the country by human means, and appear to Providence. Both the great parties have failed. I wish we might have a woman's party now, and see how that would work. I feel persuaded that, in extending the suffrage to women, this country could lose absolutely nothing and might gain a great deal. For thirty centuries history has been reiterating that, in a moral fight, woman is simply dauntless ; and we all know, even with our eyes shut upon Congress and our voters, that from the day that Adam ate of the apple and told on Eve down to the present day man in a moral fight has pretty uniformly shown himself to be an arrant coward.

(Mark Twain – Serious this time.)

Sheriff's Sale.

TO satisfy executions in my hands against Jno. W. Fairfax, for the benefit of H. Dulany and others, I will sell at public auction, in front of the Court House, in Leesburg, on

MONDAY, APRIL 13, 1874,

(1st day of the County Court,)

12 Head of Horses,

AND

COLTS,

of very superior stock, one THOROUGH-BRED STALLION, and some fine Driving Horses, double or single; also some Carriages, Phaetons, &c., and Harness.

Sale to commence about 12 o'clock, M.
TERMS CASH.

WM. F. BARRETT,
april 8-ts   Sheriff

Sheriff's Sale.

TO satisfy an execution in my hands against R. W. Thomas, Jacob and Wm. Myers, for the benefit of Daniel Miller & Sons, I will sell at public auction, in front of the Court-house, in Leesburg, on

MONDAY, APRIL 13th, 1874,

(first day of the County Court,)

2 Good Work Horses,

Sale to commence about 1 o'clock, P. M.
TERMS CASH.   WM. F. BARRETT,
april 8-ts   Sheriff.

Sheriff's Sale

OF

STOCK,

Farming Implements

AND

Store Goods.

TO satisfy executions in my hands, against John M. Orr, and C. W. Paxson and H. S. Williams, dec'd, his sureties, I will sell, at public sale, at

GORESVILLE

Loudoun County, Va., on WEDNESDAY, the 15th of APRIL, 1874,

6 HEAD OF GOOD WORK HORSES,

some of them fine driving and riding Horses; 1 very superior STALLION of the "Exile" stock; 20 head of Ewe Sheep, Lambs by their side, of superior quality; 1 very fine Ram;

2 CARRIAGES AND HARNESS,

1 Cutting Box and other Stable Fixtures, and some Farming Utensils, some

HOUSEHOLD AND KITCHEN FURNITURE.

Also a lot of store goods, consisting of a general variety usually found in a country store.

(The financial panic of 1873 might have had something to do with these ads.)

A True Story.

4/22/74 Mirror.

Tact is one of the first qualities of a business man, and the following incident in the history of C. G. one of the most successful merchants, shows a development of this trait early in his business career.

Coming to New York from the country, without friends and with very little money, he found his way to "Lower Wall Street," and walking into the store of W. & Co., passed back into the counting room and waited modestly and patiently until he should divert the attention of Mr. W., who was at that moment busily engaged with some business friends.

At last the frank, open face of the boy attracted his notice and he addressed him with :

"What can I do for you sonny ?"

"I want a place."

"Well, what can you do ?"

The boy answered eagerly, "most anything, sir."

Mr. W., partly for a joke and partly to rid himself of the almost too confident boy said :

"Ah, ah ! Well, just go out and borrow me a couple thousand dollars."

The lad placed his hat on his head, walked out of the store, then walked slowly down Front street until he came to another large store in the same line of business, our friend of the past, Messrs. S. C. & C then with a bold but honest look, he went up to the head of the house and said :

"Mr. W., of W. & Co., sent me down to borrow $2,000."

"He did, my son ? how is business down at your place ?"

The boy having seen the appearance of large shipments, answered, "Very good sir"

"Two thousand dollars, did you say ; will that be enough ?"

"Well, $2,000 is all he told me, but if you have plenty I think he would like it if you send him $3,000."

"Just give this boy a check for $3,000 for W. & Co.," remarked Mr. S. to his cashier.

The boy took the check and returned to Mr. W., and said "here it is sir.

Mr. W., taking one look at the check and then at the boy, said:

"Young man, come in here ; you are just the one I have been looking for."

THE MIRROR.

WEDNESDAY.......................May 27

MEMORIAL DAY.—Nine years have elapsed since the last gun was fired in defence of Southern independence. All over this once beautiful South-land, the green grass grows, and the perfume of flowers sheds its fragrance around the last resting place of those who fell, martyrs to a "lost cause." The struggle is ended, and those who survive the conflict have long since "clasped hands over the bloody chasm," with those who in war were their foes, and each to-day recognizes but one country and one flag. But while this is true, the heart warms with a feeling of tender affection for those who fell "wearing of the gray," and gave their young lives a sacrifice upon the broken altar of their bruised and bleeding country. Theirs were brave spirits, and so long as "virtue has a votary, or the heart of men is susceptible to the emotions of love," so long should their memory be kept green in the breasts of the living—and with each revolving year, we should esteem it our highest privilege, to strew with the early flowers of June, the graves of the Confederate dead.

5/6/74 Mirror

General Conference M. E. Church, South.

The Conference of the M. E. Church, South, is still in session in Louisville. On Friday, the Committee to whom was referred the case of Lorenzo D. Huston, expelled for immorality made a report sustaining the action of the Baltimore Conference.

The Committee on the Organization of the Colored Methodist Episcopal Church of America made a report, which was adopted, declaring that the organization of a colored church into a distinct ecclesiastical convention meets with the hearty approval of this conference, and that efforts to establish an institution of learning for the education of colored ministers deserve to be commended to the friends of the colored people.

During the day Bishops Bowman and Simpson, of the M. E. Church, North, were admitted to the Conference.

The minority report on temperance, which provides as an amendment to the general rules, that any person making, buying, selling, or using as a beverage any intoxicating liquor shall, upon conviction, be debarred from membership in the Church, was adopted by a vote of 355 to 58.

The question caused a very animated and prolonged discussion.

This action will be sent to the General Conference, and if they confirm it will pass into law.

THE CHURCH WILL NOT UNITE WITH THE NORTHERN METHODISTS

On Friday, the Committee on Fraternal Relations with the Northern Church reported that it is deemed proper for the attainment of the object sought to guard against all misapprehension to declare that the organizations are not involved in fraternity: in our view of the subject the reasons for a separate existence of the two branches of Methodists are such as to make a corporate union undesirable and impracticable; they say that the causes which

LED TO A DIVISION

in 1844 have not disappeared. On the subject of slavery they say that the position of Southern Methodism is scriptural, and that their opinions have undergone no change.—It refers to the fact that many colored persons who had been converted through their instrumentality have gone over to the Northern Church, and says: "Following the indication of Providence we have, without abandoning this work, adapted our methods to the changed condition of the African race. Many of them had been drawn away from us by appliances that we are not prepared to co interact, but a remnant remained, and, at their request, we have set off our colored members into independent ecclesiastical bodies. We have turned over to them titles and possessions of church property formerly held by us. Our Northern brethren have pursued a different plan, and they seem committed to it by honest and conscientious convictions. They have

"MIXED CONFERENCES,

mixed congregations, and mixed schools. We do not ask them to adopt our plan; we could not adopt theirs."

(Reunification happened in 1939.)

5/27/74 Mirror

NELLIE GRANT'S WEDDING.

The newspapers of last week were filled with the details of a wedding that took place in the East Room of the Presidential mansion in Washington. The parties to the entertainment, was Miss Ellen Wrenshall Grant, the only daughter of the President, and Mr. Algernon Charles Frederick Sartoris, of England.

We gather from our Washington cotemporaries, the following items. It was the third ceremony of the kind that had ever taken place in the White House, and it seems to have been conducted with simplicity and a due regard to propriety. The number of invitations was limited to 250. The guests, including the several Cabinet Ministers, the Justices of the Supreme Court and the ladies of their respective families General and Mrs. Sherman, Surgeon General and Mrs. Barnes, Miss Lizzie Sherman, Speaker and Mrs Blaine, Sir Edward and Lady Thornton, Admiral Porter, Senators Conkling, Frelinghuysen, Thurman, Stewart, &c.

The hour for the wedding was fixed at 11 o'clock. The avenues leading to the White House were thronged with curious spectators, but the gates of the enclosure were strictly guarded, and none were allowed to enter who was not provided with a wedding garment.

IN THE EAST ROOM

was a dais or platform on the east side where the marriage ceremony was performed, this splendid apartment being tastefully decorated with plants and evergreens, and brilliantly illuminated from the lighted chandeliers, the windows having been darkened for the occasion. The dais was spanned with a floral arch, and from its center was suspended a large bell composed of snow-white blossoms, under which, at the appointed time, stood the bride and groom, with four bridesmaids on each side, the officiating clergyman, Rev. Dr. Tiffany, in front, and Mr. and Mrs. Grant in close proximity to the happy couple.

SKETCH OF THE COUPLE.

Miss Nellie Grant is very popular among her friends, and will be very much missed in society. She is quite young, not yet 19, and is noted for her quiet self-possession and modesty.

Mr. Algernon C. F. Sartoris is the only son of Mr. Edward Sartoris, of Hampshire, England. He is only 23 years of age. He and Miss Grant met for the first time on the Russia, when the latter returned from her European tour, 18 months ago. He is an engineer by profession.

The ceremony was performed by Dr. Tiffany, according to the forms of the Methodist church. There were eight bridesmaids, and no groomsmen. Col. Fred Grant acting "best man" for the groom.

Miss Nellie was attired in a white satin dress, made in Brussels at a cost of $5,000 and imported expressly for the occasion. The bridal presents were very beautiful, and were valued at $60,000 to $75,000.

THE WEDDING BREAKFAST

was spread in the State dining room, which is said never to have been surpassed in this country for richness, artistic skill and systematic arrangement.

At 1.15 P. M; the couple attended by the bride's youngest brother and Gen. Babcock, proceeded to the Baltimore and Potomac depot, where, at 1.40 P. M., a special palace-car bore them away to New York, whence they sailed on Saturday for England.

While they were being driven to the depot, the chimes of the Metropolitan Church rang forth several of their sweetest airs.

intention of practicing his profession and becoming an American citizen, but the death of his brother rendered it necessary for him to take charge of the estates, and make his home in England. By the sudden death of this, his elder brother, Mr. Sartoris became heir to one of the most beautiful estates of its size in England. It is located about fifteen miles, in a southwesterly direction, from Southampton, near Nettley Abbey, and directly opposite the Queen's summer residence, on the Isle of Wight.

On Saturday, Mr. and Mrs. Sartoris, accompanied by the President and Mrs Grant, Colonel Frederick D. Grant, Jesse Grant, U. S. Grant, Jr., Secretary Babcock, ex-Collector Murphy, Mr. Pullman, and others, in carriages, left the Fifth Avenue Hotel, and passed to North river, whence they were convered on board the revenue-cutter Grant, in which, followed by quite a crowd in ferry boats, floated far out into the bay, and soon after 11 o'clock the Baltic moved out of her dock, and amid the firing of cannon, the waving of handkerchiefs, and the huzzas of the crowd, the happy pair stepped aboard the Baltic, where the most gorgeous preparations had been made for their reception and comfort—and the next moment the youthful bride had bid farewell to her native land, and ere now is far out upon the ocean's briny wave.

(It was one of the most elaborate weddings of all times with over a million dollars worth of yesterday's money in gifts.)

THE MIRROR.

VOL. XVIII.   LEESBURG. VA., WEDNESDAY, JUNE 3, 1874.   NO. 50.

Nellie Grant's Husband not a Rich Man—Intended for a Drummer.

From the Chicago Post and Mail

The enterprising young Briton who has captured our President's daughter is not a man of wealth. On the contrary, he is barely well-to-do. In this matter I speak by the card, my information coming direct from Mrs. Grant. His father, Edward Sartoris, has a small estate in Southampton, and is somewhat interested in a Sheffield manufactory. Algernon originally came to this country with an idea of serving the Sheffield house as a travelling salesman. He had comparatively little education and no profession. It has been reported that he was a civil engineer, but this is untrue. If he ever studied engineering at all, it was only for a short time, and entirely too little to acquire a knowledge of the science.

The death of his elder brother made him heir to his father's estate, but as Sartoris, Sr., still lives, it can do him no good for the present. All the income he has is such as his father allows him; and may be cut off at any moment. He is also sadly deficient in morals, his chief pleasure being apparently the society of a party of jovial fellows over a glass of good wine. Unless he mends, it will be a sorry alliance for Miss Nellie.

The house in England, also, which has been the subject of so many glowing descriptions, is nothing but a neat little cottage on the elder Sartoris's grounds. It is by no means an elegant building, and can only be maintained as Sartoris, Sr. permits. Nevertheless, I am told by people who know the family, that Algernon Charles Frederick's mother is a splendid woman, and that she will make it very pleasant for Nellie.

(Unfortunately, this rather mean spirited assessment of the groom proved largely true. Sartoris was a self centered philandering husband to Nellie who was then America's sweetheart. In this country he was a very unpopular man.)

A COLLISION ON THE POTOMAC —*Narrow Escape from a Wawaset Horror.*—On Saturday the steamer Lady of the Lake left Washington with an excursion party of one hundred and thirty persons. They were taken to or near the Wawaset cemetery.— Toward evening the steamer started on its return to Washington, and upon reaching Fort Washington, at 7:40 P. M., met the United States steamer Gettysburg, which was going down the river. The necessary signals, two blasts of the whistle, were given by the Lady of the Lake to request the Gettysburg to turn to the left, but no notice was taken of it, although the Gettysburg responded, though kept on. The captain of the Lady of the Lake saw this, and repeated the signal, and still the Gettysburg kept on, knowing that there would be a collision, and to break the force of it as much as possible the Lady of the Lake reversed its motion and retreated. Then the Gettysburg officers woke up to the alarming situation and reversed its engine, but it was too late, and soon the prow of the Gettysburg was imbeded about nine feet into the guards of the Lady of the Lake, and but for her having an iron hull might have resulted very disastrously. While this was going on there was the greatest excitement on the Lady of the Lake. Miss Kate Irving was seated at the piano in the saloon cabin, at the time of the shock, remained calm, and continued playing, thus preventing an unusual scare in that portion of the steamer. Passengers male and female, ran here and there in the greatest terror in search of life preservers, but none could be found. It was afterwards ascertained that these necessary equipments were hid away behind some door or in some out-of-the-way box. In a short time it was apparent that the danger was passed, and the excitement cooled down. The injuries sustained by the Lady of the Lake were not of a very extensive character. The Gettysburg kept on without inquiring the nature of the injury, and the Lady of the Lake returned to Washington.—*Sun.*

6/18/74 Mirror

Col. Mosby – War Not Over.

[Correspondence of the Baltimore Sun]
VERNON MILLS, Fauquier county, Va.,
June 13, 1874

An altercation occurred at Salem, Fauquier county, between Col. M by and R. F. Rixey, ex-State Senator on Thursday, June 4, in which a cane and a carriage whip were freely used. The parties were separated by friends. Politics were being discussed at the time.   D

6/18/74 Mirror

How to Choose a Good Cow.—A crumply horn is a good indication : a full eye another. Her head should be small and short. Avoid the Roman nose, which indicates thin milk and little of it. See that she is dished in the face—sunk between the eyes. Notice that she is what stock men call a good handler—skin soft and loose, like the skin on a dog. Deep from the loin to the udder, and a very slim tail. A cow with these marks never fails to be a good milker.
Northwestern Farmer.

As a former dairyman, I will reject everything the above paragraph says. It was interesting though.

THE MIRROR.

BENJ. F. SHEETZ, Editor.

Wednesday Morning, June 24,

HYDROPHOBIA. -The melancholy death of Mr. Butler, the well known dog-fancier, who for some thirty years has sold dogs in this city, is a severe blow to the theory that hydrophobia is purely an imaginary disease. Mr. Butler held this theory, and insisted that men who die of hydrophobia were simply the victims of their own imaginations. A week ago he was bitten by a rabid dog, and in spite of his theory contracted the disease. When to the case of this cool-minded disbeliever in hydrophobia are added the two cases on record in which an infant and idiot are reported to have died of the disease, it is hardly possible for an unprejudiced person to deny its existence. Doubtless nine out of ten dogs that are called rabid are suffering from some other disease. Nevertheless, no person ought to be needlessly exposed to the danger of death in its most horrible form. The clearing of the streets of homeless curs is a duty that no clamor should induce the city authorities to neglect. If people will keep dogs in the city let them keep them in their houses. The law forbidding any dog to appear in the street without a muzzle should be extended to all seasons of the year. Poor Butler was one of those who held the law to be a needless and cruel provision against an imaginary disease. His fate ought to confirm the authorities in their purpose of ridding the city of the class of dogs who are most subject to rabies ; and perhaps the shortest and easiest method to attaining that end would be an order directing policemen to shoot any dog that may be found on the street without a muzzle.—*New York Graphic.*

Mr. Butler's Case Not a Case of Hydrophobia.

In Plympton Hall Friday evening Mr. G. Will Johnson said that Mr. Francis Butler's was a case of death from tetanus and not hydrophobia. The speaker was an intimate acquaintance of Mr. Butler, and knew that he was bitten by rabid dogs twenty years ago.

The Tilton-Beecher Affair.

For a year or two past ugly rumors have from time to time been put afloat relating to a matter of scandal between Rev. HENRY WARD BEECHER and THEODORE TILTON, in which the Rev. Henry was the offender. The matter had nearly passed from the public mind, when Tilton last week appeared in a long letter, charging Beecher with a grossest offense, but in no part of it says what it is, and the general reader is left to his own conjectures; but from the manner in which Mr. Tilton is alluded to, there is little reason to doubt that the gravamen of Tilton's action, lay in Beecher's conduct toward Mr. T. While no specific charges are made he places Beecher in a most unenviable position, from which nothing can relieve him in public estimation, but a clear and emphatic explanation of the whole matter—silence under Tilton's implied accusations, is equivalent to an open confession of guilt, either of which must destroy his usefulness as a minister. We think it clear that Beecher is conscious of his guilt, else he would never have penned the following :

"BROOKLYN, January 1, 1874.

"I ask Theodore Tilton's forgiveness, and humble myself before him as I do before my God. He would have been a better man in my circumstances than I have been. I can ask nothing except that he will remember all the other breasts that would ache. I will not plead for myself; I even wish that I were dead. * * *

H. W. BEECHER."

These recent disclosures of Tilton's are said to have been brought out by brother minister's of Mr. Beecher's denomination, envious of his great reputation, one of whom, Dr. Bacon, by lauding the "magnanimity" of Mr. Beecher at the expense of Mr. Tilton's behavior, contributed to sting him into these disclosures. The public will look upon the whole affair with feelings of regret if not of repugnance. The most serious aspect of it is the discredit which the misconduct of professors of religion tends to bring on it.

THE pleasantest feature of the Beecher-Tilton matter is the immovable confidence shown by Mrs. Beecher in her husband's innocence. She says bravely : "I don't believe a word of it : I know my husband."

THE MIRROR

BENJ. F. SHEETZ, Editor.

Thursday Morning, July 30

THE "BEECHER-TILTON SCANDAL."

We publish elsewhere in to-day's paper, a few extracts from the voluminous letters that for the past week have monopolised the space of our city exchanges, relative to the great scandal between Rev. Henry Ward Beecher and Theodore Tilton. These extracts by no means contain the full text of the disgusting epistles, and are merely intended to convey to the general reader a faint idea of the depths of of shame to which these so-called "christians" have descended. An exhibit, which for damning hypocrisy, criminality, and shame, on the one side, and brazen disregard of all the tender feelings of humanity on the other, and the triumphant gusto with which the vices of the wife and mother, are paraded before the world by the pen of the husband and father, and the apparently utter indifference with which he covers himself with the scorn and contempt of every right thinking mind, in making his disclosures stand without a parallel in the world of scandal.

For Theodore Tilton individually, we have no respect whatever. Better for him that he had ten years ago slain the accused destroyer of his domestic happiness, and then by his own hand put an end to his "free-loving" life, or with manly purpose, his puny heart swelling with a sense of the wrong done him, paid the penalty of violated law. But he did neither. And to-day, in the quiet seclusion of his own study— his soul steeled to all the noble impulses

of a generous nature, with the cold fiendishness of a savage, or the complacency of a dog returning to his vomit, he prepares a bill of indictment against the woman he had sworn to love cherish and defend" and her pastoral paramour, every line of which bristles with charges of crime, the moral blackness of which captivates the curiosity while it shocks the sensibilities of those who read it—until the very name of TILTON is a stench in the nostrils of men.

But, however base and unworthy Tilton may have proven himself, loathed and scorned as he may be for his perfidy—there is another side to the picture, and it is that to which we want to call attention.

For more than a week the newspapers of the land have been occupied with the details of the filthy quarrel of these two Reverend or semi-reverend persons, who have made their pulpit and sanctum mere buzzard roosts, befouling every one who approaches within reach of their emanations. The journals of New York and other cities of their vicinage have teemed with their obscenities, so that decent females are afraid to take up a newspaper, or even to ask the news of the day, while in the veins of the vast multitudes who have sought the narrative the corrupting poison has run like the virus of the Cobra.

How these publications have escaped the penalties of the law against obscene books it is hard to tell, for the evil effect of the worst "sensation" novels which are limited in number and are read in secret is nothing to the universal taint spread by the public narration of the crimes of these two individuals, the one claimed to be the "St. Paul" of the modern pulpit the other the editor of one of the "Journals of Civilization," both of whom claim to be in the highest station of intellectual life—

Why is it that these two men should be allowed to thrust upon the public *their* personal jealousies and their lasciviousness—as if it were of more public moment than the brothel experiences of any Five Point thief or drab?

Now a man occupying the place which Beecher has, in fact any clergyman, should be like Cæsar's wife, above suspicion—or if so shining a mark could not hope for immunity from slander, he ought at once to vindicate, not himself so much, but his office, by the most effectual mode. Beecher should have promptly cited Tilton to a court of law, in a suit for slander, and have forced him to the most rigid investigation. He should have said to his people, I cannot minister here save in spotless garments—and I will not occupy this pulpit until all imputation on my purity has been fully removed.

But if he plead that he was stayed from this course by consideration for Mrs. Tilton—that difficulty was not in the way of his raising a committee of "investigation" nor is it in his way now when the whole story has been spread broadcast. The Congregation of Plymouth Church—the "Church of the Puritans," should say to him, "Mr. Beecher we will not desert you, we will not condemn you, on mere ex-parte testimony, we will stand by you, with money and confidence, until (if such be possible) you are fairly proved to be guilty, and we will rejoice with exceeding great joy and with no surprise, at your perfect vindication—but, sir, you owe it to yourself, to us your people, to our church, to religion, to the vast multitudes who have admired you and who have sat under your teachings, to have this matter thoroughly sifted by a tribunal whose power and whose impartiality can force out the exact truth of the case. Now, sue Tilton without an hour's delay, or leave us. Instead of that he says humbly that he has suffered the torments of the damned for years—sleepless nights and agonized days—which made it the hardest of tasks to keep up a seeming cheerfulness, and to be fresh and vigorous "on Sunday."

So long as Beecher and the "Church of the Puritans" are content with an "investigating" committee of themselves, organized to acquit him, a court and jury of his own selection, who cannot compel adverse evidence if they wished, nor elicit that evidence under the threat of punishment for perjury—who cannot be entrusted with the custody of documentary evidence, nor be open to any public audience—he and they must be convicted by the jury of sinners of the world.

Separate the great cause from those who disgrace it. Realize that in a state of society where true religion is held in reverence and where its profession is "the highway to trust and confidence"—there always will be those who use its semblance for corrupt purposes. When Constantine made the Christian religion the state religion of the Roman Empire, and a profession of christianity became profitable, corruption came in as a flood—but true christianity did not expire. Then do not lose faith in the reality of goodness or holiness, because its exterior is assumed and its uniform put on by the scouts and spies of the Devil. And learn too, by this Beecher-Tilton scandal—that no matter how high the sinner or how hidden the sin, there is inexorable and *practical* truth in the Bible where it says: "Be sure your sin will find you out"

Preliminary Statement of Beecher – His Defense of Mrs. Tilton and Himself An Indignant Denial of the Charge of Mr. Tilton, &c.

I have no doubt that Mr. Tilton found that his wife's confidence and reliance upon my judgement greatly increased while his influence had diminished in consequence of a marked change in his religious and social views which were taking place during those years, Her mind was greatly exercised lest her children should be harmed by views which she deemed virtually false and dangerous.

I was suddenly and rudely aroused to the reality of the impending danger by the disclosure of domestic distress, of sickness perhaps unto death, of the likelihood of a separation and the scattering of a family, every member of which I had tenderly loved.

The effect upon me of the discovery of the state of Mr. Tilton's feelings and the condition of his family, surpassed in sorrow and excitement anything that I had ever experienced in my life. That my presence, influence and counsel had brought to a beloved family sorrow and alienation, gave, in my then state of mind, a poignancy to my suffering which I hope no other man may ever feel.

Even to be suspected of having offered, under the privileges of a peculiarly sacred relation, an indecorum to a wife and mother could not but deeply wound any one who is sensitive to the honor of womanhood.

There were peculiar reasons for alarm in this case on other grounds inasmuch as I was then subject to certain malignant rumors, and a flagrant outbreak in this family would bring upon them an added injury, derived from these shameless falsehoods.

Believing at the time that my presence and counsels had tended, however, unconsciously, to produce a social catastrophe represented as imminent, I gave expression to my feelings in an interview with a mutual friend, not in cold and cautious self-defending words, but eagerly taking blame upon myself, and pouring out my heart to my friend in the strongest language, overburdened with the exaggerations of impassioned sorrow.

Had I been the evil man Mr. Tilton now represents I should have been more prudent. It was my horror of the evil imputed that filled me with morbid intensity at the very shadow of it. Not only was my friend affected generously, but he assured me that such expressions, if conveyed to Mr. Tilton, would sooth wounded feeling, allay anger and heal the whole trouble.

He took down sentences and fragments of what I had been saying to use them as a mediator.

7/30/74 Mirror

TILTON'S STATEMENT:

Astounding Charges Against Henry Ward Beecher.

NEW YORK, July 21.—The letter of Theodore Tilton to the investigating committee has been published. He says that while Beecher possessed a perfect knowledge of both his offence and apology, he has chosen to put on a public affectation of ignorance and innocence concerning them, and has conspicuously appointed a committee of six of the ablest men of his church, together with two attorneys, to inquire into what he leaves the committee to regard as the unaccountable mystery of this offence and apology, as if he had neither committed the one nor offered the other, but as if both were the mere figments of another man's imagination, thus adroitly prompting the public to draw the deduction that Tilton was a person under some halluciniation or delusion, living in a dream and forging a fraud. "Furthermore, in order to cast over this explanation the delicate glamour which always lends a charm to the defence of woman's honor, Mrs. Elizabeth A. Tilton, lately my wife, has been prompted away from her home to reside among Mr. Beecher's friends and to co-operate with him in his ostensibly honest and laudable inquiry into facts concerning which she, as well as he, has for years past had perfect and equal knowledge with himself. The investigation, therefore, has been publicly pressed upon me by Beecher, seconded by Mrs. Tilton, both of whom, in so doing, have insisted in assuming before the public the non existence of the grave and solemn facts with which they have conspired to investigate for the purpose, not of eliciting, but of denying the truth.

The first assumption by them which has seemed to the committee to be in good faith has naturally led the committee into examination which the committee expect to find on their part nothing but innocence, and on Tilton's part nothing but slander. Tilton then says it is now his unhappy duty to give the facts and evidences to the committee for reversing their opinion. He charges Mrs. Tilton with joining Beecher in a conspiracy which cannot fail to be full of peril and wretchedness to many hearts. The last opportunity for reconciliation and settlement has passed.

Tilton says of Beecher : "This desperate man must hold himself only, and not me, accountable for the wretchedness which these disclosures will carry to his own home and hearth as they have already brought to mine ; and I will add that the original documents referred to in the Beecher sworn statements are for the most part in my possession, but that the apology and a few other papers are in the hands of Francis D. Moulton.

Tilton then swears to statements, among them the following : First, that on the 2d of October, 1855, at Plymouth church, Brooklyn, a marriage between Theodore Tilton and Elizabeth M. Richards was performed by Rev. Henry Ward Beecher, which marriage thirteen years afterwards was dishonored and violated by this clergyman through the criminal seduction of this wife and mother, as hereinafter set forth. Second, that for a period of about fifteen years, extending both before and after this marriage, an intimate friendship existed between Theodore Tilton and Rev. Henry Ward Beecher, which friendship was cemented to such a degree that in consequence thereof the subsequent dishonoring by Mr. Beecher of his friend's wife was a crime of uncommon wrongfulness and perfidy. Third, that about nine years ago the Rev. H. W. Beecher before and thereafter had a friendship with Mrs. Elizabeth R. Tilton, for whose native delicacy and extreme religious sensitiveness he often expressed to her husband a high admiration visiting her from time to time, for years, until 1870, when, for reasons herein stated, he ceased such visits, during which period, by many tokens and attention, he won the affection and love of Mrs. Tilton, whereby, after long moral resistance by her and after repeated assaults by him upon her mind with overmastering arguments accomplished the possession of her person ; maintaining with her thenceforward during the period hereinafter stated, the relation called criminal intercourse.

8/6/74 Mirror

AUGUST COURT This day of famous memory is again upon us. It will be ushered in on Monday next, but whether attended with the pomp and circumstance of days lang syne, ye local saith not. Time was when August Court was one of the institutions of Loudoun : Leesburg was scarcely visible for the people and from every section of the county friend met friend face to face, on the Court-green, and the whole town was one vast auction room, wherein was exposed for sale wares of every imaginable description, from the heaviest thresher to the inevitable small-beer, ginger-cake and water-melon,—and as the shades of evening gathered over the busy scene, the motley crowd dispersed, each one feeling that it was good to have been here. But time and circumstances have wrought sad changes in the manners and customs of the people since those halcyon days of the past—Not only have many of those who gave life and zest to these annual reunions been gathered to their fathers, but the very features of our system that rendered an August Court necessary have been so distorted by the innovating hand of legislation, that they are scarcely recognizable

But a truce to the past. Court square has been greatly enlarged and improved, and the county seat generally so thoroughly renovated in many places, that were a citizen of the past generation to revisit the scene he once knew so well, he would scarcely know them now. Let us, therefore, on Monday, have a genuine, old-fashioned outpouring of the people, and symbolize in appearance, at least, what we lack in substance of an August Court in Loudoun. Let us—

"Revive those times, and in our memories
Preserve, and still keep fresh, like flowers in
water"

It was just a few years ago when the historic section of Leesburg was sectioned off and the last of this unique and ancient ritual was celebrated.

8/13/74 Mirror

AUGUST COURT.— August Court has come and gone. Another of Loudoun's ancient holydays, a mile post on the course of Time, has been passed. On Monday last scores and hundreds of the people of this county, with the same joyous tread that inspired their fathers in ye ancient times, made their annual pilgrimage to the County-seat, bringing with them their children and their children's children, thus perpetuating in the minds of the rising generation a sacred love for a simple custom as ancient as the County itself, and beautiful because of its antiquity We know not in what it originated—we are ignorant of the causes that set apart August Court as pre-eminently entitled, above all the other Courts of the year, to such distinguished consideration—and perhaps the oldest citizen now living would be as much puzzled as we are, to answer the question. Still, it is pleasant to contemplate its recurrence. To consider that amid the ravages of Time— "Father did it." Long may it survive.

The crowd on Monday was not as large as we have seen, but was amply sufficient to attest that the people still retain a lively admiration for one of the landmarks of the past. At an early hour every available space around the public square, was occupied by men, women and children, with tables and stands from whence to deal their small wares, principally of something to eat, and soon the crowd began to swell in numbers until our streets were thronged with white faces, and black of both sexes, until there was before us a solid mass of living, breathing humanity. The usual amount of melons and other edibles and fluids were disposed of but we have never seen a more quiet gathering on similar occasions. There were few drunken men, no boisterous ones, and throughout the day there was not a solitary arrest for a breach of the peace and dignity of the Commonwealth.

The arrival during the day, of the Tankerville Band, seated in their wagon drawn by four handsome horses, and filling the air with sweet sounds, added greatly to the life and animation of the occasion.

8/13/74 Mirror

MIXED SCHOOLS IN WASHINGTON.—The new public school board of Washington city, organized Monday night. A resolution to revise the school rules and discipline, was referred to a committee of three colored and two white trustees. George W. Dyer, a white member, announced boldly that he was in favor of mixed schools, and no dissent was expressed from his views. The colored members favored the same thing, if the law will carry them out. An effort will be made by the late board to restrain the new board from proceeding further upon the ground that they have no right to break up the public school system.

8/20/74 Mirror

CAMP MEETING—AN EXTRA TRAIN OF CARS WITH A BIG CROWD AND BAD ACCOMMODATIONS.—A camp meeting of the M. E. Church, South, was commenced near Vienna station, on the W. & O. Railroad last Thursday. As everybody likes to go to camp meeting, and they all want to be there on Sunday, an extra train of cars was advertised to run that day for their accommodation.

THE CROWD.

At 8¼ o'clock, the train, consisting of engine, tender and *three* passenger cars, hove in sight, from Purcellville, all filled as full as three cars cars ought to have been, while an anxious crowd of at least 250 souls stood upon the platform of the depot waiting transportation. As soon as the cars stopped, a great rush was made to board them, and a scene of almost indescribable ludicrousness followed. Another camp meeting, under the auspices of the negroes, was in progress the same day, at Falls Church, consequently the crowd here was divided in color, about 'alf and 'alf. Mothers with babies, women with baskets, men and boys with cigars in their mouths and umbrellas and canes in their hands, pressed on until seats, aisles, platforms and every available spot was occupied. Two freight cars that happened to be standing on the switch were tackled on to the train, which relieved the jam slightly. The engine finally moved on carrying with it not less than 500 people — while not a few who desired to go, were afraid of the pressure, and returned home.

We think the railroad authorities stand greatly in their own own light, in not providing suitable accommodations on occasions of this sort. Nothing but their *religious zeal*, and a determination to patronize the road could have induced so many people to submit to the inconveniences of that Sunday morning ride —we know it was nothing else —and such devotion ought to be rewarded with comfortable seats. The return trip was made more pleasant by having an additional number of cars.

We learn from those who persevered to the end, that the encampment near Vienna, is quite large, there being between 70 and 80 tents. The crowd on Sunday is pronounced immense. Rev. Mr. GARDNER preached in the morning, and Rev. Dr. HEAD in the afternoon.

From the Alexandria Gazette of Friday

Threatened Duel Between Col. Jno. S. Mosby and Capt. A. D. Payne.

The Mosby Payne difficulty has been the all absorbing topic of conversation in this city since the first intimation of it reached here yesterday afternoon. The particulars of the affair, as reported, are substantially as follows: Col. Mosby, when in this city, on Wednesday last, was informed, by letter, that Capt. A. D. Payne had exhibited a paper signed by H. C. Bowen, of Rappahannock Township, Fauquier county, certifying that Col. Mosby had declared to him that votes for Barbour would be as satisfactory as votes for himself, and that he desired certain friends of his to be elected at the meeting of the Conservatives of that township, to be held at Bealton tomorrow, delegates to the Congressional Convention to meet in this city next Wednesday, but that Bowen stated that Payne, who wrote the paper, had colored it too highly. Upon the reception of this letter, Mosby started at once for Warrenton, and meeting Mr. James Barbour at Warrenton Junction, intrusted to him a note to Payne demanding a denial of the statement or a resort to arms. The note having been delivered, Mr. Barbour was referred by Payne to his relative, General W. H. Payne, who, with Judge Thomas Smith, and in the office of the latter, accepted the challenge for the principal, appointed a place of meeting, and selected rifles as the weapons. Their preliminaries having been settled, Mr. Barbour wended his way to the railroad depot, and while there was approached by Judge Keith and a constable and arrested as a party to the contemplated duel. Mr. Barbour, being anxious to take the train Judge Keith bailed him at once in the sum of $5,000, Dr. John Ward going on the bond. Immediately thereafter Gen. Payne and Judge Smith were also arrested and likewise placed under bonds. Capt. Payne having heard of these arrests left Warrenton in a buggy with Mr. L. S. Helm, who was substituted as the second in the place of the General.

Col. Mosby returned to this city yesterday on the freight train and went on the three o'clock train to Washington, and when the train from Warrenton came in he was joined by Mr. Barbour and young Mr. Brooke, of Warrenton. Fearing an arrest there, the party seeking to avoid recognition, loitered about the Capital grounds, and as night approached took seats on the steps of the east front of the Capitol, in the shade of the pillars, talking over the matter until after eleven o'clock, at which hour Mr. Barbour proposed some refreshments, and they repaired to Sanderson's restaurant, southeast of the capital, but hardly had they entered the door, when a Washington detective advanced, and placing his hand on the Colonel's shoulder said: You are Col. Mosby and my prisoner. The Colonel denied his identity and appealed to his two friends to substantiate his assertion, but the manner in which the denial was made was unsatisfactory, and so the whole were marched off to a Magistrate's office, where the Colonel was bailed in the sum of $5,000 for his appearance at half past ten o'clock this morning.

Capt. Payne and Mr. Helm left their horse and buggy at Greenwich, near Catlett's Station and concealed themselves to avoid arrest last night.

Capt. Payne was the commander of the famous Black Horse Cavalry and is now practicing law.

The arrest of Mosby, in Washington by order of Judge Keith prevented him keeping the appointment. Payne got on ground with difficulty. No thought is entertained of an indisposition on the part of either to fight. The affair has terminated more fortunately than was to have been expected. It ought not to have been commenced. It should not be continued.

THE FINIS

WARRENTON, VA., August 24.— The following is forwarded for publication:

The difficulty between Colonel J. S. Mosby and Captain A. D. Payne has been this day amicably and honorably adjusted.

EPPA HUNTON.
JAMES KEITH.

August 24, 1874.

NEW ADVERTISEMENTS.

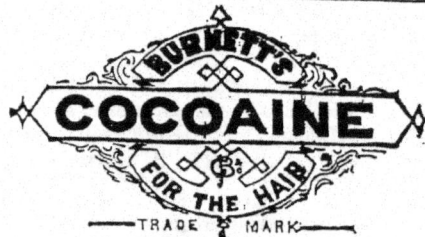

A RAINY DAY ON A CAMP GROUND

The rain of Saturday afternoon. having cooled the atmosphere and laid the dust, we like many others were inspired with a zeal to attend Camp Meeting. Accordingly, a pair of us set out at an early hour Sunday morning and after a drive of three hours, through a region of country blistered and parched by the severe drought, we reached the camp ground near Middleburg, at half-past 9 o'clock, where we found a large crowd already assembled and more coming.

Rev. J. C. Dice was just finishing from the regular stand, the 8 o'clock services. which were followed by an earnest and persuasive exhortation in the altar from that veteran of the church, JOHN A. CARTER, ESQ. —Bishop DOGGETT was to have preached from the stand at 11 o'clock, but the fast falling rain not only prevented any thing of that sort, but drove every body under shelter, who was fortunate enough to find one. The Bishop finally repaired to the "Tabernacle," a board tent large enough to accommodate a couple hundred persons —and beneath which double that number had already taken refuge, many, no doubt, to hear the sermon. and many more to avoid the rain, which fell in torrents. He proceeded, however, as well as the unfavorable surroundings allowed, to preach an able and interesting discourse, based on the 25th verse of the 5th Chapter of John.

We listened for a while, but despairing of hearing much of the discourse, we sought a boarding tent and something to eat. We found both in abundance and very good; but neither prepared for the contingency then going on. In taking your seat you were in danger of landing in a puddle of water,—at the table the "beautiful rain. sifted in your plate, and entered largely into the condiments of the meal, and if you sought rest in the sleeping apartments, it was sure to find you out, so that we finally accepted the situation, and acting probably on the old maxim that misery loves company. spent the afternoon enjoying the discomfort of others.

Good clothes were at a discount, and a yard and a half of black cotton stretched over a few steel ribs, was at a decided premium. Ladies who in the morn appeared arrayed as never was of a Solomon in his most glorious day presented a sorry sight. Their hair wet and dishevelled, hung down their backs in magnificent disorder. Crinoline that erst rivalled the snow in its purity, trailed ingloriously in the black mud of the lob-lolly aisle, while ever and anon a "maiden all-forlorn" flitted by with a "love of a bonnet" safely deposited beneath the folds of her shawl, while a dainty little handkerchief afforded the only protection for the head bared to the storm.

All these, of course, were outsiders, who had visited the ground for the day, many of them in open vehicles. Those domiciled for the season, fared better. We have never seen more perfect arrangements for comfort and protection on a camp ground in Loudoun. The tents numbered about sixty five, and many of them were built of boards, and were very substantial. It seems like a pity to pull them down The ground is admirably adapted to the purpose and a good idea would be to buy or lease it, and add to the cabins already standing, others that would bid defiance to every storm.

At four o'clock we left the Rev. Dr. Poisal holding forth in the "Tabernacle" to a miscellaneous group of men and women, interspersed with divers "crying babies," while we wended our way to the horse pound, to find that some scamp had villainously cut the bit from our bridle.— In the woods, eighteen miles from home. wet, muddy and generally uncomfortable, still pelted by a cold, drenching rain, and an important item for facilitating our movements in getting away, missing—formed a concatenation of perplexing events by no means calculated to inspire proper thoughts for a Sabbath evening's contemplation. However, a gentleman who seemed to sympathize with us in our misfortune, kindly loaned us a bridle. and we took our departure, and after a half mile drive found shelter beneath the hospitable roof of "Montpelier," where we remained. until Monday afternoon, when we set our face homeward

August 18, 1874 · Mirror

Virginia vs. Mob Law.

It is worthy of note that while in some of the southern States mob-law reigns supreme, and atrocities, outrages, and murders have so increased within the past few months that the President has felt it his duty to send troops to the South to protect the lives and property of the colored people, in Virginia there has been nothing of the sort. While the kuklux and white leaguers have run riot in many of the States lately in rebellion, the Old Dominion has maintained a dignity of action and self-respect worthy of the mother of States and statesmen. That her people sympathized with their southern brothers in the rebellion there is no denial on their part; that many of her citizens fought for the cause of secession they admit, but it is due them in justice to say that while there are isolated cases of ostracism on account of birth, &c., the generality of the people have shown by their actions that they accept the past as past, and are ready and willing to aid in building up a good government.

8/29/74 Washingtonian

☞ Mob-law is too commonly enforced for the good order of many localities in the country. It looks badly for a people who boast of their good government and high standard of morals and religion, to give way to the tempory flush of passion, and murderously take the lives of individuals—in some instances without a pretext for the outrage, as occurred recently, as we have it reported, in a Kentucky village, where the wrong man was executed and the intended and guilty victim made his escape. While the outrage upon individual rights of such a practice, is a most serious wrong, the most lamentable consequences which flow from it are engendering and disseminating among the people, a want of that high regard and reverence for the law, essential to all well ordered and peaceful communities.

When public sentiment becomes so demoralized as to regard infractions of the law as necessary for temporary grievances, the popular mind is rapidly maturing for the inauguration of anarchy and the introduction of that code which gives to the stronger the power to rule. A sound, healthy public sentiment which secure to the laws of the country their true influence and demands their strict enforcement, is the only firm basis upon which government and good order can rest. When the law loses the support which a healthy public sentiment gives it, we are loose from the anchor which holds us secure amidst the storms of passion and prejudice, which are the common infirmities of our nature, and confusion and disorder follow, resulting in the most disgraceful tragedies, such as are too frequently occurring in this country.

THE MIRROR.

THURSDAY...................Sept. 3

ALMOST FATAL.—Mr. Chas. E Lacey, of this county, a young man about 18 years of age, met with an accident on Friday last, that came very near proving fatal. It appears that Mr. L. was driving a two-horse wagon, loaded with plank, in the vicinity of Clark's Gap. The jolting over the rough road threw the plank forward against the horses, which set them to running and kicking. The driver was thrown from his seat, and the horses, after running some distance and completely demolishing the wagon, themselves became entangled and fell, and in this condition remained until some colored men at work close by were attracted to the spot by the noise of the struggling horses. They found young Lacy lying in the road, insensible, and as they supposed, dead. They carried him to his father's house, and Dr. Cross was summoned to his aid. He was badly cut and bruised about the head and it was not until after daylight Saturday morning that he became conscious. His injuries, though painful, were not serious, and he is now, we are glad to learn, entirely out of danger.

ONE NIGHT last week Mr. H. C. CHAMBLIN hitched his horse and buggy to the fence of a friend near Snickersville, while he went in the house. On his return horse and buggy were both missing. Immediate search was instituted, and kept up for three days, at the end of which time, the horse was found grazing in a field about two miles from where he started, detached from the buggy, but with the harness still on him. The buggy was found a short distance off, in the woods, and strange to say, the total damage done to horse, buggy and harness, did not exceed five dollars. The horse is a spirited one, and has the reputation of running almost at the drop of a hat, and yet a portion of the route taken, by him, in his lonely march, was through a dense woods, and over a rugged road.

THE WATERFORD CAMP MEETING of the M. E. Church, commenced last Friday week, closed on Monday morning, having been extended over two Sundays. The encampment was not a large one, but the meetings were generally well attended. On Thursday, the Rev. Mr. SCOTT, one of the preachers in attendance, was attacked and roughly handled by a young man named Tavener, whom Scott had previously insulted. The largest crowd seen on the ground during the meeting was there on Sunday. During the assembling of the congregation that morning to listen to a sermon from Rev. Mr. PHELPS, a brace of colored damsels thought to illustrate the practical workings of promised Civil Rights, by taking seats in the circle among white ladies. Some little commotion was excited for a moment, but the prompt appearance of special officer Johnson, who speedily removed the offenders, put an end to further excitement, and the regular services were proceeded with.

We heard of several collisions and break downs among the wilderness of carriages and horsemen, but "nobody was hurt," except one fellow on the suburbs, who late in the evening, instigated, probably, by strong drink, and forgetting that regard due the presence of ladies, and not having the fear of the brawny arm of a " big " father before his eyes, was subjected to the painful effects produced by a phrenological examination of the head with a fence rail.

8/29/74 Washingtonian

[From the New York Tribune.]

A Review of the Beecher Case

All the testimony in the Beecher-Tilton case likely to be made public pending the deliberations of the Committee has now been printed, and our readers are in a position to form a judgment on the evidence to be considered in the final report. Mr. Moulton may have further supplementary charges to add to the disgusting mass of scandal which has grown so steadily under his care during the past four years.

First let us look at the charge itself. Mr. Tilton asserts that in July 1870, his wife confessed to him that she had committed adultry repeatedly with Mr. Beecher that in the following December she repeated this confession in writing; that the confession was shown to Mr. Beecher, who acknowledged his sin to both Tilton and Moulton, and signed an apology, taken down by Moulton from his lips. To this Mrs. Tilton and Mr. Beecher both interpose an emphatic denial. The alleged written confession is not in existance, and since Mr. Moulton refuses to testify, its character rests on the unsupported word of Mr. Tilton. The so called apology is admitted to be genuine, but it does not expressly refer to adultry, and Mr. Beecher declares that it refers to something else.

While every letter and circumstance thus far cited as indicative of Mr. Beechers guilt can be readily reconciled with his innocence, there is a bit of testimony on the other side with which Mr. Tilton will find it impossible to explain away. We have shown that the charge with which Mr. Tiltons winds up his pursuit of Mr. Beecher in 1874 is not the same with which the pursuit began in 1870. It is not the same with which he forced his wife to put in writing in December of the latter year and which she withdrew in her letter to Mr. Beecher immediately afterwards. It is not the same which he mentioned to Mr. Bowen, to Dr. Storrs, to fifty other persons, so late as last year. It is not the same which he embodied in the "True Story" that he drew up in 1872. It is not the same even which he indicated in his recent letter to Dr.

Bacon. It was never brought forward until Tilton refused to sustain her husband any longer in the warfare which that letter brought to a crisis. Then, in order to ruin Mr. Beechers most valuable witness, Tilton abandoned the original indictment for improper solicitation and substituted the graver accusation of long continued adultry. But But the testimony which he had prepared to support the first accusation he forgot to change so as to fit the second.

Of the manner in which Mr. Tilton has conducted this prosecution and the sordid spirit which seems to have animated every stage of it we shall speak herafter. We have only to add to our present argument a few few words as to character. The man at whose door the shame sin is laid is a clergyman whose name has been honored wherever the English language is spoken. Over sixty years of honest life bear witness for him. The lady denounced as his paramour has been universally praised as a fond wife and mother and woman of such strong religious feeling and devout impulses that her husband can only account for her alleged fall on the supposition that she did not suppose adultery with a minister to be any sin. Mr. Tilton on the other hand, has pursued during the last few years the most discreditable courses. He has consorted with loose women. He has written a scandulous biogryphy of a notorious she devil, and afterward confessed that he knew it to be a pack of lies. He has lied about these very charges. He has taken money from the man whom he accuses of dishonoring his wife. His career has been afront to social decency, and a grief to his friends. His character for veracity in particular is said by those who have known him long to be extremely bad. All the presumptions are against him, and he has only himself to blame if the world refuses to take his word.

From the St. Louis Republican.]

It confirms all but universal judgment as to Beecher's guilt.

From the Louisville Courier-Journal.]

It presents extraordinary chains of circumstantial and documentary evidence in support of the original charge of Tilton

[From the New York World.]

Not one actual evidence or trustworthy evidence has been brought forth by Moulton which add new difficulty or inconsistency to the explanation already put forth by Beecher.

9/3/74 Mirror

THE GREAT SCANDAL.

Beecher Declared Innocent.

A Stormy Scene.

The committee charged with the investigation of the Tilton-Beecher scandal, have at last made their report—and done what they were probably chosen to do—acquitted him. The report makes several columns of the daily papers, and winds up with a full vindication. The report was read in Plymouth Church on Friday night. The scene is thus reported.

Plymouth Church was densely crowded to-night. After introductory religious exercises, the business meeting was opened with Mr. Jas. Freeland chairman. The members of the investigating committee were invited to come on the platform and were received with cheers. The report of the investigating committee was then submitted by the examining committee, with their approval and indorsement, without one dissenting voice. In their brief report the examining committee say :

We find nothing in the evidence to justify the least suspicion of our pastor's integrity and purity, and everything to justify and demand on the part of Plymouth Church and society a greater degree of confidence and affection toward its pastor if possible than it has ever yet felt toward him. It is not the office of this committee to review his errors of judgment in managing a complex trouble and struggling against the most infamous conspiracy known to the present age. It is for us simply to consider what moral culpability if any is developed upon his part, and of this we find no proof, although under a delusion artfully brought about by his enemies, our pastor was for a long time made to believe himself in fault.

The committee, in conclusion, recommend the adoption by the church of the following resolutions :

Resolved, That the evidence laid before the examining committee not only does not furnish any foundation for putting the pastor of this church, the Rev. Henry Ward Beecher, upon trial, but on the contrary, establishes to the perfect satisfaction of this church his entire innocence and absolute personal purity with respect to all charges now or hereafter made against him by Theodore Tilton.

Resolved That our confidence and love for our pastor, so far from being diminished, are heightened and deepened by unmerited sufferings which he has so long borne, and that

we welcome him with sympathy more tender and trust more unbounded than we ever felt before to his labors among us, to our church, our families, our homes and our hearts.

The report of the investigating committee was read by Professor Raymond. During the reading of the report frequent interruptions were caused by applause which followed certain passages sustaining Beecher, and outbursts of laughter were drawn out by any allusions to Moulton and his participation in the matter. The concluding portion of the report and the summing of the committee were received with waving of handkerchiefs, hats, &c., and the applause which greeted its ending was almost deafening.

At this point Moulton took his seat in the front portion of the church as if to take notes. Before the vote was taken, R. W. Raymond made a speech, in which he stated that Moulton had tried to poison the minds of the people against Mr. Beecher. Moulton called him a liar, and for a while a lively time was anticipated. Quiet was finally restored, and Raymond closed his speech by stating that come what might they would all stand by the man who had stood up so nobly for them.

The chairman then put the questions on receiving the report of the committee and adopting the resolutions. On motion, it was passed by a standing vote, with the waving of hats and handkerchiefs, when the ayes were called for, but when the nays were called Frank Moulton only rose, and was greeted with a perfect storm of hisses and another uproar succeeded, but was calmed in a slight degree.

A motion was made to adjourn, but Mr. Halliday anounced that the proceedings would terminate with the singing of the doxology.

At this juncture Mr. Moulton rose from his seat and pushed his way toward the door through the surging crowd which blocked the passage. During his route he was hustled on every side and when he reached the hall, hands were stretched out to wreak vengeance upon him, but they were kept off by the police officers who hurried him down an alleyway to where a carriage was in waiting, into which he was pushed rather than helped and with a police officer standing on each step of the vehicle was driven rapidly away.

9/17/74 Mirror

George C. Harding's Opinion of the Seducer of His Daughter.

It is hard to kill certain beasts. The hyena who has been tossing on a bed of pain for the past fortnight, with two bullets in his fool carcass, has lacked the decency to die and sink to the hell that is yawning to receive him. He will be out again in a short time, free to walk the streets, free to breathe the air that is breathed by decent people, and free to resume the practice of his hellish arts. He will not be molested. Vile and indecent as he is, the law throws its protecting arms around him, and no one dare load a shot-gun with buckshot and blow his vile entrails out at the first opportunity. It is lawful to kill a mad dog. It is not lawful to kill a hyena. But what shall be done to this disgrace to the form of man, to this parody on human nature!

As we have said before, it is not lawful to kill him, though his life is justly forfeited to God and man. But there is one way to reach his coward heart. Let him be made to feel that he is a leper, an outcast, a pariah, a creature too vile to associate with even the vilest of human kind—an obscene beast, whose bare presence pollutes the air. Let no man speak to him, or take him by the hand. Let every woman gather up her skirts for fear of contamination in passing him on the street. Teach little children to regard him as a being accursed. Let him, in the midst of multitudes, feel the horror of solitude, and the want of companionship. His own race and religion have driven him forth as a moral leper. Let no one give him shelter from the scorn.

9/17/74 Mirror

FARMWELL TOURNAMENT.—There was a Tournament at Farmwell Station, on the W. & O. Railroad last Thursday. A large crowd was present, numbering, it is said between five and six hundred persons, and everything passed off delightfully. E. M. LOWE, Esq., charged the Knights in handsome terms, after which the riding commenced, and resulted in the success of G. N. White, of Loudoun, Knight of Leesburg; J. T. Drane, Knight of Sunny South; C. F. Burgess, Knight of Grangers, and G. O. Ferguson, Knight of Aldie.

A dancing floor had been prepared in a grove a short distance off, and thither the crowd repaired, where the Knight of Leesburg, crowned Miss Alice Atkinson, of Alexandria, Queen of Love and Beauty; Knight of Sunny South, crowned Miss Laura J. Bauckman, of Loudoun, 1st Maid of Honor; Knight of Grangers, crowned Miss Nellie Bauckman, of Loudoun, 2nd Maid of Honor; Knight of Aldie, crowned Miss Bell Elgin, 3d Maid of Honor.—Mr. CHAS. J. BROWN of this county, doing the honors of the coronation.

Dancing and other social enjoyments followed, to the great pleasure of all in attendance.

THERE will be a Tournament on the lands of Mr Jno. F Waters, two miles from Harpers-Ferry, on the Hillsborough grade, on Friday, the 25th of September. One of Charley Brown's handsome saddles is the prize to be ridden for. After the riding is over, the usual amount of dancing and other social pleasures will be indulged—for which ample preparations will be made.

(The tournament has been called Loudoun's most popular sport in the 19th century but baseball was coming on strong.)

134

Supposed Murder!

Mysterious Disappearance of the Victim.

SUSPICIOUS CIRCUMSTANCES.

Arrest of the Suspected Parties.

THEIR EXAMINATION.

NO EVIDENCE OF GUILT

A Further Investigation on Saturday, &c.

For some weeks past this community has been considerably exorcised over the sudden disappearance of a German, who went by the name of WM. REILY. Rumor was busy with her thousand tongues, and each day seemed to add fresh material to thicken the web of mystery that veiled the transaction. Heretofore we have refrained from alluding to the subject, because the whole thing appeared as baseless as the fabric of a dream,—but now that the matter has found its way into the courts and is undergoing a judicial investigation, we have concluded to give the facts as we know them from our own observation, and through the testimony already adduced in the Justices Court.

THE PARTIES.

A little more than a year ago, ALBERT SHINER, a German Tobacconist, came to this town attended by a dwarfish looking little fellow called REILY. REILY had formerly resided in Leesburg, and it was reported that he was going to marry a daughter of a hard-working, thrifty German of this place, Godfrey Shelhorn. But of this we know nothing. In a few days after their appearance here, however, Shiner, who was decidedly the best looking man of the two, wooed and won the fair Catherine, and

THEY WERE MARRIED.

Shiner, assisted by Reily, at once went to making cigars at the residence of his father-in-law, Shelhorn, where he remained a couple of months, when he took a house on King street, belonging to Shelhorn, went to house-keeping and opened a Tobacco store, under the same roof. Reily remained with him, and having been in this country much longer, and consequently a better American linguist, became a sort of business manager — making frequent pilgrimages through this and the adjoining counties of Virginia and Maryland, always afoot, selling cigars, tobacco,&c. The house occupied by Shiner, although not a large one, was adapted to the purpose, and for economy-sake, perhaps, was made to accommodate not only his own family, and afford him a place of business, but also sheltered one or two families of colored people. As may be imagined, the establishment never became famous as a place of social resort; still, the proprietor plied his vocation, and-through his own efforts and the agency of Reily, disposed of a good deal of his ware, and was supposed to be making some money.

A GERMAN LASS APPEARS.

Matters continued thus until early in June, when Shiner and his wife visited New York, and brought home with them a cheap littleGerman girl,some fourteen years old, as a sort of family help. On the 13th of July, just about one month after her arrival, this child, LOUISA SPEGER, and WM. REILY, went to the Point of Rocks, and returned

MAN AND WIFE.

Shiner having accompanied them as master of ceremonies. It soon became apparent, even to the outside world, that there was not much

CONGENIALITY OF FEELING

between Reily and his frow ; but as that was a family affair with which outsiders had nothing to do, no notice was of course taken of it, except as it gave rise to a rude jest. On Friday night, the 24th of July, however, less than two weeks from the date of his marriage,

REILY DISAPPEARED.

For a day or two his disappearance was

not noticed, and finally, when inquiries were made as to what had become of him, Shiner stated that he had disappeared on the night mentioned, and that he knew nothing of his whereabouts. Suspicions of

FOUL PLAY

came to be hinted at, and grew so thick that Maj. LEE, Commonwealth Attorney a couple of weeks ago, attempted to get them in such shape as would justify an investigation. Failing in this the matter was dropped, and shortly thereafter, Shiner and his wife

BROKE UP HOUSEKEEPING

and left, and Shelhorn, the father-in-law, had a public sale of their effects. This took place about two weeks ago. Of course the old story of foul play was revived, and trifles light as air became proof as strong as holy writ, that Reily had been murdered, and that Shiner was guilty of the deep damnation of his taking off.

LEGAL PROCEEDINGS INSTITUTED.

Public suspicion so increased, that on Saturday last Justice W. D. HEMPSTONE visited the house of Godfrey Shelhorn, a short distance from town, where he found the wife of Antoine Shelhorn, Godfrey's son, and her sister. He found that the suspicions of these two women partook of that of the community generally. They also informed him that after the sale of Shiner's goods, a lot of articles had been brought there, and among them some clothing belonging to Reily and his wife. The better portion of these goods, however, including a new suit of clothes, a pistol, etc., they knew to have belonged to Riely, had been subsequently boxed up at Shiner's suggestion, and forwarded to New York. Among the articles left behind was

A BLOODY SHIRT,

the property of Reily, and some of his old clothing. Upon consultation, Justice Hempstone deemed the circumstances sufficiently strong to warrant the arrest of the implicated parties.

THEIR ARREST IN WASHINGTON.

Accordingly the 6 o'clock train on Monday morning, bore Sheriff BARRETT, clothed with the necessary authority, to the national capitol, where he found Godfrey Shelhorn, and Shiner and his wife, at a house on 4½ street. With the assistance of some of the Washington detectives, he made their arrest and carried them to the station house, where, rather than go to prison and await a requisition from the Governor of Virginia, the trio agreed to return that evening to Leesburg, in company with the sheriff.

THEIR ARRIVAL.

The train reached here about 6½ o'clock and the party was at once driven to the Justice's office. An immense crowd soon gathered around the building, and many and varied were the conjectures as to the guilt or innocence of the accused. An hour or two was spent in listening to the statements, related separately, and under oath, of the three prisoners. Their statements seemed to be straightforward and truthful, accounting for many of the mysterious circumstances, especially the "bloody shirt," but in order to give time and opportunity for a more thorough investigation, the accused were quartered at the Reamer House for the night, under the surveillance of Sheriff Barrett.

AT 12 O'CLOCK TUESDAY,

the case was again called up in the Courthouse—Justice HEMPSTONE presiding, and Maj. C. H. LEE representing the Commonwealth, and POWELL HARRISON, Esq., the prisoner.

THE TESTIMONY.

Lawson Taylor, Amanda Moore, Milley Taylor, John Brooks and Henney Lane, five of the colored occupants of one-half of Shiner's house, were sworn.

Lawson Taylor—Had heard Shiner and Reily fussing one morning sometime after midnight—they seemed to be angry. Heard a heavy fall in Shiner's house. Couldn't tell exactly when it was.

Amanda Moore—Never saw anything suspicious about the house. Heard no noise—Smelt a bad smell—smelt like carrion—smelt awful. Had asked Reily's wife where Reily was and she said he had gone away.

Milly Taylor—Had smelt the bad smell—couldn't eat. Had also heard the noise in the house. Sounded like something falling down steps. Had not seen Reily since.

John Brooks—One morning between midnight and day heard a big noise in Shiner's house, like something rolling down stairs. Heard a groan, and some one cry, oh Lord. Mentioned the matter to his aunt Milly the next morning. Had seen Reily with right sharp money about him. Had never said anything to Shiner about the noise. Had also smelt the bad smell—appeared to come from Shiner's side of the house. Heard scouring early in the morning and saw Reily's wife empty a bucket of dirty-looking water.

Henny Lane—Heard the scrummage. A day or two after smelt the bad smell. Heard something that sounded like a wagon drive up to Shiner's door one night about midnight. Had noticed the bad smell and put lime about the place. She also heard the scrubbing.

Antoine Shellhorn—Hadn't seen Reily since harvest. Reily had told him that he was going to leave. Never saw R. with money—but heard him say that he had $700 in a bank in Baltimore. Heard Shiner say that he had struck R. over the head with a lamp. Shiner told him to send all the things to New York, which he did, including a new suit of clothes, and a pistol belonging to Reily. Found a shirt of Reily's disfigured with blood, among some rags in a box containing the clothes of Louisa Spegler, Reily's wife.

Alex. Lynch—Knew nothing, except that upon one occasion, in response to the enquiry as to where his little partner was, Shiner said that he had stolen some cigars and left. He some days afterwards told him that Reily was in business in Baltimore doing well.

Jas. F. Rinker—Knew nothing about the matter. Had witnessed some affectionate manifestations between Shiner and Reily's wife—she sitting on his lap, &c.

R. R. Attwell—Knew nothing of the case. Had seen Reily when he lived here before, a couple of years ago, in possession of several hundred dollars. Knew Shiner, who seemed to be very attentive to his business.

E. L. Bentley.—Knew Shiner. Had hired him a horse and buggy about three weeks ago. S. told him he was going to look for the little Dutchman. Said the little fellow had sold some cigars at Pt of Rocks, and he was afraid he had gone that way and collected the money, as he had none when he left, but that he had $1800 in bank in Baltimore.

Thos. McArtor—Knew nothing except from hearsay.

Shiner's Statement.

The statement of Shiner is, that Reily, whose real name is William Weeland, and his wife, did not get along well, and that during their short married life, they occupied, nearly all the time, seperate apartments, she up stairs and he down. That on Saturday, the 25th of July, Reily was going to start out on one of his usual tramps, and for that purpose got up very early. Hearing him moving about down stairs, Shiner went down, and found him ready to start. He asked him if he had cleaned the tobacco moulds as he had directed the night before. Reily said no—that he had forgotten it—Shiner then told him to look out for another boss, as he did not want him there any longer. Reily asked if he hadn't better go to Point of Rocks and Licksville and collect some money due them. Shiner said no—he didn't want him to do anything there, and went out to open the back window. His wife, who heard the conversation, looked out of the upstairs window, and saw Reily go out of the front door. She called to Shiner telling him that Reily had gone. Shiner ran to the front part of the house, saw Reily going down King street, and watched him till he turned the corner at Hough's store. That was the last he ever saw or heard of him.

$50 REWARD.

We are authorized by Mr. Shiner to say that he will give fifty dollars reward for the return of WM. REILY (or who perhaps, now goes by the name of WILLIAM WEELAND, or any information that will lead to his whereabouts.

At the conclusion of the testimony, owing to the absence of one or two witnesses Maj. Lee asked that Shiner be committed until Saturday, that the matter might be thoroughly sifted,—this, he thought, under the circumstances, was due alike to himself to the community, and to Shiner.—The motion was earnestly resisted by Mr HARRISON, who contended that there was nothing in all the testimony yet adduced to warrant such a course.

Justice Hempstone finally decided to bail Shiner in the sum of $1000 for his appearance on Saturday. The bond was accordingly executed with Godfrey Shelhorn as security, and the case adjourned over until that day.

9/24/74 Mirror.

A Copperhead Warrior Scotched

KINDNESS RECIPROCATED.

Manassas Chills his Military Ardor.

A short time ago an ex-U. S. soldier, now residing in a northern State, wrote a letter to Col. Mosby, inquiring the whereabouts of one Capt. White, who he said, had conferred upon him, in 1862, a favor which he could never forget, and that he had wished a hundred times that he might meet Capt. W. and take him to his home. This letter was forwarded to Capt. White, (Col. E. V. of this county,) who at once wrote to his unknown friend, and in reply received the following letter. We have obtained possession of this letter, and lay it before our readers, as an interesting reminiscence of "times that tried men's souls."

CITY OF —— , N. Y., Sept. 12, 1874.

COL. E. V. WHITE.—*My Dear Sir:*— Yours of 8th inst., is received. Many, and many, and many times, since Sept., 1862, I have thought of you and the great act of kindness to me. Copperhead as I had been called a thousand times, it is true, I felt constrained, early in 1861, to take the field at the head of a light battery, though past 45 years old (and now past 60). In 1862, consolidated into one of those nondescript heavy Regiments of 1250 men, we found ourselves one morning very early, at Manassas Junction, on our march to join that bag of gas, Gen. Pope. In the previous night somebody had gobbled up most of an 8 gun battery on that very spot, and the Captain, an old Albany Dutchman, who had taken good care to save his own bacon, said he had been attacked by a lot of those terrible guerrillas—(I suppose Gen. Mosby would know who were intended) One old Colonel, an old Hungarian, said "poys, we'll wip out des d—d guerrillas oursels alone, and get all te glory." So we were shelling out the corn-fields, woods, &c., in the vicinity, hoping to start up some of those terrible fellow known as Mosby's men. We saw a few soldiers off on a hill, and pitched in, hoping to capture them. The joke was, we, about 1200, undertook to capture Stonewall Jackson's corps—and the result—as *might have been expected.* We then and there commenced the 2d Bull Run battle. Over 100 of us were captured, and among them your humble servant. Some days after, and while the battle was in progress all over that terrible field, we prisoners were lying upon the little grass plot at Sudley Church. Hungry is no name for the then condition of my stomach—not a mouthful (I believe) had I eaten from the time of my capture. You appeared to me, saying that I looked badly, and was doubtless hungry—you tendered a small buttered biscuit, with two or three tiny pieces of ham inside, saying my chances for finding food were not as good as yours, and insisted I should accept it—at first I declined, but my stomach plead so strongly that I accepted the offer of so splendid a breakfast, dinner and supper,—you said it had been given you by a lady at Aldie the day before. You gave me a description of an affair you had had a day or two before at Aldie, with a Capt. Means and his Company—and after my return from Richmond I met a lad who was at Aldie and confirmed your statement, &c.

I have ever since felt a large measure of gratitude toward you—I was so terribly hungry—and that biscuit was my last meal for nine days.

Shall ever be glad to hear from or see you—so please write.

Very truly, yours,

——

P. S.—That Bull Run affair used me up and finished my service.

The letter writer was incorrect in his reference to Mosby's band. Mosby's 43rd Virginia Cavalry did not become active until 1863.

Lige White survived the war, despite being wounded several times. Afterwards, he was successful in a number of pursuits. At various times he was a sheriff, bank president, and ordained minister. He also operated a farm and grain supply business, as well as the ferry which bears his name and is still heavily used.

10/1/74 Mirror

THE MURDER WITHOUT A CORPSE SHINER DISCHARGED AND THE NINE DAY'S WONDER COME TO GRIEF.—The case of supposed murder in this town the particulars of which we published last week, has almost ceased to be remembered The further hearing of the case as will be recollected, was adjourned over until Saturday, at which time, the Commonwealth having failed to learn any new facts calculated to implicate Shiner in any criminal offense against the missing Reily, abandoned the prosecution without again calling it up before the Justice, and the accused was permitted to go on his way rejoicing.

The action of the authorities in this matter was fully justified by the suspicious circumstances with which the tongue of rumor filled the air, and in instituting the investigation the officers of the law discharged their duty to themselves and to the public, which at the same time resulted in the thorough vindication of the prisoner, so far as any charge of a criminal nature yet made, is concerned. We congratulate not only the parties immediately implicated, but our community generally upon their happy deliverence from so terrible an imputation

10/15/74 Mirror

The Blue and the Gray.

At the annual gathering last week, at Gallatin, Tenn., of the Second Tennessee Confederate regiment, presided over by General W. E. Bate, the following significant resolutions were unanimously endorsed

As such meetings are often misconstrued by certain parties, both North and South, and used to the damage of the South.

Resolved, 1. That our reunion has no political significence whatever, and is simply a meeting of comrades, who desire to review in peace the many scenes of the past.

2. Having surrendered to superior numbers in good faith, it is our intention to perform our part of the contract faithfully, our chief desire being peace, and that the majesty of the law may be maintained.

3. We send greetings to our former enemies, and an invitation for them to come and live among us, promising to all lawabiding citizens the right hand of fellowship.

(The Civil War reunions had begun.)

10/8/74 Mirror

☞ The Beecher-Tilton scandal is now about to be reproduced in the Courts of Brooklyn. On Saturday last the Rev. Henry Ward appeared before the grand jury of that city in regard to the indictment of Tilton. The indictment, which charges that Tilton "wickedly and maliciously, with intent to injure and scandalize the Rev. Henry Ward Beecher in his good name and character, did publish a false, scandalous and malicious scandal concerning him," was read to Beecher, and pronounced by him to be correct. Tilton, on the other hand, solemnly reaffirms the literal and absolute truth of his charges against Beecher, and demands immediate trial.

The next day, Sunday, Beecher's church was crammed to its utmost capacity, with as many more on the outside unable to gain admittance. A dispatch says

The church was opened at 9.30 A. M for members only and newspaper men, and at 10 o'clock a few outsiders were admitted. The church was decorated with flowers and evergreens from desk to door, in a style that was the very perfection of artistic taste.

Mr. Beecher ascended the platform at 10.30, looking as well as ever he did for ten years past. Two or three persons attempted to get up a demonstration by clapping hands, but others checked it. The opening prayer was a master-piece of pathos."

This is what the congregation of Plymouth Church calls "Religion." How appropriate the refrain, "from all such, good Lord, deliver us."

10/8/74 Mirror

A HARD CASE.—There is now, and has been for nearly a year past, confined in the jail of this county an insane white woman, whose condition is most pitiable, and appeals loudly to the humanity of our State authorities for redress. Repeated applications, we understand, have been made to both the Asylums in Virginia to take charge of her; but poor, friendless, and hopelessly insane, the response has ever been "no room." If such be the case, it is high time that the accommodations of these institutions be promptly enlarged, or, if needs be, another established. The mental condition of the unfortunate creature whose case we are now considering, is such as to require close and constant confinement. There she is afforded in her present quarters, but from the necessity of things she can receive nothing more,—and although our humane jailor does all in his power to render her as comfortable as circumstances will allow, yet his best efforts are fruitless, and her real condition, could it be published to the world, would shock the sensibilities of every virtuous mind.

We are glad to learn that the matter will at an early day be brought to the attention of the court by the committee charged with the examination of the jail, which we hope will lead to some steps for the immediate amelioration of the condition of this most unfortunate woman.

10/8/74 Mirror

WILD STEERS.

A Grand Cattle Hunt in the Streets of New York—Many Persons Knocked Down and Gored—Great Excitement in the Bowery.

NEW YORK, October 5.—While a small drove of Texas cattle were quietly plodding through Bleecker street, between Broadway and the Bowery, last evening about 7 o'clock Officer Wayne observed that they were without a driver. At the corner of Elizabeth street something startled the steers, and two of them ran down Elizabeth street. Immediately a crowd of men and boys started in pursuit of them, shooting and gesticulating violently. Others made similar demonstrations toward the rest of the herd, who had continued their way toward the Bowery, and they, too, became excited and wild. At the Bowery, where another noisy demonstration met them, they scattered in all directions, each pursuing his career with uplifted tail, plunging head and fiery eyes.

The crowds increased behind each one as his antics became more exciting. Policemen and private citizens, with an armory of weapons sprang at once to the front and began plying the luckless steers with lead and steel. Some persons even attacked them with bayonets and swords. But their tough hides appeared to be impervious to such onslaughts, and thoroughly maddened by so vigorous and unprovoked an attack they began tossing and goring all who opposed them, and for a time rendered the precincts which they invaded remarkably lively.— Two took their way up the Bowery, and into fourth avenue, being smartly chased by a demonstrative crowd; one turned on his pursuers about Fourteenth street, and after receiving four shots from Officer Broderick, rushed toward East river. Two others turned out at East Houston street, dashed through that narrow thoroughfare to East river, broke through the gate of the Williamsburg Ferry-house, plunged together off the pier, and were drowned.

Ten bulls altogether were shot. The series of scenes produced by the chase after these wild animals wherever they appeared were very stirring. The crowds of men and boys, with the exception of the policemen, and occasionally a daring citizen kept well out of reach of the threatening steers, but kept up a continual cheering, evidently enjoying the fun. The street-cars would be stopped by the crowd, and the drivers, conductors, and outside passengers usually crowded themselves rapidly inside.

In many instances the daring citizens, who volunteered to empty their revolvers into the bulls hides, emptied them instead into the crowd. Between twenty and thirty persons were injured a few severely.

11/12/74 Mirror

A Startling Scene in the Streets of Baltimore—Four Mad Cows at Large—A Man Disembowelled, Another Tossed in the Air, and others injured.

About 11 o'clock on Saturday morning four wild cows were being driven along Charles street, and when crossing Baltimore street they escaped from the rope which bound them and from their drivers, and ran at a furious pace down Baltimore street, taking the full width of the street, tossing their heads and lashing their tails, as if in enjoyment of their newly-acquired liberty. The streets at that hour were filled with pedestrians, who ran in affright into the adjacent stores for safety, while a large crowd of men and boys followed after the cattle. Two of the enraged animals turned down Light street toward the wharf, knocking down a lady and injuring her slightly. One continued down Baltimore street to Calvert, when it was caught and secured by Sergeant Parks, Officer Mitchell, and several citizens. The other ran out north Calvert street, creating an alarm along that street, until Monument street was reached, which the animal selected as its route to the east, and no one interrupted its career until at Aisquith street, when a colored man named Alexander Freeman interfered with the further progress of the infuriated animal.

It made a sudden plunge at him, tossing him in the air and across the street upon the sidewalk. When he was reached it was found he had been terribly gored in the leg and abdomen. He was assisted to the house of his wife, in Jew alley, but she not being in, he was taken in a wagon to his mother's residence, No. 6 Spring Garden avenue, where he was attended by a number of physicians, who were of the opinion that his injuries were of a most serious character, he having been literally disembowelled.

Several other persons were knocked down by the animals in their progress through the streets, but the cows that ran southward were secured before they had done any special damage.

141

"WILD BILL."

A Day's Ride with a Noted Western Character—The Scout as he Really is.

A correspondent returning from Colorado had an interview with the noted scout, Wild Bill. He notes: One of the pleasantest things in the Colorado tour is that you are liable to be thrown in contact with some distinguished person at any time without knowing it. Still I was really much surprised when the train boy whispered in my ear, as the gentleman walked leasurely away, that "He was the reg'lar old Injon fighter, Wild Bill."

I have hertofore clung to the stage conception of the Western desperado—a being some six and a half feet high, with long, flowing hair, scarred face, tobacco-stained mouth, and buckskin vestments adorned at all available points with some offensive or defensive weapon. So, when I was informed that the mild, gentlemanly young man, looking exactly like a clerk out on holiday, was the celebrated scout and Indian fighter, Wild Bill, I naturally supposed that the train boy was exercising his propensities for mischief upon me by endeavoring to perpetrate a "glorious sell," and it required the united assertion of several passengers and the conductor to convince me that this was really the veritable "Wild Bill."

Actuated by a pardonable curiosity I seated myself by his side and proceeded to interview him according to the best known models. In this I succeeded far beyond my expectations, as Wild Bill is usually very shy and reticent with strangers.

He informed me that he was then on his way to an Eastern city to meet a large party of English gentlemen, to whom Buffalo Bill, Texas Jack and himself were to act as guides, during a three months' hunt in the Yellowstone country and in the Rocky Mountains. They were to receive for their service the small sum of $8,000. These famous scouts are always well paid for their skilful guidance and are frequently the recipients of valuable presents from generous tourists. Wild Bill wore in his breast at the time I met him a magnificent diamond pin, presented to him by an English nobleman.

Wild Bill is a man of mark on the frontier, chiefly on account of his generally hitting the mark (no pun intended.) Wonderful stories are told of his proficiency with his favorite weapon, the pistol. It is said, though with what truth I know not, that he can hit a nickel at thirty yards, or a man at 100 without difficulty. I, myself, saw him shatter small objects, not larger than my hand, at the distance of twenty or thirty yards, while the train was moving slowly, which I consider pretty fair shooting. He uses a pair of heavy Smith & Wesson revolvers, which shoot nearly as accurate as rifles. The remarkable quickness and dexterity with which he wields them is the secret of the wholesome respect in which he is held on the frontier. No man can get the "drop" on him, although I suppose plenty have tried, as he is said to have killed only the trifling number of forty-two men already, and as he is only about twenty-seven, he has plenty of time to add to the bloody catalogue.

I could not help wondering, as I looked in the face of the quiet resolute man beside me whether remorse had ever laid her envenomed lash upon him, or if memory did not sometimes call back his victims from an untimely grave, to haunt him with their awful presence. And I was afterward informed, on creditable authority, that he lives in constant fear of assassination, and that he frequently suffers under some horrible nightmare, when, after uttering the most dreadful groans, he will gradually awaken in an agony of fear. We passed through a little town in Kansas, where it it said Wild Bill could not show his face without being shot or strung up. He was once United States Marshal there, and ruled the town with a strong and heavy hand.— It is said he killed four United States soldiers there in one drunken squabble.

He was far too modest to speak at length of his adventures, but gave me a graphic account of the first occasion on which the Indians felt the effect of the terrible repeating rifle. A little band of scouts were returning from some expedition, when they saw a large body of Indian charging down upon them at full speed. Now, one good shot armed with a repeating rifle is more than a match for half a dozen Indians equipped with bow and arrows, or even the old fashioned musket. So they quietly stopped and awaited the arrival of the deluded savages. As they came within long range the scouts discharged a volley. At this the Indians, thinking the whites had only rifles, came rushing on, confident of a speedy victory. Nor were they greatly discouraged by a second well aimed fire, for thinking that if the whites had double barrels, their guns were certainly completely emptied, they came on with redoubled ardor. But when on coming into close range they were greeted with a third and fourth discharge, they were evidently completely demoralized, and at the fifth, they fled as though the evil spirit himself was after them.

(He was, of course, Wild Bill Hickock. Many are aware of the "dead man's hand" of aces and eights he was holding at his demise. His friends said that it was the first time they remembered him not sitting with his back to the wall.)

RATES OF TOLL

ON LEESBURG & ALDIE TURNPIKE.

ON and after NOVEMBER 16th, 1874, the following tolls will be charged, and cash demanded in all cases.

For 20 Sheep or Hogs, and at that rate for more or less........... 5 cts.
For 20 Cattle, and at that rate for more or less................... 10 cts.
Each Horse, Mare, Mule or Gelding 3 cts.

RIDING CARRIAGES.

Two-Wheeled .... 10 cts.
Four-Wheeled, with one horse.... 15 cts.
Four-Wheeled, with two horses. 20 cts.

WAGONS OR CARTS.

Tire under four inches, each animal..................... 6 cts.
Tire from four to seven inches, each animal................. 3 cts.
Tire over seven inches.......... 1 ct.

THERE ARE NO FREE PASSES WHATEVER.

Persons living on Ball's Mill Road can obtain tickets at one third of these rates, all trans cut travel pay full tolls. Return is free if on same day.

By order of the
BOARD OF DIRECTORS.

Nov 5, 1874-3t

11/12/74 Mirror

— WHILE a case was being heard in court on Monday evening a quarrel sprung up on the outside of the Court House, between a party of sovereigns who had been imbibing two freely of the ardent, which soon led to a sort of "free fight." The "noise and confusion" attracted those on the inside the house, and the Sheriffs went out to quell the disturbance; in less time than it has taken us to write this paragraph, the jury box was emptied, the bar deserted, and the Court, under the impression, no doubt, that the roof was tumbling in, rushed to the window, "to see." One of the beligerents having been taken to jail, and quiet otherwise restored, the jurors resumed their seats, the most innocent looking set of men you ever saw, and the course of Justice flowed on.

The Court tried to find out the offenders, but as there were none to tell the tale the bolt was attributed to the natural desire of human nature to "see a fight," and a *nolle prosequs* was entered by consent of parties.

12/17/74 Mirror

HELP THE POOR. — The weather the past few days has been more indicative of winter than any we have yet had. The howling winds, the frozen ground, the crusts of ice, and the snow of Tuesday, all serve to remind us of the presence of the dread monarch. To those upon whom Providence has smiled bounteously, the cold fierce winds of winter have no terrors—but upon the ears of the poor and the unfortunate, they fall with mournful sadness. And in the language of another, "now is the time for true philanthrophy to display itself.

And we may add, a load of wood, a barrel of flour, a piece of bacon, a few vegetables or other articles of consumption from the plentiful stores of those who have and to spare, would also serve to cheer many poor families that may be in actual want of the necessaries of life.

Senator Conkling Has a Friendly Bout with the Sad eyed Mr. Howard.

"Cr" of the Pittsburg Leader relates the following :—Chandler's great hobby is his skill as a pugilist. Roscoe Conkling is also a great boxer. He has a private gymnasium in his residence at Washington, where after dinner he invites such of his friends as are gymnastically inclined for a friendly little bout with the gloves. Conkling is a very good amateur boxer, and as he is a very large, powerful man, he generally has it in his own way with the guests who are bold enough to put the gloves on with him. For some time it was an open dispute between Chandler and Conkling which was the better boxer of the two.—Chandler would, after every dinner party of which he was a member, calmly assert that he could lick any man of his weight in the United States.

One day last winter Chandler dined with Conkling and the latter inveigled the great war senator into the private gymnasium.—The gloves were donned and the doughty champions began to make graceful senatorial passes toward one another according to the most approved rules of the P. R. The bout, however, was of very short duration. Chandler suddenly received a blow between the eyes, which caused the huge senatorial form to go over backward ; his trusty legs failed him and then he sat down so hard that tears came out of his eyes. It took four men to get the war senator upon his legs, but he threw up the sponge at once without any further effort to punish Conkling. The only remarks he was heard to make was, "Damstrange!" and "I'll fix him yet."

Conkling and Chandler were much together in a social way and it was no long after the above occurrence when Chandler received another invitation to come up to his house and spread his legs under Conkling's social board.

Chandler sent back word that he regretted very much his inability to be present, but he had at his house a guest, a valued constituent from Michigan, and he could not leave him. Conkling sent back word, 'Bring your friend along.'

With this form of invitation, Chandler consented to come up. He brought his friend with him and introduced him as Mr. Howard, of Detroit, Michigan. Howard was a sad-eyed man of diffident manners, who contented himself with paying a very close attention to the themes of the bill of fare, rather than to join in the general conversation at the dinner table.

Conkling was in a great glee during the dinner. He told over and over again the story of Chandler's discomfiture as a boxer, and never seemed to the of asking him what he thought about his ability to lick any man in the United States.

Chandler took all these remarks in an absent minded way, as if suddenly he had become lifted above any such petty ambition of considering himself a fine athlete.

After dinner, Conkling led his guests into the gymnasium for a general smoke and chat. "Come," said he, pleasantly to Chandler "don't you want another bout with the gloves ?" and then Conkling laughed again in his most cheerful turkey gobbler style, as he put on a pair of gloves.

"No, I don't want to box," said Chandler ; "but perhaps my friend here would consent to amuse you." Turning to Mr Howard, Chandler remarked "You box, do you not ?"

Mr. Howard still looked sad-eyed and absent minded. He did once know something about it, but it was such a long time ago.

"Come, come," said Conkling, "let us have a friendly bout. I won't hurt you. Evidently the great New York senator was pining to knock some one down.

The sad-eyed Mr. Howard, evidently flattered at the prospect of being even knocked down by so distinguished a man, began to lowly put on a pair of gloves. As he was drawing on the glove Chandler was observed to walk down a little to the background. A contented look was upon his face, and every now and then he would raise his huge right foot up under his swaying voluminous coat-tail and give himself a congratulatory kick, expressive of rapture.

The sad-eyed man now came forward and the round began. Conkling was for proceeding at once to knock his opponent down and would have done so had he not found great difficulty in getting anywhere near the sad eyed man. The affair culminated by the sad eyed man' suddenly rushing forward and landing a thunderbolt of a fist between Conkling's eyes. the senator went over like a great tree. and rolled into the corner of the room. where he lay for a moment stunned by the concussion. He was heard to say afterward that he thought a house had fallen on him. Conkling had enough of boxing for once.

Chandler made several pleasent little remark about the skill of his friend Conkling, which were not received in the most cheerful way.

Judge of Conkling's feelings the next day when he learned that Chandler had played a joke upon him by giving Mr. Howard $100 to come up and bounce Conkling! The Mr Howard, of Detroit, Michigan, was none other than the notorious pugilist, Jem Mace.

12/24/74 Mirror

MILL BURNED—EIGHTY BARRELS OF FLOUR AND TWO THOUSAND BUSHELS OF WHEAT CONSUMED—HEAVY LOSS AND NO INSURANCE. We regret to hear that the valuable Mill Property of Mr. JAMES M. DOWNEY, near Taylortown in this county, was on Saturday night entirely consumed by fire. The property embraced a flour and grist mill, distillery and saw-mill, and from its thorough repair and favorable location was not only valuable to its owner, but a great convenience to a large and populous section of the county.

12/31/74 Mirror

A few weeks ago we took occasion to call public attention to the pitiable condition of an unfortunate lunatic, Jane Holliday, confined in the jail of this county, because the institutions of the State designed for the accommodation of such, contained "no room" for her. God the Creator, in his wisdom had seen fit to crush the casket that held the priceless jewel of his own bestowment, and poor, friendless and bereft of reason, this wretched creature, "one of Eve's family," without a felon's stain upon her soul, was compelled to drag out a miserable existence, in a felon's cell. Lost to all sense even of her own misery, winter and summer, day-time and night, she hugged the floor of her prison-house an object both of loathing and of pity, but sunk so low in her wretchedness as to be beyond the reach of individual aid.

But it is all over now. Jane is dead!—On Saturday night, while the echoes of the chiming bells that announced the anniversary of the birth of the "Prince of Peace" still floated upon the mid night air, that messenger came and spoke peace to her troubled soul, and her spirit, freed from its dark and cheerless tabernacle on earth, found an "Asylum" in that house not made with hands, where the weary are at rest.

1/2/75 Washingtonian   Communicated.

MR. EDITOR.—The universal cry of hard times is being proclaimed and heard by all, and no doubt, in many regards, there is more truth than fiction, in the assertion, and yet in our county a plenty of the good things of life abound, as no doubt the most of our citizens can testify. As the Christmas festivities drew nigh, the parishioners and friends, of the writer of this brief article, were preparing to enjoy their abundance at their homes, they were not unmindful of the wants of a *poor country Parson.*

For some weeks past, in the form of creature comforts, have been finding their way to the parsonage—such as sausage, spare-ribs, chine-bones, chickens, butter, apples, cakes, etc., etc.

The day before Christmas, a kind lady of this immediate neighborhood, sent in a nice fat turkey, sugar, tea, coffee, etc. I have also received a new hat, and a pair of nice slippers, the latter highly prized—as they will give ease to my *corn'd* toes.

All of the articles mentioned, with many others not named, have been thankfully received—and duly appreciated.

For the two years preceding this, I am indebted, to my friends of the Rock-Hill, appointment, for a turkey each year, and numerous good things besides.

It is said, "It is more blessed to give than receive." I trust all concerned will fully realize the truthfulness of that declaration.—And may the richest benefactions of heaven rest upon us all—through Him whose nativity we should all, in humbleness of mind, and gratitude of heart, celebrate.

Respectfully yours, &.,

         L. D. NIXON.

Farmwell, Va., Dec. 30th, 1874.

1/7/75 Mirror

☞ The Rev. Henry Ward Beecher's New Year's levee on Friday surpassed all its predecessors, the number of callers reaching twelve hundred. These included members of the bar, bench, officers of the army and navy divines, merchants and members of the medical profession.

And on Monday the courts opened suit against him, upon the charge of being guilty of one of the worst offences ever brought against a minister of the gospel. with a good chance of proving it. Well!

1/7/75 Mirror

AN EXPERIMENT.—Mr. George Hughes, a northern gentleman, proprietor of the magnificent estate of White Marsh, in Gloucester county, has determined to dispense with mule and negro labor on his place for the present year. He has introduced white laborers and a steam-plough, and means to try farming in that style by way of an experiment—*Fredericksburg Star.*

1/14/75 Mirror

HINTS ABOUT MILKING.—Always manage to have the cow eating when she is being milked, for when thus occupied she lets down her milk freer, and is less liable to kick and move about than when she can giver her whole attention to the milker. It is best to milk diagonal teats at the same time, but always take of the off teat first, for if the cow is going to kick at all, she will kick from the side you commence to milk. In milking diagonal teats the left hand milks a third teat, and thus the left hand serves as a fender in case she kicks or steps about. The best stool is made by nailing a foot-square piece of pine board on a piece of 4x4 one foot long. The knees are the most convenient bucket-holder.—Get close under the cow; work the bucket well under the udder, and the milk will not be near so apt to be spilled as when you put the bucket on the floor and sit as far off as possible. Milk quickly, steadily, gently, and never leave a cow until you have her last drop. Above all things, never yell at her or beat her. Kindness is a cow's most effective master.

EARACHE—Perhaps some mother may thank the household for my remedy for ear-ache. I take a piece of salt pork, say an inch or more long and half an inch square, cut down one end to fit the ear, and insert it, taking care not to slip in. I use it in my family, and always find it gives almost instant relief. Tie handkerchief to keep it in place, if the child will allow it. I also use pork for sore throat, croupe, and lung colds. Cut slices full half an inch thick, dip in warm water, sprinkle on a little pepper, and sew on flannel.—*Rural New Yorker.*

1/21/75 Mirror

CIRCUIT COURT.—The January term of the Circuit Court for Loudoun county, Judge KEITH presiding, was commenced in this town on Monday.

There was an unusually large attendance the first day, and after the usual preliminary forms were gone through, CHARLES DAVIS, (better known as Mississippi Charles) an athletic, bad-countenanced negro, who drifted to our shores during the war, was arraigned for a murderous assault made sometime in August last upon Mrs. APPLE, an aged white female, living in this county opposite the Pt. of Rocks. The assault was made on the public highway with a stout stick, and almost, if not entirely, without provocation. Davis was fully identified as the perpetrator of the outrage, and the jury spent but a few minutes, after hearing the testimony, in finding him guilty and fixing his term of imprisonment in the penitentiary at *ten years*. C. H. Lee for the Commonwealth and L. Chancellor for defence.

The next case called was that of the Commonwealth vs. JOHN GHEEN, *alias* HARRISON. Gheen is a young white man—not more, we should think, than 23 or 24 years of age—rather good-looking, but from his levity in the prisoner's box during the pendency of his trial, indicated a moral depravity sad to witness in one so young. Sometime in November, Mr. THOS. BURCH, lost from the Exeter estate, near Leesburg, eight head of cattle. A storm during the night had blown down the fencing that enclosed the field where the cattle were grazing. The next morning the cattle were missing, and nothing was heard from them for several days, when it was ascertained that the day after their disappearance Gheen appeared with them at a drover's stand some five miles this side of Georgetown, where he sold them to a Mr. Marstello for $140—(Mr. B. valued them at $300). After selling the cattle and getting his money, Gheen returned to this neighborhood and remained until his arrest a few days af-

ter charged with the theft. The cattle were fully identified as those lost by Burch, and Gheen as the man who sold and received the money for them. When the case was called Gheen was without counsel, and the Court assigned Maj. J. M. Orr, to conduct the defence. No witnesses were summoned for the defence, and Mr. Orr, in his argument before the jury contended that before the prisoner could be convicted, the fact must be established that the cattle had first been *stolen*, and of that there was no evidence. That the simple fact that the cattle were found in the possession of Gheen afforded no such proof as the law required, that he had driven them from the field. It was proven, however, that Gheen had told different stories both as to his absence and also as to the ownership of the property and the jury, after a few minutes consultation found him guilty and affixed his term of service in the penitentiary at *eight years*: which the Court said ought to be ten. Maj. Orr moved for a new trial, upon the ground that the conviction was not in accordance with the law in the case. The Court overruled the motion, and at 8 o'clock, P. M. the prisoner was remanded to jail to await sentence.

1/30/75 Mirror

ABRAHAM LINCOLN'S DUEL

In 1842 there was great public excitement caused by the refusal of the State officers, among whom was General James Shields, then State Auditor, now residing in Missouri, to receive the bills of the State Bank in payment of taxes; the said bills being worth in specie only about fifty cents on a dollar. The measure provoked universal denunciation, and Mr Lincoln, then a comparatively unknown lawyer, wrote a communication on the subject, which was published in the *Sangamon Journal*, the Whig organ Springfield, over the signature of "Rebecca," dated Lost Township, Sept. 2 1842. It was in the form of a dialogue between "Aunt Rebecca" and her Democratic neighbor, in which he handled the officers of the State savagely for their order refusing the State Bank money, and was particularly severe on Shields, calling him a liar and a fool, "dull as a cake of tallow." Shields was a bachelor, and very vain, and his appearance at a fair in the city was caricatured, his demeanor criticised, and he denounced as a "conceited dunce."

The article soon became the talk of the town, and the exciteable Irishman fairly foamed with rage. He proceeded at once to the editor of the *Journal*, Simeon Francis, demanded the name of the author of the offensive communication, and that of Mr. Lincoln was given him. Lincoln was at that time attending court at Tremont, Tazewell County, but thither Shields hastened, accompanied by his "friend," Gen. Whitesides, and immediately on his arrival sent a note to Lincoln stating that his name had been given to him as the author of an insulting article signed "Rebecca," and requiring "a full, positive and absolute retraction of all offensive allusion to him personally, and an ample apology for the insults conveyed."

It so happened that two friends of Mr. Lincoln, Dr. Merriman and Wm. Butler, learned of Shield's departure for Tremont and its object, and mounting their horses rode all night, and communicated with Mr. Lincoln before Gen. Shields did; so he was in a measure prepared for the hostile note. The same evening he replied refusing to offer any explanation, on the ground that Shields assumed the fact of the authorship of the article in question, and while not pointing out any particular part to which he objected, demanded a general retraction, accompanying the same with threats and menace, in case of refusal.— One or two other notes were exchanged. Then Shields sent a final rejoinder, designating Gen. Whitesides as the friend selected to arrange for the meeting, at which the satisfaction he demanded should be tendered. Mr. Lincoln promptly responded, and named Dr. Merriman as his friend.

Further proceedings were, however, adjourned to Springfield; but the fact that a hostile meeting with the parties was imminent soon became known, and in order to avoid arrest Mr. Lincoln suddenly retired to Jacksonville, leaving with Mr. Butler a paper expressing his willingness to say to Gen. Shields:

I did write the "Lost Township" letter, but had no participation in any form in any other article alluding to you. I had no intention of injuring your personal or private character or standing as a man or a gentleman, and did not then think, and I do not now think, that the article could produce or has produced that effect against you, and had I anticipated such an effect I should have forborne to write it.

If this was not satisfactory, he laid down the following preliminaries for the fight:

1. Weapons—Cavalry broadswords of the largest size, precisely equal in all respects, and such as are now used by the cavalry company at Jacksonville.

2. Position—A plank ten feet long and from nine to twelve inches broad, to be firmly sixed on edge on the ground as the line between us, which neither is to pass his foot over on forfeit of his life. Next, a line drawn on the ground on either side of said plank and parallel with it, each at the distance of the length of the sword and three feet additional from the plank, and the retreating of his own accord over such line by either party during the fight shall be deemed a surrender of the contest.

3. Time—On Thursday evening, at 5 o'clock if agreeable; but in no case to be deferred longer than Friday evening at 5 o'clock.

4.—Place—Within three miles of Alton, on the opposite side of the river, the particular spot to be agreed on by you. Any details coming within the forgoing rules you are at liberty to make at your discretion; but you in no case to swerve from these rules or pass beyond the limits.

ABRAHAM LINCOLN.

Shields' friends declined to discuss the terms of settlement until they should meet in Missouri. All parties now left for Alton. Lincoln's friends met him at Jacksonville, where the weapons were procured, and a surgeon—Dr. A. T. Bledsoe—joined the party. When Shields and his party arrived all crossed into Missouri, and the work of laying off the ground was commenced.

Fortunately, at his juncture, Col. J. J. Hardin and Dr. R. W. English, warm personal friends of both parties, arrived on the scene, having come all the way from Springfield for the sole purpose of bringing about an accommodation, and immediately presented the following proposition:

To Messrs. Whiteside and Merriman:

Let the whole difficulty be submitted to four or more gentlemen of your own choosing, who shall consider the affair and report thereupon for your consideration.

This was laid before the principals and accepted. Gen. Shields promptly named Gen. Whitesides, W. L. D. Ewing, and the surgeon who had accompanied him, T. M. Hope, to conduct the negotiations on his behalf. The demand for an apology and all other belligerent papers were withdrawn, when Mr. Lincoln tendered the explanation he had already promised, which proved satisfactory, the parties were reconciled, shook hands, and returned together to Springfield.—So ended Lincoln's first, last and only duel. But the affair did not end with Lincoln's withdrawal from it. The blood of all the parties who had been connected with it was up, and nearly half a dozen challenges grew out of it, nearly as many as have occurred in the whole history of the State, either before or since.

(Lincoln, who stood at least 6 feet, 4 inches had an obvious advantage according to the terms of the duel.)

"TERRIBLE SLAUGHTER OF SHEEP BY DOGS.—On the night of the 18th instant the sheep-fold of Mr. E. W. Crocket was visited by worthless dogs, and twenty-two fine sheep killed. A few days before they were killed he refused ten dollars per head for them. We have always advocated a dog-tax for the protection of sheep, which is very profitable to the country when properly managed; but as there is no protective law it is almost useless to call attention to the subject. The people can straighten the thing by sending no man to the legislature who is opposed to a heavy dog tax. By doing this the farmer will be enable to raise sheep. Otherwise he cannot."

ANDREW JOHNSON IN THE U. S. SENATE.
—The action of the Tennessee Legislature
last week, in electing ANDREW JOHNSON a
United States Senator for six years from the
4th of March next, marks an era in the politics of the country. While there may be
some things in the past history of the irrepressible Andy that men do not admire, his
election at this time and under the circumstances, cannot be regarded otherwise than
opportune. No one will question his ability. No man ever ascended the ladder of
fame, steadily, round by round, as he has
done, until he reached the very zenith of
ambition in American citizenship, who was
not endowed with abilities of the highest
order. So, likewise, he is an aggressive
creature, of whom it cannot be said, he "has
no enemies to punish."

DEPUTY SHERIFFS. Noland, Summers
and Nixon, left on the six o'clock train
Monday morning, for Richmond, carrying
with them Golden, Gheen, and Chas. Davis:
alias "Mississippi Charles," convicted at
the last term of the Circuit Court, respectively, of murder, theft, and assault and
battery, and sentenced to the penitentiary.
The aggregate of their terms of imprisonment, is thirty-six years.

SHEEP STEALING.—One night last week,
some daring rogue or rogues, entered the
sheep-fold of Mr. Thos. Burch, near Leesburg, and caught and slaughtered three
fine sheep. The heads and hides were left
upon the ground. As yet no clue to the
thieves.

GEN. LONGSTREET RETIRES — One prominent man has shaken the mud of Louisiana
politics off his feet in disgust, and gone in
search of fresh fields and pastures new. It
is General Longstreet, while a Confederate
commander, and since a Republican politician in the distracted State. He has bought
a farm near Gainesville, Georgia, and there
proposes to spend in peace and quiet the
remainder of his days.

TO LET.—THE JAIL OF LOUDOUN COUN-
TY.—Its gloomy cells are to-day without a
solitary tenant, the first time since 1868.
We don't know whether the present condition of affairs is attributable to the high
state of morals prevailing in the community, or the vigilance of our almoners of justice, who somehow rarely see a poor devil
looking through its unpretending iron
grating.

IN ERROR.—Last week we published a
five line paragraph, upon the authority of
a gentleman direct from the neighborhood,
to the effect that Mr. HATCHER, of this
county, had detected, in the persons of two
young men, THOMAS and SILCOTT, the mysterious stoners of his house. It appears
that our informant had been misinformed,
and that the statement was without foundation, and we embrace the first opportunity to correct the error. We regret exceedingly that we should have been the medium, (though of course wholly uninten-
tionally, on our part,) of doing the two worthy young gentlemen the injustice contained in the paragraph alluded to. We cheerfully give place to the following cards published in the Washingtonian:

FEBRUARY 18th, 1875.
MR. LYNCH.—There appeared a publication
in yesterday's Mirror, in regard to capturing
two young men in the act of throwing stones
in our house which is incorrect.
Mr. Thomas was not captured, nor in any
way suspicioned of having anything to do with
the stone throwing.
T. A. HATCHER.

3 /4/75 Mirror

— There is a clamorous cry coming up for some abatement of the dog nuisance, and we have heard of some instances where persons have undertaken the repression of the evil by an indiscriminate slaughter of the animals in their vicinity—this action is of course intemperate and ill-advised, and leads to reprisals and feuds which cannot be too strongly deprecated. There is no doubt but that our county is over-run with dogs; and ninety-nine of every hundred are worthless curs whose only birth-right seems to be that of irresponsible marauders on the best interests of the country. A heavy tax on them will force out of existence all except the better breeds, and the best specimens of their kind, and the canine race will be perpetuated in these lines, purely bred well trained, well cared for, and a nuisance to no man.

An Ordinance

FOR THE COLLECTION OF THE TAXES ON DOGS AND BITCHES.

BE it ordained by the Common Council of the Town of Leesburg, in Virginia,

1st. That all Dogs and Bitches owned, kept or found within the Corporate limits of said Town, (except such as may be found with their owners who may reside without the limits of said Town,) whether assessed or not, shall be subject to the Tax imposed from year to year, on dogs and bitches.

2d. It shall be the duty of the Town-Sergeant or Collector of Taxes, within ten days after the tax shall be fixed by the Council, in each year, to collect the Tax on the Dogs and Bitches specified in the first section, and upon the payment of such Tax, shall furnish to the owner or person in whose possession such Dog or Bitch may be, a Tag—hereinafter provided for—which Tag shall be attached to such Dog or Bitch by a collar around the neck as an evidence of the payment of such Tax, the collar to be furnished by the owner of, or person holding the Dog or Bitch. And it shall be the duty of of the said officer to keep a register of the name of the owner of such Dog or Bitch, together with the number.

3/6/75 Washingtonian

MR. EDITOR—The wholesale destruction of sheep this winter, and a consequent incursion on the canines, has been a very fertile subject for comment in our usual quiet community. Whenever a flock of sheep is mangled and crippled or destroyed, a good deal of your sympathy is, "well, if you keep sheep, you must expect to lose some by dogs," or, why don't you put them in your barn yard, "or build a rail pen around them." How is it when a dog dies? What a howl goes forth, and the lamentations are often long and loud over poor old Tray, and if the demise takes place within a talking radius of Hamilton: "Well, Ike Hoge killed him." Perhaps this knowledge is the natural sequence, from the complacency with which I usually listen to a *dog story*, or from my determination and persistent efforts, at various times, for an efficient dog law, from my advocacy of a preference of sheep to dogs, and from my unrelenting manner of dealing with offenders on my own premises. Ordinarily I take the charge as a joke; but recently it is infamously and persistently circulated, that I am responsible for the death of dogs at public sales, on other's premises and most anywhere they occur, which is without any foundation but prejudice, or malice, and false in each and every particular, since notwithstanding my decided opinion of the general worthlessness of curs, I never molest any but those sneaking, or prowling around my premises. The farmers of Loudoun county have made up their minds that sheep pay just as good a profit on the investment as dogs, and they intend to raise them and take care of them too. And if masters would kennel their dogs, as carefully as owners are compelled to fold their sheep, for protection, then both dogs and sheep might lie down in peace.

ISAAC C. HOGE.

Pleasant Valley, March 2, 1875.

151

"Them Grasshoppers."

THE TALE OF A CHAMPION SUFFERER.

He looked into the waiting-room at the Central Depot, saw an elderly lady come there waiting to go West, and then after making sure that the special policeman was not around, he entered the room. He was a man who had seen other days, that was plain. His plug hat was years old, his coat shone with age and grease, and there was no collar on his neck. A policeman would have mentally recorded him as a "vag" without a moment's hesitation, and the fellow would have stood a chance of being trotted to the Central Station.

"My good friend," he commenced, as he approached the innocent old couple from Vermount; "for heaven sake, help me a little.'

"Who are you?" asked the husband, struck with the bummer's lonesome voice and general hard look.

"Name's Jones—Kansas—grasshoppers." replied the man, turning away his head as if deeply affected.

Be you one of those poor unfortunates who were almost eat up by the grasshoppers?" exclaimed the woman, her sympathies all aroused.

"The same madam," sighed Jones: "had to leave the State—going to New Hampshire—got as far as here and money gave out ; Heaven only knows what will become of us."

"Are you marred ?" she asked.

"Yes'um—wife'n nine children; they'er out here on the commons in a wagon, all sick and shivering with the cold.

"I've herd about them grasshoppers: were they very thick ?" asked the man.

"Thick !" echoed Jones, "you couldn't tell the difference 'twix day and night and the roaring of their wings made us deaf."

"My grashus! wasn't that awful." sighed the woman.

"I had a hundred acres of corn, fifty of wheat, thirty of oats—nice meadow lots of fruit, but the grasshoppers made a beggar of me in five hours !" continued Jones.

"They eat the stuff right up, did they !"

"Eat ! Why the farm looked as if a fire had passed over it !

'And you had to leave ?"

"Yes, sold my land for eleven dollars got my family into a wagon and started east. Been 180 days coming this far, and buried two children on the way. Lord only knows what's to become of us ! I wish I was in this river out there ; then my heart wouldn't be bustin' with grief and trouble !"

"Poorman !"sighed the woman. Ebenezer, let's us give him two dollars."

"Two dollars is a pile of money," mused the man.

"But it's an auful sad case, Ebenezer —nuff to tech a heart of flint.

"The Lord loveth a cheerful giver,' added Jones, as he drew his sleeve across his nose.

"Well I s'pose it's a hard case, and we won't be any pooer for giving two dollars," said the husband, as he pulled out his wallet and handed out a $2 bill.

"Thanks my kind friend," replied Jones. "I hope you will never see the trouble I am having. This'll buy us medicine and provisions, and kinder help us along like; and I feel as if I could throw my arms around ye and hug ye for your kindness.

"That is all right," said the husband.

"I wish it was ten," said the woman, as she shook Jones outstretched hands.

He slid out, and ten minutes afterwards might have been seen in a saloon pouring bad gin out of a tall decanter, and remarking to the bar keeper,

"Say, old pard, was it in Virginia or Kansas that the grasshoppers was so thick ?"

3/11/75 Mirror

Baltimore Annual Conference
M. E. Church, South.

The Baltimore Annual Conference, M. E. Church, South, Bishop E. N. Marvin, of Missouri, presiding, commenced its annual session in Mt. Vernon Place Church, Washington, D. C., on Wednesday, March 3d. The Bishop addressed the Conference, saying this was his first appearance among them officially—and that their greeting had been most kind. He congratulated the members upon the success with which Divine Providence had blessed their efforts, and hoped that the services could be conducted to the religious edification and improvement of all, and especially, of those connected with the Church in which they were meeting. He made allusion to the unministerial practice of chewing tobacco, and hoped that the members would refrain whilst in session, as in furnishing the church no provision had been made, very properly, for the use of tobacco.

The consideration of the 20th question, the characters of the ministers, was proceeded with, and Washington district being called, the presiding elder, Rev. Nelson Head, gave a cheering account of the condition of the district, stating that the amounts received by the preachers was in advance of the amounts received last year. (The Bishop.) That is very cheering considering the financial depression of the country.) Class-meetings and love-feasts were better attended than formerly.— There have been over 500 accessions during the year.

The Bishop, after questioning the presiding elder at length, and receiving satisfactory answers, said that it was necessary to enforce the rules and regulations of the discipline.— You may preach for years against dancing, but without effecting anything, unless the rules are carried out. He urged that the members enforce the rules with firmness, and at the same time with love.

The names of the other ministers of Washington district were called and their characters passed.

When the name of Rev. James Higgins was called the presiding elder, Rev. Mr. Gilbert, stated that he had not served Alleghany circuit, to which he was appointed.

The Bishop called for an explanation, and Mr. Higgins explained that he had served forty years in the ministry and went to this appointment, but found that he had no place to live and nothing to live on, and the traveling was very difficult, being obliged, in going to some appointments, to ford streams eighteen or nineteen times.

Rev. Mr. Gilbert and Rev. S. Rogers spoke in behalf of Mr. Higgins, and the conference sustained him in his action by unanimously passing his character.

When the name of Rev. S. R. Snapp, of Franklin, was called, the presiding elder related that Brother Snapp had had the misfortune to have his horse stolen, and it was sold, but brother Snapp had received from the party to whom the horse had been sold another horse, with the understanding that he was to keep it if his own horse was not returned.— [The Bishop.—It was not such a bad snap, after all.] He had, however, incurred an expense of about $100.

The characters of Revs. Norval Wilson, Thomas B. Sargent, Henry Hoffman, P. S. E. Sixeas, William H. Wheelright, J. N. Tongue, W. H. D. Harper, Jason P. Etchison, and Thomas Briley were passed, and they were continued on the superanuated list.

Rev. J. S. Martin asked for a superanuated relation for Rev. A. A. Eskridge. Mr. Eskridge, in a few feeling remarks, said that he had been in the active ministry for forty-five years. His first circuit, with 24 appointments, requiring 300 miles of travel, and he had in his first year received 400 into the church.— Although he could preach as long and as well as ever, yet he was not able to ride a circuit, and he felt that he should get out of the way and make room for younger men.

The Bishop said that there might be something in what brother Eskridge has said as to the old men, and he urged that the people should always cherish the old. There was no reason why good and effective men should be shoved out of the way for the young.

Several ministers spoke of the effectiveness of Mr. Eskridge as a minister.

The conference granted Mr. Eskridge a superanuated relation.

THERE are at present only two occupants of the jail; Robt. E. Buggy, charged with stealing $250 from G. V. Sagle, in the neighborhood of Harper's Ferry, and Henry Taylor, colored, charged with burglary and larceny. The Colonel's establishment, we believe, makes "no distinction on account of race, color, or previous condition of servitude," and there is none of that foolishness about troubling a man for his little bill if he happened to drop in over night without his baggage. Then the fastenings about the windows and doors seem to be so secure that no one could go pestering your things if you should happen to step out; besides the Colonel totes the keys around at night, so that, if you walk in your sleep you can't wander about and hurt yourself. We have never staid to dinner, but without meaning any disparagement of of the bill of fare there, we believe we had rather take our chances at one of George's setouts at the "Eagle."

Cock Fight in Frederick County

FREDERICK, MD., March 12.—Probably some of the most revolting and brutal scenes ever occurring in Frederick county were witnessed yesterday and to-day at the Point of Rocks, on the Baltimore and Ohio railroad, in a series of cock fights arranged by persons from this State and Washington city. The sporting fraternity from Baltimore, Philadelphia, Washington and elsewhere were represented to the number of several hundred, and among them were not a few old men. Fourteen battles, it is said, were fought, the Washingtonians gaining a majority of two. "Sweat cloths" and "French pools" were in operation, and large amounts of money changed hands. The The barrooms were crowded and drunken brawls numerous. The horrid spectacle of the many fowls with eyes torn out by sharp steel gaffs, legs and necks broken.&c., seemed only worthy the cruelties and barbarisms practiced in the darkest ages. Many of our people feel outraged, and will take measures to prevent a recurrence of such disgraceful scenes within the borders of this county.—Balt. Sun 12th inst.

THE RICHMOND DUEL.

On Thursday Mr. Jas. P. Cowardin and Col. Fulkerson were before the police court of Richmond on the charge of being about to engage in a duel. The following communications passed between the parties:

RICHMOND, March 16, 1875.

Colonel Abram Fulkerson:

DEAR SIR—You have seen fit recently to assail my father's person and character in a most unjust and untimely manner. His honor is dearer to me than my own life, and unless there is some retraction on your part, you must answer to me for your wanton attack upon one of the purest and best men in this Commonwealth. My friend, Mr. H. Tate Evans, will act for me and receive any reply you may have to make to this communication. I am, sir, yours, very respectfully,

JAMES P. COWARDIN.

RICHMOND, VA., March 17, 1875.

James P. Cowardin, Esq.:

DEAR SIR—Your note of the 16th instant was handed me at a late hour last night by your friend, Mr. Tate Evans. I will reply at an early date. Very respectfully,

A. FULKERSON.

EXCHANGE HOTEL and BALLARD HOUSE. }
Richmond, March 17, 1875. }

James P. Cowardin, Esq.:

DEAR SIR—Your note, dated 16th of March, was received through your friend, Mr. H. Tate Evans, after 10 o'clock last night. I do not consider that I have assailed unjustly or *untimely* either the character or person of your father, but have simply vindicated a wrong done to myself by him, for which he admitted his responsibility in the columns of his paper. If your father was in any wise incapacitated from redressing a grievance which he provoked, and will confess an unwillingness, by reason of such inability or incapacity to seek redress for such, then it would be time enough if *I* chose to dignify your intrusion by your note handed me by Mr. Evans, as stated above. This note will be handed you by my friend, General Bagwell. Very respectfully,

A. FULKERSON.

RICHMOND, March 17, 1875.

Colonel Abram Fulkerson:

DEAR SIR—Your note of this morning has been handed me by my friend Mr. Evans—it is entirely unsatisfactory. You should know enough of the ways among gentlemen to appreciate this fact. I am in the city on a visit to settle the matter, and it must be settled at once. You must make ample apology for the assault made upon my father, or hold yourself responsible to me. An immediate and definite reply would greatly oblige.

Yours, very respectfully,

JAMES P. COWARDIN.

At this point, Mr. James Cowardin, senior editor of the *Dispatch,* asked the justice to allow him to say a few words to which the justice readily assented.

Mr. Cowardin said he wished it to be understood that he was entirely ignorant of his son's connection with the affair until he heard of his arrest. Could he have seen him in time he would have prevented the occurrence of anything of the kind. He had requested his other sons not to take any steps in the matter; and they had obeyed him; and he knew if he could have seen his son James that he, too, would have heeded his request.

Justice White then said he would be constrained to bind over both parties in the sum of $1,000 to keep the peace. Mr. John Purcell became the surety of Mr. Cowardin, and Mr. S. Longley, General Bagwell and General J. H. Greever sureties for Colonel Fulkerson.

THE MIRROR.

THURSDAY...................... Apr. 1

MR. JOHN HOFFMAN lost about forty pieces of bacon from his meat-house on Saturday night. The miscreants after stealing the meat, pressed several of his horses into service and they were found straggling about town on Sunday morning. We suspect that our people will have to inaugurate those wholesome Western institutions, "vigilance committees," to protect themselves against these midnight marauders. There is scarcely a week that we do not hear of similar depredations.

DEATH OF AN OLD CITIZEN—We regret to learn of the death of Mr. JOHN GRUBB, SR., which occurred at his residence, near Lovettsville, in this county, on Monday last in the 85th year of his age.

Mr. Grubb enjoyed in the fullest degree the confidence and esteem of all who knew him as a man of sterling integrity and worth. He represented this county in the Legislature at one time, and was most useful in promoting the business affairs of his neighbors and fellow citizens.

ISAAC WATERS, colored, was committed to jail on Monday, for threatening to stone J. W. Richie on the highway near Waterford, was subsequently bailed to answer at Circuit Court. Isaac says "he didn't 'tend on doing nothing, and 'twas only a little Easter spree."

William Harris and John Gregg "sent up" by Mayor Head for disturbing the peace by boisterous language, on Monday.

Amos Hunter "pinted his "old army" at a snow-bird and she fetched one of Mr. Rhodes' hens."—5 days in jail.

On Thursday night "the fire-bell's clanging dissonance" startled the quiet of our town with its dread alarm. Fortunately it proved to be merely a burning chimney of the house lately occupied by Rev. Mr. Follansbee, which soon burned out without other damage to the property. Again on Saturday night an alarm was given, and the lurid glare which lit up the sky, this time, indicated something more serious. The bright reflection of the conflagration upon several buildings in the immediate vicinity of the fire inspired the apprehension at first that they were also afire, but upon arriving on the grounds we found the fire confined to the stable of the Binns' house and that of Mr. Powell Harrison, adjoining. The fire is supposed to have originated from accidental causes in the stable in use by Joseph Waters, who was so unfortunate as to lose a mare by the flames. Mr. Harrison was lucky enough to get out his horses, cow, buggy, and cutting-box; we learn since his cutting box was loaned out. (Moral:—Be neighborly.) Our fire department was on hand with commendable promptness, but some little delay was caused in adjusting a section of hose, rendered necessary by the distance of the burning buildings from a reservoir. We have not enough cisterns to meet an emergency of this kind, and if the water supply is inadequate the best efforts of the most efficient fire department would be neutralized. This reference is not designed as a captious fling at our authorities, but they will not fail to recognize the justice of protecting that class of our citizens whose premises are somewhat remote from facilities of this kind.

THE MIRROR.

THURSDAY.....................Apr. 8

THE LONG LOST ONE HEARD FROM AT LAST.—It will be remembered that last September, ALBERT SHINER, of this town, was arrested, and an examination held before a Justice of the Peace, on the charge of murder committed on one WILLIAM RIELY, who had been in S's employ and had suddenly disappeared without leaving any intimation as to where he had gone. For the time being, the affair was a sort of nine day's wonder—but as it was necessary to produce a corpse before they could establish a murder, Shiner was released, and that was the end of it, until Friday last, when Mr. S. received a letter from his supposed victim, WILLIAM RIELY, who writes from Lawrenceburg, Indiana, the letter being postmarked Vevay, in that State, in which the defunct Riely says he has plenty of work and plenty of money—two things by the way, that dead men are generally supposed to be entirely relieved from, and affords the best evidence that Riely wasn't murdered. Mr. Shiner says he will not rest satisfied until he has brought the missing Riely back to the sight of those who insisted on his death.

MORE STEALING.—Last week we chronicled the stealing from Mr. JNO. HOFFMAN near this town, of between 30 and 40 pieces of bacon, a few pieces of which have since been found, concealed in a straw rick. A night or two after Mr. H. lost his bacon, the smoke-house of Mr. LEMUEL WATSON, in this town, was entered, and several pieces of bacon taken therefrom ; and on Thursday night, a live shoat was stolen from the pen of Mr. T. W. EDWARDS, near town.—This is rather a hoggish business, and ought to be rooted out.

On Saturday last, a negro man whose name we did not learn, had a hearing before Justice KEENE, at Guilford, and was found guilty of chicken-stealing. The Justice sentenced him to 30 lashes, which were duly administered. After the whipping, the fellow made threats against the officer who executed the sentence, for which, in default of $100 bail, he was committed to jail.

☞ The Beecher-Tilton trial is still attracting large crowds to the halls of justice in Brooklyn. H. W. B. has been on the stand for several days, in the course of which he gave an emphatic denial to all the charges brought against him in which a consciousness of guilt might be inferred. Portions of his testimony were delivered with such dramatic effect, that the spectators applauded. Judge Neilson cautioned the crowd against a repetition of the offence. The saddest commentary on the chasteness of the proceedings, is found in the Judge's advice to the *ladies* present, when he told them they had better stay at home for a few days. And yet the very next day hundreds of them flocked to Plymouth Church to hear Beecher preach.

4/22/75 Mirror

At a meeting of Confederate soldiers the other day in Atlanta, so many were dubbed with titles that the following appropriate resolution was introduced : 'Resolved, That the president appoint a committee of one to inquire whether there are any surviving privates of the late war.'

4/8/75 Mirror

ABOUT ten days ago a dog laboring under an attack of *rabies* made his appearance in the vicinity of Ish's Tanyard, in the lower portion of the county. Several persons made narrow escape from his fangs; fortunately he devoted his attention mainly to the dogs which attacked him on his route. We understand as many as fifteen dogs were killed by their owners to prevent them contracting the terrible malady to which inoculation rendered them liable. The dog was finally killed by Mr. Ludwell Hutchison, after an exciting chase, several miles from the point at which he was first noticed.

4/15/75 Mirror

BITTEN BY A MAD DOG.—A son of Mr. Jacob Workman, living near Ball's Mill, in this county, was severely bitten on Saturday last, by a dog supposed to be mad. The young man went to a straw rick, where he was seized by the infuriated animal. The dog, we understand, was known to have been bitten by a mad-dog several days previous, and it is supposed that he also was laboring under the distemper. The young man was at once taken to Mrs. Tyler's, where the famous mad-stone was applied, but with what results we have not learned.— "The dog is dead."

(In researching these old newspapers, I have found occasional use of this stone over a great span of years. It was apparently used into the 20th century. If the stone stuck to the wound, the patient was allegedly cured.)

4/29/75 Mirror

MAD-DOG AND FIRE.—The cry of mad-dog and the alarm of fire are two things that never fail to attract attention, and whenever and wherever uttered are sure to produce a commotion in the best regulated families, or in the most staid and quiet communities, but when the two come together, the effect is simply appalling, as was evidenced in this town Saturday. About 9 o'clock on the evening stated, a cur of majestic stature, made his appearance on King street, and from his eccentricities and disposition to bite his canine fellows, led to the very natural belief that he was, to say the least of it, *mad*. After biting quite a number of other dogs that he found on his nocturnal promenade, he repaired to his owner's domicil, to which place he was pursued by an officer of the law, captured, and "shot upon the spot."

Several victims of his bite shared a similar fate, and for awhile mad dog was on the tongues of affrighted men, women and children—in the midst of which, the alarm of fire was given, caused by the burning of some rags stored in a back shed on the premises of Mr. JOHN SMALE. The hour was unseasonable for a mad-dog, and the wind unfavorable for a fire—but the latter was speedily extinguished, and the fear of the former subsided, and so far no serious damage has resulted from either.

We do not know whether the animal above referred to was really afflicted with *rabies* or not, but it would be well for owners of dogs knowing them to have been bitten by him to make some *safe* disposition of them, in order not only to allay public apprehension, but probably to prevent serious results. Our attention has been called to the following law upon the subject of rabid dogs, taken from page 867, Code of 1873, viz:

Mad dogs or dogs that worry Sheep, to be killed

5. Any justice, on proof that any dog is mad, or has been bitten by a mad dog, or has killed or worried any sheep, shall order such dog to be killed.

6. If the owner of any dog so ordered to be killed, shall conceal him, or cause him to be concealed, to prevent the order from being executed, he shall forfeit four dollars for every day such dog shall be so concealed.

THE MIRROR.

THURSDAY..................... May 6.

RELIGIOUS. The Rev. HENRY BRANCH will preach at Catoctin in the morning and in Hamilton at night on Sabbath, the 9th of May.

RUNAWAY ACCIDENT.—Mr. Geo. S. Ayre, of Loudoun county was thrown from his carriage near Leesburg, yesterday, and badly, though not seriously injured. The horse attached to the buggy in which he was riding became alarmed at the sight of a gipsey encampment on the side of the road and ran away, entering a piece of woods near by, smashing the buggy against the trees, and throwing Mr. Ayre out, and stunning him so badly that he lay there exposed to the rain for a long time, and until he recovered his consciousness, when his groans were heard by people passing along the road, who went to his assistance.

SUSAN B. ANTHONY is mad again. She has discovered an Illinois woman hitched up beside a cow in front of a plow, and she wants somebody shot.

There was quite an ovation at Plymouth Church, Brookyn, on Sunday. The New York Sun says that Beecher in all of his twenty seven years service as pastor of that church never before witnessed anything like the eager throng that tried to crowd within its walls. It was the first of May and communion day and the building was beautifully loaded with flowers. On Mr. Beecher's right stood the tall glass vase filled with calla lilies, ferns, ribbon grasses, and orchids. In front of the pews a table was spread with the sacrament upon it, and loaded with silver plates. Before this was another tall glass was filled with spotless white lilies. As the pastor stood up, the lower part of his body was in some degree hidden behind the wealth of flowers between him and his congregation; and these floral decorations, together with the great assembly, the noble music and the solem-

nity attaching to the communion table combined to make up a scene probably never before seen in Plymouth Church."

After the usual ceremonies one hundred and five new members were admitted to church fellowship – twenty six of the number, young men and women, knelt before Beecher and were baptized. Of such is the Church of Plymouth.

The following communication very fully explains itself:

To the Editor of the Richmond Enquirer
In your issue a few days ago I saw an advertisement with the caption "So So," inviting the reader to send 25 cents and receive instruction how to write without pen and ink. I did so. My 25 cents was donated and I received an answer to the following effect: "Write with a lead pencil you d—d fool."
(Signed) H. H. BUZZARD.

5/20/75 Mirror

THE PIONEERS.—We understand that the advance guard of the dreaded Grass-hopper, so destructive in late years to vegetation in various parts of the country, has reached our borders. Several persons have encountered them, and one gentleman, thoroughly familiar with the animal and its destructive habits as developed elsewhere, assures us that the specimens seen here are unquestionably the Grasshopper of the Northwest,—that there is no mistaking him, find him where you will. They are said to be two or three times larger than our ordinary grasshopper—they hop or fly from fifty to one hundred yards, without lighting and feed not alone upon the tender blade, but upon stout, tough vegetation, as well, such as is never attacked by the little fellow with whom we have heretofore been acquainted.

5/27/75 Mirror

The Grasshopper Scourge.

Great alarm is felt in the west at the ravages of the grasshoppers. They have already overrun the western tier of counties of Missouri and appear to be eating their way eastward.

A despatch to the Chicago *Tribune* states that everything in some counties has been destroyed, and the farmers have been obliged to drive their stock into Arkansas for pasturage.

It is feared they will pass through the entire State of Missouri and infect southern Illinois during the present season.

Ten thousand square miles of Missouri land has already been laid waste, and the farmers are utterly discouraged.

Every effort is being made to exterminate the plague, but all seems futile. It seems nothing short of a miracle can avert famine and bankruptcy.

All the wholesale houses of St. Louis are receiving letters by hundreds from western Missouri, creditors declaring their total inability to meet their paper on account of the plague. The formation of relief committees are already being agitated. So great is the alarm and so utterly helpless are the people to avert the danger, that the Governor has issued a proclamation designating the 3d day of June next as a day of humiliation and prayer throughout the State, to implore the interposition of Providence against this new calamity that threatens them.

EDWARDS
&
HUTCHISON,
DRUGGISTS & APOTHECARIES.

LEESBURG.

KEEP constantly on hand, a complete stock of Drugs and Medicines, Patent Medicines, Soaps, Perfumery, Combs, Brushes, (Tooth, Hair and Nail,) Knives and Scissors, Tobacco—Chewing and Smoking, Cigars, Pipes, &c.

PRESCRIPTIONS CAREFULLY COMPOUNDED.

Stimulating Liniment,
INVALUABLE FOR
Rheumatism, Neuralgia, Spinal Affections, Chilblains, Sprains, Stiff Joints, Bruises, Enlarged Glands Swellings of all Sorts, Sore Throat, Toothach, &c.,

IN MAN OR BEAST.

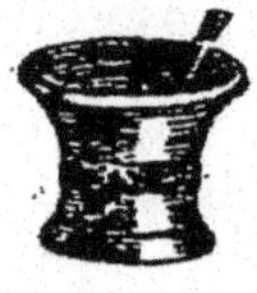

5/27/75 Mirror

MRS LINCOLN— HER REPORTED ATTEMPT to COMMIT SUICIDE. Chicago, May 20.

The *Times* has information that Mrs Lincoln attempted to commit suicide by poisoning. After being removed from the court room where she was adjudged insane yesterday, she was put under the strictest surveillance, it being feared she might do injury to herself. To-day she escaped from her room and hurried to the drug store of Frank Squires, under the Grand Pacific Hotel. She ordered a compound of camphor and laudanum, ostensibly for neuralgia.

The clerk informed her it would take about ten minutes to prepare it whereupon she took a carriage and drove to two other stores. She was followed by Squires who in each case prevented the druggist from giving her the compound. She finally returned to the first place and procured a mixture which she supposed was what she wanted but which was harmless. She drank this as she left the store, and as it had no effect, she tried to leave her room again to obtain a larger dose, but was prevented. She was removed to a private hospital at Batavia, Illinois this afternoon, where she will have every attention.

5/27/75 Mirror

OPINION OF VIRGINIA.—The following letter needs no comment. Its author is a Northern gentleman who settled in this county several years ago—in good faith casting his lot with those amongst whom he came—becoming in fact as well as name, a citizen of the Commonwealth, not to enrich himself by assuming the control and direction of the political destinies of his neighbors, but by his strong arm and well directed energies to aid them in building up the broken fortunes of the State.— How well he has succeeded his own letter tells. And so it is with every man who comes amongst us imbued with the same honesty of purpose :

BROAD RUN, LOUDOUN Co., VA. }
May 8, 1875. }

Hon. Lewis McKenzie :

DEAR SIR,—In answer to your inquiries as to the opinion I have formed of Virginia since I have resided in it, I would make the following statement :

I came here four years last Christmas from New Jersey, and bought 205 acres of land in Loudoun county, near Guilford Station, on the Washington and Ohio railroad, for which I paid $30 per acre. I have worked this land ever since, and am well satisfied with it, as well as with all my surroundings. I have since bought 197 acres adjoining for $18 per acre, and about 60 acres more near Herndon, on the railroad for the same price. These tracts are both woodland. I have worked my farm to corn, wheat and oats, and have done quite as well with it, as to profit, as I did upon my New Jersey land. I have also cut and sold the railroad company about $5,000 worth of wood.

With good land, good water, and a fine climate, and surrounded by good, kind neighbors, I think I would be unreasonable if I were not contented with my lot. My lines have been cast in pleasant places.— The Guilford neighborhood is not as well supplied with churches as we would wish, but hitherto the country has been thinly peopled, and as it fills up we shall be better off. We have plenty of good free schools.

I am about eight miles from Leesburg, the county town, and 30 miles from Washington city, Alexandria and Georgetown, and find in these places good markets, by rail, for everything I have to sell.

The winters are mild here, snows not frequent and never heavy, and cattle need not be housed and fed more than four months in the year. H. S. SMITH.

P. S. Lazy people and paupers had better stay away. The people about here are frugal and industrious, as a general thing and have little sympathy for those who are not.

May, 1875

MRS. ABRAHAM LINCOLN.

The Question of Her Insanity in Court She is to be Sent to an Asylum.

CHICAGO, May 19.—In the county court the trial of the question of the sanity of Mrs. Lincoln, widow of Abraham Lincoln, came up to-day. The proceedings were based on a petition led by Robert L. Lincoln setting forth that his mother Mary L. Lincoln, has property and effects exceeding $75,000; that she is *non compus mentis* and incapable of managing her estate.

Several witnesses testified eccentricities in the conduct of Mrs. Lincoln which commenced at the time of the assassination of President Lincoln, and which have become more marked as time progressed. She imagines she hears voices in the walls that strange beings accost her in the entries of her hotel; that she was the victim of poisoning plots. etc. Her closets are full of unopened packages of goods which she had ordered to be sent to her room. After short arguments the case was given to the jury who brought in a verdict in accordance with the facts elicited. Mrs Lincoln will be removed to the hospital at Batavia.

"Oh! Robert. to think that my son would ever have done this."

The widow of the late President Lincoln has given such evidences of insanity that a Chicago jury has felt itself justified in committing her to an insane asylum. The saddest misfortune that can befall a human being in this life is, insanity, and the sufferings of the victim so afflicted, appeal strongly to our sympathy and commisseration. There is an inexpressible sadness in the condition of one bereft of reason. that at once touches the finer feelings of human nature. even in the breast of a stranger. But there are occasional instances in which the weight of the affliction becomes more and more painful to the senses.

A few years ago Mrs. Lincoln was a happy wife and mother in a contented western home. whose affections entwined themselves around her household idols, and whose sweetest ambition was the promotion of the happiness of those of her family circle. But she was suddenly transferred from the calm and quietude of that home to gayer scenes, where she was flattered, not because of any high intellectual merit of her own, but simply because she was the wife of a President.

The transition proved too much for her. For five years she revelled in the giddy maize of fashionable society and soared amid the dreamy realms of power, until she fancied herself a star, whose brilliancy gave light, and life and joy to a universe; but just as she was about to rise higher in the firmament of fame, a change came. Suddenly, and without warning, a bolt as deadly as it hurled from the avenging hand of Deity, was aimed by an assassin, and Mrs. Lincoln was recalled from the dizzy heights to which she had been wafted, to weep over the lifeless remains of her murdered partner. Then, ere the tear stains of grief had dried upon her widowed cheek. she beheld the hollowness and vanity of what the world calls fame.

Since then, her career has been little observed by the world, but her conduct in the language of the verdict of the jury has been erratic and to such a degree "eccentric." that upon *the motion of her own son.* she was adjudged a lunatic, and sent to a mad house. The scene, when the verdict was rendered. is said to have been an affecting one, as the demented mother, taking the arm of her child. addressed him, not in the wild incoherent utterances of a maniac but in the tender, gentle words of a losing mother's heart "Oh ' Robert, to think that my son would ever have done this."

An Ordinance,

TO REGULATE THE LIGHTING OF
LAMPS, SUPPLY OF OIL, &c.

BE it Ordained by the Common Council of
the Town of Leesburg :

1. That the Street Lamps shall be lighted
by dark every night, and kept burning until
daylight, at which time they shall be extinguished, provided, however, that after the
full of the moon the light shall be put out at
the rising of the Moon, if clear, until the
moon shall rise after 12 o'clock, P. M.

II. It shall be the duty of the Mayor, from
year to year, to advertise for at least two successive weeks prior to the first regular meeting in July, for bids as follows :

1st. To supply the Town with as much Oil
as the town may require for its Lamps, at so
much per gallon for the next ensuing year.

2nd. To light the aforesaid Lamps and extinguish them, and keep them in order, including the supply of Wicks, Chimneys and
Lamps. should any be broken, according to
the provisions of this Ordinance.

3d. To light the aforesaid Lamps and extinguish them, and keep them in order, according to the provisions of this ordinance,
and to furnish all the Oil, Wicks. Chimneys
and Lamps (should any be broken) and every
thing required to keep said Lamps in good
order for the next ensuing year.

III. The Mayor shall at the first regular
meeting of the Council in July, after such
bids shall have been received. report the same
to the Council. and the Council may thereupon reject all of such bids, or accept such
bid or bids as they may deem most advantageous to the interests of the town; and enter
into a contract with such bidder or bidders.
according to the tenor and provisions of this
ordinance.

IV It shall be the duty of the Mayor to inspect said Lamps, at least once a month,
and report any delinquency he may discover
on the part of the party contracting to light,
extinguish and keep said Lamps in order as
aforesaid : and whenever it shall appear to
the Council that said party is not doing his
duty, or complying with the said contract the
Council may. upon two weeks notice, terminate said contract and pay such party pro
rata for so much of the year as he may have
discharged the requirements of his said contract.

This Ordinance shall be in force from its
passage.

Passed June 8th. 1875.

H. O. CLAGETT, Recorder.

6/10/75 Mirror

☞ The Washington *Capital* tells a good
story about a dog, a dog catcher and President Grant. Bowser, the dog, is the property of Marshal Sharpe, and the *Capital* says
knows more than an average Congressman,
and is therefore permitted to hang around
without a muzzle. A day or two ago a dog
catcher passing Sharpe's yard, and seeing
Bowser minus the badge of doggish citizenship, began whistling for him with the
hope of enticing him into the street that he
might make a capture. The balance of the
story is thus told by the *Capital* :

Marshal Sharpe appeared upon the
ground, followed by the Administration,
that happened to be making a visit to its
brother-in-law.

"Let that dog alone," cried the indignant
Sharpe.

"I'se ordered to catch dogs dat has no
muzzle," was the response of the scooper,
still struggling with Bowser.

"You whistled him out of my yard, you
scoundrel."

"Dah now—dah now, don't yous talk dat
way, I'se an officer."

"Let the dog alone," sternly cried the
President.

"What you foolin' in dis bizness for, eh ?
You mind yer own bizness," responded
scooper, not recognizing His Excellency,
and as he said this he mildly elbowed the
Administration. The Administration. in a
twinkling of a telegraphic click, shot its
right arm out from the shoulder and scooper stopped the blow with his countenance,
and immediately went to grass. Gathering
himself up, he said in wrath :

"I'll have you scooped for dis violence ;
I'll complain. I will. Who is you, anyhow ?"

"This fellow," interposed Marshal Sharpe,
"is General Grant, President of the United
States."

Consternation fell upon the army of invaders. The dog-catcher, the dog-catcher's
deputy, the dog-catcher's assistant deputy,
were filled with horror and amazement, and
left, while the administration retired to
Marshal Sharpe's and refreshed.

6/24/75 Mirror

The farm of John M. Scott, known as
Farmington, near Chantilly, in Fairfax
county, containing six hundred acres, has
been sold to Thomas N. Latham, of Fauquier county, for four dollars and fifty cents
per acre.— *Gazette.*

THE MIRROR.

BENJ. F. SHEETZ, Editor.

Thursday Morning, June 17.

"THE MIRROR."—In looking over our files a few days ago, we were reminded that this issue of the "*Mirror*" completes the nineteenth year of its existence, and its first decade since the war. As we pore over its pages, and read the local record of those nineteen years, reflected in its columns, there wells up in our bosom mingled emotions of gratitude and of sorrow.

Its present proprietor, younger then than now, witnessed its birth into the family of journalism—he rocked the cradle of its infancy, and supported it through the struggling years of its early life, and to-day he rejoices over its healthy condition and encouraging prospects for a ripe old age.— And whilst he returns his sincere gratitude to the numerous friends in this county and elsewhere, whose pabulum gave it strength in its weakness and nourishes it as it grows older, a feeling of sadness steals over the heart, as he reads the departure for realms unknown, of many of those with whom he was wont to take counsel when the clouds were dark and the skies lowering. Its original founder and editor has long since crossed the dark river, as have also many of its early friends and supporters ; the children of those who then were children, now read and criticise its "make up," until he almost feels that he, too, is "growing old."

Nineteen years ago ! But a drop in the wave of time, yet what mighty changes have convulsed the world since then.— changes, the effects of which are not merely visible upon us as individuals and as a community, but which have left their impress upon the history of nations to be studied with wonder and amazement by generations yet unborn. Governments of the old world, renowned for the splendor of their appoint-ments—and imperious because of their supposed stability—have gone down under popular outbreaks ; while in our own land and nation a sectional war has been waged —the fiercest and most disastrous that ever crimsoned the soil with the blood of the slain.

But it was not to talk of these things that we began to write, but simply and more particularly to note the fact that this issue of the *Mirror* ends its first decade since the war. On the 14th day of June, 1865, under many difficulties and disadvantages, we commenced its republication, and during the ten years that have followed, have sought to make it a faithful chronicler of passing events, and a welcome visitor to every hearth.

(The Livery Stable was a ubiquitous and necessary institution in those days before the automobile supplanted the horse. The purpose of livery stables was to provide boarding for private horses. Wagons, carriages, and horses were rented and other transportation services provided.)

The Coonton Family After Church.

It was after the evening service. Mrs. Coonton and the three Misses Coonton had arrived home. They sat listlessly around the room with their things on. Mr. Coonton was lying on the lounge asleep. It had been, undoubtedly, an impressive sermon, as the ladies were silent, busy with their thoughts.

"Emmeline," said Mrs. Coonton, suddenly addressing her eldest, "did you see Mrs. Parker when she came in?"

"Yes, ma," replied Emmeline.

"She didn't have that hat on, last Sunday, did she."

"No," said Emmeline. "It is her new hat. I noticed it the moment she went down the aisle, and I says to Sarah, 'What on earth possesses Mrs. Parker to wear such a hat as that?' says I."

"Such a great prancing feather on such a little hat looked awful ridiculous. I thought I should laugh right out when I saw it," observed Sarah.

"I don't think it looked any worse than Mary Schuyler's with the flaring red bow at the back," said Amelia.

"I don't see what Mrs. Schuyler can be thinking of to dress Mary out like that," said Mrs. Coonton, with a sigh. "Mary must be older than Sarah, and yet she dresses as if she was a mere child."

"She's nearly a year older than I am," asserted Sarah.

"Did you see how the widow Marshall was trucked out," interrupted Emmeline. "She was as gay as a peacock. Mercy, what airs that woman puts on. I would like to have asked her when she's going to bring back that pan of flour?" and Emmeline tittered maliciously.

"She's shining around old McMasters, they say," mentioned Amelia.

"Old McMasters?" ejaculated Mrs. Coonton, "Why he is old enough to be her father,"

"What difference do you suppose that makes to her?" suggested Emmeline. "She'd marry Methuselah. But I pity him if he gets her. She's a perfect wild cat."

"Say, Em, who was that gentleman with Ellen Byxby?" inquired Amelia.

"That's so," chimed in Sarah, with spirit, "who was he?"

"What gentleman?" asked Mrs. Coonton

"Why, I don't know who it was," explained Emmeline.

"They came in during the prayer. He was a tall fellow, with light hair, and chin whiskers."

"It couldn't have been her cousin John from Brooklyn," suggested Mrs. Coonton.

"Bother, no," said Sarah, pettishly. "He is short, and has brown hair. This gentleman is a stranger here. I wonder where she picked him up?"

"She seemed to keep mighty close to him," said Amelia, "but she needn't be scared.— No one will take him unless they are pretty hard pushed. He looks as soft as squash. Did you see him tumbling up his hair with his fingers. I wonder what that big ring cost—two cents?" and the speaker tittered.

"Well I'm glad if she's got company," said Mrs. Coonton, kindly. "She's made efforts enough to get some one, goodness knows."

"I should say she had," coincided Emmeline. "She's got on one of them Victoria hats, I see. If I had a drunken father I'd keep in doors, I think, and not be parading myself in public."

Just then there was a movement on the lounge, and the ladies began to take off their things.

"Hello, folks," said Mr. Coonton, rising up, and rubbing his eyes. "Is church out?"

"Yes," said Mrs. Coonton with a yawn, which communicated itself to her daughters.

"Did you have a good sermon?"

"Pretty good," accompanied by another yawn all around.

"See many good clothes?" was the next query.

"I suppose you think, Mr. Coonton, that is all your wife and daughters go to church for to look at people's clothes," said Mrs. Coontom tartly.

"That's just like pa," said Emmeline with a toss of her head, "he is always slurring church people." —*Danbury News.*

MARK TWAIN LOSES AN UMBRELLA.— The following advertisement appears in the Hartford Courant :

Two hundred and five dollars reward.— At the great base ball match on Tuesday, while I was engaged in hurrahing, a small boy walked off with an English-made silk umbrella belonging to me, and forgot to bring it back. I will pay $5 for the return of that umbrella, in good condition, to my house on Farmington avenue. I do not want the boy, (in an active state,) but will pay $200 for his remains.

SAMUEL L. CLEMENTS.

7/1/75 Mirror

THE BEECHER-TILTON TRIAL. This case, which has now occupied the time of the Brooklyn court for nearly seven months is still undisposed of. After the examination of witnesses closed, Porter spoke for six days; he was followed by Evarts in an eight days effort, both for Beecher. Then came Beach on behalf of Tilton, and he consumed ten days, in one of the most powerful and convincing arguments, and splendid forensic efforts ever listened to by a Brooklyn audience: and which, whatever the verdict of the jury may be, has not failed to confirm the belief of every unprejudiced mind that either heard or read it, of the unworthiness of Plymouth's idol. The case was given to the jury last Friday, but up to this time no verdict has been rendered—the members standing at is understood, nine (Beecher says eleven) for acquittal, and three for conviction.

At his last Friday night prayer meeting, Beecher, for the first time since the commencement of the trial, alluded to the investigation—proclaimed his innocence, and avowed his determination to remain pastor of Plymouth church, be the result of the trial what it may: expressed his assurance of the confidence and sympathy of his congregation, who he knew would stand by and sustain him. During the delivery of his discourse he was several times applauded.

On Sunday he preached to an immense congregation—the platform on which he stood was decked with flowers more profusely than usual, and he read out the names of twenty-three persons to be admitted to Church fellow-ship next Sunday.

7/1/75 Mirror

A CENTENNIAL INCIDENT.—The Boston Herald tells this · "The day following our centennial festivities the following incident occurred in a south end saloon : A friend had invited one of the South Carolina soldiers into the saloon to put another turf on the buried hatchet. While standing at the bar a stranger came in. The Carolinian suddenly dropped his glass and closely eyed the stranger. His gaze was so steady and peculiar that the friend began to be alarmed and to fear that the hatchet was about to be dug up again. Directly the Carolinian asked the stranger if he knew him: There was no recognition, whereupon the Carolinian asked him if he was in the late war. 'Yes,' was the reply. 'And you were once stationed at such a place?' 'Yes.' 'And took part in such a skirmish?' 'Yes.' 'Well, I thought so,' replied the Carolinian, and raising his hat showed a large scar on his forehead, saying, 'There's your sabre mark, my boy; come up and take a drink.'"

THE MIRROR.

BENJ. F. SHEETZ, Editor.

Thursday Morning, July 8.

THE FOURTH.—The anniversary of Independence was celebrated in Baltimore on Monday with little or no attending excitements, and the larger portion of the inhabitants remained quietly within doors, or found a refuge in the coolest place to be had. In the city the event calling forth immense crowds of spectators was the reception of Boston pigs given by Mr. Baker to the Fifth Regiment, and a burlesque parade by members of that command.

The day was celebrated at Washington, D. C., by the Old Inhabitants Association, before when after the reading of the Declaration of Independence, an oration was delivered by Jos. H. Bradley, Esq. At Philadelphia there was a succession of brilliant military and civic events, chiefly occurring in Fairmount Park. New York and other cities celebrated the day with heartiness. Even the Indians in the Indian Territory got up a patriotic demonstration, the first in the history of the United States.

In Memphis. Tennessee, the colored people presented Gen. N. B. Forrest with a banner, in token of reconciliation.

In Richmond there was a more general suspension of business than since 1860. Several military companies, both white and colored, paraded and spent the day in festivities.

THE FOURTH OF JULY falling on Sunday this year, Monday the fifth was generally adopted by those desiring to celebrate the 99th year of American Independence.— Hereabouts it passed off pretty much as other days,—with the exception of a few who went fishing, everybody attended to their business as usual—the chief aim of all being, apparently, to keep cool.

SEVERE ACCIDENT.—On Monday evening last, as the Rev. Mr. CANNON, of this town, was buggy-driving over the mountain road between Leesburg and Waterford, accompanied by Miss MARY WISE of Prince William county, the breechband and lines both gave way, leaving the occupants of the buggy entirely at the mercy of a somewhat fractious horse. After travelling a short distance in that unpleasant condition, and at a rather disagreeable speed, the buggy came in contact with a large stone, by which it was overturned, the occupants dashed out with considerable violence, and the vehicle rendered a complete wreck.— Mr. Cannon received a severe cut on the back of the head, and his lady companion an ugly gash on the forehead, both of them besides, sustaining severe contusions.

INSANE.—Mr. WILLIAM BIRKETT, of this county, was committed to the jail in Leesburg on Tuesday, as a lunatic.

7/1/75 Mirror

—Mark Twain says: "I have seen slower people than I am—and more deliberate people than I am—even quieter, and more listless than I am. But they were dead."

July, 1875

7/8/75 Mirror

FINIS— The Beecher-Tilton trial has at last been brought to a close. The jury, after listening for six months to the testimony of witnesses and arguments of counsel, and quietly considering the whole for six days in their private room, on Friday arrived at the conclusion that it was utterly impossible for them to agree, and were discharged. They stood nine for acquittal and three for conviction.

This, we suppose, will be the end of the matter—as it is not at all likely that another trial will be instituted. Tilton will, probably, *a la* Dan Sickles, return to the embrace of Elizabeth, and Henry Ward, rescued from the "ragged edge," will seek consolation in the bosoms of Plymouth Church.

The New York *Sun* says:

Mr. Beecher mounts the pulpit after this distrusted by a majority of his countrymen, not having been able, after his best efforts during a long investigation and with the aid of able counsel, dexterous attorneys, and vast money resources, to clear his character from reproach. In fact, the doubt which encompassed him are much stronger than they were before the trial began. His own sworn testimony did not carry conviction. His light behavior under legal scrutiny awakened disgust. His proved cowardice and deceit long ago pulled him down from his lofty pillar of influence. His method of meeting the assault of Tilton by personal abuse of his accuser, of unprecedented virulance, checked the Christian sense of the community. Yet he essays to preach to men about manliness, charity, truth, honesty, spotless Christianity, and an exalted morality !

If he had been a man of sensitiveness, we should have been spared his flippancy during the trial, both in the court room and in Plymouth Church. That he has the effrontery to show himself in the pulpit after the revelations of the last year, shows that he has the hide of the rhinoceros. What ever he does, however, he is a ruined man, and — very sadly we say it — he deserves his fate.

7/15/75 Mirror

THE WAGES OF SIN IN PLYMOUTH.—On Monday evening last a meeting of the pew-holders of Plymouth Church, was held in the lecture room — Mr. J. B. Hutchison was called to the chair, and stated that the meeting had been called for the purpose of considering the question of increasing Mr. Beecher's salary.

Mr. Henry W. Sage then offered a resolution to the effect that the salary of the pastor for the ensuing year be fixed at $100,000 instead of $20,000, which it has heretofore been.

Mr. S. B. White then delivered a brief and pertinent address in favor of the passage of the resolution. He said that while the investigating committee were sitting, Plymouth Church had made no effort to influence them in any way and so it had been all through the trial. They had made no move whatever towards influencing the jury or anybody else in Mr. Beecher's behalf. Their time had not come until to-night, and now, said the speaker, "We will show to the world that Plymouth Church can spend millions in the defense of her pastor's innocence, but not one dollar for blackmail or bribery."

The resolution was then put to a vote and passed unanimously, there being not one dissenting voice.

7/15/75 Mirror

LETTER FROM COL. MOSBY.—Col. John S. Mosby, of Virginia, has declined the invitation to deliver an address in Tremont Temple, Boston. He says: "Although circumstances compel me to decline it, I assure you that I do so from no want of sympathy with the noble object you profess a desire to promote—the restoration of fraternal relations between the people of the long-estranged sections of our country.— For the soldiers of the Union I cherish no feelings of bitterness, but on the contrary sentiments of the highest respect, and I trust the day is not far distant when the soldiers of both armies will receive from the whole country the credit due to their valor and patriotic devotions in the big wars that made ambition virtue.'

(Mosby, the famed confederate partisan leader, has had at least five biographies written about him. He lived in a neighboring county and occasionally practiced law in the Leesburg courts.)

169

WHAT NEXT   *The President of the United States Visits Tom Murphy's Stable to Witness a Glove-Fight Between His Son-in-law and a Stock-broker.*—To say nothing of his political course, and its influence upon the country, it is doubtful whether any President of the United States ever before provided such numerous and varied feasts of amusement for the "fancy," as Gen. GRANT. His well known fondness for fast horses has long been the admiration of the turf. His peregrinations a year or two ago, to all the agricultural shows that he could reach, gratified the morbid curiosity of the multitude. Later, his son went gunning for Don Piatt, in Washington, but gave up the chase without attaining much glory. Next, and only a few weeks ago, the President himself exercised his muscle by knocking down a darkie who was trying to toll off Marshal Sharp's dog,—and now his son-in-law, Sartoris, gets licked like blazes in endeavoring to establish his reputation for expertness in the highly necessary and intellectual science of the ring.

At Long Branch, the other day, a number of young gentlemen of sporting proclivities, were boasting of their muscle, the arms of Mr. Sartoris and Mr. Goicouria, a stock broker, were the most muscular, and the result was an agreement between the two to test their strength and skill in a glove-fight, in *Tom Murphy's stable.* The New York *Sun* furnishes the particulars :

At 10 o'clock on Monday morning the friends of the contestants drove from the West End Hotel to Mr. Murphy's stable, six coaches being well filled with sport-loving young men. It is said also, that President Grant, Mr. Thomas Murphy and his son, George Washington Childs, A. M. and other cottagers in the aristocratic neighborhood, walked over to the scene and manifested great interest in the sport.

At about 11 o'clock the men stripped to the buff, both showing magnificent muscle, and both being in good fighting condition. Although rather below the size of his opponent, Mr Sartoris seemed to be harder in flesh and able to stand more punishment ; and in the preliminary sparring it was plain that his knowledge of the noble science of self-defence was greater than that of his adversary. But in point of strength and in quickness of foot Mr. Goicouria had all the advantage.

The first round was a cautious one on both sides, although Mr. Goicouria got in a left-hand facer, which Mr. Sartoris reciprocated with a neat clip on the side of the head, administered with his right. Then followed a series of feints and parries, and the round ended.

Mr Sartoris opened the second round with a bold attack, which Mr. Goicouria skilfully parried, and seeing that his opponent in his eagerness, relaxed his guard, he went for him right and left, the result being a knock down.

From this time out the game was all in the hands of Mr. Goicouria. After getting first knock down he drew first blood, and for six or seven rounds battered the President's son-in-law unmercifully. Mr. Sartoris stood up round after round with bull-dog courage and endurance, but at length his friends saw that his chance of winning was less than nothing, and persuaded him to retire.

Departure of the Grasshoppers.

Kansas has been at last relieved of the presence of the terrible plague, the grasshoppers, with which the young State has been so sorely afflicted during the past year, and the people are greatly rejoiced at the prospect which now opens before them of saving their crops this year. The singular method of their departure, which was as sudden and unlooked for as their coming, is related by a correspondent of the St. Louis *Democrat*, who says:

The grasshoppers are gone from Kansas, if we except a few discouraged and undecided swarms here and there, not numerous enough to cause noticeable trouble, and apparently remaining here because they lacked energy to join in the general flight. The exodus commenced in earnest last Sunday week, and continued for four days. During all that time the upper air was filled with the contemptible pests, all moving due north. The flight seemed to have been preconcerted. They commenced to rise at about the same time all over the State, and once on the wing, they showed no disposition to alight again. Their route took them directly over some of the richest grain fields in Kansas, but they resolutely sailed on into the blue beyond, without so much as a slackening of speed, which was very nice behavior, indeed, and won a great deal of hearty commendation. They moved at the rate of twenty to thirty miles a day, just near enough to the earth to be seen with the naked eye, and the sight was at times queerly interesting; in fact, we haven't seen anything in the last twelve months that was so generally and so thoroughly enjoyed.

COUNCIL MEETING.—The first meeting of the new Council for the town of Leesburg was held on Monday night, and the members sworn in.

The contract for furnishing oil, lamps, chimneys, and wicks, and cleaning, lighting, extinguishing, and keeping in order generally, the lamps of the corporation for one year, was awarded to M. B. Steadman Price paid $230.

The following committees were appointed for the ensuing year:

On Finance.—Bradfield, Shafer and Foster.

On Church and Fayette Street — Lynch, Hough and Wildman.

On King Street and Town Sewer.—Shafer, Foster, Wildman and Dibbrell.

On Liberty and Ayre Streets.—Birkby, Orrison and Bradfield.

On Wirt.—Mott, Birkby and Orrison.

Market.—Hough, Mott and Lynch.

Loudoun.—Norris, Birkby, Orrison.

Cornwall.—Shafer, Orrison, Dibbrell.

North and Union.—Dibbrell and Shafer.

Royal.—Birkby and Wildman.

Highway.—Mott, Norris, Wildman.

The next regular meeting of the Council will be held on Friday night, at which time they will elect a *Town Sergeant.*

PROPERTY ASSESSED.—The assessors of the property within the Corporation of Leesburg and liable to taxes, have just completed their work, with the following result:

Horses	$ 8 353
Carriages, &c	3,815
Books, &c	7.490
Tools	1.175
Clocks	770
Watchs	5.829
Bank Stock	39.000
Musical Instruments	7.315
Bonds	105,005
Capital Invested	6.850
Furniture, Plate, &c	31.945
Town Lots	420,760
Church Property	14.400
Total	$736,337

The books show but 86 dogs in the Corporation, subject to tax.—we had thought there was nearly that many thousand.

THE MIRROR.

THURSDAY...................... July 15

KILLED.—HENSON McKENZIE, (colored,) better known in this community as "Binn's Henson," was killed by a passing train of cars on the B. & O. Railroad at Flemington, W. Va., about ten days ago. He was in the employment of Mr. Chas. Powell, and had gone with that gentleman for a drove of cattle. While the cattle train was laying over at Flemington for a few minutes, the deceased walked up the track a short distance, and as he faced about to return, an express train came thundering along, and striking him in the back killed him instantly. His mutilated remains were gathered together and decently buried at Flemington. Henson was a quiet, inoffensive, reliable man, and enjoyed the respect and confidence of his employers. He has a wife and several children living in this county.

RANAWAY.—Mr. Frank Poulton left a pair of fine young horses, hitched to a wagon, standing alone at the lower end of King street on Monday afternoon. During his brief absence, the animals became frightened and ran for nearly a mile before they were arrested. Strange to say, no damage was done. Look well to your horses in fly time.

A NEGRO CHILD, three years old, living with its parents on the farm of Mr. Nathan Brown, in this county, last week fell in a well 38 feet deep. The father climbed down the well, rescued the child from three feet of water, threw it over his shoulder, and again climbing up by the sides of the well, brought it to the top, strange to say, without the slightest injury to either father or child.

Two excursions over the W. & O. Railroad are advertised to come off on the 17th and 24th of this month. The first for the benefit of the colored M. E. Church, of this town, and the other by the "O. of G. S.

PT. ROCKS, JULY 12th, 1875.
EDITOR MIRROR—*Dear Sir:*—Please put the following notice in your issue of this week:

Drowning of an Unknown Man near the Pt. of Rocks, Md.—On Friday morning at about eleven o'clock the body of an unknown man was found in the canal, near the 28th lock. It is supposed that he fell from a boat during the night of Thursday. He was apparently about 50 years of age. He was without coat or waist-coat, nor was there anything found upon the corpse to identify his person. The coroner was sent for, but after viewing the body it was thought that an inquest was unnecessary, and the remains were interred in the Methodist burying ground and the place designated, so that they can be removed if they should hereafter be identified. Subsequent circumstances have led to the impression or supposition that the remains are those of a man by the name of William Wicks, of Hillsborough, Loudoun county, Va.

Respectfully,
R. W. TRAPNELL.

[The unfortunate man alluded to above, was WM. WICKS, of this county. Mr. W. was an intelligent, kind-hearted, obliging man; and those who knew him best will bury with him in his lonely grave the foibles of his life, and remember only the generous traits that marked his erratic nature. He was a son of the late Rev. Dr. Wicks of the M. E. Church, and was in about the 63d year of his age.]

7/22/75 Mirror

General Lee on Gen. Sherman.
(From the Charleston News.)

When General Lee visited this State (not long before his death) a gentleman who knew him well asked his opinion of Sherman's conduct. This, it must be remembered, was several years after the war, when the same means that there are now of forming a true judgment. What passed is given as follows:

D. H.: "General Lee, I desire to ask a question, which you will please not reply to if there is any impropriety in it."

General Lee: "Ask it, sir."

D. H.: "Was General Sherman, in his march through the country, justified, *under the usages of war*, in burning our homes over the heads of our women and children while we were in the field?"

General Lee rose from his chair, with his eyes brightened, and said: "*No, sir! no, sir! it was the act of a savage.* He was not justified under the usages of war."

DEATH OF ANDREW JOHNSON.

Ex-President ANDREW JOHNSON, is no more. He died at the residence of his daughter, Mrs. W. R. Brown, in Carter county, Tennessee, at about 2 o'clock on Saturday morning. Mr. Johnson had not been very well for some time, but on Wednesday, rode seven miles on horseback, to his daughter's, and the same afternoon was rendered insensible by paralysis. On Thursday he was a little better, became conscious, and had partial use of his body—but he soon relapsed, and died as stated above, on Saturday morning. He peacefully breathed his last, surrounded by his wife, children and all his grandchildren, except the son and daughter of ex-Senator Patterson. One of his last wishes was that his winding sheet should be the flag of his country.

As soon as his death was made known in Washington, the President announced the fact in the following executive order :

"Washington, July 31, 1875.—It becomes the painful duty of the President to announce to the people of the United States the death of Andrew Johnson, the last survivor of his honored predecessors, which occurred in Carter county, East Tennessee, at an early hour this morning. The solemnity of the occasion which called him to the presidency, with the varied nature and length of his public services, will cause him to be long remembered and occasion mourning for the death of a distinguished public servant. As a mark of respect for the memory of the deceased it is ordered that the executive mansion and the several departments of the government at Washington be draped in mourning until the close of the day designated for his funeral, and that all public business be suspended on that day. It is further ordered that the War and Navy Departments cause suitable honors to be paid on the occasion to the memory of the illustrious dead. U. S. GRANT.

His body will be buried with Masonic honors, in Greenville, on Tuesday.

DEATH OF ANDREW JOHNSON. The announcement of the death of ex-President ANDREW JOHNSON, will be received with sorrow by the people of the United States with whom his name and his fame have long been familiar. No man in this country ever had a more remarkable or a more successful career. And if he was at times obstinate, self willed and a little given to vanity, there was that in his history that made them more excusable in him, than they would have been in most of his compeers. His whole life is a brilliant example for the encouragement of the poor and friendless youths of the land, and one that may be profitably studied by the more favored children of fortune. No man ever achieved what ANDREW JOHNSON accomplished, upon whose brow nature had not set her seal of noblest manhood. Orphaned at the early age of four years—at ten apprenticed to a tailor for seven—never attending school a day in his life—but working at his trade, and supporting his dependent mother—whom to his lasting honor be it said, he never neglected; he found himself at the early age of 20, with a wife and mother to support, and himself up to that time barely able to read. His wife taught him penmanship arithmetic, and grammer, and yet upon that foundation he reared a structure of intelligence and usefulness that commanded the respect and admiration of all with whom he came in contact. Holding the position of Alderman of Greenville when he was but twenty years of age—successfully filling the office of village Mayor,—a member of the House of Delegates of Tennessee,—Presidential elector in 1840, encountering successfully on the stump, many of the leading spirits of the old whig party, a member of the State Senate,—a representative in the Congress of the U. States for ten years,—twice elected Governor of Tennessee,—U. S. Senator for six years,—Vice President, and finally President of a nation of 40,000,000 of people, and at the time of his death, again a U. S. Senator-elect from the State that had so often honored herself, in doing honor to her distinguished son by adoption.

Whilst there were many things in the later years of his life that many of us, perhaps, could not approve, there was so much innate goodness and greatness in his composition, that we are bound to acknowledge his superiority. and honor him for the virtues that ennobled his manhood — and at his death mournfully feel that the grave closes over one of the brightest intellects, and most remarkable men, that has in this country adorned the present century.

8/5/75 Mirror

DEATH OF GEN. GEO. E. PICKETT. Geo. E. Pickett one of the most distinguished officers of the late Confederate army, died in Norfolk, Va., one day last week, in the fiftieth year of his age. His division bore throughout the war a reputation for intrepid courage, which found, perhaps, its most brilliant illustration on the second day of the disastrous battle of Gettysburg. Pa., July 3, 1863. He was a graduate of West Point, but on the breaking out of the war took the side of his section, and was soon in command of a brigade, and subsequently of a division in Longstreet's corps of General Lee's army. He led his troops into nearly every principal battle fought in Virginia, and was especially distinguished in the battles around Richmond, Fredericksburg, and Manassas. Va., and also at Antietam, Md, and Gettysburg. Pa; at Knoxville. Tenn., and in the stubbornly fought and final battle of the war around Petersburg, Va.

(What is not mentioned is that in the final days of the war Lee removed him from command. At a critical time, Pickett was absent and allowed his men to be flanked precipitating the retreat to Appomatox. He did not obey but continued with his men and was there at the surrender ceremonies causing Lee to remark "Who is that man?")

The funeral of ex-President Johnson took place at Greenville. Tenn., on Tuesday. attended by about 5000 people. He was buried with masonic honors.

8/5/75 Mirror

AN EMBRYO DIPLOMATIST. The other day when a Vicksburg boy had trouble with a neighbor's boy and came out first best, he realized that something must be done at home, and he slid into the house and said:

"Mother, you know how kind and good you have been to Mrs. B —— , next door ?"

"Yes, I have tried to be a good neighbor to her."

"Well, do you know that she says you clean your teeth with a whitewash brush, and that father ought to have a pension for living with you?"

He did out, and when Mrs. B —— reached the gate, on her way to the house to ask why her boy must be pounded in that way, she heard a shrill voice calling her :

"Vile wretch, don't you enter that gate or you'll get scalded."

She returned home, and the young statesman dropped down under a shade tree, kicked up his heels and softly chuckled.

Vicksburg Herald.

8/5/75 Mirror

AN ESTRAYED NORTHERNER writes home from Virginia that no one from this section should venture into that fate at present unless he is prepared to be "waylaid, seized upon and carried off to houses, and kept and stuffed and filled and put through a course of mint julep, and buttermilk, and johnny cake, and fried chicken, and mush, and old ham and cabbage, and Powhatan pipes with reed stems and the finest tobacco in the world." Yankees are ku-kluxed in this way at sight, he says.

THE MIRROR.

THURSDAY............................ Aug. 12.

PROF. BIRCHARD is stopping at the Osburn House, in this town, where he will be pleased to see those of our citizens who desire a phrenological chart of their own or childrens' heads. The Professor spent some time in Hamilton a short time ago, and is thus spoken of by the *Enterprize* of that town :

PHRENOLOGY.—Prof. C. A. Birchard, the eminent phrenologist, whose reading of human character, and whose counsels to the young in relation to the formation of character, and social and conjugal relations in life, have gained for him a reputation second, perhaps to no man is this country, is now in Hamilton, where he expects to remain for a short time. We commend the professor to our friends as a gentleman of high repute, and our friends to him for phrenological examination, with the injunction, "man, know thyself."

Phrenology was a pseudo-science popular in the 19th century. It essentially determined or predicted a person's intelligence, character, and other traits by the size and shape of the cranium. The question regarding the eminent professor was whether he actually believed this outlandish theory or was an articulate charlatan pursuing profitable lecture opportunities.

THE CAMP MEETING in Benton's woods, near Middleburg, commences to-morrow. The encampment promises to be a large one ; a number of the most eloquent Divines of the Church are expected to be present.

THE Camp Meeting (colored) commenced in Carr's woods, near the Dry Mill, on Friday last is still in progress. We understand that there are about twenty tents on the ground, and that good order generally has been observed.

ROUND HILL CAMP MEETING. — The Camp Meeting at Round Hill, in this county, which was commenced on Friday last, has been well attended ever since. The encampment is in a beautiful grove on the lands of Mr. HENRY HEATON, within a few hundred yards of the depot and consequently exceedingly convenient for visitors who go by rail.

The heavy rain of Friday night, was a perfect dust-settler, and on Sunday, notwithstanding from 3000 to 4000 people threaded the avenues of the Camp, the day was delightfully pleasant, and in every way enjoyable.

An extra train of cars that day, brought from Alexandria, Washington, and the intermediate stations, a large invoice of visitors, while another extra train from Leesburg, added about 400 to the crowd.

"Dirty Camp," a mile off, was the scene of some excitement, but no violence. Several members of the sporting fraternity, had the "working tools" of the craft, money and all, gobbled up by the police.

CAMP MEETING —Sunday last was a beautiful day, and a pair of us decided to go to Camp Meeting. We started about 7 o'clock in the morning, and a delightful drive of sixteen miles, a portion of it through the most charming section of old Loudoun, and the whole of it just new, magnificently studded with a wilderness of corn, that gracefully saluted each passer-by, filling the breast, even of those who like herself causing "no foot of land do we possess," with a feeling of admiration and thankfulness, over the abundant fruitfulness of the earth.

The camp ground is located in Benton's grove, a lovely strip of woods almost on the extreme southern border of the county, a locality as yet undisturbed by the thundering footsteps of the steam engine; consequently the only means of reaching it are by those primitive ones that conveyed the early fathers to similar gatherings, Hence from morning's early dawn, the public roads and by-ways leading to camp, were thronged with people of all sizes, sexes, color and religious creed, some on foot others mounted on steeds of fiery metal, or astride the back of a "meek and lowly" mule. Yonder went the family carriage, which for years, it may be, had borne to the house of worship, the grey-haired sire, surrounded by the youthful gems of household treasure, while following in the rear or speeding in the front, dashed the gay cavalier, taking advantage of the clattering hoofs of his proud stepping Bucephalus, to breathe words of love into the open ear of the fair companion seated by his side. In the distance slowly moved the jaded horse and dilapidated wagon, of the honest son of toil, who with wife and children, arrayed in Sunday attire, with clean hands and pure hearts, were wending their way to the sacred retreat, while by their side rolled the grandly elegant equipage of their more favored neighbor, who reckoned his fortune by the hundreds of thousands—all wending their way to a common centre, where, beneath bending boughs and singing birds, songs of rejoicing were filling the air.

But, we are loitering too long by the way side. We reached the ground at 10 o'clock and had time before morning service to stroll around and take a bird's-eye view of the encampment. There are about seventy large substantial, well arranged tents with every necessary convenience to make their occupants comfortable, while the extensive arrangements about Pickett's well kept hotel affords abundant accommodations for outsiders. In front of the preacher's stand is a large canvass-covered awning about forty feet in length, and capable of seating beneath its shadow, we should think, a congregation of 300 or 400 persons. The ground is beautifully lighted. Some forty or fifty oil lamps, made for the purpose, swing beneath the pavillion, several large lamps fixed on posts stationed around the circle, a half dozen fire stands with an immense head-light of a steam engine planted a little to the left of the stand, combine to throw over the circle a "flood of light," and clothe it with a weird beauty rarely seen on a "country" camp-ground. We think there were at least 5,000 people on the ground Sunday and according to our estimate from 2,000 to 2,500 of them were seated or standing within the circle during the delivery, in the morning, of an excellent discourse by Rev. Dr. Rosser, from the words, "Why will ye die, oh! House of Israel. The Dr. preached with his accostomed vim and power, and was listened to with marked attention.

The meeting is still in progress, with, we understood the most encouraging results.

THE Camp Meeting in Benton's woods, closed on Monday, having been kept up for twelve days. The attendance was large, and characterized throughout by remarkably good order, while the main object of the meeting was a decided success—adding to the church numbers of such as shall be saved.

8/19/75 Mirror

Camp-Meetings and their History.

Camp-meetings originated in the United States. The Baltimore *Sun* says:

"The first camp-meeting in the United States was held in 1790, on the banks of the Red river, in Kentucky. The common idea that it was exclusively of Methodist origin is erroneous. The manner in which it began was this: There were two brothers by the name of McGee, one a Presbyterian and one a Methodist preacher. Being on a religious tour from Tennessee, where the former was settled, to a locality near Ohio, they stopped at a settlement on the river to attend a sacramental occasion with the Rev. Mr. McGeedy, a Presbyterian. Sermons were delivered on the occasion by the brothers McGee and by three Presbyterian clergymen, and the excitement created seems to have been as great among those present as that which has followed the preaching of Moody and Sankey in England. When the news of the extraordinary movement reached the surrounding country the people having never heard of the like before, rushed in such crowds to the meeting-house that it was immediately overflowed, and the religious services were therefore transferred to the forest. Many came from every direction, with provisions and other necessaries for encampment, and continued several days, dwelling in tents. Sectarian divisions seemed to have been entirely forgotten in this first camp-meeting. The services were conducted by Presbyterians, Baptist and Methodist. The result was so extraordinary that it suggested another meeting of the kind, and from this unpremeditated beginning these meetings extended, increasing in power and usefulness, under the special direction of Presbyterians and Methodists. Because of this union of sects in their support they were called 'general camp-meetings.' At length, however, the Presbyterians gradually retired from the field, but the Methodists carried them into other parts of the country, till they became general in the connection.

8/26/75 Mirror

Mrs. Lincoln Released from the Asylum.

CHICAGO. Aug. 21.—A correspondent of the *Evening Post and Mail* writing from St. Charles, in the vicinity of Bellevue Asylum, says "You will be glad to learn—and this is the first public intimation of the fact—that Mrs. Lincoln is pronounced well enough to leave the asylum and visit her sister, Mrs. Edwards, at Springfield. It is not likely that she will return to Bellevue Asylum, as there is some feeling evinced in the matter of her incarceration by friends who refuse to believe her insane. A leading lady lawyer of Chicago has been with her much of late, and will assist in Mrs. Lincoln's restoration to the world. She is decidedly better, sleeps and eats well, and shows no tendency to any mania.

8/12/75 Mirror

ICE MAKING IN THE SOUTH.—At Montgomery, Alabama, there is a manufactory of ice in full operation. Some one writing from that city gives a glowing and interesting account of what is done, and the manner of doing it. Twelve thousand pounds of ice are made daily, which takes seventy thousand gallons of water, and the cost, when placed in the ice house, is about three-eighths of a cent per pound, which is cheaper than the freights from the north, if the ice should be put in the cars gratis.

We summarize the process. The water is distilled, put in rectangular tin cans, thirty inches long and nine and a half inches wide, and three-fourths of an inch thick. These are placed in rows, in tanks filled with salt water, coming not quite to their tops. Ether, which has been liquidized in an adjoining room under a pressure of from 70 to 110 pounds to the square inch, is then forced into about 100 pipes in each tank, filling all the tubes as it expands into a gas. The ether extracts the caloric from the water surrounding the tubes, equalizes the temperature and brings the whole below freezing point. The distilled water congeals readily, and the salt water is brought down several degrees colder than ice without freezing. The gas passes on to a receiver and is again made to do service. It is difficult to confine it, but if not allowed to escape, the same quantity can be used continually. It is claimed that ether is better than mercury, as the latter eats out copper and iron pipes quickly, while the former does not affect the metals. Three times a day the cans are taken out, dipped into hot water which loosens the cake inside, and slabs of ice are produced weighing twenty-five pounds each. Four of these are piled on top of each other and allowed to freeze together.

A LITTLE MISTAKE.

9/2/75 Mirror

From the Huron County (Ohio) Chronicle.

He took the evening train up from Cleveland, and in looking through the cars discovered a female sitting alone in a seat, and it instantly occurred to him that she might be lovely. A veil dropped over her face, but there was no reason to suppose that she was not good looking, and he gallantly raised his hat and sat down beside her, remarking with a lovely smile:

"It's lonely travelling alone."

She just murmured a reply, but the accent was captivating, and he was won at the start.

He was practiced in all the arts of polite tactics, and spoke to her softly of this great, desolate world, with appropriate allusions to human hearts. He told her how he hungered and thirsted after the affection of a true heart, and had yearned to feel the breath of the heavenly flame of love.

No, he sighed, he had no wife, no one to love and caress him, and mend his suspenders; and when he inquired if she was treading the path of life single and alone, she murmured so pensively and sad that he felt compelled to put his arm on the back of the seat lest she should fall out of the window—which was closed.

They reached Norwalk, and just as the train stopped he heard a grating, hissing sound close to his ear, and then the words:

"Y-o-u villain; y-o-u old hypocritical s-i-n-n-e-r, I'll make you think you've been struck by a breath of heavenly flame, you old owl."

He looked around just far enough to get a glimpse of a pair of flashing eyes and the face of his wife, who had murmured so fondly to him along the journey. A sudden spazm seized him, but he managed to accompany her from the train, and as they moved into the darkness toward home her flashing eyes lit up his pale face with a spectral effect.

A COW IN THE GARDEN.

Danbury Bailey's friend, Mr. Cobleigh, is again in trouble. The *News* says : A cow got into Mr. Cobleigh's garden, Sunday afternoon. Cobleigh was lying down at the time, thinking of this very garden, over which he had labored all the spare time since the first of May. Mrs. Cobleigh discovered the animal. It was feeling its way across the lawn to a row of early cabbages. Mr. Cobleigh was aroused at once, and, without stopping to put on his hat or his boots, he hastened out to the yard, with a very lively sense of impending danger.— The boy in the next house saw the cow, but discreetly forebore to call attention to it until he saw Mr. Cobleigh appear ; then he hastened upon the scene with commendable speed. The owner of the garden was horrified on gaining the yard to see the cow with her front teeth resting upon the lettuce bed, and her tongue just licking in the top of a drumhead.

"Whey, there ;" he shouted, dashing at her and flourishing his arms.

The cow looked around, and seeing Cobleigh, and not recognizing him as an acquaintance, immediately set about extricating herself from the dilemma by immediately turning around and backing out ; but just then the boy came up with all the fire and ardor of youth, and a chunk of coal, and the poor animal dashed off in another direction.

"Woosh ! woosh ! you beast," yelled Mr. Cobleigh, in an agony, as he saw her carom on the tomatoes. "Drive her back " he shouted to the boy. That young man instantly complied by hitting her with the lump of coal, and sending her over the beets.

"Woosh ! woosh ! yelled Cobleigh.

"Hi, there !" screamed the boy.

"Si, boy ! si, boy !" shrieked Cobleigh, as the animal suddenly dropped its horns and threw two dollars worth of pea-vines into the air.

But the animal would not be directed.— It either lost all control of itself, or was determined on revenge. Cobleigh grabbed up a clothes pole and dashed at her with desperate fury ; the boy snatched up another, and put after her in an opposite direction ; whereupon Mrs. Cobleigh, who had been an excited observer of the battle, caught up a hoe, with the evident intention of joining in the pursuit, but becoming mysteriously tangled in the handle, was precipitated in the grass, to the ill concealed disgust of her husband. But she was on her feet in an instant, and would have undoubtedly rendered efficient service, had not Mr. Cobleigh abruptly intimated that he'd put an ounce of lead in her if she did not clear into the house. Thereupon she gained the stoop at once, where she remained, eagerly looking for an opportunity to hurl the hoe at the devastating beast, which she finally did, and with such marvellous precision as to hit her husband and the boy both at the same time, the former in the middle of the back, with the handle, and the latter on the top of the head, with the blade. The boy was just on the point of jumping up to give a stroke at the cow, but instantly changed his mind, and emitting a yell of poignant distress, lost no time in getting over the fence into his own yard, where he stood rubbing his head and staring at Mrs Cobleigh as if fascinated. What remarks Mr. Cobleigh intended to make will never be known, as probably just as the hoe struck him, the animal suddenly raised both hind legs and hit him square in the face with a hill of cucumbers, blinding his eyes, choking his speech, and filling his neck with earth. Then the beast dashed through the peas, over the lawn and through the gate, with a prize tomato plant on each horn, and swinging her tail in vindictive triumph, while the unfortunate Mr. Cobleigh, sitting on the ground, was making strenuous endeavors to catch his breath.

When he went into the house to get the dirt out of his mouth and neck, Mrs. Cobleigh was telling the woman in the next house that she had been a month at Cobleigh trying to get a catch put on the gate. She guessed it would be attended to now

It has been.

10/7/75 Mirror

ANDERSONVILLE PRISON. — Although more than ten years have elapsed since the close of the war, certain northern people persist in misrepresenting the treatment of federal prisoners by the Confederates, and notably those at Andersonville. Recently the St. Louis Globe-Democrat contained an article, which charged Jefferson Davis and other prominent Confederate officials with conniving at the alleged cruelties practised on the federal prisoners at that point, and refusing an exchange. In reply to this Judge Ould, of Richmond, who was the Confederate Commissioner of Exchange, has written a letter to Col. Wood, of St. Louis, in which he fully exculpates the Confederate authorities, and clearly proves that whatever blame attached to the mode of treatment received by Federal prisoners confined at Andersonville, was directly traceable to the United States authorities. In regard to those prisoners, he says:

"I offered them for nothing—that is, without requiring a delivery of equivalents—to the federal authorities in August, 1864, and urged them to send transportation for them quickly. The offer was accompanied by an official statement of the monthly mortality then, and set forth our utter inability to provide for the prisoners. It was after that time that the principal mortality occurred. The prisoners were not sent for until the following December, and then they were promptly delivered, without our ever receiving the equivalents for them."

We concur in the conclusion of the Baltimore Sun, that it is time that the miserable prejudice which prevents honest admissions on this subject, resulting in continued injustice to Jefferson Davis and other Confederates, had ceased, and that the truth be admitted.

(The prisons in the north were almost as bad with less excuse for it. The suspension of the prisoner exchanges was mostly responsible although it may have shortened the war.)

9/9/75 Mirror

HOW TO REMOVE WARTS.—Warts are not only very troublesome but disfigure the hands. Our readers will thank us for calling their attention to the following perfect cure even the largest, without leaving a scar. Take a small piece of raw beef, steep it all night in vinegar, cut as much from it as will cover the wart and tie it on ; or, if the excrescence is on the forehead, fasten it on with strips of plaster. It may be removed during the day and put on every night. In one fortnight the wart will die and peel off. The same prescripwill cure corns.

10/21/75 Mirror

Hundred Years' Progress in Agriculture.

When we look back from one year to another, we sometimes think that little progress has been made in our agriculture. It has sometimes been remarked that notwithstanding our numerous farmers' clubs throughout the state, county, and town, agricultural papers and books, that we are going on in about the same old plodding way. It is true that from day to day, from year to year we can scarcely perceive the advance that is really taking place. The huge elm which stands by the wayside, yearly and daily adds to its size, yet we are unable to perceive it. But when we turn back twenty-five years or a hundred years, and learn what was the size of the tree then, we are astonished at its increase in size.—

Could we be placed back upon a Massachusetts farm in the year 1771, we should almost feel ourselves in a half civilized age.

The farm implements were few in numbers and of rude construction. There were no mowing machines, no cultivators, no iron plows, and no cast steel hoes. The plows were made of wood with a few iron bolts to hold them together and a few strips of iron nailed upon the parts of wood which were most exposed to wear. The plows were so clumsily made that it took almost twice the amount of team to draw them which would be required for our plows, and required a strong man to hold the handles to keep the plow in the ground, and another man to ride upon the beam if it was desired to plow to a good depth. The hoes were made of iron, heavy and clumsy. The threshing was done with flail and winnowing by the wind.

The admirers of nice fruit would find little to please the eye or tempt the taste in the Colonial orchards. Very little attention was given to the raising of fruits except for making cider. Even so late as 1825 there was not a nursery for the sale of apple and pear trees in New England.

The cattle were inferior to our poorest specimens. Even in England at that time there was no stock which was comparable with our native cattle of to day. The average gross weight of the neat cattle sent to Smithfield for slaughter did not exceed three hundred and seventy pounds each, and the average weight of sheep was twenty eight pounds. Now the average weight of sheep in that same locality is eighty pounds and the average weight of neat cattle eight hundred pounds, showing what a vast improvement has been made since that day. The wool of the sheep was coarse and the fleece light. During the last fifty years great improvement have been effected in our sheep husbandry. So great has been this improvement, that at the World's fair in London, in 1851, the fleece which commanded the highest prize for the fineness and beauty of staple in a free competition with Spain, Saxony, and Silesia, and other parts of Germany, was grown on the green pastures of Tennessee. At the international exposition at Hamburg, in 1863, Vermont merinoes took the prizes.

Even the grass crop was little attended to a century since. The principal resource for wintering the stock was the natural grasses of swales, meadows and salt marshes. Even in England the cultivation of grasses was not attended to until the latter part of the eighteenth century, and it is a noteworthy fact that the modern improvement in cattle did not began till after the systematic culture of the better qualities of grass. Timothy grass was a native of America and was named after Timothy Hannon, who is said to have cultivated it extensively and taken the seed of it from New York to Carolina. This grass was introduced into England from this country only a little more than a century ago. Now our grass crop is our most valuable crop, and its importance annually increases.

At the time of the outbreak of the revolution there were no agricultural journals, very few newspapers of any kind, not many books, and no mail and no regular communication between the colonies. There were no mails until 1790, and in 1791 there were but eighty-nine post offices and less than two thousand miles of post roads, and upon nine-tenths of these, the mail service was done on horseback. With the exception of four short "Essays on Field Husbandry," by the Rev. Jared Eliot, of Connecticut, no agricultural book had been printed in the colonies previous to the revolution. The *American Farmer* was started in Baltimore in 1819, and was the first agricultural newspaper published in the United States. Now we have over one hundred periodical devoted to the various branches of agriculture.

During the past fifty year the improvement in farming and farm apparatus has been remarkable. The mowers, reapers, horse rakes, cultivators, seed drills, horse hoes, thrashing machines and other valuable implements which have come into existence during this time have excited an all powerful influence upon the production, and capacity of our farms.

A Painful Scene and a Touching Confession.

We find in the Maroa (Ill.) *News* of the 25th of September, an account of the resignation of Elder J. V. Beekman as pastor of the Christian Church of that village. For some time past the Rev. gentleman's habits have been such as to cause great grief to his friends and bring reproach upon the church. At the close of the sermon, which was preached by a neighboring pastor, Elder Beekman made the following address, which we give as a warning to all men, both young and old, to avoid the sin and shame which have come upon this man :

As a man, I have the highest conception as to what the life and character of a minister of the Gospel should be. I know that he should lead a consistent and an upright life, that can be looked to by the community as an example of purity and righteousness. Knowing that my life has not been such in all respects, I desire to tender to this church for which I have labored so long, my resignation.

You are aware that I refer to my sin of intemperance. This may be my last opportunity of addressing you, and I want to ask you that you will not charge this great shame to the religion of Christ. It teaches better things. Charge it all to my own depravity and sinful nature. To you who have not this habit, it is strange that I should thus yield to temptation. I well remember the time when I thought it strange that others drank and ruined themselves with alcohol. I am glad that there are so many young men here this morning, that I may lift my voice in warning, and beg them to profit by my example. You think now that you are strong and in no danger. I well remember the time when I believed the same. Twelve years ago when I reached forth my inexperienced hand and took the intoxicating cup, I thought I was strong, but I developed a habit that holds me in chains, and in the most awful slavery that humanity was ever subjected to. It holds me in its embrace when I seek my bed for repose; it disturbs my dreams during the weary hours of night, and seizes me as its prey when I rise up in the morning to enter upon the duties of the day.

Profit, oh ! profit by my example; see what it has done for me. There was a time when I stood as fair as any minister of the church in Illinois ; there was a time when I had as bright prospects and as cheering hopes for the future as any of my class-mates. But now they are all gone because of intemperance. Oh that I could bring the whole world to hear my warning voice. Young ladies you can do much to remove this curse from the world by not countenancing its use among your companions.

Brethren, I severe my connection with you as your pastor with a sad heart. It would be sad under the most favorable circumstances, but much more so as it is. But I shall remain with you in the church and labor in the community for our livelihood ; I will come to our social meetings and work with you in the Sunday school, and will do all I can to atone for the great sin I have committed.

God knows I do not wish to injure His cause. Pray for me that I may yet overcome this besetting sin. I trust that I shall be able to conquor. But, should I go down under the withering influence, I ask that you remember me kindly. Whenever you meet me, and under what circumstances, remember there was a time when you were proud of me. But treat me as you may, act towards me as you choose, I beg that you will remember my wife kindly. Do not give her pain and sorrow because of my wrong doing. Poor woman, she has already suffered enough. I married her a sweet and innocent girl. She has been a patient and painful wife. Again I ask that you will kindly remember my wife and children.

11/13/75 Washingtonian

STONEWALL JACKSON.

THE BRITISH BRONZE TO THE VIRGINIA HERO.

Unveiling of the Statue at Richmond — Imposing Ceremonies — Speeches of Gov. Kemper and Rev. Dr. Hoge.

Special Telegraphic Correspondence of the Baltimore Sun.

Richmond, Va., October 26, 1875.—The bronze statue of Stonewall Jackson, the gift of a number of eminent Englishmen to Virginia, was unveiled on its pedestal in the Capitol grounds, in Richmond, to-day. The city was thronged with visitors, including a strong delegation of Marylanders from Baltimore, many of whom belonged to the old Stonewall Brigade, and fought under Jackson's banner. There were strangers from all parts of Virginia and the South.

ELABORATE DECORATIONS.

Richmond was decorated throughout the city, few houses appearing without some token in honor of the hero who was second in command in the armies of the Confederacy when he fell. The British flag was conspicuous among the decorations everywhere, and the old Confederate flags were entwined with the stars and stripes, emblematic of the reunion and harmony of prevailing peace. Many of the Confederate flags displayed were torn and stained treasures kept in families as mementoes of the past.

THE STATUE OF JACKSON.

The bronze statue on the north side of the capitol, midway between the Washington monument and the Governor's mansion, and between the main avenues of Capitol square and Capitol street, is seven feet in height, and represents General T. J. Jackson as he was uniformed at the time of his death. His left hand is resting on his sword, which is planted on a portion of broken fortification. The head is turned to the right. The right hand holds a glove and rests on the hip. The sculptor has succeeded admirably in the expression, it being that of a man who neither knows nor fears danger. As a likeness of Jackson, however, he has not done so well. As a work of art it can not fail to add new lustre to the already brilliant fame of the English sculptor Foley, who finished it just before his death in August last. The statue is mounted on a circular base of granite, with a pedestal of five feet in height of the same material. The inscription is as follows:

Presented by English gentlemen
as a tribute of admiration for
the Soldier and Patriot,
Thomas J. Jackson,
and gratefully accepted by Virginia,
in the name of the Southern people.
Done A. D. 1875.
in the hundredth year of the Commonwealth.

"Look! there is Jackson, standing like a stone wall."

A GRAND PARADE.

A great feature of the demonstration was the parade through the streets draped in flags; the sidewalks crowded, housetops and windows filled, while the greatest enthusiasm prevailed everywhere. The line was formed on Broad and Foushee streets, the First Virginia Regiment on the right, and the students of Richmond College on the left. It took the procession an hour and a half to pass a given point. The procession was composed as follows: General Joseph E. Johnston and staff, General Harry Heth, first assistant marshal; Bradley T Johnson and aids; First Virginia Regiment Infantry, 300 men, and full band; Virginia Military Institute Cadets, commanded by Col. Scott Shipp, 200 young men; Blacksburg Agricultural College Cadets, 100; Virginia Institute Cadets and band; Monticello Guards, Charlottesville, 50; Petersburg Grays, 51; West Augusta Guard, Staunton, 50; Norfolk City Guard, 50; Norfolk Artillery Blues, 43; Richmond Howitzers, 54; a carriage containing Governor Kemper and W. W. Corcoran, of Washington, D. C.; a long line of carriages containing State and City officials, guests and army officers. Then followed veterans from various States; veterans of the Army of Northern Virginia; the Maryland Division, under General Trimble, 53 men, and survivors of the old Stonewall Brigade, who were cheered by everybody; Catholic societies of Richmond; singing societies, &c. The colored organizations decided not to turn out, although it was believed they would participate up to the last moment. Four negro men who served as cooks in the Stonewall Brigade all through the war turned out in their old camp dress and attracted much attention. Some of the veterans wore their old, ragged Confederate jackets.

UNVEILING CEREMONIES.

After parading through some of the principal streets the procession arrived at the Capitol and was massed in the vicinity of the veiled statue and the platform from which the speaking was to take place. Mrs. Jackson, the widow of General Jackson, was present on the grand stand, with her little daughter, Julia Jackson, aged thirteen years; Mrs. Osborne and Mrs. J. E. B. Stuart. The party were the guests of Governor Kemper. Among the notable persons also on the grand stand were General Joseph E. Johnston, who presided, General W. H. F. Lee, General D. H. Hill and lady, General Ransom, of North Carolina; General Lane, of North Carolina; Ex-Governor Randolph, of New Jersey; Ex-Governors Letcher and William Smith, of Virginia; R. M. T. Hunter, General G. Martin, and others.

STONEWALL JACKSON'S DEATHBED.

Interesting Reminiscences of the Great Confederate General.

A writer in the Richmond Dispatch, detailing reminiscences of Stonewall Jackson, says: A gallant gentleman who served on the staff of General A. P. Hill has recently given me a somewhat new version of the wounding of Jackson, which has never been in print, and which I will give in detail. While General Rodes' division was pressing the enemy in line of battle A. P. Hill's division was moving in column to their support, and General Hill and his staff rode to the front to assist in relieving the confusion which had necessarily ensued from charging through the thick undergrowth. After the pursuit had ceased and Hill's division was moving forward to relieve Rodes, the enemy opened a very severe fire of artillery from some thirty pieces; and just after this Hill met Jackson in the turnpike and received from him the characteristic order, twice repeated, and with General Jackson's peculiar wave of the hand in the direction indicated: "Press them and cut them off from the United States ford." Hill replied: "General, I am entirely unacquainted with the topography of this country. Have you an officer who could aid me?" Jackson then directed Captain Boswell, of his staff, to report to Gen. Hill, and he himself rode on down the road through the lines, and about fifty to seventy-five yards in front of them.

My informant thinks that there was with Jackson at this time none of his staff, and only one of the signal corps; but it would seem, from other accounts, that he was at least joined soon after by Capt. Wilbourne and Lieut. Morrison, of his staff. The contiguity of the confederate lines to the federal lines at this time was shown by the fact that some of Lane's brigade of Hill's corps brought in a federal colonel, who said that he stepped in front of his lines and only came a few feet before he found himself in ours. As soon as Gen. Hill saw Jackson ride in front of his lines he felt it his duty, as a subordinate, to join him, and accordingly he also rode forward, accompanied, by several of his staff and couriers.

When the firing first begun the party were sitting quietly on their horses, looking in the direction of the enemy's lines, and eagerly listening at the clatter of the axes felling timber and other noises indicating their movements. A smattering fire commenced on the right, possibly in response to one from the enemy,) and immediately the brigade in front of which Jackson's party were quietly sitting on their horses opened fire upon them with the most fatal results. The party at this time consisted of General Jackson, who received three terrible wounds in the arm and hand, and whose horse dragged him under the bough of a tree and lacerated his face terribly. Captain Wilbourne and Lieutenant Morrison, who saved himself from being carried into the enemy's lines by his frantic horse by throwing himself to the ground and suffering severe bruises; General Hill, who saved himself by jumping to the ground and lying there till the firing was over; Colonel William H. Palmer, whose horses was killed under him; Captain Forbes, a gallant quartermaster, who was serving as a volunteer aid on Hill's staff, who was instantly killed; Major Conway Howard, whose horse carried him into the enemy's lines; Captain Murray Taylor, whose horse was killed with five bullet wounds

Dr. Hunter McGuire, in an account of Jackson's last hours, says: About daylight on Sunday morning Mrs. Jackson informed him that his recovery was very doubtful, and that it was better that he should be prepared for the worst. He was silent for a moment, and then said: "It will be infinite gain to be translated to heaven." He advised his wife in the event of his death to return to her father's house, and added: "You have a kind and good father, but there is no one so kind and good as your Heavenly Father." He still expressed a hope of his recovery, but requested her, if he should die, to have him buried in Lexington, in the Valley of Virginia. His exhaustion increased so rapidly that at 11 o'clock Mrs. Jackson knelt by his bed and told him that before the sun went down he would be with his Saviour. He replied: "Oh, no.— You are frightened, my child. Death is not so near. I may yet get well."

She fell over the bed, weeping bitterly, and told him again that the physicians said there was no hope. After a moment's pause he asked her to call me. "Doctor, Anna informs me that you have told her that I am to die to-day; is it so?" When he was answered he turned his eyes toward the ceiling and gazed for a moment or two, as if in intense thought, then replied, "Very good, very good; it is all right." He then tried to comfort his almost heart-broken wife, and told her he had a good deal to say to her, but he was too weak. Col Pendleton came into the room about one o'clock, and he asked him, "Who was preaching at headquarters to-day?" When told that the whole army was praying for him he replied, "Thank God! they are very kind." He said: "It is the Lord's day; my wish is fulfilled. I have always desired to die on Sunday." His mind now began to fall and wander, and he frequently talked as if in command upon the field, giving orders in his old way; then the scene shifted, and he was at the mess table in conversation with members of his staff; now with his wife and child; now at prayers with his military family. Occasional intervals of return of his mind would appear, and during one of them I offered him some brandy and water, but he declined it, saying, "It will only delay my departure and do no good; I want to preserve my mind to the last if possible." About half-past one he was told that he had but two hours to live, and he answered again feebly but firmly: "Very good; it is all right." A few moments before he died he cried out in his delirium: "Order A. P. Hill to prepare for action!" "Pass the infantry to the front rapidly!" "Tell Major Hawks"— then stopped, leaving the sentence unfinished. Presently a smile of ineffable sweetness spread itself over his pale face, and he said quietly and with an expression as if of relief.— "Let us cross over the river and rest under the shade of the trees;" and then, without pain or the least struggle, his spirit passed from earth to the God who gave it.

Vice President Wilson.

A CORPSE IN THE CAPITOL

THE LAST SAD SCENE.

WASHINGTON, November 22.—Vice President Wilson died in the Vice President's room, at the Capitol, at twenty minutes after 7 o'clock this morning. His demise was quite unexpected, and a shock even to those who had been with him during his illness. Yesterday he passed a quiet day. A number of visitors called to see him, and he chatted pleasantly with them. During his illness he had been in receipt of a number of letters from all sections of the country, and he seemed to take great interest in reading and commenting upon such expressions of regard and anxiety concerning his health. Yesterday, when Dr. Baxter called, he warned him against all mental excitement, and forbade him reading letters, much to the Vice-President's dissatisfaction.

HIS CONDITION LAST NIGHT.

Shortly after three o'clock yesterday he fell into a peaceful slumber, from which he awoke quite refreshed at seven o'clock, and talked cheerfully with the attendants in the room. At eight o'clock he was advised of the death of Senator Ferry, of Connecticut. This seemed to oppress him, and before retiring for the night he alluded to the matter several times.

At half-past nine o'clock he retired. His sleep was quite sound and peaceful. About three o'clock this morning his rest was disturbed by a pain in the chest, of which he complained. Mr. Ford, one of the Capitol policemen, who was in attendance, rubbed the affected parts with an anodyne, which had been prescribed by Dr. Baxter, which gave him relief. He again fell into a profound slumber.

PARTICULARS OF HIS DEATH.

At 7 o'clock this morning precisely the Vice President awoke, and in response to inquiries of attendants replied that he had slept very soundly and felt very much refreshed.— He sat up in bed and took a glass of the bitter water prescribed for him by Dr. Baxter, and shortly afterwards arose from his bed and moved about the room. One of the attendants, Mr. F. A. Wood, of the Capitol police, was in the room with him when he observed, about fifteen minutes past 7 o'clock a change in the Vice President's condition.— He was then lying in bed and drawing short and hurried breaths, and moving about uneasily, his limbs twitching convulsively. Mr. Wood immediately called Captain E. D. Town, of the Capitol police, and telling him that the Vice President was worse, asked him to send a messenger immediately for Dr. Baxter and another for Dr. C. M. Ford, residing on Capitol Hill. This was done by Captain Town, who then joined Mr. Wood. Approaching the bed, Captain Town noticed that each breath of the Vice President grew shorter and weaker, and as he stepped around the side of the bed to support his head, he gave one long gasp, and expired at twenty minutes past 7 o'clock.

12/25/75 Washingtonian

Earthquake at Richmond, Va.

*Two Distinct Shocks— Rocking of Build-
ings— Alarm of the Inhabitants— an Exceptional Phenomenon.*

RICHMOND, Va., December 22.—A shock,
supposed to have been an earthquake, occurred here at 11.40 P. M. and lasted about ten
seconds, and was felt all over the city. The
shock was quite severe, shaking buildings
and causing many people to rush into the
streets to ascertain the cause.

RICHMOND, Va. December 22.—The shock
felt here at 11.40 lasted ten seconds, and was
quickly followed by another briefer and not so
severe, the last by a concussion in the air,
a smothered sound. The guests at the different hotels were so alarmed from the
rocking of the buildings are to
assemble in the parlors en disha-
bille ready to leave. The alarm was general,
the shock being felt in all parts of the city,
and citizens leaving their domicills in fright
and haste. Crowds gathered at prominent
points to discuss the matter, and a general
state of inquietude exists, many fearing a
recurrence of a phenomena exceptionally singular in this region. An extensive earthquake occured in Louisa county, fifty miles
off over forty years since, but none nearer
here. The vibration appeared to be from
south to north. The shock was felt in Man-
chester, across the River.

Many persons attribute the shock to an explosion at Clover Hill coal mines, thirteen miles
south of Richmond. If such is the case the
explosion must have been an extraordinary
one to have been so perceptibly felt here.

From Richmond Dispatch.

Excitement and Dismay among the People.

About 11 45 o'clock last night three severe
and distinct shocks as of earthquake were
felt in all parts of the city, and created great
consternation. Thousands of people who
were peacefully slumbering at the time were
aroused by the rattling of window-panes and
the trembling of their houses, and awoke in
great fright. The sensation lasted for about
twenty or thirty seconds, and began with a
slight rocking, which rapidly increased until
houses swayed to and fro and the earth seemed slipping from beneath the feet of those
who were on the street.

A gentleman who was quietly sitting smoking his pipe in his chamber in the western
portion of the city says he heard the rumbling noise as if of some heavy vehicle passing on the macadamized street, before he felt

THE QUIVERING SENSATION.

Then he heard the rattling of the window-
panes and the floor began to shiver, producing an unpleasant sensation, like he experienced when standing on the Supreme Court-
room floor the moment before it gave way
with such terrible destruction of human lives.
This gentleman states that looking at the
head-board of the bed in the room he clearly
perceived it vibrating like a pendulum. There
were three shocks, the two last running into
each other, not sharp or sudden, but coming
on rather slowly, swelling in force and then
quickly dying out. The gentleman ran to his
window and opened it, and almost simultaneously several other windows were raised. He
asked, "What is the matter?" and a gentleman from across the street responded, "It is
an earthquake. What shall we do?" Even
at that time the earth seemed hardly settled.
Every voice that was heard conveyed the impression of fright and of some dreaded

CATASTROPHE IMPENDING.

RICHMOND, Va., December 23.—A short
time after the cessation of earthquake shocks
last night the streets were thronged with
frightened and excited people. Many made
their way to the newspaper and telegraph
offices to learn the extent of the phenomena,
while others of more nervous temperaments
remained in the streets for hours, not daring
to re-enter their houses for fear of a repetition of the shocks. But the remainder of the
night passed off without further disturbance.
To day this remarkable epoch in Richmond's
history was the general topic of conversation,
it being discussed in all its phases, each one
having their own experience to relate. Telegrams from various points in Virginia report
shocks similar to those felt here. In some
places a greater number of shocks are reported than in others.

The shock was felt distinctly in Baltimore
Alexandria, Washington and in the section
of country along the Atlantic coast, as far
South as Weldon, North Carolina. It was
distinctly felt in Leesburg.

(Aforementioned Louisa County was the
center of a small but newsworthy tumbler
just a few years ago.)

WASHINGTONIAN.

LEESBURG, LOUDOUN COUNTY, VA.

SATURDAY, FEBRUARY 5, 1876.

CHICKEN STEALING.—There have been more chickens stolen in this town and vicinity, within the last week or two than was ever known before in one season. To name the parties who have lost their chickens would be to give the names of many of the housekeepers in some parts of the town. The rogues have reduced the practice to a profession, and with devilish daring and skill, they have taken whole coops, and cleaned out the hen houses, without leaving a single one to tell the tale of its departed companions. Mrs. White. Mrs. Henderson and Pancoast, and others, whose names we did not learn, on the Southeast square of Loudoun street, have lost all they had. In the country, convenient to town, we have heard of frequent depredations of this kind.

———

CHICKEN THIEF ARRESTED.—Our vigilant police officer, B. F. Head, on Wednesday night, arrested a colored man, named Lawson Taylor, upon the charge of stealing chickens—two of Mrs. Henderson's chickens were found in his possession. He resisted the officers, but was compelled to succumb. He was carried before Justice Powell on Thursday, examined and found guilty, and sentenced to jail three months for resisting the officer, and thirty lashes for stealing the chickens. It is suspected that he is one of the leaders of those who have been recently playing havoc with the chickens of the town. We hope the others may be caught.

———

ON Saturday night, a colored boy, stole a cap from Mr. Bassell's store, and a belt from Mr. J. A. Hammerly's store. He was arrested, tried before Justice Edward Powell, sentenced to be flogged, ten lashes for the first, and fifteen for the last offence.

Mr. J. W. Hammerly, jr., had stolen, on Saturday night, from his new clothing store, opposite Reamer's Hotel, a new coat. The thief made his escape—but he is known.

2/10/76 Mirror

Pt. of Rocks Turnpike.

MR. EDITOR—The Point of Rocks and Leesburg road, during most of this winter, has been either a mortar bed, or line of frozen ruts—either too muddy, or too rough, and all the time a hard road to travel.

The many who use it to market, to court, to church and post-office, suffered such annoyance in loss of time, and temper, in wear and tear of wagon, carriages and teams—not to name the extra profanity it occasioned—that very little clear gain could result from either market or church.

(Today, this is heavily traveled Route 15.)

2/10/76 Mirror

COMMUNICATED.

MR. EDITOR—Having had occasion on Monday afternoon to go to the jail, I found this state of things:

There are two rooms on the South side of the jail, about ten by twelve feet, separated by a partition of two inch boards, but communicating with each other by a door. They have gratings looking into the corridor that separates the Northern from the Southern half of the jail, and each has a grated window looking into the jail yard: the privy is in the eastern room; the stove in the Western one. The beds are ticks filled with straw, and the covering is composed of blankets. The prisoners were asked where they slept. The answer was, "On the floor in this room." The question was put, "Why do you not sleep in the other room?" The answer came, "It is too cold there; it is sometimes too cold here."

Now, in this room were confined two white men, one convicted and the other held for trial; five negro men, two of them held for trial, three convicted.

This state of things may suit our Board of Supervisors, but its continuance will not rebound to the credit of the County of Loudoun.

A VISITOR.

The corresponding half of the jail is occupied by a lunatic, and his rooms are warmed by a drum from the dining room of the jailor.

2/17/76 Mirror

TURNING THE TABLES ON "CRUSADERS."
—One of the heaviest cases of turning a
joke" that we ever knew took place yesterday, at Herndon, Fairfax county, on the W.
& O. railroad. Yesterday morning a party
of nine females, consisting of Mrs. Switzer,
Mrs. Brady, Mrs. Ridout, Mrs. Charles Burton, Mrs. Leanord, Misses Laura Burton,
Burbank and Williams, and one who is described us a "wash woman" (white wash?)
called at the saloon of Mr. Amos Fox, for
the purpose of praying him out. While
they were going on with their devotions Mr.
Fox quietly made fast all his windows and
doors, and slipping out himself, securely
locked the crusading party in. A tremendous excitement was the consequence. The
women, of course found the situation unpleasant, as their prayers were in a measure
wasted, and it grew more and more so as
hour after hour wore by, and Mr. Fox remained deaf to their entreaties to be released, and uninfluenced by the offers of their
husbands to ransom them. Mr. Fox required them to take the oath, before he
would consent to release them, and they did
in fact give him their word not to interfere
with him or his business, again, and the
husbands of the married ones agreed to execute bonds for their future good behavior
The negotiations for release lasted *nine
hours* during all of which time Mr. Fox held
them prisoners- *Alexandria Sentinel of Monday.*

To Those Whom it May Con-
cern :

INASMUCH as Mr. R. H. TAYLOR is trying,
by threats of prosecution, to prevent the
sale and use of the Iron Plows made by us on
the ground that they are infringements of
his rights,—this is to give notice, that we are
ready at any time, to answer Mr. TAYLOR's
charges, when called to do so before the proper tribunal; and to abide its decision. Until
then, we will continue to make and sell our
plows and castings, and will on demand, fully
indemnify all dealers and purchasers for any
loss sustained at the hands of said Taylor on
such account.
Respectfully,
LOUDOUN MANF'G COMPANY,
JNO. MILTON, President.
JNO. R. SMITH, Treasurer.
Feb. 10-tf.

3/16/76 Mirror

"ALL'S WELL THAT ENDS WELL."—A
few weeks ago we announced the arrest in
Georgetown, by Sheriff Barrett, of this
county, of Mr. S. T. UNDERWOOD, and his
return to Loudoun, upon a criminal charge
of seduction under promise of marriage.—
The case was called at the last term of the
County Court, and continued, the prisoner
giving bail for his appearance. On Monday, at the present term of the Court, the
case was again called, and all things being
ready, was proceeded with, Lee for the prosecution, and Messrs. Janney, Kilgour, and
Clarence Thomas for the defense.

A jury was empannelled, and a number
of witnesses examined, prominent among
whom was the fair Duleine, who sought the
vengeance of the law to punish her truant
lover. After several hours spent in listening to the details of a case, the like
of which is becoming quite frequent
in our courts, its further hearing was
laid over until Tuesday morning, the accused being, in the meantime, committed
to jail. Tuesday morning his counsel were
confident of a verdict of acquittal. But not
so the unfortunate accused—who seems to
have regarded his personal liberty of too
much importance to be entrusted to the
uncertain verdict of twelve men and he accordingly had another process served by the
Clerk of the Court, requiring the benefit of
clergy. So when the case was once more
called in Court a statement was made to the
following effect:

In Leesburg, on Tuesday morning, March
14, 1876, in the parlor at the jail, by Rev. R.
T. Davis, Mr. S. T. UNDERWOOD and ANNIE
B. GANT —all of Loudoun

Whereupon, by instruction from the *groom,*
his counsel entered the fact of marriage as a
bar to further proceedings, and the case was
dismissed.

2/17/76 Mirror

THE WHISKY RING—BABCOCK ON TRIAL.
—The trial of Gen. Babcock, private Secretary to President Grant, charged with complicity in the infamous whiskey rings of the West, whereby the Treasury of the United States has been defrauded out of an immense amount of revenue, was begun in St. Louis on Monday, the 7th of February.

The testimony of the prosecution is not yet all in, but so far twenty-four witnesses have been called, six of them to prove the general fact of a conspiracy, and four intended to connect Babcock directly with it.

3/6/76 Washingtonian

STARTLING REVELATION.

A MEMBER OF THE CABINET CAUGHT

W. W Belknap, Secretary of War, Accused of a High Crime and Misdemeanor—An Appeal for Mercy.

HIS IMPEACHMENT BY THE HOUSE

Special Dispatch to the Gazette

WASHINGTON, March 1.—The profoundest sensation that has startled this country since the firing on Fort Sumter will follow to-morrow when the committee on expenditures in the War Department reports to the House that W. W. Belknap, Secretary of War, has been found guilty, on his own confession, of a high crime and misdemeanor. The facts are these :

A Mr. Marsh, of New York, appeared yesterday before the committee aforesaid, in obedience to a subpoena served on him last Saturday, and testified that he had obtained a contract to post traderships at Fort Sill and other army posts in the Southwest, for which he paid the wife of Secretary Belknap $10,000 cash, and $6,000 per annum as long as he held the same—three years. To day Secretary Belknap was notified of what had transpired, and was requested to appear before the committee, which he did. The testimony of Mr. Marsh was read to him, and he did not attempt a defense, but confessed that the statements of Marsh were all and singular true. He begged mercy at the hands of the committee, and asked that he might be allowed to resign and no proceedigns further taken in the matter. To this not even the Republican members of the committee were inclined to listen. The whole transaction is so damna-

ble, and the evidence so perfectly overwhelming, that any suppression of the facts would be certain and eternal infamy to all who were privy to any such an arrangement.

3/23/76 Mirror

THE WASHINGTON SCANDAL.—Ever since the unearthing of Belknap's shortcomings, scarcely a day passes that some one else, either holding high official position under the Government, or who is regarded as one of the leaders of public sentiment in the country, is implicated in the game of addition, division and silence, until the whole atmosphere about Washington, is impregnated with the disagreeable smell of corruption—and the very garments of the President himself are tainted with the odor of "bad egg."

The Post Office Department is being investigated for fraud in awarding contracts to straw bidders,—the Emma Mine Scandal, the Alaska Fur Trade Company : the Navy Department,—the letting of contracts for furnishing tombstones for the Soldiers' graves;—the Government Printing Office, which is said to be run at a cost 50 per cent above what the work would cost in private hands;—the Interior Department, the sale of West Point Cadetships for $3,000 by a member of Congress, and the gross and palpable frauds of the war-department, known to every body, constitute a few of the many "irregularities" which are now undergoing investigation by the various committees of the House of Representatives, developing a mass of corruption and rottenness in the administration of affairs, almost unprecedented in any government, and which are a disgrace to the national character, and a sad commentary on our republican institutions.

(Grant is generally regarded today as a good general but a poor president, mainly due to the corruption in his administration. Although likable and honest himself, he seemed deficient in judging the character of associates and subordinates.)

5/4/76 Mirror

THE CENTENNIAL EXHIBITION commences in Philadelphia on Wednesday next, the 10th of May. All the arrangements for the Exhibition have been completed, and they are as ample as they are magnificent. At a meeting of the Board of Commissioners on Saturday, it was decided that throughout the Exposition, the buildings and the grounds should be closed on Sundays.

5/4/76 Mirror

MOSBY ON HOUSE-BURNERS — The correspondent of the Boston Advertiser having sent a telegram to that paper, saying that Capt. Sam Chapman had been concerned in the massacre of thirty Union soldiers during the war, Col. Mosby had authorized the same person to send another dispatch, saying, "that whatever Chapman did was under his order, and he has no apology to make for it, and moreover, that if he or any of his men are ever caught burning dwelling houses in New England, as there were by Chapman in Virginia, that they will expect to be hung or shot on the spot : and that if he should ever catch anybody from Boston burning dwelling houses in Virginia over the heads of defenseless women and children they may expect to share the same fate. It seems that in August, 1864, General Custer was camped near Berryville, and sent out a squadron of cavalry with orders to burn the dwelling houses in that vicinity. Colonel Mosby sent Chapman in pursuit of them with orders "to shoot on the spot" all he caught in the act of burning dwelling houses. Chapman followed their track, which was lighted by the blaze of the burning homes of the citizens of Clarke. Many of the men who were with him passed by the smoking ruins of their own homes and witnessed the agony of their mother and sisters driven out in the world without a shelter, and they swore bloody vows of revenge. They overtook the party of burners at the house of Col. Morgan, which was then on fire, and from which the occupants had just been driven. Chapman's men charged them with a yell and both sides fought with the savage fury of men who knew no quarter was to be given. These are the facts, and Chapman stands vindicated in the eyes of all honorable men.

5/4/76 Mirror

THE custom of appointing young lawyers to defend pauper criminals received a back set, the other day, in our District Court.— His honor Judge Noonan, had appointed two young lawyers to defend an old and experienced horse-thief. After inspecting his counsel for some time in silence, the prisoner rose in his place and addressed the bench : "Air them to defend me ?" "Yes, sir," said his Honor. "Both of them ?" inquired the prisoner. "Both of them," responded the Judge. "Then I plead guilty," and the poor devil took his seat and sighed heavily

6/17/76 Washingtonian

Dr. M. Moriarty Veterinary Surgeon and Trainer, having lost by fire his stables at Rock Spring Trotting Park, has perfected arrangements with Mr. Henry Fadely, whereby all horses, entrusted to him for *treatment* or *training,* will be comfortably cared for, in DRY AND WELL VENTILATED STALLS, in his stable at Leesburg. The reputation of Mr. Fadely is such that parties having horses or colts to train or break, may depend confidently upon the very best stable care and management; while their proper and thorough instruction in harness, *on the track or road,* (as may be preferred,) is in all cases guaranteed. (June 1-1t.

Killed by the Indians.

CUSTER CITY, May 25, 1876.

I am obliged to inform you of the worst news that could have fallen to my lot to write. Your generous, noble-hearted young brother Louis has been foully murdered by the Indians. He and two friends were overtaken en route to Mount City, with two wagon loads of goods. They were each shot five or six times and then scalped. They were surprised, and did not get a chance to return their fire. Louis was asleep at the time. * *

The Indians are becoming worse every day. Over a hundred white men have been killed. The Government must do something, or there will not be a white men north of Cheyenne.

6/8/76 Mirror

Mark Twain's Report of an Accident.

Mark Twain recently tried his hand at writing up a distressing accident for a Boston local paper, and this is how he said it:

"Last evening about 6 o'clock as William Schuyler, an old and respected citizen of Hyde Park, was leaving his residence to go down town, as has been his custom for many years, with the exception of only one short interval in the spring of 1850, during which he was confined to his bed by injuries received in attempting to stop a runaway horse by thoughtlessly throwing up his hands and shouting, which, even if he had done so a single moment sooner, would inevitably have frightened the animal still more instead of checking its speed, although disastrous enough to himself as it was, rendered more melancholily distressing by reason of the presence of his wife's mother, who was there and saw the occurrence, notwithstanding it is at least likely, though not necessarily so, that she should be reconnoitering in another direction when incidents occur, not being vivacious and on the lookout, as a general thing, but even in the reverse, as her mother is said to have stated, who is no more, but who died in the full hope of a blessed resurrection upward of three years ago, aged eighty-six, being a Christian woman without guile, as it were, in prosperity, in consequence of a fire in 1849, which destroyed every solitary thing she had in the world. But such is life. Let us all take warning by this solemn occurrence, and let us endeavor so to live that when we come to die we can do it. Let us place our hands upon our hearts and say with earnestness and sincerity that, from this day forth, we will beware of the intoxicating bowl."

6/29/76 Mirror

A FIGHT WITH THE SIOUX.

Nine Soldiers Killed and Twenty-one Wounded—The Indians Defeated.

A despatch has been received in Washington officially announcing a serious fight with the Sioux Indians. The despatch states that there was a sharp fight on Rose bud Creek, a branch of the Yellowstone in Montana, in which Gen. Crook's loss was nine men killed and twenty-one wounded.

6/8/76 Mirror

A DEADLY STROKE--A MAN AND FIVE HORSES KILLED BY LIGHTNING.—Last Saturday morning, Mr. Michael L. Hunter, a thrifty farmer, living near Morrisonville, in this county, took a load of wheat to Hamilton depot, driving his five horse team. Upon his return in the afternoon he was overtaken by the severe storm that then raged, and just as he reached his own home, and was in the act of turning into his barn yard, he was struck by lightning, and himself and every horse attached to the wagon, instantly killed. One who saw him after death, informs us that the bolt seemed to have struck Mr. Hunter on the head, tearing his hat into fragments, and ran down his face, body and left limb into the ground under the saddle horse. The horses had no marks upon them, and died without a struggle. The wagon was uninjured, but a butter firkin in the wagon was demolished.

Mr. Hunter was an industrious, enterprising man, about forty years of age, and leaves a wife and eight children to mourn his sudden and terrible death.

We also learn that a negro man, employed at Janney's Mill, in Hillsborough was so severely stunned by lightning the same evening, that he did not get over it for a day or two.

6/29/76 Mirror

BOARD OF SUPERVISORS —COUNTY LEVY— IMPORTANT ORDER, &c. At the annual meeting of the Board of Supervisors on Thursday

It was also ordered, that for medical attention rendered paupers, outside the poor house, physicians shall be allowed $1.50 for each visit, including prescription and medicine, when in the country, and 75 cents in town,—and that in all cases their accounts must be approved by the Overseer of the Poor in their respective districts.

THE CHAIN GANG.

The following order will be read with interest, as a new departure in a good direction—

Ordered, That the Sheriff of this county be directed to procure six balls and chains, with the necessary fastenings, for the use of the chain gang established in this county; said balls and chains to be placed in the charge of the jailor, when procured; that all persons required to work on the chain gang, shall work for the period of ten hours a day, that being a day's work recognized by this board; that all persons working on said chain gang shall be returned to the custody of the jailor by the party employing them, at the end of each day; that the charge for each person working on the chain gang, shall be fifty cents per day, to be paid to the county by the person or party employing the convicts; and that the jailor be allowed by this Board ten cents per head daily, for all convicts taken from the jail for work.

192

THE CINCINNATI CONVENTION.

THE PRESIDENTIAL TICKET.

6/22/76 Mirror

The republican National Convention, which met in Cincinnati on Wednesday last, adjourned on Friday evening, after having nominated the following ticket: For President, RUTHERFORD B. HAYES, of Ohio; For Vice President, WM. A. WHEELER, of New York.

Their three days session was marked by a good deal of excitement, and a vast deal of wire-pulling. Upon the assembling of the Convention, the three most formidable candidates were, Blaine, Morton and Conkling, with the chances decidedly in favor of Blaine. But when it was discovered on the first two or three ballots, that Blaine was about to distance the other two, a combination was effected between the friends of the latter, which on the 7th ballot resulted in the choice of Hayes.

6/29/76 Mirror

THE ST. LOUIS CONVENTION.—The Democratic National Convention met in St. Louis on Tuesday. At this writing we are without advices as to its action. For the past week, and even up to the day of its assembling, speculation has been rife as to its results, but so complicated and uncertain have been the signs of the times, that we are unable even to conjecture what a day will bring forth.

There is no doubt that Tilden has a stronger following to start with than either of his competitors for the nomination, and if the two-thirds rule was rescinded, he might possibly get the nomination on the first ballot. But whether the rule is rescinded or not, unless he is strong enough to win on the first heat, he will probably lose the race, notwithstanding John Morrissey, on Monday morning, bet ten thousand dollars that Tilden would be nominated.

After Tilden comes, Hancock, Hendricks, and Thurman, with a strong possibility that some as yet "unknown" man, may bear off the prize. It is too late, however, now, to indulge in speculations; we may, even before we go to press, be able to announce the St Louis ticket—and believing that whoever compose it will be men of honesty and purity of character,

THE MIRROR

BENJ. F. SHEETZ Editor.

Thursday Morning, July 6.

FOR PRESIDENT,
SAMUEL J. TILDEN,
OF NEW YORK.
FOR VICE-PRESIDENT,
THOMAS A. HENDRICKS,
OF INDIANA.

"OUR FLAG IS THERE."—The National Conventions of the two great political parties of this country having been held and the nominees of each given to the people the canvass for 1876, may be regarded as fully inaugurated, and from now until the 7th of November, the work will be active and warm. While the nominee of the Cincinnati Convention, is a *better man for the Presidency than* Morton, Conkling or Blaine would have been; it is yet a fact patent to everybody, that Mr. HAYES was only caught up when the chances for each of the above had grown desperate, and his nomination was purely the result of a combination to defeat the triumph of BRISTOW, a better man than all of them put together. Mr. Hayes was nominated because of his amiable disposition, his negative qualities and his comparative obscurity, qualities which the conspirators well knew, the better fitted him for a pliant tool in their hands; and whose administration, if elected, could be run in the same radical groove that Grant's has been. As a candidate he is emphatically the creature of Grant, Morton, Conkling, Blaine and Company. As his bed has been made, let him occupy it.

7/13/76 Mirror

WAR WITH THE INDIANS.

Wholesale Slaughter of Federal Troops—General Custer and Two Brothers Killed — Five Companies of Cavalry Exterminated.

Official advices have been received in Washington confirming the reports of a bloody fight on the Little Horn River, in Montana Territory, between five companies of United States soldiers under Gen. Custer, and an encampment of Sioux Indians commanded by Sitting Bull.

On the 25th of June, after a forced march of several days, Gen. Custer came upon the main camp of Sitting Bull, and without waiting for reinforcements, which he knew were coming, he attacked with five companies, the Indians, who are supposed to have numbered between 3000 and 4000. The fight lasted about four hours, and resulted in the entire massacre of General Custer, his two brothers, nephew, and brother-in-law and about three hundred men. Only thirty-one were wounded. Two hundred and seven were buried in one place.

General Custer found the Indian camp of twenty-five lodges on Little Horn, and immediately attacked it with five companies, charging into the thickest of the camp. Nothing is known of the operations of this detachment after the charges, as they were only traced by their dead. Major Reno attacked the lower part of the camp with the seven remaining companies.

The Indians surrounded Reno's seven companies and held them in the Hills one day away from water. General Terry's command then came in sight, and the Indions broke camp and left in the night. The remnant of the Seventh cavalry and Gibbon's command returned to the mouth of the Little Horn river, where there is a steamboat. The Indians got the arms of the killed soldiers. Seventeen commissioned officers were killed. The whole of General Custer's family died at the head of the column.

Many of the men found dead on Custer's field were horribly mutilated, and most had their skulls smashed by stone mallets. This was the work of the squaws, who swarmed to the battle field robbing and mutilating the bodies of the dead and killing the dying and wounded. There were in Custer's regiment when he went into battle 585 men and 26 officers. Of these 40 men were killed with Reno and 51 wounded.

7/20/76 Mirror

A Fearful Scene on the Battlefield—Horrible Mutilation of the Soldiers' Bodies—Sitting Bull Killed.

NEW YORK, July 14.—A Detroit dispatch says Lieutenant John Carland, of company B, 6th infantry, with General Gibbons' command, writes as follows concerning the slaughter of the 9th cavalry and General Custer. The letter is dated "Mouth of the Little River, June 29."

"Major Reno was to attack the enemy in the rear while Custer fought them in front. This would have worked all right, as Reno had got in their rear, but General Custer, marching down on the other side, saw what he supposed was the front of the camp, and made a charge on them, the Indians giving way and letting him right in the gap. The brave man rode in with his three hundred men, and would have killed the whole two thousand Sioux, I believe, if there had been no enemy behind him. But instead of charging the front he was right in the center of between three thousand and four thousand Sioux. Those that were behind him kept concealed until he was right in their midst, and then, when it was too late, he made a bold dash, trying to cut through them; but the enemy were too many.

"He fell about the first one and the horses becoming unmanageable the poor soldiers were cut down in less time than it takes to tell.

"The Sioux then turned with all their force upon Major Reno. He charged them with one company and returned with only eleven men. He then retreated a short distance, placing his men on a bluff. Out of the whole regiment only 328 men are left, and 40 of them are badly wounded.

"It makes one's heart sick to look over the battle ground and see the poor fellows. Some of them with their entrails cut out, others with their eyes dug out, and hearts laid across their face. They even stopped to cut their pockets to get their money and watches. The most fearful sight was Colonel Cook. He was a splendid looking man with long dark whiskers. They dug his face all out so as to get his fine beard, it is supposed. They did not disfigure General Custer in any way, but his brother, Tom Custer, was opened and his heart taken out.

"We estimate the loss of the enemy at 500, though it is hard to tell how many were killed, as they carried most of them away.

"Sitting Bull was killed, also a white man named Milburn, Sitting Bull's chief adviser.

Wrong about Sitting Bull — He was killed in 1890 by Indian police at the Standing Rock Reservation.

7 /27/76 Mirror

The War with the Indians—Preparations for the Conflict—Views of Gen. Sherman—A Stubborn and Bloody Campaign in Prospect—The Situation at Present.

WASHINGTON, July 23.—Great activity prevails at army headquarters in forwarding troops and supplies to the scene of war in the mountains of the Big Horn. Gen. Sherman, by judicious distribution of the troops doing duty on the Atlantic seaboard, has been able, notwithstanding the limited forces at his command, to respond to the calls of Gen. Sheridan for more troops. This will enable him to renew the operations of the army in the savage country with increased vigor and prompt and decisive results. The last of the detachments are now on their way westward. In the meantime Lieut. Gen. Sheridan reports from Chicago that everything is progressing satisfactorily, and will be in shape for a resumption of active operations in a few weeks.

According to the official intelligence received at headquarters here, as soon as the necessary preparations are made and supplies forwarded the general will take charge and superintend the operations of the troops in person, as he did in his eminently successful winter campaign of 1868 and '69 against the Cheyennes, Kiowas, Arrapahoes and Comanches, between the Platte and the Red river of the South. General Sherman will remain in Washington directing the general movements of the troops.

In speaking of the war Gen. Sherman says it will be stubborn and bloody; that the Indian chieftains will naturally have the choice of positions; that to fight them it will be necessary to take them when they offer or wherever caught; that they will not fight if they can help it unless they have the advantage of ground and numbers, and as a consequence we must suffer losses. He says that Crook and Terry have no superiors as Indian fighters, and if they get a fair chance they will make it warm for the warriors of the Big Horn. He estimates the fighting force of the Sioux now in arms at twenty-five hundred. It is the settled purpose to make the punishment of the Sioux one never to be forgotten by that yet powerful portion of our aboriginal population.

8/3/76 Mirror

BISHOP WHIPPLE—HIS VIEW OF THE CUSTER MASSACRE—Bishop Whipple, while riding across his diocese on the cars, has dashed off a characteristic letter on the Little Big Horn massacre. He seems to apprehend that the public is not in the mood for hearing a good word for the Indians, and that his strictures upon the course of the Government will be received with impatience. The venerable Bishop need never fear that he will be accused of a cowardly dread of public opinion. He is one of the noblest souls in the Northwest, and has at heart the interests of his fellow-men, red and white. He regards the degradation, the hate, and the treachery of the Indians as the result of a policy which has recognized them as independent nations, made treaties with them, and then violated them. He contrasts the sickening harvest of blood that has been reaped with the quietude and prosperity of the Indian subjects of the Dominion of Canada. "We left," he says, "the Indian without government. We placed them where no white men could live by cultivation of the soil. We established vast alm houses. Whenever any Indian became an outlaw or Ishmaelite we allowed him to escape to Sitting Bull. For months war has been imminent : the army, the agents, the friends of the Indians, have all spoken words of warning ; that unless we took steps to avert it we should have one of the most terrible Indian wars in our history.— No one heeded the warning. Congress spent months in wrangling over the appropriations at a time when the Indians on the Missouri were living on half rations. We have placed them where they must be fed, or they will have to steal or starve. It would almost seem as if by the violation of our treaty, by the withholding of supplies, we wanted to force all the Sioux into war. Our brave troops have been murdered, not by Custer's rashness, not by bad orders ; not by savage Indians but by a nation which, after one hundred years of trial, persists in a policy which sows blunders and crimes and reaps massacre and war."

Washington. Aug. 21, 1876.

WHO EQUIPPED THE SIOUX FOR WAR. —A correspondent writes to the N. Y. *Herald* a long letter from "Camp on the Rosebud," August 14th, in the course of which he pretty broadly intimates that the present administration, through its Indian Agencies, in which Orville Grant, a brother of the President, is "a chief partner," has for several years been furnishing Sitting Bull with the sinews of war, notwithstanding the remonstrances at the War Department, by the officers in command. He says:

Time permitting, I hasten to get down a few more facts for the consideration of the public. They are hastily collected scraps of information from reliable sources. It is not generally known that about a year ago the government bought and presented to the Sioux some 250 horses, which cost each $125, and if any one doubts it he has only to refer to the files of the Omaha papers and read the advertisements from the Interior Department. Sitting Bull, though notoriously hostile, has been for years allowed to provide himself with ammunition at the Fort Peak Agency, in which Casselberry, Bonnafin and Orvelle Grant are or were chief partners.

The steamboat Durfee, when ordered to bring troops up the Yellowstone, had on board immense quantities of arms and ammunition consigned to Messers. Powers & Co., at Fort Benton. It is useless to say these munitions of war were not intended for the Sioux, because Powers has been for years trading with this tribe, and it is said any one known to be a friend or agent of this house can pass safely through Sitting Bull's camp. Captain Hughes, of Terry's staff, found these munitions on board at Bismarck. He telegraphed to the War Department for permission to seize them, but it seems the military authorities can find no legal means of preventing traders supplying Indians with war material even when they are engaged in active hostilities against the United States. Two years ago an energetic officer, who was sent to Stockton from the Platte, met a train going to the the hostile Indians with 200 Winchester rifles and 80,000 rounds of ammunition, and stopped the train and telegraphed to Washington for instruction. He was surprised at receiving orders to let the train go on its way. Army officers are tired protecting

against the outrage of arming the savages with the most approved arms, when it is notorious that they are used chiefly, if not wholly, to murder unoffending citizens or to shoot down the soldiers of the United States.

(Not mentioned is the probability that George Custer was one of the "reliable sources" quoted. He was called to Washington to testify in the spring of 1876 and supplied hearsay evidence concerning Orville Grant and others. Understandably, President Grant refused to see him. Without orders, he petulantly left Washington to rejoin his unit and only the efforts of Generals Sheridan and Terry prevented him from being arrested.

Many soldiers in the 7th U.S. Calvary were not as enamored with Custer as were the New York newspapers. One fellow officer later remarked "I'm only too proud to say that I despised him.")

UNFORTUNATE.—The Acqueduct bridge at Georgetown, is said to have been in an unsafe condition for sometime past, and on Tuesday morning an accident occurred which resulted seriously to a citizen of this county. The despatch says:

Mr. Gill Furr, of Loudoun county, Va., drove over the bridge with sixty head of cattle, and while in the act of turning the bend from the Virginia side he heard a crash, and in less time than it takes to describe the scene, half his cattle were precipitated into the canal below. The remaining cattle stampeded and rushed back toward the Virginia side of the bridge. The unfortunates, twenty-six in number, struggled in the water and made the effort to get on the district side of the canal, but only two of the number succeeded in crossing safely.

In the 1840's, largely from the pressure of various merchants, the Aqueduct Bridge was built to accommodate canal boats from the C&O Canal in Georgetown to the Alexandria Canal downriver. In the Civil War, it was drained and used by the troops. Despite several changes, time took its toll, and it was closed in 1917.

9/7/76 Mirror

THE POLE RAISING ON SATURDAY.—In accordance with previous announcement, quite a large number of persons from the surrounding country, assembled in Leesburg, on Saturday afternoon, to assist in the labor of hoisting the pole prepared by the Tilden and Hendricks Club of this District.

The work was begun about 2½ o'clock, and for three hours the work was slow, tedious and uncertain—owing to the fact that it had to be elevated to an angle of about forty-five degrees, almost by main strength, before the ropes could be brought to bear upon it. In less than a half-hour, however, after the ropes took effect, the pole was placed in position, a beautiful streamer, 17 feet long, streaming from its mast, bearing upon its folds in bold, black letters, painted on either side, the talismanic words

TILDEN, HENDRICKS & REFORM. Directly thereafter, a national flag, 20×13 feet, emblazoned with stars, representing each of the present States and Territories, was run up amid the wild huzzas of the assembled multitude. Special credit is due to Messrs. Jos. L. Norris, Capt. Geo. R. Head, Thos. B. Cockey, and Wm. P. Smith, assisted by Mr. C. W. Hammerly and Mr. Samuel Boyd, of Woodgrove, for the safe and successful erection of the pole. And to-day it stands 106 feet above the ground, a very thing of beauty, commanding the admiration of all who behold it. It is planted on Market street, about mid-way between the Court-house and the Clerk's office.

The Leesburg Brass Band was present, during the afternoon, and enlivened the occasion with excellent music.

9/7/76 Mirror

FREDERICK DOUGLAS, jr., (colored) publishes a letter in the Washington Chronicle, on the causes of the troubles in the South, in which he says.

"I am not at all surprised at the State of affairs in the Southern States among the colored people when I take into consideration the class of white Republicans who have misled them ever since they became citizens, for their own selfish ends.—The colored people of the South have been made to believe from the start by their pretended Republican friends that there was money in politics, so much so that it has been impossible in very many instances to get good, honest colored men in office, because they could not be used to wink at whatever white Republicans might do that was corrupt. The most illiterate, unprincipled colored men are generally chosen for office by the white Republicans of the South because they are easier to manipulate. White men have been elected to office by negro votes who scarcely had a second shirt on their backs before being installed in office: a few months later they are sporting fine horses, gold watches and chains, smoking fine cigars, and purchasing fine dwellings, traveling, &c. The black man notices this, and immediately makes up his mind that the next time he is asked to vote he must receive something, if not he must have an office, whether competent or not."

9/14/76 Mirror

GEN. WADE HAMPTON is represented as having recently asserted on the stump in South Carolina: "The South did not fight for slavery in the late war. Gen. Robert E. Lee told me whatever way the war ended the colored people would be free."

September, 1876

9/7/76 Mirror

MAKING THE BIG BRIDGE

The work on the great bridge yesterday consisted in moving the new working rope from the "traveller" to the upper ends of the towers and anchorage. This was done by blocking it up on the towers, and then pushing it on to greased planks, down which it slipped into position. The wire at the Brooklyn anchorage could not be moved over an upright in the yard that was used to hold an iron brace. One of the professional riggers swung out on the wire, traveled down about 150 feet, and, swinging off on the perch, lifted the rope over it as it approached him, and then catching hold of it again, climbed back on the anchorage, going hand over hand. It was expected to get the second rope over the mate to the one just spoken of—but this was postponed until to-day.

Town Ordinance.

WHEREAS, accidents are frequently occurring, and the lives of the citizens of the Town are endangered, by allowing Horses hitched to Wagons and other Vehicles,

TO STAND IN THE STREETS,

without some person to Watch Over and Attend to them.

THEREFORE, Be it Ordained by the Mayor, Recorder and Common Council of Leesburg, Va., in Council Assembled,

FIRST.—That it shall not be lawful for any person to have Standing in the Streets of the Town, any Horse, Mule or Oxen; hitched or attached to any Vehicle whatever, unless properly secured, or without some person being present to watch over and attend to them.

SECOND.—Any person violating this Ordinance shall forfeit and pay to the Corporation, not less than ONE nor more than FIVE DOLLARS, for each offence.

THIRD.—It shall be the duty of the Sergeant, when such violation shall come under his notice, to arrest the Owner or Driver of such Vehicle, and take him before the Mayor or Acting Mayor, who shall give judgment for said fine, with costs of recovery and any citizen of the town may report such violation to the Mayor or Acting Mayor, who shall forthwith issue his warrant for the arrest of such person, and give judgment for the Fine and Costs of recovery. And in case the fine and Costs, in either case, shall not be forthwith paid, the Sergeant shall take possession of the Animals and Vehicles and hold the same until the Fine, Costs of Recovery, and expenses of keeping such animals shall be paid, or until he shall be ordered by the Mayor or Acting Mayor, to release the said property.

This Ordinance shall be in force after Fifteen Days from its passage.

Passed August 25th, 1876.

GEO. R. HEAD, Mayor.

H. O. CLAGETT, Recorder

aug. 31, 1876-3t.—

MR. EDITOR—In reference to a card written by some one to fame and me unknown, and signed by W. S. Summers, Deputy Sheriff of Loudoun county, I will notice but one item, in alluding to me he says: "A man who during the late war, pandered to the enemy, of his home and friends." Now, I will say, if there is a man or woman in my neighborhood that has the slightest claim or pretension to respectability, will say that I ever entertained a thought, made a remark, or committed one single act that could result to the detriment of the Southern arms—or that I ever had a wish or desire but for the independence and success of the Southern Confederacy, I will forfeit my position in society, and say I do not deserve the notice of a single respectable person. The whole statement is an infamous and malicious lie, originating in the cowardly heart of W. S. Summers, Deputy Sheriff of Loudoun county. If this cowardly creature had have been a gentleman, our difficulty would have long since been settled, and the public would not have been annoyed by a publication from either, but it is a fact as old as time and as radiant with truth as heaven is with splendor, that a coward is a liar. W. S. Summers, Deputy Sheriff of Loudoun county, has acknowledged himself guilty of the first charge and the evidence is abundantly sufficient to convict of the latter. E. M. LOWE.

Sept. 28, 1876.-1t

AN INDIAN POW-WOW.

Spotted Tail Speaks a Speech— What the Indians Want—Previous Promises to them Unfulfilled —A Treaty Made—The Black Hills to be Surrendered to the Whites.

We stated last week that a treaty had been concluded with the Indians. Prior to the signing of the treaty, there was an Indian Pow-wow, in the course of which Spotted Tail spoke a speech full of good sense and honest truth. Col. Boone, chairman of the Commission; said—

"Mr. Friends—Seven days since we sent down some propositions to you that were submitted to the people at Red Cloud. We have come now to hear your answer and decision."

SPOTTED TAIL'S SPEECH.

Spotted Tail said : "We have come here to meet you, my friends. We have considered the words you brought us from the Great Father, and I have made up my mind. This is the fifth time words have come to us from the Great Father. At the time the first treaty was made on Horse creek there was a promise made to borrow the overland road of Indians, and though I was a boy then they told me that promise was made to last fifty years. These promises have not been kept. The next conference held was with Gen. Maynadier, when there was no promise made, but we made friends and shook hands. Then there was a treaty made by Gen. Sherman, Gen. Sanborn and Gen. Harney, when we were told we should have annuities and goods for thirty-five years. They said this, but did not tell the truth. At that time Gen. Sherman told me the country was mine and I should select any place I wished for my reservation. I said I would take the country from the head of White river to the Missouri. He said they would give us cows to raise cattle, mares to raise horses, and oxen and wagons to haul logs and goods and earn money that way. He said also there should be issues of such things as we needed to learn the arts with, and besides that money to every one. He told us, each of us should have $15 for an annuity, but I told them that was a bad amount—that we did not understand money, and that it should be $20 to each one, and he assented to that— He told me these things should be carried out, and for me to go to the mouth of the White Stone and locate my people, and these promises should be fulfilled to me.— But it was not true. When these promises failed to be carried out I went myself to see the Great Father and went to his house and told him these things. The Great Father told me to go home and select any place in my country I chose for my home, and go there and live with my people. I came home and selected this place and moved here. They told me if I would move here I should receive a fulfillment of the promises made to me, but all I got was some very small cows and some old wagons that were worn out. Again, last summer you came to talk about the country, and we said we would consider the matter. We said we would leave it to the Great Father for him to settle. In reply to that he has sent you out this summer. You have come to visit our land, and we now ask you how many years there are for us to live. My friends, you who sit before me are traders and merchants. You have not come here to turn anything out of the way without paying for it. When a man has a possession that he values and another party comes to buy it, he brings with him such good things as he wishes to purchase it with. My friends, your people have both intellect and heart. You use these to consider in what way you can do best to live. My people who are here before you are precisely the same. I see that my friends before me are men of age and dignity, and men of that kind have good judgment and consider well what they do. I infer from that that you are here to consider well what shall be good for my people for a long time to come. I think each of you has selected somewhere a good piece of land for himself with the intention to live on it, that he may there raise his children. My people are not different.— They also live upon the earth and upon things that come to them from above. We have the same thoughts and desires in that respect that the white people have. This is the country where they were born ; where they have acquired all their property, their children and their horses.

"You have come here to buy this country of us, and it would be well if you would come with the goods you propose to give us, and not to put them out of your hand so we can see the good price you propose to pay for it. Then our heart would be glad. My people have grown up together with these white men who have married into our tribe. A great many of us have learned to speak their language, and our children are with them in our school, and we want to be considered all one people with them.

"My friends when you go back to the Great Father I want you to tell him to send us goods, send us yokes, oxen, and give us wagons so we can earn money by hauling goods from the railroad. This seems to me to be a very hard day, half of our country is at war, and we have come upon very difficult times. This war did not spring up here in our land. It was brought upon us by the children of the Great Father, who came to take our land from us without price, and who do a great many evil things. The Great Father and his children are to blame for this trouble. We have here a store-house to hold our provisions, but the Great Father sends us very little provisions to put into our store-house.

And when our people became displeased with our provisions and have gone north to hunt, the children of the Great Father are fighting them. It has been our wish to live here peaceably, but the Great Father has filled it with soldiers, who think only of one death. Some of our people who have gone from here in order that they may have a change, and others who have gone north to hunt, have been attacked by soldiers from this direction, and where they have got north, have been attacked by soldiers from other directions. And now when they are willing to come back soldiers stand between them and keep them from coming home. It seems to be there is a better way than this. When people come to trouble it is better for both parties to come together without arms, talk it over, and find some peaceful way to settle. You have mentioned to me two countries. The Missouri country I know. When we were there we had a great deal of trouble. I left hundreds more people buried there. The other country I have never seen, but I agree to look at it with fifty of my young men. When this trouble commenced the Great Father stopped the sale of ammunition, which has caused great suffering to my people. Notwithstanding, we are all sincere to do what is good for your people. "My friend," pointing to Gen. Van Dever, "you are a wise man. When you was here last spring you told me you would help me. I want you to do it."

Swift Bear then said they wanted to consider until to-morrow. The propositions were read for a second time and interpreted, and the council adjourned till morning.

A TREATY CONSUMMATED.

SPOTTED TAIL AGENCY, Sept. 25th, via Sydney, Sept. 26.—A treaty with the Indians of this agency was concluded this evening, after three hours' council. Spotted Tail made another lengthy speech, in which he insisted upon going down to the Indian Territory, first looking at the country and then going to Washington to talk with the Great Father and touch the pen at the same time. He also insisted upon delay in signing the treaty until the present war was satisfactorily ended. He said:

"I wish to have two men help me: one is chief minister, pointing to Bishop Whipple and the other Rev. Mr. Hinman, to settle matters. You have words of the Great Spirit and you try to live according to his will. You know this war trouble does not please the Great Spirit, and I want you to help me rub it out. Baptiste Good said a white minister (Episcopalian) has come here to teach us, but I don't think it is done properly. I would like to have some female minister come dressed in black clothes to receive girls in one house and teach them, and have white man ministers in black hat and coat and take boys to another house and teach them properly. These ministers I want to take the names of things sent to us, and when they come to see that they are all there."

Blue Teeth, Spotted Tail's father-in-law, wanted to know who was to carry their words to the Great Father, and upon Gen. Gaylord being pointed out he handed him a handsomely decorated pipe and tobacco pouch, which he said the Great Father had given him. He told Gen. Gaylord to present them to the Great Father at Washington as from a man he heard speak at the council, and ask the Great Father to be merciful to the Indians, pity them, help them, and let them remain in their own country.

Speeches were made by other Indians, and by Judge Gaylord, Col. Boone and Bishop Whipple, but the Indians are still undecided. Spotted Tail arose and left the council room. While outside, W. Raymond, a white man living with Spotted Tail's people for the last twenty-seven years, told him if he did not sign the treaty Red Cloud would get ahead of him and derive all the advantages to be had from the treaty. Raymond then went to Red Cloud and Red Dog, of Red Cloud agency, who were outside the council room, and told them to go in and urge Spotted Tail and his people to sign. They did so, making short but effective speeches, and then withdrew, whereupon Two Strike said: "The reason we are afraid to touch the pen and are silent before you is because we have been deceived so many times before. If we knew the words you tell us were true we should be willing to sign every day."

Then Spotted Tail addressed the people, saying: "If our friends up above (referring to the Red Cloud agency) have not signed the treaty I would help them in holding out, but as our friends up there have signed I ask all good men who are trustworthy to come up and sign." Half an hour later the necessary signatures were attached and the treaty was made.

The Indians here all want the present military agents removed and Gen. Howard reinstated.

10/12/76 Mirror

TILDEN AND HENDRICKS BARBECUE AT LEESBURG, THURSDAY, OCTOBER 26th, 1876.

There will be a Tilden and Hendricks Barbecue in Mr. Vandevanter's Grove, near Leesburg, on Thursday, 26th inst., at which speeches will be made by several of the most distinguished speakers of the country. Ample provision will be made for the entertainment of all who may come.

The public is cordially invited to attend, to hear the orators and to partake of the banquet spread for the multitude, which will be there.

A number of distinguished speakers have been invited to be present, among them the Hon. D. W. VORHEES, of Indiana, and the occasion promises to be one of unusual interest.

Come one, come all, and let us have a grand rally for the cause of our country

11/2/76 Mirror

VOTE, VOTE.—Do not forget that next TUESDAY, the 7th of November, is the day of Election—the result of which may determine for years to come; the weal or the woe of this country. We have tried Republicanism for the last sixteen years, and it has brought the nation to the verge of of bankruptcy and ruin. Any change must be for the better.—Therefore, vote early and vote late, for TILDEN, HENDRICKS and REFORM.

Yellow Fever and the Frost.

MEMPHIS, TENN., Oct. 2.—There was a heavy frost here last night but it did little damage. This relieves all anxiety in regard to yellow fever here.

SAVANNAH, GA., Oct. 2.—The total number of interments to-day was 40, of which 28 were from yellow fever. Thirteen of the burials were colored. H. H. Rowland, of the firm of J. C. Rowland & Co.; Chas. H. Hitt, druggist, and W. B. Griffin died to-day.

ELMIRA, N. Y., Oct. 2.—Over $1,100 were raised in this city to-day, and forwarded to the South for the relief of yellow fever sufferers at Savannah and Brunswick.

QUEBEC, Oct. 2.—Subscription lists in aid of yellow fever sufferers of Georgia, were opened in this city to-day. Donations are coming in freely.

THE PESTILENCE IN BRUNSWICK.—The yellow fever at Brunswick, Ga. exceeds any pestilence known to history. The "Mayor pro tem." telegraphs to Mayor Latrobe as follows: "In distress; ninety per cent sick. Any help will be thankfully received." The worst accounts of the plague in Greece, the black death and the spotted plague of the seventeenth century, fall short of the horror of the Brunswick pestilence. With ninety out of every hundred down with the fever, there are not enough left to bury the dead; not a tenth enough to tend the sick. Starvation must soon add its horrors to the scene; and the unburied bodies aggregate the malignity of the disease. Let all whose hearts are not stone send aid to the sufferers.—Baltimore Gazette.

(Two years later in 1878 these pages record a more serious yellow fever epidemic in the Mississippi Valley. Surprisingly, our nation has found this disease as far north as Boston. In 1793 while our federal government was temporarily located in Philadelphia, our leaders, including Washington, had to seek higher ground or go home to avoid sickness of death. In 1900, Walter Reed and others discovered that it was mosquito born.)

10/28/76 Washingtonian

Opium Eating.

RAPID INCREASE OF THE DEADLY HABIT IN A NEW ENGLAND TOWN.

Most people know that the opium habit is increasing throughout the country, but few are aware of its alarming growth in New England. In Providence the city druggists report a more or less rapid increase in the number of their opium customers, and physicians find that female patients cannot be affected by less than four times the ordinary dose of morphine.

Many acquire the opium habit during illness, when it is taken to relieve pain; others, during great mental despondency; others, from an inherited craving for it, and others still while trying to leave of drinking liquor. Its use is not a characteristic of any one class. The contracted pupil of the eye, the sallow countenance, the placid expression, the dreamy distant look, which denotes the opium eater, are found in the workshop and factory, as well as in the counting room or the boudoir. Wealthy opium eaters buy the drug through a trusted agent, whose tongue is sealed by pay; the poor usually buy theirs covertly, in the evening, usually saying that it is for some one else.

Some try to conceal their purchase of the drug by buying in different stores, until almost the whole city has been gone over; others appear as regularly at the same place, Saturday evening as the evening comes. The wish to conceal the habit is universal, and it is never taken, as liquors are drank, in a crowd and with merry making. A grain of opium, or an eighth as much of morphine, is a dose for a beginner, but the desire and ability to take it grows so rapidly that five and even ten grains of morphine are taken in a day, perhaps in three doses.

An opium eater in Providence a few months ago ate 125 grains of opium in twenty four hours, and a woman drinks a coffee cup full of laudanum without harm. There are large number of men whose weekly purchase of opium indicates that they use about twenty-five grains a day. A novel method of taking opium is by the use of the hypodermic syringe—a tiny instrument with a needle point, which is stuck through the skin, and through which the liquid is conveyed into the blood. The effect when administered in this way is much more immediately than when taken in the usual way as a powder or in little pellets. Physicians addicted to the habit (and there is a surprising number of them) usually adopt the hypodermic method, and one doctor is known whose body is in spots scarred like the traces of small-pox from the marks of his morphine syringe.

The high cost is one hindrance to its use. Really poor people cannot afford to extensively use an article which costs $5.50 to $5.80 an ounce. Nevertheless, with the habit once formed, a man or woman will do anything to get opium that the most inveterate drunkard would do to get rum. Opium eating is, if possible, more seductive than liquor drinking, and the confirmed opium eater can have scarcely a hope of escape from its power; the victim is in misery whenever he is not under the influence of the drug.

10/19/76 Mirror

LINCOLN WORSTED IN A HORSE TRADE —When Abraham Lincoln was a lawyer in Illinois he and the judge once got to battering one another about trading horses, and it was agreed that the next morning at 9 o'clock they should make a trade, the horses to be unseen up to that hour and no backing out, under a forfeiture of $25.— At the hour appointed the judge came up leading the sorriest specimen of a horse ever seen in those parts. In a few minutes Mr. Lincoln was seen approching with a wooden saw horse upon his shoulders.— Great were the shouts and the laughter of the crowd, and both were greatly increased when Mr. Lincoln, on surveying the judge's animal, set down his saw horse and exclaimed, "Well, judge, this is the first time I ever got the worst of it in a horse trade.—*Chicago Tribune*

11/2/76 Mirror.

The Grand Demonstration!

1200 People in Attendance.

NINE STIRRING SPEECHES.

A Substantial Dinner for All.

BRILLIANT ILLUMINATION and Torchlight Procession.

The Old Town Ablaze With Enthusiasm.

THE WHOLE AFFAIR A MAGNIFICENT SUCCESS.

GOOD ORDER, GOOD HUMOR, AND A GOOD TIME GENERALLY.

Everything Lovely and the Goose Hanging High.

THE "COON-KILLER" ON THE WAR PATH, &C.

As had been previously announced, last Thursday was the day for a grand Tilden and Hendricks demonstration in the town of Leesburg. The morning was dark, cloudy and disagreeable, which no doubt prevented the attendance of many who would have otherwise been present. At about 10 o'clock, however, the clouds lifted, and although the atmosphere was raw, at least 1000 to 1200 people gathered in the Court House square to listen to the speeches, and partake of the collation served for them.

THE BALL IN MOTION.

A stand had been erected and seats provided on the north side of the square, and at 12 o'clock the meeting was called to order by the Chairman of the Executive Committee, who introduced as the first speaker

DR. CHAS. P. ALLEN,

of the city of Washington. Dr. A. spoke for about one hour and fifteen minutes.— The greater portion of his remarks was directed to a discussion of finance, and kindred questions involved in the campaign, all of which he handled with decided ability and force. His delivery was good, his language chaste, and his points well sustained throughout.

THE DINNER.

At the conclusion of Dr. Allen's speech, a recess was taken for an hour, during which time the crowd repaired to the tables arranged at the western side of the yard, where an abundant supply of creature comforts was spread for their enjoyment—and for the once politics were voted a bore, and each one devoted himself to the more agreeable task of providing for the cravings of the inner man. And, thanks to the energy and untiring exertions of Messrs. McCabe, Henderson, Divine and Abbott, of the committee of arrangements, there was sufficient to have satisfied the hunger of double the number.

SPEAKING RESUMED.

Dinner over, and the air being unpleasantly cool, the crowd was invited to repair to the interior of the Court-House, which was soon filled to overflowing.

(We will omit here the summation of seven speeches.)

ILLUMINATION, TORCHLIGHT PROCESSION, &C.

At about 6½ o'clock, the streets of Leesburg began to wear an unusual air of life and animation, and by 7 o'clock, the whole town presented a fairy-like scene, the like of which had not been witnessed, scarcely in the memory of the "oldest inhabitant." Throughout the town business houses and private residences were aglow with brilliant lights, and handsome and appropriate devices, while over 600 Chinese lanterns reflected their wierd appearance over the gay spectacle. As viewed from the corner of Market and King streets, the scene was simply grand, and so suddenly and so enchantingly had the old town been transmogrified, that if the oldest citizen had been aroused from a two hours' nap, he would scarcely have recognized his own home. To specially mention each locality, where all sparkled like "stars on the brow of night," would be out of the question; but that our distant readers may form some conception of the magnificence of the display, we will tell them, that a beautiful arch spanned King street, opposite Hough & Gray's store, bearing on one side, in large black letters, the word "Tilden" and on the other "Reform," which was surmounted by a row of Chinese lanterns, that looked decidedly handsome; a similar arch and device spanned King street, opposite the Osburn House. The Reamer Hotel looked grand. The windows on the west and south sides of the house, gleaming with brilliant lights; at the upper end of Market street, the private residence of Mrs. Jane Wildman, in addition to its bright lights, had its windows and portico artistically trimmed with evergreens, flowers, appropriate mottoes, &c., most of which was designed and executed by the skilled hands of the mistress of the establishment, who had just stepped over the bounds of her four-score years.— Loudoun street, always one of the most attractive in the old town, that night shone with unwonted brilliancy and beauty—the residences of Capt. Head and Mr. Chas. P. McCabe being specially noticeable. But it is useless and invidious to try to particularize—nineteen twentieths of the business houses and private residences wore a magical expression, in the highest degree creditable to the good taste and enthusiastic devotion of our people to the cause of honesty, reform, and constitutional liberty.

THE TORCH-LIGHT PROCESSION.

At 7 o'clock a procession was formed at the east end of Market street, headed by the Leesburg Brass Band, and under the direction of Maj. J. F. Divine, W. W. Athey, Thos. Osburn, Lemuel Norris and R. B. Wildman, mounted marshals. There were several hundred persons in the procession, in the front of which was a large U. S. flag, carried by a couple of colored men, representatives from the Tilden & Hendricks Club of Lewinsville. There were over one hundred torches in the line, besides some 25 or 30 transparencies, one of which bore an excellent likeness of Tilden, another of

Hendricks, and another of Gen. Hunton, while all of them bore some appropriate motto or carricature—and all along the line of march sky-rockets, from time to time, went whirling through the air, illumining the heavens with their lurid glare.

THE COON KILLER ON THE RAMPAGE.

A small cannon belonging to Alexandria, was brought up on the evening train and played a conspicuous part in the exercises of the evening. Under the management of Messrs. M. Nash and Charles Dearbourn, who accompanied it, it woke the echoes of the surrounding hills, as it belched forth its thunderous peals. We trust the little varmint may be taken good care of, and that at an early day after the 7th of November, it may be permitted to join in firing a parting blast over the fresh made grave of defunct Republicanism.

THE SPEECHES AT NIGHT.

After traversing the principal streets, the procession returned to the Court-House and was dismissed. And at the tap of the bell, Court-Hall was again filled to repletion, by the enthusiastic crowd, which was beautified by the presence of a number of ladies. After the meeting had been called to order,

GEN. EPPA HUNTON

was first introduced, which was the signal for uproarious applause, in which we observed that the ladies lent vigorous hands, if not loud voices. The Gen. spoke well and to the point, as he always does, and the greeting he received showed the esteem in which he is held by a Loudoun audience.

(General Eppa Hunton apparently served this area well first as a Congressman and later as a Senator. During the war, he had commanded the local 8th Virginia regiment and was wounded in Pickett's charge.)

Shortly after 11 o'clock the meeting was dismissed, every body in a pleasant humor and all hands delighted with the "days doings." No untoward event occurred to mar the pleasure of the occasion, and taken all in all was a delightful affair, and can only be eclipsed by the more imposing one that will follow the election of Tilden and Hendricks on the 7th of November.

11/9/76 Mirror

The YEAR of JUBILEE HAS COME.

Tilden our Next President

"Let Us Have Peace."

LATER.

A despatch received at this office at 2 o'clock Wednesday afternoon, says :

"Tilden certainly elected. Virginia goes for Tilden by 35,000 majority.

LATEST.

WASHINGTON, Nov. 8, 4 o'clock. P. M.— Latest returns up to this hour don't change indications of last night. Democratic Committee claim 215 electoral votes for Tilden and give Hayes 154. It is understood the Republicans concede 191 for Tilden. Wisconsin, Oregon, Florida still to hear from, claimed by both parties. Latest from South Carolina gives Hampton 9,000 majority, with several counties to hear from, which will reduce it. Electoral vote of South Carolina undecided, but probably for Hayes.

The result of the Election on Tuesday has flooded the land with glory. The bright sun of peace kisses the folds of our banner as it proudly floats in the breeze and the song of rejoicing is everywhere heard.

We have neither time, opportunity nor disposition, at this stage of the game, to dilate upon the glorious issue. It is enough for us this week to know, that the reign of Fraud, Dishonesty, Corruption and Usurpation, have been brought to a stand still —and Peace, Prosperity and constitutional government will on the 4th of March be inaugurated.

a Democratic majority in the next House of Representatives. At 3 o'clock this morning we make up the following summary of the result as indicated by the voluminous returns given in detail in our columns :

FOR TILDEN.

Alabama	10	Mississippi	8
Arkansas	6	Missouri	15
Connecticut	6	New Jersey	9
Delaware	3	New York	35
Florida	4	Tennessee	12
Georgia	11	Texas	8
Indiana	15	Virginia	11
Kentucky	12	West Virginia	5
Louisiana	8	North Carolina	10
Maryland	8	Wisconsin	10
			206

FOR HAYES

Illinois	21	Nebraska	3
Iowa	11	Nevada	3
Kansas	5	New Hampshire	5
Maine	7	Ohio	22
Minnesota	5	Colorado	3
Massachusetts	13	Pennsylvania	29
Rhode Island	4	Vermont	5
			136

DOUBTFUL

South Carolina	7	Michigan	11
California	6	Oregon	3
			27

November. 1876

THE MIRROR.

BENJ. F. SHEETZ, Editor.

Thursday Morning. Nov. 16.

THE WAR IS ENDED.

The election of TILDEN is the fulfilment of GRANT's "Let us have peace." It has broken the backbone of the Republican party, whose real strength was in the passions and prejudices of the North. The "bloody shirt" has lost its power, and "the war" no longer exists as the tocsin to array section against section. The Democratic triumph is but the triumph of home rule and the equality of the States. It gives to the South the assurance it sought and failed to receive from the Republicans, that it is a component of the Union, not a vassal of the North. It welds and certifies the Union as the Union of equals. It breaks down the color-line. It makes us one people.

Let us rejoice, therefore, that once again under one and the same flag, we enter upon our second century with hearts united in the resolve to do our whole duty to our common country.— *Whig*

Thursday Morning. Nov. 23.

THE SITUATION.—Another week of suspense has elapsed, and practically, we are as far from knowing who is to be the next President as we were a fortnight before the election.

With a brazen effrontery almost unparalleled, the Radical Canvassing Board in South Carolina has already counted that State for Hayes by 600 majority, and from present indications there is little doubt but that the Board in Louisiana, composed of as unprincipled a set of politicians as ever disgraced official positions, will throw the vote of that State in the same direction.

TROOPS IN WASHINGTON—During the past few days a number of United States troops have been called to Washington by the President, and placed in quarters—and orders issued to the Depot Quartermaster at Philadelphia, to forward at once camp and garrison equipage for three thousand men.

A knowledge of the gathering of troops at the national capitol, created considerable commotion throughout the country, as to what they were there for. The President and members of the cabinet all disclaim any political significance in the matter, and state that all present army movements are mere matters of routine.

Thursday Morning. Dec'r 21

THE SITUATION PRACTICALLY UNCHANGED.—The situation in the bull dozed States of the South, practically, remains unchanged—and whilst there is scarcely any who doubt the election of Gov. Tilden by the people, it is by no means so certain that he will be permitted to take his seat.

Congress has her committees in each of the three States of South Carolina, Louisiana and Florida, and of course that body will take no decisive action until their agents return and report, so that several weeks yet will have to elapse before any intelligent understanding can be had as to results. In the meantime speculations are rife, and a thousand theories advanced for the solution of the difficulty.

The committee is at work in Florida, progressing quietly, unearthing the most positive evidences of cheating, and have disposed of several counties, but of course will make no report of their doings until the canvass of the State is completed.

In Louisiana, the committee are subjected to all manner of annoyance in the discharge of their official duties.

WASHINGTONIAN.

LEESBURG, LOUDOUN COUNTY, VA.

Saturday, November 18. 1876

PRESIDENTIAL ISSUE

We give all the news bearing upon the situation of affairs in the disputed States. The whole matter, there, is in the hands of the Returning Boards, and nothing will be definitely known until they have made their count of the votes. In Louisiana the Board is composed, as we learn from the papers, of two negroes, who will be under the control of Kellog, as unscrupulous a man as ever disgraced an official position. There is some probability of a fair return in Florida, and we think, if the matter is settled before it gets into Congress, it will be done by Florida. If Florida, however, follows the course of Louisiana, then the coming session of Congress, which will convene on the first Monday in December, will take charge of the matter.

This difficulty, which is now playing havoc with the mercantile interests of the Northern cities as purchasers will not buy in this unsettled state of our affairs, is the result of the reconstruction policy of the Republican party, in which they aimed to punish and oppress the Southern people, and at the same time, by the colored vote, fasten their party as a fixture, upon the country. And at this early day, we have the bitter fruits of their folly—the government and the whole country quivering beneath the most painful apprehensions.

Whatever may be the decision, the people must resolve that the peace of the country should be maintained, and trust to time and legal remedies for the cure of our ills. This government is not to be given to violence and the winds of passion, because a few bad men, under laws passed during the dark days of the Republic, are enabled to perpetrate a fraud upon the country.

It is worth too much to us, and those who will come after us, to be thus cheaply sacrificed. We must wait and see what Congress will do, and abide by its decision

The Election Difficulty.

The result of the election, as far as ascertained, leave the country in the same state of uncertainty, that it has been since Saturday last. The Returning Boards in Louisiana, Florida and South Carolina, which have been constituted, in those States, by the Republican governments, with extraordinary powers over the votes of the people, have the ballots there in charge, and the result will not be known until the votes have passed the ordeal of their inspection and count. In those States hangs the difficulty. The apprehensions of fraud, warranted by the character of Chamberlan, of South Carolina and Kellogg, of Louisiana, have created a high state of excitement in the country, which induced the President to order troops to Florida and Louisiana, and to invite leading Republicans to go there and superintend the counting of the vote. This made it necessary for the Democrats to send a committee of their leading men there, to watch the Republicans, as well as the partizan Returning Boards.

RUNNING FOR GOVERNOR.

Mark Twain Experiences a "Campaign of Defamation."

A few months ago I was nominated for Governor of the great State of New York, to run against Stewart L. Woodford and John T. Hoffman, on an independent ticket. I somehow felt that I had one prominet advantage over these gentlemen, and that was good character. It was easy to see by the newspapers that if they had ever known what it was to bear a good name, that time had gone by. It was plain that in these latter years they had become familiar with all manner of shameful crimes. But at the very moment that I was exalting my advantage and joying it in secret, there was a muddy undercurrent of discomfort "riling" the depths of my happiness—and that was the having to bear my name bandied about in familiar connection with those of such people. I grew more and more disturbed. Finally I wrote my grandmother about it. Her answer came quick and sharp. She said :

"You have never done one single thing in all your life to be ashamed of—not one. Look at the newspapers—look at them and comprehend what sort of characters Woodford and Hoffman are, and then see if you are willing to lower yourself to their level and enter a public canvass with them."

It was my very thought. I did not sleep a single moment that night. But, after all, I could not recede. I was fully committed, and must go on with the fight. As I was looking listlessly over the papers at breakfast I came across this paragraph, and I may truly say I never was so confounded before :

"PERJURY.—Perhaps, now that Mr. Mark Twain is before the people as a candidate for Governor, he will condescend to explain how he came to be convicted of perjury by thirty-four witnesses, in Wakawak, Cochin China, in 1863—the intent of which perjury was to rob a poor native widow and her helpless family of a meagre plantain patch, their only stay and support in their bereavement and their desolation. Mr. Twain owes it to himself, as well as to the great people whose suffrage he asks, to clear the matter up. Will he do it ?"

I thought I should burst with amazement! Such a cruel, heartless charge—I never had *seen* Cochin China ! I never had *heard* of Wakawak ! I didn't know a plantain patch from a kangaroo ! I did not know what to do. I was crazed and helpless. I let the day slip away without doing anything at all. The next morning the paper had this—nothing more :

"SIGNIFICANT.—Mr. Twain, it will be ob-

served, is suggestively silent about the Cochin China perjury."

[*Mem.*—During the rest of the campaign this paper never referred to me in any other way than as "the infamous perjurer Twain."]

Next came the *Gazette* with this :

"WANTED TO KNOW.—Will the new candidate for Governor deign to explain to certain of his fellow-citizens (who are suffering to vote for him) the little circumstance of his cabin-mates in Montana losing small valuables from time to time, until at last these things have been invariably found on Mr. Twain's person or in his 'trunk' (newspapers he rolled his traps in,) they felt compelled to give him a friendly admonition for his own good, and so tarred and feathered him and rode him on a rail, and then advised him to leave a permanent vacuum in the place he usually occupied in the camp ? Will he do this ?"

Could anything be more deliberately malicious than that ? For I never was in Montana in my life.

[After this, this journal customarily spoke of me as "Twain the Montana Thief."]

I got to picking up papers apprehensively—much as one would lift a desired blanket which he had some idea might have a rattlesnake under it. One day this met my eye :

"THE LIE NAILED !—By the sworn affidavits of Michael o'Flanagan, Esq., of the Five Points, and Mr. Kit Burns and John Allen of Water street, it is established that Mr. Mark Twain's vile sentiment that the lamented grandfather of our noble standard-bearer, John T. Hoffman, was hanged for highway robbery is a brutal and gratuitous lie, without a single shadow of foundation in fact. It is disheartening to virtuous men to see such shameful means resorted to to achieve political success as the attacking of the dead in their graves and defiling their honored names with slander. When we think of the anguish this miserable falsehood must cause the innocent relatives and friends of the deceased, we are almost driven to incite an outraged and insulted public to summary and unlawful vengeance upon the traducer. But no, let us leave him to the agony of a lacerated conscience (though if passion should get the better of the public, and in its blind fury they should do the traducer bodily injury, it is but too obvious that no jury could convict and no court punish the perpetrators of the deed)."

The ingenious closing sentence had the effect of moving me out of bed with dispatch that night, and out at the back door also, while the "outraged and insulted public" surged in the front way, breaking furniture and windows in their righteous indignation as they came, and taking off such property as they could carry when they went. And yet I can lay my hand upon the book and say that I never slandered Governor Hoffman's grandfather. More; I never even heard of him or mentioned him up to that day and date.

[I will state, in passing, that the journal above quoted from always referred to me afterward as "Twain, the Body-Snatcher."]

The next newspaper article that attracted my attention was the following:

"A Sweet Candidate.—Mark Twain, who was to make such a blighting speech at a mass-meeting of the Independents last night, didn't come to time. A telegram from his physician stated that he had been knocked down by a runaway team and his leg broken in two places; sufferer lying in great agony, and so forth, and so forth, and a lot more bosh of the same sort. And the Independents tried hard to swallow the wretched subterfuge and pretend that they did not know what was the *real* reason of the absence of the abandoned creature whom they denominate their standard-bearer. A certain man was seen to reel into Mr. Twain's hotel last night in a beastly state of intoxication. It is the imperative duty of the Independents to prove that this besotted brute was not Mark Twain himself. We have them at last! This is a case that admits of no shirking. The voice of the people demands in thunder tones: 'WHO IS THAT MAN!'"

It was incredible, absolutely incredible, for a moment that it was really my name that was coupled with this disgraceful suspicion. Three long years had passed over my head since I had tasted ale, beer, wine or liquor of any kind.

[It shows what effect the times were having on me when I say that I saw myself confidently dubbed "Mr. Delirium Tremens Twain" in the next issue of that journal without a pang—notwithstanding I knew that with monotonous fidelity the paper would go on calling me so to the very end.]

By this time anonymous letters were getting to be an important part of my mail matter. This form was common:

"How about that old woman you kiked of your premises which was beging.

POL PRY."

And this:

"There is things which you have done, which is unbeknowens to anybody but me. You better trot out a few dols. to yours truly or you'll hear thro' the papers from

"HANDY ANDY."

This is about the idea. I could continue them until the reader was surfeited, if desirable.

Shortly the principal Republican journals "convicted" me of wholesale bribery,

and the leading Democratic paper "nailed" an aggravated case of blackmailing to me.

[In this way I acquired two additional names: "Twain, the Filthy Corruptionist," and "Twain, the Loathsome Embracer."]

By this time there had grown to be such a clamor for an "answer" to the dreadful charges that were laid to me that the editors and leaders of my party said it would be political ruin for me to remain silent any longer. As if to make their appeal the more imperative, the following appeared in one of the papers the very next day:

"BEHOLD THE MAN!—The independent candidate still maintains silence. Because he dare not speak. Every accusation against him has been amply proved, and they have been indorsed and reindorsed by his own eloquent silence, till at this day he stands forever convicted. Look upon your candidate, independents? Look upon the Infamous Perjurer! the Montana Thief! the Body-Snatcher! Contemplate your Incarnate Delirium Tremens! your Filthy Corruptionist! your Loathsome Embracer! Gaze upon him—ponder him well—and then say if you can give your honest votes to a creature who has earned this dismal array of titles by his hideous crimes, and dares not open his mouth in denial of any

There was no possible way of getting out of it, and so, in deep humiliation, I set about preparing to "answer" a mass of useless charges and mean and wicked falsehoods. But I never finished the task, for the very next morning a paper came out with a new horror—a fresh malignity—and seriously charged me with burning a lunatic asylum with all its inmates because it obstructed the view from my house. This threw me into a sort of panic. Then came the charge of poisoning my uncle to get his property, with an imperative demand that the grave should be opened. This drove me to the verge of distraction. On top of this I was accused of employing toothless and incompetent old relatives to prepare the food for the foundling hospital when I was warden. I was wavering—wavering. And at last, as a due and fitting climax to the shameless prosecution that party rancor had inflicted upon me, nine little toddling children of all shades of color and degrees of raggedness were taught to rush on to the platform at a public meeting and clasp me round the legs and call me "Pa!"

I gave it up. I hauled down my colors and surrendered. I was not equal to the requirements of a gubernatorial campaign.

11/18/76 Washingtonian

A SMASH UP — On Monday evening Col. H. E. PEYTON left his span of horses standing in front of Douglas & Sellman's while he stopped in the store. A dog fight on the opposite corner frightened the horses, and they left—leaving one wheel of the vehicle against the Court-House fence—and hugging a tree in front of Mr. J. W. Wildman's residence. they came to a halt. and about put a period to the wagon. Don't tempt your horses to bad tricks by leaving them alone in the streets.

WHERE DO THEY COME FROM. — One day last week, Mr. EDGAR BURCH jr., shot and killed a fine Deer. that he found feeding among his cattle in a field near the Big Spring, about two miles from town. The animal was a buck, very fat, and weighed about 150 pounds.

(They apparently were rarely seen then – not so today.)

GROVER & BAKER'S
IMPROVED
ELASTIC STITCH
AND
Lock Stitch

Sewing Machines,
17 NORTH CHARLES STREET,
BALTIMORE, MD.

11/25/76 Washingtonian

SHEEP KILLED. — Mr. T. M. C. Paxson, had killed by dogs on Monday night last, 54 sheep and 42 wounded, some of which will die, out of flock of 104. This makes 72 killed and 49 wounded by dogs for him within the last few weeks. Cannot something be done to protect this kind of property from the dogs?

Sheep Fund.

ALL persons in the county of Loudoun who may have had Sheep destroyed by Dogs, *between the First day of February*, 1875, *and the First day of February*, 1876; are notified that they must place in my hands, on or before MONDAY, the 12th day of JUNE, 1876, their certificates of such loss, properly prepared and sworn to. After that date the business of the above named year will be closed up, and the surplus fund, if any, turned over to the School Fund of the respective Districts. Persons, therefore, who may have suffered loss by the ravages of Dogs will see the necessity for prompt action. No claim, dating between Feb. 1st, 1875, and Feb. 1st, 1876, can be considered after June 12th, 1876.
B. F. SHEETZ,
Com. Sheep Fund of Loudoun County.

Packs of marauding dogs were often a serious problem. A dog tax of 75 cents was enacted which supported a fund to partially reimburse sheep owners who suffered such attacks.

11/18/76 Washingtonian

A Texas Judge is credited with the following decision. The fact is, Jones the jail is an old, rickety affair, as cold as an iron wedge. You applied to this court for a release on bail, giving it as your opinion that you would freeze to death there. The weather has not moderated and to keep you from freezing I will direct the sheriff to hang you at four o'clock this afternoon.

Naughty little boys in Cincinnati are told that right in the centre of the hind hoofs of every live mule there is a little lump of gold, which can be easily dug out with a penknife.

210

12/30/76 Washingtonian

One of Custer's Scouts.

Frank Smith and his Beautiful Indian Wife —Six Years of the Thrilling Adventure

NORWICH, Dec. 4—Six years ago a stripling boy left the parental roof, in one of the border towns of Chenango county, to seek fortune in the far off West. The lad made his way to the Crow Agency, on Crow Creek, with a party of Western roughs whom he met, three of whom were subsequently massacred by the leader of the gang. For three years past the boy has made his home with the Mountain Crow Indians, among whom he has had a lodge, choosing his companion from among the fairest of the tribe. Last spring he went with Custer from Fort Laramie, and served as one of his scouts from that time till the terrible day that gallant soldier fell. He had been sent with despatches from Custer to General Terry and was returning with despatches from Terry to his chief, and was but a few miles from the scene of conflict, which he did not reach, from the failure of his horse, when the whole command was slaughtered in the sanguinary fight on Rosebud Creek. With a field glass he witnessed the hand-to hand encounters, the life and death struggle, and saw Custer, who held out to the last, go down. To save his own life and avoid being scalped, he had away beneath a rock about two miles from, next day when he visited the scene of carnage and assisted in burying the dead. After that he was a bearer of despatchs for Gen. Crook, often riding, by night and by day, hundreds of miles away, in the face of danger and death in the performance of his perilous mission. He wears the scars of hand-to hand contest and personal bravery. He has seen Red Cloud, Spotted Tail, Sitting Bull, Crazy Horse, Rain in the Face, and nearly all of the noted chiefs and warriors of recent Indian tragedy and story.

To-day a beardless youth of 22, tall and straight, with flowing locks, in buckskin dress ornamented with fringe and beads, and bearing the trappings of savage warefare and Indian life, appeared in our quiet village. The bright eyed, good-featured, well-formed youth was en route for the paternal roof in Lincklaen, which he left for a world of sights and scenes six years before. With the comming of spring, Frank Smith returns to his home and lodge among the mountain Crows, and to his dusky companion, whom he idolizes as the most beautiful of her tribe.

12/21/76 Mirror

[Special Dispatch to the Baltimore Sun.]

Sanguinary Rencontre with Knives—Exciting Scene at a Hotel.

WASHINGTON, December 15.—A short time before nine o'clock to-night a rencontre occurred in the lobby of the Ebbitt House between Col. J. W. Fairfax, of Virginia, and Francis M. Schell, of Indiana, which caused intense excitement, and resulted in the spreading of exaggerated rumors all over the city. For a long time after people came flocking to the scene of battle to make inquiries. In the present disturbed condition of affairs the thought in every one's mouth was that politics were at the bottom of the affair, but this was not the cause, which was of a personal nature entirely. Schell was at the last session one of the assistants of the doorkeeper of the House, and was called the brevet speaker, from his habit of mounting to the desk every morning five minutes before the meeting of the House, pounding the Speaker's gavel and peremptorily ordering all unprivileged persons off the floor. His manner was very offensive, and he was constantly getting embroiled in disputes with people who resented his conduct. On one occasion last summer, it is stated, when Col. Fairfax was on the floor of the House on the invitation of a member, Schell rudely asked him to show his authority to be there or leave, for which Fairfax told him he should bring him to account.

To-night Schell was sitting in the lobby at the Ebbitt, when Col. Fairfax, accompanied by a friend, passed by. Fairfax looked at Schell and said, "There is the damn bull dog who put me off the floor, and I have a great mind to cut him." Schell replied, "You are all right colonel." Fairfax repeated his remark, or words to the same effect, when Schell said, "If there is going to be any cutting you had better commence now," and rose from his seat and planted himself with his back to one of the pillars. Fairfax drew from his pocket his penknife and advanced with it open. Schell also drew his knife and lifted his cane, a heavy hickory stick with a crooked end. As Fairfax advanced and made a lunge at him with his knife, Schell dealt him a tremendous blow with his stick. At the same time Fairfax's heel slipped on the smooth tiling and he fell. While he was prostrate, it is asserted, Schell stabbed him three times. He fought, however, with desperation, and in the struggle the two combatants moved eight or ten feet from where they commenced. Fairfax only succeeded in striking Schell once.— Schell weighs about eighteen stone, while Fairfax, although tall, is of slender build.

As soon as Schell was struck he discontinued the attack and cried out, "I am killed!" He then was assisted to the door by one of the hotel porters and went home, where he sent for Dr. Bliss. On examining his injuries, Dr. Bliss discovered that the knife after penetrating through two coats had struck one of his ribs and then glanced off. The wound was about one inch long and one inch deep.

Col. Fairfax had received three wounds, one a punctured cut over the region of the heart, one in the region of the shoulder from behind, and a very long gash in the neck. As he rose from the floor the blood gushed from him in torrents and soon stained all his garments and wet the floor.

The encounter had been sudden and apparently so desperate that no attempt has been made to separate the belligerents. The spectators were completely absorbed in thoughts of their own safety and gave them a wide berth. Col. Fairfax did not seem to be at all alarmed at his condition, but he yielded to the entreaties of those who soon came up and went to his room, walking up four flights of stairs.

Drs Lincoln and Ashford were sent for and remained with him for some time, and on a critical examination pronounced his wounds not dangerous, if he was kept quiet. A powerful opiate was then administered to him.— Col. Mosby and a number of his other personal friends called to see him but it was thought best to admit but a few. Among those who remained with him for some time was Dr. Carter, of Baltimore, who served with him in the Confederate army. Col. Fairfax comes of a distinguished Virginia family. He was on Longstreet's staff, and was present at Lee's surrender. He is a personal friend of President Grant, who a year or two ago paid him a visit at his house in Virginia. He has many friends in Baltimore, and has a son there in business.

—The Washington *Union* of Tuesday says that Schell is under police surveillance, but will not be arrested until the wishes of Col. Fairfax are made known. It is said that he has declined to prosecute the matter. On Monday night, his physicians, Dr. Lincoln and Ashford, pronounced Col. Fairfax out of danger.

(Colonel Fairfax was a well-known Loudoun citizen who was on Longstreet's staff and later owned the James Monroe mansion.)

1/11/77 Mirror

DEATH OF COMMODORE VANDERBILT.—
Commodore Vanderbilt, who died at his home
in New York, on Thursday last, was one of
the wealthiest and most enterprising citizens
of New York. He was born in Staten Island,
N. Y. in 1794, and was raised during boyhood
in comparatively needy circumstances. He
began business as the master of a sail boat ;
became captain of a steamboat in 1817, and
later built many steamboats and steamships of
improved construction. In 1851 he established a steamship line from New York to California by way of Nicaragua : in 1862 he gave
to the U. S. Government his new steamer,
"The Vanderbilt," that cost $800,000, and for
which Congress passed a resolution of thanks.
He was, up to his death, Chief Comptroller of
the New York Central and Harlem railroad,
and had been for a number of years. His
health began to fail about eight or ten months
ago, and he has been waving between life and
death ever since. His enterprise, genius and
success are known and felt throughout the
world

A recent summary of his railroad wealth
fixed it at $45,000,000. He owned compara-
tively little real estate. His personal estate
for 1876 was assessed at $3,000,000.

On the news of the Commodore's death at
Nashville the Chancellor of Vanderbilt University sent information to all the professors,
who were at the time in the midst of their lec-
tures. Immediately the classes were dismissed, and the bell was tolled as the students
slowly marched from the building. The fac-
culty were called together, and resolutions
passed in honor of the founder's memory.—
The University exercises are suspended for
the rest of the week. The chapel is being
draped in mourning.

1/25/77 Mirror

MORE HORSE STEALING.—There appears
to be an organized band of horse thieves
operating in this county, and the utmost
vigilance should be exerted to secure their
capture and punishment. On last Saturday
night the lock on Col. A. T. M. Rust's stable door was broken, the door opened, and
one of the Colonel's finest horses, stolen — the
thief taking with him also, a wagon saddle
and blind bridle. This is the fourth or fifth
horse stolen from that immediate neighborhood within the last few months, and so systematic and perfect have been the plans of
the rogues, that in neither instance has the
owner of the stolen property ever heard of
it.

1/25/77 Mirror

WOMEN WILL SETTLE IT.

WASHINGTON, January 17.—The proceedings of the woman suffragists to-day were
marked by many humorous incidents, and
many of the speeches abounded in happy
witicisms. There was less fuss but more
feathers, for everybody had their Sunday-
go-to-meeting clothes on. Elizabeth Cady
Stanton opened the session. "There were
but three," she said, "of those who started
the question of woman suffrage still living,"
Miss Anthony, Mrs. Gage and herself, and
they purposed to still fight for right. She
wished in every church the women would
leave and the cold congregation of men be
left alone, and the narrow-minded priests
would soon feel their loss. She related an
incident when she with others educated a
young man for the ministry and gave him
a new broad cloth suit of clothes, a cane,
kid gloves and a starched shirt. They invited him to preach, and to their disappointment he took for his text : "Suffer not
a woman to speak in the church." This
satisfied those who had done so much for
him, and from that day they concluded
they would never be caught in such a trap
again.

Dr. Mary Walker was called for. She
appeared willingly, and was attired in a
new black suit of clothes. Her pants were
a little short, and the red tops of her boots
showed quite plainly. The doctor started
off by referring to the constitution, but had
not proceeded far before some person in the
rear of the hall cried out, "Doctor, pull
down your vest !" The doctor smiled, and
continued. A law was wanted to protect
woman in her rights, and woman intend to
demand it. [A voice, "How much did Van-
derbuilt leave you, Mary ?"] The remark
caused much laughter, but did not prevent
the doctor from finishing.

(Eccentric through she was, Mary Walker is
the only woman to win the Medal of Honor.)

1/18/77 Mirror

A negro was found dead in Georgia, having fallen and broken his neck while stealing chickens from a high roost. He was a
class leader in a church and his pastor, in
preaching the funeral sermon, was bothered
by the question where the soul of the dead
brother had gone. "His well-known piety,"
said the preacher, "indicates that he died a
Christian ; yet there are circumstances connected with his death that are perplexing.
If, after he fell and before he struck the
ground, he repented of his sins, there can
be no question but that he is now in glory ;
but there was mighty little time for him to
think about it."

(Actually, an important theological
question.)

GEORGE WOODS & CO'S.,
Parlor Organs.

2/1/77 Mirror

CIGARETTE SMOKING.

A Fatal Mania — Strong Argument Against the Use of Cigarettes — A Deadly Poison.

Lately a mania for cigarette smoking has developed itself. Formerly the fashion was confined principally to boys and Cubans, but within the past year or two it has been adopted by all classes, and cigarette smoking is now the rule rather than the exception. In former times it was considered *en regle* to smoke a cigarette between the acts of the play or opera, but now the paper cigars are seen on the streets and the front platform of cars, and the sale of meerschaum cigarette-holders is getting so large as to gladden the hearts of the manufacturers.— Although there are expensive brands of cigarettes, it very often happens that the tobacco from which many of them are made is of an inferior quality. These breeders of disease are frequently compounded of refuse tobacco, cut up from old butts of cigars that are picked up in the street, and the curled exquisite, puffing away at his cigarette, would probably throw it away from him in disgust, were he aware that the tobacco from which it is made is, in all probability, the remains of a cigar that has been between the lips of a man afflicted with a contagious disease. There are instances now on record where sore mouths and sometimes even worse complaints have been introduced in this way. Another objectionable feature in cigarette fillings is that they are very often made of Turkish tobacco into the composition of which opium enters largely. The effect of this constant inhalation of this narcotic is injurious beyond description. It acts directly upon both the nerves and the liver, and the constant smoker of so-called Russian or Turkish cigarettes soon becomes pale, jaundiced, and listless, the enervating drug sapping up the life of the smoker, and, at the end of a few years, leaving him unfit for work and

A VERITABLE OBJECT OF COMPASSION

in his inability to free himself from the baneful influence of the subtle poison.

THE WASHINGTONIAN.

PUBLISHED WEEKLY, BY WILLIAM B. LYNCH, LEESBURG, LOUDOUN COUNTY, VIRGINIA.

VOL. 71.   SATURDAY MORNING, FEBRUARY 3, 1877.   NO. 36.

The Great Issue.

The bill to settle the Presidential question has gone into effect, after passing the ordeal of both Houses of Congress, by a large majority. The Commission consists of Messrs. Thurman and Bayard, Democrats, and Messrs. Edmunds, Morton and Frelinghuysen, Republicans, of the Senate, and Messrs. Abbott, Payne and Hunton, Democrats, and Garfield and Hoar, Republicans, of the House, and Justice Clifford, Strong, Miller, Field, and Bradley of the Supreme Court.

Speculation as to the conclusion of the High Commission, is not in order, as no one can tell what it will be. We can only say we have great faith in the wisdom and justice of the members of the Supreme Court on the Commission, and believe they will do as they believe right, and we feel very well assurred that the members of the Commission from the two Houses, will vote as they deem right—but under a law of conscience which governs politicians, and which seldom varies, they are irresistably led to believe their side is right, and will vote accordingly. Upon the justices of the Supreme Court, in the Commission, will turn the result.

FIRE.—A dwelling house near the Leesburg Cemetery, belonging to Mr. P. Harrison, was discovered to be on fire last Wednesday about noon. The fire department was soon on duty, and in a short time put the fire out. The damage to the building was slight, and it was insured in a New Jersey company, Mr. Henry Bronaugh, agent. It was occupied by colored people, whose loss, in the destruction of their household goods, was, to them, very serious. Their misfortune was much regretted by those present. There is generally an unnecessary and indiscriminate destruction of property at fires, which the fire department, by some regulation, should endeavor to remedy.

FIRE.—A log dwelling house about two miles Southwest of Leesburg, belonging to Misses Mary and Elizabeth Saunders, and occupied by a colored family, was entirely consumed on Tuesday afternoon, the 30th instant.

☞ We are pleased to learn that Col. A. T. M. Rust has recovered the horse stolen from him a short time ago. It was captured in Baltimore. It is also reported that the thief is in custody. We hope this will prove true.

The Baltimore *Sun* of Friday says:

Wholesale Horse Stealing.—Otho T. Gant, colored, was arrested yesterday by policemen of the western district, charged with stealing four houses from persons living in the neighborhood of Leesburg, Loudoun county, Va., at intervals since the 7th of November last. Gant lived in a room on Raborg street, and would occasionally make a raid into Virginia and bring in a horse to Baltimore. Two of the horses were sold to a firm of horse dealers in the western section of the city, and had been sent by them away from Baltimore. The other two were recovered by policemen of the western district, and are held at the station house awaiting identification by the owners. One of the recovered horses had been sold to Clinton J. Cooper, colored, No. 51 China street, on the 10th of November. The other one was found at a livery stable. The policemen on the district had only been notified yesterday of the depredations, and were prompt in the arrest and recovery of two of the horses. Gant, whose alias is Gannon, is held at the western station house for a hearing.

Beating a Dead-Beat.

[From the Detroit Free Press.]

For some days past an unknown female has been in the habit of making an afternoon trip on the Woodward-avenue cars, generally getting aboard at Jefferson avenue and riding to Brady street. The first two or three times she paid her fare promptly enough, but the next trip she wrote something on a card, handed it to a gentleman and he paid her fare. The next trip she waited till the driver rang the fare-bell, and when she saw him looking through the door she advanced and held up a card on which was written:

"I am deaf and dumb."

The driver didn't want to create a scene, and she rode as a dead-head. Next day she went through the same performance, but when she boarded the car the third afternoon he was ready for her. He had every reason to believe her a fraud, as she had been heard to speak in a car coming down. When she entered the car she took a seat and began reading, seeming to have no earthly interest in the fare question. There are no conductors on the route, and the driver controls both doors. Before Brady street was reached the unknown female was the only passenger. She rose and rang the bell at the street, but the driver paid not the least heed. She rang again, and he hurried up the horse. Then she tried to pull the bell of the car, but the man never turned his head. The woman rushed to the door and pushed and tugged till she was red in the face, but not an inch would it budge. Rushing to the front door, she pounded the glass in a furious manner, and by and by the driver "accidently" looked round. She gestured wildly, and as he shook his head in a stupid way, she held up her card, which said: "I am deaf and dumb." The driver fumbled around for two or three minutes and brought out a small placard on which was printed:

"So am I!"

They were then about half a mile above Brady street, making excellent time, and the woman's indignation was so great that she shook her fist at the driver and screamed out:

"I'll have you shot for this!"

He held up his card, shook his head, and paid no further attention to her blood-curdling threats. At the turn-table, a mile and a half above Brady street, the door slid back, and the woman jumped into the mud. She blessed that man from crown to sole, and she blessed all his relatives back to the Revolution, but he did not seem to hear her. As he started off she called out:

"You are a monster, villain, sneak, and thief!"

He gave the lines a shake, got the card from his pocket, and she was not too far away to read the answer:

"So am I!"

A WONDERFUL INVENTION.

Sent by Telephone—The First Newspaper Dispatch Sent by a Human Voice Over the Wires

SALEM, Feb. 12—10.55 p. m.—Professor A. Graham Bell, the inventor of that wonderful instrument, the telephone, which has caused so much interest in the scientific world and which is now becoming so popular known, lectured on his invention at Lyceum Hall this evening. The lecture was one of course of the Essex Institute, and about 500 persons were present. The lecture was very well received and the frequent and long-continued applause showed that the audience appreciated fully and wonderful uses and the experiments made with the machines. Professor Bell briefly explained the construction of the instrument and then sketched his studies of the system of transmitting sounds. He explained that it was his first attempt before an audience to try these different experiments. An intermittent current was first sent from Boston by Mr. Thomas A. Watson, Professor Bell's associate. This caused a noise very similar to a horn from the telephone. The Morse telegraph alphabet was then sent by musical sounds, and could be heard throughout the hall. The audience burst into loud applause at this experiment. A telephonic organ was then put in operation in Boston.— "Should Auld Acquaintance be Forgot" and "Yankee Doodle" were readily heard through the hall and heartily recognized. At this point Prof Bell then explained how he learned to,

TRANSMIT THE TONE OF THE HUMAN VOICE,

and paid a grateful tribute to Mr. Watson.— Professor Bell asked Mr. Watson for a song, and "Auld Lang Syne" came from the mouthpiece of the instrument almost before his words were ended. Mr. Watson was then asked to make a speech to the audience. He expressed himself as having more confidence eighteen miles away than if he were present. His speech was as follows: "Ladies and gentlemen—It gives me great pleasure to be able to address you this evening, although I am in Boston and you in Salem." This could be heard thirty-five feet distant—that is, all over the hall, and brought down the house with applause.

"IT IS FINISHED." — 'Tis done—the foul transaction's done, and to-day RUTHERFORD B. HAYES, of Ohio, occupies the Chair once filled by Washington.

The devious processes by which Mr. Hayes has attained his present elevated position, need no recital. They are known and read of all men. At four o'clock last Friday morning, the vote of Wisconsin. the last State in the alphabet was disposed of by recording her 11 electoral votes for Hayes and Wheeler—making the necessary 185 required by the Constitution to entitle them to the offices of President and Vice-President of the United States, for four years, from the 4th of March, 1877.

The ways and means resorted to to bring about this result; are now parts and parcels of the nation's record ; and as long as time shall last, the student of our national history will read, that in the centennial year of our national existence, a man was elevated to the highest position known to our system of government, by a fraud so palpable, so gross, and so enormous, that in any other land than our own, it would have been followed by bloodshed. He will read, and wonder and blush as he reads, that in the face of a popular majority of 268,000,—an electoral majority of at least 18 or 20, and a popular white majority of nearly a million votes. a trio of Returning Boards, composed of men whose names are branded with infamy, violently set at naught the *verdict of the people of their respective* States, as expressed at the polls, and counted in the defeated candidate. And saddest of all, he will read how three members of the highest legal tribunal in the Republic, deliberately closed the eyes of Justice, and with their judicial robes hanging loosely about them—robes which in all ages have been regarded as the sacred emblems of a nation's glory, leaped from their exalted places, and plunging into the political pool, consorted with Wells, Anderson, Cassanave and Kenner, to justify a crime. and legalize a fraud — that they might thereby place in office a man repudiated by the voice of the people. These are facts that cannot be gainsaid, and will not be forgotten.

But "it is finished." Mr. Hayes sits in the Chair of Washington. He has taken the prescribed oath, and gone through the usual forms of an inauguration, and to-day wields the helm of the Ship of State. As no forcible resistance was offered to his induction into office—neither should any obstruction be thrown in the way of his proper and legitimate administration of its duties.— We are all interested in good government, and none should be so suicidal as to refuse it when tendered, even though it flows through an illegitimate channel.

LAST Sunday Grant "stepped down and out" of the Presidential mansion, and to-day is simply U. S. G. He reigned during an important period of our national history. and had it in his power to establish for himself an immortality of fame. But he wasted his opportunities, and has gone hence "unwept, unhonored and unsung." with few to do him reverence, even of that ignoble army of plundering scamps who during his eight years power. sneezed whenever he took snuff—while the country generally exclaims—

"Fare thee well,
And if forever, still farewell,"
and as a national executive, may we ne'er look upon thy like again.

THE MIRROR

BENJ. F. SHEETZ, Editor.

Thursday Morning, Apr. 5, '77

If it has not already been done, an order will be issued within the next few days withdrawing the United States troops from the State House in South Carolina, which, as everybody knew, and as Chamberlain himself acknowledges in his letter to the President, is equivalent to the recognition of Hampton as Governor of the State. Both the contestants for the Gubernatorial chair, Hampton and Chamberlain, have left Washington, and ere long it is safe to predict, peace, quietness and good government will prevail in that long-suffering State, and an impetus given to her industries such as she has not experienced lo these many years.— Let similar action speedily follow in Louisiana, and the indications now are that new life and energy will be infused into those Commonwealths that cannot but result in great good to the whole country—and go a long way towards reconciling the country to the administration of its present *de facto* President.

LOUISIANA AFFAIRS.—A Washington dispatch to the New York *Tribune*, says that the New Orleans Commission was to start for their field of labor on Tuesday. It is believed that the adjustment of the South Carolina dispute by removing the troops from the Columbia State House will have the effect of making the solution of the problem in Louisiana simpler than it would have been a week or two ago

[Special Dispatch to Baltimore Sun.]

LIBERATION OF SOUTH CAROLINA.

The Troops to be Withdrawn from the State House at Columbia—End of the Carpet-Bag Rule—Chagrin of the Patterson-Chamberlain Clique—The Victory of Conservatism.

WASHINGTON, April 2.—The decision in the South Carolina case was reached by the cabinet to-day, and was in accordance with the predictions made in these despatches for a number of days past. Secretary McCrary was directed to prepare the necessary order to Gen. Ruger to withdraw the troops from the State House at Columbia, and to send them into camp. With the issuance of this order ends the reign of the carpet-baggers in South Carolina, and the beginning of a new era for the citizens and tax payers of that State.

This result would not have been achieved had Governor Hampton shown the slightest disposition to entertain the proposition for a compromise; but the firm and unyielding spirit was too much for the diplomacy of the Chamberlain-Patterson clique, aided and abetted by two or three members of the cabinet, and the administration was forced to accept as conclusive the voluntary assurance of Gov. Hampton that he would administer the duties of his office with impartiality, and extend protection to all the citizens of the State, white and black alike.

Wade Hampton intends to leave for Columbia at half-past one o'clock to-night, and will stop at Charlotte, N. C., one day, where his daughters are at school. He will not reach Columbia before Thursday, and does not believe the order withdrawing the troops will be promulgated before that time. It is expected the instructions to Gen. Ruger will be sent by mail and not by telegraph.

[General Dispatches.]

FINAL ACTION OF THE CABINET ON THE SOUTH CAROLINA QUESTION — THE TROOPS TO BE WITHDRAWN.

WASHINGTON, April 2.—At the cabinet meeting this morning the Secretary of War was directed to prepare an order transferring the troops from the State House in Columbia, S C., to their camp.

WASHINGTONIAN.

LEESBURG, LOUDOUN COUNTY, VA.

Saturday, April 7, 1877

☞ Mr. MAX COHEN, No. 608 F. street, N. W. Washington, D. C., is the authorized gent to receive advertisements for this paper

☞ The ovation with which Hampton was greeted from his home in South Carolina to Washington, was an expression of the popular approval and admiration of his wise and honorable course since he took in hand the redemption of his native State from the reign of discord. He has gained his point, and and the birds of political prey, which have flocked there to the destruction of the State, will seek more congenial climes, and the people will become harmonious and contented, and the State will gradually, but surely, rise from her ruin to the prosperity, which the development of her natural resources will secure to her. The people of South Carolina will thank the President and Hampton for this. They will not regard it as a party triumph, but the triumph of justice and right. The receptions of Hampton, through the country, and in Washington, show the popular heart to be with him and his cause. A correspondent of the Richmond "State," in writing from Washington says :

"It would have have done your heart good to have seen the sensation that Hampton created. I have lived here near ten years, and I have never seen anything like it. We are cynical here on the subject of so-called great men, and the average. Washingtonian hardly turns his head to look at a passing celebrity, be he Prince or President; but they kindled for Hampton, and the streets in front of his hotel were thronged with crowds waiting patiently to see him pass to his carriage."

The Southern Policy.

Chamberlain Gives it up and will Leave South Carolina.

The South Carolina question is settled, and Gov. Hampton will remain in undisputed control as Governor of the State. The President, though slowly, has acted wisely in this case. He simply did his duty, and that is to be commended in these days of political degeneracy. The good men of the country will approve his course, and rejoice that he has made one firm step in the path of pacification and restoration of order and justice to those States,—and we have the assurance that he will soon follow up this wise move, by a similar course towards the State of Louisiana, which will remove, forever, we hope, this cause of complaint and irritation in the country. He has but to do right, and the approval of his countrymen will be his reward. The following correspondence gives all the facts in the case.

[Special Dispatch to the World.]

WASHINGTON April 3.—Chamberlain has decided to-day not to enter upon any legal contest with Govenor Hampton in the court over the Governorship of South Carolina, but to return to Columbia, issue an address to the Republican party of the State, and then remove from the State forever

☞ Mr. Tilden has acted wisely in declining to engage in any proceeding, looking to a legal contest over the Presidency. It is too late for that now. We want peace in politics and confidence restored in all business matters. We have had enough agitation. We must now wait with Mr. Hayes, and should have the moral courage to approve and give him credit for all the good he does, and criticise the wrong.

☞ The South Carolinians are preparing to give Gov. Hampton a grand reception on his return home. Business is reported to have brightened up very much in South Carolina since the settlement.

Wade Hampton

[In our nation's history, after every war we have witnessed successful military leaders, often generals, who have later risked their reputations in the political realm. Interestingly, after the Civil War for the remainder of the century, all but three had served as generals. President McKinley had also served in the military but as a major under Hayes.

While Wade Hampton never made it to the presidency, he was destined to serve with distinction in war and peace. Both he and Bedford Forest were the only two to rise from Private to become Major Generals. Hampton was wounded five times, two seriously, and he lost a brother and a beloved son under his command. Longstreet regarded him "as the greatest natural cavalry leader of our or any other country." Hampton took over Lee's cavalry in the final months after Jeb Stuart was killed at Yellow Tavern.

South Carolina was considered the most dysfunctional and corrupt of the reconstruction states. Concerning the election crisis described in the previous column, this area was a tinder box of potential violence since all factions carried guns. With this ex-Confederate hero's firm but benevolent eloquence, the immediate problem dissipated.

As the South's first Democratic governor, things began to turn around. First of all, honest men began to replace bribers. Blacks outnumbered whites two to one, but Hampton's relationship with the freedmen was supportive, sensible, and progressive in the context of the times. Despite the fact that his family had been the state's largest slave holders, a large portion of the blacks ended up supporting him.

On a personal level, Hampton had many difficulties. A few years before, he lost his wife and a child. In the postwar economy, this former plantation owner had to declare bankruptcy, a fate suffered by many. This meant moving to a much more modest brick house. More seriously, he suffered a hunting accident in which he almost lost his life but was saved when they amputated his leg.

The recovery was agonizing, but Hampton was talked into accepting the less demanding job as U.S. Senator. He held this for 12 years. Finally Cleveland asked him to serve as a railroad commissioner, which he dutifully performed. He was one of the South's most popular leaders, and his popularity appears well justified.]

The above opinions are those of this writer, who has researched several biographies.

4/26/77 Mirror

ALL HAIL TO LOUISIANA

The U. S. troops left the St. Louis Hotel in New Orleans at 12 o'clock on Tuesday. Everything passed off quietly, not the slightest disturbance marred the progress of events. Gov. Nicholls was to take possession of the State House on Wednesday.

"The commission sent from Washington to adjust matters has returned, and it is due to President Hayes to say that he has fulfilled the promises made by him in his letter of acceptance and his inaugural address, by restoring local self-government to the only two remaining States in the South that had been deprived of it by federal interference."

THE LAST OF THE CARPET-BAGGERS.— Under the operations of an order issued by President Hayes, the U. S. troops stationed in the vicinity of St. Louis Hotel in New Orleans, have vamosed. At meridian on Tuesday last, they marched to their barracks outside the city limits. Prior to their leaving, a number of the Returning Board members of Packard's Legislature went over and joined the Nicholls Legislature, giving to that body a full quorum, and Democratic majorities in both branches. The pretentious Packard alone remained in the State House, but Warmouth telegraphs that Packard would vacate the St. Louis Hotel soon after the removal of the troops ; and thus ignominiously ends carpet-bag rule in the South.

4/26/77 Mirror

THE WICKEDEST TOWN IN AMERICA.

What the Great American Humorist Saw in Cheyenne.

CHEYENNE, April 11.—I have seen wicked cities in my time. I have seen spreeing at the Esler in St. Petersburg, seen fellows "make a night of it" in the Oryheum in Berlin, seen the wickedness at Nijni Novgorod during the September fair, seen the Mabille packed with depravity when the empire was at its meridian, but I never expected to see hell itself. I sauntered out on the streets of Cheyenne at midnight. Fifty saloons and a dozen licensed gambling houses line the principal street, all thronged and gaily illuminated till the morning sun puts out the lights.

What makes Cheyenne the wickedest city in the world ?

I. Cheyenne is the metropolis where the rich owners and the buckskin-clad drivers of five million dollars' worth of cattle rendezvous for a weekly spree.

II. It is the nearest point where the Black Hillers can sell their gold dust and nuggets and then gamble and spree away the proceeds so as to go back to the mines.

III. It is the point to which all the Indian-fighting army officers come as a place where they can spree away a hundred dollars in a night and make up for lost time on the Big Horn.

IV. It is the stopping point for all the swell demimond from San Francisco, St. Louis, and Chicago. In a word, it is the American paradise for licensed drinking, fighting, gambling, &c.

Walk with me into one licensed house on the principal street in Cheyenne at 3 o'clock in the morning. The house is a medley. It is the Parisian Varieties on Sixteenth street, John Morrissey's Saratoga gambling house, the Argyle rooms on Sixth avenue, and the Alhambra, with its fifty waiter girls, in London, all crowded into one. The building is perhaps 50 by 130 feet, and two stories high. On the ground floor is a theatre stage, room for three hundred cow boys, soldiers, ranchmen, and waiter girls, and just out of it are the gambling tables and bars. At the tables every known game is played. Among the dealers are several French women dressed in silks and diamonds. Utterly devoid of delicacy they shuffle and deal the cards and handle the chips for the swearing, drinking crowd which throng around the tables.

On the stage there is a constant variety show going on. Skillful variety actors are employed, and there the tight rope walkers, the song and dance women in tights, the low-necked ballad singer, the clog-dancer, the negro minstrel, the model artists, and the female bathers come out in a continuous stream from ten at night till morning.

On the first floor every drink is 25 cents, and about thirty English, French, and American waiter girls keep the crowd constantly drinking. Above this motley crowd of cow boys, ranchmen, Black Hills freighters, miners, and soldiers, is a row of private boxes filled with rich ranch men, officers, tourists, and fellows who have come down with gold dust from the Black Hills. These boxes all communicate with the stage. Twenty or thirty waiter girls supply the boxes with champagne, the price of which is $5 for pint bottles. All drinks in the boxes are 50 cents. It is a common thing for a rich ranch man, after selling a thousand cattle, to come here and spend $1,000 on a spree. A Colonel in the army, who had been fighting up in the Big Horn country, came in the other evening and spent $1,000, and finally left his watch on the red, and lost that too — The proprietor of this gambling and variety saloon is a very generous man. Everybody likes him, and he is considered a good citizen in Cheyenne. Clergymen shake him by the hand, and bankers chum with him like an old schoolmate. The profits in the one building are $1,000 per day. I suppose there are a dozen houses on one block where gambling goes on day and night with open doors — Sometimes the marshal and the policeman take a hand. The judge goes out and "bucks the tiger" while the jury are agreeing on a verdict. You will see Colonels in the army standing by private soldiers, and see cow boys in buckskin dividing the chips with a Cheyenne Indian—all in the most enterprising border town in America and the wickedest city in the world.

To-morrow I'm off for the Black Hills.

ELI PERKINS.

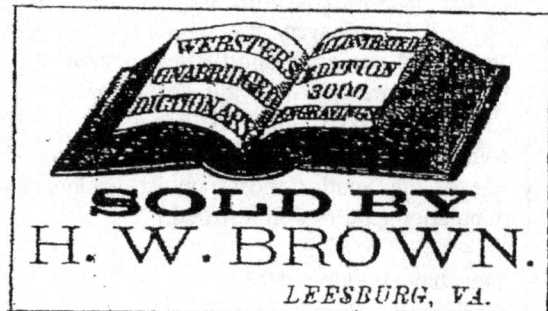

4/26/77 Mirror

Anecdote of President Lincoln.

I called upon Mr. Lincoln soon after he was first installed in the White House. In the room where Mr. Lincoln granted interviews, &c., were several persons who were waiting their turn to speak with him. I listened to the requests of several men and women, and I saw that very few were granted what they solicited. I had a seat at, or near one end of a long table. Mr. Lincoln sat at the other end. Soon after I was seated, in walked several officers in the Spanish navy to pay their compliments to Mr. Lincoln. By some means they were directed toward my end of the table, and I saw they took me for the President. Mr. Lincoln saw the same thing, and hastily signalled me to "go ahead," as he expressed it, and receive them. I rose, shook hands with each officer, and exchanged a few words with them, which would have been I suppose, appropriate had I indeed been President. The moment their backs were turned I looked toward Mr. Lincoln. He was shaking with laughter. I thought now I had paved the way to win the position I had come to ask. I made up my mind to address the President in a new way, and thus add to the hold I already had upon him. So, when my time came, I stepped up to Mr. Lincoln and said:

"Sir, I have seen the annoyance to which you are subjected by so many and often repeated requests for innumerable positions, &c. Now, if you will permit me to shake hands, I will try and smother my desire for a certain position which I had come to ask from you."

Mr. L. jumped up, and grasping my hand said:

"Sir, you are one man in a thousand. I am doubly indebted to you. You have been the means of conveying to those Spanish officers that the President of the United States is a very handsome man, and then you do not even ask an office. But," he added, "hurry home. You may repent."

It is sufficient to add that I hurried.

5/24/77 Mirror

ANOTHER FEARFUL WARNING—A HORRIBLE DEATH FROM COAL OIL.—We have another instance to add to the hundreds that have preceded it, of the horrible deaths resulting from the careless handling of coal oil, —and holding it up as a fearful warning to those whose daily use of this dangerous element should teach a lesson. On Saturday morning last, about 6 o'clock, MARY, a worthy and much respected colored woman, the wife of CHARLES CHANCELLOR, was so horribly burned by the explosion of a coal oil can, that death ensued in eight hours.

5/24/77 Mirror

How Buffalo Bill Performed the Ceremony for a Couple

A good story is told of how he performed the ceremony of marriage while he was justice of the peace. It was his first attempt, and the applicants were of of the true western type. They called upon Cody in the log cabin where he held his justice office.—Bill had a book of forms, which he took down and studied attentively to get some idea of how he should tie the knot. There were forms for nearly every transaction of life, but he failed to find what he was looking for, and finally slammed the gook down and observed to the parties."

"You two fellers join hands;" and the "two fellers" did so.

Then he said to the groom: "Are you willing to take this woman to be your lawful wedded wife, to love her, honor her, and obey her?"

"You bet your butes," was the response of the bashful hair-lifter.

"And you, Miss, are you willing to take this here man to be your wedded husband to love him, honor him, and support him?"

She giggled, and nodded in the affirmative; but this didn't suit Bill, who said: "See here, Miss, we've got to have this thing on the dead square, and we can't marry folks by halves in this country. We are bound to go the whole hog. If you want this here man for a husband you must speak out and say so, as though you meant it sure, I'll ask you again. Will you take this here man to be your wedded husband, to love him, honor him and support him?"

This time the lady responded bravely. "Yes, Sir, I will."

This satisfied his honor, and he remarked, "That settles it. Now look here, you two; you are man a wife, and whoever Bill Cody and God almighty have joined together, let no man put asunder."

"And now," added Bill, let's take another sip of tarantula juice, and drink to the happiness of the happy couple," which everybody with true western unanimity proceeded to do.

5/12/77 Washingtonian

Fighting for Life.

A Deadly Conflict at Beallsville, Montgomery County, Md. — The Assassin Killed.

The most desperate and horrible attempt at murder, resulting in the death of the would be murderer, known in this section for many years, occurred at Beallsville, Md., (a small settlement in Montgomery county, about thirty miles from this city, and three miles south of Salem station on the Metropolitan branch of the Baltimore and Ohio railroad), last Friday morning. It seems that on Wednesday night last a smoke-house was broken into and a quantity of meat stolen. Subsequently a valuable mule was stolen from the farm of Mr. Lemuel L. Beall. Mr. Beall, while speaking of the matter the next day to his neighbors, stated that he believed that one Henson Ames, a noted desperado, and of whom the residents of Beallsville stood in great fear, had committed the thefts. Later in the day Ames called at a store near the house of Mr. Beall, kept by a gentleman named John Belt, and asked for Mr. Beall, and said further that he intended to kill him for having charged him with robbing the smoke-house and stealing the mule. He then left the store. Mr. Beall called and was informed of the facts. Ames, armed with a stout cudgel, a murderous weapon, cut from a green sapling, appeared at the store again late on Thursday afternoon, and inquired for Mr. Beal, and said that he had cut the club to kill him with. Mr. Beall, being aware of the fact, kept in his house all night, and would not be induced to leave it until Friday morning about sunrise. At that hour Ames, armed with his club, called at the house and demanded that Beall come out. Beall, arming himself with a revolver, went out and met Ames, who rushed forward and dealt Beall a murderous blow on the head with the club. Beall raised his pistol, pulled the trigger, but the weapon missed fire, and Ames again dealt his victim another deadly blow upon the cheek bone. This blow was followed up by another and another, and Beall attempted the second time to shoot Ames, but again did the pistol miss fire, at which Mr. Beall threw it to the ground, and it was immediately discharged. Ames continued to pour in a shower of heavy blows.

Beall then, as a last resource, closed in upon his adversary, and with an adroit movement that no doubt saved his life, struck Ames a powerful blow just under the chin, causing him to fall backward heavily, and breaking his neck. He expired instantly, the fight having lasted thirty minutes. At the time there had collected about Beall's stable, where the affair transpired, half a dozen persons, who although able to overpower Ames, were afraid to do so. After the conclusion of the struggle Mr. Beall got on his horse and rode to Poolesville, five miles distant, and

gave himself up. As soon as the tragedy was circulated about the village, a crowd collected about the spot, and a justice of the peace living near, acting as coroner, summoned a jury and an inquest was held. After hearing a number of witnesses whose testimony was in substance as above, a verdict of justifiable homicide was rendered, and Mr. Beall, then under arrest, was released. The strange part of the affair, which shows how utterly worthless Ames was considered, is that the father-in-law and brother of the dead man who were working in a field near by, when informed of the deed, positively refused to go near the dead man or to have anything to do with the body, declaring that it served him right, and that the world was rid of a great villian. After the dead man had remained neglected nearly all day, some farmers living in the neighborhood visited Mr. Beall's, placed the body in a wagon and carried it to the house of his father-in-law, who subsequently placed it in a rough pine box and buried it without ceremony in a deserted spot at the back of his house.

(Bealleville is about 30 miles northeast of Loudoun County.)

DIED:

At his residence in Hillsboro', on the 19th of March, ROBERT F. JONES, son of the late John Jones, Sr., in the 37th year of his age.

At the beginning of the late war he offered his service as a private in the Loudoun Cavalry—was afterwards transferred to White's Battalion, and in one of the raids of that officer into Maryland, he was shot through the spine, and in consequence of the paralysis which resulted, was never able to walk or use his limbs afterward. A truer, a more chivalrous spirit never lived. Kind and generous to his friends—magnanimous to a fault with his opponents, he was a good son, and an affectionate brother. All who knew him, loved him, and sincerely mourn his death.

W. M.

5/12/77 Washingtonian

It was a very embarrassing circumstance, and it happened in a neighboring hotel. A man and his wife were stopping there. The man was subject to severe attacks of colic, and was taken sick there in the night. He told his wife he must have immediate relief or he could not live; thought a mustard draft would relieve him. She hastily robed herself, went down stairs, and found the watchman, who admitted her to the dining room, and she spread the mustard from a castor on her handkerchief, and hastened up stairs Finding the door ajar she rushed in, turned down the bed clothes and slapped the mustard draft on the unconscious man's bowels. He instantly sprang up in bed, and in a strange voice said:

"My God! madame what are you doing?"

She had got it on the wrong man.

THE MIRROR.

THURSDAY.....................May 24.

☞ Rev. HENRY BRANCH will preach at Catoctin Church, Sunday morning.

SERIOUS ACCIDENT.—We understand that on Saturday last, a young man named HOSKINSON, son of Mr. Thos. Hoskinson, of Hamilton, started from that village in a buggy for Lovettsville, when a short distance from the former place the horse became unmanageable, the buggy was overturned, and Mr. H. dragged some distance before released from his perilous situation. His injuries were of a very serious nature, and it was feared might prove fatal.

QUITE an excitement was created at Farmwell a day or two ago, caused by the absence of two little children of Mr. Jas. Havenner. It appears that the children, a girl and a boy, aged respectively 3 and 4 years, strayed from home about 2 o'clock on Monday afternoon. That evening a heavy rain fell, and night came without tidings of the lost ones. That night some forty or fifty of the neighbors scoured the country throughout the night, but day broke without rewarding their search.—About 8 o'clock, however, the little ones were found in an open field, the girl asleep and the boy keeping vigil by her side. When it is remembered that the little things had been absent through the night, and exposed to the drenching rain, we can well imagine that there was joy in the anxious household over their recovery.

THE MIRROR.

THURSDAY.....................May 31.

FIRE.— The barn, stable, shed and corn house, belonging to Griffith W. Paxson, in this county, was burned on the night of the 25th inst. The fire was evidently the work of incendiary, as Mr. P's straw rick, near the buildings, was fired only a few days previous. His loss on buildings and contents will probably reach 1,000, upon which there is an insurance of $425 in the Loudoun Mutual.

P. S. On Sunday, Deputy Sheriff HARRY RUSSELL, lodged in the jail of this county, a 12 year old paragraph of the 15th amendment—not much bigger than a pound of soap after a hard day's washing—the acknowledged author of the above mischief. He lived in Mr. Paxson's family—and says that lying in bed about one o'clock that night, he got up thinking about the matter and from some cause that he cannot account for, he got up, dressed himself, and with match in hand, went to the shed, lighted the match, stuck it in a knot hole, and then hastily returned to the house and went to bed with his clothes on, to be ready for the first alarm. The alarm was given, but too late to save the property, which was destroyed as stated above. This pocket edition of villainy can assign no reason for the crime, except that he got to thinking about it, and went and done it. The case will go before the court next Monday week, and then the trouble will be to know what to do about it.

THE contract for repairing Goose Creek Bridge, on Leesburg and Aldie Turnpike, has been awarded to Mr. R. M. Bruce, for one hundred and seventy-five dollars.

THE MAYOR of Leesburg, advertises for proposals for furnishing oil and lighting the lamps of the town for the ensuing year.

HARMON KEPHART has taken the Mt. Gilead Woolen Factory, and is prepared to exchange for money or wool, goods in his line. See advertisement.

6/21/77 Mirror

THE CONFEDERATE MONUMENT—A CONTRACT ENTERED INTO—THE UNVEILING TO TAKE PLACE ON THE 21ST OF OCTOBER.—We are glad to learn that after years of delay, the graves of the Confederate dead who lie entombed in Union Cemetery, are at last to be marked by an appropriate monument.

DEAD.—JESSIE BOOTH, of this town, died on Monday last, after a brief illness. JESSIE was an amiable, well disposed colored man, greatly respected by all who knew him. In all the bitter contests of the last few years, no amount of cajolery could swerve him from his fidelity to the white people among whom he had been raised, and with whom he had passed his maturer life. Always polite, and attentive to his duties, he won the confidence and respect of those with whom he had came in contact. As caterer for the "Eagle Restaurant" he will be sadly missed by the habitues of that establishment, with whom he was a favorite. Open and generous in his nature, his occasional imprudence, perhaps, weighed too heavily upon an already delicate constitution—but there are many nevertheless who "to his faults a little blind," will sorrow with unfeigned grief at his untimely death and long cherish the memory of his simple and unselfish virtues. Alas, poor JESSIE—peace to his ashes.

RESIGNATION OF A GOOD OFFICER.—We regret to learn that Capt. E. B. POWELL has tendered to Judge BALL his resignation of the office of Justice of the Peace in Leesburg District, not only for the remainder of the present term, but also for the term for which he has recently qualified. The reason assigned for his resignation is "the refusal of the Board of Supervisors to pay expenses incurred in execution of sentences from my (his) office as Justice of the Peace." It appears that Capt P. several times had occasion to impose stripes upon parties brought before him, and in such cases, there being no Constable to execute the sentence, he resorted to the appointment of a special officer to discharge the unpleasant duty, whom he allowed $2 for the service. This the Board refused to pay, and in consequence Leesburg District loses an efficient officer, who was a terror to evil-doers.

6/28/77 Mirror

FREDERICK DOUGLASS IN MARYLAND.—Frederick Douglass, United States Marshal of the District of Columbia, many years ago a slave on the Eastern Shore of Maryland, visited his old home and his old master at St. Michael's, Talbot county, on Sunday last, with a large party of colored excursionists.

The boat arrived at an early hour in the morning, and as soon as convenient Douglass called at Captain Auld's residence, where he was received by Judge William H. Bruff, Captain Auld's son-in-law, who addressed him as "Marshal Douglass."—"No, no," expostulated the Marshal, "I am Marshal Douglass in Washington; here let me be called Fred. Douglass again."

"I come, first of all," he said, "to see my old master, from whom I have been separated for forty-one years; to shake his hand, to look into his kind old face, and see it beaming with light from the other world. I have had great joy in shaking that hand, in looking into that face, streaked with age and disease, but aglow with the light that comes from an honest heart, and reflecting the glory from the spirit-world, upon whose border he is, and where we shall soon again meet. Forty-one years ago I left him. I left him, not because I loved Cæsar less, but because I loved Rome more."

Mr. Douglass stated that in his book written soon after his escape he had made some statements that lapse of time and reflection had caused him to feel he had better have left unsaid, and for aught that he said that was unjust to his old master. or had wounded his feelings, he begged his forgiveness. Captain Auld told him that he had never expected to keep him in slavery; that he knew forty-one years ago he was too smart to be a slave, and that when he sent him to Baltimore, after his difficulty at Freedland's instead of selling him South, it was with the expectation that he would achieve his freedom. Douglass called upon Captain Auld again in the afternoon, just before starting to the boat, to bid him good-bye, and when they parted both men wept.—*Baltimore Sun, 19th.*

7/5/77 Mirror

BROKE JAIL.—There was another jail delivery in this town on Saturday night.—Spaulding, Nickins and Wigginton, confined in a cell on the first floor, of the jail of this county, made their escape some time after midnight, and have not since been heard from. Another prisoner, confined in the same cell, who only had eleven more days to complete his term of imprisonment, did not avail himself of the opportunity thus afforded to make his escape, and from him it is learned that those who did go, found in the sink, to which they had access, a case knife, made into a saw,—where or how it ever got there, "is one of those things that no fellow can find out." With that they sawed a bar of the iron grating in the window, through the hole thus made, they had no difficulty in reaching the jail-yard, carrying with them the blankets from off their beds. Once in the yard, they tore the blankets into strips, tied them together, fastened a brick in one end, threw it over the top of the high wall surrounding the jail yard, and by this means scaled the enclosure, and as we have already stated, have not been seen since.

Spaulding was awaiting trial for entering a gentleman's house at Snickersville during the absence of the family at church, and carrying off a Sunday dinner prepared for the preacher.—Wiggington had been sent to prison for six months for stealing a pair of boots, and had served out about one-half his term. Geo. Nickens had been found guilty of stealing wheat, and the jury fixed his punishment at four years in the penitentiary—but on the motion of his counsel, who asked for a new trial, he had been granted on extension of judgment until the July term.

7/12/77/Mirror

Miss Jennie North Graduates at the Head of a Class of Thirty-Eight Young Men.

LEWISTON, ME., June 28.—It has been duly announced in the World that the salutatory and other accustomed orations at the annual commencement of Bates College, in this pleasant little city, were delivered on Wednesday last with their usual excellence and effect, in which announcement appeared the unostentatious statement that Jane Rich North spoke the valedictory. Under ordinary circumstances this might and undoubtedly would have sufficed for Bates and the people hereabouts who are interested in its affairs, but on investigation the circumstances do not appear to be ordinary. The name Jane implied a young woman—incredulous as it seemed that one of this sex should have carried off the highest honor is a class of her superiors, men—and a young lady the valedictorian proves to have been.

To her classmates, many of whom still remain in town, and who are found properly, if somewhat unexpectedly, enthusiastic upon the subject of her many and varied talents, she is known as Jennie North, and is described as a "perfect brick of a girl," whose career in college has been a continuous justification of the coeducation of the sexes.

Sabbath-School Festival.

THE LADIES OF CATOCTIN SABBATH SCHOOL, near Taylortown, will hold a FESTIVAL on FRIDAY, JULY 6th, commencing at 2 o'clock, P. M., for the purpose of purchasing a Library for said school. REFRESHMENTS of every description will be prepared for distribution. The audience will be entertained with music by the Tankerville and Point of Rocks Bands. The public is invited.
july 5, 1877-1t.

Tankerville Cornet Band FESTIVAL.

THE MEMBERS of the Tankerville Cornet Band will hold a FESTIVAL at Tankerville School House, near Hoysville, on THURSDAY and FRIDAY, the 19th and 20th of JULY, the proceeds of which will be used for the purchase of a uniform for said band. REFRESHMENTS of every description will be prepared suitable for the occasion. The audience will be entertained by the Jefferson and Point of Rocks Bands. The public is invited.　[july 5-3t.

(Tankerville Road is still there; Tankerville is not.)

7/19/77 Mirror

THE FIREMEN'S STRIKE.

Rough Work on the B. O. Railroad.

Last week the authorities of the Baltimore & Ohio Railroad passed an order reducing the pay of all employees of the company who received over $1 per day, ten per cent. The order was to go into effect on Monday, at which time there was a general strike, principally among the firemen. So far the chief difficulties exist at Baltimore, Martinsburg, Keyser, Grafton, and Wheeling, having begun on the first and second divisions which include Baltimore and Martinsburg. It is estimated that between 400 and 500 men are engaged in the movement.

The local authorities at Martinsburg finding themselves unable to deal with the rioters, the company telegraphed to Gov. Jacobs for assistance, who at once telegraphed to his aid, Col. C. J. Faulkner, jr., of Martinsburg, to use the military under his command at that place.

Accordingly at 5 o'clock Tuesday morning, Col. Faulkner had the Berkely Light Infantry in ranks, and marched to the depot, where he made a sympathetic speech to the rioters, and urged them to desist. To these appeals the crowd turned a deaf ear, and then, finding it was useless to reason with them further, Capt. Faulkner read to the assembly the Governor's orders. At the same time he made a statement of his duty as he understood it, and ordered the company to load their pieces and resist any attempt made to stop the train.

The militia company was deployed on both sides of a train which was about starting, an engineer and fireman having volunteered to work. As the train reached the switch one of the strikers, Wm. Vandergriff, seized the switch-ball to run the train on the side track. John Poisal, a member of the militia company, jumped from the pilot of the engine and attempted to replace the switch so that the train should go on. Vandergriff fired two shots at Poisal, one causing a slight flesh wound in the side of the head. Poisal returned the fire, shooting Vandergriff through the hip. Several other shots were fired at Vandergriff, striking him in the hand and arm.

When the firing was heard a very large crowd of railroaders and citizens collected, and the feeling became intense. The volunteering engineer and fireman of the train ran off as soon as the shooting began. Capt. Faulkner then made the statement that he had performed his duty, and if the trainmen deserted their posts he could do nothing more. The militia company was therefore marched to their armory and ingloriously disbanded, leaving the rioters in possession of the field.

(The B & O, the oldest track in the country was right across the river from Loudoun County. Obviously rural Loudoun was becoming alarmed at the increase of labor strife)

7/26/77 Mirror

RAILROAD STRIKERS.

The Troubles of the B. & O. Railroad.

STATE MILITIA AND U. S. TROOPS ON THE WAR PATH.

The Soldiers Fire on the Mob.

NINE MEN KILLED IN BALTIMORE, &C.

Last week we announced briefly, that the employees of the B. & O. Railroad, were on a strike. Full details of what has since transpired would occupy more space than our paper contains. We therefore epitomise from our daily exchanges the events of the week.

At the date of our last issue, the strikers were massed at Martinsburg, where several hundred freight trains had been stopped, with their cargoes for the east and the west. The Governor of West Virginia had ordered out the volunteer companies at Martinsburg to suppress the strikers, and put the wheels of the blockaded trains in motion. The State troops were found unequal to the task, and the Governor applied to the President of the United States for federal assistance.

On Wednesday morning, the arrival in Martinsburg, of 36 men of the Matthews Light Guard of Wheeling, added to the excitement, and by night the strikers and their friends numbered over several hundred, having been joined during the day by all the idle hands from the Chesapeake and Ohio Canal. The soldiers remained in the cars all day. At night they were quartered in the Court-house. Threats of violence were freely indulged in by the strikers, but none was attempted—neither was a single car removed from the yard.

Toward night it become known that President Hayes had acceded to the request of Gov. Matthews, and that about 300 U. S. soldiers from Washington and Fort McHenry, with several pieces of artillery, had been despatched to the scene of action. Copies of the President's proclamation, warning persons against aiding or abetting the riotous demonstration, and commanding the rioters to disperse by 12 o'clock on Thursday, were freely circulated among the crowd and prominently posted in the city.

About 7 o'clock Thursday morning, a train arrived with the U. S. troops, under Gen. French. No resistance was offered them by the strikers.

THE GREAT STRIKE.

The strike on the Baltimore & Ohio Railroad last week, which was at first supposed to be an outburst of passion on the part of a few restless breaksmen and firemen, has since assumed fearful proportions, and no longer partakes of an honest demand on the part of hardworked laborers for a fair equivalent for their services, which was right, but it has grown into a destructive mob, carrying anarchy and ruin and death in its pathway. The flame kindled at Martinsburg was blown into a blaze that has spread throughout the northern and western portions of the Union, until nearly all the leading lines of railroad transportation have been paralyzed, and a wild spirit of communism holds high carnival in the land, the like of which has never before been witnessed in this country, and the ultimate results of which none can foresee. Already the Governors of four States have ordered out the militia of their respective commonwealths, to suppress the disturbance, and it has even been found necessary to call in the strong arm of the United States army to aid in the preservation of law and order.

The causes that produced the strike among the workmen are understood, viz: a curtailment of 10 per cent on the wages of all who were receiving over $1 per day— From Baltimore to the Ohio river the laborers affected by this order rose as one man in open, violent resistance—not only refusing to accept the terms offered, but absolutely refusing to allow others to work for the wages they declined. Their lawless proceeding in this, is of course without justification. It was their privilege and their right to demand more wages for their labor, and to cease work unless it was paid to them ; but when they undertook to say that OTHER men should not toil for the wages they had declined, and attempted by violent and unlawful means, to enforce this communistic principle, they transcended the bounds of good citizenship, and became an armed mob, nothing else.

THE STRIKE—WHAT IT HAS DONE.

At this writing the railroad troubles have about ended—the strikers have subsided, passenger and freight trains, are running on schedule time over nearly or quite all the roads, and as a consequence business at the centres of trade is reviving, and soon all will be life, activity and bustle, where a little while ago, scarce a sound was heard, save the clangour of arms, or the measured tread of the sentinel on his round.

And now that comparative quiet has been restored, men naturally look for the fruit of this nine days wonder, and inquire what has been gained by the disturbance, or who has been benefitted by the disgraceful scenes enacted. The railroad companies, whose parsimony, it may be, aroused the slumbering fire of discontent that for months and years had been smouldering in the breasts of their employees have profited nothing. The immense destruction of property, and the heavy loss sustained by the interruption of their business, turns the balance sheet largely against them, in a pecuniary point of view, if nothing more.

The strikers certainly have made nothing by the operation. So far, while seeming concessions have been made to them in minor matters the pay has not been increased even of those who have resumed work. The time lost in their vain attempt to dictate terms, has depleted their coffers of their scanty savings, while in not a few instances, the wolf is scratching at the door where helpless women and innocent children cry for bread, to say nothing of the dead and maimed, whose misfortune will be a perpetual sorrow in many a household. So it is clear that the last condition of both the strikers and the struck is worse than the first.

But the trouble was not confined to these, For an entire fortnight the whole country has been as it were, in a state of siege.— Five States of the Union, distrusting their ability to deal with a domestic outbreak within their own borders and among their own citizens besought federal interference, thus weakening the confidence of the people in the sufficiency of the bulwark of our political and social independence, State sovereignty, and hastily setting a precedent, in this hour of apprehended danger, that future Governors of the various commonwealths may avail themselves of for the accomplishment of less patriotic purposes.

But, worse than all, it has developed the existence on American soil of a communistic spirit as wild and aggressive in its desires as ever drenched with blood the streets of some of the fairest cities of the world — and reveals the fact that underlying the peaceful calm of society, there lurks a volcano that only needs to be pricked with a single act of violence, to vomit forth a mob ready armed for the commission of any outrage.

8/2/77 Mirror

A STRIKE IN LOUDOUN.—A gentleman living a few miles from Leesburg, made preparations last week to thresh his crop of wheat. The thresher had been put in position at his stack-yard—the workmen, previously engaged, had assembled, and all things were in readiness to proceed with the work. But just then the hands employed deemed it an opportune moment to strike for higher wages, and they struck—refusing to turn a wheel unless their demand was complied with. But the demand didn't pay worth a cent. The proprietor refused to comply, and made the situation known to his neighbors, who, nobly asserting their independence, went themselves to the rescue—took the places abandoned by the laborers, threshed out that crop, and are now in turn, doing the same thing for each other. It is to be hoped that the lesson will have a good effect on the "strikers"

8/9/77 Mirror

THE RAILROAD STRIKERS, under the persuasive influences of shell and ball, have succumbed to the inevitable, and peace reigns along the public highways, and railroad business is progressing much as before the outbreak. There is no longer any obstruction to the running of trains, and apparently all is serene. And now the Governor of Maryland is turning his attention to the striking boatmen on the Chesepeake and Ohio Canal, who for a month and more have held the boats on that highway locked up to the great injury of the business of the country, and pecuniary loss of the Mining Companies; and if the obstructionists do not at once peaceably desist their unlawful interruption, the military will be employed to open the blockade.

But while this is true of the railroads and canals, matters wear an ugly aspect in the mining regions of Pennsylvania. It is said that "There are are forty-five thousand idle miners and railroad men in and about Wilkesbarro who refuse to go to work unless their demands are complied with by the employers. Among these are of course, many who would be very willing to work, but are not permitted by the rules of their trade-unions, and in going to work they would not only run the risk of being killed by their brother workmen, but would incur the odium of treason to their class. The property of the mining companies and the dwellings of the miners or workmen who disregard the threats of the desperadoes are given to the flames nightly, and the reign of terror is complete. On the other hand the companies hold out and make no effort to reach an amicable understanding.

In the meantime a large army of United States soldiers is being concentrated in Pennsylvania, along the line of the road, with their headquarters at Pittsburg. Already there are nearly three thousand regular troops in the very heart of the central State of the country."

Leesburg Va., Aug. 22nd, 1877.

MR. EDITOR: Is it not time a voice was raised in behalf of some measures for the improvement of the sanitary condition of our town, and for the promotion of Health? At this season of the year when "fevers rage" and ague shakes its victims, is it not a little remarkable that with the neglected condition of all sanitary measures the health of the place is as good as it is. In passing through the streets at many points you are greeted with a stench that is unbearable. One of the most prominent of these is on King Street, nearly opposite the P. O. where the Drain crosses said street. The course of the drain after leaving the street, is through an old decayed or decaying wooden trunk, which is sadly neglected, not having been *thoroughly* cleaned and *Limed* for *two years.* Is it strange it should become "loud"? I should think not.

To a little farther south on King, to an alley on the west side, and you will observe strong indications of *Pig-pens* in that locality, i. e. in the square bounded on the east by King, and on the south by Loudoun streets. On between King and Wirt a very unpleasant odor greets you, also corner of Market and Wirt. The "Pig-pen" odor at that point is dreadful, with strong indications of a still *greater nuisance,* (when uncared for) somewhere in some of the adjoining squares. Can not these things be remedied? Who is responsible for it? Is it the Mayor? Is it the Council? Both have been appealed to. Is it the Street Commissioners? They have had their attention called to it. What, then, must we do? Can they only be reached by Petition —if so, let us then perform that duty. Must we *beg them to act?* We would even do that, if it would secure the desired end. Whose duty is it to see that *Lime* is kept for sanitary purposes? Is it either of those above mentioned? Is it the Town-Sergeant? Is it the duty of the people? the citizens? If there is no other way to remedy the Sewer, let us, as citizens, agitate and devise means to remedy the nuisance. In vain, have we looked to the Executives of the Town—the Mayor and Council—but no relief has yet reached us. If, as citizens, we must attend to these things, ourselves, let us begin at once. Let each one constitute a "Board of Health," do all in his power to promote the Health of our Town, thereby adding greatly to our happiness and prosperity, as well as discharging a duty we owe to ourselves and our fellow-man.

Yours, &c   JUSTICE.

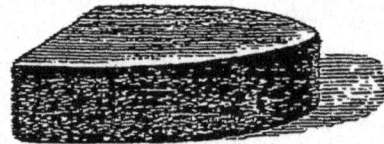

August, 1877

ORDINATION OF ELDER E. V. WHITE— INTERESTING CEREMONIES.— We understand that the services of the Baptist Association at the Valley Meeting House, in this county, on Sunday last were of an unusually interesting character. A number of clergymen and visiting brethren from a distance were in attendance, as well as a large congregation of the members and friends in the neighborhood.

The event of the day was the ordination to full powers and privileges of Elder in the church, of Col. E. V. WHITE, of this county, a gentleman well and favorably known to the people of Virginia.

The ordination sermon was preached by Rev. Dr. BEBE, of New York, who took occasion to feelingly allude to the gallantry with which the candidate before him, had in other days battled for the homes and firesides of the wives and children of his native South, but who, when "grim visaged war, had smoothed his wrinkled front," sheathed his sword, and was now about to dedicate himself to the service of the Great Master whose kingdom is not of this world. Our informant states that the ceremonies throughout were of the most impressive nature, and that during the solemn scene attending the laying on of hands, tears fell freely in that large audience from eyes long unused to weeping. In the afternoon Elder WHITE delivered a short discourse.

Col. White has for some time past been preaching, but until Sunday was not commissioned to baptise, marry, or perform certain other duties belonging to a regularly ordained Elder. We have never heard him preach, but those who have speak well of his efforts. One thing we may say, however, and that is, his church possesses no more earnest, conscientious or thoroughgoing laborer within her pale, than Elder E. V. WHITE.

(Local Confederate hero Elijah White became a very successful businessman and his ferry across the Potomac, which bears his name, is still heavily used. Now a new achievement and responsibility.)

DISTRESSING ACCIDENT—DROWNING OF LEWIS DONOHOE.—An accident occurred in the vicinity of Leesburg on Friday evening, that cast a gloom over the community, and which resulted in the death of a most worthy citizen, Mr. LEWIS DONOHOE.

There had been a heavy rain fall during the afternoon which greatly swelled Tuscarora branch, ordinarily a small stream that may be waded at its deepest point. The channel is narrow, however, and after each rain, its rise is sudden and rapid, and its fall equally so, after the rain ceases. Mr. DONOHOE came to town during the day in a one-horse wagon, and late in the evening, about 6½ o'clock, started for home, a negro boy in the wagon with him. When he reached Tuscarora where it crosses the Ball's Mill road, one mile from town, he found the creek very high, and the tide rapid. A gentleman in a buggy on the opposite side, who was waiting for the water to run down, hollered to him, and endeavored to persuade him not to venture across. The negro boy also remonstrated against the attempt. But the stream, even in its swollen condition, was not twenty feet wide,—the unfortunate man had crossed it hundreds of times, and could imagine no danger; and plunged into the rushing waters.— Almost instantly the horse and wagon were washed down, and the wagon, coming in contact with a floating log, was capsized and lodged against the foot crossing, and both man and horse were drowned—the boy having jumped from the wagon when he found Mr. D. was determined to make the venture.

The alarm was at once given, and the horse, a valuable one, was soon dragged out. Vigilant search was instituted for the body of Mr. D., which was kept up until a late hour at night, and renewed early Saturday morning —dragging the stream for more than a mile below the point where he went under— Finally, about noon on Saturday, the water was drawn off of Hempstone's dam, about two hundred yards from where he attempted to cross, and the body was discovered, lodged in an eddie, against the roots of a tree.

Mr. D. was in the 71st year of his age, and leaves a wife and several grown children to mourn his untimely end. On Sunday his remains were interred in Union Cemetery,— Rev. R. T. DAVIS officiating—and attended by an unusually large concourse of relatives and friends.

9/6/77 Mirror

MONUMENT TO OLD JOHN BROWN.—At Ossawatomie, Kansas, on the 30th of August, it is said that 10,000 people assembled to witness the ceremonies attending the dedication of the old John Brown monument. Gov. Robinson, of Kansas, was the President of the day, and the Rev. Mr. Adair, a brother in law of John Brown, offered prayer.— Resolutions were passed requesting the Legislature of the state of Kansas to make an appropriation to procure a statue of John Brown in bronze or marble, to be placed in the national hall of statuary in the capitol at Washington, as a gift to the nation, and asserting that it is the duty of the Kansas state historical society to take measures at the earliest practical moment to collect and put upon record the personal recollections of the associates of John Brown respecting his career in Kansas. Senator Ingalls was the orator of the day.

We suppose the people of Kansas, if they are so disposed, have a right to make geese of themselves after the manner indicated above, so far as their own territory is concerned. — But if the "National hall of statuary in the capitol at Washington," is to be made the receptacle for effigies perpetuating the memory of all horse-thieves, cut-throats, and border-ruffians generally that have disgraced the American character, under the guise of philanthropy and freedom, the sooner that "hall" is abolished, the better. Whatever those Kansasites may think of John Brown, or whatever the motives that prompted the above action, they yet know that the last act of his life, the crime for which he forfeited his life on the gallows in Charlestown, was the act of the insurrectionist and incendiary—a flagrant violation of both State and National law, the penalty of which was death. He invaded the soil of Virginia at midnight, fully prepared to murder her citizens and destroy their property —he and a portion of his followers were arrested in the act—they were tried, convicted and hung as they deserved to have been, and as the law directed. And if the infamous memory of such malefactors is to be perpetuated in "marble or bronze," and placed in the national gallery of art, let "Ichabod" be inscribed over the doors of the capitol.

9/6/77 Mirror

BRIGHAM YOUNG, the great Mormon prophet and head of the Church, is dead — and the probability is that Mormonism will soon follow. He was a great old scamp in his day but we very much doubt whether he has left behind him in the Mormon church any one who can successfully take his place. He was a man of rough and uncultured mind, but was possessed of strong will and sound practical sense on many objects. A son in law of Brigham says of him "he had a horror of mendicancy, and he instructed everybody who had means to give labor to the poor and not alms.

Brigham Young was the father of fifty-six children, forty four of whom are now alive — sixteen sons and twenty eight daughters. He leaves seventeen wives.

9/13/77 Mirror

DIED.—In Washington, on Sunday morning, at 2 o'clock, JOHN BIRD, of Leesburg, Va.

This simple announcement, which we find in a Washington exchange, will carry the minds of many in this county back to the primitive days long gone by, when all communication between Loudoun and the District, was carried on over the old Georgetown turnpike, and "John Bird," mounted on the old-fashioned Stage-box, held with master skill, the reins of his famous six-in-hand. John was a good "whip," and a clever fellow, ever ready with a helping-hand or a cheerful word to make pleasant the journey of his passengers, and a seat by his-side on the outside the coach was always considered the post of honor. Ah! those were halcyon days. But with the advent of rail and steam "Othello's occupation ceased, and John took up his abode at the end of his route. But he has made his last drive; he has journeyed to that far off country from whence there are no return passengers.

9/27/77 Mirror

MR. M. B. FURR, a cattle dealer of Fauquier, formerly of Alleghany county, Va., lost $1,000 one day last week, while travelling on the C. & O. Railroad, between Gordonsville and Staunton, by three professional monte players. The trio soon after left the train. Mr. Furr proceeded to Staunton, and offered $200 reward for the arrest of the montemen and recovery of his money. Pursuit was instituted, and the next day the parties were arrested. After preliminary hearing, the accused refunded Furr his money, and he not appearing against them thereafter, they were discharged. The $200 reward was distributed among the five men who made the arrest.

10/4/77 Mirror

LAST Friday night somebody entered the field of Mr. NATHAN BROWN, near Hughesville, and caught and slaughtered a very fine sheep. The next morning when the depredation became known, steps were taken to ferret out the thief. Suspicion rested on JOHN TAYLOR and JOHN RECTOR, two colored men living in the neighborhood, and warrants procured, and search instituted. About 8 o'clock Saturday night, a party of men armed with the proper authority, made a descent on Taylor's house, where they found a quarter of mutton cooking on the stove. Further search revealed the rest of the sheep buried in the cellar, a foot under ground. Justice THOS. E. TAYLOR was present, and the guilt of the parties being fully established, he sentenced Taylor and Rector to thirty lashes each, which were duly administered "by the light of the moon," by Constable CARLISLE. That is the quickest, most economical, and surest remedy for petty thieving yet devised, however abhorrent some people may pretend to regard it.

COLE'S MENAGERIE AND CIRCUS was brought to this town on Sunday night by three special trains from Alexandria, and on Monday gave two exhibitions to large crowds of people. The street procession was very fine, and the performances under the canvass came much nearer filling the bill than such things usually do.

(It seemed that every town function and church supper featured oysters. This was probably due to their availability as well as their popularity.)

10/11/77 Mirror

DROWNING OF MR. W. E. CARTER.—Only a few weeks ago we announced the death by drowning of Mr. LEWIS J. DONOHOE, of this county, who attempted to cross Tuscarora just after a heavy rain fall, when the stream was temporarily swollen, and this morning we have to record the death, under similar circumstances, of Mr. W. E. CARTER, of the firm of Kelly & Carter, Commission Merchants of Alexandria, Va. On Thursday morning Mr. C. reached Leesburg from Alexandria, and late in the afternoon, after the heavy rain of that day, he and his brother started for Aldie in a buggy. The unfortunate man expressed some doubt as to their ability to cross the streams on the route, but they determined to try it, and proceeded as far as where Sycolin creek crosses the Aldie Turnpike, just this side of Mr. Chas. Powell's residence. They drove in—but the current proved too strong—the horse and buggy were washed down and under a log footway. A little farther down, the buggy was capsized, throwing both men out—the brother, Mr. Marshal Carter, landing in shallow water, while the other, Mr. W. E. Carter, was swept downward, clinging to the overturned vehicle—Marshal Carter standing only a few feet from the terrible scene, witnessing the impending doom of his brother. but powerless to render him assistance. He gave the alarm, and in a short space of time the body was found about a quarter of a mile below the crossing, lodged against some trees or bushes. The body, we understand, was still warm, but life was extinct. The horse and buggy were both subsequently rescued without serious injury to either.

Mr Carter was raised in the neighborhood of Aldie, in this county, and was a worthy citizen. He was about 30 years of age, and we understand leaves a wife and two children

It is to be hoped that these two melancholy events, following so close upon each other, will cause people to be more cautious in their attempts to cross these treacherous little streams when swollen by heavy rains. Ordinarily, at the points where Mr. Donohoe and Mr. Carter lost their lives, the water is scarcely six inches deep, and although subject to sudden rise, an hour later, in either case, the crossing could have been made in safety.

11/1/77 Mirror

COURT HOUSE HALL was filled to overflowing on Wednesday evening, by an appreciative audience of ladies and gentlemen from almost every section of the county, to listen to a musical treat from Blind Tom, and at the close of the entertainment there was of course but one expression, that of pleasure. The offspring of pure African blood—blind from his birth, and almost, if not entirely idiotic upon all subjects save that of music—Tom's wonderful performance on the piano, executing the most difficult pieces of the classical masters, as readily as the commonest airs of the day—imitating all manner of sounds, and at one and the same time, playing Yankee Doodle with one hand, Fisher's Hornpipe with the other, and singing Tramp Tramp—are simply incomprehensible. But the musical feats of this prodigy are two well known to need rehersal. Nature has neverproduced but one Blind Tom, and in all her wild freaks, will perhaps never duplicates the original—and to duly appreciate the remarkable talent of this musical prodigy, he must be heard.

11/1/77 Mirror

THE entertainment of Blind Tom last week, made clear, if anything was needed to do it—the necessity of a suitable Hall, in this town. It was with much difficulty that the Court House could be obtained, and then it was altogether unsuited to the purpose, either for the convenience of the performer, or the comfort of the audience. We are glad to know, however, that the Council having already purchased the Bess property, will take immediate steps to erect on that eligible site a handsome building, the second story of which will be arranged for a town hall. All necessary arrangements will be made,—and the work commenced early in the spring. Let it be done with as little delay as possible.

(Blind Tom appeared in Leesburg several times, always to enthusiastic audiences. Unfortunately, in later years he was taken advantage of by unscrupulous promoters.)

11/22/77 Mirror

A TOUCHING INCIDENT OF MATERNAL LOVE.—Some months ago a lady was committed to the Western Lunatic Asylum as a patient, one phase of her insanity being almost complete silence. She appeared to know or notice no one. A few days ago her little daughter, a prattler not yet two years old, which she had not seen since she was bereft of her reason, was brought to see her. The mother had greatly altered in appearance, her hair being cut off and the change in her mental health had been reflected in her features, but the child sprang to her at once, and clasping her round the knees buried the face in her dress, crying, "It's my mamma—my own, *own* mamma!" The mother hardly noticed the child but the little one climbed into her lap and commenced stroking her hair with its little hands, all the time crooning, "My own mamma!" In a little while the mother began to notice it, and shortly the maternal feeling fully re-asserted itself in close clasps of recognition and affection. Since the visit the patient has undergone marked improvement.—*Staunton Vindicator.*

11/15/77 Mirror

A RATTLE BAND SERENADE IN LOU-
DOUN — ONE MAN KILLED AND HIS SLAYER
IN PRISON.—A most sad and unfortunate
event occurred near Lovettsville, in this
county, on Friday night last, which resulted
in the death of one man and the imprisonment, on the charge of murder, of another,
thus bringing sorrow and deep distress
upon two entire households.

It appears that they have in that neighborhood what they term a "Rattle-Band,"
whose custom it is, when a marriage takes
place, to serenade the couple by the use
of tin horns, bells, and such other instruments as are best calculated to make night
hideous.

On Thursday last, Mr. JOSEPH B. MANN
was married in Frederick city, and returned
that evening with his bride, to his mother's
residence, about two miles from Lovettsville. The Rattle-Band Club proposed to
pay him a visit that night, but was deterred
by the inclemency of the weather. On
Friday, however, they determined to carry
out their programme, and first visited a
brother of Mann, whom they persuaded to
accompany them. The brother at first
refused to go, and endeavored to persuade
them to desist, telling some of them that
Joseph had asked him that evening to
advise them not to come, as trouble might
grow out of it if they did. They paid no
attention to the warning, and went, choosing on the way, Mr. JOHN BRISLAN, one of
the number, Captain. Arriving on the
premises, they had scarcely made one circuit
of the house, when they were fired upon
three times in rapid succession, by Mr.
Joseph Mann. No one being hurt by the
firing, and the party fearing no danger,
continued their demonstration when, two
other shots were fired, one of them taking
effect in the back of the neck of theCaptain,
JOHN BRISLAN. Mr. B. fell and was carried
by his comrades into MANN's house. Medical assistance was at once summoned, and
the unfortunate man lingered until about 8
o'clock Saturday morning, when he died.
MANN fled, but on Sunday evening
returned and surrendered himself to the
officers of the law. On Monday he was
lodged in the jail of this county, and on
Tuesday had a preliminary examination
before Justice E. B. POWELL, of this town,
who committed him to jail for the action
of the next grand jury.

His counsel asked that he might be bailed,
but the Justice decided that he had no
authority to receive bail, and the County
Court being then in session, the matter was
carried at once before Judge BALL, when
the witnesses were all re-examined, and the
question of bail ably and fully argued by
Messrs. EDWARD NICHOLS and POWELL
HARRISON for the prisoner, and Maj. C. H.
LEE, Commonwealth's Attorney, and J. M.
ORR, for the prosecution, the hearing of
which occupied the Court until a late hour
in the evening. At its conclusion the Judge
refused bail, and the prisoner was again
committed to jail to answer the charge at
the next sitting of the grand jury, which
will probably not be until January.

All the parties to the unhappy transaction
resided within a mile or so of each other,
and were proven to have been on the most
intimate terms. The dead man leaves a
wife and three children to mourn his
untimely end, and the bride of a few
hours is plunged into a grief more crushing
than widowhood. The prisoner and his
victim are represented as worthy men of
steady, industrious habits, and good citizens.

11/22/77 Mirror

PRESIDENT LINCOLN AND GENERAL LEE. —*The Offer to Gen. Lee of the command of the Federal Army.*—Mr. Allen B. Magruder, of Winchester, Va., contributes to the Philadelphia Weekly Times a letter from Gen R. E. Lee, dated Lexington, Va., February 25, 1868 and addressed to the Hon. Reverdy Johnson, then a United States Senator from Maryland. The letter is in response to a charge made in the United States Senate, by Hon. Simon Cameron, of Pennsylvania, that Gen. Lee had applied to President Lincoln for the command of the Federal army destined to invade and subdue the Southern States, and that, being refused, from pique and resentment he turned and offered his sword in aid of the Southern cause, and thus was raised to the chief command of the Confederate forces. Mr. Johnson denounced the statement as untrue, saying that although he had not the authority of the accused to deny it, Gen. Lee's lofty character and unstained honor alone sufficed to repel the charge. This elicited from Gen. Lee the following letter :

"*Lexington Va.*, February 28, 1868.—Hon. Reverdy Johnson, United States Senate, Washington.—My Dear Sir : My attention has been called to the official report of the debate in the Senate of the United States of the 19th inst., in which you did me the kindness to doubt the correctness of the statement made by the Hon Simon Cameron in regard to myself. I desire that you may feel certain of my conduct on the occasion referred to, so far as my individual statement can make you so.

"I never intimated to any one that I desired the command of the United States army nor did I ever have a conversation with but, one gentleman (Mr. Francis Preston Blair, on the subject, which was at his invitation and, as I understood, at the instance of President Lincoln. After listening to his remarks I declined the offer he made me to take command of the army that was to be brought into the field, stating as candidly and courteously as I could that though opposed to secession and deprecating war, I could take no part in an invasion of the Southern States

"I went directly from the interview with Mr. Blair to the office of General Scott, and told him of the proposition that had been made to me and my dicision. Upon reflection, after returning to my home, I concluded that I ought no longer to retain the commission I held in the United States army, and on the second morning thereafter I forwarded my resignation to Gen. Scott. At the time I hoped that peace would have been preserved, that some way would have been found to save the country from the calamities of war,

and I then had no other intention than to pass the remainder of my life as a private citizen. Two days afterward, upon the invitation of the Governor of Virginia, I repaired to Richmond, found the convention then in session had passed the ordinance withdrawing the State from the Union, and accepted the commission of commander of its forces which was tendered me.

"These are the simple facts of the case, and they show that Mr. Cameron has been misinformed. Your obedient servant,
"R. E. LEE."

11/22/77 Mirror

ANECDOTE OF LINCOLN.—"One day, said Mr. Lincoln, "when I first came here, I got into a fit of musing in my room, and stood resting my elbows on the bureau. Looking into the glass it struck me what an awful ugly man I was. The fact grew on me and I made up my mind that I must be the ugliest man in the world. It so maddened me that I resolved, should I ever see an uglier, I would shoot him at sight. Not long after this Andy——"(naming a lawyer present) "came to town, and the first time I saw him I said to myself, "There's the man." I went home, took down my gun, and prowled round the street waiting for him. He soon came along. 'Halt, Andy,' said I, pointed my gun at him 'Say your prayers, for I'm going to shoot you.'

" 'Why, Mr. Lincoln, what's the matter ? what have I done ?"

" 'Well, I made an oath that if I ever saw a man uglier than I am, I'd shoot him on the spot. You are uglier, sure: so make ready to die.'

" 'Mr. Lincoln, do you really think I am uglier than you ?'

" 'Yes"

" 'Well, Mr. Lincoln,' replied Andy, deliberately, and looked me squarely in the face, "if I am any uglier, *fire away* !"

11/29/77 Mirror

TERRIBLE FLOOD.

Immense Damage to Property.

Five Lives Lost at Mason's Island.

The storm that commenced in this section on Friday night, appears to have been widespread and general in its fury and work of destruction. From the southern borders of Virginia, to as far north, certainly, as Baltimore, we have tidings of the fearful flood, and although mail facilities have been greatly interrupted, we have enough to know that Lynchburg, Charlottesville, Danville, Richmond, Harper's Ferry, Alexandria. Washington, Georgetown and Baltimore, have felt its effect in the flooding of streets, washing away of railroad bridges, telegraph wires, mills and other property. But while the general destruction of property has been immense in the localities indicated above, the

LOSS IN LOUDOUN

has been heavy and sad.

The rain of the preceding days began to tell, on the Potomac river toward night on Saturday, and by Sunday morning that usually placid stream presented a wild, terrific scene fearful to behold, and the damage done to property along its banks, in the county, from Harper's Ferry down, is very heavy, to say nothing of the destruction of human life.

FIVE PERSONS DROWNED ON MASON'S ISLAND.

This island is owned by Dr. J. F. Mason, and cultivated by Mr. John H. Howser. On Sunday morning Mr. H. found his house, containing himself, wife and three children, and wife's sister, completely surrounded by the angry flood, the water rapidly rising, and his only boat, used for communicating with the adjacent shores, swept off. They remained in that situation until another boat was procured, and about 3 o'clock Sunday afternoon, two negro men, whose names we regret we have been unable to learn, rowed from the Loudoun shore for the rescue of the water-bound family. They reached the house in safety, but as the boat was not of sufficient capacity to bring off the entire household at one trip, they

started with Miss ALICE MILBURN, (a sister of Mrs. Howser, and a daughter of Mr. John F. Milburn, of Leesburg,) and Mr. Howser's two little daughters, aged respectively 7 and 10 years. They had proceeded but a short distance when the boat became entangled in the branches of a tree and was capsized. One of the men and one of the children

WERE NEVER SEEN AFTERWARD.

Miss Milburn, the other child, and the remaining negro man were

LODGED IN THE TOP OF A TREE.

There being no other boat at their command, and night coming on, the unfortunate lady and her companions were compelled to remain where they were. From time to time they were hailed by those on the shore, to which they responded, until two o'clock in the morning. After that the only answer to the frequent calls of the anxious but impotent crowd on the banks of the river, was the sullen roar of the maddened stream. When day-light dawned the tree, with its precious freight,

WAS NOWHERE TO BE SEEN.

The sturdy oak, which for a dozen hours during that night of terror had afforded a resting place for the doomed trio had itself yielded to the fury of the flood, and

THREE MORE HUMAN BEINGS FOUND A WATERY GRAVE.

Who can depict the terror of those helpless creatures, as amid the gloom and rain. they for eight lonely hours hugged the cold branches of that tree—the darkened heavens above them, and beneath them, like a pack of ravenous wolves, the roaring waves howling for their prey.

Monday morning, as soon as another boat could be procured, it was despatched to the ill-fated island, and Mr. Howser, his wife and an infant child, who had remained in the house, were brought safely to the Virginia shore.

In addition to his deep domestic affliction, we understand that Mr. H. lost about 1,600 bushels of wheat, a quantity of corn, and every living thing in the shape of stock, &c, that he possessed, save nine head of horses, that by some means managed to keep their "heads above water." Mr. Howser is a most worthy and excellent citizen, and has the deepest sympathy of our people in his hour of sad distress.

HARRISON'S ISLAND,

just opposite "Ball's Bluff," belonging to Mr. Henry Harrison, jr., and cultivated by Mr. —— Daily, was likewise entirely submerged, and sustained serious damage in a pecuniary point of view, but fortunately no lives were lost. When Mr. Daily went out Sunday morning, like the inhabitants of Mason's island, he found the place covered with water and his boat gone. He at once ran a white cloth to the top of a tree, as a sort of flag of truce, which attracted the attention of Mr. John Auil, who launched a boat and went to his assistance, and during the day succeeded in landing Mr. Daily's family on this side of the river. Mr. D. and several of his friends, however, returned to the island and "held the fort," until the water subsided on Monday evening. Being near town, the banks of the river were visited on Sunday and Monday morning by hundreds of people, and the scene was one of terrific grandeur, as viewed from the height of the famous Bluff, and brought to mind another scene in which this island played a conspicuous part, sixteen years ago. There was on the island about 1,000 barrels of corn, a large quantity of provender, and in addition to the usual stock of the farm, about 75 head of cattle, the constant lowing of which, mingled with the roar of the water, was truly pitiful. Five head of cattle left the island, and after floating down stream some two or three miles, pulled for shore, which they reached in safety. About 400 barrels of corn were swept off—100 acres of fodder, and the straw, fencing, &c., entailing a loss on Mr. H., and his tenant, of at least several thousand dollars.

At White's Ferry the water was on the second floor of Col. E. V. White's new warehouse, and that gentleman sustained considerable damage. We understand that among other things he lost about $1,000 worth of baled hay, which was lying on the banks ready for shipment and some 3000 bushels of wheat.

The wife and child of Zachariah Reed were drowned on Sunday afternoon, near Goose Creek, opposite Edwards Ferry.— The boat in which they were crossing the river was washed over the Great Falls.—

THE FLOOD IN WASHINGTON.

The neighborhood of the Baltimore and Potomac depot, as usual suffered greatly by the overflow. The depot was surrounded by a lake all day, and the cellars of the houses on B and Sixth streets and Missouri avenue were filled.

THE WEST END.

Cumberland's boat house, foot of Twenty seventh street, was completely submerged and his boats floating about the streets. Stover's wood and coal wharves were inundated and a considerable quantity of wood washed away The Analostan boat-house was flooded.

AT THE LONG BRIDGE.

The wood and coal wharves in the neighborhood of the Long Bridge were all under water, and the loss to the different owners will doubtless be considerable.

The debris resting against the piers of the bridge was considerable, but no fears are entertained for the safety of that structure, as no dam was formed, and the water passed under the arches with perfect freedom.

TRAINS STOPPED,

All trains on the Midland Road, running South were abandoned Saturday night.

Communication was cut off between Washington and Alexandria Sunday afternoon, as the ferryboats ceased running.

AT GEORGETOWN.

The storm was the most disastrous that has visited Georgetown since April 20, 1853. The loose lumber on the wharves of Wheatly Bros. had to be removed to the north side of Water street, as did also the loose lumber in the yard of Joseph & J. E Libbey.

All of the warehouses along Water street were overflowed.

Marbury's warehouse, on Water street, was inundated and about $20,000 worth of guano was destroyed.

DAMAGE TO THE CANAL.

The water in the Chesapeake and Ohio canal rose rapidly. At the Great Falls four miles of the towpath were washed away, and reports from that point stated that the river and canal formed one body of water.

AT HARPERS FERRY,

Old inhabitants state that they never before witnessed a coincident flooding of both the Shenandoah and Potomac rivers at their confluence, nor had they ever before seen the rivers so high.

12/20/77 Mirror

Don't For Husbands.

Don't think when you have won a wife that you have also won a slave.

Don't think that your wife has less feeling than your sweetheart. Her relationship to you is simply changed, not her nature.

Don't think that you can dispense with all the little civilities of life toward her you marry. She appreciates those things quite as much as other women.

Don't be gruff and rude at home. Had you been that sort of a fellow before marriage the probabilities are you would be sewing on your own buttons still.

Don't make your wife feel that she is an incumbrance on you by giving grudgingly. What she needs give cheerfully as if it were a pleasure so to do. She will feel better and so will you.

Don't meddle in affairs of the house under her charge. You have no more right to be poking your nose into the kitchen than she has to walk into your place of business and give directions to your employees.

Don't find fault with her extravagance in ribbons, &c., until you have shut down on cigars, tobacco, whiskey, &c.

Don't leave your wife at home to nurse the children, on the score of economy, while you bolt down town at night to see the show or spend a dollar on billiards.

Don't bolt your supper and hurry off to spend your evenings lounging away from your wife. Before marriage you couldn't spend evenings enough with her.

Don't prowl in the loafing resorts till midnight, wasting your time in culpable idleness, leaving your wife lonely at home to brood over your neglect and her disappointment.

Don't think that board and clothes is a sufficient return for all a wife does for you.

Don't caress your wife in public and snarl and growl at her in private. This proves you both a hypocrite and a dog.

Don't wonder that your wife is not as cheerful as she used to be when she labors from early morn till late at night to pander to the comfort and caprice of a selfish pig who has not soul enough to appreciate her.

Don't if your wife has faults, be constantly reminding her of them while you have never a word of commendation for her virtues.

12/27/77 Mirror

CHRISTMAS has come and gone. In Leesburg the day was cloudy, damp and unpropitious. The town was pretty well filled with people, but everything, so far as we could discern, passed off quietly and in order —nothing transpiring to mar the good feeling that usually characterizes this festive season.

12/29/77 Washingtonian

Telegraphing Without wires.

The Washington correspondent of the Hartford *Times* sends the following to his paper:—

In these days of telephonic wonders, nothing, if it is within the range of anything, like probability, surprise us. Information has reached here recently that Professor Loomis who has been in the mountainous regions of of West Virginia for some months conducting a series of experiments with his proposed aerial telegraphy, has demonstrated finally that telegraphing without wires is practical. His manner of operating, which has on a previous occasion been described in this correspondence, has been endorsed by many scientists. It consists of running a wire up to certain altitude, reaching a particular current of electricity, which, according to Professor Loomis, can be found at various heights. At any distance away, this same current can be reached by a similar wire, and communication can be had immediately.

1/10/78 Mirror

PASSING the Cabinet Shop of Messrs. BIRKBY & SLACK. the other day, our attention was attracted to a beautiful vehicle, just delivered. It was of modern pattern and unique appearance, with but one seat in front, and that for the driver. The end and sides were of solid plate glass, three eighths of an inch in thickness, which gave it a decidedly handsome finish ; but alas, it was one of those melancholy evidences of grief, which none ever desire to see halted before their door, but the appearance of which at some time, is as inevitable as death itself— a *Hearse*. It was certainly a "thing of beauty," but we can't exactly see where the "joy" is to come in. Nevertheless, as it is appointed unto all men once to die, and after that the Undertaker, we suppose the smoother he can make the path-way to the grave the better. But we wish it distinctly understood that this notice is entirely gratuitous on our part, for while we commend the enterprise of the new firm to those who *mourn* for their services, we'll *die* before we'll ever avail ourself of their accommodations.

2/14/78 Mirror

"When I die," said a married man, "I want to go where there is no snow to shovel." His wife said she presumed he would.

1/24/78 Mirror

GONE.—On Tuesday last, Deputy Sheriff L. M. CARR and H. H. RUSSELL, left Leesburg for Richmond, having in charge Mr. LANDON T. LOVETT, sentenced last week to ten years' imprisonment in the penitentiary. As this is Mr. L's second appearance in that institution, the probability is that the authorities there will enforce the law, and have five years added to his term of imprisonment. Poor Landon! In early life he was handsome, intelligent, generous, and possessed of a handsome property. Liquor, cards and bad associations have brought him where he now is.

1/24/78 Mirror

—A Portsmouth man was going East with his wife last week, and the train started off very suddenly while he was talking with his friend. He grabbed hold of a woman chucked her on the train, jumped after her and away they went fifty miles an hour, with his wife shrieking and tearing her hair on the platform, and a woman he never saw before going into high pressure hysterics in the car, calling him a monster and yelling "save me." By a terrible mistake he had got hold of the wrong woman, and the conductor, refusing to listen to his explanations, kicked him out of the car, and brakeman chucked him into the ditch, the Sheriff met him before he was half way back to town and put handcuffs on him, and when at last he got home he saw his business partner holding his wife on his lap and telling her that there were men in the world who loved her much better than her faithless husband.

2/28/78 Mirror

A GOLDEN WEDDING. A correspondent of the Washington *Post* writes from Pleasant Valley, Fairfax county, Va., an account of a Golden Wedding, held on the 17th of February. He says :

At the residence of Mr. Silas Hutchinson Uncle Silas and Aunt Huldah entered upon the seventy-second year of their natural and the fiftieth of their married life. They were born in Loudoun county, and have resided in old Fairfax for the last thirty-five years. The very singular fact of both having been born when their respective mothers were exactly fifty years old, adds increased interest to this remarkable couple. There were about fifty five of their immediate relatives present, and a healthier or finer looking body of people no other county in the State could produce. Among the number were eight who had been present at the wedding ceremonies of the aged couple, six of them septuagenarians, one over eighty and the youngest over sixty,— The occasion was an enjoyable and memorable one. The aged couple are still vigorous and hearty, and time has laid his hands upon them gently, not a 'silver thread' showing on the gold of Uncle Silas' hair and not a furrow yet to mar the smiling beauty of Aunt Huldah's face.

(In sifting through the old newspaper records, I came to find this regarding my great grandparents, Silas & Huldah Hutchison. Three sons went to war and only one came back, my grandfather Joshua.

A DESTRUCTIVE FIRE IN LEESBURG—A DWELLING HOUSE ENTIRELY CONSUMED, AND A FAMILY MADE HOMELESS.—The last night of the Old Year was signalized by one of the most destructive, and for a while, most fearful conflagrations that has visited Leesburg since the memorable winter of 1855, when the alarm of fire was of almost nightly occurrence.

At about 7½ o'clock on Monday night, the cry of fire was heard on the street, and simultaneous with the alarm,

THE HEAVENS WERE ILLUMINATED

with a bright blaze, which proceeded from the dwelling house of Mr. JOHN HAMMERLY, at the northern end of King street. The house was a two-story frame building with wing attached, and was sandwiched between two other frame buildings, neither of them more than ten feet from the burning house.— The fire originated in one of the rear buildings, and when first discovered, the kitchen was in full blaze, and a strong wind blowing from the West, drove the flames directly against the main building. This, with the difficulty experienced in getting the engine in working condition, soon rendered it apparent that the most that could be done, was to save the furniture, and protect the adjacent houses. To this object the crowd present applied themselves with energy and success; nearly all the furniture in the main portion of the house, including a fine piano, were speedily, and so carefully removed, as to do very little injury to any portion of it. This end accomplished, the next was to prevent the spread of the flames, and by the constant application of water from buckets, and the long discarded little "Virginia," they succeeded.

The Hammerly house, however, was entirely consumed, from turret to foundation, and all that this morning remains of a once pleasant home, is a blackened mass of smouldering ruin.

As an occasional strong gust of wind would stir up the fire, filling the air with a cloud of flying embers, it presented a grand but alarming pyrotechnic display, that seriously threatened other and even distant portions of the town.

Too much praise cannot be bestowed upon our citizens, both white and colored, for the promptness and efficiency with which they labored to save property.

MR. EDITOR: Is not the question, "Are Fire Insurance Companies justified in taking risks in the Town of Leesburg, Loudoun Co., Va.?" a pertinent one, if it were asked just now, after the disastrous fire of 31st ulto? Will not a consideration of this question now tend to wake up the sleeping city fathers, to the importance of having an efficient fire department, properly equipped? Most persons take it that the business of Fire Insurance Companies is to make money and indeed it is, but for whom is this money made? It is useless to urge that they charge too much, and that the fact of the payment of immense dividends proves it, because their charges are regulated by competition, and the large dividends arise from the popularity of the company, which increases its business and makes its capital stock earn that much more. But to the question, What is there in the way of means for stopping or confining a fire to the point it breaks out? We have two fire engines, a hose carriage and, but I believe that is all. What are the facilities for procuring a sufficient supply of water, perhaps at certain points, in the town? A supply could not be obtained to last an hour if used upon the adjacent buildings. In the locality of the fire of 31st ulto., there was absolutely no water that could be obtained, save without difficulty and delay. But what is the use to continue this any further; people will say, "Well we hardly ever have a fire, and when we have had them, only the one building has been destroyed."— As an answer to this, it can be safely asserted, upon the judgment of experienced gentlemen, that if a single section of a hook and ladder company had been present at that fire, even after the kitchen roof had fallen in, the whole of the front of the house could have been saved, even without the use of a bucket-full of water, and if aided by an engine with proper hose, all in good order, the back building could have been preserved in such condition as to have been repaired at little cost. Not one word of complaint or blame is here meant to apply to the conduct of our paid department. If men have nothing to work with, it can't be expected they will perform a very great service. A single stream of water from an engine of perhaps ½ horse power, can't perform wonders in putting out a raging conflagration. The men did nobly, in being able to save adjoining property; they did all they could; and to put a sudden stop to this matter, I ask: Can't we have a Hook and Ladder Co., and one good serviceable hand engine with proper hose? We might then be able to sleep soundly, while the wind howls about our chimneys, feeling that our property and our lives are rendered secure, by the use of proper means, placed at the disposal of the brave men of our town. Thinking this is a sufficient answer to the query made, I will say I am not a

PAID FIREMAN.

The Lower Classes in the Carolinas.

Special Correspondence of the Philadelphia Times.

ASHEVILLE, N. C., Feb. 9.

After sojourning five or six weeks among the quaint inhabitants of that extensive mountain region, beginning in West Virginia and running through Virginia, the Carolinas, Kentucky, Tennessee, Georgia and a portion of Alabama, I have become so much interested in their peculiar folk-life that a brief review of the manners, traditions and habits of living of these people may not prove uninteresting to your readers. I find but little difference in these people, wherever I have met them. They possess pretty much the same characteristics, the same vernacular, the same boorishness and the same habits; although in different localities they are known by different names. Before the war they were usually called squatters, in the rich alluvial bottoms of the South and Southwest; in the Carolinas, and Georgia they are known as crackers or sand-hillers; in the Old Dominion, rag-tag and bob-tail; in Tennessee and some other States, people in the knobs or bonies—but everywhere, poor white trash, a name said to have originated with the slaves in *ante bellum* days, who always looked upon themselves as much better than all "po'" white folks."

To form any proper conception of the condition of the poor white trash one should see them as they are. It is true that the war, emancipation and the establishment of free schools has helped their condition somewhat, but they yet retain many of those characteristics which distinguished them in slavery times. The poor white trash are about the only paupers in the Southern States, and they are very rarely supported by either the State or community in which they reside. They are found nowhere but in the country, in hilly and mountainous regions generally, in communities by themselves, and far removed from the more refined settlements. Why it is they always select the hilly, and consequently unproductive districts for their homes is unknown. I remember to have heard an anecdote of one of this peculiar class of people sold before the war. A gentleman who had spent some time among the sand hills persuaded a youthful representative to accompany him out of the hill-country into the nearest alluvial bottom, where there were any number of plantations in a high state of cultivation. So soon as the young sand-hiller reached the open country his eyes began to dilate, and his whole manner indicated bewilderment and uneasiness. "Bedad seized!" exclaimed he, at last; "if this yere kedintry haint got nary sign ov er tree! How in thunder does folks live down yere? By G or j! this beats all that Uncle Peter tells about Karlina. Tell yer what, I'm goin' ter make tracks for dad's—yer heer my horn toot!" And he did make tracks for dad's, sure enough.

How They Keep House.

In the settlement wherein they chiefly reside, the poor whites barely live more than a mile or two apart. Each householder or head of a family, builds himself a little hut of round logs or pine poles, chinks the space between them with clay mixed with wheaten straw: build at one end a big wooden chimney with a tapering top, all the interstices being "dobbed" as above; puts down a puncheon floor and a loft of ordinary boards overhead; fills up the inside of the rude dwelling with a few rickety chairs, a long bench, a dirty bed or two, a spinning wheel (the loom, if any, is outside under a shed), a skillet, an oven, a frying pan, a triangular cupboard in one corner and a rack over the door, on which to hang old "Spitfire," the family rifle; and both the cabin and furniture are considered as complete. The happy owner then "clears" some five acres or 40 of land immediately surrounding his domicil, and these he pretends to cultivate, planting only corn, pumpkins and a little garden truck. He next builds a rude kennel for his dog or dogs, a primitive looking stall for his "nag," ditto for Beck, his cow, and a pole hen house for his poultry. This last he covers over with dirt and weeds and erects on one side of it a long slim pole, from the upper branches of which dangle gourds for the martins to build their nests in—martins being generally regarded as useful to drive off all bloody minded hawks that look with too hungry an eye upon the rising generation of dunghills. Being thus prepared for housekeeping, now comes the tug of war. Whatever may be said of the poverty of the poor whites, of his ignorance and general spiritual degradation, he rarely suffers from hunger or cold. As a class, indeed, they are much better off than the peasantry of Europe, and many a poor mechanic in your city—to say nothing of the thousands without trade or occupation wandering through the North and West—would be most happy at any time from December to March to share the cheerful warmth of the blazing pine knots which glows upon every poor man's hearth in the South; as well as to help devour the fat haunches of the noble old buck, whose carcass hangs suspended from one of the beams of the loft overhead, ready at any time to have a slice cut from its sinewy bones and boiled to delicious juiciness upon the glowing coals. Indeed, the only source of trouble to the poor white is the preservation of his yearly "crop" of corn, owing to the sterilness of his lands and deficient cultivation that sometimes fails him, running all to weeds and grass. But he has no lack of meats. Wild hogs, deer, wild turkeys, squirrels, raccoons, opossums—these and many more are at his very doors, and he has only to pick up "old Spitfire," walk a few miles out into the forest, and return home laden with meat enough to last him a week. And should he desire to purchase a little wool for spinning, or cotton ditto, or a little "sweet'ning" to put in his coffee or "sasselock" tea, or a few cups and saucers, or powder and

shot, salt, meal, or other household necessaries, a week's successful hunting invariably supplies him with enough game to procure the withal for luxuries which he soon possess himself of from the nearest village or cross-roads store. Having obtained what he wants he hastens back to his barren solitude, his wife and daughters spin and weave the wool or cotton into such description of cloth as is most in vogue for the time being while the husband, father, sons and brothers betake themselves to their former idle habits—hunting, beef-shooting, gander pulling, marble playing, card playing, and getting drunk. Panics, financial pressure, and the like, are unknown among them, and about the only crises of which they know anything is when a poor fellow is called upon to "shuffle of this mortal coil." Money, in fact, is almost an unknown commodity in their midst, and whether our currency is gold, greenbacks, or the "dollar of the daddies," concerns them not. Nearly all of their trafficking is carried on by barter alone. In their currency a cow is considered worth so much, a horse so much, a dog so much, a fat buck so much, a fat turkey so much, a coon skin so much, ect., and by these values almost everything else is rated. Dollars and dimes they never bother their brains about.

4/11/78 Mirror

A Young White Man, hailing from an adjoining county, was arrested on Saturday last, charged with stealing a pistol from a negro, and carried before Justice M. M. Rogers, at Dover. The Justice heard the case, found the prisoner guilty, and sentenced him to 30 stripes, which were duly administered by the officer charged with that duty. This is, we believe, the first instance, in a long while, in which a white man has been subjected to the lash in this county, and it should serve as a warning to others similarly disposed, as the Justices of Loudoun seem determined to act upon the suggestion of the last legislature for reducing the criminal expenses of the Commonwealth—without fear, favor or affection.

3/9/78 Washingtonian
Death of Ex-Senator Wade.

The death of Ben Wade removes another of the old school of extreme abolitionists who, narrowing their minds and their lives to one idea, mistook bigotry for liberality, incendiarism for independence, and envy, hatred and malice and all uncharitableness for philanthropy and Christian love. It has been claimed for some of these men that they were honest and that their intentions were good. But most of the mischief in the world has been done by men of good intentions and honesty is questionable when it believes in no honesty but its own. Ben Wade's honesty and good intentions led him to revile and spit upon the constitution until he found that the Southern people, all of whom he hated with a religious hate, had placed themselves on his platform when he became one of the eleventh hour champions of the constitution. Nevertheless he would not have suffered that instrument to have stood in the way of his seizure of President Lincoln's office if he could have perfected his contemplated usurpation. Since the war there has been no use for these men. Gerrit Smith became insane and died Joshua Giddings has passed away. Garrison still lives, and as there are now no slaves, occasionally quarrels with Wendell Phillips himself, finding that time hangs heavy on his hands, and being bound to obtain some subject for agitation, digs up Mr. Sumner's ashes and throws them in the eyes of General Grant.— *New York Herald.*

(Wade was a radical Republican, anathema to this region – brilliant, but contentious.)

3/23/78 Washingtonian

In a recent scandal case in Smith Co., Kansas, a lady witness declined to answer a question, and the attorney demanded her reason. 'Because it is not fit to tell decent people.' 'Oh, well, just walk up here and whisper it to the judge,' said the attorney.— *Omaha Herald.*

3/21/78 Mirror

It is a sad fact that Mrs Abraham Lincoln, the widow of the late President Lincoln, is living a secluded life in an interior town in France and declines to return to America, lest she may again be placed in a lunatic asylum. It is said that in France she still indulges to a moderate extent, in her propensity for buying things for which she has no use.

3/23/78 Washingtonian
Lightning Striking a Scoffer in Church.

A startling event that occurred on Wednesday night last in the M. E. Church at Leiter's Ford, is regarded by many people in Indiana as a direct interposition of Divine Providence for the punishment of the scoffer. A revival had been in the church for two weeks Elias Bidinger, a married man, about twenty-five years of age, and Robert King, had been disturbing the meetings by making sport of those who led the services. On Wednesday night about 75 persons were present. During the exercises Bidinger and King began to create a disturbance. Mr. Jones, the minister, went to expostulate with them laid his hand upon Bidinger's shoulder, and urged him to change his way of life. Bidinger replied with an oath that he would never change his ways. A few moments afterwards while Michael Shadle, a member of the congregation, was leading in prayer, lightning flashed into the church, extinguished all the lights, killing Bidinger, and prostrated King upon the floor.

King as soon as he returned to consciousness, called upon the spectators to pray for him, and declared himself converted.

4/18/78 Mirror

DEATH OF WM. M. TWEED.—This man, who for years robbed the city of New York of millions of dollars, but who more recently has been hounded by the minions of the law, to compel a disgorgement of his ill-gotten gains, has cancelled his villainy, so far as this world is concerned, by ending refuge in a dishonored grave. He died at noon on Friday, in Ludlow Street prison. The *Sun* says: He was only a little more than fifty-five years old, and under other conditons might have expected a long life. But the mortification of his detection and downfall, his confinement for months and years in various prisons, and the excitement and exhaustion of a mode of living most discordant with his active-energetic nature, all concurred to promote his disease and to kill him.

The most obvious reflection over the death-bed of this man is the contrast between his greatness when he was the dictator of this city, the levier and the robber of its taxes, the maker of governors, the buyer of legislatures, the ambitions and rant for the greater power and the richer opportunities which Washington and the national treasury displayed to his imagination, and the utter misery and meanness of his death. No contrast could be more impressive. His power was well nigh boundless; his crimes were on the same scale of grandeur; and his punishment, though only the smallest part of it was inflicted by the ministers of the law, was most complete and exemplary.

4/25/78 Mirror

BODY FOUND.—During the severe freshet in November last, it will be remembered that in attempting to rescue the family of Mr. JOHN HOWSER, living on Mason's Island, in the Potomac river, Mr. H.'s two children, his wife's sister, Miss ALICE MILBURN, and the two colored men who undertook their rescue, were drowned. Several days thereafter, the bodies of the two children were found, and interred in the Cemetery at this place. Diligent search was made at the time for the other bodies, but without success, and they were given up as lost. On Saturday morning last, however, as some colored men were at work on the Maryland side of the river, opposite Ault's, some three or four miles from where the unfortunate victims went down, and not more than 100 yards from where one of the children was found last fall, they discovered the remains of a human body, partially covered with brush, sand, &c. They communicated the information to others, and from portions of the dress, and a pocketbook containing private papers, found in the pocket of the dress which had withstood the vicissitude of long exposure, there was no difficulty in fully identifying the remains as those of Miss Milburn. They were properly coffined and brought to her father's home in Leesburg, from whence they were interred in Union Cemetery Sunday afternoon. It is greatly to be regretted that the bodies of the brave men who lost their lives in their heroic efforts to save others, cannot be recovered, that they may at least be honored with christian burial.

THE WM. ANSON WOOD EAGLE

Reapers and Mowers

FOR THE HARVEST OF 1878.

The Tilton-Beecher Scandal—Full Confession of Mrs. Tilton—Rev. Mr. Beecher's Reply.

NEW YORK, April 15.—The following letter from Mrs. Tilton will appear in the morning papers to-morrow:

"Mr. Ira B. Wheeler—My Dear Sir: A few weeks since, after long months of mental anguish, I told, as you know, a few friends whom I had bitterly deceived that the charge brought by my husband of adultery between myself and the Rev. Henry Ward Beecher was true; and that the lie I had lived so well the last four years had become intolerable to me.

"That statement I now solemnly reaffirm, and leave the truth with God, to whom also I commit myself, my children, and all who must suffer. I know full well the explanations that will be sought by many for this acknowledgment—a desire to return to my husband, insanity, malice, everything save the true and only one, my quickened conscience, and a sense of what is due to the cause of truth and justice. During all the complications of these years you have been my confidential friend, and therefore I address this letter to you, authorizing and requesting you to secure its publication.

"ELIZABETH R. TILTON.

"Brooklyn, April 13, 1878."

Mr. Beecher was out of the city to-night when Mrs. Tilton's letter was made public, and his whereabouts were not known save to a few friends. The New York Tribune telegraphed him a copy of the letter at a late hour to-night, and received the following reply from Mr. Beecher:

"Waverly, N. Y., April 15, 1878.—To the Editor of the New York Tribune: I confront Mrs. Tilton's confession with an explicit and absolute denial. The testimony to her own innocence and to mine which for four years she had made to hundreds, in private and in public, before the court in writing and orally, I declare to be true.—And the allegations now made in contradiction of her uniform, solemn and unvarying statements hitherto made, I utterly deny. I declare her to be innocent of the great transgression.

"HENRY WARD BEECHER."

The New York Sun "The statement Mrs. Tilton now makes is undoubtedly true. It agrees with all the evidence in the case, and furnishes the only satisfactory explanation of the otherwise marvellous and mysterious expressions of BEECHER's letters.

Henry Ward Beecher is an adulterer, perjurer, and fraud; and his great genius and his Christian pretences only make his sin the more horrible and revolting."

EDISON, THE INVENTOR.

Some Account of Him and His Extraordinary Invention.

Edison, the inventor, now so famous, is a young man, only thirty-one years of age, and comes from Ohio. He appears to have been born inventor having made his first invention when he was but twelve years of age.— In 1863 he was train boy on a Michigan railroad. In the fall of that year he began to work as a telegraph operator, and two months later he brought to the manager of the office in which he was employed a plan for a duplex telegraph arrangement which he had studied out for himself. His first recorded invention, for which, however, he did not take out a patent, was published by him in the *Telegraphic Journal* in 1858, and was also for a duplex. His first application for a patent here was in connection with the gold and stock telegraphs, and he has about fifty patents on record connected with that system, and his was in an important respect the first successful invention.

He is now a noted man at the Patent Office where his inventions recorded number about 150. He has invented many forms of duplex and quadruplex telegraphs; worked for awhile at the automatic system of Baque, which sends messages by perforated paper, and has worked also at the multiplex system, which sends, not simultaneously as the duplex, but in the minute intervals between other messages. He is the inventor of the electric pen, with which several copies of a letter or document are written simultaneously.

The telephone, aerophone and phonograph have absorbed him for some time. He has made important improvements in the first named instrument. The phonograph for practical use he is now completing, and in three or four months the practical machine, which is to consist of a flat dish instead of the cylinder now used, will be put on the market. He anticipated that it will be in demand among merchants who have a large correspondence; a man may read his mail, and as he reads speak his replies to each letter at once into the phonograph, which will work at a set speed by a clock arrangement.— When all is done the instrument will be turned over to a clerk, who setting the clock work to go more slowly, will copy from its dictation. It is also suggested that skilled readers will be employed to read novels and other works into a phonograph, and the impressions, being duplicated cheaply and made permanent, may then be sold for the use of the blind

THE MIRROR.

THURSDAY.................... May 9.

The exhibition in this town on Friday, of Old John Robinson's Circus & Menagerie, was well attended. The wagons and horses were in rather bad plight, but the display under the canvass was fully up to what is usually witnessed in similar shows, and much of the acting was really very fine. They only gave one exhibition, the manager declining to show at night, owing, as he said, to the imposition of the road tax and county levy, in addition to the regular State tax—which he regarded as excessive.

Mr. YARDLEY T. BROWN, the purchaser of the "Loudoun Enterprise," has changed its name to the "*Loudoun Telephone*," the first No. of which made its appearance on Saturday. We welcome our new cotemporary into the field of journalism, and trust that he may realize more pleasure and greater profit from his undertaking, than often falls to the lot of the craft. The *Telephone* is "Non Conservative."

(The Telephone became a prominent local weekly and was published in nearby Hamilton. It was a Republican paper opposing the political choices of The Mirror and Washingtonian and was a strong suppporter of the burgeoning temperance movement.)

5/23/78 Mirror

A CHANCE FOR A LONE WOMAN.—The San Francisco *Bulletin* thinks it is not often that a lone woman gets such a chance as is offered to her in the following, received at that office the other day:

MT. IDAHO, I. T., CAMP HOWARD, }
April 22, 1878. {

Mr. Editor: Dear Sir,—I wish to ask for a wife through your paper. I want to get married. My time is nearly out, and I intend to settle in this country. I intend starting a chicken ranch. I want a wife to take care of young chickens. I have got money. My wife will not have much to do, only milk nine cows, feed six hundred young chickens, chop her fire wood, cook three meals every day, and the rest of her time she can go out among the neighbors. Please publish.

Very respectfully,
ABERHAM MOOR.
Drummer Company K. Second Infantry.

5/16/78 Mirror
One Hundred Years Ago.

One hundred years ago not a pound of coal, not a cubic foot of illuminating gas, had been burned in this country. No iron stoves were used, and no contrivance for economizing heat was employed until Dr. Franklin invented the iron frame fire-place, which still bears his name. All the cooking and warming in town and country were done by the aid of fire kindled in brick ovens or on the hearth. Pine knots of tallow candles furnished the light for the long winter nights, and sanded floors supplied the place of rugs and carpets. The water used for household purposes was was drawn from deep wells by the creeping sweep. No form of pump was used in this country so far as we can learn, until after the commencement of the present century.

There were no friction matches in those early days, by the aid to which a fire could be easily kindled; and if the fire went out on the hearth over night and the tinder was damp so that the sparks would not catch, the alternative was presented of wandering through the snow a mile or so to borrow a brand from a neighbor. Only one room in the house was warm unless some of the family were ill; in all the rest the temperature was at zero many nights in the winter. The men and women of a hundred years ago undressed and went to their beds in a temperature colder than that of our modern barns and wood sheds, and they never complained.

5/23/78 Mirror

Bald Mountain Split in Twain.

ASHEVILLE, N. C., May 20.—Two years ago, residents of this section of the famous Bald Mountain were thrown into great consternation by continual rumbling and inexplicable noises heard in the bowels of the immense mountain. The phenomena attracted the attention of scientific men in all parts of the country. The rumbling lasted for about two weeks and then ceased. They had the effect of rendering the real estate in the neighborhood, that had been valuable, almost worthless, and the inhabitants hastened to move from the neighborhood of the mysterious mountain. Last Friday night the noises began again ; the mountain shook as in the throes of an earthquake ; immense trees and rocks were hurled down the mountain side, and sounds like intermittent thunder were heard during the night. This morning those who ventured near saw that the mountain had been literally split in twain, leaving a chasm of 300 feet in length and from 8 to 10 feet in width. So far as has been ascertained, the chasm is a bottomless abyss. As yet no smoke or lava has been thrown from the crater, but early in the morning there was a strong smell of sulphur about the place.

6/13/78 Mirror

A DARING THIEF — Last Thursday night several thefts were committed in Hamilton, in this county, which for cool villiany would do no discredit to rogues in wider fields. The *Telephone* says—"It is supposed that the thief first entered through a window, the residence of Wm. N. Everhart, and securing Mr. E's pocket book, went out-side, transferred all the money it contained—$15 or $20—to his pocket, dropped some papers upon the ground and threw the pocket-book back into the house. No one in the house was aroused. From there he proceeded to the house of Daniel Corbin, which he entered in the same manner. But Mrs. Corbin and her sister were in the room attending a sick child, gave the alarm, and the thief decamped without accomplishing his purpose. He then visited the house of Mr. Asbury Hoskinson, and by passing through a window, succeeded in getting into the sleeping apartment of Mr. Hoskinson. He rifled the room generally, and took a watch and a small amount of money, from the clothing of Mr. H., which were lying near the bed. A well-loaded double barrelled shot gun is a good thing to have about the house.

6/20/78 Mirror

THE PROBABLE THIEF. The night following the house robbing in Hamilton, notice of which was made in our last issue, a negro man broke into the house of Mr. Darby, at Germantown, in Montgomery county, Md., and while in the act of securing his plunder, was seized by Mr. D's two sons, and secured until morning, when he was turned over to an officer and lodged in the Rockville jail,—under the name of George Jones. The *Sentinel* of that place, says :

"The name he gives is evidently an assumed one, as in a conversation with him at the jail we found him particularly wary on this score. Mr. Yardley T. Brown, Editor of the Loudoun *Telephone* was present at our interview endeavoring to discover if the prisoner was connected in any way with recent robberies in Loudoun county. Mr. Brown could get no positive information in respect to the robberies in his town. He carried with him, however, an accurate description of a watch, knife, and lady's portmanteau, found in the prisoner's possession. These articles were recognized in Hamilton as belonging to citizens there, whose houses had been broken into a night or two previous to the burglary in this county The identification is so complete that there can be no doubt as to Jones being the scoundrel who has been operating there, and his operations have been on such an extensive scale that lead us to believe that there are still men at large who were accomplice in this extensive tour of plundering."

MEMORIAL DAY

THE ANNUAL FLORAL DECORA-
TION of the Graves of the CONFED-
ERATE DEAD, and the DEDICATION of
the MONUMENT erected to their memory in
the Cemetery at Leesburg, will take place on
FRIDAY next, JUNE 21st, '78, at 4 o'clock,
P. M.

Addresses will be delivered by Hon.
H. L. MULDROW, of Miss., Hon. J. C.
BLACKBURN, of Ky., and others.
Come one! Come all!!

J. W. FOSTER
President of Memorial Association.
H. O. CLAGETT, Secretary   [June 20.]

6/1/78 Washingtonian   [Communicated.

Exciting Game of Base-Ball.

The annual game of ball between Washington and Lee University, and the University of
Virginia took place on the grounds of the latter on Monday evening the 20th ult., The
former went with the determination to wipe
out two previous defeats, and the the latter to
retain their already hard earned laurels. After an exciting game of 1 hour and 57 minutes,
it resulted in a victory for the visiting nine
by the remarkable score of 12 to 0. The victory of the Washington and Lee University
nine was owing in great part to the curved
pitching of Mr. Sykes, who was ably seconded
by Mr. McElwee behind the bat. The playing
of McCleur, Randall and Davidson was excellent, the fielders having no chance to excel
themselves, as their opponents failed to send
any balls in their midst. Mr. Gaines led the
part of the victors:

The Universities fielded splendidly, but
seconded it poorly at the bat, only 7 men during the whole game reached first base, only
two the second, and none the third. The playing of Fawsett, Pocher, Jeffries and Delaney
was superb.

The Lexingtonians were courteously treated by their generous opponents during their
stay in Charlottesville. Who were offered in
return the same courteous welcome, provided
they visit Lexington in the ensuing years.

(The tournament has been called the main
sport in Loudoun County in the 1800's, but
baseball was coming on strong.)

6/8/78 Washingtonian

KILLING THE BIRDS.—Mr. J. E. Wright,
who has charge of the Leesburg Cemetery,
says he has picked up over a hundred little
birds which died from eating poison, which
had been put in a cornfield near by to kill
blackbirds. This is a misfortune. The killing of the old birds leaves a number of
young ones to perish. We have no better
friends than the birds, and they should be
protected. If parties wishing to keep black
birds out of their cornfields would soak a little
corn in whisky, and scatter it in their fields,
we are informed, it will make the birds
drunk, but not kill them, and they will leave
the field in disgust never to return again. This
is better than killing them. There is not a
bird that visits us, which does not destroy
more insects than will pay a dozen times for
all the corn it will eat.

6/13/78 Mirror

THE gentleman who spread strychnine in
his corn-field, requests us to say that he had
no design upon the birds in the cemetery.
His object was to get rid of the
black-birds which were robbing his
field of the corn as fast as it was planted,
thus subjecting him to constant inconvenience, loss and annoyance.

6/20/78 Mirror

SILVER ORE IN LOUDOUN.—For sometime
past there has been a general belief that silver
ore existed on the farm of the late JAMES C.
JANNEY, at Hillsboro', in this county—
and within the past year or two an experienced miner has had a force employed in endeavoring to open up the supposed rich store.
And now we are informed that Mr. SAMUEL
CLENDENNING, whose farm adjoins the Jan
ney tract, recently discovered similar ore on
his land, a nugget of which he has had analyzed, and pronounced very rich. Should this
be so, it will no doubt lead to further devel-
opments, and who can tell the extent of wealth
that may yet be extracted from the beautiful
hills of this lovely mountain village.

THE CRIMINAL CODE.

Some of the Prominent Features of the Revised Acts.

[From the Richmond Dispatch.]

The new criminal code of the State—that is to say the criminal laws, as revised and collected in one act at the last session of the General Assembly—went into operation on Monday.

The present seems an opportune moment to point out these changes and new provisions which are of general public interest—as follows:

NO VOTES TO BE BOUGHT.

If any person directly gives to a voter in any election any money, goods, or chattles, or pay his capitation tax, under an agreement, expressed or implied, that such voter shall give his vote for a particular candidate, such person shall be punished by fine not less than $20 nor more than $100. And the voter receiving such money, goods, or chattles, or having his capitation-tax paid in pursuance of such agreement, shall be punished in like manner

THE WHIPPING-POST—FINES

In all cases of conviction for misdemeanor the court of justice trying the case shall ascertain the punishment, where the same is not fixed by law: Provided, that not more than thirty-nine stripes shall be inflicted in one day nor more than seventy-eight for one offence, and that no fine shall be assessed by a court at less than $5, or by a justice of the peace at less than $3.50.

SECOND OFFENCE OF PETIT LARCENY.

Where a person is convicted of petit larceny, and it is alleged in the indictment on which he is convicted and admitted, or by the jury or justice of the peace before whom he is tried, found, that he has been before sentenced in the United States for like offence, he shall be punished with stripes; and, in the discretion of the court or justice, may be sentenced to work in the chain-gang, if there be one established, in the county or corporation in which he was tried, not exceeding twelve months. Chapter x., section 27.

PUNISHMENT OF FEMALES.

In any case where a female is convicted of an offence punishable by stripes, she may, in the discretion of the court, be punished by confinement in jail not exceeding twelve months, instead of by stripes.

ALLOWANCE FOR PHYSICIAN OR ANALYTICAL CHEMIST.

The court may appoint a physician to attend prisoners in its jail and make him a reasonable allowance, not exceeding seventy-five cents per day for each day he attends a patient. When he attends more than one patient a day there may be allowed fifty-cents per day, for each additional patient. A court may make an allowance not to exceed the sum of $25 as compensation to any physician or analytical chemist for making an analysis to discover poison in any criminal case.—

FEEDING JURORS—WHEN JURORS NEED NOT BE HELD TOGETHER.

When in a criminal case the jury are kept together beyond the day on which they are empanelled, the court shall direct its officer to furnish them with suitable board and lodging while so confined. The expenses thereof, not exceeding the rate of one dollar per entire day for such juror, shall be paid out of the treasury when allowed by the court.

CERTAIN PRISONERS MAY HIRE THEMSELVES OUT.

If any person is confined in jail under the preceding section [in default of payment of fine], or under a capias pro fine, it shall be lawful for the sheriff of the county or sergeant of the corporation, with the assent in writing of the prisoner, to hire such prisoner for such length of time, not exceeding six months, as may be agreed on, to any person, who will agree to pay the whole fine and costs for six months' service; with the assent of the county judge the hiring may be for a less sum. The contract shall be returned to the clerk's office of the county court, and if the prisoner refuses to comply with the contract on affidavit of the hirer a capias pro fine may issue and the prisoner be remanded to jail.—Chapter xviii.

FEES OF JAILERS AND SERGEANTS.

To a jailer, in case of the Commonwealth, for receiving a person in jail when first committed, twenty-five cents; for keeping and supporting him thereon, for each day, forty cents; but where there are as many as three and less than ten prisoners in jail, thirty cents for each; where there are ten or more, twenty-five cents for each prisoner in jail.

ALLOWANCE FOR WHIPPING.

Any officer who inflicts stripes under a judgment of a justice or court shall receives fifty cents therefor out of the State Treasury

OTHER CHANGES

There are many other changes These, however, seem the most important.

7/11/78 Mirror

THE GREAT RACE OF THE SEASON.—Last Thursday, Independence Day, had been agreed upon for the great four mile race between Kentucky's favorite, "Ten Broeck," and the California pet, "Mollie McCarthy."—The race took place on the Louisville course, and was for $10,000 a side. Twenty-five thousand people, men and women, witnessed the sport. The race is thus described.

When the bell called Ten Broeck and Mollie McCarthy to the track the excitement was intense. Mollie went away with the lead, and at the quarter pole was one length in advance. Ten Broeck kept her running and as she had the speed, the pair ran with scarcely a length dividing them to the half-mile pole, past the three-quarters pole and grand stand. Ten Broeck still kept the mare at her work, and the second mile was a duplicate of the first, the mare leading by a short length. At the quarter pole on the third mile Ten Broeck moved up and lapped Mollie, and before reaching the half-mile pole he was two lengths in front. From this point Mollie was beaten. Ten Broeck galloped away from her the remainder of the heat with pleasure, and Mollie stopped at the end of the three and three-quarters miles completely fagged out; she was distanced. The first mile was run in 1:49¼; two miles, 3:45¼; three miles, 5:53, and the four miles in 8:19¼.

(Blue grass aficionados will recognize this as the origin of the Bill Monroe classic "Mollie and Ten Broeck".)

7/18/78 Mirror

REMEMBRANCE OF A GOOD HOME.—Some ten months ago Mr. John Hilleary, living near Petersville, in this county, sold a horse to his brother in Warrenton, Virginia, his brother in the meantime having sold it to some one else. One day last week Mr. John Hilleary, whilst confined to his room by sickness, was informed by one of his children that "Bill horse" had come home; that he was found at the gate trying to get in. When the gate was opened by one of the hands the horse started off to the field where the horses were generally kept during the night. Bill appeared to be delighted, and nickered to such an extent that he attracted the attention of the other horses, and one in particular, his former mate, ran to meet him and showed every sign of being delighted at Bill's return. As yet Mr. Hilleary has been unable to ascertain how the horse got home, or from what quarter he came. He had evidently remembered his old home, and was recognized by his former companions, who received him with delight.—*Frederick, Md., Citizen.*

254

7/18/78 Mirror

—Last Sunday is said to have been the hottest day they have had in St. Louis, this season. Nearly thirty cases of sun-stroke were reported at the city hospital during the day. A despatch says: That "sixteen deaths occurred that day from sun-stroke alone, and twenty-two burial permits were granted in three days, which include only two of the fatal cases of Sunday. It is not unusual to have the same degree of heat here, but so many deaths from that cause in the same length of time, was never known before.

A *Herald* St. Louis special says that Sunday will become historic in St. Louis and will be known as the hottest ever experienced in that latitude. The day was one of terror, over forty adults being killed by sunstroke. Prominent citizens were prostrated in their stores and many favored a suspension of business until the weather becomes cooler. The scene at the morgue was never to be forgotten. At noon there were fifteen corpse in the morgue. Two horses of Undertaker Coffee fell dead in the streets while conveying the bodies of two victims to the cemetary. Undertaker Smithers lost three horses in the same service.—Among the bodies laid out in the morgue was that of John Phalen, once of the city council, and one of the most brilliant young men in the city. He had been picked up in the street dead from sunstroke. Dr. Hermann Voorster, ex-Coroner, and the most noted athlete in St. Louis, if not west of the Mississippi, fell unconscious and expired shortly afterwards. At 8 o'clock Sunday night twenty-six bodies were in the morgue, and despite the utmost care that had been taken the stench was so awful that it pervaded the atmosphere for a block away. Fifteen bodies were boxed for burial and others put on ice. Most of the victims are of the poor laboring class.—Many are unknown and destined to a quick and unceremonious burial. The coroner's office, attached to the morgue, was open all night. The coroner and deputies are devoting their time to receiving the bodies. Many ladies and young people were prostrated in their residences. Horses and mules suffered intensely from the heat. Sixth street cars on the Broadway line were side-tracked, because the teams had fallen dead or were dying.—Like casualties occurred on other lines, and animals generally were oppressed equally with men. It has been difficult to obtain an authentic list of the fatal cases of sunstroke.—The names of the dead for the day will exceed forty; besides these one hundred non-fatal cases have been treated at the public medical office, and these form only a part of hundreds treated at drug stores.

(We regard air conditioners as necessary for our comfort. In those days, they could well have been lifesavers.)

Ho! For Mt. Vernon!

GRAND EXCURSION BY THE PEOPLE OF LOUDOUN TO

The Tomb of Washington!!

THE YOUNG MEN'S CHRISTIAN ASSOCIATION, of Leesburg, Va., design having an Excursion to Mt. Vernon, on THURSDAY, JULY 18th, '78.

TRAINS will leave ALL STATIONS on the W. & O. Railroad, between ROUND HILL and ALEXANDRIA, Va., at the regular hour of morning Train.

☞ ROUND TRIP TICKETS can be secured at the following extremely low rates:

Leesburg, and all points West, to Mt. Vernon, $2 00; Leesburg, and all points West, to Alexandria, $1.50; Leesburg, and all points West, to Washington Junction, $1.50. All Intermediate Stations from Leesburg to Alexandria at proportionate Rates.

The above Rates to Mt. Vernon include admission to Grounds, Mansion, &c.

☞ All parties are expected to provide themselves with BASKETS WELL FILLED WITH PROVISIONS.

As it is necessary to know what arrangements to make, an Agent will be appointed at each Railroad Station to receive names of all who desire to attend. By order of

june 27, 1878. COMMITTTEE.

7/18/78 Mirror

A SEVEN-YEAR-OLD darkie attempted an outrage on a little white girl six years of age, in Putnam county, West Virginia, last week. The boy was arrested, the testimony was conclusive, and he was locked up in jail. That night a mob of eighty men surrounded the prison for the purpose of lynching the young culprit. A hastily summoned guard disputed their entrance, and they finally dispersed without accomplishing their purpose. The boy is still in jail.

7/4/78 Mirror

"Uncle Jimmie" Barrett, of Tazewell C. H., Va., who enlisted in the Confederate army, though then over eighty years of age, died on the 18th ult., aged one hundred years and six months.

THE first new wheat of the season, at Culpeper, was sold last Thursday for 90c per bushel.

7/18/78 Mirror

JEFFERSON DAVIS made a speech in Mississippi City, last week, in which he avowed his belief in the right of secession, and said several other things, which, however correct in theory, have long since been settled by the stern arbiter of the sword, and their discussion at this time can have no other effect than to keep alive sectional hate, and revive memories of the past that we should all strive to forget. Personally, the people of the South entertain a great respect for Mr. Davis, but they do not endorse his periodical contributions to Chandler and Blaine's scrap-book of Southern disloyalty.

7/11/78 Mirror

DRINKING ICE-WATER.—There is no more doubt that drinking ice water arrests digestion than there is that a refrigerator would arrest perspiration. It drives from the stomach its natural heat, suspends the flow of gastric juice, and shocks and weakens the delicate organs with which it comes in contact. An able writer on human diseases says: "Habitual ice-water drinkers are usually very flabby about the region of the stomach. They complain that their food lies heavy on that patient organ.— They taste their dinner for hours after it is bolted. They cultivate the use of stimulants to aid digestion. If they are intelligent they read, upon food and what the physiologist has to say about it—how long it takes cabbage and pork and beef and potatoes and other meats and esculents to go through the process of assimulation.— They roar at new bread, hot cakes, fried meat, imagining these to have been the cause of their maladies. But the ice-water goes down all the same, and finally friends are called in to take a farewell look at one whom a mysterious Providence has called to a clime where, as far as is known, ice-water is not used.

Annual Statement

OF THE EXPENDITURES AND RECEIPTS OF THE COUNTY OF LOUDOUN, FOR 1877.

THE following is a full exhibit of the Receipts and Expenditures of the County of Loudoun, for the year 1877, to wit :

To Sheriff of the County..........	$125 00
Clerk of the County Court....	400 00
Commonwealth for the County,	600 00
Members of Board Supervisors,	204 85
Registrars,......	08 50
Superintendent of Poor.	400 00
Physician at Poor-House,......	125 00
Judges and Clerks of Election ..	305 00
Support of the Poor-house.....	379 36
Stationery for Circ't & Co. cts.	100 00
Books for " " "	150 00
Fuel for Clerk's Office, &c......	100 00
Jailor, for fuel and cleaning C. H.	235 00
Comm'rs Rev., assessing tax, &c.	390 00
Att'y to Board, ...	35 00
Attorneys defending criminals by order of Court, ...	40 00
Overseers of Poor—per diem....	120 00
Physician & Medicines for Poor,	975 95
Burying paupers,..........	260 00
Surveyors and Com'rs, &c., for laying out new roads,.......	60 00
Printing....................	108 65
Jurors.....................	500 00
Repairs to Court-house........	500 00
Judge of the County Court,.....	570 00
Insurance on public buildings,..	94 50
Clerk of Board................	50 00
Ordinary expenses cleaning walks, yard, repairing jail, &c.,	75 00
Poor Leesburg District,..	850 00
" Broadrun "	375 00
" Mercer "	978 55
" Jefferson "	600 00
" Lovettsville "	400 00
" Mt. Gilead "	650 00
Small claims, ...	155 87
	$11,116 23

TRIAL OF STEAM ROAD WAGONS.—A year or two ago the Wisconsin legislature offered a prize of $10,000 for a perfect steam wagon for the general agricultural and hauling purpose, to be able to stand such tests as a board of three commissioners should propose. Among other things, the contesting machines were to make a 200 mile trip along the country roads, of the state, due north and south, haul a heavy wagon behind them, be able to plow; run threshing machines, and perform other feats such as the ingenuity or wisdom of the commissioners might suggest. The commission was duly appointed, and met at Green Bay, Wis., on the 15th inst. There were but two entries—the "Oshkosh," by Schomer & Farrand, of Oshkosh, and the "Green Bay," by Cowles Bros., of East Green Bay. The latter machine met with several accidents, which detained it on the road, but the former made the trial trip according to the conditions named, traversing the distance between Fort Howard and Madison, 201 miles, in 33 hours 27 seconds, or six hours less than the time required by the specifications, which called for an average speed of five miles an hour. At various points along the line, however, it attained a much greater speed, in one instance making 21 miles in two hours and ten minutes, and on the Oshkosh race-course doing a mile in 4:36. At Fort Atkinson it was attached to a gang of two plows, and turned over a goodly portion of a two acre field. The machine weighs 4,800 pounds; with water and coal for eight miles.

(Today, we call these tractors.)

TOO FUNNY FOR ANYTHING.—Some time ago there was a dancing party given in a certain neighborhood in Texas, and most of the ladies present had little babies, whose noisy perversity required too much attention to permit the mothers to enjoy the dance. A number of gallant young men volunteered to mind the young ones while the parents indulged in an old Virginia breakdown. No sooner had the women left the babies in charge of the mischievous fellows than they stripped the babies, changed their clothes, giving the apparel of one to another. The dance over, it was time to go home, and the mothers hurriedly took each a baby in the dress of her own and started, some to their homes, ten or fifteen miles off, and were far on their way before daylight. But the day following there was a tremendous row in the settlement. Mothers discovered that a single night had changed the sex of their babies.

To this day it is unsafe for any one of the baby mixers to venture into the neighborhood.

8/15/78 Mirror.

AUGUST COURT.—Monday last was a regular old-fashioned August Court day in Loudoun—an institution peculiar to our people, and the like of which, perhaps, is seen in no other county in Virginia. From time immemorial it has been observed and judging from the "turn out" on Monday, it improves with age. As a general thing, the August term is not a business one in court, yet year after year, is seen gathered at the County-seat, thousands of the intelligent, well-dressed, well-behaved, well-to-do citizens of the county. At this time harvest has ended, the crops have been gathered, and for the nonce, the busy season with farmers is over, and August Court becomes a sort of harvest home, —a day of reunion, when the people from all parts of the county are brought face to face with each other, comparing notes on every imaginable subject, farming, grazing, politics, temperance, religion, etc.

And just such a gathering was that of Monday. The crowd was the largest we have seen on any similar occasion, certainly since the war.

8/17/78 Washingtonian

AUGUST COURT.—This day so conspicuous in our holiday calender, has come and gone. At an early hour the people began pouring in to our town, and by mid-day, quite a large crowd had filled the streets fronting the Courthouse. There was a marked improvement in numbers over last year, and has given us the flattering hope that this time honored custom of our forefathers is not passing away, as the gradual falling off of the last few years seemed to indicate. The colored population of the county was well represented, regaling themselves as usual with half baked pies, weak lemonade, and warm watermelons. and some few with bad whisky.

8/22/78 Mirror

LOUDOUN CAMP MEETING.—Leaving home last Saturday afternoon, we passed the night at the Beverage House, in the pleasant village of Middleburg, which is but four miles from Benton's Woods, the location of the Camp-meeting of the M. E. Church, South. At early dawn Sunday morning the crowd began to move, and until 9 o'clock presented one grand caravan, people travelling in all sorts of ways,— wagons, carriages, on horseback, and every other conceivable mode of locomotion.— At the hour indicated, we joined the throng, and in a short time found ourselves within the precincts of the usually silent grove, but now made vocal with songs of praise and voice of prayer.

The grounds are admirably adapted to the purpose, and all the appointments are perfect. It was our first visit in three years, and we were charmed with the decided improvements made since that time, and the air of comfort and homelike enjoyment that characterized its surroundings. The old canvass tents had given place to substential board structures, many of them two stories high, while the grand pavilion in the centre of the circle, capable of seating, we should think, from 1,500 to 2,000 persons, was covered with canvass, where congregations could assemble, protected alike from the rays of the sun, and the pitiless peltings of the storm,—such as we experienced the last time we were there.

There are over one hundred tents, big and little, of which number, the irrepressible PICKETT has fifteen—and they, like omnibusses and street cars, though always crowded are never full. If there is anything that Pickett understands better than another, it is running a hotel or a boarding tent at Camp-Meeting. To first class talent as a caterer, he adds a suavity of manner, an evenness of temper that no amount of worry can upset, and a determination to satisfy his guests at whatever inconvenience or cost to himself. We should think that he dined on Sunday not less than 600 people,—and he did it well.

The crowd on the ground was simply immense, and was variously estimated, though to draw it mild, we are safe in saying that it exceeded 6,000 souls, of that intelligent, well behaved, thrifty, healthy type, that characterizes all large gatherings in Loudoun. Among the notables present, was the genial Gen. FITZHUGH LEE, who notwithstanding his familiarity with camp life, that day, for the first time, witnessed an old fashioned Methodist Camp-Meeting.

8/17/78. Washingtonian

POSTMASTER Rinker has had a Telephone wire erected, stretching from the post office to the depot of the W. & O. Railroad, a distance of 1,600 feet. Notwithstanding the distance traversed, the arrangement is so perfect that the slightest whisper at one end of the line is distinctly heard and answered from the other—and will no doubt prove a great convenience to those wishing to communicate with the agent at the depot, and in sending and receiving telegraphic messages to and from the office at that point.

We are informed by Messrs. Cline & Son (sole agents for the patentee,) that these Telephones are *very durable, easily put up,* and good for lines and distance up to 6000 feet. They are furnished by them at the low price of $5.00 per pair.

These Telephones are invaluable for many purposes, offices, stores, shops, may be connected with the residences of their proprietors; isolated residences may be connected with their neighbors, and afford agreeable social intercourse, or provide a means of summoning immediate help in case of fire or accident.

8/22/78 Mirror

TELEPHONE, AND TELEPHONE WIRE,— such as is now in use between the Post office and the Depot, in this town, and over which, a distance of 1,600 feet, the most delicate sound is accurately transmitted, are for sale by CLINE & SON, at their Hardware Store. The cost is trifling, and the convenient uses to which it may be applied are numerous. Mr. C., will furnish all necessary information as to their construction and management.

8/29/78 Mirror

A peddler stopping at a Shenandoah Valley farm house recently, dreamed for three successive nights that treasure was concealed in a tree, and finally prevailed upon the farmer to accompany him to the woods, where he pointed out the tree he had dreamed about. It was felled, and $5,000 in silver found secreted in a hole.— The money was joyfully divided, when the peddler bethought him that $2,500 was a large sum in silver to be carrying about, and intimated that he would like greenbacks in exchange. The farmer accommodated him; only to find out later that the silver was counterfeit.

8/29/78 Mirror

COL. JNO. S. MOSBY, was tendered the appointment of U. S. Consul to Canton, China. He at first hesitated, but subsequently "accepted the situation," which is worth from five to six thousand dollars a year. The Washington *Republican* says the Colonel accepts the new office with some reluctance and with a determination to return to the United State to take part in the next presidential canvass, especially in the event of General Grant's nomination."

Think as we may of Mosby's later course, time was when he had a warm place in the heart of all Northern Virginians, and presuming that he desired the mission to China, for memory of "lang syne," we congratulate him on his good luck; and if in his dealings with the celestials, he proves as successful in diplomacy as he was in fighting "yankees"—government will have no occasion to be ashamed of her representative.

8/29/78 Mirror

NEW MODE OF TEACHING THEOLOGY AND PHYSIC—Last May a Mrs. Woodard took a boy from the Orphan Asylum at Newark, who said she wished to adopt him and educate him as a clergyman or a doctor," and on leaving with her charge, asked the ladies of the establishment to pray for her, that she might have strength to bring the boy up right. Last week the waif ran away. Mrs. Woodard made him get up at 3 o'clock in the morning to milk the cows, and whipped him with the buckle end of a strap for going to sleep while extracting the lacteal fluid—she made him hoe corn, and when he failed to move fast enough, treated him to a whack over the hips with the iron end of the hoe, and would strike him on the back and hips with the iron prongs of a pitchfork if he didn't rake hay fast enough. The little fellow was examined by a physician and found to be terribly bruised, and the authorities of the Asylum sued put a warrent against the woman, and will have her arrested for cruelty to her young charge.—

259

9/5/78 Mirror

YELLOW FEVER HORRORS.

This dread epidemic is still ravaging the cities of the South, and death is holding high carnival in the plague stricken districts. The disease seems to be rather on the increase than otherwise ; while from lack of nurses and proper attention, the misery and suffering of the people is terrible.

9/12/78 Mirror

THE FEVER IN THE SOUTH,

No Abatement of the Epidemic.

The fever plague continues its ravages with no signs of having satiated its thirst for victims—and each day adds fresh horrors to its terrible carnival of suffering and death—adding as it does the pangs of starvation and want of attention, to the miseries of disease.

A despatch from Memphis on Monday, says : "The condition of this city grows more desperate every hour. Of new cases it is useless longer to keep a count. Whole families are stricken down within a few hours and the call for nurses is greater than can be supplied.

DEATH FROM YELLOW FEVER.—Our obituary column records the death, in Memphis, Tenn., a day or two ago, of Mr. WM. T. POWELL, a native of this county, and brother of Capt. E. B. POWELL, of Leesburg. At the time the fever broke out Mr. P. was editor of a Catholic Magazine in the ill-fated city of Memphis. About one week ago he wrote to his mother, who is now in Leesburg, telling her of the horrors that surrounded him, in consequence of which he had closed his office, and volunteered as a nurse to the sick—that having once before passed through a similar scene of suffering he thought he could be of some service—but that so terrible was the scourge, no one was safe—and whatever his fate might be, he could imagine no nobler end than dying in an effort to soothe the sufferings of his stricken fellow-men. That was the last letter received from him. In less than one week from its date, the sad tidings came that he too had fallen a victim to the terrible scourge—and helped to swell the mournful list of brave, self-sacrificing spirits who have fallen martyrs to their sense of duty, and the promptings of a noble humanity,

9/12/78 Mirror

RELIEF FOR THE SUFFERERS.—From all parts of the country it is gratifying to see the earnestness and alacrity with which all classes of people are responding to the appeals for relief that have come up from the fever stricken districts of the South.—

Last Saturday evening a meeting was called at the Court House in this town—which was presided over by Mayor Geo. R. HEAD—for the purpose of taking action looking to the relief of the sufferers. A committee of ten was appointed to canvass the town and neighborhood for subscriptions.

9/12/78 Mirror

At Memphis, Tenn., Monday, the day opened clear and warm, with the little force of workers nearly exhausted. The fever continued without abatement. Up to noon there were 48 yellow fever interments A number of negroes, some of them drunk, assembled before the commissary depot, and, becoming riotous, made a rush for the door. They were kept back by the colored militia on guard, but a second attempt being made the guards fired, perhaps fatally wounding one negro.

A despatch from Port Gibson, Miss., announces 400 cases and 50 deaths out of 550 persons remaining in town. About 1,200 have fled. The distress is very great, the sick dying with no one to give them a drink of water.

9/19/78. Mirror

THE FEVER PLAGUE.—The yellow fever continues to ravage the infected districts, and the suffering and death that follow its march is appalling in the extreme. The cool weather of the past few days has had the effect, in some localities, of mitigating the suffering and curtailing the number of deaths, to some extent, but the carnival still goes on, and the cry for relief is ever ringing in the ears of the humane citizens of the more favored portions of God's heritage, and, we are glad to know that it is not heard in vain. Last week, Leesburg and its vicinity forwarded $360 for their relief, since then $60 more have followed, and the contributions still continue. During the week some $15 or $20 have been dropped in the box at the Post-office. And the colored people of this community, to their lasting honor be it said, have raised among themselves, a purse of about $25, which will be forwarded to the relief of the sufferers,—making a total up to this time of nearly $500.

What A Washington Doctor Saw in Memphis.

[*From the Washington Post.*]

Dr. William T. Ramsey, one of the physicians who went to Memphis with the corps of Washington nurses has returned to Washington, in company with Dr. T. P. Pease and Miss Wallis. The following interview with Dr. Ramsey discloses some of the horrors and necessities of that plague stricken city :

"Before reaching Memphis, even when five miles out, the air was laden with the yellow fever poison, and as we approached the city the stench was absolutely sickening. Dr. Pease and myself went to the Peabody Hotel, the only one now open, and were shown into a room from which a dead body had just been removed. Vessels of black vomit were standing about the room, but the bed-clothes had been changed. The hotel itself is a perfect pest house, and victims of the disease are in two thirds of the rooms. Sulphur pans are kept burning in the halls, and the clothes, bedding, &c., are constantly disinfected, but they cannot get help enough in the hotel to do one half what is to be done."

"What seems to be their greatest need?"

"Provisions, clothing, physicians, money, nurses and medicines, and about in the order named. The best thing that can be done now is to send plenty of provisions and clothing. The negroes and many poor white, for a section of 150 miles around Memphis have flocked there hearing they could get something to eat, and as for clothes, hundreds of poor people are going about the streets—especially colored women—with hardly anything on at all. The sights in this respect are distressing."

"Where do these people go to who come in from the country?"

"They wander about about the city in bands, and when they find a vacant house they brake into it and take possession and appropriate whatever they want. The authorities are powerless to prevent such outrages."

"About the physicians?"

"There are seventy five there now from abroad and fully one hundred and fifty more are needed. The volunteer physicians are doing a noble work, and without pay, except such as are paid by their home friends and societies. They are not paid by any one in Memphis, and don't ask or expect it. At the same time however, a volunteer physician going there ought to be liberally supplied with funds, for he is under constant personal expense."

"On my arrival Mr. Langcaff, President of the Howard, and one of the noblest men God ever let live, urged my immediate return, but I determined to stay. Dr. Pease and myself took each of us thirty grains of quinine and 120 drops of tincture of iron every day, and the only effect it had was to increase the perspiration. Such doses could not be taken here, which leads me to believe that it is in some sense a powerful antidote to the fever. Of course, we use corbolic acid freely as a disinfectant. I wore linen suits, changing them every day, and they turned fairly yellow from the effects of the iron. At night we wore thick veils, soaked in carbolic acid, over our faces, for there is no language to describe the awful stench in the city. It is now filthy to the last degree. The bayoue which set in from the river and the surface drainage with which they are filled, the uncleansed streets and alleys, rotten wooden pavements, deep dust of the macadamized streets, dead animals and putrefying human bodies and the half buried dead all combine to make the atmosphere thick and poisonous and something fearful to endure. Bonfires of tar barrels and sulphur fires are kept burning all over the city, but with little effect. Nearly all the physicians and nurses smoke all the cigars they can. That helps them a little while visiting the sick. On Poplar, Carrol and Vance streets, for instance, where the better classes live, the plaague is not so malignant, but even there terror prevails and great suffering is experienced. On Winchester street the scene is terrible. On Monroe street I found five women all sick with the fever, whose husbands had fled,"

"Is that common?"

"Quite common among the lower classes — One can have no idea of the panic existing there. Indeed, it is no uncommon thing for the sick to be entirely deserted. When it is noticed that there are no signs of life about a house, it is broken open, and the dead are found in advanced stages of putrefaction.— The work of their removal is a job before which the stoutest quail."

"Who suffers the most—the women or the men?"

"The women by far. Of the number attacked fully 80 per cent died. They hardly ever get well, and suffer much more than the men from hemorrhages, and the children come next."

9/19/78 Mirror

LOUDOUN AGRICULTURAL FAIR. — The Eighteenth Annual Exhibition of the Loudoun Agricultural Society commenced on the Grounds near Leesburg, on Tuesday. The day opened beautifully; the bright sun, and weather sufficiently cool to make it pleasant for perambulating the grounds, affording promise of a clear sky till the close.

By ten o'clock Tuesday morning every pen and stall was filled with as fine specimens of the various breeds of Horses, Cattle, Sheep and Hogs, as any county can produce—eliciting the admiration of all beholders, and showing that our farmers are fully alive to the importance of keeping abreast of the times in the improvement of their stock. We have no room to particularize—(and might do injustice if we had,) further than to say that the thoroughbred short horns, Durhams, and Alderneys, of Washington Haines, Chas. R. Paxson, Dr. George A. Quincy, and Col. R. H. Dulany, were very handsome and attracted much attention. There is quite a large number of Horses on exhibition, many of them "pretty as a picture," and rarely excelled anywhere. The display of Sheep is also excellent—and in the opinion of competent judges, the collection of horses and stock of all kinds, this year, surpasses any former exhibition in this county—which is saying a good deal.

Swine are not numerous, but there are several pens of Essex, Chester, Berkshire, Poland China and other breeds, that can't excelled Mr. Thos. R. Smith has a Poland China pig, 15½ months old, that weighs 535 lbs.

The stock exhibited aggregates about 300 head—of which there are of horses 165,—Cattle 60,—Sheep 48 and Hogs, 30.

J. J. Stansbury and S. J. Johnston has handsome displays of Jewelry, Silver and Plated Ware. &c. Bassell has a nice array of Mayer & Stearn's Boots and Shoes. L. Schiller a fine lot of Ready-Made Clothing. A. P. Breckinridge, a beautiful set of Harness; W. M. Harrison and E. Wright, Sewing Machines; W. T. Mount and L. N. Hough, of Waterford, each a lot of Chairs; F. L. Van Auken, of Alexandria, exhibits handsome Pianos and Organs of the Estey Manufacture. Ham, Cakes, Bread, Jellies, Butter, Wine, etc., and Needle Work of various descriptions, and some of it quite handsome, filled the Hall.

LIST OF PREMIUMS.

HORSES QUICK DRAUGHT.

Sellman & Fadeley Stallion, (Anges). ...$15
do   do   do (Harold Hambræo).................c m
Romulus Furgerson, Brood mare and colt 15
Sellman & Fadely   do   do   do c m
Thornton Nichols, Stallion, 3yr old........10
Thomas B. Norris, 3yr old colt............7
Tunis Titus, Stallion, 2 yr old............5
F P Gist, colt 3 yr old....................5
J C Vansickler, colt 1 yr old..............5
Romulus Fergerson, colt, Spring 1878......5
C R Paxton pair matched horses............15
Arthur Phillips horse single harness......10
Dr C S Carter Tho bred Stallion(Ferdinand C)..............................15
Sellman & Fadeley Tho mare(Kate Wagner)10

SADDLE HORSES

Albert Chamblin Stallion...................$10
J L McIntosh Brood mare and colt..........5
J L McIntosh 3yr old colt.................5
Albert Chamblin 2yr old colt..............5
Jas Thomas 1yr old colt...................4
Col B Christian colt 1878.................4
J C Riticor saddle horse..................7

GENERAL UTILITY

Jas Laycock 3yr old Gelding...............$4
Jno G Hogeland mare and colt.............7
D N Reese colt spring 1878...............4
C R Paxton colt 1yr old..................4
Jno F Conner Stallion....................10
Hugh R Holmes do 2yr old.................4
Thomas R Smith horse 3yr old.............4
Geo H Ayre pr mules 3yr old..............4
do   do   do 2yr old...............3

HEAVY DRAUGHT

Stauffer & Brennerman stallion............$15
J M & J C Hoge stallion owned in Loudoun county................................15
Harrison Osburn brood mare and colt......15
S N Brown   do   do   do c m
J C & J M Hoge 3yr old colt...............5
Hugh R Holmes 2yr do stallion.............5
Dr G A Quinby do do colt..................5
J M McVeigh colt 1yr old..................4
Harrison Osbourne colt Spring 1878........4
N B Peacock 2 horse team.................6
E G Canfman 6 horse team................10

SPECIAL PREMIUMS

Offered by S. W. Ficklin, of Charlottesville, for the best spring colt gotten by his Imported stallion 'The Col.' Five very superior colts contested and the judges awarded the premium of $10 to J. H. Whitmore's colt.

CATTLE.

Neat Cattle.

John F Ryan, yoke oxen 1st...............$10
James Thomas   do 2nd.................5
Lewis C Helm   do 3rd...............c m
Ames Hughes, grade bull..................10
J R Beuchler, milch cow..................10
Wm Beverley   do.................c m
Geo Ball, grade heifer, 2 years old.......5
J R Beuchler, do do 2   do...........c m
Joshua Fletcher, salted beef..............7

Short Horn Cattle

4 years { W Haines, bull(Waterman) $15
old and { C R Paxton, bull thoroughbred c m
upward. { E J Smith, bull   do   c m
J C Vansickler, bull, 3 years old,........15
C P Noland,   do 2   do.........c m

C R Paxton, milch cow....................10
Wash. Haines, best herd cattle...........10
Geo Ball, bull, 2 years old..............7
C R Paxton, heifer, 2 years old..........5
Wash. Haines, do 1 year old, (Nellie Grant) 3

Holstein Cattle.

J R Beuchler, bull $15

Alderney Cattle.

Dr George A Quinby, bull, thoro 8
do   milch cow................5

SHEEP.

H. C. Gist, thoroughbred Cotswold Buck $5
do   pr   do Ewes 8
Thomas H Clagett   do do c.m.
Dr. G. A. Quinby, thoro Southdown Buck $5
do   pr   do   Ewes 8
A. H. Rogers pr   do   do c. m.
E. G. Canfman, Shropshiredown Buck......5
S. A. Campbell, pr Hampshiredown do c. m.
do   do   Ewes....8
A. H. Rogers, Shropshiredown   do.. c. m.
Edgar Burch, grade Buck
Thomas H. Clagett, grade Buck c. m.
Edgar Burch   do Ewes............8.
R E. Furr   do   do.... c m
Edgar Burch, pen mutton..................7
George H. Ayre, thro Liecester Buck......5
do......do......do Ewes.......5
T. M. C. Paxton, merino......do........8
S. A. Campbell, Shropshiredown Buck..c.m.

SWINE

Edgar Burch, grade Boar..................$5
T M C Paxton, grade Sow and Pigs.........5
Col. R. H. Dulaney, thro Essex Boar......6
do   do   do do..c.m.
James Laycock, Chester   do....6
John Norris,   do   Boar pig c.m.

S. N Brown, thro Barkshire Sow and Pigs 6
Thomas B. Smith, Poland China Boar.. 6
do do China sow & pigs 6

AGRICULTURAL PRODUCTS.

M. G. Hatcher, bushel white wheat..............$3
Jonah Nixon do red do 3
W. H. Benton do white corn in ear.... 2
D. M. Reese do yellow corn in ear.... 2
D. H. Vandeventer bushel cloverseed.... 3
do do timothy seed.. 2
G. W. Paxton do corn meal...... 1
do barrel flour.............. 2
Field of corn, not less than 5 acres W.H. Benton. 20½ bbls to acre 10

AGRICULTURAL IMPLEMENTS

Shroff & co implement for cultivating corn $2
H Vanderhoff wheat drill 3
Shroff & co Buckeye comb.mower 5
H Vanderhoff mower 5
do horse rake 2
Shroff & co straw & hay cutter 2
S Fouche two horse wagon.......... 4
R H Taylor three do plow 7
do two do do.......... 5
do one do do.......... 2
Shroff & co single shovel plow 1
do double do do.......... 1
Edgar Burch threshing machine..........10
Shroff & co corn sheller.......... 2
do wheat fan 3
do churn.......... 1
S Fouche pr trace chains.......... 2
John H Myers harrow.......... 2
Shroff & co display agricultural imp'ts....10
Edgar Burch steam engine..........10

HOME MANUFACTURES.

A. P. Breckinridge, double set Car. Harness, $5
do single Harness.......... 3
do Saddle.......... 3
G. W. Paxson, shod Horse 3
Shroff & Co., Farm Baskets.......... 1
Mrs. Tunis Titus, lot Brooms.......... 1
W. T. Mount do Chairs.......... 2
A P. Breckinridge. set 4 Horse Harness...... 5

DOMESTIC MANUFACTURES.

Mrs. John Williams, Factory Flannel..... 2
do Jane F Hogeland. Rag Carpet 3
do R. E. Furr, pr. Blankets.......... 4
do Jno. Williams, Yarn Counterpane.... 4
Miss Eliza Paxton, Cotton do 3
Mrs. Jno. H. Titus. Linen Table Cloth..... 2
do Virginia White, pr. Linen Sheets...... 2
Mrs. John Williams, Linen Towelling..... 2
W T Mount rocking chair.......... 2

HOUSEHOLD FABRICS.

Miss Jennie Littleton, hand made shirt.....$2
Ruth R. Taylor, Silk Quilt.......... 3
Miss Eliza Paxton cotton do.......... 3
" Lydia Hollinsworth, Hearth Rug.......... 2
Mrs W. B. Lindsey, Yarn Stockings 1
do M. E. Paxton, Cotton do.......... 1
do T R Moore Childs Dress.......... 2
do B Beard Worsted Quilt.......... 3
do Annie Johnston Ladies Dress.......... 2
Miss Lillie Lynch Cotton Counterpane..... 3
Mrs Cusack Specimen Needlework.......... 3
do Crochet Work.......... 2
do T Morallee Silk Netting.......... 1
Miss A C Osbourne Cotton Netting...... 1
Mrs Jno Williams Silk and Cotton Gloves. 1
do do do do.. 1
do Tunis Titus Stockings Yarn...... 1
Mrs John Williams Thread Gloves.......... 1
Miss H R Grubb set Crochet Table Mats.... 1
Mrs W B Lindsey do do Toilet do.... 1
Miss Mollie Crusen Thread Crochet Mats... 1
do Susan Yerby Oil Painting.......... 3
Mrs E A Bronaugh Grecian Painting...... 3
Miss Jannie Fergerson, Silk Embrodery...... 3
do Bertie Mott specimen worsted work... 2
Mrs Wm Giddings cotton embroidery...... 2
Mrs. John Wood, Monochromatic Drawing 2
M. E. Paxton, Pellis Work 3
Lulie Dowell, Wax Flowers.......... 2
Miss Mary Thomas, Worsted Work on Bristol Board.......... 1

CULINARY DEPARTMENT.

Mrs E A Bronaugh Pound Cake..........$2
do C F Fadeley Fruit do 2
do Ann Dowell Sponge do 2
Miss Bettie Scatterley Jelly do 2
Mrs Wm Giddings Ginger do 1
do C F Fadeley Sugar do 1
Miss Mary Thomas lot of Biscuit.......... 2
do Lilly Paxton Wheat Bread.......... 2
Mrs J C Hoge Corn do 1
do E A Bronaugh lot of Rusks.......... 1
do Jane D Wildman Walnut Catsup...... 1
do T Morallee Tomato do 1
do Jno Wood Cucumber do 1
Miss Marry Thomas canned Tomatoes.... 1
do Bettie Whitmore " Corn 1
do Freddie Hoge " Peaches 1
Mrs I C Hoge " Pears 1
do Jno Williams " Plums 1
do Wm Giddings Display canned Fruits.. 3
Miss Mary Thomas Apple Preserves...... 1
do R E Furr Peach do 1
do W B Lindsay Pears do 1
do do Quince do...... 1
do Anne White Green Sweetmeats.......... 1
do A J Souder Apple Jelly.......... 1
do W B Lindsay Peach do 1
Miss Mary Thomas Quince Jelly.......... 1
do A C Osburne Currant do.......... 1
do Fanny Edwards Grape do.......... 1
Mrs Jno Williams Raspberry do 1
do W B Lindsay Blackberry do.......... 1
do Jane D Wildman, Sour Pickle.......... 2
do Ann Dowell Sweet do 2
do do Chow-chow do 2
Miss A C Osburne Cabbage do 1
do Bettie Whitmore canned apples.......... 1
do M E Paxton variety of jellies.......... 3
Mrs Jane D Wildman Hard Soap.......... 1
do W C Saunders Soft Soap.......... 1
do Wm Giddings Bottle Vinegar.......... 1
do do Sample Lard.......... 2

VEGETABLES.

J M Hoge ½ doz Beets..........$1
S A Campbell ½ doz Carrots.......... 1
G W Paxton do Parsnips.......... 1
do do Squashes.......... 1
Alexander Murray 3 Egg Plants.......... 1
Mrs John Wood ½ doz Onions.......... 1
Wm B Clagett do Celery.......... 1
A L B Zerega Selsify.......... 1
S A Campbell ½ bush Irish Potatoes.......... 1
Massy V. Riticor do Sweat do 1
do lot Tomatoes.......... 1
Mrs Jno Wood Lima Beans.......... 1
Judge C R Ball lot Pumpkins.......... 1
Wm B Clagett lot Gourds.......... 1
Alex Murray Best Display Vegetables...... 4
C B Ball Cabbage.......... 1

DAIRY, FRUITS, &c.

Mrs Harrison Osburn Potted Butter......$3
do S A Campbell Fresh do 3
do Harrison Osburn Cheese.......... 2.50
do Wm B Lindsay Honey 1
Jonah Nixon ½ bush Apples.......... 1
Mrs Tunis Titus peck Pears.......... 1
J R Beuchler lot of Grapes.......... 1

POULTRY.

James Thomas pr Ducks..........$3
C W Fadeley pr Cochin China Fowls 2
B P Brawner pr Plymouth Rock do 2
do pr Brown Leg Horn do 2
S A Campbell pr Houdan do 2

HAMS.

Mrs R E Furr 1st premiums..........$3
do Wm B Lynch 2nd do 2

WINES.

Miss Mary Saunders Blackberry Wine..........$3
Mrs John Williams do Cordial.... 3
Miss Bettie Wildman, Elderberry Wine.... 2
do Fannie Edwards Currant do.... 2
Mrs W B Lynch Grape do.... 3
do Tunis Titus Cider.......... 2
do Brandy Peaches.......... 2

DISCRETIONARY COMMITTEE.

C Powell Noland, thoroughbred Oxforddown buck $5
Hugh R. Homes, horse general utility ....c m
Dr. Geo. A. Quinby, thoroughbred suffolk hogs.......... 6
Thomas R Smith 2 poland china pigs 4&6 months old.......... 1
Geo C Thomas 2 horse phaeton carriage... c m
do 1 horse jump seat rockaway... c m
do whitney 4 seat side bar wagon c m
D. N Reese lot factory cassimeres Fredrick manufacture 5
Mrs Mary D. Howell, feather flowers.......c m
Mrs Wm. B Sidney, worsted do.......c m
Miss Mollie Bennett Worsted Shawls...c m
do Sadie Chichester lemon butter cakes c m
M G Hatcher bushel Summerset oats......$1
Tunis Titus lot peaches..........c m
Mrs. Frank Thrift gooseberry wine.......... 1
R H Taylor & Son road scoop..........c m
Mrs Wm. B Sidney, worsted do..........c m
Miss Mollie Bennett Worsted Shawls..c m
do Sadie Chichester lemon butter cakes c m
M G Hatcher busbel Summerset oats......$1
Tunis Titus lot peaches..........c m
Mrs. Frank Thrift gooseberry wine.......... 1
R H Taylor & Son road scoop..........c m
E Wright, Stewart singer sewing machine premium..........c m
W T Shumaker corn and cob mill.......... 3
S Fouche spring wagon in the rough..c m
Monroe Graham & Co, lot wheels, spokes Loudoun make.......... 3
A M Hutchison pr twin colts.......... 4
T Carner knit counterpane..........c m
J Staub, shifting top buggy..........c m
do jump seat carriage..........c m
W T Shumaker hill side plow.......... 1
H Vanderhoff plaster sower & rake comb..c m
Col R H Dulany pen essex hogs.......... 5
W T Shumaker Hay fork and Hoister...... 1
D H Vandevanter hay fork.......... 1
L Schiller display of clothes and shoes. c m
Jno Y Eassell case of shoes..........c m
L S Howard, farm gate ....c m
W H Thomas display of stoves..........c m
J J Stansbury case plated ware.......... 3
S J Johnston do do and jewelry 3
R H Taylor & Son farm bells.......... 1
J H Vanauken pianos and organs..........c m
Geo H Ayre 6 mule team.......... 5
Mrs W B Lynch pr painted vases..........c m

FLOWERS.

Mrs Harrison Osburn Display of Flowers...$3
do E A Bronaugh do do c of M
do C R Paxson Boquet.......... 2

TROTTING.

FIRST DAY.

Trotting 4 years old—Purse $20 to first and $10 to second horse.

L. T. Jacobs, b. h., 'Arch,'	1	1	1
S. Orrison, b. m., 'Mollie'	2	2	2
J. T. Riticor, r. m., 'Kate,'	3	3	3

Time—3.46½; 3.42½; 3.48.

Racking or Pacing, $20 to first and $10 to second horse.

J. W. Dorrell's r. m. 'Sallie Hunter'	1	1	1
J. W. Riticor's s. h. 'Tom.'	2	2	2
R. W. Whittington, b. m., 'Queen,'	3	3	3
Dr. Cochran's b m. 'Jennie'	4	4	4

Time—3:01½, 3:23, 3:26½

SECOND DAY.

Three year old Trot.

H. Harrison s. h. 'Hotspur'	1	1
L. T. Jacobs b. m. 'Mollie Jacobs,'	2	2
T. B. Norris b. m. 'Lady Woodbridge,	3	Dr.

Time—3:59, 3:49.

County Trot—Wednesday.

J. A. Conklin, Bay Horse Geo. R.	3	2	2
H. J. Fadeley, s. g. Richmond	2	3	3
Sellman & Fadeley, br. s. Castleman.	1	1	1

No time taken.

THIRD DAY.

Hazel's s.m. Blanche	3	2	3
Harvey's br. g. Top	2	3	2
Moore's b. m. Halli. by Harold	1	1	1
Carter's s. g. Tom Field	4	4	4

Time—2.40, 2.46, 2.42½

(Compare the country fair of yesteryear with those of today – the number of events, the work involved, the difficulties encountered, the transportation problems.

The prizes seem meager, but remember that a dollar was roughly equivalent to $20 today.)

10/24/78 Mirror

Death of the Only Son of the Ex-President of the Confederacy.

Mr. Jefferson Davis has outlived all of his sons, and when he dies the family name will become extinct. His oldest son, Jefferson Davis, Jr., who died near Memphis the other day of yellow fever, had scarcely passed his twenty-first birthday, and though he did not inherit the intellectual ability of his father, he was a young man of considerable promise. Early in the summer, and before the fever broke out, young Davis went North with his sister and her husband. The latter returned for some purpose and was stricken down with fever. When his wife heard of it she insisted upon going to him, and young Jeff. accompanied his sister. Before the husband was convalescent his wife was attacked. Young Davis nursed his sister through her illness, and in a few days she became the nurse and he the patient. Four days later he died. In 1864, while Mr. Davis was President of the Confederacy, he returned to his residence one day from a short visit to the Capitol, and found, lying in one of the halls, the dead body of his second son, whom he had left but an hour or two before the picture of health. The child was but five years of age, and during the absence of the family fell from a rear balcony to a paved yard beneath and crushed his skull. He lived but a short while. This boy, Joseph, was the most intelligent of the family, and a special favorite with all the great men who in those days frequented his father's house. He was a bright boy, and the whole city of Richmond mourned his death. Willie, the youngest son of Jefferson Davis, was born in Richmond during the war, and died when but three or four years of age. There are now left but two children, both girls. The eldest, Maggie, was married about a year ago, and it was while caring for her that young Jeff met the terrible destroyer.

10/3/78 Mirror

When some years ago Anson Burlingame and Cassius M. Clay were stumping in the West, they returned to their hotel after a particularly warm welcome, one night and were talking affairs over. Suddenly strains of music were heard outside. "They are serenading us," said Clay; "open the window and make 'em a speech." Burlingame stepped to the window, opened it, and began, "Fellow-citizens, I hardly know how to thank you for this touching proof of your esteem and regard. Mr. Clay and myself are indeed grate—" Just at this point a voice in the crowd below was heard saying, "Boys, *that ain't the gal in red. Let's dust!*"

10/31/78 Mirror

Served Him Right.—At Lumbertown, N. C., one day last week, a young lady, Miss Amelia Linkman, called at the hotel, went into the parlor, and asked for Mr. Edward Hartman, a travelling salesman for Elhart, Witz & Co., of Baltimore, who was a guest at the house. A dispatch states that when Hartman entered the parlor, Miss Linkman rose and shook hands with him, and while he held her hand she drew a revolver, which she had concealed upon her person, and, placing it close to Hartman, shot him in the abdomen, mortally wounding him, exclaiming at the same time, "You have ruined me and I will now ruin you!"

The Wilmington, N. C., *Star* says Hartman was shot by Miss Amelia Linkman, his sweetheart, to whom he was engaged to be married. She insisted upon his fulfilling his promise, and when he refused she drew a revolver and shot him in the lower part of the body. At last accounts he was sinking very rapidly, the bullet having penetrated vital parts. Two hours after the shooting, it is said, Miss Linkman became a mother.

10/17/78 Mirror

The Washington Monument Work.—The erection of shops for workmen engaged upon the Washington monument will be speedily commenced. Proposals for material were invited from all the lumber dealers in this city.

PUBLIC SALE.

Intending to quit farming, I will offer at Public Sale at my residence, about two miles West of Hillsboro', on

FRIDAY, NOVEMBER 1st, 1878,

the following Personal Property:

3 HEAD OF GOOD WORK HORSES,

2 of them are Good BROOD MARES, the other a No. 1 Young Horse; 1 Colt, 2 years old last Spring; 1 Colt, 1 year old; and two PERCHERON COLTS, foaled last Spring;

2 Good MILCH COWS,

2 FAT CATTLE, 1 YOUNG BULL, 8 FAT HOGS, 2 Good Brood Sows and Pigs, 1 Boar, 1 HEAVY WAGON, suitable for Road or Plantation purposes; 1 Keller Grain Drill, 1 Wheat Fan, 1 Buggy Rake, 1 Cutting Box, 1 Pair Wood Ladders, 1 Stone Bed; 1 Three-horse Iron Plough, 1 Barshear Plow, 1 Harrow, Single and Double Shovel Ploughs, Wagon and Plough Gear, Collars, Bridles, &c.; also, a lot of Shovels, Hoes, Forks, Rakes, and many other articles not necessary to mention.

TERMS.—The Fat Cattle and Fat Hogs will be sold for Cash. On the remainder of the property a Credit of Six Months will be given; the purchaser giving bond with approved security; waiving Homestead Exemption.

☞ Sale to commence at 10 o'clock, A. M.

LYDIA H. JONES.

C. W. Hammerly, Auct'r.—[oct. 17-ts.

TWO BURGLARS ABROAD—ONE OF THEM WOUNDED IN THE LEG—AND LODGED IN JAIL—WHAT HIS SATCHEL CONTAINED.— A few weeks ago the Clothing House of L. SCHILLER, of Leesburg, was broken open one night, and a quantity of clothing, a couple of satchels, &c., abstracted. The neatness with which the job was executed, led to the presumption that it was done by some one familiar with such work. Divers persons remembered to have seen two suspicious looking strangers lurking around town about that time, but they were never seen after the robbery—which was held by many as "proof strong as holy writ," that they were the thieves—and so Mr. Schiller described them in advertising his loss.

Like a nine days' wonder the story of the theft had run its course, and had been almost forgotten by the majority of our people. The first of last week, however, some boys, while hunting in the mountain back of Mr. WM. BEVERLY's house, stumbled on a pile of old cast off garments, and near them a new leather satchel; the latter was brought to town and identified by Schiller as one of those taken from his store.

THE SUSPECTED ONES AGAIN IN TOWN.

Scarcely had this development been made when the cars from Alexandria on Wednesday night, brought back to Leesburg, the same suspicious characters. Of course they were at once shadowed, but little was seen of them that night. The next morning it was ascertained that they had lodged in a hay-loft on the suburbs of town, and efforts for their detection become more vigilant. About 9 o'clock Thursday night one of them made his appearance in one or two stores and made small purchases of provision—but he disappeared for the time, going no one knew where.

LOOKING FOR THE TRAIN.

Between 2 and 3 o'clock Friday morning, while Sergeant EWELL ATTWELL, who is generally pretty wide-awake in such cases, was standing at Boss' old corner, he heard two men walking up King street, coming toward him. As they approached he crossed over to Harris' corner, where he confronted them, each carrying a satchel or bundle. He called them to a halt, and inquired where they were travelling at that time of night. They replied that they were going to the train.— Upon being told that it was too soon for the train, they said a gentleman had told them the train started early, but were unable to give the name of their informant. Attwell then told them he thought they were

THE MEN HE WAS LOOKING FOR,

and as the train did not leave until 6 o'clock, invited them to go with him to the Mayor's Office, where he had fire and light, and where they could be comfortable until that hour.

DECLINING THE HOSPITALITY AND GETTING SHOT IN THE LEG.

Attwell partially turned, supposing they would follow, but instead they undertook to give leg-bail. That officer is in the habit, after mid-night, of laying aside his billy and carrying a double barrelled shot gun, loaded with B B. B shot. Finding that his game was on the wing, he again called to them to halt, which only seemed to accelerate their flight. He at once fired, the load taking effect in the knee of the larger of the two men. This had the effect of bringing the wounded man to bey, but his pard, availing himself of the confusion and darkness, made his escape.

LODGED IN JAIL.

The officer procured assistance,—carried his prisoner to jail—and immediately summoned Dr. WINCHESTER, who found about thirty large shot buried in and around the knee, a few of which he succeeded in extracting, though the majority of them are still there, causing a very painful, though by no means a necessarily fatal wound. After dressing the leg, an examination was made of the satchel, which had also been captured, and

HERE'S WHAT IT CONTAINED:

A complete burglar's out-fit, consisting of a steel drill, a steel bar about eighteen inches in length, a steel "jimmie"—a lot of steel wedges, for prizing open doors, &c., all of the best material, and neatly arranged for convenient transportation; also, a flask filled with powder; four or five feet of fuse, a long-necked funnel, evidently used to carry powder into key holes. Besides, there were four bran-new pocket pistols, carefully wrapped in a pair of white cotton socks; a small lot of chewing tobacco, and about a half box of cigars. The next morning there was found buried in the mud where he fell, when shot, a revolver, with every chamber loaded.

How the Great Inventor Made Love and Married.

The story of Edison's courtship, while it lacks the roseate tinge of romance, illustrates the man's faculty for going to the heart of things with the smallest possible amount of circumlocution. When he was experimenting some years ago, with the Little automatic telegraph perforations in paper by means of a key board. Among the young women whom he employed to manipulate these machines, with a view to testing their capacity for speed, was a rather demure young person who attended to her work and never raised her eyes to the incipient genius. One day Edison stood observing her as she drove down one key after another with her plump fingers until, growing nervous under his prolonged stare, she dropped her hands idly in her lap and looked up helplessly into his face. A genial smile, such as irreverent paragraphists have referred to as "the Edison grin," overspread Edison's face, and he presently inquired rather abruptly:

"What do you think of me, little girl? Do you like me?"

"Why, Mr. Edison, you frighten me. I—that is—I—"

"Don't be in any hurry about telling me.— It doesn't matter much, unless you would like to marry me."

The young woman was disposed to laugh, but Edison went on:

"Oh, I mean it. Don't be in a rush, though. Think it over; talk to your mother about it, and let me know soon as convenient—Tuesday, say. How will Tuesday suit you, next week Tuesday, I mean?"

Edison's shop was at Newark in those days, and one night a friend of his, employed in the main office of the Western Union Telegraph Co., in New York, returning home by the last train, saw a light in Edison's private laboratory, and climbed the dingy stairs to find his friend in one of his characteristic stupors, half awake and half dozing over some intricate point in electrical science which was baffling him.

"Hello, Tom!" cried the visitor cheerily, "what are you doing here this late? Aren't you going home?"

"What time is it?" inquired Edison, sleepily rubbing his eyes and stretching like a lion suddenly aroused.

"Midnight, easy enough. Come along."

"Is that so?" returned Edison in a dreamy sort of way. "By George, I *must* go home, then. I was *married* to day."

Marriage was an old story with him—he had been wedded to electrical hobbies for years. But in spite of his seeming indifference on "the most eventful day" in his life, he makes a good husband, and the demure little woman of the perforating machine smilingly rules domestic destinies at Menlo park, and proudly looks across the fields where the chimneys rise and her husband still works on the problems that made him a truant on his wedding day. A swarm of children pluck her gown to share their mother's smile, and lay in wait to climb into their father's lap and muss his hair with as great a relish as if he were not the greatest genius of his time.

MIDDLEBURG, Dec. 17, 1878.

DEAR SIR: By way of giving you an item or so of news, will state that Mr. Humphrey Lynn, living not far from Middleburg, lost two valuable work-horses last week, in attempting to cross Little River, at what is generally known as Cox's ford. Mr. Lynn was on the way to Leesburg, with a wagon load of wheat; the river was quite high, and very rapid. Almost as soon as the leaders got in the water they were washed under a log used as a foot bridge, and drowned in a few seconds. The other horses were saved. Quite a serious loss to Mr. L.

On last Friday night, Emory Chinn, son of Mr. R. S. Chinn, rode a large, fine roan work-horse to Middleburg, and fastened him to the rack in front of Howard Noland's store. About 9 o'clock Emory went to get his horse, but he was not there, and has not been heard of since. He and his father have searched far and near for the missing animal, but have failed to get any tidings of it. It is the impression generally that the horse was stolen. A daring robbery, indeed, and one calculated to frighten the country people out of town, and prevent them from coming to town horseback after dark. Hurriedly yours,

T. R. B.

12/21/78 Washingtonian

[From the Paducah (Ky,) Sun.]

HOW IT FEELS TO BE HANGED.

The Experience of Mr. McGee of Kentucky with a Hasty Vigilance Committee.

While the officers were searching for a clue to the whereabouts of Marks, some one, whose name McGee to this day does not know, artfully threw suspicion on Mr. McGee. This suspicion was fanned and kept alive by Sullivant. The result was that McGee was one night taken from his bed by a mob of armed men, a rope attached to his neck, the end of which was attached to the pommel of a saddle, and away he went. Arriving at a lonely spot in the woods—and one who has ever travelled the county between the rivers, as it is called, knows that there are many places in that locality peculiarly adapted to deeds of violence—the rope was detached from the saddle, and and, while these midnight maurauders gathered around, by the light of a lantern illuminated by the faint glare of one sickly candle, the line was thrown over the low-hanging branch of a tree made taut and McGee at the same time informed that he had better speedily make his peace with God, as he had but a few moments to live. He was urged by the leader to tell the whereabouts of Mark's remains, and, if any, his accomplices in the 'taking off.' As McGee was entirely innocent of the dark deed, of course he could answer that he knew nothing about it. His assertion, 'So help me God, gentleman, I never saw or heard of the man before in my life,' was answered by the remark of Sullivant himself, 'George, that is too thin!' Mr. McGee says that he distinctly saw the lantern wave twice in the air. He was lifted bodily from the ground into the air; he knew that he was being drawn up over the limb by the rope. There was no pain as long as he was ascending. When he settled back, however, with a slight jerk, his suffering was excruciating. He could feel his eyes suddenly turn into balls of fire and protrude from their sockets. He tried to scream, but no sound issued from his throat. His arms were unpinioned, and he endeavored to raise his hands, so as to grasp the rope above his head, that he might relieve that terrible shortening of his breath, which seemed, at each muscular attempt at respiration, as if the air would escape from his lungs and force itself out through the pores of skin on his breast and back. The muscles of the arm refused to obey his will. His joints experienced a sensation similar to that one would imagine the piercing of red hot needles would produce. The knees twitched and jerked convulsively. All this apparently in a minute of time. Then a delicious sensation of 'cool numbness,' to use his own words, commencing at his extremities, stole gradually over him. He lost all desire to save himself—preferred to die where he was. Almost every act of his life—no matter how trivial—flashed through his mind with the rapidity of lightning. A distant roar, as of a far-away cataract, grew gradually more and more distinct, until the fearful noise was almost deafening, then changed with the rapidity of thought itself into the most delicious music he had ever heard. Everything became as light as midday although he could distinguish nothing of his surroundings, and finally unconsciousness. 'It was not absolute unconsciousness, either,' said Mr. McGee. 'I cannot describe it intelligibly. I do not know of any words that would convey to you a correct idea of the sensation. I was myself and not myself. I seemed to be sailing away through space, as you have seen a large bird float through the atmosphere, without the apparent motion of a wing or feather. Another thing that is indellibly impressed upon my mind was the terrible, oppressive horrible silence, worse than silence—stillness, that existed above, below, about me. Still floated on and on, perfectly contented, asking for nothing, thinking of nothing, hoping for nothin—ever and with increasing rapidity moving on and upward.'

But gradually, continued Mr. McGee, this perfectly contented, devil-may-care feeling commenced to disappear. He became conscious of bodily pain again. It seemed as if iron bands had been tightened with screws about his head and chest. He consciously gasped for breath. He heard voices—the words undistinguishable at first; than one or two here and there he understood. At last, fully restored to consciousness, he heard his captors quarreling fiercely as to whether he should be strung up again or carried to the Smithland Jail. He was lying on the ground, his throat bleeding from the cruel rope, which still encircled his neck. Water was brought from a creeck near by and dashed over him. And at last he was mounted upon a horse, and still in a half dazed condition moved away.

He arrived at Smithland about daylight, was locked up in jail, where he remained three days, and was then released, Sullivant taking his place. The latter is now serving out a life sentence at Frankfort.

12/19/78 Mirror

In Wyoming, where lovely woman can vote if she will, she doesn't. Only one woman in the Territory has ever been elected to office by the people, and now official station is never demanded by any member of the sisterhood. Not half the women in Cheyenne have cast a vote since the first two elections. Although there are separate polling-places for the sex, respectable women stay away from the polls and keep out of politics. The only women who take an interest in elections are those of the baser sort.

12/26/78 Mirror

A justice of the peace in a Pennsylvania rural town married a couple the other day, and the groom asked him his terms after the knot was tied. "Well," said the Justice, "the Code allows me two dollars." "Then," said the young man, "here's a dollar ; that will make you three."

12/5/78 Mirror

GEO. JOHNSON and HENRY CLAGETT (!) two of our fellow-citizens for whom the President in his Message seems so solicitous, were before Justice Powell on Monday, charged with stealing cabbage from Col. NIXON, and had a portion of their rights guaranteed by five lashes on their bare-back, with the promise of ten additional stripes if remiss in their behavior during the next twelve months.

ARRESTED.—Deputy Sheriff Poulton, of Loudoun county, arrived here on Saturday night from Staunton, having in charge J. H. McPherson, whom he arrested in that town on the charge of seduction under promise of marriage in Loudoun. McPherson, who is very respectably connected, was confined in jail until this morning when he was carried to Leesburg.—Alex. Gazette.

Young McPHERSON was arraigned before Justice POWELL on Monday, and by him bailed in the sum of $500 to appear on Monday, the 9th inst., to answer with witnesses, &c., the charge preferred against him.

The Strange Noises That Are Heard in a Preacher's House.

[From the New York World of Friday.]

For two weeks Mr. E. Smith, of 136 Clinton avenue near Myrtle avenue, Brooklyn, has been annoyed by occasional demonstrations of a rather supernatural character, and since Monday night he has been "having 'em pretty solid," as Special Officer Wilson told a World reporter last evening. The greatest trouble has been with the front door-bell, which has insisted on ringing in season and out of season, and, not content with announcing material visitors, has gone wild over invisible callers. Knowing that the police are closely watching the door-bell to discover who was ringing it, the reporter naturally hesitated as he approached the haunted doorway last evening. The walk on both sides of the street was blocked by crowds of curious people, drawn thither by the reports of spiritual manifestations, and the efforts of a policeman to disperse the gathering was entirely unavailing.

Mr. Smith is fifty six years of age, and was formerly an orthodox clergyman. Of late years he has been a mason and builder. His family consists of a wife and two young daughters. A Mr. and Mrs. Thompson also board with him. None of these persons believe in "Spiritualism," so-called. About two weeks ago the door bell of Mr. Smith's house rang, apparently of its own accord, and the doors rattled and banged when no one was near. This conduct was repeated several times afterwards, and Mr Smith began to be uneasy over the manifestations. It grew worse, and he was at a loss to explain the noises. He would not accept the theory of Spiritualism, because it was at variance with his orthodox views. Last Monday night things grew desperate. The bell rang and the doors banged and slammed and no one could find the cause. Mr. Smith's nervousness increased and the wife and daughters were frightened. The neighbors on either side heard the queer noises. Finally Captain McLaughlin, of the Fourth precinct was notified, and, accompanied by Detective Sam Price and Special Officer Wilson, he went to Mr. Smith's house confident of capturing the ghosts.

The officers went to the house about 5:30 P. M., which was the usual hour for the beginning of the performance. Their presence appeared to be no hindrance to the noises, for very soon after they had entered the pounding began. Detective Price went outside and stood near the front door, riveting his eyes upon it and pricking up his ears. In a moment three tremendous blows shook the house and the detective's nerves. This sort of thing lasted till 10 o'clock; when it ceased the officers left and the family retired in quiet for the night. Another observation was taken Tuesday evening, and Wednesday night Captain

McLaughlin returned with reinforcements — He and Detective Price remained indoors while three officers were stationed at different points of the yard about the house.

Price stood with his hand on the inside knob of the door and his feet wide apart, ready for a spring the instant a knock should be heard, while on the other side stood a policeman whose wide-open eyes covered the whole exterior of the door. Then they were confident of their prey. Suddenly the door shook under a blow like that of a battering ram, was instantly thrown open by the detective, and the two officers stood breathlessly face to face, and swore in the clear starlight that neither of them did it. At another time, while an officer was watching the bell knob, the gong struck repeatedly and the wire rattled wildly. Finally the bell was muffled.

While Captain McLaughlin and members of Mr. Smith's family were in the dining-room there was a sound of shattering of glass and a half a brick dropped to the floor under the window through which it had unceremoniously entered. The window is shielded without by a close grape arbor, and besides that several officers were watching that side of the house for spirits The window was an old-fashioned one with twelve small panes in each sash. The brick broke three of the panes in the lower sash without injuring the sash at all. It then fell to the floor, its full force being spent. About ten o'clock this nonsense concluded, and the mystified officers retired.

Last night they returned again, less hopeful of making arrangements, but determined to see the thing out. But Mr Smith said that he had "been to the Lord with his afflictions and had received a promise of relief," and therefore he did not expect the spirits again. Sure enough they did not come, no disturbance whatever taking place. While the officers were present Mr Smith prayed to be delivered of the nuisance and sang a hymn, after which he appeared more calm. The police say that he has suffered greatly and been in a condition of nervous weakness. They would allow no one to see him. His wife and daughters are also suffering from nervous exhaustion. Mr. Smith will not, however, the police say, listen to the vulgar "spirits" theory, but thinks the whole trouble is caused by the devil himself. Why the devil should select his house he is unable to understand.

The police appear to be completely at a loss to account for the disturbance, but insist that there was no opportunity for deception.— They watched everything closely, but when two of them were standing with the door between them the door certainly resounded with loud raps. They stick to that. Mr. Smith will not leave the house if he can help it, and is inclined to think that the devil has been ordered away for good and all.

1/2/79 Mirror

DEATH OF WM. C. LYNCH.

Drowned in Attempting to Save a Friend.

The above caption tells the whole sad story of the death of our young friend. No words that we can utter will add to their force, or better illustrate the nobleness of his character, or the heroism of his death. For it is not in the power of tongue or pen to pay a grander tribute to the memory of one who has gone hence, than to say that he gave his life for his friend.

WILLIAM C. LYNCH was the second son of Wm. B. Lynch, editor of the *Washingtonian,* of this place. Had he lived until the 8th day of March, 1879, he would have been twenty-two years of age. For the past three years and a half he was a student at Washington & Lee University, Lexington, Va. Of his standing there, the testimony of those who knew him best, will be given as we proceed. Suffice it to say, it was all that his friends could desire, and gave promise of an honorable and useful future. No man in that institution stood higher or enjoyed to a greater degree the confidence, respect and affectionate regard of the faculty and his fellow students, than did the subject of this notice.

In disposition WILLIE LYNCH was from his youth up, quiet and unobtrusive, retiring almost to a fault,—and involuntarily shrinking from whatever seemed a display of self; in manner he was simple and child-like, and in feeling gentle and tender as a woman.— But beneath this there rested the stern elements of true manhood. Possessed of a mind naturally quick and bright, he was thoughtful and thorough in his studies, and as one of the editors of the *Collegian*, his writings had given evidence of rare culture; strictly conscientious in walk and conversation—devoted in his attachments, and bold and determined in the hour of trial, it is not surprising that he sacrificed his own young life in a gallant effort to save that of another.

During the year just closed, this community has been singularly afflicted in the loss of her children. In reviewing the death role for the period indicated, we find the names of these, who by reason of their abundance of years, it was not unnatural that we should find there; but anon we are reminded of those who had attained the meridian of life, and who, in the prime of their usefulness, surrounded by everything calculated to make life desirable, have gone the way of all flesh; and then in how many once happy households is the cup of joy embittered because of the absence of some little one, that to-day is not.

Such is the common heritage of our race. Day by day are we summoned to the house of mourning, where loving ears bend low to catch the farewell utterances of the departing soul, and then comes the coffin, the hearse and the grave, and the mourners go about the streets. So common are these things that we look for them as naturally as we do for the setting of the evening sun.

But in the death of Willie Lynch there is a peculiar sadness. A few brief months ago, he left the friends and the scenes of his childhood, to resume his studies at College. This was to have been his last session. He hoped, and everything conspired to assure him of success, that at its close he would engage in the active pursuits of life, with his college honors thick upon him. The plant had been well nurtured, and just as the bud was bursting and the fruit was soon to ripen, it was nipped by an untimely frost, and perished in the leaf— and that too, on the day of all others, most given to mirth and joy and pleasant recollections. At noon on Christmas Day, the mail brought a letter from the absent boy to loved ones at home which breathed words of tenderest affection, and in glowing terms told of his hopes for the future. A few hours later, when the curtain of night had fallen on the festivities of the day, and the family group were reperusing Willie's letter, there came flashing over the wires another message, announcing that the hand that had penned the *letter then being read*, was cold in death.

Upon this entire community, who knew the dead boy well, the shocking announcement fell like a thunder-bolt from a cloudless sky, and never have we witnessed a more universal manifestation of heartfelt grief, than was expressed on that sorrowful Christmas night. To his afflicted family, and especially the stricken parent, the very fibres of whose soul were entwined around the noble boy—and whose earthly plans have been so suddenly and so ruthlessly crushed forever, we can only offer the tribute of a tear. Their grief is too deep and too sacred to be soothed by human sympathy, however sincerely felt or freely offered. In the twinkling of an eye the light of a household has been extinguished,—a bright young life abruptly terminated;—but amid the night of gloom and sadness caused by his departure, there shines with the brightness of noon day, the example of a well-spent life, and the memory of a heroic death.

Willie's remains, enclosed in a metallic case, and escorted by W. S. Forrester, of Louisville, and H. C. Getzandanner, of Jefferson county, W. Va., left Lexington at 5 o'clock Thursday morning, and reached Alexandria about 10 o'clock that night—where they were met and taken in charge by Col. Bolivar Christian and Mr H. O Clagett, and by them brought to Leesburg, on the noon train Friday. From the depot here, they were attended by Prof. Williamson and a number of the former students of the Leesburg Academy, to the residence of his father, where the body remained until 3 o'clock Friday afternoon at which hour it was conveyed to the Episcopal Church, where, in the presence of an unusually large congregation, the Rev Dr Davis, assisted by Rev Theo Reed, performed the impressive burial service of that Church, at the conclusion of which, followed by a sad and mournful train of bereaved relatives and sympathizing friends, the body was taken to Union Cemetery.

HOW IT HAPPENED.

Washington & Lee University, }
Lexington, Va., Dec. 27th, 1878. }

My Dear Col.: In a letter written to our bereaved friend, Capt. W. B. Lynch, last night, I sent you a message.

The unfortunate drowning of his noble son has cast a gloom over this Institution, of which he was a highly honored member, and, indeed, over the entire community. When I passed up Main Street Xmas night, between ten and eleven o'clock, almost perfect silence prevailed, and almost everything like Xmas merriment has been suspended since noon of the 25th up to this moment.

Young Lynch was one of the most admirable young men I ever had the pleasure to know. I have felt embarrassed in writing to his father, whom I never had the honor to meet, by the effort to refrain from too much freedom of expression under circumstances so full of anguish to the friends of the poor fellow.

He died in the unselfish effort to save the life of his friend.

A number of young men had gone down to the river to take their Xmas in skating. They went up to the end of what is called "the Island," as you will understand, on the South side of the river. Young Howard Barclay who was with others, in company with our lamented young friend, informs me that Randall and one young man of Lexington were the only persons on the ice, and Randall skating across fell through the ice at a point about 30 feet from the North bank, and catching a rail that was shoved to him by a negro man, was enabled to escape. Meanwhile, William Lynch, hearing Randall's call for help, rushed to the rescue, saying to Barclay, who tried to dissuade him, that he must try and save Randall. He ran without skates, as Barclay is positive, although some one said that he had on his skates, and before he got within fifty feet of Randall he fell and broke through, lower down the river than the point where Randall was and further from the shore. The young men could do nothing where they were, and had to run down to the bridge, which you know, is several hundred yards, and up on the other side.

Meantime, several countrymen were making efforts to rescue William but failed; in fact, he must have become benumbed with cold in a few minutes, and sank, finally, in water eight or ten feet deep. It must have taken an hour, some say more, to recover his body, as a boat had to be procured and brought up from below.

The most active restoratives were applied by two physicians, but without effect—indeed, the poor fellow's life was extinct when he was taken from his watery grave.

I reached the spot about two hours, more or less, after the occurrence, and at once dispatched to my old friend, Mr. Richard Davis. As soon as the body could be properly cared for I took it in charge, myself, and brought it to the Lee Chapel, to await orders from his friends, putting the students immediately in charge of it   *   *   *

I may say to you, that I have never been more distressed by any occurrence. In fact, I was greatly attached to the dear fellow—so modest, yet so manly, so true to himself yet so unobtrusive and unselfish; so dutiful and faithful, never guilty of one single neglect of duty, to my knowledge. I wrote to Captain Lynch, Wednesday afternoon, and again yesterday, but I am so painfully conscious of my inability to afford any comfort by anything that I can say or do.

Do assure the entire family of the profound sympathy of Faculty and students.

Religion exercises will be held by the student next Sunday, in commemoration of their departed friend.   Yours, truly,
J. J. WHITE.

(The relationship between the Mirror and the Washingtonian seemed to be always amicable, rare for competing papers. Witness this kind and sympathetic account of the Lynch tragedy by Mirror editor Sheetz.)

1/9/79 Mirror

THE New Year was ushered in by a cold
snap almost unprecedented in this section—
which was likewise attended by fearfully high
winds. On Friday morning the mercury fell
to three degrees below zero, and for three or
four days successively danced attendance
around that frigid monarch. The mail coach
between Winchester and Round Hill crossed
the Shenandoah on the ice, and all along the
Potomac communication is kept up by means
of a similar bridge of nature. The streams in
this vicinity are all locked up, and if ice-
gatherers had not fully supplied themselves
ten days ago, ice could now be gotten at least
from ten to twelve inches in thickness.

We understand that during the prevalence
of the high wind last Friday night, the dwelling house of Capt. ALFRED GLASSCOCK, near
Snickersville, was partially unroofed.

On Tuesday morning the elements began to
tone down, since which time it has been comparatively moderate.

A NARROW ESCAPE.—On last Saturday
(Jan. 4th,) a newly married couple *en route*
from "The Plains" to Landmark, were considerably frightened after traveling a mile
to find their sleigh on fire. In an instant the
couple leaped forth in time to save themselves
from the blaze, that was fast consuming the
basket and blankets. The young man succeeded in unhooking the frightened horse, and
saving the runners; the basket and blankets
were destroyed by the fire.

The Bride had a considerable hole burnt in
her dress, and the Groom had a part of the
lining of his "long black" burnt out. It was
a very narrow escape. And those who have
sleighs should not allow hot *bricks* to be put
in them. That was the way the fire originated.

1/11/79 Washingtonian

A snow plow driven by five locomotives
was yesterday employed on the New York
Central in forcing a passage through the
snow drifts four miles east of Batavia. The
plow and four of the engines left track, and
two of the engines were reported as having
exploded their boilers. Thow Lawless, a fireman, was caught between the tender and
boiler, and the surgeon had to cut the bones
of his leg before he could be extricated. His
injuries are probably fatal. Four or five
others were wounded.

1/2/79 Mirror

Crockett in a Bear's Den.

"A MEMBER OF CONGRESS NEVER ROSE QUICKER IN THE WORLD THAN I DID!"

[From the New York Mercury.]

"I never but once," said Col. Crockett, "was in what I call a quandary. It was during my electioneering for Congress, at which time I strolled about in the woods so particularly pestered by politics that I forgot my rifle. Any man may forget his rifle, you know, but it isn't every man who can make amends for forgetfulness by his faculties, I guess. It chanced that I was strolling along, considerably deep in congressionals; the first thing that took my fancy was the snarling of some young bears, which proceeded from the hollow of a tree; but I soon found that I could not reach the cubs with my hand, so I went feet foremost to see if I could draw them up by the toes. I hung on the top of the hole, straining with my might to reach them, until at last my hands slipped, and down I went more than twenty feet to the bottom of that hole, and there I found myself almost hip deep in a family of young bears. I soon found that I might as well undertake to climb up the greasiest part of a rainbow as to get back—the hole in the tree being so large and its sides so smooth and slippery from the rain.—Now this was a real genuine, regular quandary. If I were to shout, it would have been doubtful whether they would hear me at the settlement, and if they did hear me the story would ruin my election, for a man that ventured into a place that he couldn't get himself out of. Well, now, while I was calculating whether it was best to shout for help or wait in the hole until after election, I heard a kind of growling overhead; looking, I saw the old bear coming down stern foremost upon me. My motto is always 'Go ahead!' and as she lowered herself within my reach I got a tight grip of her tail in my left hand, and with my little buck-hafted penknife in the other, I commenced spurring her forward. I'll be shot if ever a member of Congress rose quicker in the world than I did! She took me out in the shake of a lamb's tail!"

12/12/78 Mirror

A few days since a young gentleman, who reside in Bedford, was crossing the Blue Ridge, on foot, when he lost his way and wandered until night. Afraid to sleep on the ground he climbed a large chestnut tree which had been broke off by the wind and seeing that the hollow top was filled with leaves crawled into it. The tree proved to be a mere shell, hollow to the roots, and the young man of course went to the bottom, a distance of about forty feet.

The only aperter, through which he could breathe was a small hole not larger than his hand, and he at once commenced the work of enlarging it by picking off the wood with his fingers. Shortly before dark on the following evening he emerged from what he had first considered a living tomb.—*Lynchburg News*

1/9/79 Mirror

Elegant Habits of Some Statesmen.

A letter from Washington describes the House of Representatives as a very impressive body. It was not necessary for the writer to say that it was his first visit to the capitol. I should like, writes a correspondent from the capital, to read a letter of his, written with the same frankness and honesty, after the close of the short session. I should want him to be present in the gallery during a row, and to attend all the night sessions and the closing ceremonies. I should want him also to keep his eye on certain members I should name. If he is attentive, he will see members roaring drunk once in a while ; he will see dozens of members squirting tobacco juice over carpets that cost six dollars a yard; he will see scores of members smoking in the chamber during the sitting; he will see members stretched out on the sofas asleep, and he will hear them snore ; he will see members with both feet on their desks, sitting on their back bone ; he will see members munching apples while attending to the public business; he will see occasionally a member with his boot off, easing his corns, and he will see much else that will detract somewhat from his description of an impressive body.

1/23/79 Mirror

[COMMUNICATED.]

MR. EDITOR :—The definition of a Road is "ground appropriated for travel," and the appropriation we are now to make in the shape of Road Tax, is supposed to go to that end.

There are various ways of travel, now-a-days, but the only possible way of safely passing over our road would be by balloon, and we suggest to those in charge of spending our Road Tax, to buy or hire one, and sail out this way, to see in what splendid condition our ground appropriated for travel now lies.

We are, and have been, utterly opposed to the mode of working our Road. We believe, and so declare, that any water brake, made at right angles to the course of road is a nuisance, and should be abated. We believe any chuck-hole filled with large rock and covered with loose dirt, multiplies evil, breaking wheels, springs and axles, and breaking down beasts of burden. We believe an open ditch across a level road is a snare and a delusion, a pit into which many fall. And, finally, we believe our taxes go from us, to call into being, and support these evils we deplore, and might more profitably be employed in instructing those who handle them, as to the use for which they are paid, to mend our ways, not ruin them. VIATOR.

1/16/79 Mirror

OFF TO DAKOTA.—We understand that our young friends, D. J. MERCIER and W. P. CARR, of this county, were on Saturday last commissioned to proceed to the city of Bismark, in the Territory of Dakota, the present western terminus of the Northern Pacific Railroad, to take charge of U. S. Signal Offices in or near that city. We heartily congratulate these young gentlemen upon receiving so desirable an appointment, as it will place them in the midst of a truly enterprising community, in a fine, healthy, bracing atmosphere, and with a compensation of near $900 per annum, and a good prospect of an early material increase. By way of preparation for this position, they have been spending several months of the year just closed in acquiring a knowledge of all the different modes of distant signaling, in the practice of expert telegraphy, in pursuing the study of all the different branches of meteorology, and in familiarizing themselves with the use of the various instruments of which they will have charge in their new occupation. This course of instruction has been pursued under competent instructors, at Fort Whipple, on Arlington Heights, in this State near Washington City. We are told that they are now pronounced by the officers in charge of the Fort, expert in their several studies, and competent to take charge of the responsible positions assigned them — There are in the United States nearly two hundred Signal Stations ; and though the duties performed there are all of a civic nature, yet the Signal Service is entirely and strictly under control of the War Department.

1/16/79 Mirror

A New York Granger recently lost one of his cattle of the male persuasion. He mounted his horse and rode off a couple of miles, asking all whom he met if they had seen such an animal. At last he met a woman of whom he inquired if on her way down she had seen anything of a big red heifer with a star in its forehead and two white feet. She said she had not, but there was a bull up there answering the description. 'That's her,' said the modest Granger.

1/30/79 Mirror

James Rumsey, the Steamboat Inventor.

Col. A. R. Boteler, of Jefferson county, W. Va., recently delivered a Lecture in Charlestown, entitled "Justice to James Rumsey."

In his lecture Col. Boteler reviewed the evidence upon the subject, showing that Rumsey in 1782 finished his first model of a steamboat. Discouragement and poverty met him on every side, but he battled with them all, and in 1785 completed a steamboat, the second one he built—the first, when on the eve of completion in 1784, was carried off by a flood to Harper's Ferry, dashed to pieces and the machinery destroyed.

Col. Boteler, according to the report of the *Free Press*, described in glowing terms the scene on the banks of the Potomac at Shepherdstown, W. Va. on the 5th of December, 1785, when hundreds of the people gathered to witness the trial trip of the great invention. A few ladies, from one of whom he heard the story, were on the boat; and as the little rude structure darted out in mid stream, and then shot up the river, Gen. Horatia Gates, who stood on the shore, cried, out—"My God! she goes, she goes! The Shepherdstown mechanics did the iron work. Rumsey himself making the steampipe by twisting an iron tube around a horse-collar block at a sadler's shop, thus getting it similar to the worm of a still. Among the spectators to this trial trip were names familiar to us all—Bedinger, Kearsley, General Gates, Stephens and Darke, and hundreds of others Shepherdstown had a larger population then than now.

Testimonials were given by Gen. Washington, Major Bedinger, and many other celebrated men; and protection was applied for and obtained from the Legislature of Virginia and Maryland, the former agreeing that if the protection was withdrawn within ten years, to pay Rumsey £10,000 in gold or silver. The year after a Rumseyan *Society* was formed in Philadelphia, of which Benjamin Franklin was President, and money raised to send Rumsey to Europe. He went to London and built a steamboat to be exhibited on the Thames; but his money gave out, he was involved in debt and finally his boat was seized by his creditors and he was not allowed to loose it from its moorings but only permitted to show how its machinery would work. Finally it was suggested that he deliver a lecture in order to raise funds, to which he consented, but on appearing before an audience of London scientific men, his first attempt at public speaking, he endeavored to utter some words and failed; again tried to articulate, fell back senseless, and never spoke afterwards. The next day he died.—

Robert Fulton—the reputed inventor of steam navigation, was with him in London—was associated with him at the time of his death, and the next year applied for right of protection for a boat to be propelled by steam. The speaker stated that John Fitch, of Pennsylvania, who also laid claim to the honor of his invention, had been in Kentucky at the time of Rumsey's first effort in Bath, when Daniel Bedinger went there and evidently communicated the idea to him, though Fitch claims to have discovered it by accident, and afterwards pried about Rumsey's workshop until the citizens of Shepherdstown threatened to tar and feather him if he did not leave. Chancellor Livingston, then Minister to France, has the credit of finally bringing out the steamboat from drafts by Robert Fulton, who, however, was so ignorant of mechanical principles that the workmen laughed at him. The facts conclusively proved by Col. Boteler are, that Rumsey philosophically worked out his invention of the steamboat, and reduced it to practical use on the Potomac at Shepherdstown in 1785 when there was not a single steam engine on the Continent of America, and twenty years before Fulton's experiment on the Hudson; and that beyond a doubt both Fitch and Fulton got their ideas if not the full details of the invention, from him.

(Bath (now Berkeley Springs, WV) was my father's family home as it was for a time for Rumsey. I thus learned of this man first from the spoken word before I researched him.)

AN ANCIENT DOCUMENT.

Loudoun County a Hundred Years Ago.

Maj. B. P. NOLAND, grand-son of BURR POWELL, has put us in possession of a verified copy of the proceedings of a public meeting held in Leesburg, Loudoun County, on the 14th of June, 1774—nearly one hundred and five years ago. It is interesting, not merely for its antiquity, but as showing the spirit of independence that animated the breasts of our liberty-loving county-men, two years before the Declaration of American Independence, in 1776.

The original document was found among the papers of Col. LEVEN POWELL—at one time member of Congress from this District,—who died in 1810. His son, BURR POWELL, forwarded a copy to R. H. LEE, Esq., who in 1826, was about to publish a second edition of his memoirs of the life of R. H. LEE, of Revolutionary fame. The second edition of that work, however, never appeared, and the proceedings of the Loudoun meeting are now, for the first time, given to the public in printed form.

We publish the accompanying memoranda of BURR POWELL, as showing the authenticity of the paper in question:

PUBLIC MEETING IN LOUDOUN IN 1774.

At a meeting of the Freeholders and other inhabitants of the County of Loudoun, in the Colony of Virginia, held at the Court-house in Leesburg, the 14th June, 1774,—F. Peyton, Esq., in the Chair,—to consider the most effectual method to preserve the rights and liberties of N. America, and relieve our brethren of Boston, suffering under the most oppressive and tyrannical act of the British Parliament, made in the 14th year of his present Majesty's reign, whereby their harbor is blocked up, their commerce totally obstructed, and their property rendered useless—

Resolved, That we will always cheerfully submit to such prerogatives as his Majesty has a right, by law, to exercise, as Sovereign of the British Dominions, and to no other.

Resolved, That it is beneath the dignity of freemen to submit to any tax not imposed on them in the usual manner, by representatives of their own choosing.

Resolved, That the act of the British Parliament, above-mentioned, is utterly repugnant to the fundamental laws of justice, in punishing persons without even the form of a trial; but a despotic exertion of unconstitutional power, designedly calculated to enslave a free and loyal people.

Resolved, That the enforcing the execution of the said act of Parliament by a military power, must have a necessary tendency to raise a civil war, and that we will, with our lives and fortunes, assist and support our suffering brethren (this far is written in the handwriting of George Johnston, I think; the balance is certainly in the handwriting of the late Leven Powell,) of Boston, and every part of North America that may fall under the immediate hand of oppression, until a redress of all our grievances shall be procured, and our common liberties established on a permanent foundation.

Resolved, That the East India Company, by exporting their tea from England to America, whilst subject to a tax imposed thereon by the British Parliament, have evidently designed to fix on the Americans those chains forged for them by a venal ministry, and have thereby rendered themselves odious and detestable throughout all America. It is therefore the unanimous opinion of this meeting not to purchase any tea or other East India commodity whatever, imported after the first of this month.

Resolved, That we will have no commercial intercourse with Great Britain until the above-mentioned act of Parliament shall be totally repealed, and the right of regulating the internal policy of N. America by a British Parliament shall be absolutely and positively given up.

Resolved, That Thompson Mason and Francis Peyton, Esqs, be appointed to represent the county at a general meeting to be held at Williamsburg, on the 1st day of August next, to take the sense of this Colony at large on the subject of the preceding resolves, and that they, together with Leven Powell, William Ellzey, John Thornton, George Johnston and Samuel Levi, or any three of them, be a committee to correspond with the several committees appointed for this purpose.

A PARTY of strolling Gypsies passed through Leesburg one day last week, and are now encamped on the lands of Mr. P. H. Carr, about three miles south of town. They had with them ten or twelve wagons, some of them very handsome, 25 or 30 head of horses, and men, women and children in proportion; and all necessary appurtenances required by their nomadic course of life.

2/13/79 Mirror

About noon on Monday, the case of the Commonwealth vs. F. Foster, charged with having broken into and robbed the store of L. Schiller of a number of articles on the night of the 31st of October last, was taken up—a jury empanneled, and the hearing of the case proceeded with. Quite a number of witnesses were called, mainly by the prosecution, the examination of whom occupied the time of the Court until noon Tuesday at which time Maj. Lee opened the argument for the Commonwealth in a speech of about half an hour. He was replied to by Messrs. W. C. BALCH and J. B. McCABE, counsel for the defense. Each of them spoke for about an hour and a quarter. The testimony tending to convict the prisoner was circumstantial, and his counsel wove for him the most plausible theory the circumstances would allow, which they sought to impress upon the jury with an eloquence and zeal worthy of a better cause.

The Court took a recess until 7 o'clock Tuesday night, when the Prosecuting Attorney, Maj. LEE, in a half-hour speech, reviewed the evidence and replied to the arguments advanced by the counsel for the defence, with a clearness and force that must have carried conviction to the minds of the jurors—if they were not already convinced—because in less than half an hour's consultation they returned with a verdict of guilty and fixed Foster's term of imprisonment in the penitentiary at five years.

There were two indictments against Foster one for house-breaking and robbery, and the other for possession of burglarious implements. He will now be tried on the second indictment.

2/8/79 Washingtonian

A HOLSTEIN HERD IN VIRGINIA

Eds. Country Gentleman—I recently had the pleasure of accompanying Judge Fullerton of New York to his farm in Virginia, and was much gratified to see what his skill and energy have accomplished. The farm contains about 800 acres, beautifully situated near the old battle ground of Centerville. Between three and four hundred acres are in a truly splendid state of cultivation, producing crops of lucerne, clover, blue grass, orchard grass, timo-

thy, corn, roots, &c., which would make New York State farmers open their eyes. The farm buildings are commodious and provided with every labor saving convenience. On the ground floor of the cow house there are accommodations for 100 head of cattle stock; a never failing stream of fine clear water runs through all the barn-yards, pig-pens, &c. At this time there are about 100 head of stock on the place, eighty of which are full blood Holsteins, all of them imported or out of imported stock. At the head of the herd stands the bull 4th Highland Chief, a truly magnificent animal, weighing over 2,700 pounds. The young stock of both sexes are of the very best quality, but it is of the most remarkable yield of milk that I desire to make special mention.

(Fullerton might have been the first Holstein breeder in Virginia, but if so, Dr. Quinby or Mr. Buechler from Loudoun were a close second. Jerseys or Guernseys were the prominent dairy breeds but were then called Aldernays.)

A Woman and Something Over.

3/6/79 Mirror

The wife of a certain well-known rancher living near this place has got the true grit.—Her husband was away on business a whole week recently, and one day while he was absent the pump gave out. The nearest neighbor lived a long distance, so she hoisted up the pipe herself, and found that the trouble lay in the suction feather, which was too much worn to work properly. Away she went and cut a new one, using the old one as a pattern On returning, she found that a large hog had fallen into the open well.—Nothing daunted, she got a strong rope, a slip-noose, fished it around the squealing porker, and then lifting as hard as she could, made the end fast to the curb, thus raising the animal partially out of the water and preventing it from drowning. She then harnessed a horse, hitched him to the rope, and in less time than it takes to tell it, the hog,

All dripping with freshness, arose from the well.

But before the rescue of the parent animal two of her offspring, crowding too close to the curb, probably to sympathize with their mother's distress, lost balance and were now floundering around in the water at the bottom Instantly the hog was rescued, our heroine set about the recovery of the pigs. She procured a ladder, which, however, though long enough to touch the water, was not long enough to reach the bottom of the well. Necessity is the mother of invention, and procuring a fence rail she thrust it through the top round, resting both ends on the curb.—Then climbing down the hanging ladder she rescued the two pigs, bringing both safely to surface. This done she quietly completed the job by putting in the new suction leather, lowering the pipe into the well, closing the curb and pumping water for her week's washing.—*Livermore (Col.) Herald.*

3/20/79 Mirror

AMERICA LOSES THE BELT.—The great international walking match, which commenced at Gilmore's Garden, New York, at 1 o'cl'k last Monday morning week, ended exactly at 10 o'clock Saturday night, and the record stood; Rowell, 500 miles; Ennis, 475; Harriman, 450. Ennis was the last to leave the track, Rowell having withdraw at 9 o'clock; and Harriman fifteen minutes before Rowell did. O'Leary, who won the belt in England a year ago, and loses it now, retired from the contest on Wednesday evening, after having walked 215 miles. On the sixth and last day Rowell made 72 miles, Ennis 69, and Harriman 60.

278

3/13/79 Mirror

A young lady, after passing the Cambridge local examination, suddenly broke off her engagement with her sweetheart. A friend expostulated with her, but she replied, "I must merely say that his views on the theosophic doctrine of cosmogony are loose, and you must at once understand how impossible it is for any true woman to risk her happiness with such a person."

3/20/79 Mirror

"Mother, what is an angel?" "An angel—well, an angel is a child that flies." "But, mother, why does papa always call my governess an angel?" "Well," explained the mother, after a moment's pause, "she is going to fly immediately."

3/13/79 Mirror

There are now six female lawyers in the United States, and all are having a fair practice.

THE Pt. OF ROCKS LYNCHING,

Particulars of the Summary Execution—Scene of the Tragedy—Removal of the Inquest to Frederick City, &c.

[Special Correspondent of the Sun.]

FREDERICK, MD., April 18, 1879.

The lynching of James Carroll, colored, at Point of Rocks on Thursday night, for the outrage on Mrs Richard Thomas, Licksville, Md., on Monday night last, was the absorbing topic of conversation in Frederick county today. The cool and deliberate manner in which the preparations were made for the lynching, and the summary mode in which the prisoner was dealt with, showed a determination on the part of the residents of the county not to wait for the slower verdict of law, and if the man had succeeded in getting to Frederick City jail there were 500 armed men ready to tear or burn down the building and capture the ravisher.

Mr. Richard Thomas, the husband of the unfortunate lady who was the subject of attack, says that when he was in Georgetown, D. C., on Wednesday, walking along the canal path, he met the negro, who raised his hat to him and said, "Good morning, Mr. Thomas." Mr Thomas passed on and warned Mr. Hy. C. Volkman, a mounted policeman of the third precinct. After following the man for about seven squares Mr. Volkman became afraid he would lose his man amongst the lumber yards in the neighborhood, and, dismounting, continued the pursuit on foot and captured the fellow.

As heretofore shown the prisoner was taken to the Washington depot of the Baltimore and Ohio railroad and left for Frederick by the 4.30 P. M. train in charge of officers H. C. Volkman and B. F. Harper and in company of Mr. Richard Thomas and his brother, F. C. Thomas. About this time a number of farmers were gathered around the depot at Point of Rocks. Ever since Tuesday last there has been a vigilant search for the criminal. Men left their labor and scoured the country night and day in the hope of capturing the outrager. On Thursday afternoon a telegram was received from Sandy Hook that a colored man answering the description of Carroll had been seen at the caves near that place. While waiting to hear further as to this news the following telegram was received by Messrs Jarboe and Offut from Mr. F. C. Thomas, "Prisoner caught, will leave on 4.30 train. Send notice to Lickville.—Meet Dick at depot."

As soon as this message was received a hurried consultation was held by those present, and in a few minutes a mounted messenger, bearing the name of "Brick" Pomeroy, although not akin to the Western political economist, started to bear the message to the neighbors in the county. The fiery cross in the times of Roderick Dhu and the Scottish clans could not have been carried swifter, and in about an hour from 125 to 150 men, some on foot, others on horseback, and about 25 of them colored, had gathered near the depot. Several of them boarded the train at Tuscarora, four miles from Point of Rocks, but gave no intimation as to the object of their journey. As the train drew near the depot it stopped on the siding in order to allow the east-bound train to pass. At this juncture about twelve or fifteen men entered the car in which the prisoner was seated with his captors, and, seizing him, began to drag him to the platform. The police officers protested but uselessly, and as soon as the man had reached the platform of the car, a rope, with an ordinary noose, was placed around his neck, and he was dragged toward the ground. As he fell, with his head on the track and his feet in the air, the east-bound train passed by, narrowly missing the half strangled man, and almost striking one of the vigilantes, who was holding to him. As soon as the train was passed he was dragged across the track, in the pouring rain, towards a fence at the foot of a steep hill adjoining the track. Over the fence his captors dragged him, shouted, "Up the hill with him!"

At this juncture the rope broke, and a halt was made to refix it. Officer Volkman then appeared on the scene, and called out, "Gentlemen, I appeal to you in the name of the law and of the State of Maryland, let the prisoner go." The answer came back, "Go away from here," and the reply was, "I shall only go by force." Then half a dozen men caught the officer, lifted him bodily over the fence, and placing him in the car kept guard over him. Across the plowed field a hundred willing hands dragged the half-dead negro until they reached a thicket on the brow of the hill. Close to a tall yellow poplar stood a walnut sapling, about twelve feet in height. A youngster jumped up and threw the rope into a forked limb. With a quick jerk the man, who all this time was prostrate was dragged in the air. The rope was twisted twice around the limb and made fast, and the self-appointed executioners felt that their work was done.

After the lapse of about twelve minutes one

of the men put his finger on the dying man's pulse and found it still beating. His shirt was torn open and the throbbing of his heart was felt, but in about three minutes afterwards all motion ceased—the man was dead. Then began a scramble for mementoes of the hanging. Twigs were broken from the tree, the coat of the suspended man was torn, and a deaf and dumb colored man (who was present) fastened on his shirt with his teeth, and tore a scrap from it. Not one of the lynchers wore a mask. It was at first suggested that every face should be blackened, but this was overruled. They said they were not ashamed or afraid of what we are going to do.

Mrs Thomas is a delicate woman, 30 years of age, and the mother of seven children — Tired and worn out with her day's labor she went to bed at night, with her little babe, about ten months old. At 11 o'clock she was awakened by a hand on her throat and a voice saying, "Your money or your life." In the dim light which came through the window she recognized Carroll and saw that he was brandishing a large brass handled knife. She replied, "I have no money, spare me." At this juncture, one of the children, in another bed, began crying, and Carroll called out, "Hush up or I will kill you." Turning again to Mrs. Thomas he repeated his demand for money — Her reply was "As I am a Christian woman, I have no money" and then the fiend with a firmer clutch at her throat, dragged her across the bed, accomplished his purpose and left. All through the long night the wretched woman lay more dead than alive. When her husband returned next day she told him the story of her sufferings, and then almost collapsed from this mental and physical struggle through which she had passed. Since that time she has been in bed, a low fever burning through her system, and the humiliation which she has undergone, as she herself says, eating her very heart out. Dr. William H. Johnston, the family physician, does not entertain a very hopeful view of her recovery, especially as she has always been predisposed to heart disease. Her husband, who is well known and much respected in the community, is utterly broken down under the blow, and yesterday, as he told the story, his lip quivered and the tears came unbidden to the frank blue eyes. All day yesterday the farmers of the county were coming in on horseback to the scene of the execution, leaving quickly, after satisfying themselves that the work was finished, seemingly afraid that they might be called upon to act as jurymen. In corner groceries, at the depot and in farm houses nothing was talked of but the hanging, and not a man could be met with who denied his connection in the matter. All of them declar-

ed that they had done their duty and had benefitted society. About 4 o'clock P. M. Coroner Wallace and constable Rine arrived from Frederick City, and after cutting down the body, went back with it to that place by the next train. A jury will be summoned and an inquest held to morrow at Montevue Hospital, and it is believed that the State's attorney has determined to thoroughly investigate the lynching.

The lynchers comprised ex soldiers of both sides and persons of all political proclivities. The event was recognized in common rejoicing, and political enemies shook hands, while private feuds were buried and differences reconciled. Negroes and whites affiliated, and everywhere the event was referred to in most favorable terms. Everywhere the residents repudiated the statement that the executioners had been masked. They indignantly denied having used any disguise whatever, and said they were not ashamed of having participated in the affair.

About eighteen months ago Carroll was released from the penitentiary, where he had spent a term of imprisonment for robbery.

4/26/79 Washingtonian

ADDITIONAL DETAILS OF THE LYNCHING OF JAMES CARROLL.

The Sentiments of the Community.

[Special to The American.]

POINT OF ROCKS, FREDERICK CO., MD., April 18.—The excitement over the lynching of the negro ravisher James Carroll at this Point has not abated in the least, and in the neighboring village hotels and stores nothing else is talked about. Free expressions of opinion are given, and the general sentiment of this community, however it may be regretted, is that the lynchers were justified in their summery execution of the villian.

Carroll was about 23 years of age. Nothing was known of his antecedents. He came suddenly a short time ago from Virginia. He was employed by Mr. P. N. Leapley, at Licksville, and gave satisfaction, but was held in bad repute. Monday morning last, about twelve hours before the crime, he was sent to a neighboring blacksmith shop to have a plowshare repaird. While in the shop he got possession of several horse shoe nails. One of them, it was subsequently ascertained, he put under a rear window of the residence of Mr. Thomas, his victim's husband, in order, it is supposed, to facilitate his entrance and exit that night. During the day he overheard Mr. T say that he would remain at Point of Rock to superintend the loading of a new canal boat. At night he watched the Thomas residence from a neighboring negro shanty, and after the husband and father had left for the village he repaired there. Forcing an entrance both to the house and Mrs. T's bedroom, he brandished a case knife with a brass handle, and ordered her to remain quiet. The infant (a few week's old) he hurled from its mother's breast, and an inquiry from another child, 'Is that you papa?' brought the reply: 'Keep quiet, or I'll cut your throat, too.'

Negroes and whites affiliated, and everywhere the Lynching was referred to in most favorable terms. Everywhere the residents repudiated the statement that the executioners had been masked. They indignantly denied having used any disguise whatever, and said they were not ashamed of having participated in the affair.

The corpse of Carroll hung from the tree at the edge of the thicket until 4 o'clock Friday afternoon. Local magistrates had been notified of the hanging, but for some reason did not respond. Finally, at the above hour, Coroner Jno. Wallace, of Frederick, arrived with a coffin, into which the corpse was placed and taken to Frederick, where Mr. Wallace said an inquest would be held to-morrow morning. When asked why he did not hold it here at once, he said he could not get a jury. 'Why can you not get a jury?' asked one. 'Because I have been ordered by State's Attorney Motter, of Frederick, to take the body there and hold an inquest.' There were any number of men willing to serve on the jury, but their voluntary services were declined. This was the first case of lynching in Frederick county.

The body remained hanging all night and nearly the whole of to-day. It was in plain view of passing trains on both lines, and passengers crowded to the platforms to view it, having heard of the affair.

4/17/79 Mirror

A THREE-HORSE TEAM, belonging to Mr. THOS. MOFFETT, was "left standing alone," near Orrison's corner last Saturday afternoon, and becoming disgusted with the situation, started for home. On Wirt Street they demolished a lamp-post, but successfully turned the corner into Market; reaching the law office of Messrs. HARRISON & POWELL they brought the wagon in contact with two shade trees, barking them severely, in return for which the wagon was overturned, and considerably broken; with the tongue and two front wheels, however, the frightened animals pursued their journey for about two miles, when they were arrested and brought back to gather up the fragments. So much for letting horses stand alone in the street—against which practice there is a corporation fine of five dollars.

5/17/79 Washingtonian

[Special] Dispatch to the Baltimore Sun.]
*THE FIRES IN THE CATOCTIN MOUN-
TAINS—MORE THAN THREE THOUS-
AND ACRES BURNED OVER.*

Frederick, Md , The fires which originated about ten days ago in the vicinity of Catoctin Furnace, on the Eastern slope of the Catoctin mountain, still continues to rage with unabated fury, and so far have baffled all efforts to extinguish them, the flames only being subdued in one place to break out in another locality with even greater havoc. Up to this time they have spread across the ridge into Middletown Valley and over to South Mountain, burning over an area of probably more than three thousand acres of woodland, and extending to the vicinity of Black Rock, in Washington county The terrible but beautiful sight presents the appearance of slow burning volcanoes, and has been witnessed almost nightly by large numbers of our people.

On Saturday it was generally believed that the fires had been subdued by the strenuous efforts put forth for that purpose, hundreds of men being employed for days previous endeavoring to check the flames and save property, but last night the smouldering fires that crept so stealthily through the dry leaves and brush, again broke forth, even nearer the city than before, and burnt over a section about one mile and a half long by half a mile wide.

(These mountains across the river from Loudoun dip down in the Potomac and reform in Virginia They moderate however, in Virginia and about a mile west of Leesburg they resemble mere foothills.)

5/24/79 Washingtonian

'What does your husband do?' asked the census man. 'He ain,t doin' nothing at this time of the year,' replied the young wife.
'Is he a pauper?' asked the census man. She blushed scarlet to the ears. 'Law, no, she exclaimed, somewhat indignantly. 'We ain't been married more'n six weeks.—*Burdette.*

5/15/79 Mirror

MR. EMERSON'S MEMORY.—One evening when Ralph Waldo Emerson was engaged in preparing his new lecture,Mrs. Emerson who had that moment flattened her finger while trying to drive a nail with a smoothing iron thrust her head into his study, and said:
"See here, sir, I want you to drop that everlasting pen of yours for a minute or two, at least, and go down to the grocery and get a mackeral for breakfast."
'My dear,' replied Mr. Emerson, looking up from his work; 'my dear can't you? You see I am billed a dozen places to deliver this lecture on Memory, and it isn't half finished yet.
'And that's what you call your infernal lecture, is it?' said Mrs. Emerson sharply. 'A nice party you are, to deliver a lecture on Memory!'
'And why my love?' said Mr. Emerson, meekly.
'You never go out of the house that you don't forget to put on your hat or your boots, and you never take a letter of mine to mail that you don't carry in your pocket six months or a year, unless I find it sooner.— During the past thirty days you have carried out of this house and forget to bring back no less than seventy-five or eighty umbrellas; and you know yourself that the last time you went to church that you took out your false teeth, because, as you said, they hurt your corns, and came away and left them in the seat. I say you are a nice man to talk to a cultured audience on Memory and if you don't trot right off to the grocery I'll expose you before you're twenty-four hours older.
Mr. Emerson started on a jump for the grocery and when he got there he couldn't for the life of him recollect what he had come for.—*Cincinnati Enquirer.*

(Country editors apparently recycled some of these old anecdotes. This was also found in the 10/21/80 edition of the Mirror.)

5/22/79 Mirror

Two white and one colored man were hung at Raleigh, N. C... last Friday, and as usual now a-days, the work was inhumanly done. The ropes around the necks of two of them were too long, and their feet rested on the ground. They were raised and the rope retied, causing death from strangulation. A terrific thunder storm raged during the hanging, and the scene was wild and terrible. At least 8,000 people were present.

A Letter from the Indian Territory.

FORT HILL,
INDIAN TERRITORY, June 6th, '79.

Dear Sheetz:—I promised you some weeks since, that I would occasionally, when not busily engaged, drop you a few lines from this out-of-the-way, and to our Loudoun people, unknown land. It is useless for me to say anything of the beautiful region of country traversed by the Missouri Pacific road, from St. Louis to Fort Scott, Kansas, or of that rich and attractive portion of Kansas, the Cherokee or Choctaw country along the line of the Missouri, Kansas & Texas Railroad; other and more gifted pens have so often painted the beauties of this fertile and attractive region that I will only speak of that portion of the Indian Territory west and south-west of Caddo, a small hamlet on the line of the M. K. & T. R. R. This station is about thirty miles north of Denison, Tex., and at this point at 3 o'clock, P. M., on the 28th ult., four of us took stage, or rather a two-horse wagon, without springs, for Fort Sill, distant about one hundred and sixty-seven miles. Our wagon had no cover, the sun was oppressively hot, and the dust, which is continualy fanned by the almost constant winds of the Prairie land, did not hold out very flattering prospects for pleasure over this long and lonely road—but having come here to rough it, and with a determination to press forward with our enterprise, with a cheerful heart we took our seats, and turned our faces to the westward. For the first thirty miles our road led over a rich and beautiful prairie, through the Choctaw nation. There is no timber along this road, nor in sight, except very narrow belts of osage orange, or scrub oak, along ravines or creeks, and these belts rarely exceed twenty steps in width, except, perhaps, the belt on big Blue River, and this does not exceed one hundred yards in width; but is better timber, some of the trees growing large enough to make a saw-log—but not tall enough to obtain one of more than ten feet in length. There are some good farms on this Prairie, under fence, and in cultivation, and fine fields of corn, as high as a man's shoulder, and the wheat ready for the reaper. In one place we saw a handsome and large frame house, surrounded by a large and beautiful young orchard of several hundred trees. All of this property belongs to Choctaws—many of whom are well educated, and have made rapid strides in agriculture and the mechanical arts. After leaving this Prairie we passed, for ten miles, through what is here termed the cross-timbers—a high sandy ridge, in some places gravelly—and the gravel invariably of the blue lime stone variety. This ridge has hackberry, white oak, osage orange, (called by the natives Bow Dock, and is the timber from which they manufacture their bows. Post Oak, Black Jack, and occasionally Hickory, growing about as thick on the ridge, as an ordinary apple orchard, and the trees about the same height. This is a great Turkey region, and they may be seen here as often as the tame variety in Loudoun. During the remainder of the night we traveled over rolling prairie, much of which I thought poor, and sandy, but the next morning, after getting our breakfast at a ranch which we were told was ten miles from any other habitation, we struck the Wachita river, in the Chickasaw nation, and along this, lies for several miles, what is called Paul's Valley, the richest and most beautiful valley I ever beheld. It is owned principally by what are here called Squaw men, that is, white men who have married Chickasaw wife's, and have thus become Indians by adoption. I will describe the largest one of these fine estates:— It belongs to Mr. Smith Paul, and consists of twenty-five hundred acres of as rich land, probably, as there is in America, and as level as any river-bottom can be, to be dry—two hundred acres of this was in rank, waving oats, now in full head—two hundred in beautiful wheat, one-half in shock, and two reapers at work on the remainder—and nineteen hundred acres in corn, one-half as high as the backs of their horses, and the remainder so large that I noticed that the twenty Gang, or Buggy-Plows which I counted at work, bent the corn as they passed over the rows.— The corn raised here finds a ready market at Fort Sill. The remainder of our route was over gently rolling prairie land, in one or two places, with ridges of scrub oak, thinly scattered over the light, sandy soil. This whole country strikes a Loudoun man as being very badly watered although the people here consider it as well watered. The banks of the wet weather streams are very high, and no doubt the streams are formidable during exceedingly wet weather, but at this time great numbers were crossed by us, where the banks were from ten to twenty feet in height, and no running-water; but only miserable muddy pools enclosed between. We always enquired when we left a stage station, how far we would have to go to reach drinkable water, and in one instance we were told five miles, were generally told from ten to fifteen, and at one point, twenty-five had to be traveled before we could reach drinkable water, and then such water would be regarded as intolerable in old Loudoun. I had the pleasure of seeing but two springs between Caddo and Fort Sill, but was told that there were eight or ten within one or two hundred yards of the road. Muddy gypsum and salt pools are met with frequently, and from these the cattle drink. We made the trip in forty hours, by travelling the whole of two nights, and found, to our delight, that here we had pure limestone water, as clear as crystal, drawn from the two beautiful Wichita Mountain streams that flow by this substantial post.— Fort Sill is situated on a high limestone prairie, about four miles south-east of Washita Mountains and consists of from seventy to one hundred houses, for the accommodation of the troops stationed here. Some of the buildings are really handsome, and all are of the troops stationed here. Some of the buildings are really handsome, and all are neat and substantial—built of blue limestone rock, in the best manner, and laid off in such style as to have beautiful parade grounds, lawns and parks within the lines formed by the long rows of commissary buildings, quartermaster stores, stables, &c. The buildings are sufficient to comfortably accommodate one or two thousand troops, with all the horses, interpreters, &c., with which these frontier troops are necessarily supplied. There are really no fortifications here, as the name would seem indicate, but only quarters for the troops when not scouting. The number of troops here at this time, is less than usual, as a part of the cavalry are out on the lookout for any white settlers that may be trying to settle on this Territory, and one company started yesterday with about seven or eight hundred Keowas and Comanche Indians, to their grand annual medicine dance, a sort of religious ceremony which the Indians regard as indispensable to gain or retain the favor of the Great Spirit. The rations of beef for the present fiscal year being exhausted it is proposed on this trip to recruit their supplies of meat by killing enough buffalo to last them until July. The buffalo hunting grounds are sixty or seventy miles west of this, and they dry the meat in the sun in this high, dry climate, without the use of salt, and with but slight trouble. The troops go along to protect the Indians from the white ruffians, who hover around the borders of this Territory, and are more to be dreaded than the Indians. Since I arrived here I have been up to Wichita and passed, unarmed, through the camps of Kiowas, Comanche, Wichita, Apache, Caddo, and other wild tribes, and have met with the most friendly reception among all of the different bands. These tribes all paint and wear full Indian costume, and are as far from civilization as any on the Plains, but are peaceable, and apparently friendly, and altogether, I think I shall enjoy the wild and romantic life of this country for a year or two at least. But I must here stop, as it is late and at some future time may find time to speak of the peculiarities of these wild warriors of the Plains.   * * *

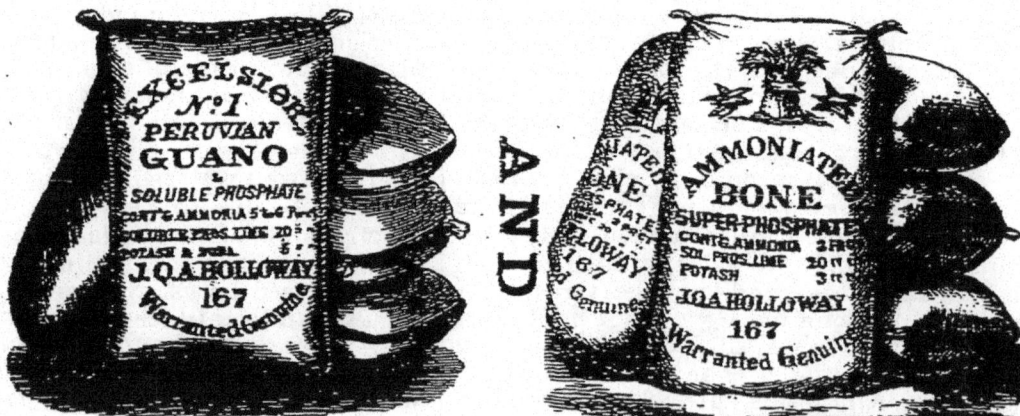

THE MIRROR.

THURSDAY..................... *June* 12

NOTICE TO LOT-HOLDERS.—In compliance with an order of Council, the Town Sergeant gives notice that he will, on Monday next, June 16th, begin an inspection of every lot in the town of Leesburg, and report all nuisances existing therein to the Mayor, whose duty it is to see that they are promptly removed. Let lot-holders, therefore, go to work on their respective premises, so that they may be able to show a clean record at his coming.

He also notifies the citizens that from 5 to 7 o'clock on Saturday morning next, Lime will be distributed from the Lime-house to all who call for it.   [june 12-1t.

We understand that while three young ladies, the Misses Brown, and a Miss Bowers were driving on the Waterford road, on Monday, the 2d inst., the shaft came off causing the horse to run. Miss Kate Bowers and Miss Brown jumped from the vehicle, sustaining severe but not dangerous bruises—Miss Mary Brown was thrown from the vehicle and very severely injured. Dr. Love rendered the necessary surgical assistance, and the young lady was conveyed to her father's at Wheatland. A little care would prevent many such accidents.

DESTRUCTIVE HAIL STORM.—The storm that passed over this town last Friday afternoon, without doing any damage, broke, we understand with destructive fury in the northern portion of the county, and played sad havoc with the growing crops. In the vicinity of Lovettsville it was attended with wind, rain and hail, the latter falling furiously in stones as large as marbles. It moved in a belt about three-quarters of a mile in width, and lasted for nearly half an hour.—Corn fields were furrowed as with a plough, and the young plants completely destroyed. Wheat fields, fast ripening for the sickle, were threshed as with a flail, many of them left not worth the harvesting.

MR. JAS. E. CARRUTHERS, our newly elected Sheriff, will ride the Leesburg District himself; his deputies will ride as follows: H. H. RUSSELL, Lovettsville District; COR-NELIUS SHAWEN, Jefferson District; T. N. CARRUTHERS, Mt. Gilead District, and WM. S. SUMMERS, Broad Run District. The Deputy for Mercer is not yet named.

Two colored men, near Waterford, were last week carried before Justice Vandevanter, charged with stealing fifteen bushels of wheat from Mr. Israel Warner. The Justice found them guilty, and sentenced them to 30 lashes each, and sixty day's confinement in the county jail. The first course was promptly administered, and they are now enjoying the luxury of the latter.

On Saturday afternoon, while a colored man was engaged in painting the gable end of the MANNING house, on Market street, he received a fall that might have been fatal.—He was standing on the end of a ladder applying the brush, and to steady himself, ran his arm down the top of the chimney. While in this position, at least fifty feet from the ground, the brick in the chimney gave way and he fell. Fortunately, a small cedar tree stood immediately beneath him the branches of which broke the force of the fall, and he picked himself up with no more serious injury than a few immaterial scratches.

6/19/79 Mirror

Smokers and Opium-Eaters in Congress.

[From the Boston Herald.]

The report that Senator Carpenter is killing himself with nicotine, by smoking twenty cigars a day, is a reminder that others are suffering from the same sort of excess. Most of the smokers in Congress smoke too much.— Some of them carry a cigar in their mouths all the time. There are senators and members who never walk down the avenue without the stump of a cigar between their fingers. One prominent man in Congress is rapidly killing himself with opium, and one of the door keepers of the House is at the point of death from the same cause. The public man I refer to is a popular and respected man, whose strange ways have long been a wonder to those who do not know of his secret habit. He is a kind and genial gentleman, but he is liable to pass his best friend with a blank stare half an hour after he has met him pleasantly in conversation. His fits of abstraction and depression amount almost to craziness. At times he is so odd and queer that his associates are puzzled by his conduct. Opium is eating up his life, and he will not last long. It is a pity, for his is one of the best intellects in Congress, and he might render much useful public service, if he would.

7/3/79 Mirror

PREDICTIONS ABOUT 1880 TO 1887.—In a pamphlet recently published the author, Professor Grimmer, asserts: "From 1880 to 1887 will be one universal carnival of death." Asia will be depopulated, Europe nearly so, America will lose fifteen million people. Besides plague, we are to have storms and tidal waves; mountains are to "toss their heads through the choicest valleys," navigators will be lost by thousands, owing to the "capricious deflexures of the magnetic needle," and islands will appear and disappear in mid-ocean. All the beasts, birds, and fishes will be diseased; famine and civil strife will destroy most of the few human beings left alive by plague; and finally, "two years of fire"—from 1885 to 1887 —will rage with fury in every part of the globe. In 1887, the "Star of Bethlehem" will "reappear in Cassiopia's Chair," the immediate results being universal war and portentous floods and shipwrecks. North America is again to be involved in civil war, unless a "Napoleon arises to quell it; but during these terrible days the Pacific States will be a veritable Paradise of Peace compared to the hellish strife that will be waging throughout the world." The few people that may manage to survive till 1887 will have reason to be thankful.

7/31/79 Mirror

FROM THE INDIAN TERRI-TORY.

KIOWA, COMANCHE, & WICHITA AGENCY)
WICHITA Indian Ter., July 17, 1879)

Dear Sheetz: Since I last wrote you I have seen much of this Territory, and, have seen the different bands of this reservation in their own camps and have, therefore, learned much (that interested me) of the wild and restless tribes of this country.

I mentioned in my last that Fort Sill was located on a high Prairie table land; this is washed on the east by Cash Creek, and on the north by Medicine Bluff Creek; up the latter there is some of the most beautiful scenery I ever saw. One mile west of Fort Sill this beautiful stream cuts through one of the ranges of the Washita Mountains, and on the stream the bluff rises perpendicularly to the height of two hundred and eighty feet, and is of solid stone, and as smooth as a stone wall. On the north side the bluff is not more than thirty feet, but of the same character as the south side. The water in the stream extends from bluff to bluff, and is from six to twenty feet in depth, and so clear that the small objects may be seen at the bottom

West of these mountains, and extending across the staked plains, into Mexico, is now about the only country producing buffalo to any great extent. Ten years ago buffalo were very abundant here, and for seventy-five miles east of this; now, they are all gone, and this valuable animal is nearly annihilated by the insatiate white hunters, who killed them almost by millions, for their robes alone, leaving their carcasses to rot upon the plains. One of these hunters, now present, informs me that he has frequently killed one hundred and fifty in a day. It seems to me that it would be wise policy in our Government to stop this wholesale waste, which the Government is now forced to make up by millions of dollars worth of beef, to prevent the Indians from starving.— I think our Government is doing right to give them the beef they are now issuing to them, but the destruction of their natural food by white men is what makes this heavy expenditure necessary. But as I have nothing to do with the Legislation of the Country I shall not waste time in moralizing on this subject.

I have been interested on two or three occasions, in watching the Kiowa and Comanche Indians killing their cattle, when issued them at Fort Sill. So soon as the issue is made they throw open the gate of the pen in which the cattle are issued, mount their horses, stampede the cattle on the broad, open Prairie, and hunt them down on the style of hunting Buffalo. After chasing them around for two or three miles they ride close to the side of the frightened animal and spear or shoot him, either with an arrow or with a pistol. They usually wound the animal in the side, and as they find one shot is not sufficient they give him the second, when the animal usually stops running and turns on his pursuers for battle, which the Indians avoid, until the animal, sickened by the loss of blood, lies down, then they leave him to die in peace, while they go off in pursuit of another. After they get all of the cattle down, the Squaws commence to skin them.

The first thing, invariably, is to secure the tongue, which they take from the under side of the lower jaw. After this they skin the animal in the usual way, and cut the flesh from the bones as fast as it is laid bare. The strips of flesh they throw in a pile, so that when they are done skinning no portion remains except the bare bones and the intestines, which are all eaten, many of them raw, and as fast as taken from the animal—the warriors enjoying this rare luxury while the Squaws are hard at work. The liver is always eaten raw, with the gall poured over it as a seasoning. I have just spoken to an old frontiersman, now by my side, and he insists that raw liver, with gall, is better than raw oysters with the usual condiments—but I have no idea of testing the matter myself, and leave it to those more curious than myself to try for themselves. After the skinning is done the bones are broken up and roasted, when they pick from them what little flesh their knives failed to get off, thus you see, nothing is lost except the head, and they take the brain from that—sometimes to eat and sometimes to be used for tanning purposes. The piles of beef are now cut into very thin strips and dried in the sun, without salt, and is done in a very short time during clear weather; when the weather is unfavorable they dry it over fires.

No labor of any kind is ever performed by the wild warriors, the whole devolving on the Squaws, and one of them told me that a child was always in luck when it was born a boy, as from infancy, up, they are reared with much more tenderness and care. Among these tribes are many Mexicans, who have been captured when very young, and are thorough Indian in all their tastes and habits.

These tribes are remarkable for their great fondness for gambling, and especially for horse-racing, which they practice to a very great extent, and are a proud of their fast ponies as any of our Eastern men of their crack horses. It is the general idea in the States that the Comanches are the best horsemen in the world, but this I find is a very great mistake. I could mention the names of great numbers of persons in Loudoun and Fauquier counties who far excel any Comanche I have met. They admit themselves that they are not a match for the Texas cowboys in horsemanship. These Indians, and the Mexicans, have always been celebrated for their skill with the lariat, but the frontier cow-boys far excel them ever at this daring method of taking wild horses and cattle.

8/7/79 Mirror

THE TRAVELS OF EGO AND ALTER.—The Richmond *Dispatch* contains another letter from "Alter," one of the Richmond "Tramps," noticed in these columns last week. He writes from Harper's Ferry, detailing the incidents of their trip from Alexandria to that place, and we extract from his letter as follows:

At Bailey's cross-roads, five miles from Alexandria, we began to strike a rolling and highly-cultivated country, smooth meadows banked with new-mown hay, fields of tall and graceful corn, and every hillock topped by a decent and well kept house. It was unnecessary to inquire, for we saw at once we were getting into the new Virginia—Virginia settled by northern people. So unmistakable are the signs of these new settlers, that in passing along the road, if the Old Virginia farmer were to be seen at all, we could say with singular accuracy where the land began and ended. Old Virginia never had his house white-washed or painted, the rotten timbers of his ancestral porch were propped up by unplaned posts from the nearest grove, the worm-eaten roof afforded a fair scope of the heavenly bodies the rich garden-spots were overgrown with weeds, the crops badly tended and generally a failure, and the uncultivated fields flooded with an ugly, stubby undergrowth. With him decorative art finds no place or encouragement. The refinement of life, the cosy, comfortable home like adornments and conveniences are—well simply

"Unwept, unhonored, and unsung."

With new Virginia, however, things are essentially different. From house to barn everything is in perfect order. The people do not seem to exist merely to eat and drink and sleep. The culture of flowers, the presence of paint and bright colors everywhere, the regularity with which the crops are laid out, the certainty of success, the neat, clean appearance of the field and meadow—all show that good taste may be combined with thrift, and that the careful cultivation of the soil does not necessarily preclude attention to those matters that relieve and delight the eye, mitigate the burning rays of the sun, and afford pleasant recreation when the severe work of the day is done. This contrast is certainly not in favor of the old resident of Virginia.— But let it be noticed that description here is made of outward appearances. The old Virginian can't adapt himself to the new order of things, but he retains the same cordial hospitality, the same kindly regard for strangers, the same *tout ensemble*, that characterize Virginians wherever they go. Our northern settler will tell you all you want to know, but he'll not ask you to linger and tell the news; or, if you drop in he'll not ask you to dinner, even though he has just risen from his table and sees you are tired and hungry. Of course there are exceptions, but in general these things are true of both classes in those walks of life where neither wealth nor advanced education abound.

Falls Church is one of the most beautiful villages we have ever seen. It occupies about two thousand acres of land, and is composed of tastefully-built cottages, each having quite an extensive lot or yard, and Flowers, birds, shade trees are associated in our memories with this pleasant little village, with its two or three hundred houses, newly painted and whitewashed, basking in the gay sunshine. Here it is the northern settler, and the office-holder from Washington finds after his short ride of nine or ten miles in the evening his home, peaceful and happy, amid the honeysuckle and the arbutus.

For several miles beyond Falls Church the same beautiful scenery extends. After that, as the northern settler becomes fewer and fewer, the country gets rougher and wilder, and before long we realize we have taken our farewell of Virginia's improvers. At nightfall after a good day's walk, we find ourselves opposite an unattractive inn, where we are compelled to spend the night. The landlord received us graciously, and, having given us a simple meal, escorted us to a room, or a loft which contained a bed with one sheet, but no chairs, no pitcher or basin, no looking-glass, no—nothing. But we had long since learned not to be over-nice, and, hastily blowing out the light, we took to bed, and calmly composed ourselves to sleep. Next morning mine host, with execrable calmness and satisfaction, inquired how we had spent the night. We *felt* as if we could have choked him, but we *looked* as if no one had spoken recently. Then began the tug of war. We were poorly prepared for the work, and the road was bad. Occasionally we got some pretty views, but for the most part the way appeared provokingly straight, and the only tune we could think of was—

"Over the hills and far away."

But it's a long lane that has no turning, and if the way was unusually tedious, certainly the terminus was exceedingly glorious. No man can approach the old town of Leesburg without feeling all his æsthetic nature thoroughly aroused. The scenery is not sublime. It does not excite the emotions of awe or wonder. But the element of the beautiful enters into everything. The fields waving with corn and grass, the rolling hills, the deep, quiet pasture-lands, the numberless cattle in long, green meadows, beautifully situated cottages shaded by the oak and aspen, the zigzag fence covered with Virginia-creeper, pursuing its maudlin course, the quiet dell and sequestered glen, and

"The decent church that topped the neighboring hill———"

these all, if they be not apparent at one sweeping glance, present themselves in rapid succession and in the most unexpected way. Leesburg is the newest town we have ever seen considering its age. It was in existence when the unfortunate Braddock passed through that section of Virginia, and the house where the brave English General stayed is still pointed out. The fact is the people take a just and proper pride in making themselves and places attractive. The contrast made above of another portion of our route does not hold true of Leesburg and the surrounding country. Here everything seemed thriving and everybody well to do. It is the boast of the Loudoun farmer in this section that every field has a stream, and the country therefore presents a smiling and fruit-laden aspect. Indeed, one can't help from wondering why people will farm elsewhere when farming can be done in Loudoun and near Leesburg. Nor is the county an unfit abode for the people. Those that we had the pleasure to meet in and around Leesburg were gracious, hospitable people, who, in extending kindness to you, made you feel you were doing them a favor to accept. We found ourselves quite well-known by the newspaper men, to whom we were formerly introduced by our friend Chas. P. Janney, Esq.

Monday afternoon we left for Hamilton, a beautiful little village six miles distant, where we had friends whom we wished to see. Next morning we started for Harper's Ferry, passing through Hillsborough, a little village perched high among the hills, in a gap between the Short Hills. Here we had the pleasure of meeting Dr. Taylor and his attractive family, with whom we spent several hours. I have no time now to speak of the blackberries, the cherries, and the green apples, but I shall ever retain the tenderest recollection of Loudoun's fruitful soil. With the Blue Ridge on our left and the Short Hills on the right, we pursued a northward course, and after a short respite now and then we descended, amid the "crepuscular adumbration," the Loudoun Heights, which overlook in eternal menace the "embrace of the lordly Potomac and the lovely Shenandoah." At sunset we entered Harper's Ferry, which has been the Italy of these two modern Hannibals, Ego and   ALTER.

Harper's Ferry, July 30, 1879.

8/2/79 Washingtonian

[From the New Orleans Democrat, July 16.]

Mrs. Sarah A. Dorsey's Will.

Mrs. Dorsey's will was probated in the Second District Court on Saturday, and is as follows:

BEAUVOIR, Harison county, Miss.,
January 4, 1878.

I, Sarah Anne Dorsey, of Tensas Parish, La., being aware of the uncertainty of life, and being now in sound health of mind and body, do make this my last will and testament, which I write, sign, and seal with my own hand, in the presence of three competent witnesses, as I possess property in the States of Louisiana, Mississippi, and Arkansas. I owe no obligation of any sort whatever to any relative of my own; I have done all I could for them during my life. I, therefore, give and bequeath all my property, real, personal, and mixed, wherever located and situated, wholly and entirely without hinderance or qualification, to my most honored and esteemed friend, Jefferson Davis, ex-President of the Confederate States, for his own sole use and benefit, in fee simple, forever; and I hereby constitute him my sole heir, executor, and administrator. If Jefferson Davis should not survive me, I give all that I have bequeathed him to his youngest daughter Varina. I do not intend to share in the ingratitude of my country toward the man who is in my eyes the highest and noblest in existence.

In testimony whereof I sign this will, written with my own hand, in the presence of W. L. Walthall, F. S. Hewes and John C. Craig, subscribing witnesses, resident in Harrison county, Miss.

SARAH ANNE DORSEY.

The scene in the court-room was very impressive. The opening of the will was witnessed by the venerable Jefferson Davis, accompanied by a large party of ladies and gentlemen. When it became known throughout the court-room that Jefferson Davis was present the clerk of the court, the lawyers and all who happened to be in the building, hastened to gaze upon and pay a tribute of respect to the honored representative of the lost cause, so that in a few minutes the room was densely crowded. When the formalities of the law had been gone through, and the illustrious legatee of Mrs. Dorsey walked away, every hat was lifted and every head was bowed in token of silent respect.

(Beavoir was his home the rest of his life and was passed on to his daughter. It has recently been renovated.)

8/2/79 Washingtonian

[Communicated.

MR. EDITOR:—Permit me to ask the attention of the 'City Fathers' to the importance of a clean board in these days of pestilence. The people of Washington, Alexandria, Baltimore and even New York, seem to be wide awake on this subject. I hope Leesburg will not go to sleep under the overpowering exhalations of hog pens, and if I must be plain, of divers *privies*, that seem to invite a visit from *Yellow Jack*—if he should come within call. Several gentlemen who recently visited this town, expressed surprise when informed that it was regarded as healthy. Their ideas in walking over it, evidently was, that it was preserved by the grace of God, rather than the care of its population. Let us remember that last year several Eastern towns, located in the remote hills, suffered from Yellow fever, from simple want of timely care.

HEALTH.

8/14/79 Mirror

AUGUST COURT.—Another August Court in Loudoun has come and gone. The day on Monday was characterized by a good deal of its ancient glory—a big crowd—thousands of water-melons—innumerable venders of pies, cakes and other small wares, and later in the evening an occasional bloody nose, the result, no doubt, of a too free intercourse with that arch-fiend whose bite is like unto that of a serpent, and whose dominion Hickman came to make war upon. But notwithstanding this commingling of the races—the reunion of friends—the destruction of melons—the discussion of the most "fittin' man" for the approaching canvass—and the hilarity engendered by the absorption of a liquid that flows not from the mountain side—the day was comparatively a peaceful one; everybody appeared in a good humor, and no county in the State, with such an outpouring of all her people, could present a more robust, healthy, intelligent, well-behaved concourse than filled the streets of Leesburg on Monday. In numbers the crowd was fully equal to that of later years, and the probability is that until the "moon turns to blood," and all of those other dire calamities spoken of in holy writ, come to pass, Loudoun will rejoice in the magnitude of her August Courts.

8/23/79 Washingtonian

A poor old tramp was entertained at Battle Creek, Mich., by a colored man whom he had once owned in the South. Times had changed for both.

Rufus McGaughey, of Munroe county, Tenn., while at work in a field left his little son, three years old, under a tree. The boy was carried off by a bear, who has cubs in the neighborhood, and all the neighbors are searching for the den.

A common way of imposing upon ignorant prospectors in the mining regions of Nevada, is to shoot gold filings into the ground from a gun. Even brass is made to serve the purpose, and by this means many a worthless claim is sold at a high price.

George Washington was recently hanged in Kentucky, now Napolean Bonaparte has mounted the scaffold in Mississippi.

8/28/79 Mirror

A MILE A MINUTE —A correspondent of the N. Y. Sun. dubious as to the possibilities of American railroad speed is thus answered by certain engineers of the Pennsylvania and Jersey Central lines : "A speed equal to a mile a minute is such an ordinary, every-day occurrence that we are beginning to consider it slow. The trains which leave Philadelphia at 7:35 A. M., and Jersey City at 3:55 and 4:05 P. M., attain a greater rate than this on every trip. A mile in 55 seconds does not excite remark even.

A patent. the invention of a Pittsburg man, has recently been tested for the use of petroleum as fuel for driving steamboats. The little steamer Billy Collins, on the Alleghany river, was enabled to raise eighty pounds of steam in her boilers without a bit of smoke in her stacks, ashes in her pans or clinkers in her fire box. By a simple arrangement, a few gallons of crude oil, costing sixty-three cents a barrel, has been allowed to run out of a barrel on her guards, and was converted into a waving flame ten feet long under her boiler, and with the steam thus produced, she made a satisfactory trip on the river.—*Baltimore American.*

A well known local preacher in a suburban town. while instructing a class of urchins in the catechism, told them that God could do everything, whereupon one of them asked :— "Can God make a rock so big that He can't lift it ?" The boy's question remains unanswered.—*New York Tribune.*

9/4/79 Mirror

THE FAIR.—We hope the people of Loudoun are preparing for the Fair of the Agricultural Society which commences on Tuesday, the 16th of September. The season has been most propitious,—the harvest was abundant—the corn never promised a better yield, the orchards are groaning under their weight of fruitage, the late rains revived the pastures to such an extent that stock of all kind is in nice order, and there is no reason way the exhibition this year should not eclipse in variety and beauty any that have preceded it, and such, we are glad to learn, is the present prospect.

CARRIER PIGEONS.—Not the least of the attractions at the approaching County Fair, will be the turning loose from the grounds a dozen Carrier Pigeons, that will be brought from Alexandria for the purpose. They will be let loose for their homeward flight, and their arrival communicated back by telegraph.

ESCAPED AND RECAPTURED.—Young Armstrong who killed a tramp at Warrenton about a year since, and who was tried last week, was on Saturday sentenced to seven years' confinement in the penitentiary. While on his way from the Court house to the jail he broke away from the officers and fled. After a long chase over fences, etc., he was recaptured by a negro man and turned over to the officers who safely secured him in jail.—

FRED. DOUGLAS IN LOUDOUN—HE AD-
DRESSES 2,000 PEOPLE AT PURSELLVILLE.—
The announcement previously made that
FRED. DOUGLAS. Marshal of the District of
Columbia, would address the colored people
of Loudoun, in the woods near Pursellville,
on Thursday last, attracted thither quite a
large crowd, numbering we suppose not less
than 1,500 negroes and some 300 or 400
whites.

A stand and seats had been erected in the
woods, and at half past twelve, the meeting
was called to order by a colored man, and
the proceedings opened with prayer by Rev.
BRYANT BROWN, colored, of Middleburg, after which

DOUGLAS WAS INTRODUCED,

and spoke for two hours. Everybody has heard
of FRED. DOUGLAS, a negro man, formerly
the property of Capt. Anthony, of Easton,
Maryland. How he ran away from his
master in 1838, went North, and by
perseverance and industry, succeeded not only
in accumulating a comfortable competency,
of this worlds goods, but also, in educating
himself—becoming a leader in the ranks of
the Republican or anti-slavery party, until,
under the administration of President Hayes,
he was appointed to one of the most lucra-
tive and honorable positions within the gift
of the Executive. Of course we shall attempt
no full or accurate account of his speech on
the occasion alluded to, but merely give our
readers a few of his thoughts. that they may
form their own conclusions as to what

MANNER OF MAN HE IS.

Douglas, we should suppose is between 65
and 70 years of age. He is a portly, well-
developed specimen of his race, and much
more than ordinarily intelligent. He began
his speech by expressing the embarrassment
he experienced in standing before a mixed
audience on the soil of Virginia. He came to
offer his advice to the people, and while he
had somethings to say that would be appropriate to one class of his hearers, they might
not be so to the other. He would, however,
address himself to both races, feeling that he
had a right to do so, because he was the representative of both, having in his veins as
much of

THE BLOOD OF ONE AS THE OTHER,

and he appealed to both to give him an impartial hearing, and if he uttered anything
that either might wish he had not said, to at
least accord him credit for honesty of intention, as he had no purpose to say one
word that could wound the feeling of a solitary human being.

He referred to the days gone by, when the
white men were not only the owner of the
soil, but of the bone and sinew of the negro,
from the traffic in which, in 1837, Virginia
realized $18,000,000. But he was not going
to reproach them for the past,—both races
had been the victims of a false policy. The
negro was not revengeful, and bore no malice toward his former owners, but only asked
now, that the conduct of the one toward the
other be shaped in accordance with the
changed order of things, and when the true
relations between the races were fully established, and each observed toward the other
the laws of justice and humanity, the South
would become as great and prosperous as the
North ; and there was no reason why she
should not. He alluded to the

"GOOD OLD TIMES" OF SLAVERY,

which he said were not altogether made up
of "paddles" and cat-o ninetails. They had
their seasons of joy and merry-making,
when the negro looked forward with rapture
to Whitsontide Easter, and especially to
Christmas; when he reveled in sweet-pota-
toes, cider and slavery. He touchingly alluded to the ties of friendship that existed between the races in those days, when Mass
Bob and Jim had nursed at the breast
of a colored "mamma." But notwithstanding all that, it was a devilish system, and he
was glad it was gone.

He said that the late war and the consequent abolition of slavery, was not the result
of the teachings of Garrison, Calhoun, Phillips, nor none of that class of agitators. It
was brought about simply by the logic of
events. When the war began, neither the
heads of the department at Washington, the
Generals of the federal armies, nor the soldiers in the ranks, were moved by any regard
for the negro, and in support of his assertion cited the orders of McClellan, Ben. Butler, etc.
forbidding slaves to take refuge within the
the lines of their armies ; and also to the
report made to the Court of St. James by Seward
in which he declared that however the war
might end, the status of no State was to be
changed ; and that if the Northern soldiers,
when they first invaded the soil of Virginia,
could have seen the end from the beginning,
and realized that their victory was to free
the negro and place in his hands the ballot,
they would have thrown down their muskets
and their knapsacks, and gone home. That
it was not until the federal armies had become

depleted, and northern homes were made houses of mourning because of the loss of their fathers, sons and brothers, that a change was wrought, and they cried aloud, "help, negro, or I sink." That through affliction God revealed to them that if they would be successful; they must break the chain of slavery. And, said the speaker, whoever had first struck the blow in that direction would have been the victor. Gen. Lee was ready for it—and had the Southern authorities sustained him, and said to the negro, fight on our side and freedom is yours, there would to-day, have been

A SOUTHERN CONFEDERACY.

He thought, however, that it was well they didn't see it. At all events he for one was glad they had not.

He advised the white people, in their dealings with the negro, to bear in mind their changed relations; that as while in a state of slavery it was perhaps proper that they should have been held in ignorance; now, that they are free men and voters in this great Republic, they should endeavor to aid them in cultivating their minds, that they might thus become better citizens. That while States Rights might have been necessary at one time, the safety of the people now was in a strong government. He acknowledged the greatness of a State, but thought the U. S. was greater. That there was no danger of centralization so long as the people held the ballot, with which to remove unworthy rulers.

After some further remarks, addressed more particularly to the white people, the speaker turned to

THE COLORED POPULATION

and gave them some excellent advice. He asked them whether, as freemen, they are doing as well for themselves as they did for their masters when they were slaves—did they rise as early in the morning as when old master blew the horn, and do as many days' work in the year as then? If not, their liberty was a failure. He reminded them that whatever they might be naturally—and he believed, with the Declaration of Independence, that all men were born equal—practically they were inferior to the white man; and whatever they might become they were not yet his equal.—That the white man had already piled up for himself centuries of civilization, refinement and culture, while the negro had just started in the race of moral improvement—and if they would enjoy the blessings of freemen, they must live soberly, honestly and truthfully—They must waste no time—buy nothing that they could do without—and quit running off on every excursion that was gotten up. He also urged them to marry and cultivate a higher regard for the sanctity of family relations—that the pride of family name was one

of the strongest incentives to virtuous living. He said once they had no family name—that when he was a slave they used to call him Capt. Anthony's Fred, and illustrated what he meant by relating an incident that he said occurred during the ministry of the late GEORGE ROSZELL, whom he knew well and had often heard preach. He said that on a certain occasion, at the close of services at the church, a baptizing of children took place, and after all the white babies had been attended to, a colored woman approached with her sable offspring in her arms, and requested that the sacrament of baptism be administered. "Certainly," said Roszell, "what is its name?" "John Wesley," answered the proud mother. "John Wesley, a negro has no business to be called John Wesley," said the preacher, and immediately proceeded—"In the name of the Father, the Son and the Holy Ghost I BAPTIZE THEE POMPEY." But, said Douglas, you have family names now, and you ought to be proud of them, and seek to perpetuate them. Work hard, be economical, and secure an interest in the soil. There must be no communistic feeling—no conflict between capital and labor; one is dependent on the other—the white man has the money and the brain and you have got the muscle, and you must use it, and thus accumulate property, and become respected, and unless you do that you can be of little account to society. When you make a bargain stick to it; if you contract a debt, pay it, and pay it at the time you promise—In a word, cultivate all the virtues of the white man and shun his vices. The speaker, in quite an amusing way, admonished his colored brethren against appropriating to themselves that which didn't belong to them. He said when he was a slave, although a good christian, he thought it no harm to take a goose, or a turkey or a chicken belonging to his master, and eating it for his dinner, because that was merely a *transfer of property*—the master's goose simply going to strengthen master's muscle—but all that was changed now, and he abjured them that if any of them had contracted that habit to abandon it at once. Taken all together the speech was a fair one—and was listened to with unusual attention by all present—it was, as the speaker said he intended it should be, free from anything particularly offensive—and the impression he made was favorable, and his advice good. It was just forty-one years ago that day, he said, since he ran away from his old master.

Mr. Douglas was accompanied by —— GREENER, colored, Prof. of Law in Howard University, Washington.

October, 1879

10/9/79 Mirror

Indians Again on the War-Path

On the 29th of September, Maj. Thornburg's command of U. S. soldiers, composed of three companies of cavalry, was met a mile south of Milk River, Colorado, by several hundred Ute Indians, who attacked and drove the troops to their wagon train, with great loss. Maj. Thornburg was killed and the command devolved upon Capt. Payne, who telegraphed to the department at Omaha, the death of Maj. T., the painful but not serious wounding of Lt. Haddock and Dr. Grimes, the death of ten enlisted men and wagon-master, with the wounding of about twenty men and teamsters. He continued—"I am corralled near water, with about three-fourths of my animals killed." Some 500 or 600 troops from the surrounding stations were hurried to his relief, and he was in hopes of sustaining himself until their arrival.

10/23/79 Mirror

DEATH OF JOHN L. RINKER.—This gentleman died at his home in Leesburg, on Saturday last, October 18th, in the 71st year of his age. Few men were better known in this community than the subject of this notice, and few forms more familiar or voices more frequently heard than his. He was for a long number of years constable in the Leesburg district, in which capacity he was ever careful, prudent and prompt. In later years he devoted himself almost exclusively to the duties of Auctioneer, and who that has attended the courts of this county during the last forty years, does not remember his oft repeated "going, going, gone." He was a kind and indulgent father—a good citizen, and a useful man, whose genial face and kindly offices will be greatly missed in this community, where for almost half a century he has been so well and favorably known.— For a year or two past, his health was so infirm as to almost wholly retire him from the active pursuits of life, but it was only during the last few weeks of his existence that he was confined to his bed. On Sunday afternoon his remains were laid away in Union Cemetery, amid the lamentations of his immediate family, and the deep sorrow of a very large concourse of friends.

10/11/79 Washingtonian

THE UTE REBELLION.

WASHINGTON, Oct. 5.—The following has been received at the Indian bureau from Agent Stanley, at Los Pinos, Colorado, dated Oct. 2.

'To *Commissioner Hayt.*—A runner just in from the White River Agency reports that the agent and employees are killed There has been a fight with the troops, in which the officers in command were killed. The troops are surrounded, away from any water supply,and their trains have been captured. Chief Owray, the head of the Ute nation, sends the following order to his people by a runner: 'To the chiefs, captains, headmen, and Utes at White river: You are hereby requested and commanded to cease hostilities against the whites,injuring no innocent persons or any others further than to protect your own lives and property from unlawful and unauthorized combinations of horse thieves and desperadoes, as anything further will ultimately end in disaster to all parties.''

(Special dispatch to the Post.)
THE UTES AT BAY.

BATTLE-FIELD, MILK RIVES, Oct. 5, 6 A. M.— Merritt has just reached us, and the surrounding hills resound with cheers of welcome. We have tried for three days to send out a courier, but the Indians have been alert and constantly watching and firing. The red devils have surrounded us ever since the battle, pouring in an effective fire from the bluffs at a distance of five or six hundred yards,having a cross-fire upon our position, which position was chosen hastily on the first day of the fight. All our horses and all but twelve mules have been killed. We sheltered them as best we could with wagons, but to no purpose. Captain Dodge and Lieut. Hughes, with company D, 9th cavalry, came to our rescue Thursday morning at daybreak,after a forced march of thirty five miles from Bear river. Cheer upon cheer rent the air from our trenches when ascertained who were coming. A lull in the firing enabled them to come in and shelter horses as well as possible, taking to the fortifications quickly, when the attack redoubled its fury. Had the heights been accessible Capt. Dodge would have charged them with his company while we covered him from our rifle pits, but this being utterly impossible, the ascent being nearly perpendicular,all we could do during the day was to keep a good lookout from the loop holes, and return the fire when an Indian showed his head. This, however, was a very rare occurrence as the Indians have rifle pits and loop holes. Before dark every horse but three of Capt.Dodge's command was shot down. A very fortunate thing for us has been that the Indians have left us unmolested at night, with the exception of an occasional shot to make us scatter our pits. We have been able at great risk to haul off our dead animals every night, otherwise the stench would be intolerable. A sally is made every night for water, a distance of two hundred yards from our entrenchments. Wednesday night Private Erser, of company F, was shot in the face while out with a party after water. The Indians were only a few yards away, and were driven off by a volley from the guard and trenches. Captain Dodge brought us cheering news that our dispatches reached Bear river safely, and would undoubtedly reach Rawlins. We all agree that Gen Merritt, from Fort Russell, with the companies of the Fifth cavalry there and all other available troops, will be ordered to our rescue, as they will all be needed to finish the campaign.

CAPTAIN PAYNE.

The Richmond (Va) State says: 'Capt Payne, the young hero who is in command of the small remnant of calvalry left after Maj. Thornburgh's disaster, and which is now surrounded by the enraged Ute Indians in Colorado, is a young and cherished brother of Gen. Wm. H. Payne, of Warrenton, Va. He passed throught West Point since the war, and has risen rapidly by promotion to his captaincy. The fact that the gallant officer,who, though twice wounded, still remained on the field and incommand, and is in charge of the beleaguered camp , for whose relief an army is now on the march, is a Virginian, and brother of one of her most distinguished sons, will lend new interest here to the fate of the brave troops who are now exposed in so perilous a position.

RAWLINS, WY, T. Oct. 7.—A letter received this morning from Lt. Price at Fortification creek, bearing date of the 3d inst., says: 'I have seen no Indians in this vicinity. With my 29 men I can stand off 300 Indians. A company of the 9th cavalry, 50 strong,reached Payne yesterday morning, the 2d inst.' From the above, which is entirely reliable, there is probably no doubt but what Payne's command still exists. The news creates a great deal of rejoicing here. The letter was written by Lt. Price to his wife, and the above is all the war news it contained.

WASHINGTON, Oct. 7.—The following telegram, corroborative of to-day's press dispatch, and furnishing additional statements of the interest, was received this evening:

'CHICAGO, Oct 7.- Gen. E. D. Townsend, Adjt. General, Washington: Lt. Price, from Fortification creek, writes October 3 that Payne has been able to hold the Indians in check, that he has been joined by Dodge's company of the 9th cavalry,and that Merritt must have reached him next day, 4th inst.   P. H. SHERIDAN,
                                                'Lt. General.'

Capt. Dodge's company is composed of the colored troops belonging to Col. Hatch's regiment, who were scouting in the same general region at the time of the battle, who, it was feared,had been intercepted by the hostile Indians before news of the disaster could have reached them.

THE INDIAN TROUBLES.

A Peace Commission Proposed by the Indians— Justice First Proposed by the Government— Merritt's Advance to White River Agency

WASHINGTON, Oct. 13.—Official information from Agent Stanley, at Los Pinos Indian Agency. Colorado, is to the effect that messengers had arrived and state that the women and children of the White River Agency were in charge of Chief Douglas, and that one or more of the white men employed there were not killed. The murder of Mr. Meeker is confirmed. The report that Chiefs Sapavaneiro and Shavano took part in the fight is untrue, and it is not true that Chief Douglas led the White River Utes. Chief Ouray thinks that Jack, a White River Ute, commanded the Indians in the charge on Thornburgh's command. No further trouble is anticipated unless the troops advance. Chief Douglas sends word to Chief Ouray that the women and children, the money and papers of the agency will be sent to Los Pinos when it is safe to do it. Ouray endorses a recommendation made by Agent Stanley to the department for a peace commission to investigate the trouble, and let the blame rest where it belongs. A council has been held at Los Pinos, and the Utes will abide by Ouray's decision. They want peace and will have nothing to do with the White River trouble, and request Ouray to inform the White River Utes of their decision. A later dispatch (October 9) from Agent Stanley, at Los Pinos, announces the arrival of employee Brady and an escort of Indians from White River, who say the Utes recognized and obeyed Ouray's order, and will fight no more unless forced to do so. They favor a peace commission to settle the trouble.

It will be observed that Agent Stanley's suggestion for a 'peace commission' meets with no approval from either of the two branches of the government immediately connected with Indian affairs. Opinions differ widely as to the probabilities of a continuance of the hostilities. The general impression at the War Department is that there will be some more hard fighting, but Secretary Schurz and Commissioner Hayt both think that the hostile Utes will speedily surrender and throw themselves upon the mercy of the government.

MERRITT'S ADVANCE—SCENE AT THE WHITE RIVER AGENCY.

RAWLIN'S, WY. T., Oct. 13.—Emil Webber and Geo. Fuhr, two couriers, have just arrived from what was a few days ago the White River Agency. From them is learned the following particulars: Gen. Merritt advanced upon the agency on the 11th inst. On his way he found many dead bodies. Among others he found the bodies of Carl Goldstein, an Israelite, who left here with government supplies for the Utes at White River Agency. He was found in a gulch six miles this side of the agency. He was shot twice through the shoulder, and was about two miles from his wagons. A teamsters named Julius Moore, formerly from Bainbridge, Mass., who was with him when he left here, was found about 100 yards from Goldstein, two bullet holes in his breast and his body hacked and mutilated with a knife or hatchet. As the command advanced through the canyon they came to an old coal mine, and in it was found the dead body of an agency employee named Dresser. He had evidently been wounded and crawled into the mine to die. His coat was folded up and placed under his head for a pillow. Beside him lay a Winchester rifle containing eight cartridges. In one of his pockets a letter was found, which, as near as the courier can remember, was as follows:

'White River, Sept. 29, 1 P. M.:—Maj. Thornburgh: I will come with Chief Douglas and and another chief and meet you to-morrow. Everything quiet here, and Chief Douglas is flying the United States flag. We have been on guard three nights, and will be to-night. Not that we expect any trouble, but because there might be. Did you have any trouble coming through the canyon?

N. C. MEEKER, U. S. Indian Agent.'

On entering the agency a scene of quiet desolation presented itself. All the buildings, except one, were burned to the ground, and not a living thing was in sight except the command. The Indians had taken everything except the flour and decamped. The women and children were missing, and nothing whatever could be found to indicate what had become of them. They had either been murdered and burned or else taken away as hostages. Their dreadful and unmentionable fate calls forth the most profound sympathy. The dead body of Father Meeker was found about one hundred yards from his house, lying on his back, shot through the head. The left side of his head had been smashed in with some blunt instrument, a piece of a barrel stave driven into his mouth and one of his hands and arms badly burned. The dead body of Mr. W. H. Post, Father Meeker's assistant, was found between the building and the river, a bullet-hole through his left ear and one under his ear. He, as well as Father Meeker, was stripped entirely naked. Another employee, named Eaton, was found dead. He was stripped naked, and had a bundle of paper bags in his arms. His face was badly eaten by wolves. There was a bullet hole in his left breast. Frank Dresser, a brother of the man found in the coal mine, was found badly burned. He had, without doubt, been killed instantly, as a bullet had passed through his heart. The bodies of Eaton, Thompson, Price, Eskridge, and all other employees not before named, were also found. Eskridge was found two miles this side of the agency, naked and with a bullet hole through his head. In the position occupied by the Indians during Thornburgh's battle, in a breastwork made of stone, was found the dead body of an unknown white man, dressed in buckskin. He was sitting on his knees, and had his gun in position to fire. He was shot through the forehead. From this it appears the Indians are not alone in their hellish work. The supposition is the Indians have gone South to join the Southern Utes, and the impression among the officers of Merritt's command is that the Indians who fought Thornburgh numbered at least 700.

Lieuts. Burke and Schuyler arrived here this morning. They state that on the afternoon of the day on which Gen. Merritt reached Capt. Payne's camp he had a fight with the Indians, and had to move camp about a mile from Payne's old position that night, on account of a fearful stench created by the dead animals. Merritt moved upon the agency, and reached there Saturday. The Indians are retreating Southward, and it is expected that in small bands they will drop into the several agencies, and thus covering up themselves, it will never be known who were the warriors opened battle on Maj. Thornburgh. The dismounted companies and the wounded will be here in seven days.

10/30/79 Mirror

THE INDIANS AND THEIR GRIEVANCES:— The three white women and two white children whom the Utes carried off from the White River Agency came into Gen. Merritt's camp on Friday. They report that the Indians have treated them with respect and kindness. After the killing of Meeker, Chief Douglass and two others took Mrs. Meeker and the rest under their personal protection until such time as they should be able to restore them to their friends. Compare the conduct of these so-called savages with that of the United States troopers who shot down the Cheyenne women and babies with as little compunction, apparently, as though they had been so many rabbits.

As to the killing of Meeker and the agency employees, the White River Utes tell a consistent story, which is corroberated in part by other testimony. The ill-fated agent's hobby was to make these red men work, white man fashion, and the more sullenly they resisted the more imperiously he insisted. According to the Indians, he withheld their supplies, scolded them, threatened to put them in irons, and even to hang them if they did not go to work. Finally, he told them, they say, that Major Thornburgh was coming with a supply of chains to be used in binding them, as a preliminary to hanging them. This explains the chain found on Meeker's dead body. A committee of the Indians went to meet Thornburgh. They say that he met them haughtily, would not say anything to

want a fight. Presently runners brought the news to the Indians at the agency that the fight had begun, and that fifteen of their brethren had been killed. Then the more hot-headed of them, against the remonstrances of Douglass and other chiefs, killed Meeker and his white workmen, sparing, as we have seen, the woman and children.

But for the prompt action of the head chief, Ouray, other branches of the tribe would have gone to the help of the White River Utes, and we should have had a bloody and costly war on our hands. The army officers and the Indians are agreed on this point.

What a queer return it would be to rob Ouray and Douglas and all the other friendly Utes of their homes, and march them off as prisoners to some unhealthy corner in the Indian Territory.

10/16/79 Mirror

Sam Patch.

HIS LAST LEAP AS DESCRIBED BY AN EYE-WITNESS.

I will premise by saying that he was no impostor, but that in his brief career he always performed all that he promised in a straight-forward and honest way. He never resorted to the use of rubber straps, coils of wire, or a parachute, in order to render his leaps from apparent danger. Sam Patch, as he was familiarly called, was a native of Paterson, N. J., the son of "poor but honest parents," and for some years lived there alone with his widowed mother. He is said, by some persons to have been a lazy shiftless and dissipated fellow, but I was assured by an old and reputable merchant of the place a few years ago, who knew Sam well, that this was not so. The same gentleman kindly took me to the place where he made his first leap into the Passaic river, of some eighty or ninety feet, and which he repeated several times.—During the summer of 1829 Patch went to Niagara Falls and made one or two successful leaps into the seething waters below. In October of the same year he came to Rochester, and gave out that he would leap from a small island above the upper falls. This was the last of October, and was an occasion that called together more people than Rochester ever saw before.

Fully fifty thousand were on hand to witness for the first time a daring feet that no other man had ever attempted in this country. On this occasion I took my stand below the falls close to the water's edge, and nearly under the projecting rock from which he was to jump. Promptly at the hour announced Sam made his appearance on the spot, and was greeted with cheers and a tiger such as any human might be proud of.—After surveying the vast assemblage for a moment, he removed his out-side garments and tied a red bandana around his waist.

Soon he waved a farewell to the the people on all sides, which no doubt sent a chill through many a bosom, and, with arms extended, leaped into the waters below. I shall never forget the sensation as I looked up and saw him coming down. Just as he reached the water he brought his arms to his side, and went in without a ripple upon the surface. In an instant he reappeared and swam to shore, with no injury save a slight bruise on his shin against a sunken tree. He was taken on the shoulders of some present and carried up the bank, where he received the hearty congratulations of all the vast, admiring crowd.

On the 9th of November following, he made another and his last leap; this time from an elevated platform 25 feet high making the whole distance of the leap 125 feet. It was chilly, unpleasant day, with some ice in the river, and, to protect himself from the cold, he drank rather too freely of brandy, as we noticed in following him close on the island, from which he was destined never to return. He ascended to the place of leaping with apparent ease and coolness, and, after looking out upon the sea of heads for a moment, he, as before, removed all his garments except pants and shirt, and, tying the bandana again around his body, he motioned to all a last farewell, and walked off to almost instant death. He struck the water on his breast, and as it closed over him we felt sure that for him this was "the last on earth."—Diligent search was at once made for his body, but all in vain. Early the next spring, however, it was found floating at the mouth of the river at Charlott, with the handkerchief still on.

10/23/79 Mirror

—Blondin, in his Vienna exhibitions, uses a rope stretched at a height of 130 feet, and walks blind-folded, without a balance pole.—No net is spread to break a fall, and death would be inevitable if he tumbled. In this respect his feats are more dangerous than at Niagara, where a drop into the water might not have killed him.

10/16/79 Mirror

An Incident of the Last Engagement.

Gen. Gordon, who commanded the last effort of the Confederates against Grant, gives this incident of the advance :

The hour had come, and when everything was ready I stood on the breastwork of Colquitt's salient and ordered two men to my side with rifles, who were to fire the signal for attack. The noise of moving our own obstructions was going on and attracted the notice of a Federal picket. In the black darkness his voice rang out :

"Hallo, there ! Johnny Reb ! what are you making all that fuss about over there ?"

The men were just leaning forward for the start. This sudden call disconcerted me somewhat ; but the rifleman on my right came to my assistance by calling out in a cheerful voice :

"Oh ! never mind us, Yank ; lie down and go to sleep ; we are just gathering a little corn ; you know rations are might short over here."

There was a patch of corn between our lines, some of it still hanging on the stocks — After a few moments there came back the kindly reply of the Yankee picket, which quite assured me. He said :

"All right, Johnny go ahead and get your corn, I won't shoot at you."

As I gave the command to "forward," the man on my right seemed to have some compunctions of conscience for having stilled the suspisions of the Yankee picket, who had answered him so kindly, and who the next moment might be surprised and killed. So he called out to him :

"Look out for yourself now, Yank ; we're going to shell the woods."

This exhibition of chivalry and of kindly feeling on both sides and at such a moment touched me almost as deeply as any minor incident of the war. I quickly ordered the two men to "fire."

Bang ! Bang ! The two shots broke the stillness, and "forward men !" I commanded The chosen hundred sprang forward, eagerly following the axemen, and for the last time the Stars and Bars carried to aggressive assault.

10/31/79 Washingtonian

"William," said one Quaker to another, "thee knows I never call anybody names; but William, if the Governor of the State should come to me and say, Joshua, I want thee to find me the biggest liar in the State of Virginia, I would come to thee and say, William, the Governor wants to see thee particularly.

10/11/79 Washingtonian   [Communicated.

A certain bass voiced Cow goes serenading around Leesburg every night. She waits till all is still and "O'er the one half earth nature seems dead," then she opens with the national air of Cows, and in deep monotone makes the night hideous till morning. We are fond of the "lowing herd" when it is "O'er the lea," but under our windows at three o'clock in the morning, it is a nuisance. Can this Cow's complaints not be attended to ? they have been heard often.

SUFFERER

[Communicated

MR. EDITOR :—As Horse Thieves have commenced operations again in this county, the Society for the Recovery of Stolen horses, should be reorganized and put in working order at once. A few years ago, several valuable horses that were stolen from farmers near this place, were recovered by the Society, the thief arrested, tried, convicted, and sent to the Penitentiary. Would it not be advisable to call a meeting and organize as soon as practicable ?

A FORMER MEMBER.

11/22/79 Washingtonian

A FALLING BRIDGE—MIRACULOUS ESCAPE
—An accident, that might have been serious,
occurred at the Leesburg and Aldie Turnpike
Bridge over Little River, on Monday afternoon. Mr. GEO. SURVICK, butcher, of this
town, was crossing the bridge with a two
horse wagon in which were fourteen hogs,
secured in a crate. When about half way over,
the bridge gave way, and the entire structure
fell with a tremendous crash, landing SUR-
VICK, his horses, wagon and hogs into the
stream below a distance of some ten feet. The
horses were thrown on their sides and held
fast by the entangled harness,—the wagon
lay upside down—the crate, caught by the
debris, kept the hogs secured, while Mr. S.,
wedged in amongst the broken timbers, with
the breath almost knocked out of his body
remained in that position for several minutes,
until the noise of the falling bridge attracted
the attention of a number of persons in the
neighborhood, who ran to his assistance, and
succeeded in rescuing, man horses, wagon and
hogs,—and strange to say, beyond a few immaterial bruises and a severe stunning by Mr.
SURVICK, no further damage was sustained.
Dr. Quinby was soon on hand, and administered to Mr. S. the necessary restoratives, after which his team was harnessed up and he
proceeded home.

The bridge was comparatively a new one, and
in addition, we understand, had been recently painted and otherwise repaired. It was in
constant daily use, persons crossing and re-
crossing continually with all sorts of vehicles
and with the utmost feeling of security. The
accident, all things considered was most remarkable, not only because of its unexpected-
ness but also miraculous escape from serious
injury, if not death, of the party crossing.—

11/20/79 Mirror

A Case of Mistaken Identity.

If the trunk manufacturers do not quit making so many thousands of valises exactly
alike, somebody is going to get into some awful trouble about it sometime, and some trunk
maker will be sued for damages enough to
build a court-house.

The other day an omnibus full of passengers drove up town from the Union depot.—
Side by side sat a commercial traveler, named
William Mackaby and Mrs. Winnie C. Dum-
bleton, the eminent lady temperance lecturer,
When the omnibus reached the Barrett
House the commercial missionary seized his
valise and started out. The lady made a grab
after him, and he halted.

"I beg your pardon," she said, "but you
have my valise."

"You are certainly mistaken, madam," the
traveler said, courteously, but firmly, "this is
mine."

"No, sir," the lady replied firmly, "its mine.
I would know it among a thousand. You
must not take it."

But the traveler persisted and the lady insisted, and they came very near quarreling.—
Presently one of the passengers pointed to a
twin valise in the omnibus, and asked:
"Whose is that?"

"It isn't mine, said the traveler; it is
just like it, but this is mine."

"And it isn't mine," said the lady; "he has
mine, and I'll have it or I'll have the law on
him. It's a pity if a lady can't travel alone
in this country without being robbed of her
property in broad daylight."

Finally the traveler said he would open
the valise to prove his property. The lady
objected at first saying she did not want her
valise opened in the presence of a crowd of
strangers. But as there was no other means
of settling the dispute she at length consented. The traveler sprung the lock, opened
the valise, and the curious crowd bent forward to see.

On the very top of everything lay a big
flat flask half full of whiskey, a deck of cards
and one or two things that nobody knows the
name of.

The traveler was the first to recover his
self possession and speech.

"Madam," he said, "you are right. The
valise is yours. I owe you a thousand apolo—'

But the lady had fainted, and the traveler
relocked his valise with a quiet smile. Early
in the afternoon a sign painter down town
received a note in a feminine hand, asking
him to come to the Barrett House to mark a
red leather valise in black letters a foot and a
half long.

Miss Meeker's Story of Her Capture.

Mrs. Meeker, her daughter, Josephine, and Mrs. Price and her two children have been detained here two days on account of Mrs. Meeker's illness, caused by nervous reaction, after a terrible journey of five hundred miles on stages and Indian ponies, bareback and with poor saddles, over mountains and alkali deserts. During this ordeal she was only half clad in a calico dress and a single shawl, without blankets, and had only the bare ground to sleep on in the Indian camp. The party leave for Denver in a day or two, going thence to their home in Greeley. Miss Josephine Meeker was threatened with death, and her escape was a narrow one. She is a blonde, with blue eyes and light hair, and is tall in statue, and vivacious in manner and conversation. She was a teacher at the agency and a great favorite among the Indians. She taught the boy of Chief Douglass, and had half a dozen offers of marriage from the Ute braves. Her quick wit and knowledge of the language undoubtedly saved her life.

HOW THE MASSACRE BEGAN.

Miss Meeker says: "I was in the kitchen with my mother washing the dishes. It was afternoon. I looked out of the window and saw the Utes shooting the boys who were working on the new building.

We ran into the milk room, which had only one small window, and locked the door and hid under a shelf. Firing went on for several hours at intervals. There was no shouting, no noise, but frequent firing. While waiting in this horrid suspense Dresser said he had gone to the employes' rooms, where all guns were stored, but found them stolen.— In the intervals of shooting Dresser would exclaim: 'There goes one of the government guns.' Their sound was quite different from those of the Indians.

We stayed in the milk room until it began to fill with smoke. The sun was half an hour high.

I took May Price, three years old, and we all ran to father's room. It was not disturbed. The papers and books were just as he left them. 'Pepy's Dairy' lay open on the table. We knew the building would be burned and ran across Douglass avenue for a field of sage brush beyond the ploughed ground. The Utes were so busy stealing the annuity goods that they did not see us at first. About thirty of them, loaded with blankets, were carrying them toward Douglass' camp, near the river. We had gone one hundred yards when the Utes saw us. They threw down the blankets and came running towards us, firing as they came. Bullets whizzed as thick as grasshoppers around us. I do not think they intended to kill us—only to frighten us—but they tried to shoot Frank Dresser, who had almost reached the sage brush.

Mother was hit by a bullet, which went through her underclothing and made a flesh wound three inches long. As the Indians came nearer they shouted: 'We no shoot! Come to us!' I had the little girl, and the Indian named Pursune said for me to go with him. He and another Ute seized me by the arm and started toward the river. An Uncompahgre Indian took Mrs. Price and her baby and mother was taken to the headquarters of Douglass. We came to a wide irrigating canal which father had the Indians build. I said I could not cross it. The Indians answered by pushing me through the water. I had on only moccasins, and the water and mud were deep. The baby waded, too, and both of us came out wet to the skin.

As we were walking in Chief Joseph came and pushed away Pursune and in great anger, told him to give me up. I understood some of the language. Pursune refused to surrender me. Hot words ensued and I feared the men would fight for a moment. I thought I would ask Douglass to take me, but as both were drunk I kept silent and afterward was glad I did not go.

ties. The Indian, Pursune, took me to where his ponies were standing by the river and seated me on a pile of blankets while he went for more. The Indians were now on all sides. I could not escape. Pursune packed his effects, all stolen from the agency, on a government mule which was taller than a tall man.

He had two mules stolen from the agency. It was now sundown. Packing was finished at dark, and we started for the wilderness of the south. I rode a horse with a saddle, but no bridle.— The halter-strap was so short that it dropped continually. The child was lashed behind me. Pursune and his assistant rode each side of me, driving the pack mules ahead. About twenty other Indians were in the party.

Mother came later, riding bareback behind Douglass, both on one horse.— She was sixty-four years old, feeble in health, wounded and not recovered from a broken thigh, caused by a fall two years ago. Chief Douglass gave her neither horse, saddle or blankets. We followed the river, and on the other side Pursune brought me a hatful of water to drink. We trotted along until nine o'clock, when we halted for a half an hour. All the Indians dismounted and blankets were spread on the ground and I laid down to rest, with mother lying not far from me.

Chief Douglass was considerably excited, and made a speech to me with many gestures and great emphasis. He recited his grievances and explained why the massacre began. He said Thornburgh told the Indians that he was going to arrest the head chiefs, take them to Fort Steele and put them in the calaboose—perhaps hang them. He said my father had written all the letters to the Denver papers, and circulated wild reports about what the Indians would do, as set forth by the Western press, and that he was responsible for all the hostility.

While Douglass was telling this he stood in front of me with his gun, and his anger was dreadful. Then he shouldered his gun and walked up and down before me in the moonlight and imitated the employees who had kept guard at the agency for three nights after the massacre. He mocked them and sneered and laughed at them and said he was a heap big Indian. Then he sang English songs which he had heard the boys sing in their rooms at the agency. He sang the negro melody, 'Swing Low, Sweet Chariot,' and asked me if I understood. I told him I did, because he had the words and tune perfectly committed.

Then the brave chief, Douglass, who had eaten at our table that very day, walked off a few feet, returned and placed his loaded gun to my forehead three times and asked me if I was going to run away? I told him I was not afraid of him nor of death, and should not run away.

When he found his repeated threats could not frighten me, all the other Indians turned on him and laughed at him.

We urged our horses forward and journeyed in the moonlight through to the Grand Mountains with the Indians talking in low tones among themselves. The little three-year-old May Price, who was fastened behind me, cried a few times, for she was cold and had had no supper, and her mother was away in Jack's camp but the child was generally quiet. It was after midnight when we made a second halt in a deep and sombre canyon, with tremendous mountains towering on every side. Mother was not allowed to come up. Douglass kept her with him half a mile further down the ravine. Pursune had plenty of blankets, which were stolen from the agency. He spread some for my bed and rolled up some for my pillow, and told me to retire.

I fell into a doze, and did not awake until the sun was shining over the mountains. Next day Pursune went to fight the soldiers, and he placed me in charge of his wife with her three children.

That same day mother came up to see me, in company with a little Indian girl. On Wednesday, the next day, Johnson went over to Jack's camp and brought back Mrs. Price and her baby to live in her camp. He said he had made it all right with the other Utes.

On Wednesday and on other days one of Supanzisquait's three squaws put her hand on my shoulder and said: "Poor little girl, I feel so sorry. You have no father and you are away off with the Utes so far from home." She cried all the time and said her own little child had just died and her heart was sore. When Mrs. Price came into camp another squaw took her baby, Johnny, into her arms and wept over him and said, in Ute that she felt very sorry for the captives.

I asked the Indians before Brady came where the soldiers were. They replied that they were "still in that cellar," and the Indians were killing their ponies when they went for water in the night. They said: "Indians stay on mountains and see white soldiers; soldiers no see Indians. White soldiers not know how to fight."

[Most modern newspapers receive more profits from their advertisements than from subscriptions.

Perhaps it was the same then.]

THE WASHINGTONIAN

LEESBURG, LOUDOUN COUNTY, VA

SATURDAY................December 27, 1879

CHRISTMAS.

We should all feel grateful that we have been permitted, once more to, witness the return of this season of enjoyment for the young, and pleasure and consolation for those of riper years.

Throughout the christianized world millions of light, merry, little hearts are to-day happy and joyous in the bountiful display of the evidences of parental affection, which show the kindly and softening inspirations drawn from the remembrance and associations of the great event we celebrate. Unlike the events which note epochs in the civil history of the world, it never wearies in its commemoration—nor is the joy which greets its coming diminished by the lapse of time. Ages have passed, centuries have piled the archieves of nations with the records of their events, and yet the Christmas morning is welcomed with the same full, fresh gush of joy.

OUR CARRIER.—There have been great complaints, since the so called resumption of specie payment, of silver being locked up in the treasury vaults, and of the difficulty the government experiences in getting silver in circulation.—Now our Carrier who has faithfully in all sorts of weather carried your paper regularly to your door, has no prejudies against the pale metal at all, and will gladly receive from the patrons of this paper his customary quarter *in silver*. He will make his call on New Year's Day.

On Christmas Eve, the children of the Sunday School of St. James' Episcopal Church, were presented with their usual Christmas Gifts. The Church had been tastefully dressed for Christmas day, and was filled with a crowd of the expectant young folks—A handsome tree lighted up with tapers, and hung with holiday ornaments and packages of all that delights the hearts of children, stood in the Chancel. Dr. Davis in his robes conducted a simple service with an address explanatory of the observance of the day and then the presents to the scholars were distributed. A package of books, sent to the school by Mrs. Western a kind friend who has often shown her interest in the children, was distributed among the pupils who had been most punctual. The bright happy faces of the children made even old bachelors smile.

THE PHONOGRAPH.—Edison's Phonograph was exhibited in Leesburg, at Hammerly's Hall, on Monday night last, before a large audience. The almost miraculous performance of this instrument gave more than satisfaction to all who saw and heard it talk, laugh, &c. For a piece of machinery to be made to perform such feats, proves that the reach of science has not yet, by far, attained the verge of its success in the discovery and revelations of the mysteries of nature, and the application of inventions to practical and useful purposes. Those who saw and heard it, state that to appreciate its novel and wonderful performance it must be heard and seen.

304

www.ingramcontent.com/pod-product-compliance
Lightning Source LLC
Chambersburg PA
CBHW080413270326
41929CB00018B/3012